INTRODUCTION TO FINANCIAL MANAGEMENT

Lawrence D. Schall/Charles W. Haley

Professors of Finance
University of Washington

McGraw-Hill Book Company

New York   St. Louis   San Francisco   Auckland   Bogotá
Düsseldorf   Johannesburg   London   Madrid   Mexico   Montreal   New Delhi   Panama
Paris   São Paulo   Singapore   Sydney   Tokyo   Toronto

Library of Congress Cataloging in Publication Data

Schall, Lawrence D
    Introduction to financial management.

    (McGraw-Hill series in finance)
    Includes index.
    1. Corporations—Finance. I. Haley, Charles W.,
joint author. II. Title.
HG4011.S33   658.1'5   76-41826
ISBN 0-07-055097-2

**INTRODUCTION
TO FINANCIAL
MANAGEMENT**

    34567890 DODO 78321098

This book was set in Times Roman by Progressive Typographers.
The editors were J. S. Dietrich, Marjorie Singer, and Michael Weber;
the designer was Anne Canevari Green;
the production supervisor was Leroy A. Young.
The drawings were done by J & R Services, Inc.
R. R. Donnelley & Sons Company was printer and binder.

contents

PART TWO. THE FIRM'S INVESTMENT, FINANCING, AND DIVIDEND DECISIONS

preface

Our primary goal in writing this text is to provide students with a thorough foundation in finance. The book is designed for undergraduate one-quarter or one-semester courses. If supplemented with cases and readings, however, it is suitable as the primary text for courses extending two quarters or more. Instructors using this text for an introductory course for M.B.A. students will find that the appendixes to Chapters 5 through 9 enable them to approach basic finance on a more advanced level.

The introductory course is the only exposure to finance for many students, and we have covered all the material that we believe is essential to a comprehensive understanding of financial management. We have included, therefore, discussions of financial markets and institutions, personal finance, and even a touch of public finance, while maintaining the primary emphasis on problems of business financial management. However, students who will be taking additional courses in finance are not neglected. Basic principles, techniques, and institutional aspects needed for effective analysis of business finance cases are well covered. A foundation for more advanced theoretical courses is provided in the chapter appendixes and in the more difficult problems, and we have tried to ensure that our approach here is consistent with current theory. Students completing a course of study using this book should be well prepared for courses in investments because of our stress on risk and return in the financial markets and our coverage of the basic characteristics of securities and markets.

Although an unusually wide range of topics and issues is examined in the book, we have in all cases treated the material at an introductory level. Topics such as the cost of capital are stripped of the complications often found in other books. Our preference has been to explain carefully the fundamental issues and then to discuss how managers in practice come to grips with the problem. The importance of managerial judgment and experience in actual decisions is stressed throughout the book.

We have made a special effort to provide an integrated discussion of the topics covered. The concepts are related to one another rather than treated as a potpourri of disconnected ideas. However, we should emphasize that this book is designed so that the instructor has wide flexibility in choosing the order of presentation of most chapters. Furthermore, most chapters have one or more sections that can be deleted without any loss of continuity. To enhance the usefulness of the book, appendixes are used in several chapters to explore major concepts in greater depth. These appendixes are intended as supplements to the basic coverage of the text and are designed for use by well-prepared undergraduate and beginning graduate students. The *Instructor's Manual* explains the numerous options for sequencing and deleting material.

The first five chapters provide an introduction to the book and an introduction to finance in general. The organization of Part 1 is unique. Chapter 1 introduces the book and the topic and discusses the role of the corporation in society. Chapter 2 is a description of the financial system, focusing on financial institutions, securities, and markets. It is intended to ease the student into the world of finance. Chapter 3, which covers taxes and business organization, is not essential for students with good accounting backgrounds. Others will find it a valuable reference, since a general understanding of personal and business income taxes is assumed in many of the later chapters. Chapter 4 provides a thorough treatment of compound interest calculations, focusing on personal finance problems. The student is shown why interest calculations are made as well as how they are made. Chapter 5 is an extensive introduction to risk and market valuation. Appendixes to this chapter provide a more advanced treatment of diversification and the capital asset pricing model.

Part 2, which consists of Chapters 6 through 10, provides the basic foundation of business finance—the investment, financing, and dividend decisions. The material in these chapters is highly integrated so as to emphasize the interrelationships between these three decision areas. The appendixes of Chapters 6 through 9 amplify and extend the discussion. The topics covered in the appendixes include the following: the relationships between the capital asset pricing model and the cost of capital (Appendix 6A) and investment risk (Appendix 8A); the validity of net present value as an investment criterion (Appendix 7A); the reinvestment rate assumptions of the present value and internal rate of return methods (Appendix 7B); and a proof by example and discussion of the Modigliani-Miller cost of capital propositions (Appendix 9A). The text presents a very basic discussion of these concepts, which then are explored in depth in the appendixes.

Chapters 11 through 15 form Part 3 of the text. Here we deal with ratio and break-even analysis, forecasting, and working capital management. In addition to presenting the basic tools of analysis, these chapters explore the fundamental concepts underlying the techniques, how they should be used in practice, and their shortcomings. Some instructors may wish to delete Chapter 12 on break-even analysis and the measurement of operating and financial leverage if this material has been covered in other courses.

Part 4 offers a detailed discussion of the characteristics of the different securities issued by business firms and the procedures for issuing securities. Chapter 16 explains the procedures involved in raising capital through direct arrangements with a financial institution e.g., a bank or insurance company, or through a public offering of securities. Chapter 17 describes various forms of leasing arrangements, discusses the rationale of leasing, and explains how the financial manager decides whether to lease or to purchase a particular asset. Chapters 18, 19, and 20 cover common stock, various types of long-term debt, preferred stock, convertible securities, and warrants. The characteristics of each type of security are examined from both the investor's viewpoint and the firm's viewpoint and are related to the firm's decision as to which type of security provides the best means of financing. Special care is taken to provide a clean and intuitive explanation of the more complex and difficult concepts, such as the consequences of a rights offering, refunding decisions, and the valuation of convertible securities and warrants.

Part 5 contains material that should normally be covered at the end of the introductory finance course. Chapter 21 looks at mergers and discusses how to analyze a potential acquisition. Chapter 22 presents a basic introduction to the field of international business finance. This chapter is unusual in its breadth of coverage. Chapter 23 deals with bankruptcy and reorganization.

Although this book is written so that the instructor has substantial latitude in selecting which chapters to cover and their order of presentation, we suggest that certain chapters be taught in a given order. Chapters 4, 5, 6, 7, 9, 11, 13, and 14 are prerequisites for certain other chapters. Specifically, Chapter 4 should precede Chapter 5, and Chapters 4 and 5 should precede all of Part 2 (Chapters 6 through 10). We recommend that the chapters in Part 2 be taught in sequence. However, these chapters can be rearranged to suit the needs of the individual instructor. A complete discussion of the possibilities for alternative sequences is included in the *Instructor's Manual* for the text. Many instructors may choose to assign early in the course Chapters 11, 12, and 13, which cover financial statement analysis, break-even analysis and forecasting, respectively. This can be done with no difficulty, although the discussion of financial leverage in Chapter 12 is most effectively taught if it is presented after Chapter 9. Consistent with the above sequencing guidelines would be a course with Chapters 4 through 9, 11, 13 through 15, and one or more of Chapters 16, 17 and 21; other chapters could be intermingled with these. Several alternative course outlines are provided in the *Instructor's Manual*.

Students come into the basic finance course with a wide range of prior preparation in accounting, mathematics, and economics, all of which serve as foundation areas for finance. We have assumed minimal background in these areas; but we do expect that students have had at least one quarter of accounting shortly before taking the class. Able students should be capable of mastering the material almost without regard to their previous formal course work. We have tried to make the book as self-contained as possible and, through extensive use of examples, to make it suitable for self-study.

As an aid to students, many instructors recommend a study guide to their classes when such is available. The *Study Guide* written by Tom Stitzel serves as an excellent review and supplement to this book. It contains additional solved problems as well as questions in a programmed learning format. We believe that many students will find this supplement helpful.

Many people have aided us in this project. Our students have provided us with numerous comments that have resulted in substantial improvements over earlier versions of the text. Colleagues at the University of Washington and elsewhere have reviewed drafts of the manuscript, and we are very grateful for their help. Our thanks go to Eugene F. Drzycimski of the University of Wisconsin, Oshkosh; George W. Hettenhouse of Indiana University; Lee Hoover of Iowa State University; Michael H. Hopewell of the University of Oregon; James Hugon of Portland State University; John B. Major of California State University, Hayward; Donald A. Nast of Florida State University; Michael Rice of the University of North Carolina, Chapel Hill; Ralph Ringgenberg of the University of Colorado; Timothy Sullivan of Baruch College; Ernest W. Walker of the University of Texas, Austin; and J. Kenton Zumwalt of the University of Illinois, Urbana, for their help with various stages of the manuscript. We are indebted to Charles D'Ambrosio, who provided encouragement throughout the development of the book and helped us over many rough spots. Charles Henning gave us special assistance on the discussion of international finance in Chapter 22 and provided us with an initial draft of the chapter. Jean-Claude Bosch, Gregg Brauer, Susan Doolittle, and John Settle developed many of the end-of-chapter questions and problems and checked over the answers to them. They also provided us with many helpful suggestions for improving the text based on their teaching of this material.

The editorial staff at McGraw-Hill has been a very useful resource for us at all stages of preparation. Marjorie Singer diligently read the entire manuscript and made copious suggestions for improving the clarity of the text. We owe her a tremendous debt for the increase in quality that resulted from her advice and prodding. Stephen Dietrich, Michael Weber, and Michael Elia have all contributed in important ways to this effort. Finally the book could not have been written without the support of Anne Haley.

Many people have been engaged in this project over the past four years. We hope that the net present value is positive from your point of view as well as our own.

Lawrence D. Schall
Charles W. Haley

introduction to financial management

PART 1

THE ENVIRONMENT OF FINANCIAL DECISIONS

Part 1 consists of five chapters in which we present the general background for individual and company financial decisions. Chapter 1 is an introduction to business finance and to this text. Here we discuss the nature and objectives of financial management. In Chapter 2 we examine the American financial system: the network of financial institutions and markets which is an important part of the financial manager's environment. Chapter 3 covers other aspects of this environment, the legal form of business organizations, and the tax laws which affect financial decisions. Whereas the material in the first three chapters is largely descriptive, in Chapter 4 we develop a fundamental financial concept, the time value of money. We show here how to solve a variety of basic financial problems involving time and money. In Chapter 5 we discuss a second fundamental concept, risk, and show how risk affects the value of financial assets.

The material in Part 1 is important not just to the managers of business firms. Most of the topics covered are of equal importance to an individual concerned with such financial problems as borrowing money and choosing alternative ways of investing personal savings. The remainder of the text is almost exclusively concerned with problems faced by financial managers; but these first five chapters cover financial concepts that are useful to everyone.

financial management and goals

This is a book about financial decisions—the financial decisions of a company. A company can be a large corporation such as General Motors or Sears Roebuck. It can be a medium- or small-sized firm—an advertising agency or a commercial printer. It can be a "Mom and Pop" business such as a small bookstore, or even a person on his or her own—a lawyer, a writer, or an accountant.

The financial decisions of large corporations sometimes have a strong element of drama, for the risks and rewards involved may be measured in hundreds of millions of dollars. A case in point was Eastman Kodak's announcement, in 1974, that it was preparing to enter the field of instant photography, until then the private preserve of another large corporation, Polaroid. But the financial decisions of even the smallest enterprises are no less vital to their welfare, and the procedures involved are basically the same: there are facts to be considered, goals to be defined. *This book explores those facts and develops those goals within the framework of important contemporary issues and the practices of modern financial management.*

For example, when a paper company or an oil refinery is thinking of expanding its productive capacity, it must now consider—among other things—the ecological problems. When Playboy Enterprises was contemplating a new magazine, *Oui,* it had to consider whether the magazine would be competing against *Playboy* itself; what the reaction of advertisers would be; what goals could realistically be set for circulation. A basic rule is that all important consequences of a financial decision must be taken into account.

The financial decisions of a company can affect the interests of many groups in society. In this chapter, we will be concerned with the two most controversial relationships: between the stockholders (owners) and management (which makes most of the decisions), and between the company and the rest of society. Each of these relationships can involve mutual benefit or serious conflict. The first part of this chapter will identify and clarify the problems that can create conflicts, and it will suggest how these differences are resolved. Once this is done, we will inquire into the nature of finance as a discipline, and into the functions and objectives of the financial manager as a practitioner of this discipline.

THE CORPORATE OBJECTIVE

To perform effectively, the financial manager must have a clear understanding of the company's goals. We will begin by distinguishing between policies and goals. We then ask who determines the policies and goals of a company—its stockholders, management, or society—and, equally important, what goals are ordinarily pursued by firms in practice.

The objectives or goals of a company are usually defined in terms of maximizing the value of the owner's interest in the firm (maximizing the value of the corporation's shares),[1] though nowadays social considerations can also be an important company objective—for example, helping to save energy or minimizing pollution. The policies of a company are *the strategies it employs to achieve its goals.* Company policy may involve such questions as whether to try to speed up growth by buying existing businesses, how much to invest in research and development, and what degree of risk to accept in launching new products or entering new markets.

A company's goals and policies are determined—theoretically—by the owners (the shareholders or stockholders) as represented by an elected board of directors. The board's responsibility is to make major policy decisions affecting the firm and to hire the day-to-day management team. In practice, however, the board of directors usually consists of a slate that is proposed by the company's management and which includes the top echelon of the management team. Thus, in reality, the shareholders delegate to management enormous powers to "run the company"—that is to say, to set its goals and shape its policies. There are two good reasons for this. The first is that it would be extremely impractical and inefficient to transmit to management the views of every stockholder on every issue—there are hundreds of companies which have literally several thousand stockholders, and a giant such as American Telephone & Telegraph has nearly 3 million. Secondly, the owners recognize that professional managers, because of their training and expertise, are better qualified than they are to operate the business. This delegation of authority is acceptable to most stockholders, so long as the company's performance is satisfactory in terms of dividend payments and earnings progress.

Owner and Management Objectives

Small businesses are usually managed by their owners. For such firms there cannot be any conflicts between owners and managers, since they are the same people. However, we have noted that most large firms are run by professional managers who, by law, represent the stockholders.

---

1. As explained in Chap. 3, a corporation is a company whose owners are called "shareholders or stockholders." Each shareholder owns pieces of paper called "stock certificates" or "shares" which represent the owner's interest in the company. If a company has a total of 100,000 shares outstanding, the owner of 1,000 shares owns 1 percent of the firm.

The duty of the management team is to exercise the authority delegated to it in such a way as to pursue the goals of the stockholders in a manner consistent with the law.

Conflicts between management and shareholders may arise because the managers place their own interests ahead of those of the shareholders. They may, for example, grant themselves excessive salaries and perquisites. Or the shareholders may feel that management, in order to maintain its position, has painted an unrealistically rosy picture of the company's performance. There are many well-known cases in which stockholders belatedly discovered that management had been concealing major mistakes, and even illegal acts. A notorious example was the Equity Funding scandal of 1973, in which audacious frauds and other hocus-pocus committed by management remained hidden from the stockholders—and from government regulatory authorities—for as long as nine years. The exposure of this historic swindle revealed that the company's reported profits were nonexistent and that more than $100 million of its assets had been faked. The stockholders' losses amounted to several hundred million dollars. Equity Funding's president and eighteen officers and employees of the company eventually pleaded guilty to charges brought against them and were sentenced to varying jail terms.

But quite apart from the issue of wrongdoing, it is extremely difficult for the average shareholder to know what marks to award to management. On the one hand, a great many errors and inefficiencies remain unrecognized or at least unpublicized. On the other hand, difficulties and misfortunes occur which are due to circumstances beyond management's control. For example, one cannot really blame hat manufacturers for not foreseeing that, within a relatively short span of years, the majority of American men would simply give up wearing hats. Moreover, if the company does moderately well, it is impossible for a stockholder without exceptional expertise to know how much better the firm's performance might have been if different policies had been adopted.

The question that naturally follows is: What assurances are there that management will serve, rather than exploit, the stockholders? There are several mechanisms which protect the shareholder's position. **Stock option** plans, which make it easy for operating officers to become part owners of the company, encourage managers to align their interests with those of stockholders. Publicity by a disgruntled stockholder can create embarrassment for management and discontent among other shareholders, if the grievances are well founded. Most importantly, stockholder complaints can result in a change of management, especially if the stockholder leading a movement for change is a major investor in the company. A month after industrialist Norton Simon protested that Burlington Northern was foolishly delaying the development of its natural resource holdings, a corporate reorganization occurred, and new emphasis was placed on resource development. Norton Simon owned (among other things) 5 percent of Burlington Northern stock.

The possibility of an outside takeover of the company can also be a powerful deterrent to mismanagement. Although the small shareholders may not have the requisite knowledge to judge management's performance, there are others who do have such knowledge, notably the managers of other companies and those people in the financial world referred to as entrepreneurs (or, less politely, as "wheeler-dealers"). Such parties are constantly on the lookout for opportunities to purchase a company with unrealized potential.

What tells them that a company is not realizing its potential? The simplest indications are a poor record of sales and earnings and/or substantially lower margins of profit (the percentage relationship between profit and sales) than those of companies in a similar line of business. Such unfavorable performance usually results in a depressed price for the company's stock. And the depressed stock price provides an opportunity for another company, a group of investors, or a well-financed individual to buy enough of the company's shares to obtain representation on the company's board of directors and thus press for changes of policy or even a change of management.

Alternatively, an outsider who senses strong dissatisfaction among a company's shareholders can mobilize a drive for election of a new slate of directors. If the drive is successful, the new directors will presumably institute new policies and changes in management.

Thus, the possibility of an outside takeover or a stockholders' revolt is a sword hanging over the heads of management. In practice, the sword falls infrequently, because a takeover requires a great deal of money, whether the parties involved are outsiders or an insurgent group of stockholders. If the takeover is attempted through large purchases of stock, the price offered will have to be substantially above the current market price in order to induce existing stockholders to sell out. This premium above market price may be unacceptably large from the outsider's standpoint. If the takeover is targeted at electing a new slate of directors without massive purchases of stock, all the company's stockholders have to be contacted and persuaded individually to cast their votes at the annual meeting for the newly proposed slate of directors. The promotional, legal, and other expenses involved in such an undertaking run to large numbers. What's more, the chances of success—judging from the historical record—are not encouraging. To begin with, the existing board of directors has a significant advantage; it is entitled to use the company's funds to defend its position through mailings to stockholders. More importantly, the inertia of stockholders—coupled with their normal distrust of insurgents or acquisitive outsiders (often referred to as "raiders")—usually ensures victory for the incumbent board, unless it is guilty of dishonesty or company performance has been conspicuously bad.

Having emphasized the odds against stockholder revolts and takeover attempts, we should point out that they are, occasionally, successful. A prominent example was the takeover, in late 1974, of a well-known television manufacturer, Magnavox, by North American Philips. Originally, Magnavox's management expressed strong opposition to the takeover bid, but it capitulated when the offering price for the stock was raised from $8 to $9 per share.

The Corporation and Society

To Harvard economist John Kenneth Galbraith, many large corporations are exploitative, polluting, resource-wasting parasites that often demand and receive excessive prices for their products. Galbraith's solution is to impose strict governmental regulations and controls (if not nationalization) on corporations to ensure that they behave themselves.

A sharply contrary view is held by the University of Chicago's free enterpriser, Milton Friedman, who maintains that a corporation's function is simply to maximize profits by producing products demanded in the marketplace. He espouses an economic environment free of most government controls. Friedman's position is that "social good" is extremely hard to define and subject to wide disagreement: it is better to set very general rules of conduct and then allow each individual or firm the freedom to pursue a chosen course within these rules. In contrast to the Galbraithian philosophy, there is no presumption by the Friedman school that the corporation is wrong and relatively little reliance on direct government intervention to influence behavior; there is a greater faith that the "invisible guiding hand" of a competitive marketplace will ultimately lead to the best achievable state of affairs. Although the debate between the Galbraith and Friedman camps has not been resolved—at least at the philosophical level—in actual practice the pendulum seems to have swung in favor of increased government involvement.

It would, literally, take pages simply to enumerate the areas in which governmental authorities exercise regulatory controls and the scope of their activities. Among the major industries subject to extensive regulation are the public utilities, railroads, airlines, shipping, the securities industry, and the drug companies. Governmental agencies set forth regulations or "guidelines" applicable to such diverse matters as labeling of food products, door-to-door selling practices (e.g., for encyclopedias), "truth in lending" (making clear to the borrower the full amount of interest charges involved in a loan or installment contract), and more recently, automobile safety. The Federal Trade Commission is empowered to file complaints against companies deemed guilty of unfair, misleading, or "monopolistic" selling practices. The Justice Department takes court actions to block company mergers which, in its view, will diminish competition or to force large companies which have allegedly acquired a monopolistic share of their market to be split up into independent, competitive entities. A case in point with potentially far-reaching implications for American industry was the Justice Department's suit against IBM, on which court hearings began in February 1975. Quite frequently, companies successfully employ stalling tactics to fend off the regulatory agencies, or they manage to persuade them to settle for modest concessions. Nevertheless, government regulation is a central fact of life for large areas of American industry, and it is therefore a matter of major concern to financial managers.

What policies should a firm adopt and what goals should it pursue in such an environment? From a moral standpoint there is no generally acceptable answer, for people differ on what is or is not moral. From a legal standpoint, the answer is much clearer: Management should adopt policies that are lawful and that satisfy stockholder wishes. Stockholders want the value of their ownership interest to be as great as possible, which means a company policy that emphasizes earnings. Indeed, such a policy appears to be the one commonly followed by corporations, although there are exceptional cases in which some profitability has been sacrificed to pursue social ends. Aetna Life and Casualty, a firm not noted for radical causes, voted against the management of companies in which it held stock by favoring such changes as the disclosure of business operations in South Africa, ending investment in the South African territory of Namibia, and revealing corporate lobbying activities. Other companies that have similarly voted against management on social issues, or have set up committees to consider such a move, include Teachers Insurance and Annuity Association, Bank of America, Morgan Guaranty & Trust, Prudential Insurance, and Travelers Insurance. However, in spite of such efforts by a few companies, the primary, and often sole, standard of performance used by stockholders and management is profitability. Of course maximization of share values usually means obeying the laws, such as antipollution statutes, that compel firms to protect society's interest. For violation of such laws can be very expensive in terms of government fines and hostile consumer reactions. Since share value maximization is the most important target for management, let us take a closer look at this objective.

The Firm's Objective

We have stated that shareholders are primarily interested in maximizing the monetary returns from their ownership interest in the company. Stockholders' dollar returns are in the form of dividends (regular dollar payments from the company to stockholders) and the dollars received if the owners eventually sell their shares. The greater are expected dividends from the stock and the higher is the stock's expected future price, the more valuable are the company's shares and the happier are shareholders. The market value of the company's stock is the price investors are willing to pay for the future monetary benefits from owning the stock.

We will assume in this book that shareholders and management (which represents shareholders) prefer policies that maximize the market value of the company's shares.

Share values depend on the firm's earnings, since earnings are used to pay dividends and to reinvest in productive assets which will generate earnings in later years. But the risk as well as the level of earnings is important to shareholders. It is true that stockholders always prefer that the company achieve greater earnings per share than less. However, when a particular policy is adopted, the *future* effect on earnings is ordinarily uncertain. Shareholders may, for example, prefer policy A that provides completely safe (certain) future company earnings of $50,000 per year over "risky" policy B that will result in earnings as high as $100,000 or as low as zero, with an equal chance for all amounts between zero and $100,000. Both policies imply an average of $50,000 per year in the firm's earnings, but B is clearly less certain than A.[2] It is likely that in a market of investors who do not like risk the value of the firm's shares will be greater under policy A than under policy B. Later chapters in the book will examine in detail the impact of risk on company policy.

It should be noted here that using share value maximization as the objective does not mean that management is concerned with day-to-day fluctuations in the stock market. It is true that as long as existing stockholders and other investors in the market have accurate and timely information on the firm's activities, better performance will mean a higher market price for the stock. However, information may not be immediately available to investors, and furthermore, there may be different views as to what the available information implies about the firm's future performance. Hence, the real concern of management is to maximize share value over the long term.

Figure 1-1 illustrates in general terms the interactions between a firm's owners, its management, and society. The exact nature of these interactions will differ from company to company. And for virtually all firms the relationships will vary over time as a result of changes in our social and economic institutions.

THE KEY ROLE OF FINANCE

The Financial Manager

The financial manager plays a central role in the company. As summarized in Table 1-1, the manager's duties include budgeting, raising funds in the capital markets, selecting and evaluating investment projects, and planning the company's marketing and pricing strategies. An individual manager is often a specialist, with a knowledge of many areas of

---

2. The average earnings under policy B are computed by simply taking the midpoint between the highest ($100,000) and lowest (zero) possible earnings outcomes, since all outcomes from zero to $100,000 are equally likely. The $50,000 is therefore a middle estimate of the earnings outcome of policy B.

Figure 1-1. Formulation of company objectives and policies. The firm's objectives are primarily based on owner preferences and on the economic and legal environment; however, the objectives that are sought by the firm may be affected by management attitudes. The policies to achieve the objectives are developed by management and influenced by legal and economic factors.

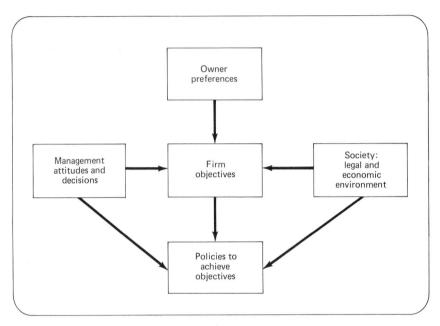

finance but particular expertise in one or two specialities. The breadth of the finance function is so great that in many companies it includes personnel from several departments and involves many echelons of management.

The crucial role played by the finance staff has not gone unrecognized in executive promotions. Richard Gerstenberg, previously an executive vice president for finance, emerged as chairman of General Motors after a reorganization of management in 1971. Another person with financial expertise, Thomas A Murphy, was named to the number two post of vice chairman. Finance people have headed many well-known corporate giants, including Republic Steel, Anaconda, and CBS. This ascendency of finance people to top corporate positions is not surprising. Finance is concerned with the lifeblood of a company, money: how it is obtained to finance the business and how it should be used to assure the business's success. Clearly, skill in this area is an extremely valuable asset in managing a company.

Corporate Organization

The assignment of finance functions to individuals and departments will depend upon the size of the company. The larger the company, generally the greater the degree of specialization of tasks, and the greater the proliferation of positions and departments. A smaller firm would consolidate many duties into fewer departments.

Table 1-1. Finance functions in a firm

1. Financing and investments: supervising the firm's cash and other liquid holdings, raising additional funds when needed, and investing funds in projects

2. Accounting and control: maintaining financial records; controlling financial activities; identifying deviations from planned and efficient performance; and managing payroll, tax matters, inventories, fixed assets, and computer operations

3. Forecasting and long-run planning: forecasting costs, technological changes, capital market conditions, funds needed for investment, returns on proposed investment projects, and demand for the firm's product; and using forecasts and historical data to plan future operations, e.g., planning services and uses of cash

4. Pricing: determining the impact of pricing policies on profitability

5. Other functions: credit and collections, insurance, and incentive planning (pensions, option plans, etc.)

Generally, corporations are required by state law to have a president, a secretary, and a treasurer. Historically, the chief finance officer has been the treasurer. In recent years, two other positions have evolved—the controller and the financial vice president. The controller supervises most of the accounting and control functions listed in Table 1-1, whereas the treasurer supervises or participates in most of the remaining finance functions. The treasurer oversees or manages the company's liquid assets, liabilities, payroll and cashier activities, credits and collections, forecasting, capital budgeting and investments, and financing. The treasurer is an active participant in long-range financial planning. In the corporate hierarchy, the financial vice president is above the usually coequal controller and treasurer. It is the financial vice president's task to supervise all financial operations and planning and to advise the board of directors on financial matters.

Although the finance functions shown in Table 1-1 are generally performed by staff specifically assigned to those tasks, nonfinance personnel in other areas also frequently participate in the financial decision-making process. For example, although cost recording and control are accounting and finance functions, the determination of standard costs and the responsibility for correcting for variations from realizable standards rests with the production department. Similarly, it is the task of the sales department (and any marketing consultants hired by the firm) to estimate the level of sales for various pricing policies; this information is then utilized in financial planning to estimate profit levels for each price structure. Pricing policy is jointly determined by the marketing or sales department and the financial planning staff. Planning funds for operations and capital budgeting is also a joint decision-making process conducted by the production, sales, and finance personnel. Thus, the need for a new machine might be determined by the production department, which submits its request to the division head (who is in part a financial manager). If the expenditure is not greater than a prescribed dollar amount, say $20,000, the decision as to whether to acquire the machine would be made at this point. If the outlay is above that amount, the requisition would be submitted for approval to the home office with the division head's recommendation (and supporting data). The home office financial staff, and perhaps the board of directors, would then approve or disapprove the proposed investment, based upon data relating to projected production and sales, and the availability of funds to finance the investment.

FINANCE AS A DISCIPLINE

The focus of this text is on the financial management of business firms; however, the field of finance is much broader. Put simply, finance is a body of facts, principles, and theories dealing with the raising (for example, by borrowing) and using of money by individuals, businesses, and governments. You will find courses in colleges and universities entitled personal finance, business finance, public finance, investments, financial markets, financial institutions, international finance, etc. These titles indicate the wide range covered by finance. Although our primary concern here will be with managerial finance, essential aspects of individual financial planning and of financial institutions will be covered.

The individual's financial problem is to maximize his or her well-being by appropriately using the resources available. Those resources can be invested or can be spent on consumption goods (for example, food, clothes, or rent on a home). An investment might be in real estate (e.g., purchase of a home), in one's education, in stocks or bonds, or in a savings account. Finance deals with how individuals divide their income between consumption and investment, how they choose from among available investment opportunities, and how they raise money to provide for increased consumption or investment.

Firms also have the problem of allocating resources and raising money. The firm must determine its investment opportunities and be able to select from among them by using certain criteria of choice. A company must also select the best means of acquiring the funds to finance its investments—for example, by selling new stock or bonds or by borrowing from a bank. Just as the individual seeks to maximize his or her happiness, the firm seeks to maximize the wealth of its owners (stockholders).

Finance also encompasses the study of financial markets and institutions, and the activities of governments, with stress on those aspects relating to the financial decisions of individuals and companies. Financial transactions are conducted within the confines of laws and conventions, which are enforced by the state and by private institutions and customs. A familiarity with the limitations and opportunities provided by such an environment is crucial to the decision-making process of individuals and firms. In addition, financial institutions and governments have financial problems comparable to those of individuals and firms. The study of these problems is an important part of the field of finance.

The central topic of this text is business financial management. In addition to a knowledge of strictly company financial affairs, an appreciation of the individual's investment behavior and preferences is critical to a full understanding of managerial finance. Managers are representatives of existing shareholders; they must contract with new stockholders and creditors in raising funds. They are also concerned with investors because they conduct the firm's activities in financial markets. A sensitivity to the financial attitudes and desires of these various parties is crucial to management's effectiveness.

THE ORGANIZATION OF THIS BOOK

This text provides the background and tools required for effective financial management. Of course, topics can be dealt with here only on an introductory level. Additional readings are recommended for those interested in pursuing a topic. Part 1 provides a description of the general environment for individual and company financial decisions. Financial institutions, markets, and securities, as well as basic finance concepts such as the time value of money, risk, and valuation of securities, are introduced here. Part 2 examines the long-term investment and financial structure decisions of the company. The chapters cover the concept of risk and its relationship to capital budgeting and firm financing. Capital budgeting techniques and investment risk evaluation are explained in detail. The characteristics of alternative financing methods and the problem of choosing the appropriate methods are covered. Also included is a discussion of dividend policy and its relationship to a firm's financing policy. Part 3 describes tools of analysis that are particularly useful for evaluating company performance and planning company operations. Part 3 also discusses management of short-term assets and liabilities, and the relevance of short-run planning to long-term financial and marketing strategies. Part 4 describes the process by which the company raises money to finance its operations and its relation to long-term financing sources. The various types of securities issued by a corporation and the rights of the security holder are examined. Part 5 deals with special problems confronting some firms, such as mergers, financial management in multinational business, and bankruptcy.

SUMMARY   The primary objective of shareholders and management is generally maximization of the value of the owners' interest in the company (maximization of the value of the firm's shares). Sometimes, there is conflict between the company policies favored by stockholders, those favored by management, and those favored by society at large. However, differences between stockholders and management are minimized by various factors, including the possibility of the company's takeover by an outside group or the election of a new board of directors which would replace the existing management. These factors tend to encourage management practices which are in harmony with the owners' preferences. Socially oriented company policies are sometimes encouraged by prodding from stockholders but more often by laws (e.g., antipollution statutes). Any such laws are ordinarily viewed by management as constraints within which the company seeks to maximize profits.

The financial manager is a key person in the business organization, frequently rising to the top post in the firm. The finance function includes a wide variety of responsibilities, including budgeting and investing funds, accounting, product pricing, and forecasting.

The field of finance embraces many subareas, including personal finance, financial institutions, and managerial finance. This is a text on managerial finance, that is, on the financial management of business firms. However, we will touch upon other finance areas to the extent that they provide the financial manager with the understanding necessary to perform effectively.

Environmentalism and the Corporation

The past fifteen years of American experience—perhaps more than any other comparable time period—have confirmed the adage that society's only enduring quality is the tendency to change. Although many people still pay only lip service to social problems, a rapidly growing segment of the population, particularly among the post–World War II generation, feels deeply about society's problems. Adam Smith's eighteenth-century concept (which has survived into the twentieth) that economic self-seeking and unbridled competition always serve the social interest has been tempered with the view that there can be areas of conflict between the social good and business policies designed to maximize profit. This realization has led to the enactment of laws which limit corporate discretion in such areas as ecological impact, equal opportunity employment, and consumer protection. The law is likely to impose increasingly broad and well-defined constraints on the choices available to business. Our concern here is the impact of environmental protection laws on the firm's financial planning.

THE PEOPLE VERSUS THE CORPORATION

Pressure on firms to consider the environmental impact of their actions has generally been exercised through legal channels. Individuals or groups can sue for pollution damages or file for injunctive relief against the offending party. Citizens may also sue public officials who are negligent in discharging their duty to enforce antipollution regulations, or they may sue to force officials to reconsider past decisions in the light of newly available information.

In addition to citizens' legal suits, the public can act against polluters through the pollution agencies established under state and federal antipollution statutes. These agencies enforce effluent standards and can impose penalties for violations. The Clean Air Act of 1963 began a federal regulatory effort which was extended by the Air Quality Act of 1967 and by the National Air Quality Standards Act of 1970. The National Environmental Policy Act of 1969 expanded federal concern to other environmental areas; Section 102 of this act requires the filing of environmental impact statements for certain types of projects and has been the basis for many citizen suits against corporations. The Environmental Protection Agency (EPA) was created in 1970 by Executive order and has the power to set and enforce water and air purity standards.

Many states have set their own pollution standards, some of which have been more stringent than those of the EPA. Montana, for example, forced the Anaconda Company to install pollution abatement facilities costing the company $30 million more than would have been necessary to meet the standards of the EPA.

ROLLING WITH THE PUNCHES

The American corporation is a flexible institution and has adjusted, albeit at a cost, to the necessity for environmental protection. Firms have been affected in several ways:

Huge capital outlays for pollution control equipment. For the period 1973–1977, approximately 6 percent of all capital outlays have been for pollution control; this amounts to an annual outlay of between $6 and $8 billion.

Planning and preparation costs. The need to conform with local, state, and federal antipollution requirements has increased project planning and evaluation costs and has lengthened the lead time required by investments because of the frequent need for pollution agency approval. Projects may be challenged in court by governmental agencies or by citizen groups, further delaying or even preventing the project. For example, Delaware's environmental laws blocked Shell Oil Company's $200-million refinery and petrochemical complex.

Increased uncertainty. In addition to pollution control increasing the known costs of a project, new environmental laws present another element of risk to an investment. A classic case is that of the problems of the Alyeska Pipeline Service Company in obtaining approval of the Alaska oil pipeline after substantial outlays had been made by the company. Class action suits by Friends of the Earth, Sierra Club, and other environmental groups delayed the project for over two years until 1973, when court and congressional approval were obtained. The outcome of the suits for Alyeska were increased construction costs because of inflation during the delay period and additional outlays for ecological protection.

THE BENEFICIARIES

Environmental protection is meant to benefit the general public. Some businesses particularly benefit, since the added cost to firms acquiring antipollution equipment is added income for firms that manufacture the equipment. Indeed, an entire industry has arisen to engage in the research, development, production, and marketing of an array of devices to protect the environment from industrial damage. There are five types of pollution control: air, water, thermal, noise, and solid waste—with air by far the major sector. Forty or so firms dominate a pollution control industry comprising several hundred companies of varying size. The market for air pollution equipment alone is expected to reach annual sales of $600 million by 1980, up from $185 million in 1972.

Turning pollutants into "gold" has not been as easy for the pollution control industry as was once supposed. The demand for antipollution products is a reluctant one; firms will invest in the facilities only when forced to do so. Increased domestic and European competition, technological problems, and the easing of some governmental restrictions have meant that the pollution control industry has had to scramble to maintain profitability.

FINANCING POLLUTION CONTROL EXPENDITURES WITH PCRBs

The federal government has allowed companies to use highly accelerated depreciation schedules for pollution control facilities in order to compensate firms forced by the law to install such devices. A more significant subsidy, however, has been the federal income tax exemption allowed on interest paid to holders of pollution control revenue bonds (PCRBs). The buyer of the bonds pays no income tax on the interest and therefore demands a lower pretax yield than would be the case if the bonds were taxable. PCRBs are issued by municipalities, and the proceeds are used to purchase pollution control equipment, which is then sold or leased to local firms. Under the provisions covering PCRBs, if the equipment is purchased by the user firm, and often even if it is only leased, the user is entitled to the depreciation deductions, the investment tax credit (see Chapter 3), and an interest deduction (the firm can charge off interest on the PCRBs) in computing taxable income.

The main attraction of PCRBs is their lower interest cost in raising capital to purchase the antipollution equipment. Since the interest is not taxed, investors are willing to receive a lower interest rate on the bonds. The lower interest cost for the municipality means that the municipality which just seeks to cover its costs will charge the user firm a lower fee for using the facility. The interest savings are sometimes over 2 percent relative to ordinary debenture financing and can mean a huge dollar saving. Among the largest issues made to date was $27 million worth of thirty-two-year bonds issued by Tampa Electric. The bonds had a net interest cost of 5.79 percent annually. Comparable corporate financing would have required a rate of 7.75 percent and would have involved $17 million in extra interest cost over the life of the bonds. Not a trivial benefit!

If the user firm has insufficient income to benefit from the depreciation and other income tax advantages of ownership, a **leveraged lease** arrangement is sometimes used. The municipality issues bonds for perhaps 80 percent of the pollution equipment's cost, and an outside investor puts up the remaining 20 percent, which entitles the investor to the depreciation, tax credit, and interest tax deduction for tax purposes. The user firm leases the equipment from the investor, with the tax benefits passed on to the user in the form of lower lease payments than would be involved if PCRBs were not used to finance the equipment.

OTHER FAVORABLE MEANS OF ACQUISITION

A limited effort has been made by banks to extend low-cost loans for financing pollution control outlays. In 1970, First Philadelphia Bank issued 5 percent ninety-day and $5\frac{3}{4}$ percent two-year "earth bonds," using the proceeds for pollution loans. The idea was that some bond investors would be willing to sacrifice yield if they knew that their funds were being used for a socially beneficial purpose. A number of other banks followed suit by issuing similar bonds or by lending at a lower than usual interest rate for pollution control investment. In general, the success of this approach has been quite limited, both because other pollution financing methods have been more attractive to companies and because bank effort has been less than vigorous.

In the area of water pollution, publically owned effluent treatment facilities are sometimes shared by local companies. Significant economies can be generated by spreading the costs of the waste treatment plant among many users. An illustration is the 1973 arrangement by five industrial firms on the Houston Ship Channel to form the nation's first regional water treatment facility. A state agency created by the Texas legislature, the Gulf Coast Waste Disposal Authority, owns and operates the plant. The companies pay a fee to use the facility and, primarily because of economies of scale, are expected to save 10 to 25 percent on the cost of waste treatment.

THE FUTURE

There is general agreement in most quarters that our air, water, and land should be clean. The meaningful debate centers on degree and equity: How stringent should the environmental quality standards be, and who should pay the price for keeping the environment pure? Stalwart environmentalists favor very strict standards, usually financed out of the corporate purse. Business would prefer lax standards, with the costs of meeting those standards covered by government (taxpayer) subsidies. The sympathies of any given citizen may lie with either of these extreme positions or somewhere in between. It is the in-between that will likely prevail—with a slight tilt, in the long run, toward the environmentalist position of tight standards and business paying the bill. The citizens of this country increasingly view our natural surroundings as the property of the community, to be protected from polluters. This concept holds that business must pay a price or even desist if it is impairing that property. Of course, one could just as logically (although the logic would be less popular) argue that the environment is "owned" by everyone, business included, to be "used up" on a first come, first serve basis. This would imply no liability on the part of polluters, and society would have to pay a firm to stop it from polluting. This latter philosophy has not been widely accepted, although some government assistance has been extended to business (accelerated depreciation and nontaxability of interest on PCRBs). The primary antipollution cost has been, and will probably continue to be, borne by industry and by the consumers of goods made by pollution causing firms (since the added antipollution costs are passed on to the consumer through the price of the product). And the standards will be tough. Environmental protection is not a flash-in-the-pan issue. It has become a permanent concern for society as a whole and for business in particular.

the american financial system: an overview

Before we can examine the role and functions of a financial manager, we must be familiar with our financial system, which provides the background for all business enterprises. This system consists of the institutions and markets which serve companies and individuals in financing the acquisition of goods and services, in investing capital, and in transferring the ownership of securities. A knowledge of our financial system is important not only for financial managers, but for informed citizens as well.

An efficient financial system is essential to a healthy economy. Its primary role is the distribution of capital in the economy. For example, the personal savings of an individual, placed in a bank, can be loaned to another individual to buy a house or to a business firm to build a plant. Thus the activity of the financial system affects every citizen.

Technically advanced nations, such as the United States, the Soviet Union, the European countries, and Japan, have complex and highly developed financial systems. In contrast, most of the nations of Asia and Africa have poorly developed financial systems. There is a clear relationship between the financial sector of a country and the development of its economy.

We will begin our study by outlining the nature of the services provided by the financial system and the institutions providing them. We will then look at the various types of securities which are issued and traded in the financial markets. Finally, we will discuss the factors which determine the general level of interest rates in the economy.

In order to appreciate the nature of the services provided by the financial system, we must understand the general role of the system in the economy. This general role is to aid in transforming the **savings** (income minus expenditures on goods and services in a given time period) of some individuals and companies into **investment** (purchases of physical assets which are used to produce goods and services) by others. *The financial system provides the principal means by which a person who has saved money out of current income can transfer these savings to someone else who has productive investment opportunities and needs money to finance them.*[1] This transfer of money almost always results in the creation of a

SERVICES PROVIDED BY THE FINANCIAL SYSTEM

---

1. The "persons" described in this section can be individuals, business firms, farmers, governmental units, or whatever.

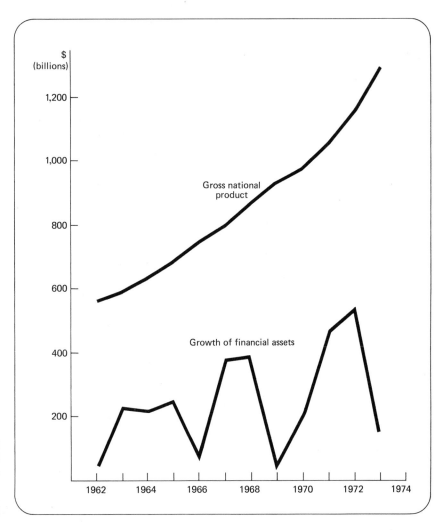

Figure 2-1. Historical trends in gross national product and growth in financial assets. (Source: Federal Reserve Bulletin.)

financial asset, which is a claim against the future income and assets of the person who issued the asset. From the viewpoint of the issuer, this claim is a **financial liability.** Therefore, for every financial asset owned by someone there is a corresponding financial liability for the issuer. Financial assets are the basic "products" of the financial system.

Figure 2-1 shows the annual increases in financial assets for the United States since 1962 compared with the gross national product. Notice the wide variation from year to year. This is due to the sensitivity of financial asset creation to general economic activity.

Types of Financial Assets   Financial assets fall into three general classes: money, debt, and stock. At the present time, money is issued by the federal government as paper currency and coins, by commercial banks as demand deposits (in the form of checking accounts), and by certain other financial institutions.[2] Debt is issued by practically everyone including governments, whereas stock is issued only by business firms. Our emphasis in this chapter will be on the creation of debt and stock because they are issued by individuals and business firms, whereas money is issued only by the federal government and financial institutions and is the medium of exchange for transactions in goods, services, and the other financial assets. Debt and stock are very important in managerial finance. The issuer of debt promises to pay the creditor a specified amount of money at a future date, whereas the issuer of stock is selling ownership of the corporation. A stockholder is entitled to a share of the profits once the claims of the debtholders are satisfied. The precise amount of money to be paid to the owner of stock is not spelled out in advance as it is in the case of debt. Thus the stockholders (owners of stock) of a firm receive income from the firm after its creditors (owners of debt) are paid what is owed them.

There are many different types of debt assets in the financial system. We will examine the major types issued by individuals, governments, and businesses in this chapter. Chapters 15, 17, 19, and 20 will discuss in detail the kinds of debt used by business firms. An important part of financial management is the intelligent use of debt in raising money for the company.

The two basic types of stock are **common stock** and **preferred stock.** Common stock is the security which represents the ownership of corporations. The owners of the common stock of a firm are the owners of the firm. The extent of ownership by any person depends on the number of shares of common stock held by the person relative to the total number of shares outstanding. For example, if the firm has 1,000 shares of common stock outstanding, someone owning 100 shares would own 10 percent of the firm. Preferred stock is much less significant than common stock in terms of the amount outstanding and as a method of financing. The owners of preferred stock are paid dividends before any dividends can be paid to the common stock owners. Many financial managers think of preferred stock as being similar to debt. When we say "stockholders" we always mean the owners of common stock not the owners of preferred stock.

Table 2-1 shows the major types of financial assets in the economy and their owners. These data indicate both the relative magnitudes of the financial assets and their distribution among the various ownership categories. Note the importance of financial institutions as represented by

2. By 1976 mutual savings banks and savings and loan associations in some states had acquired the legal right to issue demand deposits or NOW accounts. NOW stands for "negotiated order of withdrawal" and are essentially interest-bearing demand deposits. Demand deposits could be classified as debt, since they represent money which must be paid by the issuing financial institution on the demand of the owner. However, since checks drawn on demand deposits are widely used as a means of payment, they are usually classified as money.

Table 2-1. Financial assets, Dec. 31, 1973
(Amounts outstanding in billions of dollars)

Asset	Ownership				
	Individuals	Businesses	Financial institutions	Governmental units	Total
Demand deposits and currency	170	55	19	27	271
Time and savings deposits	636	21	1	45	703
Life insurance reserves	150	—	—	—	150
Pension fund reserves	308	—	—	—	308
U.S. government securities	105	5	141	115	366
State and local government securities	50	4	133	2	189
Corporate bonds	54	—	191	—	245
Home mortgages	10	—	343	34	387
Consumer credit	—	32	149	—	181
Other loans and mortgages	34	33	520	40	627
Corporate stock	744	—	199	—	943
Total	2,261	150	1,696	263	4,370

Source: *Federal Reserve Bulletin*.

the first four categories of assets. Except for currency, all these assets are liabilities of financial institutions. Financial institutions are the primary suppliers of credit to the rest of the economy as reflected by their holdings of the debts (mortgages, bonds, consumer credit, and other loans) of individuals, business firms, and governmental units.

The Creation and Transfer of Financial Assets

So far we have said that the general role of the financial system is to serve the saving-investment process of the economy. The basic instruments in this process are the financial assets created when money is transferred from one person to another.

A direct transfer of money occurs when a person who wants to acquire money issues a financial asset (debt or stock) and sells it to someone
who has money available. For example, a person starting a small business
might issue shares of stock to friends and relatives in exchange for
money. He or she might also borrow money from them (issue a debt claim
in exchange for money). The financial asset issued in this process is simply
a piece of paper which indicates the nature of the asset and which meets
legal requirements for establishing the claim (debt or stock) in case dis-
agreements arise between the two parties involved. Financial institutions
such as security **brokers** and **dealers** are often used to facilitate direct
transfers. A broker is in contact with people who have money and wish to
own financial assets.[3] Thus a borrower can approach a broker who will arrange for the actual transfer of money from the investor to the borrower in
exchange for financial assets. A dealer actually purchases the financial
assets of borrowers and then sells them to investors. Brokers simply act
as "go-betweens"; they don't actually own the financial assets but they
charge a commission for their services. Dealers buy and sell financial
assets and their income depends on the difference between the price they
pay for an asset and the price they sell it for.

Sales of financial assets by the issuer, regardless of whether brokers or
dealers are involved, are called **primary market transactions.** In contrast,
most of the activity of brokers and dealers involves financial assets that
have been issued *in the past* and are being sold by someone other than the
person who originally issued them. There are **secondary markets** for existing financial assets just as there is a market for used cars. In these secondary markets people who own the assets are able to sell them to others.
The existence of secondary markets provides advantages to everyone.
For an investor who has funds today there is a greater choice of financial
assets to purchase, since the investor isn't limited to purchasing newly issued ones. Also, someone who purchased the asset in the past can raise
money now by selling it rather than having to wait until the original issuer
pays it off. The secondary markets are of particular importance to the
owners of common stock, since these securities need never be paid off, so
long as the corporation that issued the stock continues in existence.

As noted above, primary markets are those in which financial assets
are originally issued. Since the amount of existing financial assets is much
greater than the amount of new ones being issued, there is a great deal
more activity in the secondary markets.

Indirect methods for transferring money involve the use of a group of
financial institutions called **financial intermediaries.** These include banks
and insurance companies. These institutions purchase the financial liabil-

---

3. These people are often called "investors" since they wish to invest in financial assets. In
   order to distinguish between people who *have* money to invest and people who *need*
   money, we shall refer to people who have money as "investors" and people who need
   money as "borrowers."

ities of firms and individuals; they also borrow by issuing their own financial liabilities, including money, as in the case of commercial bank demand deposits. As a simple example, consider a bank which has loaned money obtained from savers to a person who is buying a house. The new financial assets which have been created here are a home mortgage owned by the bank and savings accounts owned by savers. In a direct transaction there would be only one financial asset—the mortgage owned by savers.[4] There are several advantages to money transfers performed by financial intermediaries.

1. Flexibility and liquidity: The intermediary is able to provide large sums of money to a borrower by pooling the savings of several investors. Moreover, the intermediary can provide investors with financial assets which may be money or readily convertible into money at the same time that it is making loans which will not be repaid for a long time.
2. Diversification: By purchasing the debt issues of many different borrowers, the intermediary is able to increase the chances that most of the money lent will be repaid. Therefore, it is able to provide relatively low-risk assets to investors. The federal government further decreases the risk by insuring against loss accounts in commercial banks, savings and loan associations, and savings banks.
3. Convenience: Intermediaries offer a variety of financial services to their customers besides loaning money and creating financial assets. It is convenient for a single person (individual or business) to deal with a single firm which can supply whatever services are needed.
4. Expertise: The intermediary, because it is continuously purchasing financial assets issued by many borrowers, becomes expert in the process. A single person, whether borrower or investor, is apt to be much less knowledgeable as to exactly what the proper form of the assets should be.

Since the 1920s there has been a general trend toward increasing utilization of financial intermediaries. However, in recent years the trend has been interrupted on several occasions. When investors reduce their holdings of the financial assets issued by financial intermediaries (withdraw money out of a savings account, for example) to purchase the financial assets issued directly by borrowers, the process is called **disintermediation.** It occurs whenever the interest rates on financial assets available in the primary and secondary markets rise enough above the interest rates

---

4. Technically, a mortgage is a pledge of property as collateral for a loan, and the debt instrument (e.g., a note) represents the financial asset. Following common usage, we use the term "mortgage" here to refer to the financial asset backed by the collateral.

paid by financial intermediaries to offset their other advantages. A dramatic example of this was the net flow of funds from savings and loan associations in the summer of 1974.

There is an unfortunate aspect to disintermediation. Small borrowers, both individuals and business firms, are often unable to make direct issues of securities and they rely heavily on financial intermediaries. If financial intermediaries are unable to acquire money to loan, such borrowers are adversely affected. In particular, disintermediation makes it extremely costly and difficult—in some cases impossible—to obtain home mortgages. This, in turn, has a disastrous effect on the housing market.

In response to disintermediation, the intermediaries have issued financial assets (for example, savings certificates) that compete more effectively (pay higher rates) with the direct issues available. In addition, there has been active government intervention, especially to aid individuals who wish to obtain mortgages to buy houses. These recent developments have increased the alternatives available to borrowers and investors and have also increased the complexity of the financial system.

The services provided by the financial system and its component institutions also include various forms of insurance (life, health, fire, etc.), the facilitation of consumer and business transactions through the monetary system, and loans to consumers for purchase of goods and services (as compared with financing investment in productive assets). Now that we have a general idea of the nature of the services provided by the financial system, we will examine some of the financial institutions which play a vital role in that system.

FINANCIAL INSTITUTIONS

The financial system is composed of the financial markets and the financial institutions which, in many respects, create the markets. It is difficult to separate these two aspects of the system; however, we will look first at the financial institutions themselves and then describe the markets and the securities that are bought and sold in them. We will concentrate here on the private financial institutions of most interest to individuals and business firms. However, there are many governmental agencies which play an important role in various parts of the financial system. Table 2-2 indicates the range of governmental activity in financial affairs. Some of these organizations such as the Federal Reserve System are probably familiar. Others, such as the Federal Credit Administration, are too specialized to be of much general importance. The Securities and Exchange Commission and the Small Business Administration are particularly relevant to business firms and will be discussed in Chapter 16. Then there are some that will be mentioned in the discussion of a specific topic but will not be discussed in detail.

Table 2-2. Governmental organizations in the financial system

1. U.S. Treasury
2. Agencies which regulate and supervise the financial system[a]
   a Federal Reserve System
   b Federal Home Loan Bank System
   c Federal Deposit Insurance Corporation
   d Comptroller of the Currency
   e Securities and Exchange Commission
   f State regulatory agencies and supervisors
3. Agencies supporting housing and urban renewal through loan and insurance programs
   a Federal Housing Administration
   b Veterans Administration
   c Federal National Mortgage Association
   d Government National Mortgage Association
   e Federal Home Loan Mortgage Corporation
   f Public Housing Administration
   g Housing and Home Finance Agency
4. Financial agencies supporting agriculture
   a Farm Credit Administration (includes Federal Land Banks, Federal Intermediate Credit Banks, and Banks for Cooperatives)
   b Commodity Credit Corporation
   c Farmers Home Administration
   d Rural Electrification Administration
5. Federal agencies providing loans and insurance to business firms
   a Small Business Administration
   b Export-Import Bank
   c Agency for International Development
6. State and local government retirement funds

[a] Many of these agencies have other major functions; for example, insuring deposits and making loans to financial institutions.

Deposit-Type Financial Institutions

There are four types of financial institutions that accept demand or savings deposits—commercial banks, mutual savings banks, savings and loan associations, and credit unions. They accept the money deposited by individuals, businesses, and governmental units and lend this money to other individuals, businesses, and governmental units.

Commercial banks are by far the largest type of financial institution measured in terms of the amount of financial assets they hold. There were over 14,000 commercial banks in the United States as of the end of 1976. Table 2-3 provides some insight into the diversity of their activities. They hold substantial numbers of securities issued by governmental units, lend heavily to individuals both for purchases of homes and for other needs, and are a major source of credit to business firms (as represented by "other loans and mortgages"). Commercial banks sometimes refer to themselves as "department stores of finance."

Table 2-3. Financial assets held by deposit-type financial institutions

(In billions of dollars)

Assets	Commercial banks		Savings and loan associations		Mutual savings banks		Credit unions	
	1963	1973	1963	1973	1963	1973	1963	1973
Money	21	38	3	3	1	1	1	1
U.S. government securities	68	89	7	23	6	7	—	3
State and local government securities	30	96	—	—	—	1		
Corporate bonds	1	6	—	—	3	13		
Home mortgages	25	68	79	188	25	44	6	20
Consumer credit	27	81	1	3	—	2		
Other loans and mortgages	93	306	12	44	12	30		
Miscellaneous	17	71	6	11	3	10	—	1
Total financial assets	282	755	108	272	50	108	7	25
Annual growth in financial assets, 1963–1973	17%		15%		11%		26%	

Source: *Federal Reserve Bulletin.*

Savings and loan associations and **mutual savings banks** acquire the majority of their funds in the form of savings deposits by individuals. They then lend those funds to finance home purchases. Both make mortgage loans on apartment houses and on some commercial real estate, but primarily they (1) lend to individuals who wish to buy homes and (2) accept the deposits of individuals. Savings and loan associations are found in every state. They are now second only to commercial banks in assets among all financial institutions and have been growing faster than the commercial banks. Mutual savings banks are found in only eighteen states, because they are state-chartered institutions and not all states have laws permitting their establishment.[5] In the Northeast, where they are very active, mutual savings banks have aggressively expanded the financial services provided to individuals.

5. Commercial banks are owned by shareholders just like business firms; however, they may be chartered by the federal government (national banks) or by state governments (state banks). Savings and loan associations may also have federal charters or state charters and they may be owned by shareholders (stock associations) or by their depositors (mutual associations). Almost all federal savings and loan associations are mutual associations. Credit unions may have state or federal charters and are also nonprofit cooperative institutions.

Credit unions are institutions established to provide credit to individuals who share some common bond, such as working for the same firm. While they are a relatively small financial institution, there are many of them throughout the country (over 24,000 at the end of 1976). The members of the credit union provide the funds in the form of savings accounts to lend out to other members who need money. Credit unions usually provide the least expensive consumer credit available.

Insurance Companies

Insurance companies can be divided into two groups—life, and property and casualty. Both play distinctly different roles in the financial system and must be examined separately. To see why this is so, we must understand the nature of insurance.

A basic insurance contract or **policy** involves the payment of a periodic fee or **premium** to the company in exchange for a promise to pay the insured if the peril which is being insured against occurs. For example, if a person insures a house against loss through fire for $30,000 and the house burns down, he or she will collect $30,000 from the insurance company. The insurance company collects premiums from a large number of people to provide funds to pay the small number who actually have losses. Similarly, one can purchase an insurance policy on one's life. If the insured person dies during the period or term for which the policy is in effect, the beneficiaries of the policy collect. The insurance companies can predict fairly accurately the number of people who will die in a given age group. They then can set premiums which will provide enough money to pay off the policies of those who die. All basic insurance policies sold provide the insurance companies with investable funds, since the premiums are paid in advance. However, these funds are relatively temporary. To illustrate, suppose an insurance company collected $1 million in premiums at the beginning of the year on basic insurance policies and sold no more insurance thereafter. By the end of the year, if the losses or deaths were as predicted, the only money left in the insurance company would be the profit on the insurance—perhaps $30,000 or so. The rest of the money would have been paid out in claims to policyholders and in operating expenses.

The distinctive features of most life insurance policies compared with basic insurance is that life insurance policies often *incorporate a savings element*. A portion of the premium paid is set aside just as if it were a savings deposit in a bank. This portion earns interest, and the total accumulates over time as more premiums are paid and interest is added. The total amount saved is called the **cash value** of the policy. Policyholders who wish to cancel their insurance get the cash value paid to them. Moreover, they can borrow the cash value instead of canceling the policy. Although they must pay interest on such borrowing, the interest rate is usually low and is specified in the policy. There are additional financial aspects of life insurance policies, but it is sufficient for our purposes to note that because of the savings element life insurance companies accumulate large amounts of money available for investment. In this activity they perform financial intermediation just like the deposit-type financial institutions. The importance of life insurance companies to the financial system is based more on their ability to accumulate funds for investment than on their stated business of providing insurance.

As one would expect, life insurance companies as a group are much larger in total assets than are property and casualty insurers, which only issue basic insurance. Table 2-4 provides some information on the asset composition and growth of the two types of insurance companies. These data might also be contrasted with those for deposit-type institutions in Table 2-3. Life insurance companies hold large amounts of corporate securities and are a major source of business financing. They invest heavily in mortgages—both home mortgages, which they acquire through mortgage companies (discussed later in this chapter), and mortgages on shopping centers—and in other commercial real estate. About 95 percent of the "other loans and mortgages" category are commercial mortgages.

Table 2-4. Financial assets held by insurance companies
(In billions of dollars)

Asset	Life insurance companies		Property and casualty insurance companies	
	1963	1973	1963	1973
Money	2	2	1	2
United States government securities	6	4	6	3
State and local government securities	4	3	11	30
Corporate bonds	56	92	2	7
Corporate stock	7	26	10	20
Home mortgages	27	22		
Consumer credit[a]	6	23		
Other loans and mortgages	24	59		
Miscellaneous	5	14	2	7
Total financial assets	137	245	32	69
Annual growth in financial assets, 1963–1973	8%		12%	

[a] Policy loans.
Source: *Federal Reserve Bulletin.*

Table 2-5. Financial assets held by other financial institutions

(In billions of dollars)

Asset	State and local government retirement funds		Private pension funds		Mutual funds		Finance companies	
	1963	1973	1963	1973	1963	1973	1963	1973
Money	—	1	1	2	—	1	2	3
United States government securities	7	5	3	4	1	1		
State and local government securites	3	1						
Corporate bonds	13	50	20	30	2	4		
Corporate stock	1	19	28	90	22	38		
Home mortgages	—	—	2	3	—	—	3	12
Consumer credit	—	—	—	—	—	—	20	43
Other loans and mortgages	3	7	—	—	—	2	10	29
Miscellaneous	—	—	2	5	—	—	—	—
Total financial assets	27	83	56	134	25	46	35	87
Annual growth in financial assets, 1963–1973	20%		14%		8%		15%	

Source: *Federal Reserve Bulletin.*

Other Financial Institutions

There is a wide variety of other private financial institutions operating in the financial system. Some of the more important remaining financial institutions and the types of financial assets they hold are shown in Table 2-5. We will briefly discuss each of them in this section.

Pension funds are established to provide income to retired or disabled persons in the economy. The Social Security System and other federal pension funds invest largely in nonmarketable issues of the United States government and do not directly affect the financial system. Pension funds for the employees of state and local governments are significant, as they invest heavily in corporate bonds and stocks and some mortgages. Private pension funds established by business firms are most often managed by the trust departments of commercial banks and to a lesser extent by life insurance companies. As can be seen in Table 2-5, the principal type of financial asset held by private pension funds is corporate stock.

Mutual funds are financial institutions established to invest the money of numerous individuals in securities of various types for the benefit of the individuals. The fund pays a fee to a management company consisting of professionals in the field of investments. These professionals manage the fund's assets, which are derived from selling "shares" to individuals. Mutual fund shares are a financial asset whose value equals the value of the securities and cash owned by the fund. The distinctive feature of mutual funds is that persons owning shares in the fund have a right to sell them back to the fund at their current asset value whenever they wish to do so. The fund is obligated to redeem the shares it issues, and mutual fund shares are not traded in secondary markets. The importance of these institutions in the financial system is that they provide an easy way for individuals to invest in a diversified portfolio of stocks and bonds. They are primarily active in the secondary market for corporate securities.[6]

The assets of mutual funds are invested primarily in corporate stock. However, there are bond funds and so-called "balance funds," which maintain a mixed portfolio of stocks, bonds, and sometimes government securities.

In recent years, a new type of fund has come into being—the "liquid assets" fund—which invests only in the money market instruments (assets) discussed later in this chapter. All told, there are more than 400 mutual funds in the United States, ranging in size from giants such as Massachusetts Investors Trust and Investors Stock Fund with assets of well over $1 billion to minifunds with assets of a few million dollars. Stockbrokers usually classify mutual funds in terms of their investment objectives which, broadly speaking, fall into three basic categories. The so-called "income funds" seek primarily to provide their shareholders with a high level of current income; within certain limits, they are mainly concerned with high, stable dividend yields. The so-called "growth funds" pursue investment policies primarily oriented toward capital appreciation; their objective is to make their shareholders' money grow over the years, and dividend yield (current income) is quite a minor consideration. "Income-and-growth" funds, the third major category, adopt a middle-of-the-road posture. They seek to strike a reasonable compromise between two generally incompatible investment objectives: current income and growth.

Within this general framework, there are literally dozens of specialized funds—funds which concentrate in broad investment areas such as energy or science and technology, funds which specialize in a particular industry (e.g., insurance), funds for investing in foreign securities, and so on. Broadly speaking, the very large funds tend to be conservative. Because of their size, they are more or less compelled to concentrate their investments in the stocks of the large, well-established blue chip corporations which are the backbone of American industry. The smaller funds tend to be more adventurous in the hope of achieving an exceptional profit performance and thereby attracting more shareholders. Many of

6. Mutual funds are a type of investment company. They are sometimes referred to as "open-end" investment companies because they are continuously selling and redeeming their shares. Mutual funds are much larger than other types of investment companies (such as "closed-end" investment companies, which do not redeem their shares) and therefore are the only type covered here.

them did just that—in some cases spectacularly—in the speculative investment climate of the middle and late 1960s. They were known on Wall Street as the "go-go" or "performance" funds, and their top managers became overnight celebrities in the Wall Street firmament—the rock-and-roll superstars of the financial world. But with very few exceptions, the "go-go" funds and the financial "swingers" who ran them took a brutal shellacking in the period from 1969 to 1974, when stock prices *as a whole* suffered a decline of more than 60 percent from the peak levels of 1968. Indeed, the generally unfavorable experience of investors during that five-year period caused considerable disillusionment even with the more staid segments of the mutual fund industry which—many people had naïvely assumed—offered a perfectly "safe" way to participate in the stock market. Nowadays, it is widely recognized that most mutual funds will reflect the fortunes—bad as well as good—of the stock market as a whole. The case made by the proponents of mutual funds is that they probably do better than small or average investors with no expertise could do on their own. As noted earlier, they enable investors with limited amounts of money to obtain (at a rather modest cost) the advantages of professional management and diversification (shares in a large number of companies).

Finance companies raise their money by issuing securities and borrowing from commercial banks. They use their funds to make short- and intermediate-term loans to individuals and business firms. Finance companies can be broken into three types, which are grouped together in Table 2-5. **Sales finance companies** make consumer installment loans, especially for automobiles; the largest sales finance company is General Motors Acceptance Corporation, a subsidiary of General Motors. They also, as a group, lend some money to business firms. **Personal finance companies** make small cash loans to individuals. Most people are aware of their activities from their substantial advertising programs. Household Finance Company and Beneficial Finance Company are personal finance companies. Finally there are companies which might be termed **business finance companies.** These firms make large cash loans to individuals and loans to business firms. Their activities are largely confined to high-risk customers who find it difficult to obtain financing from commercial banks.

There are several other financial institutions which are not represented in Table 2-5. **Personal trust funds** are funds belonging to individuals or the estates of individuals which are being held "in trust" and are managed by someone else. Commercial bank trust departments dominate the personal trust business. The majority of personal trust funds are invested in corporate stock. The amount involved is large. It is estimated that in 1970 personal trusts amounted to approximately $200 billion; however, data comparable to that for the other financial institutions are not available.[7]

---

7. See Federal Reserve Bank of New York, *Monthly Review* (October 1972), for additional information on personal trust funds.

Since 1964 there exist financial institutions called **real estate investment trusts** (REITs) which invest money in real estate and mortgages. REITs are still a relatively small part of the financial system. A number of them got into serious financial trouble in 1974, and it is not clear whether there is a future for this type of financial institution. There are also some specialized financial institutions which are important sources of money for business firms which will be discussed in Chapters 15 and 16.

FINANCIAL MARKETS AND SECURITIES

Financial markets exist wherever a financial transaction occurs. By financial transaction we usually mean the creation or transfer of a financial asset. This contrasts with the exchange of money for real goods or services, which would not be categorized as a financial transaction. By our definition of financial markets, a person who transfers funds from a checking account to a savings account is operating in the financial markets just as if he or she were buying savings bonds, common stock, or any other financial asset. From this example we can see that the financial markets are pervasive throughout the economy. Indeed, if you include purchases of goods on credit, virtually everyone in the country is active in them.

We can classify the financial markets in several ways. Most often classification is based on the nature of the financial assets being traded. Just as we can speak of the automobile market, we can speak of the savings market or the corporate bond market. We will divide the financial markets into two general classes—money markets and capital markets. *Money markets deal in short-term debts whereas capital markets deal in long-term debts and stocks.* The only markets we will examine are those which are national in scope. The stock market is a national market. It is very easy for a miner in Butte, Montana, to purchase General Motors stock which was previously owned by a seventy-two-year-old woman currently residing in Fort Myers, Florida. The basic transaction might take place within five minutes after the miner placed an order to buy and the woman placed her order to sell the stock, although the paperwork would take several days to complete.

In contrast to the stock market, the markets for savings accounts are primarily local ones, despite attempts by some financial institutions (especially in California) to attract depositors across the country. For individuals and small firms, local financial markets can be quite important; however, medium-sized and large firms are more concerned with the money and capital markets presented here.

The Money Market

Knowledge of the operations of the money market is a measure of sophistication in the financial world. The securities traded are among the most esoteric of financial assets: federal funds, commercial paper, Treasury bills, banker's acceptances, certificates of deposit, and other short-term debt instruments. To be considered a money market security, a financial asset must have little or no risk of loss to the purchaser. The money market is centered in New York but operates through a national network of commercial banks and securities dealers. It serves as the basic glue that holds the financial system together because it is the part of the financial system which acts most directly in preventing appreciable differences in local and regional interest rates. The existence of the money market, more than any other single aspect of the financial system, makes it possible to speak of a general level of interest rates which applies to the economy as a whole. In order to understand this, let us examine the financial assets which are issued and traded in the market.

Federal funds   Commercial banks which are members of the Federal Reserve System (77 percent of the bank deposits in the country are held by member banks) hold most of their required reserves on deposit in the Federal Reserve Banks. A bank can write checks drawn on its deposits with the Federal Reserve just as individuals and firms write checks against deposits at their banks. The unique thing about bank deposits at the Federal Reserve is that they can be transferred from one bank to another almost instantaneously by wire. This means that a bank in Portland, Oregon, can transfer $1 million of its deposits at the Federal Reserve to a bank in New York at 1 P.M. Eastern Standard Time on January 5 and the bank in New York will have the funds available at 1:15 P.M. Federal funds are simply these deposits which can be "bought" and "sold" in the money market. A "sale" of federal funds is a *loan* by one bank to another. The loan is for one day only or over the weekend. The total volume of such loans can exceed $20 billion per day, and the basic trading unit is $1 million.

The interest rate on federal funds is one of the most volatile interest rates in the economy. Since the rates are for one day only, they reflect daily, even hourly, changes in the financial markets. Remember that most transactions in the economy for goods and services as well as for financial assets involve the use of checks drawn on demand deposits in commercial banks. As funds are withdrawn and deposited throughout the economy, some banks accumulate more deposits with the Federal Reserve than they need to cover their reserve requirements. Other banks have shortages. Federal funds provide a mechanism for banks with excess reserves to provide them to banks with shortages. Therefore, the demand and supply of federal funds depends on transactions throughout the economy and is sensitive to all kinds of changes in the financial system. Also, the Federal Reserve itself operates in the money markets as a means of implementing monetary policy by buying and selling United States government securities. The actions of the Federal Reserve have appreciable impact on the federal funds market, because a purchase of securities by the Federal Reserve is paid for by increasing the reserve accounts of member banks, and a sale results in a decrease in those deposits. The Federal Reserve uses the interest rate on federal funds as an index of the impact of its activities in the money markets.

Treasury bills Every Monday at 1:30 P.M. (New York time), the U.S. Treasury closes the bidding on its weekly 91-day and 182-day debt issues. Later in the afternoon the successful bidders, primarily financial institutions, will be told how much of some several billions of dollars in bills being sold they have just bought. Payment is due and the actual bills will be delivered on Thursday. Once a month a similar process will occur for nine- and twelve-month bills. The United States government is continuously borrowing money to pay for expenditures in excess of tax receipts and to pay off maturing debt issues. Treasury bills are short-term (less than one year) debts of the federal government of the United States. The **par value** or **face value** of a bill is the amount of money that will be paid to the purchaser when the bill is due. The interest return to an investor is provided by the difference between the par value of the bills and the price the investor pays for them. This difference is called the **discount** on the bill. For example, a bill might initially be sold by the Treasury for $950 to be redeemed for its par value of $1,000 a year later. The original purchaser would earn $50 on an investment of $950 if he or she held it for a year. There is an active secondary market in bills, and the investor can also sell the bill before it matures. Of course, the investor who does this will receive the current market price of the bill, which will be less than the par value of $1,000.

U.S. Treasury bills are the most popular of the money market securities in terms of total volume outstanding and also in terms of their use by many different types of investors, because they are backed by the United States government and they have short maturities. The minimum unit of purchase is $10,000, which puts bills within the reach of many individual investors and most business firms.

Banker's acceptances Banker's acceptances are the oldest form of money market paper. Their equivalent was first used in the Roman Empire, and during the Renaissance the banking houses in Italy brought them to a high stage of development. A banker's acceptance (or just acceptance) is a short-term debt issued by a business firm on which a large commercial bank has guaranteed payment to the investor. In other words, a bank has backed the debt with its own credit standing. The purchaser of an acceptance does not have to worry about the risk of the borrower but only whether the bank is strong.

These securities vary in face value depending on the size of the underlying commercial transaction. They are sold at a discount from face value similar to Treasury bills. Acceptances are usually created as the result of a sale of goods from one business firm to another when the goods will be in transit for a few months as is typical in international trade, and they arise primarily from import and export activity.

Commercial paper   Commercial paper is a short-term debt (usually three to six months maturity) of a business firm or financial institution which has been sold in the market. It is also issued at a discount from face value. This type of financing instrument is discussed in more depth in Chapter 15. As for its place in the money market, we will only point out that commercial paper is a debt issued by a private firm and that private firms (both financial and nonfinancial) have been known to fail. In 1970, Penn Central had $82 million of commercial paper outstanding when it filed for bankruptcy. Since that experience, investors have been more cautious about purchasing commercial paper, and interest rates on commercial paper have stayed well above the rates on Treasury bills.

CDs and other money market securities   Since 1961, commercial banks have been issuing negotiable certificates of deposit (CDs) to corporations. These securities are interest-bearing deposits at the bank which issued them and have a minimum size of $100,000. They have fixed maturities, normally under one year, and they pay interest at maturity. They cannot be withdrawn from the bank prior to their maturity date. The owners of the certificates can sell them in the money market prior to maturity, and there is an active secondary market for them. During times of tight money when banks are aggressively seeking money for loans, CD rates can get quite high. Three-month CDs were paying a rate of 12 percent per year in the fall of 1974.

In addition to the securities discussed so far, there is another set of securities which are part of the money market—the maturing bonds of governmental units and corporations. A bond issued in 1946 which matures on December 31, 1976, was at the time of issue a long-term debt with a thirty-year maturity. However, on January 1, 1976, it was due in one year and thus in the money market. The distinction between the bond market and the money market is somewhat arbitrary. The two markets merge for low-risk debt issues with maturities somewhere between one and three years. Also there are debt securities issued by state and local governments which have original maturities of less than one year. The United States government issues notes with maturities ranging from one to ten years, and corporations sometimes issue notes with maturities of three to ten years. Consequently, there is no way to draw a firm line which distinguishes the bond market from the money market; they blend together and strongly influence each other.

The capital markets consist of the markets in which the intermediate- and long-term securities of individuals, business firms, and governmental units are issued and traded. They are frequently subdivided into three parts—the bond market, the mortgage market, and the stock market. There are some fairly important differences among them. We will describe briefly each of the three components, focusing on obligations of individuals and governmental units.

The Capital Markets

Issuing capital market securities Before examining the capital markets in detail, it is useful to consider the procedures by which money is raised in the primary markets. There are four general methods of issuing debt and stock. One way is direct in the sense discussed earlier: the firm, individual, or governmental unit goes to someone else, usually a financial institution, and borrows the money or sells stock. More money is raised directly than by all other methods combined, and this is the only way individuals can borrow. A second way is the **auction approach** used by the U.S. Treasury described earlier in the discussion of Treasury bills. The Treasury invites bids by investors, who submit both the prices and amounts they wish to acquire. The Treasury then accepts as many bids as it needs to raise the amount of money required, taking the highest bids first.[8] The Treasury is the only user of this method in the United States to our knowledge. A third method used heavily by state and local governments, and to some extent by business firms (primarily gas, electric, and telephone companies) is **underwriting through competitive bids.** The borrower announces that it wishes to issue, say, $20 million in bonds to mature in twenty-five years. A single financial institution or a group of financial institutions (called a **syndicate**) can submit a bid for the entire issue. The bidder with the lowest interest cost to the issuer wins the entire issue and will then try to sell it in smaller portions to investors. The aspect that makes this procedure ''underwriting'' is that the winner is buying the issue to sell to someone else rather than lending the money directly. Commercial banks cannot legally bid on corporate issues; but they are able to do so on state and local government debt and tend to dominate the market in those securities. Financial institutions whose primary business is underwriting are called **investment bankers.** The fourth method, negotiated underwriting, is normally used only by business firms, and both bonds and stock are issued by this method. It will be discussed extensively in Chapter 16 in conjunction with the activities of investment bankers.

---

8. Bids are on the basis of price rather than interest rate since there is no interest payment on bills, and notes and bonds are issued with fixed coupon rates (refer to the next section for a definition).

The bond market   Bonds are debts of federal, state, and local governmental units and large corporations. They normally are issued in units of $1,000 maturity or par value and have a fixed-interest payment made semiannually. The total annual interest is expressed as a percentage of the maturity value and is called the **coupon rate.** For example, a 7 percent coupon bond would pay $70 (0.07 × 1,000) per year in two semiannual installments of $35 each until maturity, when the bond is to be redeemed for $1,000.

While the money market is fundamentally centered in New York City, the bond market is somewhat more widespread. The issues of state and local governments in particular are traded throughout the country as are, to a lesser extent, the bonds issued by business firms. However, the focus of activity in these obligations is still New York, as it is for the issues of the federal government.

Governments and agencies   In the language of the bond market, there are two groups of federal securities—"governments" and "agencies." "Governments" are notes and bonds issued by the U.S. Treasury and guaranteed by the federal government. They are considered to be the safest long-term debt securities available. The distinction between a note and a bond is maturity. Notes have original maturities of up to 10 years, and bonds have original maturities of over 10 years. Also, notes are usually issued in units of $5,000, whereas bonds usually have $1,000 as the minimum unit. At the present time Congress has limited the interest rate that can be paid on bonds to $4\frac{1}{4}$ percent. Notes can be issued at higher rates. Since interest rates on long-term bonds generally have been much higher than $4\frac{1}{4}$ percent for the past several years, the Treasury (with a couple of special exceptions) has been forced to issue notes rather than bonds. A major portion of the bonds outstanding in 1976 were issued prior to 1965.

"Agencies" are securities issued by various federal agencies which have been established by the federal government to issue their own debt securities and use the money for a variety of purposes. The major issuers are the Federal National Mortgage Association, Federal Home Loan Banks, and Federal Land Banks. The bonds issued by these federal agencies have become an important part of the bond market in recent years. The major organizations and their bonds are listed in the *Federal Reserve Bulletin*. Generally the interest rates on these securities are slightly higher than comparable rates for government bonds.

Municipal bonds   People who deal in the bond market refer to the debt issues of state and local governmental units as **municipal bonds** or "munis." The major distinguishing feature of these securities compared with all other securities in the financial markets is that the interest paid to investors is not taxed by the federal government. Since the interest is exempt from federal income taxes, these bonds are also referred to as **tax-exempt bonds.** This tax-exempt feature means that most state and local governments are able to issue bonds at lower interest costs than the federal government since investors gain from the lack of taxation.

There are several types of municipal bonds. The most common are the **general obligation bonds** issued by a town, city, county, or state. These bonds are backed by the taxing power of the governmental unit involved and therefore can be considered a debt of everyone who lives in that area. Another type is **revenue bonds.** These bonds are to be paid off from the revenues derived from a specific public project. For example, roads and bridges may be financed with revenue bonds to be repaid with tolls. Dormitories and student centers at state colleges and universities are also frequently financed with revenue bonds, and student fees are used to pay them. There is a third type, **industrial development bonds,** which is of interest to business firms. These bonds are issued to build plants to attract new industry to an area. A business firm rents the plant, and the rental payments are used to repay the bonds. In effect, the local government is using the tax-exempt feature of the bonds as a way to provide cheap financing to a business firm. Because so many people benefit from the tax-exempt feature of municipal bonds, this ''tax loophole'' stays open. Of course the general taxpayer foots the bill since taxes are not collected on the bond interest.

Corporate bonds   Business firms issue many types of debt; however, only large firms issue bonds. Smaller firms deal directly with lenders such as banks and insurance companies. If you look back at Table 2-1, the dollar amount of bonds outstanding is much less ($245 billion versus $627 billion) than the amount of ''other loans and mortgages.'' These ''other'' loans are primarily the debts of business firms, large and small, borrowed directly from financial institutions. Bonds generally have longer-term maturities than direct loans, in some cases 100 years, and are usually issued to pay for capital expenditures such as new plant and equipment. The many different types of corporate bonds are described in Chapters 19 and 20.

The mortgage market   Although local primary mortgage markets have existed for a long time, an appreciable national secondary market for the mortgages on individual residences has developed only within the last few years. The federal government established three major organizations to purchase mortgages from the financial institutions that originally made the loans. The three organizations are the Federal National Mortgage Association (''Fannie Mae''), which is now a semiprivate corporation; the Government National Mortgage Association (''Ginnie Mae''); and the Federal Home Loan Mortgage Corporation (''Freddy Mac''). A national market for mortgages provides several benefits; among these are the reduction of regional differences in mortgage rates and the increased availability of mortgage financing even in periods of tight money.

Most mortgages today are paid off in equal monthly (residential mortgages) or quarterly (commercial mortgages) installments over the life of the debt, which may extend to thirty or forty years. The interest rate on residential mortgages is usually somewhat higher than the rate on low-risk corporate bonds. A specialized type of financial institution, the **mortgage company,** operates in this market, as do commercial banks, savings and loan associations, and mutual savings banks. Mortgage companies are different from the other financial institutions in that they normally do not own the mortgages they originate but rather sell them in blocks to large investors such as life insurance companies and pension funds. The mortgage company collects the monthly payments and forwards them to the ultimate owner of the mortgage. Mortgage companies, therefore, act as the investment bankers of the mortgage market.

Despite the increased trend toward a national mortgage market, some regional differences in mortgage rates persist. Interest rates in the South and West tend to be somewhat higher than in the Northeast and Midwest. Presumably the continued development of the mortgage market will eventually eliminate most of the differences in rates.

The stock market   When the stock market is mentioned, most people think of the New York and the American Stock Exchanges. As of mid-1975, the stocks of 1,555 companies with a total market value of $634 billion were listed on the New York Stock Exchange, "The Big Board." An additional 1,220 companies whose stock had a total market value of $34 billion were listed on the "Amex." These two stock exchanges plus ten regional stock exchanges and the over-the-counter market constitute the secondary markets for the stock issues of private corporations. The primary market for corporate stock is not nearly so active as the secondary markets mentioned above. In the primary market, investment banking firms underwrite the stock issues of corporations and sell them throughout the country to individuals and institutional investors. These distributions of securities, which are critical to the financing of business firms, are discussed later, as are the securities themselves. Here we shall focus on the nature of the secondary market in corporate stock.

The organized stock exchanges are themselves only a way to bring buyers and sellers together via their representatives, the brokerage firms. Stock brokers are the financial institutions which buy and sell securities at the orders of their customers. Most large brokers are members of the stock exchanges and have representatives of their firm on the "floors" of the exchanges to make purchases and sales. However, the stock issues of several thousand smaller firms do not meet the criteria required for a listing on the New York Stock Exchange or the somewhat less demanding requirements of the other exchanges. A network of brokers and dealers has evolved to undertake transactions in unlisted stocks. This is the **over-the-counter** market. (It should be noted that some large companies which do qualify for listing on the stock exchanges have chosen to remain in the over-the-counter market.)

Trading in the stock issues of companies listed on the stock exchanges is not confined to the exchanges. There is a **third market** of dealers who buy and sell large blocks of stock. In 1974, $7 billion worth of stocks listed on the New York Stock Exchange were traded in the third market, while total volume on the NYSE amounted to $99 billion. The customers in the third market are primarily financial institutions such as banks, insurance companies, and mutual funds. Indeed, about two-thirds of the trading in the stock market overall (exchanges, over-the-counter, and third market) is due to the activities of mutual funds, pension funds, insurance companies, and other financial institutions. Thus, in the last decade, financial institutions have become the dominant force in the stock market. This is so despite the fact that over 75 percent of outstanding stock issues are owned directly by individuals.

Now that we have looked at the structure of the financial system, let us examine the basic prices in the system—interest rates.

INTEREST RATES

Interest rates are the *prices* of credit. They are usually measured as an annual percentage rate of the amount borrowed; for example, 6 percent per year is $6 interest per year per $100 borrowed. Interest rates also are the earning rates on financial assets. One person's liability is another person's asset. Therefore, interest rates as prices of credit are equivalent to interest rates as earning rates—it just depends on whether you are borrowing or lending.

Different types of financial assets will have different interest rates. However, all interest rates usually vary together over time. This means that we can speak of "high" or "low" interest rates without having to be specific about the interest rate of a particular financial asset. For example, if interest rates are "high" on corporate bonds, they will usually also be "high" on home mortgages, state and local bonds, etc. On the other hand, interest rates on a particular asset, such as U.S. Treasury bonds, can be used as an indicator for other interest rates. In the 1950s, when U.S. Treasury bonds paid 3 percent interest, the interest rates on home mortgages were about 5 percent. In 1975, when interest rates on Treasury bonds were about 7 percent, interest rates on home mortgages were about 9 percent. The general level and variation of interest rates over the past fifty years is illustrated in Figure 2-2. Even though corporate

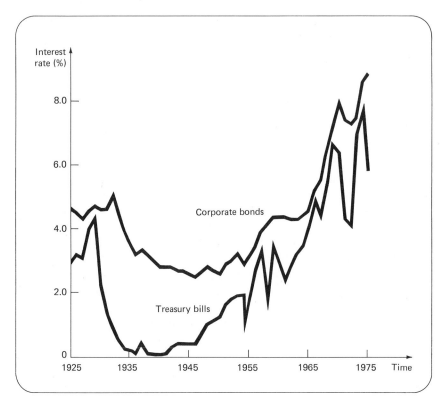

Figure 2-2. General changes in interest rates. (Sources: Economic Report of the President; Federal Reserve Bulletin.)

bonds differ greatly from Treasury bills, the interest rates on these two financial assets do show similar general trends.

What causes interest rates to change over time? There are several theories that seek to explain this phenomenon. The most popular one, which is most often used by financial managers, is based on fluctuations in the supply of and demand for loanable funds. In addition, the prospects for changes in the general level of prices for goods and services, inflation or deflation, will affect the level of interest rates.

Loanable Funds   Loanable funds are the dollars available for purchases of new financial assets in the current period. Loanable funds, like any other commodity, are subject to the laws of supply and demand. Thus, if large amounts of dollars are available for investment, the interest rate will be low, just as the price of oranges decreases when there is a bumper crop.

The **supply** of loanable funds comes primarily from savings, that is, current income less current expenses. In addition, the supply of loanable funds can be altered by the banking system, which can create money by expanding demand deposits. Increases in the money supply are limited, however, by the actions of the Federal Reserve Board. In any case, the total supply of loanable funds consists of the savings of individuals and business firms in the economy plus any increases in the money supply provided by the banking system and the Federal Reserve.[9]

The **demand** for loanable funds comes primarily from those persons who wish to borrow money to finance investment. They may include business firms that want to expand their operations or increase their productivity through modernization; federal, state, and local governments that usually spend more than they take in from taxes and must borrow funds to make up the deficit; and individuals who require funds for the purchase of houses or other durable goods. In addition, firms and individuals may wish to increase their holdings of money relative to other financial assets. This also is part of the demand for loanable funds.

As you might expect, an increase in the demand for loanable funds without a corresponding increase in the supply causes interest rates to rise until supply and demand are in balance. The general level of interest rates at any time is primarily determined by individuals' desires for current expenditures relative to their income (which determines savings) and the amount of investment opportunities available.

Inflation

The expectation of future inflation may alter the level of interest rates by changing the supply of and demand for loanable funds. If people expect prices to rise in the future, there is an incentive to purchase goods and services now rather than later (at higher prices). This has the effect of reducing savings and increasing investment in productive assets.

People owning existing financial assets sell them to get money to purchase physical assets, thereby pushing down the prices of financial assets and pushing up the rates of return (interest rates) paid on financial assets. Lenders require higher interest rates because the dollars they will receive in the future in repayment of the debt will have less purchasing power due to the inflation. The result is that interest rates are higher when people expect high rates of inflation than when people expect low rates of inflation.

SUMMARY

The primary role of the financial system is to facilitate savings and investment in the economy. Financial assets (and corresponding liabilities) are the basic products of the system. There are three general classes of finan-

9. The federal government can increase the money supply by printing more currency. The Federal Reserve does it by increasing the reserves of commercial banks on deposit with the Federal Reserve.

cial assets—money, debt, and stock. Each of these classes may be subdivided into several types. Money consists of currency and demand deposits, and stock consists of preferred stock and common stock. There are many different types of debt categorized by the issuer (individuals, businesses, governmental units, or financial institutions) and by the nature of the debt contract (loans, mortgages, bonds, etc.).

New financial assets are created in the primary markets. Money or goods are exchanged for a financial asset. Savers may deal directly with those persons needing money for the purchase of goods and services or indirectly through financial intermediaries.

Financial intermediaries create financial assets desired by savers, and they lend money to those who need it. The major financial intermediaries are the commercial banks, savings and loan associations, mutual savings banks, life insurance companies, and credit unions.

Many of the financial transactions in the economy do not involve the creation of financial assets. Instead, existing financial assets are purchased and sold in the secondary markets. In practice, little distinction is made between primary and secondary markets, and financial markets are most often described by the types of assets issued or traded in them. The money markets and capital markets are national in scope in contrast to the markets for savings, consumer installment loans, etc., which are local.

Short-term debt securities of business firms, governmental units, and financial institutions are issued and traded in the money markets. Money market financial assets include federal funds, Treasury bills, banker's acceptances, corporate CDs, and commercial paper. The money market serves an important role in eliminating regional differences in interest rates.

The capital market is often divided into the bond market, the mortgage market, and the stock market. The long-term debt issues of governmental units and business firms are traded in the bond market. Mortgages on residential property owned by individuals are the principal security traded in the mortgage market. The stock market is almost completely a secondary market where previously issued shares of stock in business firms are traded. In recent years the stock market has come to be largely dominated by financial institutions investing the money provided to them by individuals or investing in the behalf of these individuals.

Interest rates are the prices of credit. They differ according to the type of financial asset, and they vary over time. The general level of interest rates changes due to changes in the supply of and demand for loanable funds. Changes in expectations regarding the rate of inflation are an important factor in causing interest rates to change.

The financial system is a network of institutions and markets with pervasive effects throughout the economy. The total number of financial institutions is very large, and no single institution or even type of institution dominates. The highly developed financial system of the United States is a major contributor to the economic health of the nation.

1. What is a financial asset? How are financial assets created and transferred?

2. Explain the differences between money, debt, and stock. How does preferred stock differ from common stock?

3. If you obtain a student loan, is this a primary or a secondary market transaction? Explain.

4. Sandra L. withdraws $1,000 from her savings account at a bank paying 5 percent per year interest and uses the money to buy a United States government bond which will provide 7 percent per year interest. What is the word used to describe Sandra's actions? Is she doing something that is wrong?

5. The United States government issued a bond with a $6\frac{3}{4}$ percent coupon rate that matures in 1993. How much interest would you receive every six months if you bought five of these bonds which have a maturity value of $1,000 each?

6. On Wednesday, August 20, 1975, the *Wall Street Journal* reported the following quotations (New York Exchange):

Bonds	Current yield	Vol	High	Low	Close	Net Chg
Du Pont 8s81	8	76	$99\frac{1}{8}$	$98\frac{7}{8}$	99	—

1975 High	Low	Stocks	Div	P-E ratio	Sales 100s	High	Low	Close	Net chg.
$133\frac{1}{2}$	$87\frac{1}{8}$	Du Pont	5.25c	30	296	$121\frac{1}{2}$	$119\frac{3}{4}$	$119\frac{7}{8}$	$-1\frac{1}{4}$

What do these figures mean? (See Appendix A, page 751, for help with this question.)

7. Distinguish between brokers and dealers. In which type of secondary market would you expect to find each?

8. Distinguish between money markets and capital markets. What types of assets are traded in each?

9. At the time of this writing there were four "stock markets." Three are mentioned in the text. The "fourth market" involves the direct sale of stock from one institutional investor to another.
   a) Why do you suppose the third and fourth markets, which are relatively recent phenomena, developed?

b) In which market are the following transactions probably taking place?

  i. Sam Jones buys 100 shares of AT&T stock through his local stockbroker.

  ii. Ponderous National Bank's trust department buys 100,000 shares of AT&T stock from GoGo Mutual Fund.

  iii. GoGo Mutual Fund buys 20,000 shares of IBM stock through a broker who is not a member of the New York Stock Exchange.

  iv. Sam Jones buys 100 shares of Speedy Inc. stock through his stockbroker. Speedy is a local department store, "home owned and operated."

10. Why is there a difference between the interest rates on corporate Aaa bonds and U.S. Treasury bills shown in Figure 2-2?

11. "During periods of inflation it is better to be a borrower than a lender." Discuss.

PROJECT   Collect the most recent twelve weekly values for interest rates on federal funds, ninety-day Treasury bills, the $7\frac{7}{8}$ percent Treasury notes due in 1982, and the $8\frac{1}{4}$ percent Treasury bonds due in 2000–2005, using Tuesday's *Wall Street Journal* as a source. Plot the values on a graph (rate versus date). What conclusions can you draw? Why are the rates changing? (For the interest rate on the notes and bonds use the values reported as "yield.")

Benjamin Franklin once wrote, "In this world nothing is certain but death and taxes." By choosing a suitable form of organization, a business firm can outlive its original owners; however, even these firms cannot escape taxes. Taxes are an important consideration in the financial problems faced by individuals and businesses, and a general knowledge of taxation in the United States is necessary before we can discuss the problems of financial management. The form of business organization— proprietorship, partnership, or corporation—affects the taxes paid on the earnings of the business, and, therefore, the tax structure influences the choice among the alternative organizational forms. This choice is primarily a problem for owners of small businesses; as we shall see, there are sound reasons for large firms to be incorporated. Since the topics of taxes and business organization are closely related, we will discuss them both in this chapter.

First, let us look briefly at the overall tax structure in the United States and the role of taxes in government finance.[1] Given this general background on taxes, we then describe the various forms of business organization and discuss the factors to be considered by owners of a business in choosing among them. In the remainder of the chapter, we discuss more fully the federal income tax and its impact on personal and business financial decisions.

TAXES AND GOVERNMENT FINANCE

Federal, state, and local governments must raise money to pay for their expenses and programs. Of all the methods available—including borrowing, selling goods and services (garbage disposal, electricity, water, liquor, timber, mineral rights, etc.), license fees (motor vehicles, hunting, establishing various types of businesses, etc.), printing money (federal government only), and selling land—the levying of taxes provides the largest revenue. Taxes on expenditures (sales taxes), taxes on income, and taxes on property are the three basic types. They are used by all

1. Governmental units have their own financial problems. Although we do not treat these problems in this book, some of the general principles discussed are used in government finance. For example, the analysis of government investment decisions is comparable in many respects to the analysis of business investment decisions. See chaps. 7 and 8 in *Public Finance in Theory and Practice* by R. A. Musgrave and P. B. Musgrave (New York: McGraw-Hill, 2d ed., 1976).

levels of government, although the importance of each may differ. For example, local governments rely on property taxes as their largest single source of revenue. The majority of state governments use sales taxes as their major revenue source (though some states still do not have sales taxes). There has been an increase in the number of states using income taxes; in New York, the state income tax actually provides more revenue than the sales tax. Generally, however, the income tax is a federal tax. Indeed, the federal tax on individual and business incomes accounts for over 40 percent of all taxes paid in the United States. The money raised from this one tax is greater than the *total* taxes (property, sales, and income) received by state and local governments.

The Federal Income Tax

Taxation of the incomes of individuals and businesses by the federal government was not permitted under the U.S. Constitution until passage of the Sixteenth Amendment in 1913, which specifically provides for a federal income tax. Congress enacts the laws which specify how the tax is to be determined, and a federal agency, the Internal Revenue Service (IRS) administers them. The IRS collects taxes and issues regulations implementing and interpreting laws passed by Congress. There is a special court, the Tax Court, in which taxpayers may contest the rules and decisions of the IRS. This system has one primary purpose—to make sure that those taxes that are owed the federal government are assessed fairly and are collected.

The income tax is determined as a percentage of **taxable income,** which is defined as total or gross income less exemptions and deductions. The tax laws define a concept of gross income, which for an individual is primarily wages, salaries, dividends, and interest from securities and savings accounts. For a business firm, gross income is primarily the revenues from selling goods and services plus interest on securities owned. Both individuals and firms are permitted various deductions from gross income. For individuals these deductions may be either a set amount based on gross income (standard deduction) or itemized deductions such as interest payments, sales and property taxes, and contributions to charities. The choice between taking the standard deduction or itemizing deductions is at the option of the individual. Businesses deduct the expenses of doing business—wages, salaries, costs of purchased goods, interest, and so forth. Individuals are permitted an exemption ($750) for each person in the family, and additional ones if they are blind or aged. The tax owed to the government is calculated as a percentage of taxable income. Since the percentage depends on the amount of taxable income, the actual computation is usually based on formulas supplied by the IRS. The complicated aspects of the tax are in the determination of what items are included in gross income, the special treatment accorded some types of income such as dividends and capital gains, and the identification of deductions. One aspect of financial management is to avoid paying any taxes that the firm is not legally required to pay, which means that all legitimate deductible expenses must be identified.

The determinants of taxable income and the percentages that apply to different types of income have important consequences for personal and business financial decisions. These issues will be discussed in more depth after we look at the forms of business organization.

The three principal types of business organization are proprietorships, partnerships, and corporations. A proprietorship is a business owned by one person, a partnership is owned by two or more people but rarely more than ten, and a corporation may be owned by any number of people from one to several million. Corporations differ from partnerships and proprietorships in that the firm itself is a legal ''person'' apart from its owners. In a proprietorship or partnership the owners are the business. This distinction is important, as we will see as we look at each of the three types.

BUSINESS ORGANIZATION

Most businesses are owned by one person and are proprietorships. A proprietorship can be established simply by beginning to sell a product or perform some service. Except for the licensing required of many businesses, proprietorships are very easy to establish and are subject to very little government regulation. The owner is responsible personally for any debts incurred in business activity as well as personally. The income of the business, less expenses, is part of the personal income of the owner and is taxed accordingly. Any profits are the owner's alone to keep and use as he or she sees fit.

In a partnership two or more people are the owners. They must agree on how much time and money will be contributed by each one to the business and how the profits are to be divided. Partnerships also are not regulated to any great extent by the government and are very easy to establish. In a **general partnership** each partner is responsible for debts incurred by the business; however, profits of the business and the ownership of its assets may be divided in any way agreed on by the partners. Usually there is a formal written agreement specifying the arrangement. The income of the partners after deduction of business expenses is taxed as personal income to each partner. Doctors, lawyers, accountants, and other professional people frequently form partnerships.

Another type of partnership called a **limited partnership** is permitted in many states. In a limited partnership there must be at least one person who is a general partner. This individual would be held personally liable for any debts incurred by the business. The limited partners usually contribute money to invest in some venture, such as oil wells or real estate.

Table 3-1. Business organizations, 1970

Type	Number (thousands)	Percent	Revenues (billions)	Percent
Proprietorships	9,400	78	$ .238	12
Partnerships	936	8	90	5
Corporations	1,665	14	1,621	83
Total	12,001	100	$1,949	100

Source: Internal Revenue Service, Statistics of Income 1970, *Business Income Tax Returns.*

They share in the profits but cannot lose any more money than they have invested.

Proprietorships and partnerships share a common problem. If one of the partners or the proprietor dies or becomes incapacitated, the business itself is threatened. Most partnership agreements have special provisions for the purchase of the ownership interest of a partner who cannot continue in the business. In a proprietorship a member of the family must take it over, or the business must be sold or discontinued.

Corporations are the most important form of business organization in the United States because of their large assets and income. Table 3-1 shows the distribution of the three basic types of business organization. Although only 14 percent of all businesses are corporations, they account for 83 percent of the total revenues of firms. Corporations are established by obtaining a charter from a state, usually the state where the primary operations of the business are located. Large firms often choose to be chartered in Delaware because its charter provisions are more flexible than those of most other states. The corporation can own assets, borrow money, and perform business functions without directly involving its owners, who are also called **shareholders** or **stockholders.** The stockholder's ownership interest in the corporation is determined by the shares of common stock he or she holds. Corporations are taxed differently than other types of businesses, and the owners are not responsible for the debts incurred by the corporation. The corporation is a legal method of permitting the affairs of a business to be separated from the personal affairs of its owners. Let us explore in more depth the problem of choosing the form of organization based on an imaginary situation.

Choosing an Organizational Form

Sam "Hot Dog" Harris and his sister Mia are thinking about establishing a ski shop. Sam would be in charge of promotion and handling customers, and Mia would be the business manager. If the shop were to be a proprietorship, either Sam or Mia would have to be the owner and the other would be an employee. If Mia were the proprietor, she would pay Sam a salary and perhaps a commission on sales. Mia would then have as personal income any money left after paying Sam, paying for the merchandise, and paying for rent and other business expenses. She would also be responsible for any debts incurred by the business and would have to raise the money needed to get it going.

Sam and Mia could also form a partnership. They would have to come to some agreement as to how they would share in the profits of the business and the amount of money that each would invest in it initially. In this case the choice between having a proprietorship or a partnership would depend primarily on the personal preferences of the two people. Furthermore, they could form a corporation instead. Suppose that Mia and Sam are trying to decide whether to set up the ski shop as a corporation or as a partnership. There are several factors which they must consider.

Limited liability   If the ski shop is incorporated, any debts incurred are liabilities only of the ski shop, not of Sam and Mia personally. Therefore, creditors of the corporation cannot go after their personal assets if the shop gets into trouble and folds. (This may not be a realistic consideration in this particular situation since major creditors of the corporation might ask for personal endorsement of its debts by Sam and Mia. Requirements that loans be personally endorsed are common for small businesses.)

If Sam and Mia wished to expand their business and needed additional money to do so, it would be much easier to sell shares in their corporation to other people than to bring others in as partners since the personal assets of the new investors would not be jeopardized if the business gets into trouble. *Limited liability is an extremely important factor in enabling corporations to raise money from investors.*

Transferring ownership and continuity   If the ski shop were a partnership, Sam couldn't sell his part of the business without Mia's permission. However, if the business were a corporation, Sam would be completely free to sell his share of ownership. Therefore, the corporate form makes it much easier to transfer ownership interests in a firm. This feature of corporations also facilitates the raising of additional money since new shareholders know they will be able to sell their part of the business more easily later on, if they so wish.

Since the existence of the corporation does not depend on the particular owners, the business can go on indefinitely. If Sam and Mia are partners and one of them dies or gets into personal financial troubles, the other might not be able to keep the business going. But, if they were incorporated and Sam died, Mia could continue the business by hiring someone to take Sam's place. Sam's heirs would get the shares that he owned and would be entitled to have their say in how the shop was operated, but the business would continue. This continuity is helpful both in selling shares to other people and in borrowing money. Both new shareholders and lenders feel more secure if the business cannot be faced with a crisis due to the death of one of the original founders. Continuity is, therefore, an advantage of incorporating.

Other factors Depending on the particular circumstances of Sam and Mia, the income tax laws may affect the decision to incorporate. Those laws which are most relevant as to the type of business organization chosen will be pointed out in the next section. In the case of Sam and Mia it is not possible to say without further information about them whether the tax treatment of income from the ski shop would make it advantageous or disadvantageous to incorporate.

Since the corporation is a legal entity chartered by the state, legal help is needed to obtain the necessary permission, and fees must be paid to the state. In addition, corporations must have boards of directors, hold annual meetings, establish bylaws to govern them, and meet other requirements that vary from state to state. The result is that setting up and maintaining a business as a corporation imposes additional costs and restrictions.

We have discussed most of the factors affecting business organizations with the exception of the taxation of income. We are now in a position to look at the federal income tax as it applies to individuals and corporations.

THE FEDERAL INCOME TAX

The federal tax on the incomes of individuals and corporations constitutes the largest single source of revenue received by any governmental unit. The federal income tax is also the most important tax because it affects more people than any other tax. Individuals and owners of business firms would prefer not to pay any more taxes than they are legally required to pay. Moreover, the tax laws influence business decisions as to investment and financing in several ways which will be discussed in Chapters 7 and 9. In this section we will examine some of the basic characteristics of the federal income tax. State and local income taxes vary considerably but generally follow similar patterns.

We will first look at the corporate income tax, which, in many respects, is simpler than the individual income tax. We will also comment briefly on the taxes of an individual owning the securities issued by a corporation. Then the taxation of individuals who are owner-managers of small businesses will be discussed. In the last section we will consider some of the tax considerations involved in business expenditures for plant and equipment.[2]

2. The material presented here is an *introduction* to income taxes, not a complete explanation. The laws regarding taxes are extensive and complex, and they change from year to year. For example, for 1975 and the first half of 1976 the corporate income tax was 20 percent on the first $25,000 of income, 22 percent on the next $25,000, and 48 percent on in-

The percentage of income that must be paid in taxes is called the **tax rate.** In 1974 the corporate income tax rate was 22 percent on the first $25,000 of taxable income and 48 percent on taxable income in excess of $25,000. Therefore a corporation with taxable income of $100,000 would pay

Corporate Income Taxes

$$0.22(\$25,000) + 0.48(\$100,000 - \$25,000) = \$41,500$$

The figure $41,500 would be the annual income tax of a corporation earning $100,000. Corporations are required (as are all taxpayers) to pay taxes essentially on a current basis. Payments of estimated taxes are made quarterly on April 15, June 15, September 15, and December 15. Thus, a corporation estimating its taxes at $41,500 for the year would pay $10,375 in each quarter. If its income actually turned out to be less or more than $100,000, the corporation would either get a refund or pay more taxes.

Taxable income for corporations is determined in essentially the same way as for all businesses. Business expenses including wages, salaries, material costs, depreciation allowances, and interest expenses are subtracted from the firm's revenues for the year. Other deductions include losses from previous years and depletion allowances for oil, mining, and other extractive industries. Some types of revenues are excluded from taxable income in whole or in part; for example, interest earned on the debt securities issued by state and local governments is not subject to federal income tax. One difference between corporations and other businesses is that only 15 percent of dividends received from a corporation's ownership of stock in other United States corporations is included in taxable income. The exclusion from taxable income of 85 percent of dividends received is made because the corporation paying the dividends has also been paying corporate income taxes on its income, and the exclusion eliminates most of the double taxation.

Business losses If taxable income for a firm is negative (i.e., expenses are greater than revenues), the firm has a loss for the year and pays no income taxes. In addition, the loss becomes a potential deduction from income in other years. Business losses for the current year may be deducted from income in past years or *carried back.* Losses may also be deducted from income in future years or *carried forward.* If the loss is carried back, the firm will receive a cash refund of taxes paid in past years. If the loss is carried forward, less taxes will be paid on income in future years than would otherwise be paid. The 1975 tax laws permitted losses to be carried back no further than three years and carried forward no further than five years.

come over $50,000. The rates were due to revert to those in effect in 1974 after June 30, 1976. However, as of July 1976, Congress was still debating whether the 1975 rates should continue in effect. Decisions that have tax consequences should be made only with the advice of tax experts.

The laws required losses to be first deducted from the earliest year (three years ago); if taxable income in that year was insufficient, the remaining loss would be deducted from the second year back and so on out to five years in the future. To see how this works consider the following example. For simplicity we will assume that there is a single tax rate of 50 percent on business income.

Suppose a firm has a loss of $50,000 in 1977. It had taxable income and paid taxes in the three preceding years as follows:

	1974	1975	1976
Taxable income	$10,000	$20,000	$30,000
Taxes paid	5,000	10,000	15,000

The firm would send amended tax statements to the IRS for these three years, deducting as much of the $50,000 loss as possible. The amended tax returns would be as follows:

	1974	1975	1976	Total
Original taxable income	$10,000	$20,000	$30,000	$60,000
Less part of 1977 loss	10,000	20,000	20,000	50,000
Amended taxable income	0	0	10,000	10,000
Taxes on amended income	0	0	5,000	5,000
Taxes paid	5,000	10,000	15,000	30,000
Tax refund	$ 5,000	$10,000	$10,000	$25,000

The firm in this case would get an immediate tax refund of $25,000. The entire loss of $50,000 has been deducted from income in the three prior years.

If taxable income in the three preceding years were less than the loss in 1977, any unused portion of the loss would have to be carried forward. If taxable income in 1976 had only been $10,000, we would have the following:

	1974	1975	1976	Total
Original taxable income	$10,000	$20,000	$10,000	$40,000
Less part of 1977 loss	10,000	20,000	10,000	40,000
Amended taxable income	0	0	0	0
Taxes on amended income	0	0	0	0
Taxes paid	5,000	10,000	5,000	20,000
Tax refund	$ 5,000	$10,000	$ 5,000	$20,000

The firm has only been able to deduct $40,000 from prior years' income, so it would receive an immediate tax refund of $20,000. The unused portion of the loss, $10,000, would have to be carried forward and applied as a deduction from income in 1978. If income in 1978 were insufficient to use up the loss, the balance could be carried forward until 1982. If the firm did not earn at least $10,000 in those next five years (i.e., 1978–1982), the unused portion of the $10,000 loss carryforward would be lost as a possible deduction.

These same general rules apply to all businesses, regardless of the form of organization. However, the actual application to proprietorships and partnerships can be fairly complex when the owners have sources of income other than the business. In such situations a tax expert should be consulted.

There are several other important features of the corporate income tax which affect business decisions. However, these features also apply to proprietorships and partnerships and they will be discussed after we have examined the individual income tax.

Individual Income Taxes

The individual income tax in the United States has a **progressive rate structure.** This means that the higher the taxable income someone has, the higher is the tax *rate* that applies to it. The corporate income tax also has this feature, the first $25,000 of income being taxed at 22 percent and income over $25,000 being taxed at 48 percent; however, the progressiveness of the individual income tax is much greater. The tax rate varies from 0 percent to 70 percent depending on the amount of income. The tax rate also depends on the marital status of the person and whether a married couple calculates their taxes on their joint income or separately on each income. Interest on securities issued by state and local governments is exempt from federal income taxes for individuals as well as corporations. Individuals also must make quarterly payments of their estimated tax for the year and on the same dates as for corporations, except that the last payment is due on January 15 instead of December 15. People who are employees of a firm or other institution rarely have to worry about estimating their taxes since the employer is required by the government to withhold part of their wages or salaries for payment of taxes. Self-employed persons and those who have substantial income from interest or dividends do have to make these quarterly payments.

Individuals who are proprietors or partners in a business have special tax problems. Since 1969, there has been a distinction between **earned income,** such as salaries, and **capital income,** such as rent, dividends, and interest. Capital income is to be distinguished from **capital gains,** which are the net gains (or loss for a capital loss) from selling an asset; this will be discussed in the next section. Earned income is subject to a maximum tax rate of 50 percent, while capital income is subject to a maximum tax rate of 70 percent. A single person reaches the 50 percent bracket at taxable income of $32,000, while married people filing a joint tax return reach the 50 percent rate at a taxable income of $44,000. These income figures are well within the reach of owner-employees of small businesses. Generally, only part of the income from a business can be considered earned income; the result is to make the impact of taxes difficult to evaluate for people earning over $30,000 from several sources. We will look at two simple cases to illustrate the general principles: (1) an individual who holds stock in a corporation purely as an investment and (2) an owner-employee of a small business. And we will show generally how they would be taxed.

Taxes on stockholders A corporate stockholder can profit from ownership of shares in two basic ways—through dividends and through increases in the value of the stock. The stockholder pays taxes on dividends when they are received and is taxed on any increases in the value of the stock only when the stock is sold or, at death, as part of his or her estate (through estate taxes).

The first $100 of dividend income to a person is not taxed. Any dividend income over $100 per year is taxed as capital income at increasing tax rates, reaching 70 percent when total taxable income is $100,000 or more for an individual, or $200,000 for a married couple filing a joint return. The distinction between earned income and capital income does not become important until the 50 percent tax rate is reached; so, for people in the lower tax brackets, dividend income is just like any other income except for the $100 exclusion. The taxes for two unmarried individuals —one with $10,100 in dividends ($10,000 of which is taxed) and one with no dividends or interest income—are shown for selected levels of earned taxable income in Exhibit 3-1. Earned taxable income is earned income less nonbusiness deductions such as interest paid on personal debts, a

Exhibit 3-1. Individual Income Tax[a]

1. Dividend income: $10,000				2. No income from dividends or interest			
Earned taxable income	Total taxable income	Federal income tax	Average tax rate, %[b]	Earned taxable income	Total taxable income	Federal income tax	Average tax rate, %[b]
$10,000	$20,000	$ 5,230	26	$20,000	$20,000	$ 5,230	26
20,000	30,000	9,390	31	30,000	30,000	9,390	31
40,000	50,000	20,000	40	50,000	50,000	19,290	39
100,000	110,000	51,290	47	110,000	110,000	49,290	45

[a] Single person, 1974 tax rate schedule.
[b] Income tax divided by total income.

portion of medical expenses, sales taxes, taxes on personal property, and charitable contributions.

Gains and losses from selling stock are treated differently from dividend income. If the stock has been owned less than six months, the difference between the amount received when sold and the amount paid for the stock is a **short-term capital gain or loss.** A capital gain results when the stock is sold for more than it cost; a capital loss results when it is sold for less. Short-term gains are simply considered part of the person's ordinary capital income for the year. If the stock has been owned more than six months and is sold for more than it cost, the stockholder has a **long-term gain.** Similarly, if the stock is sold for less than it cost, the stockholder has a **long-term loss.** Long-term gains are taxed at significantly lower rates than are short-term gains in order to provide an incentive to long-term investments. Roughly speaking, a long-term gain is taxed at half of the marginal income tax rate on capital income. The treatment of losses is rather complicated, and we will not go into this here.

The main point is that there is a tax advantage to a stockholder's receiving returns from ownership of shares in the form of long-term capital gains rather than dividends. A dollar of long-term capital gains is taxed at a lower rate than a dollar of dividends, assuming that the investor has more than $100 in total dividend income. This fact has some important implications for corporate financial decisions, as we will discuss in later chapters.

Taxes on owners of small businesses   Net business income (revenues less expenses) earned by a proprietorship or partnership is treated as personal income to its owners. If a small business is incorporated, the owners may have the option to be taxed either as a partnership or as a corporation.[3] If they choose to be taxed as a corporation, the corporate income tax must be paid. Any salaries and dividends paid to the owners will be taxed as their personal income; however, the salaries would be deductible in determining the corporation's taxable income but the dividends would not be deductible.

It would appear that there is little benefit in being taxed as a corporation, since the same net business income is being taxed twice—once as corporate income and again as received in the form of dividends by the owners. However, suppose the owners wish to retain some or all of the profits in the business in order to invest in additional assets and expand the firm. In this case, there is often an advantage to being taxed as a corporation.

3. A small corporation with less than ten shareholders can generally elect to be taxed as a partnership provided it meets certain other rules. Corporations taxed as partnerships are called "small business corporations" by the IRS, and 2 percent of all businesses in 1970 (257,000 firms) were being taxed in this way.

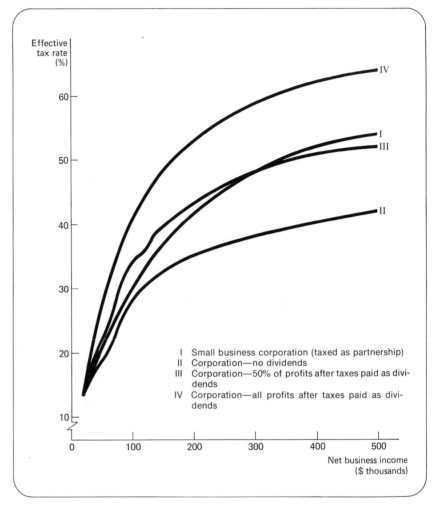

Effective tax rate (%)

I   Small business corporation (taxed as partnership)
II   Corporation—no dividends
III Corporation—50% of profits after taxes paid as dividends
IV   Corporation—all profits after taxes paid as dividends

Net business income ($ thousands)

Figure 3-1. Taxation of a two-person business. (Figure assumes each owner draws a salary equal to $7,000 plus 15 percent of net business income and has personal deductions of $1,000 plus 15 percent of his or her salary.)

To illustrate the nature of the issues here, Figure 3-1 shows the effective tax rates for four situations. Figure 3-1 is based on a firm owned by two people, Sam and Mia, for example, each with a half interest in a ski shop. Both are married and file joint returns, and their only income is from the business. The effective tax rates shown are the total taxes paid by the ski shop, Sam, and Mia divided by the net business income before taxes and salaries. Notice that paying out all corporate profits after taxes as dividends (IV) subjects Sam and Mia to the highest taxes. They would be better off being taxed as a partnership (I). Cases II and III show the tax effects of retaining all (II) or part (III) of the profits within the business. Of course, in cases II and III the money available to Sam and Mia for personal expenditures is less than in cases I and IV, since the higher the divi-

Exhibit 3-2. Taxes and Income for Net Business Income of $320[a]

Case	Personal taxes	Corporate taxes	Total taxes	Aftertax personal income	Retained earnings	Effective tax rate, %[b]
I (small bus. corp.)	$155	0	$155	$165	—	48.4
II (corp. — no. div.)	30	94	124	80	116	38.8
III (corp. — 50% div.)	61	94	155	107	58	48.4
IV (corp. — 100% div.)	95	94	189	131	0	59.1

[a] Dollar figures in thousands.

[b] Total taxes divided by $320.

dends paid, the greater is their total personal income. Salaries are assumed to increase with business income but to be the same for cases I through IV for each level of business income.

Exhibit 3-2 illustrates some of the information used to construct Figure 3-1. Business income of $320,000 was used, since this is the point where cases I and III show equal taxes. Notice, however, the fact that in case I Sam and Mia are free to retain as little in the business as they wish, whereas in case III they are investing $58,000. When only a few people own and operate a business, they must consider carefully the tax aspects of what they do. In particular, if the owners plan to expand the business by retaining most of the profits (case II), they would be better off incorporating. If they plan to draw out most of the profits (case IV), they would be better off to be taxed as a partnership. For situations between the extremes (case III), their decision will depend on the size of the business.

Since Sam and Mia have the option, if they incorporate the ski shop, to be taxed as either a partnership or a corporation, the existence of corporate income taxes would not be a disadvantage to incorporation. As their business grows, the ability to protect some of the income from high personal tax rates by retaining money in the business provides an advantage to the corporate form of organization. The larger the firm, the more beneficial incorporation is likely to be for this reason and the easier will be its access to financing, which was discussed earlier.

Although business investment decisions will not be treated in depth until Chapter 7, it would be helpful to note here the tax treatment of investment expenditures. Four topics will be covered in this section. First we will discuss the concept of depreciation and its tax effects. Second, we will look briefly at the depletion allowances of the extractive industries (oil, mining, etc.). Third, the treatment of gains and losses from the sale of

Tax Factors in Business Investment Decisions

business assets is presented. And finally, the investment tax credit is discussed. Since the specific laws affecting these four areas are highly changeable, we will be most concerned with the general concepts involved rather than with detailed calculation. The appendix to this chapter provides more information on methods of depreciation.

Depreciation Most physical assets do not last indefinitely. Machine tools, buildings, and apple trees, for example, may have productive uses for many years, but eventually they will wear out or become obsolete and have little value to anyone. **Economic depreciation** is the decrease in the market value of an asset over a period of time, such as one year. We are concerned here, however, with the depreciation allowances provided for in the tax laws. Depreciation is an expense that can be deducted from total income in determining taxable income. You will recall that business expenses in general are deductible. If a firm pays its employees $20,000 in a year, that amount can be deducted from the firm's total income. However, if a firm spends $20,000 on a new machine, it will be able to treat only a portion of the initial cost as a deductible expense each year. The expenditure of $20,000 must be deducted in installments over several years, the minimum length of time being specified for most assets by the tax laws. Those installments are the depreciation allowances for the machine. For tax purposes any expenditure can be placed in one of three categories: expenses, plant and equipment expenditures, and nondeductible expenditures. Expenses can be deducted in the year that they occurred. Plant and equipment expenditures are deducted as depreciation over the useful lives of the assets. Some expenditures, such as purchase of land, are generally not deductible.

The three most common methods of computing depreciation allowances are the straight-line, double-declining balance (DDB), and sum-of-the-years digits (SYD). Each method is based on a given **depreciable life** for the asset, that is, the number of years over which its cost must be depreciated. The appropriate lives for various assets are generally specified by the IRS. In addition, the IRS requires the firm to estimate **salvage value,** which is the amount it expects to realize from disposal of the asset. Only the difference between the cost and the salvage value may be depreciated.

Figure 3-2 illustrates the annual depreciation that would be allowed using each of the three methods for a machine which costs $20,000 and has a depreciable life of ten years and no salvage value.[4] The actual calculation of depreciation under the three methods is discussed in the appendix to this chapter. Notice that the DDB and SYD methods provide for higher depreciation deductions in the first few years after purchase of

4. The amount of depreciation shown for the DDB method in year ten is based on continued applications of the formula for depreciation in the earlier years. In fact, a larger deduction would be permitted in the last year, as explained in the appendix to this chapter.

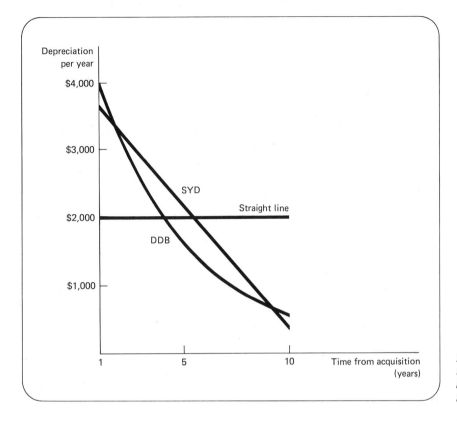

Figure 3-2. Depreciation allowances over the life of a machine under three different methods.

the asset. DDB and SYD are often referred to as **accelerated depreciation** methods because more depreciation is taken in the early years than under straight-line depreciation.

Businesses do not have complete freedom to select the depreciation method they can use for a given type of capital expenditure. The IRS provides rules based on the tax laws passed by Congress which determine what can be done. Generally, one of the two accelerated methods is permitted. A firm using an accelerated method will pay less taxes in the early years of an asset's life and more taxes in the later years. The total tax over the life of the asset will be the same under all methods, unless the firm's tax rates change either because its income changes and thus a different tax rate applies or because new tax laws are passed by Congress. Firms using accelerated depreciation generally benefit from deferring taxes because money has time value. This will be brought out more clearly in Chapter 4.

Depletion The product of some industries is a natural resource which is either completely used up after a period of production (mineral deposits) or replenished very slowly (timber). For example, after all the gold in a mine has been extracted and sold, the owner must either find another mine or go out of business. The government provides a special deduction from federal income taxes called **depletion** to encourage investment in and development of natural resources. There are two ways in which depletion allowances may be calculated: the **cost method** and the **percentage method.**

The cost method can be used for all types of depletable assets. Under this method the owner is permitted to deduct in each year the cost of the assets sold that year. Suppose that the gold mine is estimated to contain 10,000 ounces of gold and was purchased for $200,000. The cost of the gold in the mine is $20 per ounce. The owner cannot deduct this cost until the gold is actually sold.[5] If the owner sells 1,000 ounces in a year, he or she is able to deduct $20 × 1,000 = $20,000 that year as a depletion allowance, plus whatever it cost to mine the gold.

The other method of determining depletion is more controversial. The percentage method permits the owner to deduct a percentage of gross income from the property as depletion. If the owner of the gold mine has sold 1,000 ounces for $200 per ounce and the percentage permitted in the tax law is 15 percent, the owner could deduct 15 percent of the gross income, or 0.15($200,000) = $30,000, which is equivalent to $30 per ounce. Notice that the acquisition cost of the mine does not affect the depletion allowance when the percentage method is used. Instead, the higher the price received per unit produced, the higher the depletion allowance. The higher the depletion allowance is, the less are the taxes that will be paid on a given income. In some cases the cost method will provide higher deductions; in others, the percentage method. There are restrictions on the amount of depletion allowances that can be taken using the percentage method, and the percentages differ depending on the type of mineral in question. The percentage that applies to a given mineral is specified in the tax law and subject to change, as happened in 1975 to the depletion allowance for oil. Timber depletion cannot be figured using the percentage method.

Capital gains and losses   When an asset is sold, a capital gain or loss may result. The tax treatment of gains and losses on depreciable assets differs from the treatment of securities discussed earlier. The sale of a depreciable asset at a price above its book value results in "recapture" of excess depreciation. Suppose a firm purchases a machine for $20,000, depreciates it using the straight-line method with a ten-year life and sells it five years later. Total depreciation on the machine has been $10,000 (assuming zero salvage value estimated originally), since depreciation

---

5. This differs from depreciation in that if the gold mine were a depreciable asset, depreciation deductions could begin when the mine is purchased. However, the expenditure for the mine is not deductible; only the depletion allowances on the gold mined are deductible.

was $2,000 per year for five years. The **book value** (initial cost less accumulated depreciation) of the machine is now $10,000. If the machine is sold for more than $10,000 but less than $20,000, the gain (price minus book value) is considered ordinary income. For a corporation with taxable income greater than $25,000, the applicable tax rate would be 48 percent. If the machine is sold for more than its original cost of $20,000, the difference between the selling price and the original cost is a capital gain taxed at 30 percent and the $10,000 difference between the cost and the book value is ordinary income, taxed at 48 percent. If the machine is sold for less than $10,000, the difference between the book value and the price is an ordinary loss and is therefore similar to a business expense and is deductible from income.

Capital gains and losses frequently result from the sale of nondepreciable assets used in a business, e.g., land or securities. In general, whenever a firm has capital gains and losses, it must deduct all capital losses from all capital gains for the year. Any loss "left over" can be carried back three years or forward five years to offset net capital gains in those years. If there were insufficient gains in these years to offset the losses, then the remaining loss is lost as a tax deduction.

The investment tax credit   To encourage investment by business, Congress has provided the **investment tax credit.** It is effectively a gift by the federal government to the investing firm of part of the cost of the new asset and applies to all assets used in the production of goods and services except real estate. The firm's tax bill is reduced by the amount of the tax credit, which in 1974 was equal to 7 percent of the cost of the asset if the asset is owned for seven years or more.[6] To illustrate, suppose that a corporation purchases a machine for $10,000 and plans to hold it for at least seven years. Assume that the firm has a taxable income of $100,000 from its other operations and owes $41,500 in income taxes on this income. The tax credit on the $10,000 investment is $700 (0.07 × $10,000). This credit is deducted from the taxes owed for the period; i.e., the firm's taxes become $40,800 ($41,500 − $700). Thus, the benefit is $700 lower tax expense, in the year the machine is purchased.

The investment tax credit has been an "on again–off again" feature of the tax laws. Proposals have been made to make it discretionary on the part of the President. The reasoning behind such proposals is that the investment tax credit provides needed encouragement to businesses when the economy is weak, but that it might be desirable to remove it when the economy is strong and businesses do not need encouragement to invest. To date the President does not have this power.

6. From January 22, 1975 to December 31, 1976, the investment tax credit was 10 percent. In 1976, the 10 percent tax credit was extended by Congress to apply through 1980.

SUMMARY   This chapter has been concerned with taxes and the forms of business organization.

A proprietorship is the simplest type of business organization. This type of business is owned by an individual who is responsible for all its debts. The income from the proprietorship is taxed at personal income tax rates. There are usually no legal requirements for establishing a proprietorship, although some types of business require a license.

Partnerships are businesses owned by several people who share in the profits or losses. Usually professionals such as doctors and lawyers form partnerships. The income from the partnership is treated as personal income to the partners, and each partner is taxed according to the proportion of the business that he or she owns.

Corporations are legal entities established by obtaining a charter from the state in which the business operates. A corporation may have one or more owners, who are called stockholders or shareholders because their ownership interest in the business is determined by the shares of stock each one owns. Corporations are taxed separately from the owners. The stockholders of a corporation enjoy limited liability in that creditors of the corporation cannot require payment of business debts from their assets or personal incomes. Because the corporation exists apart from its owners, some stockholders can sell their shares to other people without involving the rest of the owners. The corporation can continue to exist even if the owners die. Limited liability for stockholders and continuity of existence make it easier for the corporation to raise money from new shareholders or creditors than it is for a proprietorship or partnership.

The costs of establishing and maintaining a corporation and the requirements imposed by the charter are disadvantages of the corporate form of organization. Large firms are usually corporations, and small firms are usually proprietorships or partnerships.

Corporations are taxed by the federal government on their net income after expenses at a rate of 22 percent for the first $25,000 and 48 percent on income over $25,000. Individuals are taxed on their total income less a variety of exemptions, deductions, and exclusions. There is a maximum rate of 50 percent on earned income, whereas the rate on capital income (rent, dividends, interest, business income) can reach 70 percent. Personal income tax rates depend on marital status and are progressive in that the rates increase as income rises.

If a business incurs a loss for the current year, the loss may be carried back as a deduction from taxable income of the three prior years and the firm would receive a refund of taxes previously paid. If taxable income in the past is less than the loss, losses may be carried forward as deductions from income for the next five years.

A corporation having no more than ten stockholders can elect to be taxed as a partnership if certain other provisions are met. Because of the complexity of tax laws, the advice of a tax expert is generally necessary for proper tax planning and for choosing the appropriate form of business organization.

There are several aspects of the tax laws that affect business investment decisions. These include depreciation and depletion allowances, capital gains and losses on sale of assets, and the investment tax credit.

Depreciation allowances are tax deductible expenses for owners of certain types of business assets, including fruit orchards, machinery, buildings, and the like. The three most common ways to compute depreciation are the straight-line method, the double-declining balance method, and the sum-of-the-years digits method. The latter two are called accelerated depreciation methods, since they provide higher allowances during the initial years of ownership of the asset. All depreciation methods involve taking part of the initial cost of an asset and deducting that part from yearly income. Depreciation allowances permit the owner to treat the costs of acquiring the asset as tax deductible expenses spread out over the period in which the asset is used.

Depletion allowances are deductions from income based on the using up of a mineral resource or harvesting of timber. The cost method and the percentage method are used to determine depletion allowances. The cost method is based on the original cost of the resource and the percentage method is based on the income from sale. The percentages vary for each type of mineral.

Capital gains and losses on depreciable assets are computed differently than gains or losses on nondepreciable assets. A capital gain results only when the asset is sold for more than its original cost, whereas a capital loss results when it is sold for less than its current book value.

The investment tax credit is a tax benefit provided by the federal government to firms that invest in productive assets. Its purpose is to encourage such investment.

QUESTIONS

1. Compare and contrast the three types of business organizations. Why are large businesses almost always corporations?

2. How does being a limited partner differ from owning stock in a corporation, assuming that the percentage of ownership is the same in both cases?

3. For tax purposes how do earned income, capital income, and capital gains income differ?

4. What are the tax advantages to a corporate stockholder of having the stock appreciate in value instead of receiving cash dividends?

5. List the advantages and disadvantages to a business of being taxed as a corporation rather than as a partnership.

6. If the total depreciation over the life of a machine is equal under all depreciation methods, what is the advantage of accelerated methods over the straight-line method?

7. Explain the cost and percentage methods of depletion.

8. Since it was first established, the investment tax credit has been repealed, reinstated, increased, and decreased. Under what economic conditions do you suppose it has been repealed or decreased? Reinstated or increased?

PROJECT

Research and prepare a table showing percentages in terms of numbers and gross revenues (sales) accounted for by proprietorships, partnerships, and corporations for the following lines of business: grocery stores, airplane manufacturers, construction contractors, men's clothing manufacturers, and security brokers and dealers. Evaluate the variations in percentages. (Use the IRS publication *Business Income Tax Returns* for the most recent year available.)

PROBLEMS

1. Alan N. Basket, on March 5 of last year, invested his entire savings of $16,000 in common stock of Majestic Futures, Inc., at a price of $40 per share. The tax rate for any income from this transaction is 40 percent. The capital gains tax rate is 20 percent.

   a) What additional taxes on this investment would Alan have paid if he sold the stock in July of that year at a price of $48 per share, having received dividends of $1.20 per share? [Ans.: $1472]

   b) What would his taxes have been on the transaction if he had waited until November to sell at a price of $48 per share and received $1.80 per share in dividends? [Ans.: $928]

2. The Flub Company forecast taxable income for 1978 as $92,000.

   a) Using the tax schedule on page 53, compute Flub's estimated tax for 1978 and its expected quarterly payments.

   b) Through the third quarter Flub made payments according to the estimates made in **a** above. However, at the end of the year Flub discovered that it had only earned $72,385 total for the year. What was the firm's fourth quarter tax payment? [Ans.: 0]

3. The Up–N Down Corporation has a seven-year history of income and expenses as shown below. What would their actual taxes paid (or

Year	1	2	3	4	5	6	7
Income	$15,000	$25,000	$120,000	$60,000	$80,000	$90,000	$40,000
Expenses	$25,000	$30,000	$ 55,000	$60,000	$60,000	$80,000	$80,000

received) in each year have been, making use of tax carrybacks and carryforwards? Assume a tax rate of 50 percent.

4. Five years ago the Alberts Company purchased a $50,000 machine. The depreciable life of the machine is ten years with an expected salvage value of $10,000. Straight-line depreciation is used.

   a) What is the depreciation per year on the machine?

   b) What is the book value of the machine today?

   c) If the firm sells the machine for $40,000 today, what is the recapture of depreciation?

   d) How much taxes must be paid on the sale if the firm sells the machine today and has a marginal tax rate of 50 percent?

   e) If Alberts Company sells the machine today for $60,000 instead of $40,000, will the tax bill be different from **d** above? Why?

5. Sam and George opened a movie theater and decided to incorporate. The business qualifies as a small business corporation, so they can elect to be taxed either as a corporation or as a partnership. Taxable income from the theater is expected to be $36,000 next year. They each own half the business. They are planning to open a new theater which would require a non-tax-deductible expenditure of $20,000 next year. Any money remaining after this expenditure and payment of taxes will be paid out to the partners. Calculate total taxes (personal and corporate, if any) that will be paid out of business income under the assumptions below. Should they elect to be taxed as a partnership or as a corporation to minimize taxes? Use the corporate tax rates stated on page 53.

   a) Assume both Sam and George have a personal tax rate of 30 percent.

   b) Assume both Sam and George have a personal tax rate of 50 percent.

   c) Assume Sam has a personal tax rate of 30 percent and George has a personal tax rate of 50 percent. Analyze the problem from each partner's point of view. How do you suppose they will reconcile their differences?

calculating depreciation allowances

The straight-line method of depreciation is the easiest to calculate because the depreciation allowance for a given initial cost for an asset is the same for each year of the asset's life. It is called "straight-line" because the amount of depreciation is a constant and therefore a "straight line" over the life of the asset, as was shown in Figure 3-2.

The formula for the annual depreciation allowance under the straight-line method is

$$\text{Annual depreciation} = \frac{\text{cost} - \text{salvage value}}{\text{depreciable life}}$$

For example, a machine costing $20,000, having a salvage value of $4,000, and having a depreciable life of ten years would provide annual depreciation of ($20,000 − $4,000)/10 = $1,600 per year.

The double-declining balance method is more difficult to calculate and provides higher depreciation allowances in the early years of the asset's life than it does in the later years. It is called "double-declining balance" because the depreciation is double what the straight-line depreciation would be on the undepreciated balance of the asset and that balance declines over the life of the asset as depreciation is deducted. The undepreciated balance is the book value of the asset, the initial cost of the asset less total depreciation to date.

The easiest way to calculate the depreciation allowance using the double-declining balance method is to divide the current book value of the asset by the original life of the asset to get the straight-line amount then double that value. The formula can be expressed as

$$\text{Current depreciation} = 2 \left(\frac{\text{current book value}}{\text{depreciable life}} \right)$$

where current book value = initial cost − total depreciation to date

For example, a machine costing $20,000 and having a depreciable life of ten years would have a depreciation allowance of 2($20,000/10) = $4,000 in the first year. Notice that we do not need to consider salvage values initially and that the initial book value is simply the cost of the machine. For the second year we calculate the new book value as the initial book value less depreciation previously taken or $20,000 − $4,000 = $16,000. Depreciation for the second year is then computed as 2($16,000/10) = $3,200. Later years are treated in a similar fashion until book value reaches salvage value, at which point no further depreciation is deducted. However, salvage value can be ignored if it is less than 10 percent of the original cost of the asset, according to current IRS regulations. This is true regardless of the method of depreciation.

If the book value of the asset in the last year of its original depreciable life is greater than the salvage value, the entire difference can be taken as depreciation. In the example above, the machine would have a book value of $2,684 at the beginning of the tenth year ($20,000 initial cost − $17,316 total depreciation[7]). If the salvage value is zero (or less than $2,000, 10 percent of $20,000), the entire book value can be taken as depreciation in the last year. This is equivalent to a change from the double-declining balance method to the straight-line method in the last year of the depreciable life of the asset. It is possible to make this change in earlier years as well, and many firms do this because a change to straight-line in the last few years of the asset's life will provide higher depreciation deductions than continuing under double-declining balance.

The sum-of-the-years digits method determines the depreciation in each year as a proportion of the original cost less salvage value. This method also provides higher depreciation in the early years relative to the later years. The proportion applicable to a given year is found by dividing the number of remaining years of life by a constant factor equal to the sum-of-the-years digits, which is how the method is named. For example, the factor for an asset being depreciated over four years is $4 + 3 + 2 + 1 = 10$. The factor may also be computed from the following formula:

$$\text{Factor} = \text{depreciable life} \left(\frac{\text{depreciable life} + 1}{2} \right)$$

or, as in the above example:

$$\text{Factor} = 4 \left(\frac{4 + 1}{2} \right) = 10$$

7. The book value at the beginning of any year can be calculated directly using the following formula:

$$\text{Book value}_t = \left(1 - \frac{2}{n} \right)^{t-1} (\text{initial cost})$$

where n is the depreciable life in years and t has a value of 1 for the first year. Depreciation in any year t under the double-declining balance method is therefore

$$\text{Depreciation}_t = \frac{2}{n} (\text{book value}_t)$$

Depreciation in year t is now determined as

$$\text{Depreciation}_t = (\text{cost} - \text{salvage value}) \left(\frac{\text{depreciable life} + 1 - t}{\text{factor}} \right)$$

where the first year is considered year 1 ($t = 1$). For the example of a $20,000 machine with $4,000 salvage value and a ten-year life,

$$\text{Factor} = 10 \left(\frac{10 + 1}{2} \right) = 55$$

The depreciation for the first year would be

$$\text{Depreciation}_1 = (\$20,000 - \$4,000) \left(\frac{10 + 1 - 1}{55} \right)$$

$$= \$16,000 \left(\tfrac{10}{55} \right)$$

$$= \$2,909$$

For the second year

$$\text{Depreciation}_2 = \$16,000 \left(\frac{10 + 1 - 2}{55} \right)$$

$$= \$16,000 \left(\tfrac{9}{55} \right)$$

$$= \$2,618$$

The depreciation for the tenth and last year would be

$$\text{Depreciation}_{10} = \$16,000 \left(\tfrac{1}{55} \right)$$

$$= \$291$$

A History of Finance[1]

ANCIENT TIMES

When a Neolithic farmer some 7,000 years ago borrowed additional seed grain so that he could expand the land he had under cultivation, he had no idea what he was starting. By 3000 B.C. loans of grain and silver were commonplace in ancient Sumer. Going interest rates were $33\frac{1}{3}$ percent per year on barley loans and 20 percent per year on silver loans. Not long afterward groups of merchants established trading associations that were the predecessors of the modern corporation.

The Code of Hammurabi (about 1800 B.C.) regulated financial transactions in Babylon. Such banking operations as deposits, transfers to another party (checks), and loans were widespread by this time. Business partnerships of various types were codified, and requirements for security arrangements in loans (assets pledged to the lender) were set out. During the sixth century B.C., merchant bankers were active in Babylon. These firms engaged in activities similar to those of the great European merchant bankers of the nineteenth century, the Rothschilds: making loans to individuals, businesses, and governments; entering into partnerships with other firms to engage in some joint commercial venture; accepting, transferring, and paying interest on deposits; and purchasing existing loans secured by land (equivalent to buying a mortgage in twentieth-century secondary markets). Interest rates on loans in this period were 10 percent to 20 percent per year depending on the type of loan. Thus the Babylonians developed relatively sophisticated financial capabilities quite early in history, and, as we shall see, there were few significant advances beyond this point for the next 2,000 years.

The Greeks' contribution to finance was minimal compared with their contributions in other areas. They did develop and extend the types of loans made. By the fourth century B.C., unsecured loans became common. Interest rates were generally lower than in Babylon. A well-secured loan in second century B.C. Athens could be obtained at an annual rate of 6 percent. On the other hand, many of the city-states of Greece had very poor credit ratings, and loans made by individuals to some cities carried interest rates as high as 48 percent per year.

A common financial arrangement throughout the Mediterranean area in ancient times was the "sea loan." Typically this was a loan secured by a ship or by its cargo made at the beginning of a voyage. If the voyage was successful, the lender was repaid; otherwise he was not. During stable periods the interest rate charged was about 30 percent. When there was active warfare or piracy, interest rates were 60 percent to 100 percent. This financial arrangement was essentially a partnership with one partner (the lender) being limited in the amount received but having first claim on any proceeds from the voyage.

The Romans, whose economy was based on agriculture and tribute from other nations, were not particularly interested in business and finance. It is known that joint stock companies with limited liability for the owners existed in Rome, but it is not clear where they originally

1. The major sources for this essay are Sidney Homer, *A History of Interest Rates* (New Brunswick: Rutgers University Press, 1963); Samuel Eliot Morrison, *The Oxford History of the American People* (New York: Oxford University Press, 1965); and Arthur Stone Dewing, *The Financial Policy of Corporations* (New York: Ronald Press, 1953).

were developed. The Romans were the original "cheap money" people. Low interest rates were considered desirable as a goal of public policy. They established a legal maximum on interest rates of $8\frac{1}{3}$ percent per year. After 443 B.C., a creditor charging more than this rate was liable for quadruple damages under Roman law. Later the maximum rate was raised to 12 percent, where it remained for several hundred years. During prosperous times the actual rates charged were usually well below the maximum, down to 4 percent on occasion.

One shouldn't conclude from this discussion that finance in those early times was not very different from the present day. Organized financial markets did not exist. Borrowing was usually undertaken to finance trade or for personal needs, and loans were short-term—one year or less. Large private corporations did not exist, and governmental units were infrequent borrowers, in part due to their generally poor credit standing. Temples in Babylon and Greece were heavily engaged in lending. Relatively few private banking firms existed. The penalties for default on a loan were severe—personal slavery in Babylon and Rome.

EARLY CHRISTIANITY AND USURY

The early Christian doctrine of usury—the tenet that charging interest on a loan is immoral—had a profound influence on the development of finance for 1,000 years. Loans were viewed as an aid to a neighbor in distress. To profit from a neighbor's distress by charging him interest was viewed as evil. This concept, which has philosophical appeal, was applied to loans for commercial purposes as well. The secular authorities vacillated between the absolute prohibition against interest demanded by the Church and the Roman tradition of regulation and legal maxima. Therefore, although individuals could bond together in business partnerships and share in the profits from commercial activities, borrowing money to engage in such activities was inhibited.

In time some of the obvious differences in the purpose of loans became apparent. Commercial activity began to increase during the twelfth century, and this forced the development of financial arrangements which avoided the doctrine of usury while serving the basic purpose of providing compensation to a lender. Some leaders of the Protestant Reformation—Luther, Zwingli, and Calvin—defended interest on loans as proper, provided the rate was not injurious or extortionary. Calvin fixed the maximum legal rate in Geneva in 1547 at 5 percent per year.

THE DEVELOPMENT OF SECONDARY MARKETS FOR SECURITIES

During the twelfth and thirteenth centuries, two types of long-term "securities" developed which could be resold. The first was the "census," which originated early in the Middle Ages. A census was the right to obtain a portion of the returns from agricultural property. Originally the returns were a share in the harvest; later annual money payments were substituted. A landowner could sell a census (borrow money) on his property without the buyer (lender) being considered a usurer. A variety of different types developed. A census might have fixed payments and a fixed maturity and resemble a mortgage loan of today. Some censuses were perpetuities, paying a fixed amount forever. Others ceased with the death of one of the parties. A secondary market of sorts existed for these contracts. The owner of the census could sell it to another person, but trading in these securities was not active.

A more extensive secondary market developed in Venice. The Republic of Venice forced its wealthier citizens to "loan" money to the government in order to finance its defense budget. In return the Republic paid 5 percent per year interest. Principal repayments were made occasionally, depending on the condition of Venetian finances, but interest payments on these loans were made regularly for 100 years. Essentially the loans were government bonds. No paper certificates were issued, but a record of the owner of the "bonds" was kept and the ownership was freely transferable. The prices of these securities were quoted daily as an active market for them developed. Over the period in which they were outstanding, market prices varied from 20 percent of face value during wartime to over 100 percent during prosperous periods when they were being repaid.

FINANCE FROM 1100–1750

The financial development of Western Europe, beginning in the twelfth century, is characterized by increasing trade and the resulting demand for short-term commercial loans and for methods of dealing in foreign exchange. Long-term debt contracts of various sorts arose in this period, including the equivalent of mortgages on real estate and of government bonds which were often perpetuities without promise of principal repayment. These government securities were issued by the independent cities of Italy and Germany and by Holland, and secondary markets developed for them. This period also saw the development of government-sponsored banks. The Bank of England was established in 1654.

What distinguishes this period from modern times were the limited nature of the financial institutions and the lack of large private corporations. Most of the banking activities were carried out through partnerships, often within a single family. Banking per se was often incidental to the basic purpose of the business—to engage in trade and commercial activities. The Medicis of Florence, who were leading bankers in the fifteenth century, are a well-known example of this. The family contained merchants, bankers, princes, and popes. They maintained offices throughout Europe, North Africa, and the Near East and engaged in a wide range of international trading and banking activities, while acquiring large land holdings and political power in Italy.

By 1750 financial affairs in Europe could be characterized as well-developed in the areas of government finance and the financing of international trade. Business finance was dominated by speculators. Many companies were promoted, and their stock was actively traded. Amsterdam was the financial capital of Europe. The stock of the Dutch East India Company was traded on the Amsterdam Exchange, along with commodities and the bonds of local and foreign governments. Trading methods such as margin purchases, short sales, and futures contracts had been developed. Insurance, invented in the seventeenth century, had become a means by which private investors speculated on shipping ventures.

THE NINETEENTH CENTURY

In many respects the nineteenth century was the "golden age" of finance. The industrial revolution brought heavy demands for capital investment. New companies were formed in great numbers to exploit new technologies. Preferred stock was developed in the first half of the century, and limited liability for corporate stockholders was common by the middle of the century. The railroad boom in the United States attracted large amounts of British capital. Even the Bank of England held some American railroad bonds. Long-term interest rates were fairly low (2 to 4 percent), despite the demand for money. The invention of paper currency in the eighteenth century combined with large gold discoveries kept the money supply expanding, while rapid increases in productivity kept inflation rates down. London replaced Amsterdam as the world's major financial center.

During this period the major consumer financial institutions were established: savings banks, "building societies" (savings and loan associations), and cooperative credit associations (credit unions). Commercial banks were almost exclusively concerned with the affairs of their business customers.

Prior to the American Revolution there were no banks in the thirteen American colonies. Money was in generally short supply, and many business transactions were based on the barter of commodities. After the Revolution several private banks were founded, and in 1791 the first Bank of the United States was chartered at the urging of Secretary of Treasury Alexander Hamilton. The Bank was founded to expand the credit available in the economy, but its charter was not renewed in 1811 because it had been badly managed and agricultural interests in the country were opposed to renewal.

In 1816 the second Bank of the United States was chartered. As a financial institution serving the interests of the growing country, it was well-conceived. Unfortunately, the Bank fell prey to Andrew Jackson's mistrust of "monied interests" and its policies of keeping the paper money issued by private local banks within bounds aroused intense antagonism. The second Bank's charter expired in 1836. The bankers of New York City picked up the left-over pieces of the Bank (which had been headquartered in Philadelphia) and proceeded to construct a vastly greater stronghold of financial power than had been dreamed of by its management. The ultimate result was that the farmers and frontiersmen who had opposed the Bank gained nothing, but the financial center of the United States moved from Philadelphia to New York. There was not to be another central government bank in this country until the Federal Reserve Bank was established in 1913.

The period 1836 to 1863 was the era of "wildcat banking." Anyone could start a bank and issue currency. The currency of most of these banks was not considered to be worth its face value. The most beneficial thing that wildcat banking did was to encourage the development of the American engraving industry. With every bank issuing its own paper currency, there was a lot of engraving work to do.

In 1863 the National Banking Act provided for the federal chartering of commercial banks (national banks) and imposed a tax on private bank currency issues that effectively eliminated them.

Nineteenth-century interest rates in the United States varied widely from one part of the country to the other. A tradition of 5 percent to 6 percent interest on long-term debt became established in the East, and rates stayed mostly in this range for secure debt instruments. In the West things were different. In specific cases mortgages on ranchland were obtained at 36 percent annual interest. Savings banks in Los Angeles at midcentury were paying 15 percent on deposits. The problem was the lack of a well-developed financial system to ease the movement of money from East to West. The discrepancies in rates spawned several political movements as well as a distrust in the West of "Eastern bankers" that persists to some extent today.

UNITED STATES FINANCE IN THE TWENTIETH CENTURY

The nineteenth century was the heyday of private financiers. In the twentieth century the fed-

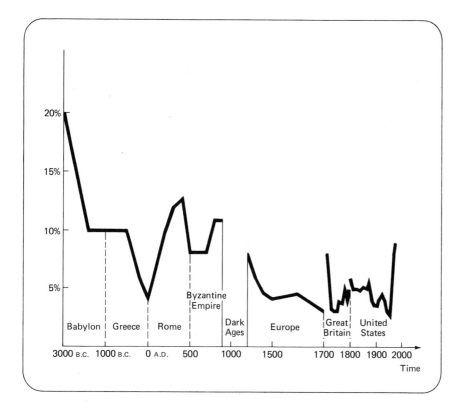

Historical interest rates. (Rates shown after 1200 A.D. are for long-term, low-risk securities. Earlier interest rates are for short-term debts.) Sources: Homer "A History of Interest Rates," and Federal Reserve Bulletin.

eral government assumed a dominant role in the American financial system. The stock market collapse of 1929 to 1932 wiped out the fortunes of many people and dispelled the notion that Wall Street financiers had financial matters well under control. Legislation passed during the 1930s made the stock market less of a private club of speculators and stripped financial power from the major banking houses of the time by forcing a division between commercial banking and investment banking. The House of Morgan—the great banking firm established by J. P. Morgan that dominated the financial scene in the early part of the century—was split into two firms still active today as major financial institutions: Morgan, Stanley, and Company, investment bankers; and Morgan Guaranty Trust, the sixth largest commercial bank in the United States.

Financially the twentieth century is also characterized by the dispersion of financial power, the proliferation of financial instruments, and an emphasis on personal finance. The stock market is dominated by financial institutions that rely on individual investors for their funds. Commercial banks woo consumer accounts with all the marketing skills they can bring to bear. Until the mid-1930s mortgage loans to individuals had maturities of five years or so, with a "balloon balance" which the borrower hoped to be able to renew for another five years when the loan became due. Now thirty-year mortgages paid off in equal monthly installments are commonplace. The average person can borrow money to finance cars, boats and appliances. Such financing was not widely available until after World War II.

Interest rates, after staying fairly low during

the early part of the century, dropped to minimal levels during the 1930s and stayed relatively low until 1965. Since then we have been living in a complex and rapidly shifting financial environment. In August 1974 the U.S. Treasury had to pay over 9 percent to borrow money for ninety days. Eighteen months later it was paying around 5 percent. Long-term United States government bonds have provided interest rates in the 1970s that exceed any paid since 1800. New York City obligations were paying 14 percent per year—free of federal income taxes—in late 1975. We have seen the bankruptcy of a major railroad (Penn Central) and the collapse of two large banks during what otherwise might be considered a period of prosperity. What is in store for us in the last quarter of the twentieth century? We cannot say. Some historical times have been better than others. We can only hope that we are heading into a quieter period.

the time value of money

A well-known fact of economic life is that money is not free and can be downright expensive. In this chapter, we look at some methods of comparing **cash flows** which occur over time. The ability to make such comparisons is very useful for both business managers and individuals in making financial decisions. Some examples of the use of time-value techniques in dealing with business and personal financial problems are provided to illustrate the concepts.

In Chapter 2 we discussed the factors which determine the general level of interest rates in the economy. Essentially three elements were noted as being of major importance: (1) attitudes of individuals with respect to the importance of current consumption over future consumption, (2) the availability of opportunities for productive investments, and (3) inflation. From the viewpoint of an individual or business firm, the practical consequences are apparent. If you have some spare cash now, you can invest it in liquid and relatively riskless assets such as a savings deposit in a bank and receive more money later. If you borrow money now, you must repay a larger amount in the future (the amount borrowed *plus* interest). The result is that $100 in hand today is worth more than $100 to be received a year from now because $100 today can be invested to provide $100 plus interest next year. The existence of interest rates in the economy therefore provides money with its time value quite apart from the attitudes of any one person or the investment opportunities available to a particular firm.

In the first part of this chapter we will assume that we know the interest rate which gives money its time value. The last section is devoted to the problem of determining an unknown interest rate on a loan or investment when all the cash flows are known.

WHY MONEY HAS TIME VALUE

If you borrow $200 for one year and agree to repay the lender $220 at the end of the year, the interest cost of borrowing is $20. The rate of interest is $20/$200 = 0.10 or 10 percent per year. All the mechanics of compound interest are illustrated in this simple example. Let's examine the basic cash flows of the example. There are really only two cash flows of impor-

BASIC CONCEPTS
Compound Interest

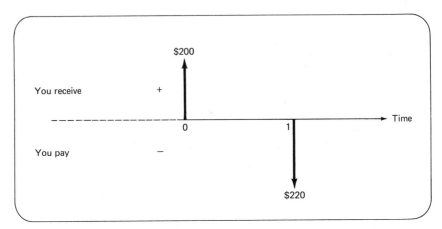

Figure 4-1. The cash flows associated with borrowing $200 for one year at an interest rate of 10 percent.

tance here, your initial inflow of cash of $200 and the payment of $220 one year later. If we take the date of borrowing as time 0 and the date of repayment as time 1 (one year from time 0), these flows can be represented in the cash flow diagram shown in Figure 4-1. This diagram is drawn from the viewpoint of the borrower. If you were the lender instead of the borrower, your cash flows would be as shown in Figure 4-2.

The general relationship among the variables in the example can be expressed as

Repayment = amount borrowed plus interest payment

and, since the interest charged is usually expressed as a rate or percent of the amount borrowed

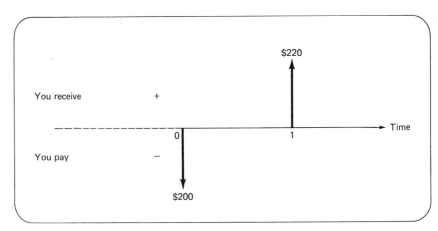

Figure 4-2. The cash flows associated with lending $200 for one year at an interest rate of 10 percent.

Repayment = amount borrowed + (rate × amount borrowed)

or, by rearranging the terms,

$$\text{Repayment} = (\text{amount borrowed})(1 + i) \qquad (4\text{-}1)$$

where i is the interest rate. In our example,

$$\$220 = \$200 \, (1 + 0.10)$$
$$= \$200 \, (1.10)$$
$$= \$220$$

Suppose that you just purchased a used Honda from Friendly Dan, the Cycle Man for \$200. He is kind enough to give you up to one year to pay off the purchase price with only 1 percent *per month* interest charge on the outstanding balance. At the end of the first month, you would owe $\$200(1.01) = \$202$. What if you didn't pay this amount at the end of the first month? Since you owe \$202 at the end of the first month, you would owe $\$202(1.01) = \$204.02$ at the end of two months. At the end of three months you would owe $\$204.02(1.01) = \$206.06$. Another way of showing the amount owed at the end of three months is

First month: (1.01)(\$200)
Second month: (1.01)(1.01)(\$200)
Third month: (1.01)(1.01)(1.01)(\$200)

or

$$(1.01)^3 \, \$200 = (1.0303) \, \$200 = \$206.06$$

The interest is being compounded monthly. At the end of twelve months you would have to pay $(1.01)^{12} \, \$200 = (1.1268) \, \$200 = \$225.36$. This example illustrates the following general relationship.

If P is a present or initial amount
  F is a future amount
  i is the interest rate *per time period*
  n is the number of time periods

then,

$$F = P(1 + i)^n \qquad (4\text{-}2)$$

In the example, P is the amount borrowed now and F is the future payment (amount borrowed plus interest). However, the formula also applies when P is the amount invested now and F is the amount received in the future (initial investment plus interest). Equation (4-2) is the basic relationship in time value of money methods. All the other relationships we will discuss later are developed from this one.

The only difficult part of Eq. (4-2) is raising $(1 + i)$ to the nth power. Unless you have a calculator handy, finding $(1.01)^{12}$, for example, takes quite a while. For this reason, there are many published tables available giving values of $(1 + i)^n$ for various values of i and n. Appendix B in the back of this book contains a fairly complete set of tables of interest rate factors. Table 4-1 shows some typical values for $(1 + i)^n$. The time periods in the table can be days, months, quarters, years, or whatever time period is appropriate for your problem.

Returning to the example, if you wished to know how much you would owe on the motorcycle at the end of four months at an interest rate of 1 percent per month, you would go to the table and look across the row for four periods and under the 1 percent column, finding this value of $(1.01)^4 = 1.0406$. The amount owed at the end of four months is therefore $(1.0406)\ \$200 = \$208.12$.

Example problem In 1626 Peter Minuit purchased Manhattan Island from the Indians for about \$24 worth of trinkets. If the Indians had taken cash instead and invested it to earn 6 percent compounded annually, how much would the Indians have had in 1976, 350 years later?

Table 4-1. Future compound value of \$1
$(1 + i)^n$

Number of periods (n)	Interest rate per period (i)						
	1%	2%	4%	6%	8%	10%	12%
1	1.0100	1.0200	1.0400	1.0600	1.0800	1.1000	1.1200
2	1.0201	1.0404	1.0876	1.1236	1.1664	1.2100	1.2544
3	1.0303	1.0612	1.1249	1.1910	1.2597	1.3310	1.4049
4	1.0406	1.0824	1.1699	1.2625	1.3605	1.4641	1.5735
5	1.0510	1.1041	1.2167	1.3382	1.4693	1.6105	1.7623
10	1.1046	1.2190	1.4802	1.7908	2.1589	2.5937	3.1058
12	1.1268	1.2682	1.6010	2.0122	2.5182	3.1384	3.8960
15	1.1610	1.3459	1.8009	2.3966	3.1722	4.1772	5.4736
20	1.2202	1.4859	2.1911	3.2071	4.6610	6.7275	9.6463
25	1.2824	1.6406	2.6658	4.2919	6.8485	10.835	17.000
50	1.6446	2.6916	7.1067	18.42	46.90	117.4	289.0
100	2.7048	7.2446	50.505	339.3	2,200.0	13,780.0	83,522.0

Since Table 4-1 doesn't go out to 350, we must solve this problem in steps.

First, how much would the Indians have in 1726 at the end of the first 100 years, which is the highest value for n in the table. We see that the value of $1 at 6 percent per year for 100 years is $339.30; therefore, the value of $24 compounded at 6 percent per year for 100 years is

$$F_{100} = \$24\ (1 + .06)^{100}$$
$$= \$24\ (339.3)$$
$$= \$8,143$$

We can now consider the $8,143 as invested at $t = 0$ and see what its value would be at the end of the next 100 years compounded at 6 percent per year. At the end of the second century (1826) the $8,143 invested in 1726 would again have grown by a factor of 339.3.

$$F_{200} = F_{100}\ (1.06)^{100}$$
$$= \$8,143\ (339.3)$$
$$= \$2,762,919.90$$

or approximately $2.763 million. By 1926, at the end of the third 100 years, the value would have increased another 339.3 times.

$$F_{300} = F_{200}\ (1.06)^{100}$$
$$= \$2.763\ \text{million}\ (339.3)$$
$$= \$937.5\ \text{million}$$

For the fifty years from 1926 to 1976 the $937.5 million would grow to

$$F_{350} = F_{300}\ (1.06)^{50}$$
$$= \$937.5\ \text{million}\ (18.42)$$
$$= \$17.27\ \text{billion}$$

This value is approximately $28 per square foot of Manhattan Island! Given current prices for Manhattan land, maybe Peter didn't make that good a buy.

Note that this problem could have been solved more simply by observing initially that $(1.06)^{350} = (1.06)^{100}(1.06)^{100}(1.06)^{100}(1.06)^{50}$. We could have just multiplied (339.3) (339.3) (339.3) (18.42) to arrive at[1]

$$(1.06)^{350} = 719.517 \times 10^6$$

This factor multiplied by \$24 provides us with \$17.27 billion, the same answer as above.

Double your money   If you look at Table 4-1 in the 6 percent column, you see that the factor for twelve periods is 2.0122. This means that \$1 invested at 6 percent per year will grow to \$2.01, or very nearly double, in twelve years. This is an example of a rule of thumb called the **rule of 72.** This rule works as follows: If you wish to know how long it will take to double your money at a given interest rate, divide the rate into 72 and the result is the number of years it will take. In this case $\frac{72}{6} = 12$. The rule works pretty well for most interest rates.[2] For example, the rule of 72 would say that it will take seventy-two years to double your money at 1 percent per year. In fact, it will take about seventy years. The rule says that it would take 3.6 years to double your money at 20 percent ($\frac{72}{20}$); in fact, it will take 3.8 years. The rule works the other way too. You can estimate the interest rate required to double your money in a given number of years by dividing the number of years into 72. For example, you must earn about 7.2 percent per year to double your money in ten years. The rule of 72 is a handy thing to remember.

Present Value   In the problems discussed above we were calculating the future value (or payment) of an amount invested (or borrowed) at a given rate of interest. In many problems, you would like to know the present amount which will grow to a given future value. Suppose you are faced with the following problem. You wish to save a portion of the earnings from your summer job this year to make your first tuition payment next fall, a year from now. Tuition will be \$500 and the bank will pay you 5 percent compounded annually. How much must you put in the bank now in order to have \$500

1. This is an application of the rule for combining exponents which says that

$$N^{A+B} = (N^A)(N^B)$$

For example,

$$2^5 = (2^3)(2^2) = (8)(4) = 32$$

2. A more accurate method is the **rule of 69:**

$$\text{Number of periods to double} = 0.35 + \frac{69}{\text{interest rate}}$$

For a development of the rule of 69 and a comparison with the rule of 72, see J. P. Gould and R. L. Weil, "The Rule of 69," *Journal of Business,* 49(3) (July 1974), pp. 397–398.

next year? The future amount you need is $500 and the interest rate is 5 percent. Let P be the amount put into savings now. From Eq. (4-2) we know that

$$F = P(1 + i) \qquad (4\text{-}3)$$

Solving Eq. (4-3) for P, we get

$$P = \frac{F}{1 + i} \qquad (4\text{-}4)$$

and

$$P = \frac{\$500}{1.05}$$
$$= \$476.20$$

The amount $476.20 is called the **present value** of $500 to be received one year from now at the interest rate of 5 percent per year. The general relationship for the present value of a future amount to be received n periods from now at an interest rate of i per period is derived from Eq. (4-2) just as the one-period relation was. Equation (4-2) was

$$F = P(1 + i)^n \qquad (4\text{-}2)$$

Solving for P,

$$P = \frac{F}{(1 + i)^n} \qquad (4\text{-}5)$$

In solving problems where P is the unknown amount, if you know the value of $(1 + i)^n$, you can remember to divide the future amount by that factor in order to find the present value. Alternatively, note that Eq. (4-5) can be expressed as

$$P = F \left[\frac{1}{(1 + i)^n} \right] \qquad (4\text{-}6)$$

Tables generally provide values for the term in the brackets so that when you wish to find the present value of a future amount you can *multiply* by the present value factor $1/(1 + i)^n$ rather than *dividing* by the compound amount factor $(1 + i)^n$. This is done because it is easier for people doing hand calculations to multiply than divide. To take a trivial example, if $(1 + i)^n = 1.05$, then $1/1.05 = 0.9524$. Which is easier to calculate, $0.9524 \times \$100$ or $\$100/1.05$?

We can use the value of $1/1.05 = 0.9524$ to solve the previous example. From Eq. (4-6) the present value of $F = \$500$ is

$$P = \$500 \ (0.9524)$$

$$= \$476.20$$

We now have two interest factors to keep track of, the **compound amount factor** $(1 + i)^n$ and the **present value factor** $[1/(1 + i)^n]$. As a way of remembering what these factors do, we use a special notation to express them. The compound amount factor is

$$(F/P, \ i, \ n) = (1 + i)^n \qquad (4\text{-}7)$$

This factor is used to find the future value of a present amount at i percent for n periods. The compound amount factor is always greater than 1.0 for i greater than zero, indicating that a present amount will always grow to a larger future value.

The present value factor is

$$(P/F, \ i, \ n) = \frac{1}{(1 + i)^n} \qquad (4\text{-}8)$$

This factor is used to find the present value of a future amount. The present value factor is always less than 1.0 for i greater than zero, indicating that a future amount has a smaller present value. A dollar in the future is worth less than a dollar today, as we said at the beginning of the chapter.

The headings in the tables of Appendix B are based on the symbols defined above. If you look at the table for 5 percent under the column headed P/F, you will find 0.9524 in the row for $n = 1$. We will be discussing the use of these tables after we look at some more difficult problems.

Annuities   An **annuity** is a series of periodic payments or receipts of equal amounts; for example, $100 per year for ten years. A typical house mortgage repayment schedule is an annuity. Figure 4-3 shows the cash flow diagram for an annuity of $A for n periods contrasted with present (P) and future (F) amounts. As an example of one type of problem involving annuities, suppose you plan to save $1,000 each summer for the next three years. You can earn 5 percent per year on this money. How much could you with-

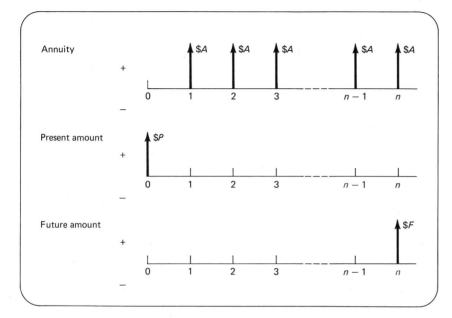

Figure 4-3. Cash flow diagrams.

draw from the bank three years from now? A cash flow diagram of the problem we are describing is shown in Figure 4-4, where F is the unknown amount to be determined. From the cash flow diagram you can see that the first savings deposit planned is one year from the present. At the end of the summer two years from now you will have that $1,000 plus the interest earned on it as well as a newly deposited $1,000, or $1,000(1.05) + $1,000. Therefore, the total in the account at the end of two years will be $2,050. At the end of the third summer you will have accumulated savings and interest of $2,050 (1.05) = $2,152.50

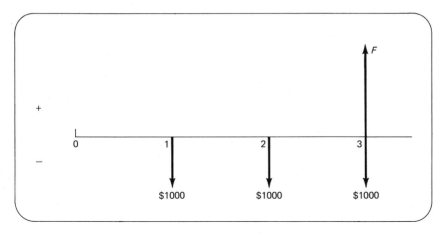

Figure 4-4. The cash flows associated with a savings program.

plus an additional $1,000 in new savings. You would therefore have a total future amount of $3,152.50, that is,

$$F = \$3,152.50$$

Future values and annuities   There is an easier way to solve such problems. To see how, let's look at the savings program a different way. At the end of the third summer the $1,000 saved in the first year would have been earning interest for two years. Therefore, the first summer's savings contributed $1,000 (1.05)^2 = $1,000 (1.1025) = $1,102.50. The savings from the second summer earned interest for one year, $1,000 (1.05) = $1,050. The savings from the third year were just deposited and earned nothing. Adding them together,

$$F = \$1,000 \ (1.05)^2 + \$1,000 \ (1.05) + \$1,000$$

$$= \$1,102.50 + \$1,050 + \$1,000$$

$$= \$3,152.50$$

We can express the computations above in terms of an annual amount A (which was $1,000 in the example) and the interest rate i.

$$F = A(1 + i)^2 + A(1 + i) + A$$

Alternatively, we can write the relationship as

$$F = A[(1 + i)^2 + (1 + i) + 1] \tag{4-9}$$

The term in the brackets is another interest factor which is sometimes called the **annuity compound amount factor.**[3] It expresses the value at the end of three periods of a three-period annuity of $1 per period invested at an interest rate of i percent. We can represent this factor for n periods and i percent per period in our notation as $(F/A, i, n)$. It is used to find the future value of an annuity and always has a value greater than 1.0. Notice from Figure 4-3 that the future value F occurs at the same point in time as does the last annuity amount A; the last annuity amount therefore earns no interest. Values for the annuity compound amount factor are also found in tables such as the ones in Appendix B.

In the example above, the factor is

$$1.1025 + 1.05 + 1.0 = 3.1525$$

---

3. The general form of the annuity compound amount factor $(F/A, i, n)$ is the sum of a series of individual compound amount factors:

$$(F/A, i, n) = (1 + i)^{n-1} + (1 + i)^{n-2} + \cdots + (1 + i) + 1.0$$

To solve our problem, we would need only to look in the 5 percent table in Appendix B under the column headed F/A and along the row for $n = 3$ to find the value of 3.1525 and multiply it by $1,000 to get our answer of $3,152.50.

Now suppose you wanted to have $3,152.50 available to you at the end of the summer three years from now. How much would you have to deposit each summer at an interest rate of 5 percent starting one year from now assuming that you save equal amounts each year? We know the answer is $1,000 per year, but how can we calculate it? It's simply the reverse of the problem above. Now we are given the future amount and wish to know the annual amount.

There is a factor used to find the annuity that must be invested to provide a future value. It is called the **sinking fund factor** and is expressed as $(A/F, i, n)$. This factor is a number between zero and 1.0. In order to solve our problem, we need to know $(A/F, 5\%, 3)$. If you now look in the 5 percent table of Appendix B down the column headed A/F and along the row for $n = 3$, you will find

$$(A/F, 5\%, 3) = 0.3172$$

To determine the annual savings required to accumulate to a future value of $3,152.50, you need to perform the following calculations:

$$
\begin{aligned}
A &= \$3,152.50 \ (A/F, \ 5\%, \ 3) \\
&= \$3,152.50 \ (0.3172) \\
&= \$1,000
\end{aligned}
$$

In general, to find the annuity A given the future amount F, use the sinking fund factor.

$$A = F(A/F, i, n) \tag{4-10}$$

It is worthwhile to note that the sinking fund factor is equal to the reciprocal of the annuity compound amount factor:

$$
\begin{aligned}
(A/F, 5\%, 3) &= \frac{1}{(F/A, \ 5\%, \ 3)} \\
&= \frac{1}{3.1525} \\
&= 0.3172
\end{aligned}
$$

The sinking fund factor is very useful in developing savings plans designed to reach a particular goal; such an example is developed later in this chapter. Many corporate bond issues require the firm to make regular payments into a sinking fund set up to retire the bonds at the end of a specified number of years. This is where the factor gets its name, since it is used to find out how large the payments (annuity) must be to make the sinking fund equal the amount of the bond issue when the bonds must be paid off.

Present values and annuities In many problems you will want to know the present amount which must be invested today in order to provide an annuity for several periods. For example suppose your grandmother wished to deposit enough money now to meet your tuition payments for the next three years of $2,000 per year. The interest rate is 5 percent per year. The cash flows are shown in Figure 4-5.

One way to solve this problem is to treat it as three smaller problems of finding the present values given the future amounts.

1. How much must be invested today to provide $2,000 one year from now?

$$P_1 = \$2,000 \ (P/F, \ 5\%, \ 1)$$

$$= \$2,000 \ \frac{1}{1.05}$$

$$= \$2,000 \ (0.9524)$$

$$= \$1,904.80$$

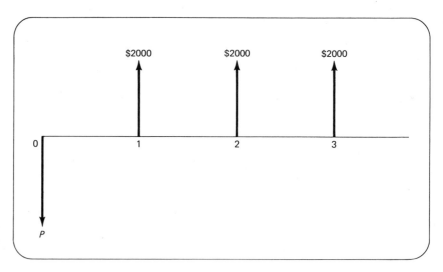

Figure 4-5. The present value of three annual amounts.

2. How much must be invested today to provide $2,000 two years from now?

$$P_2 = \$2,000 \; (P/F, \; 5\%, \; 2)$$

$$= \$2,000 \left[\frac{1}{(1.05)^2} \right]$$

$$= \$2,000 \; (0.9070)$$

$$= \$1,814$$

3. How much must be invested today to provide $2,000 three years from now?

$$P_3 = \$2,000 \; (P/F, \; 5\%, \; 3)$$

$$= \$2,000 \left[\frac{1}{(1.05)^3} \right]$$

$$= \$2,000 \; (0.8638)$$

$$= \$1,727.60$$

The total amount that must be deposited is the sum of the three values calculated above; so

$$P = \$1,904.80 + \$1,814 + \$1,727.60$$

$$= \$5,446.40$$

This computational scheme can be written in a more general form as

$$P = \frac{A}{1+i} + \frac{A}{(1+i)^2} + \frac{A}{(1+i)^3}$$

$$= A \left[\frac{1}{1+i} + \frac{1}{(1+i)^2} + \frac{1}{(1+i)^3} \right] \qquad (4\text{-}11)$$

The terms in the brackets are a simple sum of single-payment present value factors. Values for such sums are tabulated as an interest factor called the **annuity present value factor.**[4] We can denote the factor as $(P/A, \; i, \; n)$, the present value of an annuity. The annuity begins (the first A

4. The general relationship for the annuity present value factor is

$$(P/A, \; i, \; n) = \frac{1}{1+i} + \frac{1}{(1+i)^2} + \cdots + \frac{1}{(1+i)^n}$$

occurs) one period *after* the present amount P occurs (this was illustrated earlier in Figure 4-3). The value for $(P/A, 5\%, 3)$ is

$$(P/A, 5\%, 3) = 0.9524 + 0.9070 + 0.8638$$
$$= 2.7232$$

This value can be found in the 5 percent table in Appendix B. For our problem above we could have determined P as

$$P = A(P/A, i, n)$$
$$= \$2,000 \ (P/A, 5\%, 3)$$
$$= \$2,000 \ (2.7232)$$
$$= \$5,446.40$$

This brings up another issue: How accurate do you really need to be in calculating such values? The answer is: Not nearly so accurate as we have been in our calculations. For most practical purposes in solving interest rate problems three-place accuracy is sufficient. An answer of $5,450 is usually just as good as $5,446.40. There are some business situations in which greater accuracy is desirable, but you should be able to identify them when they are encountered. The values in the tables of Appendix B are accurate to four or five figures to permit more precise results if you want them. Most of the time it is safe to round off the factors to three places.

In some problems you might want to know the annuity that can be provided from a given present amount of money. For example, suppose your grandmother (a lovely person) gave you $5,446.40. You plan to deposit it in a savings account paying 5 percent and spend the entire amount plus interest over the next three years. How much could you withdraw each year with equal annual withdrawals? You know the answer already to be $2,000 per year. After the third withdrawal, the deposit balance would be zero since $2,000 per year is equivalent to (has the same present value as) $5,446.40 today. In this case we wanted to know the annuity that results from a given present amount. The general representation for this interest factor is $(A/P, i, n)$. It is the reciprocal of the annuity present value factor.

$$(A/P, i, n) = \frac{1}{(P/A, i, n)} \tag{4-12}$$

In our previous example $(P/A, 5\%, 3) = 2.7232$. The corresponding value for $(A/P, 5\%, 3)$ is $1/2.7232 = 0.3672$. You can check this by looking in the 5 percent table of Appendix B under the column headed A/P at $n = 3$.

$(A/P, i, n)$ is sometimes called the **capital recovery factor** since it can be used to determine what income is necessary to recover a capital investment given the rate of interest on the investment. It can also be called the **loan repayment factor,** since it is used to find the payments needed to pay off a loan. For example, suppose you worked for "Friendly Dan, the Cycle Man," and wished to set up monthly payment plans for motorcycle purchases. In order to find the monthly payments that would pay off a given purchase in twelve months at an interest rate of 1 percent per month, you would need to know $(A/P, 1\%, 12)$. The value of this factor is 0.0888, which you can get from the 1 percent table in Appendix B. The required payments (A) given the purchase price (P) would be

$$A = 0.0888\ P$$

For a motorcycle costing $200, the purchaser must pay $(0.0888)\$200 =$ $17.76 per month. If the cycle costs $500, the monthly payment would be $(0.0888)\$500 = \$44.40$.

Summary of Interest Factors

Three pairs of interest factors are useful in solving problems involving money paid or received at different points in time. If you are using electronic calculators or slide rules to solve problems, it is as easy to divide as it is to multiply and you would need to have available only one factor from each of the three pairs. But, when you are doing hand calculations, all six factors are helpful. Values for all six factors are included in tables in Appendix B under the appropriate headings. The examples given below all use the 5 percent table at $n = 5$.

Single payments or receipts To find the future value of a present amount, use the compound amount factor:

$$F = P(F/P, i, n)$$

where

$$(F/P, i, n) = (1 + i)^n$$

This is the amount $1 will grow to in n periods invested at i percent per period. The future value of $100 invested for five years at 5 percent is $F = \$100(1.2763) = \$127.63$.

To find the present value of a future amount, use the present value factor:

$$P = F(P/F, i, n)$$

where

$$(P/F, \; i, \; n) = \frac{1}{(F/P, \; i, \; n)}$$

This is the amount that must be invested to have \$1 n periods from now at i percent per period. The present value of \$127.63 to be received five years from now given a rate of 5 percent is $P = \$127.63(0.7835) = \$100$.

Annuities (equal payments or receipts in each period) To find the future value of an annuity, use the annuity compound amount factor:

$$F = A(F/A, \; i, \; n)$$

where

$$(F/A, \; i, \; n) = (1 + i)^{n-1} + (1 + i)^{n-2} + \cdots + (1 + i) + 1$$

This is the amount (F) accumulated by investing \$1 each period for n periods at an interest rate of i per period. F is the amount accumulated at the time the last investment is made; therefore the last investment earns no interest. The future value of \$100 per year for five years at 5 percent is $F = \$100 \, (5.5256) = \$552.56$.

To find the annuity required to accumulate to a future value, use the sinking fund factor:

$$A = F(A/F, \; i, \; n)$$

where

$$(A/F, \; i, \; n) = \frac{1}{(F/A, \; i, \; n)}$$

This is the amount (A) which must be invested each period for n periods at an interest rate of i per period to obtain \$1 in period n at the time the last investment is made. The last investment of amount A earns no interest. The annual savings required to accumulate to \$552.56 in five years at 5 percent is $A = \$552.56(0.1810) = \$100$.

To find the present value of an annuity, use the annuity present value factor:

$$P = A(P/A, \; i, \; n)$$

where

$$(P/A, \; i, \; n) = \frac{1}{(1 + i)} + \frac{1}{(1 + i)^2} + \cdots + \frac{1}{(1 + i)^n}$$

This is the amount which must be invested to provide an annuity of $1 per period for n periods at a rate of i percent per period. The annuity begins one period after the investment is made. The present value of $100 per year for five years at 5 percent is

$$P = \$100(4.3295)$$

$$= \$432.95$$

To find the annuity provided by a present amount, use the capital recovery or loan repayment factor:

$$A = P(A/P, i, n)$$

where

$$(A/P, i, n) = \frac{1}{(P/A, i, n)}$$

This is the annuity provided for n periods by investing $1 at a rate of i percent per period. The annual income for five years provided by a present investment of $432.95 at 5 percent is $A = \$432.95(0.2310) = \$100$.

We have been using the tables in our examples above, but now let's examine them more carefully. Table 4-2 is a copy of the table of factors in Appendix B for an interest rate of 6 percent per period. There is one such table for each interest rate included in the Appendix. The range of rates provided is from $\frac{1}{3}$ to 50 percent. Each of the six factors is included in the table. In order to use the tables, you merely look up the value of the factor for the rate and number of periods desired. Note that each column in Table 4-2 is headed by the descriptive notation for the factor. The second column is headed F/P. This column contains the values of $(F/P, 6\%, n) = (1.06)^n$ for the values of n shown in the first column. For example, what is the value of $(F/P, 6\%, 5)$? Find the number in Table 4-2 that corresponds to $(F/P, 6\%, 5)$. The correct value is 1.3382.

Let's look at a problem using Table 4-2. Suppose you are trying to decide whether you should buy four tires expected to last for 20,000 miles or a set expected to last for 40,000 miles. You drive an average of 10,000 miles per year and expect to keep the car at least another four years. The 20,000-mile tires will cost $90 now and the 40,000-mile tires will cost $160. The cash flow diagrams for this problem are shown in Figure 4-6. Figure 4-6a shows the cash costs of buying 20,000-mile tires now at $90 and as-

SOLVING PROBLEMS WHEN THE INTEREST RATE IS KNOWN

Using the Tables

Table 4-2. Interest rate of 6.00*

n	F/P	P/F	F/A	A/F	P/A	A/P
1	1.0600	.9434	1.0000	1.0000	.9434	1.0600
2	1.1236	.8900	2.0600	.4854	1.8334	.5454
3	1.1910	.8396	3.1836	.3141	2.6730	.3741
4	1.2625	.7921	4.3746	.2286	3.4651	.2886
5	1.3382	.7473	5.6371	.1774	4.2124	.2374
6	1.4185	.7050	6.9753	.1434	4.9173	.2034
7	1.5036	.6651	8.3938	.1191	5.5824	.1791
8	1.5938	.6274	9.8975	.1010	6.2098	.1610
9	1.6895	.5919	11.4913	.0870	6.8017	.1470
10	1.7908	.5584	13.1808	.0759	7.3601	.1359

* The complete table for a 6 percent interest rate can be found in Appendix B.

sumes that the same set is expected to cost you $90 two years from now. Figure 4-6b shows a single purchase of 40,000-mile tires. We will transform the two cash flows for the 20,000-mile tires to their present value. This gives us the cost of 20,000-mile tires in terms of dollars today which can be compared with the cost today of 40,000-mile tires. The present value of $90 today and $90 two years from now assuming an interest rate of 6 percent is

$$P = \$90 + \$90(P/F, 6\%, 2)$$

Look up $(P/F, 6\%, 2)$ in Table 4-2. Its value is 0.89. The present value of the cost of buying 20,000-mile tires is therefore

$$P = \$90 + \$90(0.89)$$
$$= \$90 + \$80.10$$
$$= \$170$$

Since the present cost of the 40,000-mile tires is $160, they are a better deal.

Beginning students usually encounter several difficulties in solving interest rate problems. One such difficulty is recognizing the factors and tables to use in solving a particular problem. This difficulty is easily overcome with the familiarity gained from solving practice problems and reviewing the example problems on a step-by-step basis. Another difficulty arises when the cash flows in the problem are complicated and don't fit the simple examples we have been using. Here, too, practice helps, but that is not enough. There is a section later on (pp. 96–98) about what to do when the cash flows vary from period to period.

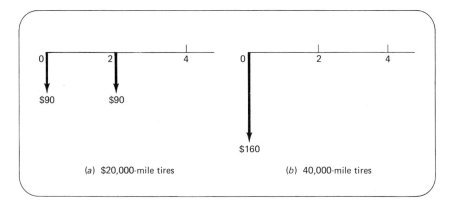

Figure 4-6. Cash flows from alternative tire purchases.

A further difficulty arises when the available tables don't have the exact factor you need to solve your problem. For example, we don't have a table here for an interest rate of $7\frac{1}{2}$ percent. If your problems involve this rate, you can use any of three methods. First, you can compute the factors you need using a calculator or a computer. Formulas for the factors are provided in Appendix 4A at the end of the chapter. Second, if your problem doesn't require a high degree of accuracy, you can interpolate in the tables you do have. Interpolation is sort of like averaging two numbers to get an "in-between" value. For example, if you wish to know the compound amount factor for five years at an annual rate of $7\frac{1}{2}$ percent, you are looking for $(F/P, 7\frac{1}{2}\%, 5)$. The tables provide the following values (look them up to check):

$$(F/P, 7\%, 5) = 1.4026$$

and
$$(F/P, 8\%, 5) = 1.4693$$

The value for $(F/P, 7\frac{1}{2}\%, 5)$ will be in between these two values. Figure 4-7 illustrates the problem. Since $7\frac{1}{2}$ percent is halfway between 7 and 8 percent, the value for the $7\frac{1}{2}$ percent factor will be approximately halfway

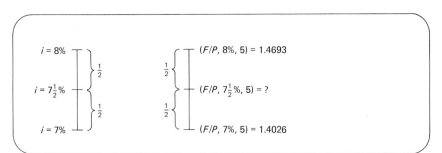

Figure 4-7. Interpolation illustration.

between the 7 percent factor and the 8 percent factor. The distance between the two factors (difference in their values) is

$$1.4693 - 1.4026 = 0.0667$$

One half of the difference is $0.0667/2 = 0.0333$. The value for $(F/P, 7\frac{1}{2}\%, 5)$ is therefore (approximately) $1.4026 + 0.0333 = 1.4359$. Interpolation can also be used when the number of periods in your problem is not in the tables. For example, if you want $(P/A, 6\%, 41)$ and all you have is $(P/A, 6\%, 40)$ and $(P/A, 6\%, 44)$, you can interpolate between the two known values to find the unknown one. Try this problem using the 6 percent table in Appendix B. Note that 41 is one-fourth of the distance from 40 to 44. The correct answer is $15.0463 + 0.0842 = 15.1305$. Interpolation is also useful in finding unknown interest rates, as we show later in the chapter. Third, you can try to find someone who has a more complete set of interest tables. Banks and libraries frequently have good tables.

Variable Cash Flows

When you come up against a problem that doesn't fit the simple situations we have been looking at, the first thing to do is to draw a cash flow diagram. Since any interest problem can be solved by applying the proper set of factors, once you identify the cash flows you can decide what factors you need. Take the example as shown in Figure 4-8a. If you wish to find the present value of the annual cash flows shown given an interest rate of 6 percent per year, either of the following two methods will work.

The first method is to consider the cash flows as being a $20 per year annuity beginning in year 2 plus a single amount of $80 in year 1, as shown in Figure 4-8b. We can first calculate the present value (P_1) of the $20 per year annuity in years 2, 3, and 4 as of the end of the first year. At 6 percent,

$$P_1 = \$20(P/A, 6\%, 3)$$

$$= \$20(2.673)$$

$$= \$53.50$$

The annuity has now been converted to a value equivalent to a cash receipt of $53.50 at the end of year 1. We can add to this figure the $80 receipt in year 1 to get the total equivalent cash receipt at this time, $80 plus $53.50 = $133.50.

$$P_0 = \$133.50(P/F, 6\%, 1)$$

$$= \$133.50(0.9434)$$

$$= \$126$$

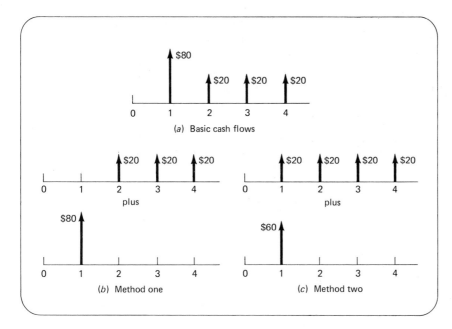

Figure 4-8.

The alternative method is to evaluate the cash flow as being an annuity of $20 beginning at the end of the first year plus a receipt of $60 at that time as illustrated in Figure 4-8c. The present value is then the sum of the present values of the two cash flows.

$$P = \$20(P/A,\ 6\%,\ 4) + \$60(P/F,\ 6\%,\ 1)$$

$$= \$20(3.465) + \$60(0.9434)$$

$$= \$126$$

As another example, suppose you wished to know what the cash flows of Figure 4-8a would accumulate to at the end of four years from today (time 0 in the figure) if deposited to earn 6 percent. Using the second method, the future value would be

$$F = \$20(F/A,\ 6\%,\ 4) + \$60(F/P,\ 6\%,\ 3)$$

$$= \$20(4.375) + \$60(1.191)$$

$$= \$159$$

Note that the $60 is only compounded for three periods since the deposit will only be in the account for that length of time from year 1 to year 4.

The annuity factor, $(F/A, 6\%, 4)$, is for four periods since there are four $20 payments, one in each period.

If the cash flows vary from period to period, then you must handle each period's cash flow individually. For example, suppose you wish to find the present value of the cash flows shown in Figure 4-9. At an interest rate of 6 percent per year the present value of all the cash flows is simply the sum of the present values of each one.

$$
\begin{aligned}
P &= \$20(P/F, 6\%, 1) + \$25(P/F, 6\%, 2) \\
&\quad + \$30(P/F, 6\%, 3) + \$28(P/F, 6\%, 4) \\
&= \$20(0.9434) + \$25(0.8900) + \$30(0.8396) + \$28(0.7921) \\
&= \$18.87 + \$22.25 + \$25.19 + \$22.18 \\
&= \$88.49
\end{aligned}
$$

Finding future values would be done in a similar fashion but using $(F/P, i, n)$ instead of $(P/F, i, n)$. If you wish to transform a set of variable cash flows into an annuity, the easiest thing to do is to first find the present value of the cash flows, as done in the example. Then use the capital recovery factor $(A/P, i, n)$ to convert that present value into its equivalent annuity. If, for example, you wished to know the annuity equivalent to the cash flows of Figure 4-9, it can be determined by using the present value of $88.49 that we have already found.

$$
\begin{aligned}
A &= \$88.49(A/P, 6\%, 4) \\
&= \$88.49(.2886) \\
&= \$25.54
\end{aligned}
$$

That is, the cash flows of Figure 4-9 are equivalent to an annuity of $25.54 per year for four years at 6 percent.

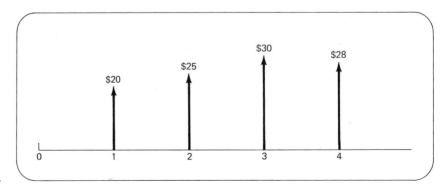

Figure 4-9.

Example problem Assume that you are twenty-five years old and wish to retire at age sixty. You expect to be able to average a 5 percent annual rate on savings over your lifetime. You would like to save enough money to provide $5,000 per year beginning at age sixty-one in retirement income to supplement other sources (social security, pension plans, etc.). You would also like to have some extra money to spend when you retire at age sixty. One problem you face is estimating how long you wish the $5,000 per year to continue on retirement. Suppose you decide that the extra income need only be provided for twenty years (up to age eighty). The problem is how to organize your savings program prior to retirement so that you will have enough money to support a retirement income of $5,000 per year for twenty years.

The initial part of this problem is fairly simple. You should find the amount of money you must have at age sixty in order to provide $5,000 per year for twenty years. In other words, you need to know the present value (as of age sixty) of a twenty-year annuity of $5,000 per year. The factor needed is therefore $(P/A, i, n)$, the annuity present value factor.

$$P_{60} = \$5,000(P/A, 5\%, 20)$$
$$= \$5,000(12.462)$$
$$= \$62,300$$

At age sixty a savings account of $62,300 earning 5 percent interest per year will permit you to take out $5,000 per year beginning one year after retirement and continuing for twenty years. Notice that we are making the simplifying assumption that you draw out $5,000 annually. In practice, you would probably withdraw smaller amounts more frequently, for example $400 or so per month beginning at age sixty. However, the assumption of annual withdrawal is a fairly good approximation and makes the problem easier to solve. If you wished to be able to withdraw some money immediately on retirement—to buy a camper, for example—you would need more than $62,300. So, let's use $70,000 as our target savings goal for age sixty. This would provide you with $7,700 to spend right away. In practice, you should estimate this amount as carefully as you can. Here we have rounded to an even $70,000 for illustrative purposes.

A simple savings program would be to deposit the same amount each year. To find out the annual amount invested at 5 percent needed to accumulate to $70,000 at age sixty, thirty-five years from now, what factor should be used? We wish to find the annuity that will accumulate to a future value, $(A/F, i, n)$, the sinking fund factor.

$$A = \$70,000(A/F, 5\%, 35)$$
$$= \$70,000 (0.0111)$$
$$= \$777$$

Therefore, you would have to save $777 per year for thirty-five years to have $70,000 at the end.

Suppose you felt that the most you could afford to save presently and until age forty-five would be $500 per year. See if you can figure out how much you would have to save each year from age forty-five to sixty in order to end up with $70,000. [Hint: The $500 saved per year for the first twenty years would be worth $500(F/A, 5%, 20) = $16,500 at age forty-five. By age sixty this amount would grow to $16,500(F/P, 5%, 15) = $34,000.] The answer is $1,667 per year needed to be saved from age forty-five to age sixty.

Time and Timing In this book, in problems where the cash flows cover several years, we simplify our calculations by putting all the cash received or paid during a given year at the end of the year. This is an approximation to simplify the problem. The savings-retirement problem shown earlier is an example. You would probably be making monthly deposits into your savings account during the savings period and variable withdrawals during retirement. Unless there is some reason to want a high degree of accuracy, treating the cash flows as single annual amounts is a reasonable way to keep down the complexity of a given problem. Of course, some problems demand that months or quarters or some other period be used—for example, finding the monthly payments on a mortgage. Usually, however, when we say that some amount of money is to be received in year 5, what we really mean is that the money is assumed to be received five years from now as a single receipt.

FINDING AN UNKNOWN INTEREST RATE In many problems you will know the amounts of all the cash flows and would like to determine what the interest rate is. Prior to the "Truth in Lending" Act, which went into effect in 1969, finding the true interest rate on a consumer loan was of particular importance. Now lenders usually state the rate; however, they have the option simply to tell you the total dollar finance charge, which they often do instead of giving the interest rate. Business investments are often evaluated using their **rate of return,** which is the interest rate expected to be earned by the investment.

Essentially we can identify two general situations in which you might wish to find the interest rate based on the cash flows—a loan agreement and an investment opportunity. When you are borrowing money, you generally receive an amount of money today in return for an agreement to pay more money back in the future. When you invest, you pay money out today in the expectation that you will receive more money in return sometime in the future. When you deposit money in a bank savings account, you are lending money to the bank with the expectation that the bank will pay you back with interest. Similarly, when the bank loans money to you, the bank is making an investment and expects you to pay the money back with interest.

The result is that, except for the direction of the cash flows, a loan is like an investment. The rate of return the bank earns on its investment in a loan to you is the same as the interest rate you will pay to the bank. The point is that finding interest rates on loans is the same as finding rate of return on investments. We will begin by showing how to perform the analysis of different sorts of loans and then give examples of finding the rate of return on an investment.

There are three payment schedules or cash flow patterns for which we can find the interest rate without using tables. These are very handy to know.

Simple Cash Flows

The first case: *You borrow money and repay the loan within one year or less with a single payment.* In this case, let P be the amount borrowed now (principal) and F be the amount repaid later. We wish to find the interest rate i given P, the principal, and future payment F.

$$F = (1 + i)P$$

$$F = P + iP$$

$$F - P = iP$$

$$i = \frac{F - P}{P} \qquad (4\text{-}13)$$

or

$$i = \frac{F}{P} - 1 \qquad (4\text{-}13a)$$

In other words, if you borrow $50 and repay $55, you are paying ($55 − $50)/$50 = 0.10 or 10 percent per year. If the loan were for less than a year, you compute the interest rate as in Eq. (4-13), then scale up to an annual basis. For example, if you borrowed $100 for six months and repaid $105, the rate would be $5/$100 or 5 percent for six months or 10 percent per year.

The second simple case: *You borrow money and promise to pay an equal annual amount of interest every year forever.* This is called a "level perpetuity" and is not a very common type of loan. This type of loan or investment is used for illustrative purposes both by us and other authors. (The British government has issued perpetual bonds, however.) The rate of interest is

$$i = \frac{A}{P} \qquad (4\text{-}14)$$

where A is the annual amount.[5] Therefore, if you borrowed $50 on the promise to pay $5 per year forever, the interest rate would be $5/$50 = 0.10 or 10 percent per year.

The third simple case: *You borrow P dollars today, pay A dollars every year for n years, and at the end pay back P dollars.* The interest rate for this type of loan is also computed according to Eq. (4-14). Corporate bonds have payments like this. For example, if you borrow $50 now and pay $5 a year for six years (beginning one year from now) then pay back the $50 at the end of the sixth year, your interest cost is 10 percent per year ($5/$50). It's like a series of one-year loans. Think of it in this way: at the end of every year you pay the interest of $5 and pay back the original $50 borrowed, then turn around and immediately reborrow the $50. You end up on balance just paying $5 per year until the last year when you no longer borrow.

There are two more simple cash flow patterns for which the interest rate can be determined fairly quickly. However, both require the use of the tables.[6] The first of these is where there is *a single payment but the loan is outstanding longer than one year.* Suppose you borrow $1,000 and agree to pay off the borrowing three years from now with a payment of $1,260. What annual rate of interest are you being charged? We know that the compound amount factor can be used to find the future payment equivalent to the principal of a loan made today.

$$F = P(F/P, i, n)$$

5. This can be proved mathematically using the formula in Appendix 4A for the annuity present value factor and letting the value for n approach infinity.

6. In the case of a single-payment loan (or investment) when the future payment will be made n years from now, the interest rate can be determined easily using a calculator with a power function (y^x). The procedure is as follows:

$$F = P(F/P, i, n)$$
$$F = P(1 + i)^n$$
$$(1 + i)^n = \frac{F}{P}$$
$$1 + i = \left(\frac{F}{P}\right)^{1/n}$$
$$i = \left(\frac{F}{P}\right)^{1/n} - 1$$

Find the ratio F/P and then calculate $(F/P)^{1/n}$ using the y^x function where $y = F/P$ and $x = 1/n$. In the text example, $F/P = 1.26$ and $n = 3$.

$$i = (1.26)^{1/3} - 1$$
$$= 1.080 - 1$$
$$= 8.0\%$$

and in this case,

$$\$1,260 = \$1,000(F/P, i, 3)$$

Solving for the value of the factor, we get

$$(F/P, i, 3) = \frac{\$1,260}{\$1,000}$$

$$= 1.260$$

We now need to find that interest rate which provides a value for the compound amount factor of 1.260 at $n = 3$. To do this, you must go to the tables and look through them until you find the right value or one close to it. A good starting point can be found by noting that the average annual interest cost is $\$260/3 = \$87$ or roughly 8.7 percent of $\$1,000$. The exact annual interest rate will be less than the average rate since you are not really paying anything until the end of three years. If you try 8 percent first, you will find that $(F/P, 8\%, 3) = 1.260$. Therefore, the rate you are paying is 8 percent per year.

However, what if the payment were $\$1,275$? The factor you would be looking for is 1.275, which is greater than the value for 8 percent yet less than the value for 9 percent, $(F/P, 9\%, 3) = 1.295$. The rate must be between 8 percent and 9 percent. If you wish to be more accurate than that, you can interpolate to provide a fairly good approximation. This is similar to the procedure followed earlier in the chapter, except that now we are trying to find the interest rate rather than the factor. The answer by interpolation is 8.43 percent.

The second payment pattern which can be analyzed easily using the tables is *an annuity*. For example, if a loan of $\$1,000$ requires annual payments of $\$250$ per year for five years, what is the interest rate being charged? We know that the loan payment can be found by using the loan repayment factor $(A/P, i, n)$. Therefore,

$$\$250 = \$1,000(A/P, i, 5)$$

and
$$(A/P, i, 5) = \frac{\$250}{\$1,000}$$

$$= 0.250$$

Now go to the tables and try to find a value for $(A/P, i, 5)$ equal to 0.250. You know the rate will be less than 25 percent ($\$250/\$1,000$) since that would apply to a perpetuity and these payments stop after five years. Try a much lower rate, say 12 percent. $(A/P, 12\%, 5) = 0.277$. That's too large a value, and so you know the interest rate must be lower than 12 percent. The lower the interest rate, the lower the payments must be. You will find that $(A/P, 8\%, 5) = 0.250$. The answer is, therefore, 8 percent. If the value of the factor for the unknown rate lies between two rates, simply interpolate.

Now let's find the interest rate on an installment loan when the lender doesn't provide one. Friendly Dan advertises that you can buy a $200 motorcycle for $9 down and $9.50 per month for twenty-four months. The finance charge is the difference between the total amount of your payments and the amount you owed (borrowed) initially, or $(24 \times \$9.50) - (\$200 - \$9) = \$37$. What interest rate are you paying? The solution to this problem is similar to the one just above. You are dealing with an annuity and therefore use the formula

$$A = P(A/P, i, n)$$

Substituting in the appropriate values, we have

$$\$9.50 = \$191(A/P, i, 24)$$

$$(A/P, i, 24) = \frac{\$9.50}{\$191}$$

$$= 0.0497$$

Looking through the tables for a value of $(A/P, i, 24) = 0.0497$, we find that $(A/P, 1\frac{1}{2}\%, 24) = 0.0499$. The value for the next lowest rate in the table is $(A/P, 1\frac{1}{4}\%, 24) = 0.0485$. The interest rate therefore is between $1\frac{1}{4}$ and $1\frac{1}{2}$ percent per month. Interpolating to get a more exact rate,

$$\left(\begin{bmatrix} 0.0499 \\ 0.0497 \\ 0.0485 \end{bmatrix}\right) \quad \left(\begin{bmatrix} 1.5\% \\ (1.25 + x)\% \\ 1.25\% \end{bmatrix}\right)$$

$$\frac{0.0012}{0.0014} = \frac{x}{0.25\%}$$

$$0.86 = \frac{x}{0.25\%}$$

$$x = 0.22\%$$

$$(1\frac{1}{4} + x)\% = 1.47\%$$

Therefore, Friendly Dan is charging 1.47 percent per month, or $12(1.47\%) = 17.6$ percent per year.

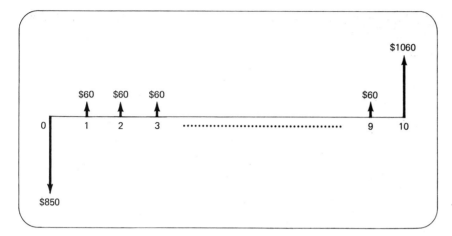

Figure 4-10. Cash flows from buying a bond and holding it to maturity.

Variable Cash Flows

Finding an unknown interest rate when the cash flows do not match one of the simple patterns shown above is more difficult. You must first set up an equation expressing the time-value equivalence of the cash flows. This equation will usually contain two or more interest factors in it involving the unknown rate.[7] Then you must try out different interest rates until you find one for which the equation will balance. This procedure is illustrated by the following example of an investment-type problem.

Suppose you would like to determine the interest rate you would earn from buying a bond and holding it to maturity. This interest rate is called the **yield to maturity** of the bond. The cash flows from buying and owning the bond are shown in Figure 4-10. The bond's current price is $850, it pays an annuity of $60 per year for ten years, and it will mature in ten years paying its par value of $1,000 at that time. If the price of the bond were $1,000 today, we know that the yield to maturity (interest rate) on the bond would be $60/$1,000 = 6 percent per year from our earlier discussion. However, since the price is only $850, we know that the yield to maturity must be greater than 6 percent. The time-value equation for the cash flows is

$$\text{Present price of the bond} = \frac{\text{present value of}}{\text{interest payments}} + \frac{\text{present value of}}{\text{principal payment}}$$

$$\$850 = \$60(P/A, i, 10) + \$1,000(P/F, i, 10)$$

The problem is to find that interest rate which will make the right side of the equation equal $850. The right side of the equation is the present value (P) of the future cash receipts from owning the bond given the interest

7. If it contains only one factor, you must have a version of one of the simple cases.

rate. We can think of the problem as finding that interest rate which will make $P = \$850$. Since we know the rate is greater than 6 percent, let's try 7 percent.

$$P_{7\%} = \$60(P/A, 7\%, 10) + \$1,000(P/F, 7\%, 10)$$
$$= \$60(7.024) + \$1,000(0.5083)$$
$$= \$930$$

This value of P is too large. In order to get a lower present value, we need to use a higher interest rate. Suppose we try 10 percent.

$$P_{10\%} = \$60(P/A, 10\%, 10) + \$1,000(P/F, 10\%, 10)$$
$$= \$60(6.145) + \$1,000(0.3855)$$
$$= \$754$$

Since the present value at 10 percent is too low, the correct rate must lie between 10 percent and 7 percent. Now that we have bracketed the true rate, we can either try some more values (8 or 9 percent) or we can interpolate. Let's interpolate.

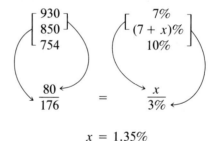

$$x = 1.35\%$$

The estimated rate is therefore 7 percent + 1.35 percent = 8.35 percent. If we wanted to get a more accurate estimate of the true rate, we could compute P at 8 and 9 percent and interpolate between those values instead of between 7 and 10 percent. The narrower the spread is, the more accurate is the interpolation. If we did this, our new estimate would be 8.26 percent. This answer is accurate to the second decimal place.

The rate of return on common stock As a final example of finding an unknown interest rate, let's look at the problem of finding the rate of return earned on an investment in common stock. Suppose you purchased ten shares of stock in a company four years ago at a price of $50 per share. Your total investment was $500(10 × $50). The company paid you the following dividends.

	First year	Second year	Third year	Fourth year
Dividend per share	$2.00	$2.00	$2.50	$3.00
Total dividends received	$20.00	$20.00	$25.00	$30.00

The current price of the stock is $60. What rate of return have you earned on your investment if you sell the stock now? The proceeds from sale of your shares will be $600(10 × $60). The cash flow diagram for the investment is shown in Figure 4-11. We are assuming that you have just received $30 in dividends for the current year, four years after the stock was purchased. Time is measured from the date of the original investment. To find the rate of return earned on the investment, we must find that interest rate which makes the present value of the cash receipts in years 1 to 4 equal to the amount invested. A direct expression is to treat each cash receipt as a single future amount:

$$\$500 = \frac{\$20}{1 + i} + \frac{\$20}{(1 + i)^2} + \frac{\$25}{(1 + i)^3} + \frac{\$630}{(1 + i)^4}$$

$$\$500 = \$20(P/F, i, 1) + \$20(P/F, i, 2) + \$25(P/F, i, 3) + \$630(P/F, i, 4)$$

This is the most general approach and will work for any set of future cash flows. However, using this approach, you must work with as many dif-

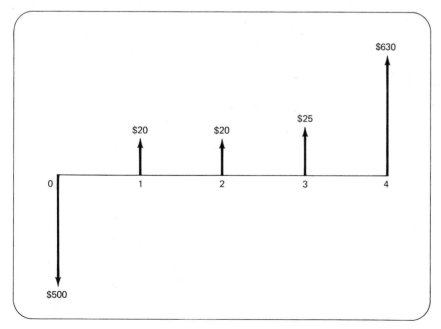

Figure 4-11. Cash flows from a common stock investment.

ferent interest rate factors as you have future cash flows, four in this example. Often the problem can be reduced somewhat by separating out any annuities in the flows. In this case we have a two-period annuity of $20; so the following expression is also correct:

$$\$500 = \$20(P/A, i, 2) + \$25(P/F, i, 3) + \$630(P/F, i, 4)$$

Now we only need to work with three factors instead of four.[8]

As we did in the previous example, we must try out different interest rates until we find two that bracket the true rate. Then we must interpolate between the two to estimate the value of the true rate. How can we know where to begin? There is no simple answer to the question. As you gain experience in solving these problems, your initial guesses will improve. Generally one examines the cash flow pattern and compares it with one of the simple cases discussed earlier. In this example we received $95 in dividends plus $100 capital gains for an average annual return of $49 per year. This is an average return of approximately 10 percent ($49/$500) on our investment. Since the true interest rate must be lower than 10 percent as most of the returns were not obtained until the fourth year, let's try 9 percent as a starting rate and go from there.

$$\begin{aligned} P_{9\%} &= \$20(P/A, 9\%, 2) + \$25(P/F, 9\%, 3) + \$630(P/F, 9\%, 4) \\ &= \$20(1.759) + \$25(0.772) + \$630(0.708) \\ &= \$500.52 \end{aligned}$$

That is very close to $500, the initial investment. The true rate must be slightly over 9 percent, and in many practical problems you could stop here. To get a better estimate, we must use the next higher rate in the tables, 10 percent.

$$\begin{aligned} P_{10\%} &= \$20(P/A, 10\%, 2) + \$25(P/F, 10\%, 3) + \$630(P/F, 10\%, 4) \\ &= \$20(1.736) + \$25(0.751) + \$630(0.683) \\ &= \$483.79 \end{aligned}$$

---

8. Although there is no advantage in this example, the following expressions are also equivalent and in many situations can be used to simplify problems:

$$\$500 = \$20 (P/A, i, 3) + \$5 (P/F, i, 3) + \$630 (P/F, i, 4)$$

and

$$\$500 = \$20(P/A, i, 4) + \$5(P/F, i, 3) + \$610(P/F, i, 4)$$

In general, if you have a stream of future cash flows $F_1, F_2, F_3, \ldots, F_n$, their present value can always be expressed as

$$P = A(P/A, i, n) + (F_1 - A)(P/F, i, 1) + (F_2 - A)(P/F, i, 2)$$
$$+ (F_3 - A)(P/F, i, 3) + \cdots + (F_n - A)(P/F, i, n)$$

This rate is obviously much too high. We can try interpolation at this point

$$\begin{bmatrix} 500.52 \\ 500.00 \\ 483.79 \end{bmatrix} \qquad \begin{bmatrix} 9\% \\ (9+x)\% \\ 10\% \end{bmatrix}$$

$$\frac{0.52}{16.73} = \frac{x}{1\%}$$

$$x = 0.03\%$$

This gives us an estimated rate of return of 9 percent + 0.03 percent or 9.03 percent per year. A still more exact figure would require use of a calculator or (preferably) a computer program. The actual rate is 9.046 percent.

SUMMARY

Interest rates give money its time value. Compound interest methods are used to solve problems when money is to be paid or received at different points in time. The basic principles of compound interest were described and illustrated through examples which serve two purposes: (1) to show how to solve problems involving compound interest and (2) to illustrate the range of problems requiring the use of compound interest techniques in real life. There are two general types of decisions that require some consideration of time value. One type of decision involves investing (or saving) money now in order to receive future cash benefits. The other type involves borrowing (or dis-saving) now to make current expenditures at a cost of having less money in the future. Intelligent financial management whether in business or in personal affairs requires familiarity with the concepts of compound interest.

One of the most useful concepts is the present value of future income. Beginning with the next chapter, the present value concept will be used extensively through this book. Present value provides a way to compare alternative income or costs streams which differ in timing and/or amounts. As we shall see, it is one of the key concepts of finance.

Interest rate factors are used to provide numerical solutions to financial problems. The six major interest factors are:

The **compound amount factor** (F/P, i, n): This is the value n periods from now of $1 invested today at a rate of interest of i percent per period. To find the value F of P dollars invested today, multiply P by (F/P, i, n):

$$F = P(F/P, i, n)$$

The **present value factor** (P/F, i, n): This is the value today of $1 to be received n periods from now given an interest rate of i percent per period.

To find the present value P of F dollars to be received n periods from now, multiply F by $(P/F, i, n)$:

$$P = F(P/F, i, n)$$

The **annuity compound amount factor** $(F/A, i, n)$: This factor is the value at the end of n periods resulting from an investment of $1 per period for n periods at a rate of i percent per period. To find the future value F of an annuity of A dollars per year, multiply A by $(F/A, i, n)$:

$$F = A(F/A, i, n)$$

The **sinking fund factor** $(A/F, i, n)$: This factor is the amount that must be invested each period for n periods at i percent per period to produce $1 at the end of n periods. To find the annuity A needed to accumulate to F dollars in n periods, multiply F by $(A/F, i, n)$:

$$A = F(A/F, i, n)$$

The **annuity present value factor** $(P/A, i, n)$: This factor is the value today of an annuity of $1 provided at the end of each period beginning one period from now and ending n periods from now given an interest rate of i percent. To find the present value P of A dollars per period, multiply A by $(P/A, i, n)$:

$$P = A(P/A, i, n)$$

The **capital recovery** or **loan repayment factor** $(A/P, i, n)$: This factor is the amount of money which must be paid each period for n periods in order to pay off a loan of $1 given an interest rate of i percent. It is also the amount of money that must be received in each period for n periods to provide an interest rate of i percent on $1 invested today. To find the annuity A equivalent to P dollars, borrowed or invested today, multiply P by $(A/P, i, n)$:

$$A = P(A/P, i, n)$$

Values for the six factors at several interest rates and numbers of periods are provided in Appendix B. In Appendix 4A there is an algebraic formula for each factor and instructions for using calculators to compute the factors directly.

The interest factors are also used to find unknown interest rates. If the cash flow pattern does not fit one of the five simple cases shown in the chapter, then a trial-and-error procedure must be used to determine the rate.

QUESTIONS

1. "A bird in the hand is worth two in the bush." Does this saying imply anything about the time value of money? Explain.
2. Two banks offer savings accounts with a stated interest rate of 4 percent per year. For bank A the actual rate is 1 percent per quarter compounded quarterly. For bank B the actual rate is $\frac{1}{3}$ percent per month compounded monthly. Will one of the two banks provide more interest than the other assuming that no withdrawals are made from the account for one year? Why?
3. What happens to the present value of an annuity if the interest rate rises? What happens to the future value?
4. Why is $(A/F, i, n)$ called the sinking fund factor?
5. Given an investment which will provide a stream of future cash flows, what is the relationship between the present value of the future cash flows and the rate of return on the amount invested?

PROJECT

Obtain information on savings and savings certificate accounts offered by at least two financial institutions in your town (the number to be assigned by your instructor). Which one would appear to be the most desirable if (1) you may wish to withdraw money at any time; (2) you will not withdraw any money for at least one year; (3) you would like to withdraw interest every three months, but the principal can remain in the account for at least 4 years; (4) you do not intend withdrawing any money for six years.

PROBLEMS

1. What is the present value (today) of the following cash flows at an interest rate of 8 percent per year?
   a) $100 received today. [Ans.: $100]
   b) $100 received five years from now. [Ans.: $68.06]
   c) $100 received 10,000 years from now. [Ans.: $0.00]
   d) $100 received each year beginning one year from now and ending ten years from now. [Ans.: $671]
   e) $100 received each year beginning one year from now and continuing forever. [Ans.: $1250]
2. Determine present values for the following cash flows and interest rates:
   a) $100 is received each year beginning two years from now and ending eleven years from now. The interest rate is 8 percent per year. [Ans.: $621.28]
   b) $100 is received each year for five years beginning one year from now (years 1–5), nothing is received for the next five years

(years 6–10), then $100 is received each year for five more years (years 11–15). The interest rate is 10 percent per year. [Ans.: $525.22]

c) $100 is received each month for five years (60 months). The interest rate is 12 percent per year (1 percent per month). [Ans.: $4,495.50]

3. What is the value five years from now of the following investments at an interest rate of 6 percent per year, $1\frac{1}{2}$ percent per quarter, or $\frac{1}{2}$ percent per month depending on the compounding period:

a) $100 invested today with interest compounded annually. [Ans.: $133.82]

b) $100 invested today with interest compounded quarterly. [Ans.: $134.69]

c) $100 invested today with interest compounded monthly. [Ans.: $134.89]

4. Find the future value of the following investments. The interest rate is 6 percent per year, compounded annually:

a) $100 is invested each year beginning one year from now and continuing through year ten, when the proceeds are withdrawn. [Ans.: $1,318.08]

b) $100 is invested each year starting today and continuing through year ten, when the proceeds are withdrawn. [Ans. = $1,497.16]

c) $100 is invested each year beginning one year from now and continuing through year nine. The proceeds are to be withdrawn in year ten. [Ans.: $1,218.08]

5. a) If you put $1,000 into a savings account today paying interest of 6 percent per year, how much money will you have in the account after ten years if no withdrawals are made from it until then? How much of this is interest?

b) Suppose you withdraw the interest every year. What will be your total interest earnings? Why does this differ from the interest earned in **a**?

6. If you wish to have $1,791 ten years from now, how much money should you place in a savings account today which pays 6 percent interest per year?

7. How much money should you put in a savings account each month in order to have $1,800 in the account at the end of ten years? Assume equal amounts saved each month and interest paid at a rate of 6 percent per year compounded monthly ($\frac{1}{2}$ percent per month). [Ans.: $10.98]

8. Calculate the following:

a) The monthly payments required on a $2,000 loan bearing a 12 percent per year interest rate (1 percent per month). The loan is to be paid back in eighteen equal monthly installments.

   b) The total amount of interest paid over eighteen months for the loan in **a**.

   c) The monthly payments on a thirty-year mortgage for $25,000. The interest rate is 9 percent per year ($\frac{3}{4}$ percent per month).

   d) The total amount of interest paid over thirty years for the loan in **c**.

 9. The day you were born your parents bought a ''baby bond'' for $100. This bond repays its purchase price plus 6 percent per year interest, compounded annually, on your twenty-first birthday. You have just turned twenty-one. Happy birthday. How much money will you be getting from your ''baby bond''?

10. If you put $100 per month into a savings account paying 6 percent per year ($\frac{1}{2}$ percent per month) compounded monthly, how much money will you have in the account after twenty-five years?

11. If you cash in your life insurance policy at age sixty-five, you will receive $50,000. You expect to invest the money to earn 8 percent per year.

   a) What is the maximum equal annual amount that you can spend out of this fund for twenty years. [Ans.: $5,095]

   b) Suppose you only spend $4,440 per year. How long will the money last? [Ans.: 30 years]

12. You own an apartment house that provides a net income to you of $300 per month. What is the maximum twenty-year mortgage loan you could obtain such that the payments on the loan could be made entirely from the apartment income. Assume a 9 percent annual interest rate ($\frac{3}{4}$ percent per month) and monthly payments on the mortgage.

13. You are the parent of a four-year-old girl and plan to begin saving next year for her college education. You wish to provide $7,500 per year for four years beginning when she is eighteen. How much money in equal annual installments must be invested each year until she is seventeen to meet this goal if you earn 6 percent on your investment? [Ans.: $1,377]

14. You work for a company that provides a pension plan for which the company contributes 50 percent of the amount you contribute. For example, if you specify that $100 of your monthly salary is to go into the plan, the company will add $50 to make the total contribution $150 per month. The plan guarantees an annual interest rate of 6 percent (compounded monthly). If you believe you can safely earn 8 percent per year (compounded monthly) by investing the money yourself, is it worthwhile belonging to the company plan? Assume that you plan to retire in thirty years and that you will set aside $100 per month regardless of the approach used.

15. Claude Foote has decided to save money to provide for his own retirement and for the college education of his son, Bonzo. Bonzo is three years old and is expected to begin college at age eighteen. He will need $20,000 a year for four years starting fifteen years from now. ("Bonzo's going FIRST CABIN"—Claude.) Claude is thirty now and wants to retire at age sixty with a retirement income of $60,000 per year starting thirty-one years from now for twenty-five years. ("If you think big, you can live big"—Claude.) Assuming an interest rate of 10 percent per year, how much money must Claude invest each year (equal annual amounts for thirty years beginning one year from now) to provide for his retirement and Bonzo's education? [Ans.: $5,082]

16. Compute the annual interest rate or rate of return that you will earn on the following investments.
    a) A U.S. Treasury bill which has a current price of $950 and will pay $1,000 at maturity one year from now. [Ans.: 5.26 percent]
    b) A U.S. Treasury bill which has a current price of $960 and will pay $1,000 at maturity six months from now. [Ans.: 8.33 percent]
    c) A U.S. Treasury note selling at its maturity value ($1,000), paying 8 percent coupon interest per year, and maturing in five years.
    d) An acre of vacation property with a current price of $5,000 which you expect to be able to sell for $7,350 in five years. There are no other expenses or income from this property. [Ans.: 8 percent]
    e) A bond with a current price of $80 (per $100 maturity value), paying 6 percent coupon interest, and maturing in twenty years.
    f) A preferred stock with a current price of $80 paying $6 dividends per share per year forever. [Ans.: 7.5 percent]

17. Determine the annual interest rate on the following debt contracts:
    a) A $25,000 mortgage with monthly payments of $209.80 to be paid off in twenty-five years.
    b) Solve the problem in a considering that the lender is charging a 2 percent fee at the time the loan is taken out so that the actual amount being lent to you is less than $25,000. [Ans.: 9.29 percent]
    c) An installment loan for $2,000 which has (low, low) monthly payments of $66 for thirty-six months and an additional "balloon" payment of $150 in the last month.

18. You are considering taking out a $2,400 loan from the Friendly Finance Company. They are charging a "low 10 percent annual interest rate" on a loan for twenty-four months. Your payments are determined as follows:

Annual interest = 10% of $2400 = $240 per year

$$\text{Total due} = \text{principal plus 2 years interest}$$

$$= \$2400 + 2(\$240)$$

$$= \$2880$$

$$\text{Monthly payment} = \frac{\$2880}{24} \text{ months}$$

$$= \$120 \text{ per month}$$

This procedure is called "add on" interest. What is the annual interest rate on this loan?

19. You are considering investing in one of the following two United States government bonds:

Coupon	Maturity	Price/$100 maturity value
6%	20 years	$80
8%	20 years	$100

Your income tax rate is 40 percent and your capital gains tax rate is 20 percent. Capital gains taxes are paid at maturity on the difference between the purchase price and the maturity value. What will be your aftertax yield to maturity (rate of return after taxes) from owning these bonds to maturity?

20. Suppose that you purchased ten shares of Standard Brands, Inc., common stock in December 1968 at a price of $45 per share. You sold the stock for $60 per share in January 1975. The following dividends per share were paid during the period you owned the stock:

1969	1970	1971	1972	1973	1974
$1.50	$1.57	$1.60	$1.66	$1.75	$1.87

a) Did the rate of return you earned from owning this stock depend on the number of shares you bought? Why or why not?

b) What was your rate of return before taxes from owning this stock?

c) Assume that your income tax rate was 20 percent in each year from 1969 to 1975 and that the applicable capital gains rate on the sale of the stock was 10 percent. What was your aftertax rate of return on the stock?

21. One year ago you invested $1,000 in a six-year maturity savings certificate account in a bank that pays an annual rate of 8.0 percent compounded monthly. Since that time interest rates have risen and you are considering withdrawing the money to invest in a higher interest rate asset. However you will be severely penalized if you withdraw

the money before the six-year period is up, five years from now, because of regulations of the Federal Reserve Board acting under authority provided by the U.S. Congress. The penalty is that the interest rate for the period you have held the certificate will be reduced to the passbook savings rate (currently 6 percent annually compounded monthly), and you will get no interest for the last three months.

a) Assuming all interest has been left in the account, what is your current balance?

b) How much will you have in the account five years from now, when the certificate matures?

c) How much money will you receive now if you close out the account?

d) How high must the interest rate earned on an alternative five-year investment be, to make it worthwhile for you to switch from the certificate? Assume annual compounding in the alternative investment. [Ans.: 9.06 percent]

e) Would the interest rate calculated in **d** be higher, lower, or the same if instead of owning the certificate for one year, you had owned it for two years? Why?

formulas and computational methods

This appendix serves as a reference and an aid to solving problems when tables are not available that fit a particular problem. Here we provide mathematical formulas for calculating the basic interest rate factors presented in Chapter 4. These formulas can be used to calculate the values for a factor for any given interest rate and time period. We also provide formulas for the present value of growing or declining streams which were not discussed in the chapter. Finally we discuss some methods to compute the factors using the formulas.

1. a) Compound amount factor:

$$(F/P, \; i, \; n) = (1 + i)^n \qquad (4\text{-}15)$$

FORMULAS FOR THE BASIC INTEREST RATE FACTORS

b) Present value factor:

$$(P/F, \; i, \; n) = \frac{1}{(1 + i)^n} = (1 + i)^{-n} \qquad (4\text{-}16)$$

2. a) Annuity compound amount factor:

$$(F/A, \; i, \; n) = \frac{(1 + i)^n - 1}{i} \qquad (4\text{-}17)$$

b) Sinking fund factor:

$$(A/F, \; i, \; n) = \frac{i}{(1 + i)^n - 1} \qquad (4\text{-}18)$$

3. a) Annuity present value factor:

$$(P/A, \; i, \; n) = \frac{(1 + i)^n - 1}{i(1 + i)^n} = \frac{1 - (1 + i)^{-n}}{i} \qquad (4\text{-}19)$$

b) Capital recovery (loan repayment) factor:

$$(A/P, \; i, \; n) = \frac{i(1 + i)^n}{(1 + i)^n - 1} = \frac{i}{1 - (1 + i)^{-n}} \qquad (4\text{-}20)$$

The formulas are grouped into the three pairs of factors for which one member of the pair is the reciprocal of the other.

There are two major advantages to knowing the factors rather than re-lying on tables. First you may not have tables available for the interest rate i and time period n that you require. The formulas apply to any inter-est rate, for example, 8.375 percent, or time period, for example, eighteen years. The second advantage is the ease with which the formulas can be programmed into programmable calculators or computers. If one of these devices is available, there is no need for tables at all when you know the formulas.

FORMULAS FOR GROWING OR DECLINING STREAMS

In many situations the future stream of cash payments or receipts grows or declines at even rates. We will examine two types of growth and decline—arithmetic and compound.

Arithmetic Growth or Decline

Arithmetic or *linear growth* occurs when a stream of cash increases by a constant *dollar* amount each period. For example, Figure 4-12*a* shows a stream of cash receipts growing at a rate of $10 per period. Similarly, Fig-ure 4-12*b* shows a stream of cash receipts declining arithmetically at a rate of $10 per period. This is also called linear growth or decline because if the figures are plotted on a graph, the points lie in a straight line, dollars versus time.

The most straightforward method of evaluating such streams is to split them into two pieces—an annuity plus (or minus) the growth (decline) ele-ment. For example, the stream of Figure 4-12*a* can be considered an annuity of $20 per period for five periods plus a growth element of $10 per period. Similarly the stream of Figure 4-12*b* is an annuity of $50 per

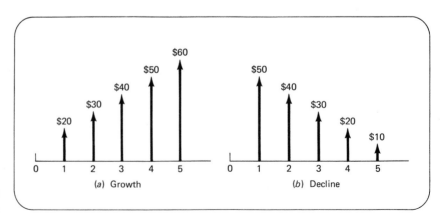

Figure 4-12. Arithmetic growth and decline.

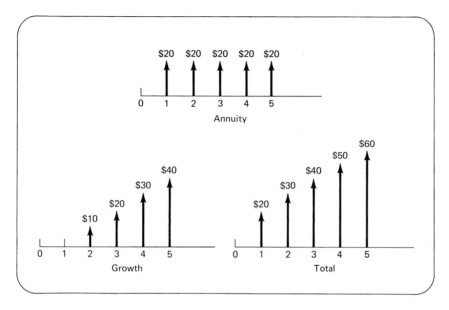

Figure 4-13. Annuity + growth = total.

period for five periods less a decline element of $10 per period. The present value of the total stream is therefore the present value of the annuity portion plus the present value of the growth element or minus the present value of the decline element. This is illustrated in Figure 4-13 for the growing stream of Figure 4-12a. Once we calculate the present value of the stream, we can compute the equivalent annuity or future value if they are desired. Let G be the amount of growth or decline per period, $10 in the examples. We can represent the present value per dollar of growth or decline as an interest rate factor (P/G, i, n) so that the present value of the growth element is

$$P = G(P/G, i, n)$$

The formula for this factor is

$$(P/G, i, n) = \frac{1}{i} \left[\frac{1 - (1 + i)^{-n}}{i} - n(1 + i)^{-n} \right]$$

$$= \frac{1}{i} [(P/A, i, n) - n(P/F, i, n)] \qquad (4\text{-}21)$$

Therefore, values for this factor can be easily calculated using tables for the two basic present value factors when they are available. Otherwise, the formulas can be used.

For example, suppose $i = 10$ percent. Then, using the tables,

$$(P/A, 10\%, 5) = 3.791$$

$$(P/F, 10\%, 5) = 0.621$$

$$(P/G, 10\%, 5) = \frac{1}{0.10} [3.791 - 5(0.621)]$$

$$= \frac{1}{0.10} (0.686)$$

$$= 6.86$$

The present value of the growing stream in Figure 4-12a is

$$P = A(P/A, 10\%, 5) + G(P/G, 10\%, 5)$$

$$= \$20(3.791) + \$10(6.86)$$

$$= \$144.42$$

The present value of the declining stream in Figure 4-12b is

$$P = A(P/A, 10\%, 5) - G(P/G, 10\%, 5)$$

$$= \$50(3.791) - \$10(6.86)$$

$$= \$120.95$$

Compound Growth or Decline *Compound* growth occurs when a stream of cash payments or receipts grows at a constant *percentage* rate per period. For example, the rate of growth might be 10 percent per period. If the initial (period 1) value is $100, and the stream grows for five periods, the values would be as shown in Figure 4-14a. Note that the dollar increase in each period is not constant as in the case of arithmetic growth but increases instead. Similarly a compound rate of decline of 10 percent per period is illustrated in Figure 4-14b.

The formulas for the present value of such streams depend on the relationship between the growth rate g and the interest rate i. Let x be the amount of the cash flow in period 1. This is the base value on which growth or decline occurs. That is, the cash flow t periods from now is $x(1 + g)^t$.

1. If the growth rate g is greater than the interest rate i, define a new interest rate i^* where

$$i^* = \frac{(1 + g)}{(1 + i)} - 1.0 \qquad (4\text{-}22)$$

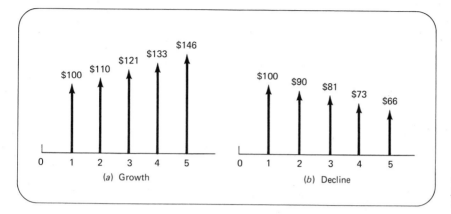

Figure 4-14. Compound growth and decline.

then the present value of the stream is

$$P = \frac{x}{1 + i} (F/A, i^*, n) \qquad (4\text{-}23)$$

2. If $g = i$, then $P = nx/(1 + i)$.
3. If g is less than i, define a new interest rate

$$i^* = \frac{(1 + i)}{(1 + g)} - 1.0 \qquad (4\text{-}24)$$

and

$$P = \frac{x}{1 + g} (P/A, i^*, n) \qquad (4\text{-}25)$$

Case 3 applies to all declining streams since g is negative for these streams. In Figure 4-14b $g = -10$ percent.

The formulas in cases 1 and 3 require the calculation of a rate i^* that depends on the growth rate and the interest rate. This rate is used just like an interest rate in obtaining values for the factors needed. However, in practice it is unlikely that the calculated rate i^* will be available in tables; therefore the formulas must be used. For example, suppose the interest rate is 8 percent. Then for the growth case of Figure 4-14a

$$i^* = \frac{1 + g}{1 + i} - 1$$

$$= \frac{1.10}{1.08} - 1$$

$$= 1.9\%$$

We would have to find $(F/A, 1.9\%, 5)$ to use the approach given here. Of course, we could always take the present value of the individual cash flows, but the purpose of the formulas is to simplify the calculations. In the declining example of Figure 4-14a, case 3 applies and

$$i^* = \frac{1 + i}{1 + g} - 1$$

$$= \frac{1.08}{0.90} - 1$$

$$= 20\%$$

Therefore we need to find $(P/A, 20\%, 5)$, which is readily available, and the present value can be calculated as

$$P = \frac{x}{1 + g} (P/A, 20\%, 5)$$

$$= \frac{\$100}{0.9} (2.991)$$

$$= \$332.33$$

Calculating Interest Rate Factors

If you examine the formulas presented above, you will see that the only difficult part to calculate is $(1 + i)^n$ or $(1 + i)^{-n}$. These are the compound amount factor and the present value factor, respectively. Therefore all the other factors can be calculated easily once one of these has been found. Although there are extensive tables for the compound amount factor available (Union Carbide Corporation publishes one, for example), a small calculator will be most useful here.

Three types of calculator available at relatively low cost will be examined.

1. "Financial" or "business" calculators often contain $(P/F, i, n)$ as a built-in function. As we noted above, once you have a number for the present value factor $[(P/F, i, n) = (1 + i)^{-n}]$, finding any other factor is easy using the appropriate formula. These calculators usually have $(P/A, i, n)$ or $(A/P, i, n)$ available as well so that they are very useful for solving interest rate problems.
2. "Scientific" calculators usually have a function described as a^x, y^x, or similar notation. Let $a = (1 + i)$ and $x = n$; now $(1 + i)^n$ can be calculated with this function.
3. Calculators lacking the needed functions can also be used to compute $(1 + i)^n$ by successive multiplication. That is,

$$(1 + i)^n = (1 + i)(1 + i)(1 + i) \cdots (1 + i)$$

n times. This process is greatly facilitated if the calculator has the capability of retaining a constant multiplier. The value of $1 + i$ is used as the constant to multiply the results of the previous multiplication until $1 + i$ has been multiplied n times. Once the first multiplication has been performed and the constant entered, $(1 + i)^n$ can usually be calculated by pressing the $=$ button $n - 2$ times. [The first multiplication gives you $(1 + i)^2$.] The most common problem with this procedure is losing count of how many multiplications have been made.

risk and value

Financial decisions require consideration of three basic factors: money, time, and risk. In Chapter 4 we developed methods of evaluating money and time; now we will look at the risk factor. You should realize at the start that the concept of risk and its effect on financial decisions is a subtle and difficult topic—but fascinating when properly understood. Almost every successful business owes its success in part to judicious risk taking, which is not the same thing as gambling. Indeed shrewd risk taking has played a crucial role in the formation of many of the world's great fortunes. The late Aristotle Onassis, after amassing millions in various business ventures, risked a large part of his wealth in assembling a fleet of supertankers. His assessment of a coming surge in global demand for tanker space proved correct, and the profits he reaped made him one of the world's super tycoons.

Three major aspects of risk are covered in this introductory chapter; more depth will be provided later. First we will look at the fundamentals of security prices, ignoring risk. Second, we will discuss the nature of risk—what it is, why it exists, and how it can be measured. Third, we will look at the impact of risk on interest rates and discuss how the market values of risky financial assets are determined. We are particularly interested in the question of what determines the value or market price of common stock. Recall that in Chapter 1 we said that the objective of a firm's financial management was to produce as high a price for its common stock as possible, given legal and other constraints. In order for management to know what decisions to make, it must know how stock prices are determined in the market. The basic principles of valuation are presented here. In later chapters, using these principles, we show how specific decisions by management affect stock prices.

The lessons of this chapter can be stated succinctly as follows:

1. The current market price (or value) of a financial asset (for example, a stock, a bond, or a mortgage) is the present value of the future payments to the owner of the asset.
2. The risk in owning a financial asset depends primarily on how well you can predict the future cash receipts from owning it. The risk of owning a United States government bond is less than the risk of owning common stock, because you can predict the interest paid by the government to the bondholder and eventual repayment of the principal

much better than you can predict the dividends that will be paid by a corporation to its stockholders and the future value of its stock.

3. The interest rate which is used to determine the present value (price) depends on[1]

   a) The current level of interest rates in the economy
   b) The attitudes of investors toward risk
   c) The riskiness of the income provided by the asset

With these points in mind, let's look first at the relationship between prices and present values. We will assume throughout this next section that all income streams are riskless in order to establish the basic points before we examine the problems posed by risk.

PRICES AND PRESENT VALUES

The benefits from owning a financial asset are the future cash flows you get from it. Obtaining these future cash flows (such as interest payments, principal payments, and dividends) is the reason you would want to own this type of asset. The current market price of the asset is the amount of money you have to give up now to obtain the future cash flows. The question is: What is the relationship between the market price of an asset and its future cash flows?

A fundamental principle of finance is the following:[2]

In an idealized world of no risk, no taxes, and perfect markets for financial assets, all financial assets provide the same interest rate or rate of return to their owners. This principle is crucial because it permits us to answer the question of the relationship between present values and prices in a simple situation before we look at the more complicated problems of why and how interest rates differ among financial assets. In order for all assets to provide the same interest rate, *the price of each asset must be the present value of the future cash flows.* To see why this is so, let's look at an example.

Suppose that the interest rate *i* is 6 percent per year and you are considering purchase of a U.S. Treasury bill which will pay $1,000 to the owner one year from now. The present value of $1,000 one year from now at a

---

1. There are other factors which affect market values of financial assets, but they are important primarily in specific cases. For example, interest on state and local bonds is usually exempt from federal income tax, and so these bonds usually provide a lower interest rate than United States government bonds which are fully taxable.

2. A perfect securities market is one where there are many buyers and sellers with equal access to information and no costs of buying or selling securities. Also, we are assuming a stable economy in which interest rates don't change over time.

rate of 6 percent per year is

$$\text{Present value} = \frac{\$1,000}{1 + i}$$

$$= \frac{\$1,000}{1 + 0.06} = \frac{\$1,000}{1.06}$$

$$= \$943.40$$

If you purchased the bill at a price of $943.40, what interest rate will you earn for the year?

$$i = \frac{\$1,000 - \text{price}}{\text{price}}$$

$$= \frac{\$1,000 - \$943.40}{\$943.40} = \frac{\$56.60}{\$943.40}$$

$$= 0.06 \text{ or } 6\%$$

Purchasing the bill at a price equal to the present value at 6 percent provides a rate of interest equal to 6 percent. If the price were not equal to the present value, then the rate of interest earned on the bill would not be 6 percent, which is contrary to the fundamental principle.

We know from Chapter 4 that two different cash flows with the same present value are equivalent, that is, of the same desirability. We now have a corresponding relationship between financial assets with different prices. Two financial assets with the same interest rate are equivalent even though their prices are different; however, this relationship applies only when there are no differences in risk of the cash flows provided by the assets.

If the interest rate is the same for all riskless securities, then dollar prices will differ among securities only to the extent that the cash payments differ in timing or amount. Exhibit 5-1 shows the market prices for several securities assuming that they all provide an interest rate or rate of return to the owner of 6 percent per year. The only things the securities shown in Exhibit 5-1 have in common are the rate of return of 6 percent provided to the purchasers of the securities and that all future payments are known for sure.

Now let's see how prices change to adjust to a given interest rate.

Price Adjustments For a given stream of future payments, the lower the price which is paid, the higher is the interest rate or rate of return received. This basic characteristic is illustrated using a security which pays $10 per year to the owner forever. Suppose the current price is $200; investors would be earning

---

Exhibit 5-1. Example of Security Prices at an Interest Rate of 6 Percent per Year

---

1. One-year bill ($100 maturity value)

$$Price = \frac{\$100}{1.06}$$

$$= \$100 \ (P/F, \ 6\%, \ 1)$$

$$= \$100 \ (0.9434)$$

$$= \$94.34$$

2. Five-year note (7 percent coupon rate,[a] $100 maturity value)

$$Price = \frac{\$7}{1.06} + \frac{\$7}{(1.06)^2} + \cdots + \frac{\$107}{(1.06)^5}$$

$$= \$7 \ (P/A, \ 6\%, \ 5) + \$100 \ (P/F, \ 6\%, \ 5)$$

$$= \$7 \ (4.2124) + \$100 \ (0.7473)$$

$$= \$104.22$$

3. Twenty-year bond (5 percent coupon rate, $100 maturity value)

$$Price = \frac{\$5}{1.06} + \frac{\$5}{(1.06)^2} + \cdots + \frac{\$105}{(1.06)^{20}}$$

$$= \$5 \ (P/A, \ 6\%, \ 20) + \$100 \ (P/F, \ 6\%, \ 20)$$

$$= \$5 \ (11.4699) + \$100 \ (0.3118)$$

$$= \$88.53$$

---

[a]The coupon rate is the interest payment expressed as a percentage of the principal value.

---

an interest rate of 5 percent per year if they purchased the security at that price.

$$Rate = \frac{\$10}{\$200} = 5\%$$

If the market rate of interest is 10 percent, not 5 percent, then the price of this security will fall, as no investor will want to buy the security at a price of $200. The new price will be

$$Price = \frac{\$10}{0.10} = \$100$$

At a price of $100, investors will earn 10 percent on this security. In a similar fashion, if the price of the security initially were only $50, investors would be able to earn $10/$50 = 20 percent. If the market rate of interest is 10 percent, everyone would want to own the bond and bid the price up until it reached $100, where the rate of return is 10 percent.

New securities issued in the market are subject to the same conditions as securities already being traded. The decisions by investors as to whether or not they wish to buy the new security, and the self-interest of the issuer, cause new securities to have the same interest rate as old securities. For example, suppose that the market interest rate is 6 percent, but a company issues bonds with a coupon rate of 5 percent. The bonds have $100 maturity value per bond and will mature in twenty years. In other words, the firm will pay $5 interest each year and $100 in year 20 to the purchaser of the bonds. From example 3 in Exhibit 5-1 we know that investors will earn 6 percent on these bonds if they pay $88.53 per bond. Since investors can earn 6 percent on other securities in the market, no one would pay the firm more than $88.53, as the rate of return would be less than 6 percent if a higher price were paid. On the other hand, if the firm offered the bonds at a price below $88.53, everyone would like to buy them since the bonds would provide a higher rate of return than available in the market. However, it would be foolish for the firm's financial managers to do this, since the firm would be paying a higher interest rate than is necessary to raise money.[3]

All securities, new and old, should provide a rate of return to investors equal to the interest rate in this idealized world of no risk. The particular value of the interest rate will depend on the overall supply and demand for money in the economy, as we discussed in Chapter 2. The market price of such securities will adjust so that the price equals the present value of the future cash flows to the owner of the security.

Now let's examine the problem of risk and the way risk affects security prices. Although the interest rate will no longer be the same for each security, we will see that the equality of price and present value will still be true.

WHAT IS RISK? Whenever you are in a situation in which you are not sure what will happen next, you are being subjected to risk or uncertainty; we will use

3. If the company wants to raise $1 million, the number of bonds that must be issued to raise this much money depends on the selling price per bond. At a price of $100 per bond, $1,000,000/$100 = 10,000 bonds must be issued. At a price of $80 per bond $1,000,000/$80 = 12,500 bonds must be issued. Since the company pays $5 per year per bond in interest, the lower the price, the greater is the interest cost to the firm. Of course the best measure of the cost to the firm is the interest rate received by investors since this rate also considers the $100 payment to be made at maturity.

these two words interchangeably. We live in a world where much is not predictable or certain. That the sun will rise tomorrow is a sure thing. But how confident can you be that you will be able to *see* the sun rise tomorrow? If you live in Death Valley, you might be fairly confident; however, if you live in cloudy Seattle, you might be uncertain.

The words "risk" and "uncertainty" convey negative feelings to most people. In their financial affairs, as in most aspects of life, both individuals and business managers try to avoid risk whenever they can, and minimize risk when it cannot be avoided. However, people will accept varying degrees of risk provided they are given some incentive, the amount of incentive needed being dependent on the degree of risk.

An important part of analyzing any financial decision is assessing the degree of risk associated with the decision. We will first discuss the sources of risk and then examine the problem of measuring risk.

Personal Risks

As you get out of college and begin to plan for your future, there are several sources of uncertainty which affect your financial decisions.

One source is your family situation. There is uncertainty as to the future needs of people dependent on your income for their support. Are you married or single? If married, will your spouse be self-supporting or not? How many children must you support? Will you have to support a parent or other relative? These uncertainties involve your future needs for money.

There is another source of uncertainty—what will be your future income to meet these needs? The nature of the work you choose to do is an important determinant of the degree of risk. Being an aerospace engineer is a riskier occupation than being a college professor. However, even if you become a college professor there will be uncertainty as to future income. There is, in addition, the risk as to your own life and health and hence the length of time you will be earning income. Insurance is often used to provide protection from these risks for yourself and people who are dependent on your income for their support.

General Economic Risks

One major source of risk arises from uncertainty as to the future course of the general economy. A recession or depression brings loss of income to many individuals through shorter hours, lower wages, unemployment, and lower profits for business firms. Another area of uncertainty in the economy is the possibility of changing levels of interest rates. This is of concern to both individuals and firms.

Business firms, their employees, and their creditors are also subject to risks from changes in tastes and technology. Changes in consumer tastes shift sales from one industry to another and from some firms to others. If consumers decide they prefer products packaged in cans over those packaged in bottles, can manufacturers prosper and bottle manufacturers suffer. Clothing manufacturers and retailers must worry about style changes. Technological changes can have significant impacts on business firms. The development of electronic calculators quickly eliminated mechanical calculators. These kinds of risks are particularly acute for firms whose sales are derived from only a single type of product.

Inflation Risk
One source of risk to individuals and businesses which has become especially significant in recent years is inflation. For individuals, inflation increases uncertainty regarding both income and living expenses; for business firms, it increases uncertainty as to product prices and costs of production. People used to believe that inflation didn't hurt business firms very much since their prices would increase along with their costs. However, experience has shown that consumers react to inflation by changing their buying patterns, shifting to lower-priced products and often trying to save more money. These changes affect business firms in several ways:

1. The shift to lower-priced products lowers the average profit earned on a line of products. The automobile manufacturers felt this in the early 1970s.
2. Total demand for a given product may decrease, especially for nonessential products like pool tables, or products whose purchase can be deferred by not replacing old goods in use. A clothing manufacturer remarked in 1975 that a lot of people must be wearing ragged underwear since sales of new underwear were down sharply.
3. Government policies to "cool down" the inflation can force the economy into a recession. Certainly the severity of the 1974–1975 recession was due in part to government policies designed to lower the high rate of inflation that preceded it.

The result is that inflation risk increases the ordinary risks to which individuals and firms are exposed. This is one of the best reasons that the government should try to prevent it.

Operating Risks
Business firms are also subject to a number of operating risks. Poor management can quickly get a firm into trouble. Shareholders, creditors, and employees are always a little nervous when new management takes over a firm that has been successful in the past. Consequently, they are always concerned about management succession—who is available to take over the firm if and when present management dies, retires, or whatever. For this reason, firms run by an exceptionally brilliant or dynamic chief exec-

utive who completely overshadows his or her subordinates are often viewed with reservations by the investment community, which tends to prefer companies with "depth" of management, i.e., a strong team of senior executives.

There are also competitive risks. Virtually all firms operate in a competitive environment and the operating results of any one firm depend on what its competitors do. Another source of risk is the degree of labor militancy or unrest in the industry or in the particular firm. A strike-prone firm is more risky than one whose employees rarely "hit the bricks."

Business Risk and Financial Risk

As we noted above, there are several sources of risk facing individuals and business firms. For firms there is uncertainty regarding the markets for their products, both prices and volume, and uncertainty regarding their costs of operation. We can say, therefore, that there is inherent uncertainty regarding the operating profits (revenues minus operating and administrative costs) of a business firm. A descriptive term for the uncertainty in operating profits is **business risk.**

There is another kind of risk called **financial risk.** Financial risk depends on the degree of debt usage by the firm. A firm financed heavily with debt has more financial risk than a firm with very little debt. Since financing decisions are a major problem for financial managers, there is a detailed discussion of this topic in later chapters. For now we wish only to point out that when you borrow money, you are obligated to pay it back with interest; and if you don't make the payments, you get into trouble. The more you borrow, the greater is the chance that you will have difficulty making the required payments.

It should be clear that individuals as well as business firms can be exposed to financial risks. Just as business firms face uncertainty as to their revenues and costs, individuals are subject to uncertainty in their incomes and expenses. For this reason the principles of business financial management are relevant to personal financial decisions. We will not explore the topic further; however, you might find it helpful to reflect on this proposition as you proceed through the material.

MEASURING RISK

In financial decisions it is often helpful to have an objective way to measure or estimate the degree of risk. Such a measure should be independent of how anti-risk a given person is. In other words, we would like to be able to separate the degree of risk in a situation from the feelings of different people toward bearing it.[4] This is useful because we can then look at the

4. It is very difficult to separate the measure of risk from attitudes toward risk. The standard deviation is appropriate under some fairly restrictive assumptions. See C. Haley and L. Schall, *The Theory of Financial Decisions* (New York: McGraw-Hill, 1973), chap. 5,

question of how much risk is involved in a particular decision as a separate issue from the question of whether enough incentive is provided to warrant bearing the risk. The amount of incentive required for a given amount of risk will vary from person to person depending on how anti-risk each one is.

The main reason for having measures of risk is to enable us to make better decisions. Any evaluation of risk, if it is to be at all useful, must be able to rank alternative risky ventures (such as investments). If there are two possibilities being analyzed, A and B, then in order to make a rational decision we must be able to determine whether A is riskier than B or vice versa. A good measure of risk should also tell us *how much more risky* A is than B. Is A twice as risky or ten times as risky as B? Is B risky at all? It would be nice if the risk measure had a value of zero for a riskless venture and increased numerically as the degree of risk increased.

Although we will begin our discussion by examining the case of investing in the common stock of a single company, business firms or individuals are primarily concerned with the risk of their total investment in all the assets they own. The risk of any single asset must therefore be ultimately measured as the contribution of the asset to the risk of total investment. For now let's assume that only one asset is being acquired; in a later section we will consider the implications of investing in more than one asset.

Risk and Probability Distributions

Risk measurement procedures are usually based on a particular method of organizing financial problems—through **probability distributions.** A probability distribution is a way to describe the future values which are possible for a quantity. The approach is illustrated in the following example.

Suppose you are thinking about purchasing some of stock A, which has a current price of $50 per share and pays no dividends. If you buy it, you plan to sell the stock one year from now. The return you will get when you sell depends only on the price of the stock at the time you sell. You therefore want to consider what price the stock might sell for next year. Suppose you perform the following analysis. You ask yourself how likely is it that the price will be less than $35. You decide there is no chance at all that this will happen. You then ask how likely is the price to be between $35 and $45 and decide that there is one chance in ten or a 10 percent chance that this will happen. You associate the 10 percent chance with a price of $40 which is between $35 and $45. Using the midpoint of $40 helps to keep things simple.[5] You proceed to estimate a 20 percent

---

5. The price can take on a very large number of possible values between $35 and $45. We are approximating an essentially continuous variable (price) with discrete values for purposes of illustration. This approach is often used in practical problems since it greatly simplifies computations.

chance that the price will be between $45 and $55, a 40 percent chance that it will be between $55 and $65, a 20 percent chance that it will be between $65 and $75, and a 10 percent chance that it will be between $75 and $85. You feel that there is no chance of the price being over $85. The result of this analysis is shown in Figure 5-1a with the "chances" shown as decimals (20 percent is .2). We have labeled the vertical axis as "probability," since the "chances" are probabilities, and what you have done is develop a probability distribution for the price of the stock.[6] Note that these are *your* estimates of the likelihood of the stock having the indicated prices (falling into the appropriate range). However, it is also information that you could ask someone else about—for example, a stockbroker.

There are two characteristics of this probability distribution which are useful in deciding whether this stock is worth owning—the expected value and the standard deviation. The **expected value** or **mean** of a probability distribution measures the average value that the variable (stock price in this case) will have. The expected value is a good estimate of the future price of the stock. We calculate the expected value by multiplying the probability of getting each price times that price and adding up the results for all possible prices. The general equation for the expected value is

$$\text{Expected value} = P_1X_1 + P_2X_2 + \cdots + P_nX_n \qquad (5\text{-}1)$$

where P_1 is the probability of obtaining amount X_1, P_2 is the probability of obtaining amount X_2, etc. In this example

$$\text{Expected value} = .1(\$40) + .2(\$50) + .4(\$60) + .2(\$70) + .1(\$80)$$

$$= \$60$$

Therefore the expected price is $60. However, we know that we may not be able to sell the stock for $60. There is uncertainty as to what the price really will be.

The **standard deviation** of a probability distribution measures the dispersion or variability around the expected value. The standard deviation can be considered a measure of the reliability of the expected value and therefore a measure of the risk or uncertainty of the stock price. In other words, given an estimate of the future price as $60, the standard deviation measures how "fuzzy" that estimate is. The higher the standard deviation, the more fuzzy or spread out is the probability distribution. For example, the price of stock B in Figure 5-1b has a greater standard deviation

6. You do have to follow some rules to develop a probability distribution: (1) all possible outcomes (results) must be accounted for; (2) all probabilities must be greater than or equal to zero; and (3) the sum of the probabilities must equal 1.0. See Haley and Schall, op. cit., pp. 73–78, for a more elaborate discussion.

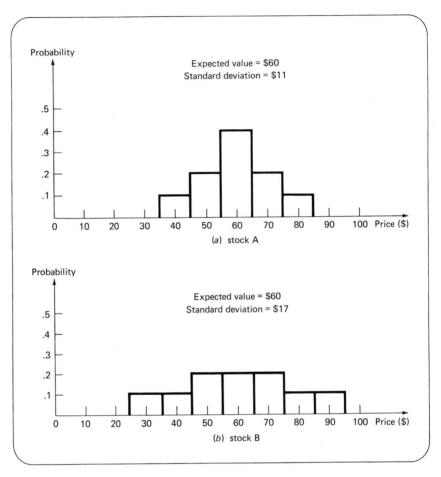

Figure 5-1. Probability distributions for two stocks' prices.

than the price of stock A in Figure 5-1*a*. We are less certain about the price that will be achieved by stock B.

The standard deviation is computed by taking the difference of each possible price from the expected value of $60, squaring the differences, weighting the squared values by the probability of getting that price, summing the weighted squares, and then taking the square root of the sum.[7]

7. The sum is called the **variance** of the distribution and can also be used to measure risk. The formula for the variance in symbolic terms is

$$\text{Sum} = \text{variance} = P_1(X_1 - \bar{X})^2 + P_2(X_2 - \bar{X})^2 + \cdots + P_n(X_n - \bar{X})^2$$

where P_1 is probability associated with X_1
P_2 is probability of X_2, etc.
$\bar{X}$ is mean of distribution

The square root of the variance is the standard deviation. In the example the variance is 120 (measured as dollars squared) and the standard deviation is $\sqrt{120} = \$10.95$.

$$\text{Sum} = .1(40 - 60)^2 + .2(50 - 60)^2 + .4(60 - 60)^2$$
$$+ .2(70 - 60)^2 + .1(80 - 60)^2$$
$$= .1(400) + .2(100) + .4(0) + .2(100) + .1(400)$$
$$= 120$$

and

$$\text{Standard deviation} = \sqrt{120}$$
$$= \$10.95$$

So the standard deviation of the price is approximately $11.

The standard deviation as a risk measure   There are four important features of this measure of risk:

1. Only differences between the expected value of $60 and the various possible values the price can take on affect the size of the standard deviation. If only one value is possible, say $60, it would have a probability of 1.0. The expected value would be 1.0 ($60) = $60 and the sum and standard deviation would be zero as 1.0 ($60 − $60)^2 = 0. Since there is no fuzziness to your estimate of $60, you are certain that the price will be $60 and there is no risk in this case. When there is no risk, the standard deviation is zero. If there is any risk at all, the standard deviation is greater than zero.
2. The differences are squared in calculating the sum. This means that those prices which are far away from the expected value increase the standard deviation much more than those which are close to the expected value. (The square of a large number is very much greater than the square of a relatively small number.) Therefore, using the standard deviation as a measure of risk implies that big differences from the expected value involve much more risk than small differences.
3. The squared differences are multiplied by the probability that the actual value will deviate from the expected value. Therefore, the smaller the chance a particular value will occur, the less effect it has on the standard deviation.
4. The standard deviation is the square root of the sum of the squared differences (weighted by their probabilities). This means that the standard deviation has the same measurement units as the expected value and can be compared directly with it.[8] Therefore, in the example the standard deviation is measured in dollars.

8. The standard deviation is a more convenient measure of risk than the variance for this reason. The variance would be in terms of dollars squared (see footnote 7 for the computation).

Now that we have developed the standard deviation as a measure of risk, what can we use it for? First it tells us something about how uncertain the price is. As a general rule there is very little chance that the actual value will be more than twice the standard deviation away from the expected value. In the stock A example, two times the standard deviation of $11 is $22. Therefore the actual price is very likely to be between $60 − $22 = $38 and $60 + $22 = $82. We can also look at the standard deviation relative to the expected value.[9] In the example the standard deviation is 18 percent of the expected value ($11/$60 = 0.18). This tells us that the actual price is likely to be fairly close to the expected price of $60. There is only moderate uncertainty. If the relative magnitude were 1 percent instead of 18 percent, the price would have very little uncertainty and would almost surely be very near the expected value. If the figure were 50 percent, then there would be a great deal of uncertainty.

The standard deviation can also be used to compare two alternatives. Suppose you evaluated stock B in Figure 5-1b and came up with the probability distribution shown in Figure 5-1b. A comparison with the probability distribution for stock A in Figure 5-1a should lead you to the conclusion that the future price of stock B is more uncertain than the future price of stock A.

Stock B has an expected value of $60 and a standard deviation of $17, as compared with the same expected value for stock A and its standard deviation of $11. The standard deviation for B is larger, which reflects the greater "spreading out" of the probability distribution of B's future price. Therefore, much more uncertainty exists about the actual future price of stock B than about that of stock A.

Rates of return   The above examples illustrate the uncertainty in future prices. However, this uncertainty is also directly translated into uncertainty about the rate of return which will be earned by an investor. For example, given that the current price of stock A is $50, let's convert the *future* prices in Figure 5-1a into rates of return. An actual price of $40 would provide a rate of return of ($40 − $50)/$50 = −0.2 or −20 percent. That is, we had $50 invested in the stock at the beginning of the year and end up with only $40 at the end. The percentage loss is therefore 20 percent. We can convert all the prices into their equivalent rate of return as shown below.

Future price	$40	$50	$60	$70	$80
Rate of return, %	−20%	0%	20%	40%	60%
Probability	.1	.2	.4	.2	.1

9. The ratio of the standard deviation to the expected value is called the **coefficient of variation** and is sometimes used as a separate measure of risk. However, it must be used with care if the expected value is a small number (close to zero) as the coefficient of variation can become very large and not meaningful. The coefficient of variation is discussed further in Chap. 8.

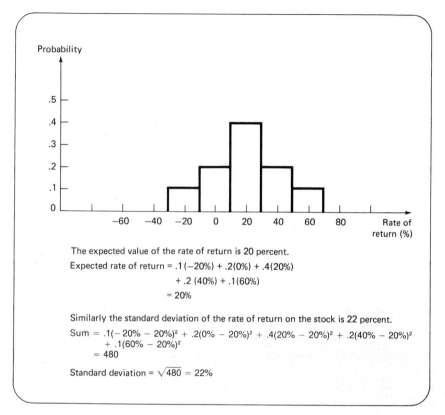

The expected value of the rate of return is 20 percent.

Expected rate of return = .1(−20%) + .2(0%) + .4(20%)
                         + .2(40%) + .1(60%)
                         = 20%

Similarly the standard deviation of the rate of return on the stock is 22 percent.

Sum = .1(−20% − 20%)² + .2(0% − 20%)² + .4(20% − 20%)² + .2(40% − 20%)²
      + .1(60% − 20%)²
    = 480

Standard deviation = $\sqrt{480}$ = 22%

Figure 5-2. Probability distribution of rates of return for stock A.

We now have a "new" probability distribution as shown in Figure 5-2. Again the standard deviation is in the same units (percent) as the expected rate of return, and the figure of 22 percent measures the uncertainty as to the expected rate of return of 20 percent.

In this chapter, we will usually work with rates of return. However, in some business finance problems discussed in later chapters, it will be more convenient to work with the cash flows themselves. The basic point here is that we can translate uncertain future dollar values into their corresponding percentage rates of return given the price of the asset.

Risk and Diversification

"Don't put all your eggs in one basket" is a simple way to express the desirability of **diversification**. Diversification means owning more than one asset with uncertain returns. If all your money is invested in one risky asset, the rate of return you earn depends solely on what happens to the income and market value of that one asset. However, if you invest in two risky assets, in order for you to get a low or negative return on your money, both investments must turn out badly. Taken individually, each asset might be equally risky. However, if you put half of your money in one and half in another, you may come out with less risk on your total investment than you would have by investing all your money in a single asset. This is so because high returns from one asset may offset low returns from the other.

Investors, both individuals and firms, are concerned with the risk of their total investment, and diversification reduces this risk. Business firms diversify by producing more than one product. For example, a firm might produce both commercial airplanes and naval ships. Then even if one market is weak, the other may be strong. We will be discussing diversification by business firms in Chapter 8. Individuals diversify in many ways—such as owning stock in several firms; investing in real estate as well as financial securities; or purchasing shares in mutual funds which are themselves diversified. Let's explore the implications of diversification for individuals by measuring the risk of single assets.

Portfolio risk and correlation   If an investor owns a **portfolio** of many different assets, then the overall risk of the portfolio is more important than the risk of any single asset in the portfolio. We can measure the risk of the portfolio by estimating the standard deviation of the rate of return on the portfolio. However, to determine the risk impact of a single asset, the investor must consider how the asset affects the risk of the entire portfolio. In measuring the risk of any asset being evaluated as a potential addition to the portfolio, knowledge of the standard deviation of the rate of return on that asset is not sufficient. The change in risk due to the addition of an asset to an existing portfolio of assets depends on the standard deviation of the rate of return on the asset *and* the degree to which returns on the asset are related to returns on the portfolio. The degree of relationship is measured by the **correlation** (or coefficient of correlation) between the returns on the asset and on the portfolio.

The correlation measures the degree to which two variables, such as the returns on two securities, move together. It takes on numerical values that range from -1.0 to 1.0. For example, if the correlation between the future prices of two stocks is 1.0, when you obtain a high price from one stock you obtain a high price for the other. Conversely, a low price for one stock will mean a low price for the other. This is illustrated in Exhibit 5-2. The prices of stock X and stock Y have a correlation of 1.0. Both stocks have relatively high prices during boom and low prices during recession. At the other extreme, when the correlation between the prices of two stocks is -1.0, the prices move in opposite directions. In Exhibit 5-2 stock Z has a correlation of -1.0 with both stock X and stock Y. In general, correlations greater than zero mean that two variables tend to move in the same direction; correlations less than zero mean that the two vari-

Exhibit 5-2. Positive and Negative Correlation of Stock Prices

Economy[a]	Stock X	Stock Y	Stock Z
Boom	$60	$50	$30
Normal	$50	$40	$40
Recession	$40	$30	$50

Correlation between stock X and stock Y = 1.0
Correlation between stock X and stock Z = −1.0
Correlation between stock Y and stock Z = −1.0

[a] Assume equal probabilities of boom, normal and recession.

ables tend to move in opposite directions; and zero correlation means there is no particular tendency one way or the other.

The effects of diversification depend on the correlation. For example, consider two possible portfolios: owning one share of stock X and one share of stock Y compared with owning one share of stock X and one share of stock Z. The future values of these two portfolios are shown in Exhibit 5-3. The portfolio of X and Y together is risky; however, all risk has been eliminated by combining X and Z. Regardless of the economic conditions, the portfolio of X and Z will provide a future value of $90. Risk is not eliminated (or even reduced) by combining X and Y into a portfolio because the returns from the two stocks have a correlation of 1.0. This is as close a relationship as possible. There are no diversification

Exhibit 5-3. Diversification with Two-Stock Portfolios

Economy	Portfolio of X + Y			Portfolio of X + Z		
	X	Y	X + Y[a]	X	Z	X + Z[a]
Boom	$60	$50	$110	$60	$30	$90
Normal	$50	$40	$ 90	$50	$40	$90
Recession	$40	$30	$ 70	$40	$50	$90

[a] Assume one share of each stock is owned.

benefits from combining securities whose returns have a 1.0 correlation. At the other extreme, X and Z have a -1.0 correlation. In this case it was possible to eliminate all risk, and the maximum benefit from diversification was achieved.[10]

Negative or even zero correlation among security returns is a rare phenomenon in the world. The returns of most securities available to investors are positively correlated (but less than 1.0) due to the dependence of security returns on the behavior of the overall economy. When the economy is doing well, most securities will provide relatively high returns. When the economy is weak, most securities will provide relatively low returns. However, there are risk reduction benefits to diversification as long as the correlation is not 1.0, and the lower the correlation is, the greater is the benefit.

A complete analysis of correlation and its impact on portfolio risk is beyond the scope of this book; however the problem is developed somewhat further in Appendix 5A. Here we wish to point out the following:

1. Investors are primarily concerned with the riskiness of the returns provided by their total portfolio of assets, and the standard deviation of the portfolio's returns is a measure of this risk.
2. For an investor owning a diversified portfolio of assets, the risk of any single asset depends on the impact of acquiring that asset on the risk of the entire portfolio.
3. For a given standard deviation of an asset's returns, the lower the correlation of the asset's returns with the returns from all the other assets in the portfolio, the lower is the risk of the entire portfolio.
4. For a given positive or zero correlation of an asset's returns with the returns from all the other assets in the portfolio, the lower the standard deviation of the asset's returns, the lower is the risk of the entire portfolio.[11]

Therefore, from the standpoint of a diversified investor, the risk of a single asset is not measured solely by the standard deviation of the returns from that asset. The risk of a single asset depends on both the standard deviation of its returns and the correlation of the asset's returns with the returns of the portfolio owned by the investor. This correlation is, for

---

10. A portfolio of two assets with a -1.0 correlation of returns is not necessarily riskless. See footnote 11.
11. The problem is more complicated with negative correlation. The impact on risk depends on the correlation, the standard deviations of the asset and the portfolio, and the amount of the investment in the asset relative to the original portfolio. A large standard deviation for the asset reduces risk more than a small standard deviation under some conditions. This is a topic for advanced courses.

highly diversified investors, approximately equal to the correlation of the single asset's returns with the general economy. For highly diversified investors, the uncertainty in the returns of their portfolios is essentially the inherent uncertainty of the general economy, and the returns from such diversified portfolios move closely with the economy. All risks not due to general economic trends can be eliminated by diversification. Thus, the risk of a single asset is measured by the correlation of the asset's returns with the returns of all other assets in the economy as well as by the standard deviation of the asset's returns. The correlation with the economy and the standard deviation of the returns for a single asset are numbers that can be estimated for the asset without knowing the particular composition of investors' portfolios of other assets. As we will see in Chapter 8, this is helpful in assessing the riskiness of business investments for capital budgeting analysis.

THE IMPACT OF RISK ON VALUE

If people dislike risk, why would anyone wish to own a risky asset such as common stock? Obviously because the expected returns from owning the stock are sufficient to outweigh the risk. To put it another way, given an asset's expected returns and risk, the price of the asset must be no greater than the value of those returns to investors. Otherwise, no one would buy the asset. The problem is to specify how the price or value is determined.

We will be discussing the valuation of assets that are traded in financial markets where there is a large number of buyers and sellers. Therefore the price of an asset at any time reflects the current average opinion of the marketplace as to the value of the income produced by that asset. Individual investors and financial managers may disagree with the markets' assessment of particular values, but an understanding of the underlying process is necessary for everyone.

We will look at two types of assets separately. The first type consists of fixed-income securities, such as bonds. The second type consists of variable-income securities, such as common stock.

Fixed-Income Securities: Bonds

A fixed-income security provides a stream of cash payments to its owner which have been promised by the issuer (borrower) at the time the security was originally issued (when the money was borrowed). Debt contracts such as bonds and mortgages are the most common fixed-income securities, although preferred stocks are also of this type. The promised stream of cash payments was fixed at the time of issue, and the payments are the *maximum* amounts that the issuer will pay. However, if the payments are at all uncertain (risky), there is a chance that the promised payments won't be made.

Let's get a better idea of what fixed-income securities are all about by looking at two bonds that are traded on the New York Exchange. One bond was issued by LTV Corporation. It has a 55 percent coupon rate and matures in 1988. The other bond was issued by Pacific Gas and Electric Company (PGE) with a coupon rate of 5 percent and maturity of 1989. Both bonds promise to pay the owner $5 per year per $100 maturity value until maturity and both promise to pay their maturity value (principal) on maturity. Prices for the two bonds early in 1976 were $50 for the LTV bond and $72 for the PGE bond.[12]

The yield to maturity on each bond is the interest rate on the bond given the current price and the promised payments (coupon interest and principal) for that bond. The general equation used to find the yield to maturity, i, on a bond maturing in n periods is

$$\text{Price} = \frac{\text{interest}}{1 + i} + \frac{\text{interest}}{(1 + i)^2} + \cdots + \frac{\text{interest} + \text{principal}}{(1 + i)^n} \tag{5-2}$$

or, equivalently,

$$\text{Price} = \text{interest } (P/A,\, i,\, n) + \text{principal } (P/F,\, i,\, n) \tag{5-3}$$

At the date of these prices (1976) the LTV bond had twelve years until maturity ($n = 12$) and the PGE bond would mature in thirteen years ($n = 13$). To determine i for the LTV bond, we use Eq. (5-3) as follows:

$$\$50 = \$5\ (P/A,\, i,\, 12) + \$100\ (P/F,\, i,\, 12)$$

The yield to maturity, i percent, is the interest rate that makes the equation balance. Applying the procedure of Chapter 4, we find that the yield to maturity of the LTV bond was about 14 percent (13.7 percent). Similarly for the PGE bond, the relationship was

$$\$72 = \$5\ (P/A,\, i,\, 13) + \$100\ (P/F,\, i,\, 13)$$

and the yield to maturity of the PGE bond was found to be about 9 percent (8.7 percent).

Why would anyone have paid $72 for the PGE bond when the LTV bond was only $50? If you bought the LTV bond and held it to maturity *and* if LTV made all the promised payments, you would have earned 14 percent per year on your investment, 5 percent more than from the PGE bond. Why? Because investors must have believed that there was significant risk that LTV would *not* make all the promised payments.

12. These prices were reported in the *Wall Street Journal* Jan. 16, 1976. Bonds usually have maturity values of $1,000 per bond. Therefore a price of $50 per $100 maturity value implies actual price of $500 per bond.

If any of the payments are not made when due to the owners of a bond, the owners will earn less than the yield to maturity on their purchase price. The yield to maturity on a bond is the *most* you can earn by holding it to maturity. For many bonds there is some risk that you will earn less than the yield to maturity. In the case of LTV, investors apparently assessed the probability of earning less as fairly large.

Bond ratings and yields   There are several ways to analyze or compare how the degree of risk affects the prices of bonds. One widely used method is based on the yield to maturity. Two bonds of the same "quality" or risk should have the same yield to maturity. Under this approach, risk is not measured precisely. Instead, bonds are classified or organized into risk groups; all the bonds within the same group should have approximately the same yield. Two financial service firms provide widely used classification systems—Standard & Poor's and Moody's.[13] Their classifications differ somewhat; but the two services provide comparable ratings in the lower-risk classes, as shown in Table 5-1.

The PGE bonds were rated AA and Aa by Standard & Poor's and Moody's, respectively; the LTV bonds were rated B by both. As Moody's says about its B-rated bonds, they "generally lack characteristics of a desirable investment." By this Moody's means that a conservative investor

13. The formal names are Standard & Poor's Corporation and Moody's Investor Services.

Table 5-1. Bond classifications

	Standard & Poor's		Moody's
AAA	Highest grade	Aaa	Best quality
AA	High grade	Aa	High quality
A	Upper medium grade	A	Higher medium grade
BBB	Medium grade	Baa	Lower medium grade
BB	Lower medium grade	Ba	Possess speculative elements
B	Speculative	B	Generally lack characteristics of a desirable investment
CCC, CC	Outright speculation		
		Caa	Poor; may be in default
		Ca	Speculative to a high degree; often in default
C	Income bonds		
DDD, DD, D	In default; rating indicates relative salvage value	C	Lowest grade

should avoid B bonds since they are fairly risky. Generally speaking, the lower the rating for a bond, the higher will be its yield to maturity. This is so because the ratings reflect the risk of bonds as evaluated by the rating firms who are experts in this area. However, all bonds of a given rating (A, for example) don't necessarily have the same yield to maturity. Some A bonds will yield about the same as Aa bonds, and some will have yields close to those on Baa bonds. The reason is that the classification scheme is only approximate, and many investors do their own "rating." Thus, if the A-rated bonds of a particular company appear more risky than the average A-rated bond, they will have a higher yield than the average A-rated bond and vice versa.

Furthermore, the yields required on bonds of a given rating are not constant over time but vary due to changes in the general level of interest rates. Also the "spread" or difference between the yields on bonds of different ratings varies over time, depending on the general outlook for the economy. Figure 5-3 shows the average yields to maturity for a sample of Aaa bonds and a sample of Baa bonds since 1929. Note that during times of general economic uncertainty such as the 1930s the difference between the yield on the two classes of bonds widens, as investors require a much

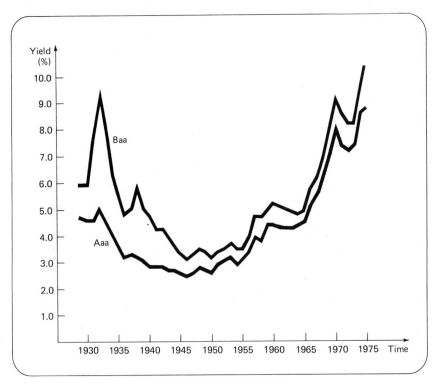

Figure 5-3. Historical interest rates on Aaa- and Baa-rated bonds.

higher yield on the more risky Baa bonds than on the safer Aaa bonds. Compare the situation in 1933 with that of 1970. In both years the yield on Baa bonds was over 9 percent. In 1933, the high rate on Baa bonds was due to concern over the risk of the bonds, as the Aaa rate was only 5 percent. In 1970 it was primarily due to the high general level of interest rates as reflected by the correspondingly high rate on Aaa bonds of over 8 percent.

A bond's expected rate of return   There is a more general approach to valuing risky assets than the yield to maturity. The yield to maturity is calculated assuming that all the promised payments are made. However, in the case of risky bonds, there exists by definition some chance that the payments will not be made when due, and perhaps never. An alternative approach is based on the concept of the expected rate of return on the bond. This approach takes into account the possibility that the actual returns on the bond may be less than the yield to maturity.

Let's consider the probability distribution of possible rates of return from purchasing LTV bonds at a price of $50 shown in Exhibit 5-4. This is a hypothetical set of probabilities of earning the indicated rates of return. Assuming that investors are planning to hold the bond until maturity, the highest rate of return is 14 percent, which is the yield to maturity on the bond.[14] However, someone buying the bond in 1976 would earn 14 percent only if the corporation pays the interest and principal when they are due. If the firm gets into trouble between 1976 when the bonds are purchased and 1988 when the bonds mature, investors might not get all the payments that have been promised and they would therefore earn less than the 14 percent yield to maturity. For example, if the firm paid $5 per year for five years and then went bankrupt and bondholders only received one additional payment of $25 per $100 maturity value, the total receipts

14. The problem is more complicated than the discussion indicates. Some investors may be planning to own the bond for only a year or two, others for a longer period of time. Essentially, we are assuming that the general level of interest rates and the risk of payments are not expected to change.

Exhibit 5-4. A Possible Probability Distribution for the Rate of Return on LTV Bonds

Rate of return	−30%	−20%	−10%	0%	14%
Probability	.02	.03	.05	.1	.8

would be $50. Investors who paid $50 for the bond would have earned a rate of return of 0 percent. The only rate that investors observe directly in the market is the 14 percent yield to maturity, which is based on the current price and the interest and principal payments promised by the issuer. Based on the probability distribution, the *expected* rate of return is considerably less. Using Eq. (5-1) and the data from Exhibit 5-4, we can calculate the expected rate of return for the LTV bond.

$$\text{Expected rate of return} = .8(14\%) + .1(0\%) + .05(-10\%)$$
$$+ .03(-20\%) + .02(-30\%)$$
$$= 9.5\%$$

The yield to maturity is not irrelevant. After all, it is directly related to the current price of the bond. Both the yield to maturity and the expected rate of return are worth considering; however, the expected rate of return is more fundamental to the problem of valuation. The difficulty with the expected return is that you cannot observe it or calculate it except by making your own judgments as to probability distributions. You can never know precisely the expected return in the market for a bond. There are two guidelines, however. First, the expected rate of return on a risky bond is always less than the yield to maturity. This is so because, if the firm defaults on its bonds, you will earn less than the yield to maturity since the firm will either delay or not make the payments promised. The expected rate of return takes into account the possibilities for lower returns.

Second, the United States government issues bonds which have virtually no uncertainty in the cash payments to the owners of those bonds. At the same time that LTV bonds were selling at $50, investors could buy United States government bonds maturing in 1988. These bonds had a yield to maturity of 7.7 percent.[15] Therefore, investors would not have been interested in the LTV bonds unless their expected rate of return was greater than 7.7 percent. Since investors were buying LTV bonds, their expected rate of return must have been somewhere between 7.7 and 14 percent. Similarly, the expected rate of return for PGE bonds must have been between 7.7 percent and their yield to maturity of 9 percent.

If investors didn't care about the riskiness of their returns, then expected rates of return on all bonds in the market would be the same and equal to the yield on United States government bonds. However, investors do not like risk; therefore risky bonds must provide an expected rate of return that is higher than the United States government yield, and

15. Yields to maturity for United States government securities are reported in the *Wall Street Journal;* therefore you don't have to calculate them for yourself.

the greater the risk, the higher the expected rate of return must be. For example,[16] the expected rate on the PGE bonds might have been 8.5 percent—a little less than the yield to maturity of 9 percent but still an appreciable premium (0.8 percentage point) over the United States government yield of 7.7 percent. The expected rate on the LTV bonds might have been 9.5 percent (as per the example), which is well below the yield to maturity of 14 percent, reflecting the degree of uncertainty, and also at a substantial premium (1.8 percentage points) over the United States government yield, reflecting the degree of aversion to risk on the part of investors.

Our two guidelines are therefore the yield to maturity on the bond and the interest rate on United States government securities.[17] The expected rate of return on the bond must lie between these two rates.

Earlier in the chapter we stated the principle that in the absence of risk all assets would provide the same rate of return to investors. We are now able to state a second fundamental principle:

The interest rate that determines the value of a risky asset depends on the general level of interest rates (measured by the interest rate on United States government securities) plus a premium that depends on the risk of the income from the asset. The more risk there is, the higher will be the premium. Notice that this principle applies not only to the expected rate of return but also to the yield to maturity. The more risky the payment stream, the higher will be both the yield to maturity and the expected rate of return on the bond.

We have found that the rate of return which the average investor in the market expects to earn from buying a security depends on the level of interest rates plus a premium for the risk of the cash payments provided by the security. The greater the risk, the greater is the premium. We can represent this relationship graphically as in Figure 5-4.

The **security market line** (SML) shown in Figure 5-4 indicates the rate of return required by investors to compensate them for bearing risk. The

The Security Market Line

16. The expected rates are provided for illustrative purposes. They cannot be calculated from data presented here.

17. Throughout this chapter we have assumed that interest rates are not changing over time. Changing interest rates cause the time to maturity to affect the interest rate required on an asset. A ninety-day Treasury bill normally does not have the same yield to maturity as a twenty-five-year government bond even though there is no uncertainty as to interest and principal payments for both securities. Explanations of the maturity structure of interest rates are covered in courses dealing with financial markets or monetary economics. For our purposes here it is sufficient to use as a measure of the level of interest rates applicable to a given asset, the interest rate on a United States government security of approximately the same maturity as the asset.

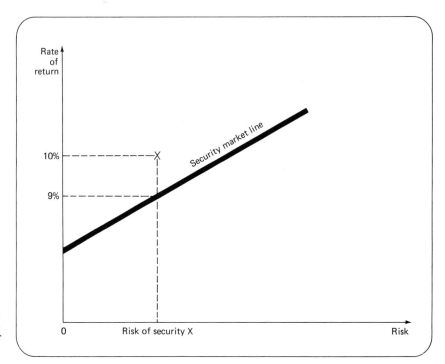

Figure 5-4. The relationship between risk and expected rate of return.

relationship between risk and required rate of return is shown as a straight line for simplicity. The precise form of the relationship, including the measure of risk to be used, is a topic of considerable debate among finance experts. Modern financial theory does indicate that both the standard deviation of a security's future return and the correlation of that return with the returns of other securities and assets in the economy are important components of a security's risk. In particular, securities whose returns have high positive correlations with the economy are more risky than those securities whose returns are less correlated, given similar standard deviations. And, as always, the greater the risk is, the larger is the required rate of return. We discuss one important theory of the security market line in Appendix 5B.

For a given amount of risk, the security market line indicates the "going" rate of return in the market. Every security having that amount of risk should provide the same expected rate of return to investors which is equal to the required rate of return for that risk taken from the security market line. If for some reason a security provides a different rate, investors will tend to buy that security, if its rate of return is high, and sell it, if its rate of return is low relative to the going rate. For example, security X is expected to provide a cash payment to the owner of $5 per year for ten years plus $50 in year 10. (This could be the LTV bond with LTV

Corporation going bankrupt in ten years and paying its bondholders only 50 percent of the $100 maturity value of the bonds.) The current price of security X is $50; therefore, the expected rate of return is $5/$50 = 10 percent. We can use the simple formula in this case because the price is equal to the expected future principal payment of $50.[18] Suppose that for the amount of risk of these payments the market rate of return is 9 percent. This situation is shown in Figure 5-4.

Investors would prefer to own this security X rather than others which are available because it offers an unusually high expected rate of return for the risk involved. Therefore the price of security X will increase. As the price increases, the expected rate of return will fall and soon the expected rate of return will equal 9 percent. Given the expected interest payments of $5 and principal payment of $50, the price of the security will now be

$$\text{Price} = \frac{\$5}{1.09} + \frac{\$5}{(1.09)^2} + \cdots + \frac{\$55}{(1.09)^{10}}$$

$$= \$5 \ (P/A, \ 9\%, \ 10) + \$50 \ (P/F, \ 9\%, \ 10)$$

$$= \$5 \ (6.418) + \$50 \ (0.4224)$$

$$= \$53.21$$

At a price of $53.21 the expected rate of return on the security is 9 percent.

Think of the rates of return indicated by the security market line as interest rates which have been adjusted for risk. Their values are determined in the security market by the activities of all the investors in the market, and they reflect the attitudes of investors toward bearing risk. These rates are not constant over time. As the general level of interest rates change (measured by the United States government bond rate) so do the risk-adjusted rates. Figure 5-5a depicts an increase in the level of interest rates. All rates shift upward by the same amount, and the prices of all securities fall. Changes in investor attitudes toward risk also affect the risk-adjusted rates. Figure 5-5b shows an increase in the premiums for risk as might occur when investors experience an increase in uncertainty as to their personal income or living costs. In this case, low-risk securities would not be much affected whereas the rates of return required on high-risk securities would increase substantially and their prices would therefore fall by large amounts.

Throughout the rest of the book we will use the special symbol k for the risk-adjusted interest rates required by investors in the security markets. These rates are outside the direct influence of an individual investor or

18. See p. 102 in Chap. 4.

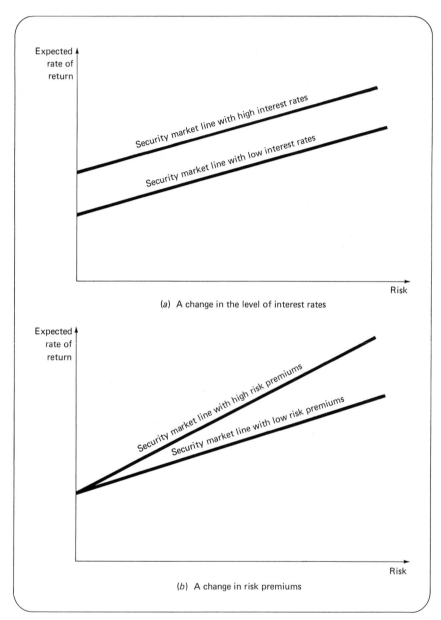

Figure 5-5. Changes in the security market line.

business firm and, as we will see, serve as standards or guides for many financial decisions.

Variable-Income Securities: Common Stock

Fixed-income securities promise to provide a set of cash payments. Variable-income securities, such as common stock, do not. Therefore, with a fixed-income security it is possible to calculate the yield to maturity based on the known set of promised payments. There is no ambiguity or uncertainty as to the value of the yield to maturity, only uncertainty as to whether it will be realized. The yield to maturity provides a reference point for fixed-income securities. There is no such reference point for variable-income securities. There is also no ceiling on how much you will earn from owning variable-income securities.

The financial returns from owning any asset come from two basic sources: periodic income (dividends on stock or interest on debt) and the amount you realize at the end of your ownership (selling price or maturity payments). In order to determine the value of the asset, you must estimate both the periodic income and the ultimate receipts from sale or maturity, and both are usually not precisely known. The returns from common stock ownership are especially uncertain since there is no promised interest or maturity payments. Future dividends are uncertain; and, since common stock has no maturity, the owner usually must sell the stock at an uncertain future price to recover his or her investment.

Let's look at the problem of determining the value of the common stock of a corporation. Suppose you were to purchase one share of stock in the XYZ Company at $50 per share. One year from now you receive a dividend of $3 and sell the stock for $57. You earned $3 in dividends plus $7 in capital gains on the sale for a total of $10. Your rate of return is $10/$50 = 20 percent. Now suppose you kept the stock for two years and received dividends of $3 the first year and $4 the second year. At the end of the second year you sell the stock for $64.44. What rate of return did you earn? To find out you must find the interest rate that makes the following equation balance.

$$\$50 = \frac{\$3}{1 + i} + \frac{\$4}{(1 + i)^2} + \frac{\$64.44}{(1 + i)^2}$$
$$= \$3\ (P/F,\ i,\ 1) + \$4\ (P/F,\ i,\ 2) + \$64.44\ (P/F,\ i,\ 2)$$

The rate is again 20 percent. We can express the relationship shown in a more general form. Let P be the price of the stock, D_1 be dividends for the first year, D_2 be dividends for the second year and P_2 be the price at the end of the second year. Then

$$P = \frac{D_1}{1 + i} + \frac{D_2 + P_2}{(1 + i)^2}$$

$$P = D_1(P/F,\ i,\ 1) + (D_2 + P_2)\ (P/F,\ i,\ 2) \qquad (5\text{-}4)$$

Equation (5-4) applies to any stock held for two years. The use of our notation $(P/F,\ i,\ n)$ is a little cumbersome so we will stop using it. Suppose a stock was held for three years. The relationship would be

$$P = \frac{D_1}{1 + i} + \frac{D_2}{(1 + i)^2} + \frac{D_3 + P_3}{(1 + i)^3} \qquad (5\text{-}5)$$

In general, if you owned the stock for n years,

$$P = \frac{D_1}{1 + i} + \frac{D_2}{(1 + i)^2} + \cdots + \frac{D_n + P_n}{(1 + i)^n} \qquad (5\text{-}6)$$

What we have developed here is a general expression to obtain a rate of return i given the purchase price of the stock, dividends paid on it, and the selling price at the end of n periods. This expression will help us determine the value of a stock.

First we might look at the stream of dividends and the future price as being expected magnitudes as of today. Associated with these expectations is uncertainty; no one can be sure what the future dividend payments and the price of common stock for a company will be. Nevertheless, investors must expect to earn a reasonable rate of return from owning the stock or else they wouldn't own it. The rate of return required by the average investor in the market depends on the uncertainty of the dividends and future price; it is the risk-adjusted interest rate k from the security market line. Thus the rate of return expected by the average investor must equal the required rate, k.

For example, suppose that the average opinion of investors in the market is that the price one year from now of a share of stock in the ABC Company will be $55 and the company is expected to pay a dividend of $2.50 next year. Also suppose that the required rate of return k is 15 percent based on the market's assessment of the uncertainty as to what the dividend and price will actually be. The price today would be

$$P = \frac{\$2.50 + \$55}{1.15}$$

$$= \$50$$

There is one more problem that has to do with the expected future price. If you are an investor planning to own stock for one year, you would be most concerned with estimating its price one year from now. If you plan to sell the stock forty years from now when you retire, you want to estimate the price at that time. However, the future price of the stock depends on what income (dividends) the stock is expected to provide people buying the stock in the future. Therefore the price of the stock today is the present value of all expected future dividends, using the interest rate k required to compensate the owners of the stock for the risk of those expected dividends. If the last payment to any owner is at time m, then[19]

$$P = \frac{D_1}{1 + k} + \frac{D_2}{(1 + k)^2} + \cdots + \frac{D_m}{(1 + k)^m} \qquad (5\text{-}7)$$

After time m, the price of the stock (or asset) would be zero since there would be no further income to the owners. At time m either the assets of the firm are being liquidated or the firm is being sold in entirety to someone and all cash received from the sale is paid out. In any case, D_m is the last payment to the stockholders of the company. For many companies the last dividend may be many years into the future—m is very, very large. Huge, well-established firms such as IBM and General Motors are expected to continue in existence for a long time. But even for large firms, there may be considerable uncertainty as to when time m is. For example, dividends may cease due to the firm's bankruptcy, and the firm might go bankrupt any time in the future.

Equation (5-7) expresses in mathematical form the proposition that the market price (or value) of an asset is the present value of all expected future receipts (the D's) from owning the asset. This is so, regardless of whether the people now owning the asset plan to continue owning it until time m, since the value at any future time (3, for example) will depend on the expectations regarding receipts in period 4 and thereafter. Let's look

---

19. As proof of Eq. (5-7), suppose you were planning to own the stock for only one year, Then

$$P = \frac{D_1}{1 + k} + \frac{P_1}{1 + k} \qquad (1)$$

The price of the stock one year from now, P_1, must be based on what investors expect to receive in future years; for example,

$$P_1 = \frac{D_2}{1 + k} + \frac{P_2}{1 + k} \qquad (2)$$

Substituting Eq. (2) into Eq. (1), we get

$$P = \frac{D_1}{1 + k} + \frac{D_2}{(1 + k)^2} + \frac{P_2}{(1 + k)^2} \qquad (3)$$

Now we can look at P_2 as being

$$P_2 = \frac{D_3}{1 + k} + \frac{P_3}{(1 + k)} \qquad (4)$$

Substituting Eq. (4) into Eq. (3), we get

$$P = \frac{D_1}{1 + k} + \frac{D_2}{(1 + k)^2} + \frac{D_3}{(1 + k)^3} + \frac{P_3}{(1 + k)^3} \qquad (5)$$

We can continue this argument until we reach D_m, which is the last payment made to owners and we arrive at Eq. (5-7).

at a special case of Eq. (5-7) which is used widely in finance and which we will use in Chapter 6, constant growth.[20]

The constant growth model   We know already that if investors expect dividends to be a constant amount, D dollars per year on the average forever, Eq. (5-7) reduces to a much simpler relationship, which is the present value of a perpetual annuity:

$$P = \frac{D}{k} \tag{5-8}$$

This formula applies when there is no growth expected in the firm's dividend payments; however, there is a more general relationship that applies when the rate of growth is constant.

Suppose that dividends per share for a firm are expected to be $1 next year. Two years from now the expected dividend is $1.06 per share. In three years the dividend is expected to be $1(1.06)^2 = $1.1236, in four years $1(1.06)^3 = $1.1910, etc. These dividends are expected to grow at a compound rate of 6 percent per year. If this growth is expected to continue for the foreseeable future (forever, to be precise), then we have an example of the constant growth case.

Let D_1 be the dividend expected in the coming year and g be the expected growth rate. The dividend in any year t is expected to be

$$D_t = D_1 (1 + g)^{t-1} \tag{5-9}$$

Equation (5-9) summarizes the general situation. In our example we had:

t	1	2	3	4	. . .
D_t	$1.00	$1.06	$1.1236	$1.1910	. . .

The series of dividends D_t in this example can be expressed compactly using Eq. (5-9) as

$$D_t = \$1(1.06)^{t-1}$$

If the expected stream of dividend payments fits the pattern of Eq. (5-9), then we have constant growth. The present value of this stream of dividends is

20. Many firms experience very high rates of growth for a while which then decrease as the firm "matures" and gets large. For such firms a forecast of the dividend stream and application of the general formula, Eq. (5-7), will be best. There are formulas for such cases, but they are much more complicated than the constant growth equation.

$$P = \frac{D_1}{k - g} \qquad (5\text{-}10)$$

Note that when $g = 0$, Eq. (5-10) reduces to Eq. (5-8), the no-growth case.

The derivation of the formula is provided in Appendix 5C. The important things to know about the derivation are (1) that it is purely a mathematical result given the assumptions of constant perpetual growth and (2) that the growth rate g must be less than the rate of return k in order for the model to make sense. If g is greater than k, the formula implies an infinitely large price for the stock.

If we substitute a 6 percent growth rate and a dividend next year of $1 into the formula, we get

$$P = \frac{\$1}{k - 0.06}$$

In order to do anything more, we need a value for k (or P). Suppose $k = 10$ percent. Then the price of the stock would be

$$P = \frac{\$1}{0.10 - 0.06} = \$25$$

The formula can also be used to estimate the rate of return on the stock. Suppose the current price is $25 and that dividends of $1 and a growth rate of 6 percent are anticipated. What rate of return would you expect to earn on the stock? The answer is 10 percent from the correspondence between interest rates and rates of return in present value relationships.

The formula can also be used to illustrate the relationship between future prices and dividend streams that we discussed earlier. Suppose that expectations do not change from this year to next year and that $1 in dividends is actually paid. What will be the price of the stock next year? The price next year will be the present value of expected future dividends. Next year, the expected growth rate in dividends remains 6 percent by assumption. Also, the expected dividend one year from then will be $1.06. If k is 10 percent, the price next year will be

$$P_1 = \frac{\$1.06}{0.10 - 0.06} = \$26.50$$

As of now (time 0), we are expecting a dividend of $1 and a price for the stock of $26.50, both to occur one year from now. If the required rate of return is 10 percent, what should the current price be? The present value at 10 percent of $1 plus $26.50 received in one year is

$$P = \frac{\$26.50 + \$1}{1 + k}$$

$$= \frac{\$27.50}{1.10} = \$25$$

We get the same price as before, which demonstrates the consistency of the "stream of dividends" approach with the "dividend plus future price" approach to stock valuation.

A final point is that Eq. (5-10) can be rewritten to express k in terms of prices, dividends, and growth rate:

$$k = \frac{D_1}{P} + g \qquad (5\text{-}11)$$

The first term on the right-hand side of the equation is called the dividend yield of the stock, dividend over price. The dividend yield is often discussed by itself. The dividend yield in our example was $\$1.00/\$25.00 = 4$ percent.

The second term, the growth rate in dividends, is also the expected rate of growth of the stock price. In our example the price of the stock was expected to grow from now to next year by 6 percent, which is the same as the dividend growth rate.

$$\frac{\$26.50 - \$25}{\$25} = \frac{\$1.50}{\$25} = 6\%$$

We can therefore consider the expected rate of return k as being composed of two parts: (1) dividend yield, D_1/P, and (2) the rate of price appreciation or capital gains rate, g.

SUMMARY   This chapter has been devoted to two topics which are fundamental to the field of finance—risk and value. If all income streams were certain, the value of any stream could be found by calculating the present value of the stream using the market rate of interest. Under such conditions all securities sell at prices equal to the present value of their income.

The sources of risk to business firms and individuals in their financial affairs create uncertainty about both incomes and expenses. There are many sources of risk. We can categorize the risk of business firms into two types. Business risk results from the nature of the business and is due to uncertainty as to the income and operating expenses of the firm. Financial risk arises from the financing decisions of management and increases as the amount of debt used increases.

In dealing with future monetary payments or receipts, a probability distribution is often useful in assessing the degree of risk. Two of the more important quantitative measures of risk are the standard deviation and the correlation. The standard deviation measures the uncertainty as to the returns of an asset or portfolio of assets. The correlation measures the degree to which the returns of one asset vary with the returns of another asset or portfolio. The total risk of a portfolio of assets depends on the standard deviations and correlations of the individual assets.

Fixed-income assets, such as bonds, have a stated promised stream of cash payments to the owners; variable-income assets, such as common stock, do not provide a promised stream, but instead may pay more or less than the income that they are currently providing. One method of valuing fixed-income securities is based on the yield to maturity. Two fixed-income securities with the same degree of uncertainty in their payments should have the same yield for the degree of risk involved, then the value of a fixed-income security would be the present value of the promised payments using that yield as the interest rate.

The second method of valuation is applicable to all types of income-producing assets. The value of an asset can be thought of as the present value of the expected stream of payments using the rate of return that is appropriate for the degree of risk of the payments. In particular, the value of common stock can be thought of as the present value of the expected dividends which will be paid to present and future owners of the stock.

The risk-adjusted interest rate or required rate of return that should be used in valuing the expected income from an asset depends on the general level of interest rates in the economy and the degree of risk. The security market line expresses the relationship between risk and the required rate of return. The greater the risk, the higher must be the expected rate of return.

QUESTIONS

1. In nineteenth-century England, economic conditions were very stable. Some English landowners leased their property at a fixed annual rental fee for 999 years. Today a transaction like this seems very foolish. Why?

2. In a world of no risk, explain why financial assets might have different prices. What is the common element to all financial assets in such a world?

3. In the world of idealized certainty (i.e., no risk, no taxes, and perfect markets for financial assets), would the following situations be possible? (In each case, support your answer.)
   a) Two financial assets providing the same cash flows selling at different prices
   b) Two financial assets selling at the same price but providing different cash flows to the owner

    c) Two financial assets selling at the same price but providing different rates of return (interest rates)

4. There are two general sources of risk to the owners of a business firm. What are they? Briefly describe each one.

5. Why do all businesses have some "business risk"?

6. Try to rank the following investment portfolios in order of the degree of diversification.
   a) Common stock and bonds issued by International Telephone and Telegraph (a company with a wide range of business activities in the United States and overseas)
   b) Shares in a large mutual fund
   c) General Motors stock plus Firestone Tire stock
   d) Common stock of three Eastern railroad companies
   e) IBM stock plus McGraw-Hill stock plus American Hospital Supply stock
   f) The stocks of three companies selected by throwing three darts at a newspaper listing of stock prices
   g) The stocks of ten companies recommended by an investment advisory service
   h) Shares in a large mutual fund plus an acre of land on a lake plus a painting by Picasso plus a collection of the coins of ancient Rome plus United States government bonds

7. If the price of a share of common stock depends on the dividends paid to the stockholders, why do we find stocks of companies that have never paid a dividend selling at prices greater than zero and in many cases at a high multiple of the company's earnings per share?

8. Should an aeronautical engineer who works for Boeing own stock in Boeing? Why or why not? Consider the likely correlation between the engineer's income and Boeing's stock price in your answer.

PROJECT   Suppose that you have $10,000 to invest. Explore several alternatives open to you, using the *Wall Street Journal* and other sources of information to find the going rates of return. Try to rank these investments in increasing order of risk according to your own judgment. Estimate the risk premiums in these investments using the rate on Treasury bills for the riskless rate. Which investments would you make?

PROBLEMS   1. a) Suppose that the market interest rate is 8 percent per year. You purchase a U.S. Treasury bill that pays $1,000 to its owner one year from now. How much would you pay at the most for the bill? [Ans.: $925.90]

b) If you purchase the bill at a price of $925.90, what interest rate will you earn on the bill for the year?

2. A U.S. Treasury note is available in the market that pays $80 in interest per year and $1,000 at maturity two years from now.

   a) If the yield to maturity on the note is 8 percent, what is its current price? [Ans.: $1,000]

   b) Given that the current price is $1,000, at what price must you be able to sell the note for one year from now (after the first year's interest is received) to earn 8 percent on your investment if you buy the note today? [Ans.: $1,000]

   c) At what price would the note sell for today if the interest rate is 6 percent per year? [Ans.: $1,036.67]

   d) Given that the current price is $1,036.67, at what price must you be able to sell the note for one year from now to earn 6 percent on your investment if you buy the note today? [Ans.: $1,018.87]

   e) Suppose that you purchase the note at a price of $1,000 to yield 8 percent per year. One year later the market interest rate has changed to a new rate of 6 percent. What will be the price of the note at that time? [Ans.: $1,018.87]

   f) Given your answer from **e**, what interest rate would you obtain if you sold the note after one year (after receiving interest)? [Ans.: 9.89 percent] What rate will you earn if you hold it to maturity instead of selling it?

   g) Suppose that you purchase the note at a price of $1,036.67 to yield 6 percent per year. One year later the market interest rate has changed to a new rate of 8 percent. What will be the price of the note at that time? What interest rate will you earn if you sell it then? What rate will you earn if you hold it to maturity?

3. In 1972 the Ecosystems Company raised $1 million by selling bonds. These bonds had a maturity of ten years, a maturity value of $1,000 each, and a coupon rate of 8 percent. The bonds could be considered riskless because the company had signed a ten-year research contract with the government that would insure solvency. In 1972 the riskless rate of interest was 8 percent.

   a) How many bonds did the company have to sell in 1972 to raise $1 million?

   b) What would have been the price of the bonds in 1975 if the interest rate had remained constant at 8 percent?

   c) In fact three years later in 1975, the rate of interest decreased, mostly because of a lowering of the inflation rate. The 1975 riskless rate of interest was 6 percent. What maximum price were investors willing to pay for the Ecosystems bonds at that time?

   d) Explain the role played by the price in relation to interest rate changes.

4. Consider a security which will pay $1,000 for sure a year from now. The rate of interest is 7 percent per year.
   a) How much should an investor pay for that security?
   b) How much should the investor pay for a security which pays $1,000 for sure two years from now and nothing at the end of the first year?
   c) How much must a security pay at the end of two years to entice the investor to pay the same price as in **a**? (Nothing is paid at the end of the first year.)

5. You are considering purchasing stock in Swinger Manufacturing Company. The current price per share is $20. You have the following expectations regarding the price of the stock one year from now (no dividends are expected):

Future price	$10	$15	$20	$25	$30	$40
Probability	0.1	0.2	0.2	0.2	0.2	0.1

   a) What is the price expected to be one year from now? [Ans.: $23]
   b) If the price turns out to be $23, what rate of return will you have earned? [Ans.: 15 percent]
   c) Determine the probability distribution of the rates of return on this stock. What is the expected rate of return as calculated from this probability distribution? Compare this answer to the rate of return calculated in **b**. Should the two be equal? Why or why not?
   d) Using the probability distribution of **c**, calculate the standard deviation of the rate of return on the stock. [Ans.: 42.13 percent]

6. The stock of the Schnitzelburg Beer Company (SBC) is widely considered to perform well relative to other stocks during depressions. On the other hand the stock of Executive Toys, Inc., (ETI) tends to do well during boom periods. The following represents your assessment of the probabilities of various economic conditions next year and of the dollar returns (dividend plus price) the two stocks will have. Both stocks are currently selling for $100 per share. Compare the expected returns obtained from investments of 1) $1,000 in SBC stock, 2) $1,000 in ETI stock, 3) $400 in SBC stock and $600 in ETI stock, and 4) $600 in SBC stock and $400 in ETI stock. Evaluate the

Economic conditions next year

	Boom	High growth	Low growth	Depression
Return of SBC stock	$105	$120	$110	$100
Return of ETI stock	$150	$125	$100	$ 60
Probability	0.3	0.4	0.2	0.1

risks of the alternative investment strategies. Which would you prefer? Why?

7. Consider a $100 (maturity value) bond that is currently sold at a market price of $80. The bond is due to mature in five years and pays interest of $10 per year.

a) Compute the yield to maturity for the bond.

b) The firm that floated the bond is in the process of penetrating a new market, and there is some possibility for failure, which will decrease over time. The estimated rates of return that would be received by bondholders and their probabilities are as follows:

Rate of return	16%	10%	0%	−20%	−50%
Probability	0.8	0.02	0.03	0.05	0.10

Calculate the expected rate of return for the bond and compare with the yield to maturity.

c) Is the relationship between the two rates what you would expect? Why?

d) Which rate would be most useful for deciding whether or not to invest in that bond? Why?

8. Petroleum Engineering, Inc., (PEI) is a firm which builds oil pipe lines. A new pipeline has been proposed to carry oil from Alaska's North Slope to the Midwest and PEI has a good chance to work on at least part of the project if it is undertaken. Western Oil Company (WOC) is the other major firm engaged in building oil pipelines. It too has good prospects of being engaged in the project; however industry experts consider PEI as more likely to obtain the major portion of the work. The profits and stock prices of these two firms will be greatly affected by the final determination of how much work each firm will obtain. The results are crucial to the firms because there are no other major pipelines planned at the present time.

a) There are two major sources of risk affecting the current stock prices of PEI and WOC. What are they?

b) Is it possible for you to invest in one or both of these two firms so that one of the two risks is largely eliminated for you? How could you invest and what risk is being eliminated?

c) PEI's current stock price is $100 per share and WOC's stock price is $50 per share. After a careful evaluation of the situation, you have arrived at the following estimates of next year's stock prices for the two firms and their probabilities depending on whether or not the pipeline will be built. Neither firm will pay a dividend next year. Calculate the expected rates of return for each stock for each of the two situations.

Pipeline built			Pipeline not built		
Probability	PEI	WOC	Probability	PEI	WOC
0.1	$100	$120	0.3	$50	$30
0.2	$120	$ 90	0.5	$60	$36
0.4	$150	$ 60	0.2	$75	$40
0.3	$200	$ 40	1.0		
1.0					

d) Using your answers from **c**, what are the expected rates of return from each stock if the probability that the pipeline will be built is .8 and the probability that it will not be built is .2? [Ans.: PEI: 35.2 percent; WOC: 19.6 percent]

e) Suppose that you invest $1,000 in each of the two stocks. What is your expected rate of return from the portfolio? [Hint: Assume that you will sell the stocks after one year and will earn the expected rate of return on each stock.]

(*Note:* Parts **f**, **g**, and **h** are more difficult and require a substantial number of calculations.)

f) Develop the overall separate probability distributions for the prices of each of the two stocks given the probabilities that the pipeline will or will not be built. [For example, the probability of obtaining a price of $100 for PEI is the probability the pipeline will be built (.8) times the probability of obtaining a price of $100 if the pipeline is built (.1), which equals 0.08.] From these probability distributions, calculate the expected rate of return for each of the two stocks, which should equal the results obtained in **d** above. Also calculate the standard deviations of the rates of return. Based on this information, which of the two stocks is more risky?

g) Suppose that you invest $1,000 in each stock. Find the expected rate of return and standard deviation of the rate of return on the portfolio. To do this you will have to develop a probability distribution for the rate of return on the portfolio or a probability distribution of the future value of the portfolio. Be sure to include all possible combinations of the prices (or rates of return) from the two stocks.

h) Given your results from **f** and **g**, rank the following investment strategies: 1) $2,000 invested in PEI stock; 2) $2,000 invested in WOC stock; and 3) $1,000 invested in PEI stock and $1,000 invested in WOC stock.

9. In 1976 the riskless rate of interest (rate of return on government securities) was about 7 percent. Assume that we have a valid measure of risk for a security that can be expressed by a number such as 0

for a risk-free security), 3, 7, etc. Suppose the expected rate of return required by the market for a security with risk 10 is 16 percent.

a) Draw the security market line.

b) What would be the expected rate of return on stock A with a risk measure equal to 5?

c) Suppose that the riskless rate of interest increases to 10 percent. What then would be the expected rate of return on stock A? Assume that there is no change in the premiums for risk.

d) Suppose now that the riskless rate remains at 7 percent, but the market requires an expected rate of return of 18 percent for a security with risk 10. Draw the new security market line. What could cause such a change in risk premium?

e) You are considering the purchase of a share of stock at a price of $80. The stock is expected to pay a dividend of $4 next year and to sell then at a market price of $85. What would your expected rate of return be if you purchased the stock now and were to sell it next year?

f) The stock risk has been evaluated to be 8 units of risk. Is the stock rightly priced by the market given the security market line of **a** above? Overpriced? Underpriced? If enough people believe as you do, what will happen to the price of the stock?

10. The Shakey Shingle Company is issuing $20 million of $1,000 (maturity value) bonds due to mature in twenty years with a coupon rate of 9 percent. You have analyzed the company and have decided one of the following *three* eventualities are possible:

1. The terms of the bonds are met in full and on time (probability of 85 percent).

2. All interest payments will be made on time, but the company will go bankrupt because it is unable to retire the bonds at maturity, and you will receive only 54¢ on the dollar for your bonds at that time (probability of 5 percent).

3. The company will encounter some years of operation at a loss and will be unable to meet the interest payments on time. To make the analysis simple, assume this eventuality may be summarized by a scenario in which interest payments of $450 are paid in years 5, 10, 15, 20, and the full maturity value of $1,000 is paid in year 20 (probability of 10 percent).

a) If the bonds are actually being sold at their maturity value, what is the expected rate of return?

b) Suppose the market's required rate of return (k) is given by a security market line such as those in Figure 5-5, the riskless rate is 6.6 percent, and the market risk premium is 2 percentage points for each unit of risk. The risk of the bonds is estimated to be 0.2 unit.

    c) In view of **a** and **b** is it reasonable to believe that the bonds will sell for $1,000?

11. Investors currently expect that the dividends per share of Super Industries, Inc., will grow at a rate of 10 percent per year for the foreseeable future. Dividends next year are expected to be $2.80 per share. The risk of Super's dividend stream is such that investors require a 12 percent rate of return on the stock.

    a) What is the price per share of Super Industries' common stock? [Ans. = $140]

    b) Suppose that new information on Super comes into the market such that the expected growth rate is reduced to 5 percent per year (but the expected dividend next year is still $2.80). What will be the new price of Super Industries?

    c) Do your results from **a** and **b** tell you anything about the sensitivity of stock prices to changes in expectations? What do they tell you?

diversification and correlation

The purpose of this appendix is to present the formulas for the expected rate of return and standard deviation of the rate of return on total investment when a single asset is added to a portfolio or to another asset. We then use these formulas to show how the risk of the total investment varies with the correlation and standard deviation of the asset.

The expected rate of return on any combination or portfolio of assets is the weighted average of the expected rates of return on the individual assets in the portfolio. The weights are the proportions of each asset in the portfolio. Therefore, when one asset I is added to an existing portfolio P, the expected rate of return on total investment T is

THE RATE OF RETURN ON INVESTMENT

$$\text{Expected rate on } T = \alpha \text{ (expected rate on } I)$$
$$+ (1 - \alpha) \text{ (expected rate of } P) \qquad (5\text{-}12)$$

where α is the proportion of total investment represented by asset I. For example, if the portfolio has an expected rate of return of 10 percent, an asset with an expected rate of return of 20 percent is added to it, and 40 percent of the total is invested in the asset:

$$\text{Expected rate on } T = 0.40 \, (20\%) + (1 - 0.40) \, (10\%)$$
$$= 14\%$$

The general formula for the standard deviation of a portfolio of assets is somewhat complicated. Here we show only how to calculate the standard deviation of the rate of return on total investment for a combination of one asset with a portfolio (or another asset). The standard deviation SD_T of the rate of return on total investment in security I and portfolio P is calculated by taking the square root of the following expression:

THE STANDARD DEVIATION

$$(SD_T)^2 = \alpha^2(SD_I)^2 + (1 - \alpha)^2(SD_P)^2$$
$$+ 2\alpha \, (1 - \alpha) \, (\text{Corr}_{IP}) \, (SD_I) \, (SD_P) \qquad (5\text{-}13)$$

where SD_I is standard deviation of rate of return on asset I
SD_P is standard deviation of rate of return on portfolio P

Corr$_{IP}$ is correlation between rates of return on asset I and portfolio P

α is proportion of total investment made in asset I

$(1 - \alpha)$ is remaining proportion invested in portfolio P

For example, suppose we invest in two stocks, one having a standard deviation of 20 percent, the other having a standard deviation of 30 percent. The correlation between their rates of return is 0 and we invest half our money in each ($\alpha = 0.5$). The standard deviation from this combination is

$$(SD_T)^2 = (0.5)^2(20)^2 + (0.5)^2(30)^2 + 2\,(0.5)(1. - 0.5)\,(0)\,(20)\,(30)$$

$$= (0.25)\,(400) + (0.25)\,(900)$$

$$= 325$$

$$SD_T = \sqrt{325} = 18.03$$

Therefore, $SD_T = 18.03\%$.

RISK REDUCTION THROUGH DIVERSIFICATION

To see how the risk on total investment is affected by diversification, let's look at some simple cases. The standard deviations presented below are calculated using Eq. (5-13); however, we do not show the computations. Only the results are given.

Suppose you currently own stock A, which has a probability distribution of its rate of return as was shown in Figure 5-2. All your money is invested in this stock; thus the expected rate of return on your total investment is the expected rate of return on stock A, 20 percent. The standard deviation of the rate of return on stock A, and therefore on your total investment, is 22 percent. You are considering diversifying your investment by selling half of the shares you own in A and purchasing stock C. Half your investment will be in stock A and half in stock C. Stock C has an expected rate of return of 20 percent and a standard deviation of 22 percent, the same as for stock A. Will you gain any advantage from this restructuring of your portfolio of stock?

First you should note that the expected rate of return on the new portfolio of A and C will be 20 percent because both securities have an expected rate of return of 20 percent. The weighted average rate of return is 20 percent. Any benefit from diversification in this case must result from a reduction in risk as measured by standard deviation. If there is to be a benefit, the standard deviation of the rate of return on the portfolio of A and C must be lower than 22 percent, which is the standard deviation of each of A and C owned individually. Will any reduction occur? The answer depends on the correlation between the rate of return on A and the rate of return on C.

If the returns from stock A and stock C have a correlation of 1.0, then the rate of return on a portfolio of A and C together has the same standard deviation as the rate of return of stock A by itself. In this case purchasing stock C is no different than keeping all your investment in stock A because stock C achieves the same rate of return that stock A does. For example, if A has a rate of return of − 20 percent, C also has a rate of return of − 20 percent.

In practice, the returns from two different assets will never be perfectly correlated; most likely the correlation of returns will be greater than zero but less than 1.0. The positive correlation of asset returns is due to the dependence of returns of most assets on general economic conditions. Suppose the correlation between the returns on stock A and stock C is .5. In this case the standard deviation of the returns on the portfolio of A and C is 19 percent, less than the standard deviation of the individual assets. Thus there is an advantage to diversifying by owning two stocks rather than one. Indeed, such an advantage will obtain for all correlations less than 1.0. Standard deviations for other values of the correlation are shown below:

Correlation between A and C	1.0	.5	0	−.5	−1.0
Standard deviation of A + C, %	22%	19%	16%	11%	0%

Therefore we see that the correlation of the returns from a single asset with the returns from the other assets held by the investor strongly influences the risk of the total portfolio. Indeed, if the correlation is − 1.0, we see that a riskless portfolio is obtainable. Of course perfect negative correlations (− 1.0) are just as unlikely to be found in practice as perfect positive correlations (1.0), but the point is still valid. The lower the correlation, the more effective is diversification.

The asset's standard deviation is also an important influence on the resulting risk of the portfolio. Suppose we take a stock D whose expected rate of return is also 20 percent. Let's assume that the correlation between the returns on D and the returns on A is .5 and look at the standard deviation of a portfolio with half the money invested in A and half in D. The expected rate of return on the resulting portfolio will again be 20 percent. The standard deviation of the portfolio depends on the standard deviation for stock D as shown below:

Standard deviation of D	5%	10%	22%	30%
Standard deviation of A + D	12%	14%	19%	23%

Therefore the higher the standard deviation of the asset being added to the portfolio is, the larger the resulting standard deviation of the combined portfolio of old and new assets is so long as the correlation between the asset and the old portfolio is not negative.

If the correlation between an asset and the portfolio is negative, the impact of a larger standard deviation for the asset on the standard deviation of the combined portfolio is more difficult to specify. Under some conditions adding an asset with a large standard deviation may provide greater risk reduction than adding an asset with a small standard deviation. This is a topic for more advanced courses and is not especially important, since negative correlations are rare.

a model of risk and return in the security market

In this appendix we present a model that provides a precise relationship between the risk of a security and its required rate of return.[21] Even though the theory presented here is highly abstract, it has received substantial support from statistical examination of the historical rates of return on securities. Many of the concepts derived from it are being applied by security analysts and financial managers.

ASSUMPTIONS

Consider a world in which securities are bought and sold in a highly competitive market. Information as to the characteristics of securities and the prospects of the firms issuing them is freely available. There are no costs, such as brokerage fees, of buying and selling securities. Investors, large and small, can borrow freely at a given rate of interest which is equal to the interest rate that they can obtain from investing in a riskless security.

Investors would prefer to earn as high a return as possible on their investment, but dislike risk as measured by the standard deviation of the rate of return. However, some investors may be more willing to tolerate a given degree of risk than are others. All investors will choose the security that offers the highest expected rate of return for a given amount of risk and would prefer the lowest-risk security offering a given expected rate of return.

In general, individual investors may differ in their wealth and attitudes toward risk, but they have the same opportunities to invest and the same expectations regarding the future. They all dislike risk and view standard deviation of the return of their investment as an appropriate measure of risk. They can freely invest in any combination of securities and can borrow, if they so desire, to finance securities purchases.

Under these assumptions investors will come to own only highly diversified portfolios containing a large number of securities (for example, shares in large mutual funds). The only risks retained by those portfolios are those resulting from changes in general economic activity which cannot be diversified away. The result is that the risk of any single security depends only on its contribution to the risk of these large portfolios and its required rate of return is a function of that risk and basic market parameters. This relationship between risk and return is the security market line.

---

21. The model is often referred to as the "Capital Asset Pricing Model" since that was the term used by one of its originators, William Sharpe.

RISK PREMIUMS AND THE SECURITY MARKET LINE

In this model the required rate of return on any security I equals the riskless rate of interest plus a premium for risk.

$$\text{Required rate of return}_I = \text{riskless rate} + \text{risk premium}_I \quad (5\text{-}14)$$

The riskless rate of interest is one market parameter. Its value affects the rates of return on all securities. The risk premium can be expressed in several different, but mathematically equivalent, ways. One way to express it is in terms of the correlation and standard deviation of the rate of return on the security.

$$\text{Risk premium}_I = (\text{constant})\,(SD_I)\,(\text{Corr}_{IM}) \quad (5\text{-}15)$$

where SD_I is the standard deviation of I's rate of return and Corr_{IM} is the correlation between the rate of return on security I and the rate of return on all securities in the market.[22] Accordingly, in this specification of the model, risk for a single security is measured as the product of its standard deviation and its correlation with the market. Notice that the model implies the general results discussed in the body of Chapter 5. Namely, for a given positive correlation, the greater the standard deviation is, the greater the risk and therefore the larger the required rate of return. Also, for a given standard deviation, securities with low correlations have low required rates of return. Indeed, securities whose rates of return are negatively correlated with the market have "negative risk" and will have required rates of return that are less than the riskless rate. This is due to the benefits provided by such securities in reducing risk. However, as we have commented before, negative correlation is rare.

BETA

Although Eq. (5-15) is helpful in understanding the nature of the model and ties it to our main discussion, an alternative form is much more widely used. We can express the risk of a security as a single quantity called Beta. Beta equals the product of the security's standard deviation and its correlation with the market divided by the standard deviation of rate of return on the "market portfolio" SD_M

$$\text{Beta}_I = \frac{(\text{Corr}_{IM})\,(SD_I)}{SD_M} \quad (5\text{-}16)$$

The market portfolio is the portfolio comprising all securities in the market.

22. The constant in Eq. (5-15) is the same number for all securities and equals $(k_M - k_R)/SD_M$. See Eq. (5-17).

We can now express the security market line in terms of Beta and some additional notation.

$$k_I = k_R + (k_M - k_R)\text{Beta}_I \qquad (5\text{-}17)$$

where k_I is expected rate of return on security I
k_R is riskless rate of interest
k_M is expected rate of return on the market portfolio (average rate of return on all securities)

We now have a precise, compact equation for the security market line. The rate of return required by investors on a given security depends on its risk as measured by Beta, the riskless interest rate, and the average rate of return on all securities in the market. However, the advantages of Beta as a risk measure are not primarily due to the neatness of the security market line that results. Let's examine its characteristics more closely.

There are two major advantages to Beta as a measure of risk for securities compared with other measures derived from this theoretical model. First, it has a convenient numerical magnitude which is easy to interpret. Second, it can be easily estimated from historical data.

Beta as a Measure of Risk

Beta can be used as a measure of risk for any single asset or portfolio of assets. The value of Beta for the market portfolio is 1.0. We can see this from the definition of Beta for a security I, Eq. (5-16), and applying it to the market portfolio M,

$$\text{Beta}_M = \frac{(\text{Corr}_{MM})\,(\text{SD}_M)}{\text{SD}_M} \qquad (5\text{-}18)$$
$$= 1.0$$

since the correlation of the rate of return on the market with itself (Corr_{MM}) is 1.0. Therefore a security or portfolio which has a Beta = 1.0 is as risky as the total market. If Beta for a security is less than 1.0, the security is less risky than the market and vice versa.

Values for Beta are often estimated from historical data. Suppose we plot the rates of returns actually earned on a security for each of several periods (days, months, quarters, years) against the rate of return on the market for the same period. Typically the rate of return of some market index such as the Dow-Jones Industrial Average or Standard & Poor's Stock Index is used as representative of the market. Figure 5-6 shows this for the common stock of General Electric Corporation (GE) and the Dow-Jones average for several years. A straight line is fitted to this data either by hand or, more commonly, by statistical methods (linear regression

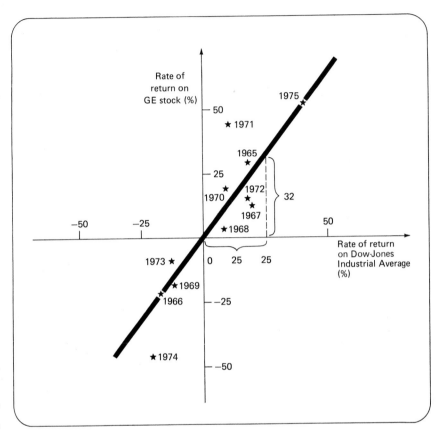

Figure 5-6. Estimating Beta from historical data. Slope of line = $\frac{32}{25}$ = 1.28. Estimated Beta = slope = 1.28.

analysis). If the Betas for many stocks are desired, computers are used to do the job. The slope of this line is an estimate of Beta for the stock.[23] The estimated value of Beta for GE is therefore 1.28.

The combination of convenient interpretation and ease of estimation has made Beta the most popular measure of risk for securities. It is used by managers of investment portfolios (mutual funds and pension funds) and by security analysts. You may have even seen advertisements by security brokers referring to the Betas of common stocks. We shall use Beta in the Appendix to Chapter 6 when we estimate the required rate of return on the common stock of an actual company. It is an important concept in finance.

23. The *Value Line Investment Survey* provides estimates of Beta for stocks. Their estimate for GE's Beta is 1.1 (*Value Line Investment Survey*, Nov. 21, 1975, p. 1016).

the constant growth formula

In the body of this chapter we observed that if the cash receipts from an asset are expected to grow at a constant rate forever, then the present value of those receipts is

$$P = \frac{D_1}{k - g} \qquad (5\text{-}19)$$

where P is the present value (price)
  D_1 is the cash received one period from now (dividend next year)
  k is the interest rate (required rate of return)
  g is the growth rate

The purpose of this appendix is to show how this formula is derived.
  We begin by assuming that the cash receipt or dividend in any period t, D_t, is

$$D_t = D_1(1 + g)^{t-1} \qquad (5\text{-}20)$$

The stream of receipts is thus assumed to be growing at a constant compounded rate g. The present value of a cash flow is

$$P = \frac{D_1}{1 + k} + \frac{D_2}{(1 + k)^2} + \frac{D_3}{(1 + k)^3} + \cdots + \frac{D_m}{(1 + k)^m} \qquad (5\text{-}21)$$

where the last payment is received in period m. Equation (5-21) is the basic valuation equation from the chapter, Eq. (5-7). If we use Eq. (5-20), our general expression for D_t, as $t = 2, 3, \ldots , m$ to substitute for each receipt $D_2, D_3, \ldots , D_m$, in Eq. (5-21), we get

$$P = \frac{D_1}{1 + k} + \frac{D_1(1 + g)}{(1 + k)^2} + \frac{D_1(1 + g)^2}{(1 + k)^3} + \cdots + \frac{D_1(1 + g)^{m-1}}{(1 + k)^m} \qquad (5\text{-}22)$$

At this point we have the present value or price of the stream of cash receipts or dividends expressed as a series of terms involving the first dividend D_1, the growth rate g, and the interest rate k.
  Equation (5-22) has a special mathematical structure that permits us to rearrange it and get a much simpler form of the right-hand side.
  Suppose we multiply both sides of Eq. (5-22) by the ratio $(1 + g)/(1 + k)$. We get

$$P\left(\frac{1 + g}{1 + k}\right) = \frac{D_1(1 + g)}{(1 + k)^2} + \frac{D_1(1 + g)^2}{(1 + k)^3} + \frac{D_1(1 + g)^3}{(1 + k)^4}$$

$$+ \cdots + \frac{D_1(1 + g)^m}{(1 + k)^{m+1}} \tag{5-23}$$

Now subtract Eq. (5-23) from Eq. (5-22). Almost all the terms disappear except those shown below.

$$P - P\left(\frac{1 + g}{1 + k}\right) = \frac{D_1}{1 + k} - \frac{D_1(1 + g)^m}{(1 + k)^{m+1}} \tag{5-24}$$

If the interest rate k is larger than the growth rate g, as the number of periods m approaches infinity, the right-hand term in Eq. (5-24) approaches zero. If we drop the right-hand term, Eq. (5-24) reduces to

$$P - P\left(\frac{1 + g}{1 + k}\right) = \frac{D_1}{1 + k} \tag{5-25}$$

Multiplying both sides of Eq. (5-25) by $(1 + k)$ and solving for P, we get our original formula, Eq. (5-19).

$$P(1 + k) - P(1 + g) = D_1$$

$$P[(1 + k) - (1 + g)] = D_1$$

$$P(k - g) = D_1$$

$$P = \frac{D_1}{k - g} \tag{5-19}$$

Bulls, Bears, and the "Nifty Fifty"

To a visitor from outer space, Wall Street in New York City is just another concrete canyon, similar to the central business district of most large cities on our planet. Throngs of people crowd the sidewalks during the day, but the street is silent and deserted at night and on the weekends. To Earth people, Wall Street is the financial center of the world. The name "Wall Street" itself connotes money and power. Many large financial institutions are located on Wall Street or close by—commercial banks, insurance companies, investment banks, securities brokers and dealers, mutual funds, and stock exchanges. Such institutions set the tone of "The Street." These participants in the stock market seem to live in a special world, populated by bulls, bears, and other diverse, unusual inhabitants. A bull is one who expects stock prices to rise; a bear expects them to fall. There are also the "random walkers," who expect prices to wander randomly in the short run and to trend upward in the long run.

The early 1970s was a traumatic time for the stock market. There were dramatic swings in the prices of most stocks. Financial institutions became the most important buyers of stocks, as individual investors sold out. In May 1975 the 183-year-old system of fixed minimum fees for stocks bought or sold through the stock exchanges was abolished, and many brokerage firms merged, cut back employees, or shut down. Let's look at this period of change in the stock market to gain some insight into some of the factors that influence stock prices which are not obvious from the simple concepts of risk and return.

INSTITUTIONAL DOMINATION

The importance of financial institutions in the stock market increased steadily throughout the 1960s. Most employers offer pension programs to their employees. The money committed to pension plans increased rapidly, and an increasing proportion was invested in stocks to obtain higher long-run returns than was provided by bonds. Individual investors began favoring mutual funds over investing directly into individual securities. Mutual bond portfolios also shifted to stocks to provide higher returns to their investors. Back in 1961, institutions accounted for 39 percent of the dollar trading volume (stock purchases and sales) on the New York Stock Exchange, while individuals accounted for 61 percent. By 1975, institutional trading had soared to 70 percent, while that of individuals was only 30 percent. Institutions also accounted for 45 percent of the dollar volume of stocks traded elsewhere (other exchanges and over-the-counter). This development has radically affected the market.

Financial institutions deal in large, sometimes gigantic, sums of money. They therefore must invest primarily in companies which have a large market value (number of shares outstanding multiplied by share price). Out of the 2,800 or so companies listed on the major exchanges, only a few hundred are suitable for *large-scale* investment by financial institutions. In the early 1970s, the leading money managers (the people who decide what stocks to buy and sell for the institutions) came to a rare unanimity of opinion: The best investment strategy was to buy—and keep on buying—the stocks of the large, well-managed "growth" companies, such as Avon, Eastman Kodak, Polaroid, IBM, Xerox, and the major drug manufacturers.

These favored companies were facetiously dubbed "the nifty fifty." This created what was called "the two-tier market." The top tier consisted of the "nifty fifty" and a few other large companies, such as General Motors, whose stock was favored by the institutions. The second tier consisted of all other stocks.

Inevitably the strategy was successful for a while. Large amounts of money were invested in these stocks, pushing prices upward. High rates of return were earned on these investments.

Meanwhile the economy was showing signs of serious problems. High rates of inflation and low corporate profits made many investors nervous about the future. Interest rates on bonds and debt of all sorts rose, causing prices of fixed-income securities to fall. The prices of the second tier of stocks were similarly affected. In January 1973, the Dow-Jones Industrial Average, which is an index of the prices of thirty largely top-tier companies, reached a record high value of 1051.70. At that time the average price for *all* stocks listed on the New York Stock Exchange was 40 percent *below* the average at the end of 1968. The price drop for American Stock Exchange stocks over the same period was almost 70 percent.

However, even the top-tier stocks could not keep rising in the face of the worsening economic outlook. In the fall of 1973, when the Arab oil embargo darkened the economic outlook, the top tier came crashing down. Between late October and mid-December 1973, the Dow-Jones Industrial Average fell 199 points. This was the largest short-term point decline in history, exceeding that of the "great crash" in 1929. When the market hit

bottom in December 1974, the average decline in the prices of New York Stock Exchange stocks from 1968 was a whopping 73 percent.

CAUSES OF THE MARKET TUMBLE

From 1968 on, stock market prices had been adversely affected by a number of significant events. The extent to which prices in general had fallen was obscured for some time by the behavior of the few but very important large companies whose prices were supported by the buying activities of institutional investors.

The 1969–70 recession aroused fears that some major corporations might follow the Penn Central Railroad into bankruptcy. Although these fears were not realized, investors were put on notice that even large firms could fail, wiping out their investment. The economic recovery that followed was not reassuring. It turned into an inflationary boom, which a noted economist aptly described as "the unhappiest boom I have ever lived through."

Investors were beset with one thing after another that undermined their confidence in the future:

1. Accelerating inflation and rising interest rates.

2. A succession of international monetary crises, casting a shadow over the future of world trade and undermining confidence in the United States dollar.

3. The government's fuzzy game plan for wage and price controls. This increased the uncertainty of expected corporate profits. Dividends were also restricted in this period.

4. A progressive erosion of public confidence in our government as the Watergate-Nixon drama unfolded in the manner of a serialized horror story.

5. The shock of the energy crisis, which was precipitated by the oil embargo that fol-

lowed the Arab-Israeli war of 1973. The quadrupling of oil prices that resulted from the embargo destroyed the profits of user industries, such as the airlines.

For six years noxious emissions from the political and economic scene cast a blanket of pollution over the stock market. At the close of 1974, the Dow-Jones Industrial Average, which since 1958 had averaged 14 to 24 times the aggregate earnings of its component companies, was at only about 6 times the aggregate earnings. Indeed, one Wall Street commentator observed that "[investors] appear to have discounted every possible disaster short of the end of the world." In 1975 investors collectively realized that the world was not coming to an end and that the economy was improving. Stock prices rose just as dramatically as they had declined. By the spring of 1976 the Dow-Jones Average had risen more than 400 points and was once again over 1,000.

Whatever the future holds for the stock market, some lessons have been learned from this experience. Despite the purported expertise of government officials, the economy and the biggest, best-managed corporations can get into difficulty. Moreover, even highly paid talented managers of the big institutional portfolios can make mistakes. There is risk in owning stocks so long as economic uncertainty exists. One of the major adverse factors affecting stock prices is inflation. So long as the economy is subject to high and variable inflation rates, we will see severe fluctuations in the market, as investors become first pessimistic and then optimistic regarding the future.

THE FIRM'S INVESTMENT, FINANCING, AND DIVIDEND DECISIONS

Part 2 comprises five chapters which deal with the firm's fundamental considerations in making its investment, financing, and dividend decisions. The sequencing of these chapters roughly follows the sequence of decisions made by the financial manager. In the light of past investment, financing, and dividend decisions, the financial manager estimates the firm's cost of capital for use as a standard to evaluate proposed investments. The cost of capital is the rate of return investors require on their investment in the firm. Procedures for estimating its numerical value are presented in Chapter 6. Management then uses the cost of capital to evaluate investments of the same risk and financed in the same way as those historically undertaken by the firm. The techniques used in this process are covered in Chapter 7. Procedures for dealing with investments that differ in risk are covered in Chapter 8.

Application of the methods of business investment planning covered in Chapters 7 and 8 results in a planned capital expenditure program for the firm. The financial manager must now consider how these expenditures are to be financed. Chapter 9 examines the major sources of financing used by business firms and explains how management decides which sources to use. If this financing method differs significantly from that used in the past, the cost of capital estimate may be revised, and a change may be made in the capital budget that was initially chosen. The final financing and investment program followed by the firm depends on the cost and availability of financing.

A major source of financing is earnings retained by the firm instead of being paid out as dividends. Chapter 10 discusses the factors that influence policies for dividend payments to shareholders and how the firm formulates the policy best suited to its particular situation.

the cost of capital

The cost of capital is the minimum acceptable rate of return on new investment made by the firm from the viewpoint of creditors and investors in the firm's securities. Undertaking an investment which is not expected to earn the cost of capital will reduce the value of the firm to its owners, the common stockholders. From the viewpoint of the financial manager, the cost of capital is also the average rate of return the firm must provide to investors in the firm's securities so that money can be raised to finance new investments. In this chapter we analyze the cost of capital and show how it can be calculated.

A primary responsibility of the financial manager is raising money. There is a variety of ways to do this. Debt can be issued in the form of bonds or loans. Earnings can be retained rather than paid as dividends. Additional common stock can be issued, creating new owners. Other types of securities can be issued, such as preferred stock. We will examine these methods in more depth in later chapters; here we need only observe that each form of financing will have its own cost. To determine an overall or average cost of capital, the costs of individual types of financing must be combined. In this chapter we will describe the costs of each type and then show how the overall average cost of capital can be estimated. We'll begin with an explanation of the average cost of capital.

THE AVERAGE COST OF CAPITAL

A value for the cost of capital is determined as a weighted average of the costs of the types of capital used to finance the firm's investments. The cost for each type of capital is multiplied by its proportion (which sum to 1.0) of the total amount of all capital issued by the firm. For example, suppose that the firm uses debt costing 5 percent and stock costing 15 percent. If the proportion of debt used is 40 percent and the proportion of stock used is 60 percent, then the average cost of capital k_a is

$$\text{Average cost of capital} = \text{debt proportion} \times \text{debt rate}$$
$$+ \text{stock proportion} \times \text{stock rate} \quad (6\text{-}1)$$
$$k_a = 0.40 \times 5\% + 0.60 \times 15\%$$
$$= 2\% + 9\%$$
$$= 11\%$$

There are two questions raised by use of this procedure: (1) why is it a valid measurement of the cost of capital and (2) how can the components (proportions and costs) be determined? Let's first discuss the validity of the procedure, as this will provide the basis for specifying precisely how the components should be determined.

Basic Assumptions   There are two basic assumptions which are necessary in order for the average cost of capital to be used in evaluating new investments:

1. The new investments under consideration have the same risk as the typical or average investments undertaken historically by the firm.
2. The financing policies of the firm are not affected by the investments being undertaken.

The first assumption means that the average cost of capital being determined here is not appropriate for investments of differing risk. The procedures used to evaluate new investments which will be developed in Chapter 7 are based on this assumption as well. In Chapter 8 we show how to evaluate investments with different risks, and the general procedure is useful for these more complex problems.

The second assumption is that the firm's financing policies are given and will not be changed as a result of any new investments being undertaken. Financing policy is the specification by the firm's management as to what types of capital will be raised to finance the firm's investment. The average cost of capital is determined for given financing policies; thus if the policies changed, the cost of capital would also change. This is a difficult problem and will be discussed briefly after we examine financing decisions in Chapter 9.

Given these two assumptions, let's see why the average cost of capital is a proper measure of the minimum acceptable rate of return on investment.

An Illustration   Suppose a firm is considering an investment such as purchasing a new machine costing $1,000 that will be financed with a debt issue of $400 and a stock issue of $600. Assume that the interest cost of the debt is 5 percent and that the stockholders require an expected rate of return of 15 percent on their investment of $600. If the cash returns from the investment are expected to continue at the same level forever and all of it is paid out in interest and dividends, how large must the annual cash flow be to justify the expenditure of $1,000?

The cash flow from the investment must cover at a minimum the interest cost of the debt and provide a satisfactory dividend return to shareholders.

$$\begin{aligned}
\text{Minimum acceptable cash flow} &= \text{interest cost} + \text{minimum dividends} \\
&= \text{debt rate} \times \text{debt issue} \\
&\quad + \text{stock rate} \times \text{stock issue} \\
&= 5\% \times \$400 + 15\% \times \$600 \\
&= \$20 + \$90 \\
&= \$110
\end{aligned} \tag{6-2}$$

The minimum acceptable rate of return on this investment is therefore the minimum acceptable cash flow divided by the amount of the investment or $110/$1,000 = 11 percent. Since Eq. (6-2) expresses the minimum acceptable cash flow in terms of the financing used, let's divide both sides of that equation by the amount of the investment.

$$\begin{aligned}
\frac{\text{Minimum acceptable cash flow}}{\text{Investment}} &= \frac{\text{debt rate} \times \text{debt issue} + \text{stock rate} \times \text{stock issue}}{\text{investment}} \\
&= \text{debt rate} \times \frac{\text{debt issue}}{\text{investment}} \\
&\quad + \text{stock rate} \times \frac{\text{stock issue}}{\text{investment}} \\
&= \text{debt rate} \times \text{proportion of debt} \\
&\quad + \text{stock rate} \times \text{proportion of stock} \\
&= 5\% \frac{\$400}{\$1,000} + 15\% \frac{\$600}{\$1,000} \\
&= 5\% (0.4) + 15\% (0.6) \\
&= 11\%
\end{aligned} \tag{6-3}$$

Therefore we can compute a minimum acceptable rate of return using Eq. (6-3). Now compare Eq. (6-3) with our initial statement of the average cost of capital, Eq. (6-1). The minimum acceptable rate of return and the average cost of capital (k_a) are equal. If the project has an expected rate of return higher than 11 percent, it should be accepted since the cash returns from the investment will provide shareholders with dividends in excess of their minimum requirements.

We have shown by means of a simple example that the *minimum acceptable rate of return on an investment is equal to an average cost of capital.* What is this average cost of capital that we are measuring? It is the average rate of return that investors require on the securities that they

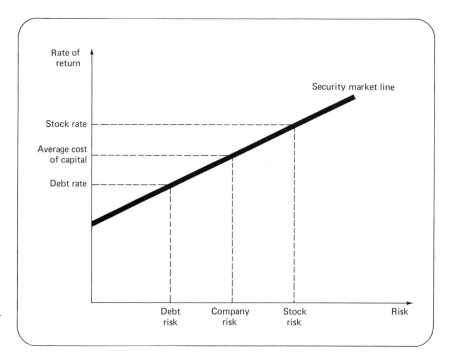

Figure 6-1 The average cost of capital and the security market line.

own.[1] The concept is illustrated in Figure 6-1. This figure shows the security market line of Chapter 5 with the risks and market rates of return of the debt and stock as indicated. The average cost of capital reflects the average risk (business and financial risks) of the total company and is therefore based on the risk-return relationship in the security markets as represented by the security market line.

General Formula for the Average Cost of Capital

Now we have the basic concept of the cost of capital and why it is a valid measure. Let's express it as a general formula. If the firm uses n different types of financing, each type j with its own costs k_j and in proportion p_j, then the weighted average cost of capital k_a is

$$k_a = p_1k_1 + p_2k_2 + \cdots + p_nk_n \tag{6-4}$$

So if the firm uses three types of financing (for example bonds, preferred stock, and common stock) with costs of 5, 8, and 12 percent each and in proportions 30, 20, and 50 percent respectively, then

1. In the numerical illustration above, the debt rate used was effective rate on debt adjusted for corporate income taxes. Figure 6-1 ignores corporate tax effects.

$$k_a = p_1k_1 + p_2k_2 + p_3k_3$$
$$= 0.30(5\%) + 0.20(8\%) + 0.50(12\%)$$
$$= 1.5\% + 1.6\% + 6\%$$
$$= 9.1\%$$

Despite the apparent precision of the formula, the cost of capital is not a very easy number to estimate exactly. The cost of capital is a theoretical concept, and there are several ways to calculate it in practice. The average cost of capital is the most widespread general method of determining a minimum acceptable rate of return for business investment decisions, but there are a number of variations on the definitions of the proportions and the costs used in the same general formula. Our stress here is on the underlying logic of the procedure and the basic estimates needed to determine the general magnitude of a firm's cost of capital. At this point we know that the proportions used are to be based on the financing plans of the firm and that the costs depend on the market interest rates required by investors in the firm's securities. We need now to identify the proportions and the costs more precisely so that they can be estimated from real data. Let's look at the costs first.

DETERMINING THE COST RATES

We need to know how to estimate the percentage cost rates [the k's in Eq. (6-4)] of each type of financing source used by the firm in order to calculate the average cost of capital. We will look at three types of financing used by firms: debt, preferred stock, and equity where equity includes common stock and retained earnings. Although the details of each type differ somewhat, our basic procedure is similar for all of them.

The rates we wish to estimate are those which the firm must provide to investors in order to finance the firm's investments in new plant, equipment, etc. However, we don't know what those investments will be yet, since the cost of capital is used as a criterion for determining what investments to undertake. This would seem to pose a dilemma. We need to know the financing rates in order to get a cost of capital to evaluate investments. However, we don't know how much money will be needed and therefore can't plan the financing until we evaluate the investments. The solution to the problem is based on our two basic assumptions as to investment risk and financing policies.

We estimate the rates of return that investors in the firm's securities currently require. These security market rates reflect the current business and financial risks of the firm. The current business risk of the firm is the same as the risk of the typical or average investment made by the firm historically. Recall that the average cost of capital is only appropriate for evaluating investments of this degree of risk. Similarly, the current financial risk of the firm is determined by past financing decisions. We assumed that the financing policies of the firm will not change so that we could use current market rates which reflect current financial risk.

Our procedure is, therefore, to estimate rates of return required by investors in the firm's securities. Under some circumstances this will be very difficult to do, and alternative approaches will be suggested to deal with these cases. However, it is important to know what the desired result is, namely, the market rates of returns which are required by the investors who supply money to the firm.

The Rate on Debt   In measuring the interest cost of debt financing, two questions arise:[2]

1. How should the use of several different types of debt be handled?
2. How should income taxes be taken into account?

The first question raises the possibility that the firm may use more than one type of debt. For example, there are several different kinds of bonds that the firm could issue. The interest and principal payments on a bond issue may be subordinated to those in other debt issues so that the investors in the subordinated bonds get paid only after the others have been paid. Since these bonds are more risky than ordinary bonds, a higher interest rate must be paid on them.

When there is more than one debt issue outstanding, we can estimate the current rate on debt by calculating the average rate.[3] For example, suppose the firm has two long-term debt issues outstanding—a "senior" bond and a "subordinated" bond where the holders of the subordinated bond get paid only if the holders of the senior bond have been paid first. Let's examine a specific case. The following data are assumed.

	Senior bonds	Subordinated bonds
Maturity value	$20 million	$10 million
Market value	$18 million	$10 million
Coupon rate	6%	8%
Yield to maturity	7%	8%

2. A third issue that will not be explored here is whether the promised rate (yield to maturity) or expected rate on the debt should be used. In theory, the expected rate discussed in Chap. 5 is more appropriate. However, we will use the interest rate promised to the firm's creditors for three reasons. First, the expected rate is difficult to estimate, whereas the promised rate can always be calculated. Second, in most practical situations, the promised rate produces sufficiently accurate results. Third, the promised rate is used in actual business practice.

3. An alternative to computing the average rate on debt is to consider each type of debt a separate financing source and include it as a part of the average cost of capital calculation. However, there are advantages to estimating an average rate on the debt, as will be shown when the method is applied to an actual firm later in the chapter.

The average interest rate required by the bondholders of the firm is calculated using the *market values* of both kinds of bonds and their *yields to maturity* as follows.

$$\text{Total market value of bonds} = \$18 + \$10 = \$28$$

$$\text{Average rate on bonds} = 7\% \left(\frac{\$18}{\$28}\right) + 8\% \left(\frac{\$10}{\$28}\right)$$

$$= 7.36\%$$

We use current market value and yield to maturity in this calculation because these reflect current interest rates in the market. Maturity values and coupon rates reflect interest rates at the time the debt was originally issued, and these historical values are not relevant to current decisions.

Income tax effects Our second question concerned the impact of taxes on the debt rate. The answer is that the effective cost of debt is lower than the interest rate paid to creditors because the firm can deduct interest payments in the determination of taxable income, thereby reducing taxes. The amount of the reduction in taxes and the effective cost of debt depend on the tax rate. The higher the tax rate, the lower the effective interest rate on debt. For example, look at the data in Exhibit 6-1. There are two firms, A and B, which have identical earnings before interest and taxes. Firm A has no debt, whereas firm B has $2,000 in outstanding debt and pays an interest rate of 10 percent. The firms' incomes are calculated

Exhibit 6-1. Tax Rates and the Effective Rate on Debt

	0% tax rate		25% tax rate		50% tax rate	
	Firm A	Firm B	Firm A	Firm B	Firm A	Firm B
Earnings before interest and taxes	$1,000	$1,000	$1,000	$1,000	$1,000	$1,000
Interest	0	200	0	200	0	200
Taxable income	$1,000	$ 800	$1,000	$ 800	$1,000	$ 800
Taxes	0	0	250	200	500	400
Net income	$1,000	$ 800	$ 750	$ 600	$ 500	$ 400
Difference[a]	$200		$150		$100	
Effective rate[b]	10%		7.5%		5%	

[a]Net income of firm A − net income of firm B.

[b](Difference in net income)/$2,000 of outstanding debt for firm B.

using three tax rates, 0, 25, and 50 percent, and the resulting values of the net incomes are compared. If no taxes were paid, the only difference between the net incomes of the two firms would be due to the interest expense incurred by firm B of $200. In this case we would say that the effective rate on the debt was equal to the interest rate of 10 percent ($200/$2,000 = 10 percent). If the tax rate is 25 percent, the impact of the debt interest on net income is only $150 due to the tax deductibility of interest. The effective rate on debt is therefore only $150/$2,000 = 7.5 percent. Similarly, at a 50 percent tax rate the effective rate is only $100/$2,000 = 5 percent. The general formula for the effective rate is

$$\text{Effective rate} = \text{interest rate} (1.0 - \text{tax rate}) \qquad (6\text{-}5)$$

where the interest rate used is the average market interest rate on the firm's debt. We therefore use the effective rate as the cost of debt in calculating the average cost of capital.

The Rate on Preferred Stock

Preferred stock is similar to common stock in that it has no maturity. Once issued, it may remain outstanding as long as the firm continues in existence. Cash payments (called **preferred dividends**) to the owners of this security are a fixed amount, for example $5 per share per year, and usually no dividends can be paid to the common stockholders unless the preferred stockholders have been paid. In this respect preferred stock is much like a bond with its fixed interest payments. However, the dividends paid to preferred stockholders are not tax deductible (as of 1976), although there has been some discussion about making them so.

The fixed cash payments to the owner plus the absence of tax deductibility means that we can estimate the rate on preferred stock by simply dividing the preferred dividend per share by the current price per share since the dividend can be considered a level perpetual payment.

$$\text{Preferred rate} = \frac{\text{dividend}}{\text{price}} \qquad (6\text{-}6)$$

For example, in July 1975, Consolidated Edison's preferred stock which pays $6 per share was selling at a price of $60. The rate was therefore $6/$60 = 10 percent.

Sometimes firms have more than one issue of preferred stock outstanding. In this situation the average current rate on all preferred issues can be used as was done for debt issues.

The Rate on Common Stock

The rate on common stock is the hardest rate to assign for any security. We need to estimate the rate of return required by the stockholders of the firm. However, as we discussed in Chapter 5, there are no fixed contractual payments for common stock as there are for other securities issued by the firm. Stockholders have expectations as to what future dividends are, but it's difficult for the financial manager to determine the expected values. Several approaches have been suggested to deal with this problem. We will examine three of them here. A fourth method is discussed in Appendix 6A. As we will see, no method is free of problems, and often more than one is used to provide the financial manager with a reasonable estimate of the rate.

Historical rate of return The first method is to determine the historical rate of return actually earned by the shareholders. Take the most recent five or ten years and calculate the rate of return earned by an investor who purchased stock at the beginning of the study period, held it to the present, and sold it at current prices. This procedure is based on the assumption that investors, on average, earn what they expect to earn. Furthermore, the method requires that (1) there were no significant changes in investor expectations as to the future performance of the firm during the study period, (2) no significant changes in the level of interest rates have occurred, and (3) investor attitudes toward risk haven't changed. Unfortunately, such conditions are very unusual, and this method must be used only with great caution. The historical rate of return often differs considerably, depending on the time period chosen.

As a simple example, suppose that five years ago the price of the firm's stock was $50. Dividends of $5 per share were paid each year, and today the stock is still selling for $50. The average rate of return for an investor who bought the stock for $50 has been $5/$50 = 10 percent per year. Using the historical method, 10 percent would be an estimate of the current required rate of return on the stock.

Estimates of future dividends The second method is for the financial manager to estimate what investors expect the future dividend stream of the firm will be and use the current price of the stock to determine stockholders' expected rate of return. The basic relationship for the price of the firm's stock was provided in Chapter 5. There we said that the price would be equal to the present value of the expected dividends given the risk-adjusted rate (k_s) required by investors. If we know the price and the expected dividends, we can determine the required rate of return from the equation

$$P = \frac{D_1}{1 + k_s} + \frac{D_2}{(1 + k_s)^2} + \frac{D_3}{(1 + k_s)^3} + \cdots + \frac{D_m}{(1 + k_s)^m} \qquad (6\text{-}7)$$

That is, given the current price P and the values for future dividends D_t, we can calculate k_s.

Determining the dividends expected by investors is very difficult in many cases. However, if the firm has maintained some regular pattern of dividend payments in the past, it is not unreasonable for investors to expect this pattern to continue in the future. Suppose, for example, that for the past ten years the firm has paid an average dividend of $5 per share per year with no trend toward higher or lower payments. Under these circumstances, it would be reasonable to assume that investors view the firm as paying a level perpetual dividend of $5 per share and therefore

$$P = \frac{\$5}{k_s}$$

If the current price of the stock is $50,

$$k_s = \frac{\$5}{P}$$

$$= \frac{\$5}{\$50}$$

$$= 10\%$$

A more typical firm would increase dividends over time. We know of a simple model of growing dividends which can be used to estimate k_s, the constant growth model of Chapter 5. In this model dividends are expected to grow at a compound rate of g per year. If D_1 is the dividend expected next year, then

$$P = \frac{D_1}{k_s - g} \tag{6-8}$$

or

$$k_s = \frac{D_1}{P} + g \tag{6-9}$$

To use this model, we must assume that investors expect the dividends of the firm to grow indefinitely at a rate of g. This would be reasonable if the firm had consistent growth in the past and no significant changes appear likely in the future. It may not be easy to estimate what investors expect as next year's dividend and the long-run average growth rate, but it is less difficult to do this than to try to estimate what investors expect in every future year.

As an example, suppose that, historically, dividends have grown at a rate of 6 percent per year and management expects to pay $2 per share next year. Assuming that nothing has changed about the firm that would warrant a change in expectations regarding future growth, those two figures can be used with the current price of the stock to estimate k_s. If the current price is $50, then k_s would be estimated as

$$k_s = \frac{\$2}{\$50} + 0.06$$

$$= 10\%$$

If the actual circumstances of the business do not fit the constant growth model, then the problem of estimating the required rate of return becomes much more difficult because it may be very hard to estimate the future dividends expected by investors. For example, what should be done for firms which are not paying dividends now and haven't paid them for years? Some very rapidly growing new businesses have never paid a dividend. For such firms some other method must be used.

Using debt rates For some firms the above methods don't work. For example, Pan American Airlines had losses in every year from 1968 to 1975. Its shareholders had a negative rate of return from their investment in the firm's shares over this period. No dividends had been paid on the shares since the losses began. Since the price of the stock was greater than zero, investors must have been expecting some positive rate of return in the future. What that figure might be is a guess. The third method, which does apply in such cases, is to look at the highest rate required on the debt issued by the firm and assume that the stockholders would require an appreciably higher rate of return than that. As a rough approximation based on historical patterns, rates of return on common stock run 4 to 6 percentage points higher than the yields on debt. In Pan Am's case that would imply that its shareholders required a rate of 16 to 18 percent, since the more risky of the firm's debt issues were yielding 12 percent in 1975.

In calculating the average cost of capital we multiply the rate for each type of financing by the proportion of that type used by the firm. Now that we know how to determine the rates, we need to specify the proportions [the p's in Eq. (6-4)].

Several alternative ways to specify the proportions are used in practice. These include using the existing proportions on the firm's balance sheet, the proportions of financing planned for the current capital budget, expected future financing proportions, and the current proportions of the market values of the firm's outstanding securities. Each of these may pro-

DETERMINING THE PROPORTIONS

vide a cost of capital suitable for investment decisions in some cases; however, we recommend the use of market value proportions for two reasons.

First, it is difficult to determine the proportions of the types of financing that will be used to provide money for current and future investments before the profitability and amount of investment expenditures are known. Yet the financial manager must estimate the cost of capital before deciding which investments would be in the stockholders' interests. The current market value proportions of the firm's outstanding securities *are* known at the time investment decisions are made; therefore there is no need to forecast the financing methods that will be used.

Second, the best estimates of the rates associated with the various financing sources are those currently required on the firm's existing securities in the market. These rates reflect investors' assessments of the current business and financial risk of the firm and, coupled with investor expectations of future income, determine the current market value of the firm's securities. The cost of capital computed with current market rates and market value proportions is the average rate of return (adjusted for the tax deductibility of debt interest) required by investors in the firm's securities. Given the assumption that the firm's business and financial risk will not be changed, the cost of capital computed with market rates and market value proportions is a valid measure of the minimum rate of return required on new investments for them to be in the stockholder's interests. Indeed, under the assumptions used here, the present value of the expected cash flow from an investment using this cost of capital is a direct estimate of the increase in the market value of the firm's common stock from undertaking the investment. This is not true of other approaches even though they may indicate correctly, under some conditions, which investments should be undertaken.

For example, we calculate the proportions in the following way, using the market values of the securities currently outstanding.

Outstanding securities	Market value	Proportion
Debt	$ 4.0 million	0.40
Preferred stock	1.0 million	0.10
Common stock	5.0 million	0.50
Total	$10.0 million	1.00

CALCULATION OF AN AVERAGE COST OF CAPITAL

Now that we know how to calculate the average cost of capital, let's do it for an actual company.[4]

A simplified set of data based on the financial statements and securities market results for Standard Brands, Inc., are shown in Exhibit 6-2. The

Exhibit 6-2. Financial Data for Standard Brands, Inc.

Outstanding debt, preferred stock, and common stock
as of December 31, 1974 (dollar figures in millions)

	Book value	Market value	Interest rate, %[a]
Bonds (6¾% due 1993)	$ 60	$ 48	8.0
Bonds (7¾% due 2001)	50	42	9.4
Bonds (9½% due 2004)	50	51	9.3
Other debt[b]	156	150	9.2
Total debt	$316	$291	9.2
Preferred stock ($3.50)	$ 20	$ 10	7.0
Common stock	$370	$833	

Common stock data, 1968–1974

	1968	1969	1970	1971	1972	1973	1974	Average growth rate, %
Dividends per share	$ 1.42	$1.50	$1.57	$1.60	$1.66	$1.75	$ 1.87	4.7
Earnings per share	2.44	2.61	2.75	2.91	3.20	3.55	4.05	8.8
Price per share	$45						$60	
Rate of return earned by shareholders, 1968–1974[c]: 8.2%								

[a] Interest rate for bonds is yield to maturity based on prices of $80, $84, and $102 for the three bonds, respectively. Prices as reported in the *Wall Street Journal* January 31, 1975 and February 3, 1975. Interest rate on other debt is the average of the yields to maturity of these three.

[b] Market value estimated based on interest rates reported in firm's annual report. This category consists of six different types of debt, none of which is traded in the securities market.

[c] Rate of return calculated assuming stock purchased at end of 1968 at a price of $45 and held to January 1975, when sold at $60. Dividends assumed received from 1969 through 1974.

---

4. Any operational method of measuring the cost of capital for a firm involves some degree of approximation, and the suggested procedure is no exception. We are ignoring such problems as the impact of taxes on the dividend income and capital gains of stockholders, costs of issuing securities, and the likelihood that new security issues may have to provide higher expected rates of return than the current market rates on existing securities. These are all relevant to investment decisions; however they cannot be incorporated easily and correctly into a single average cost of capital figure. We discuss the implication of these problems for investment decisions in Chap. 9.

consumer products manufactured by this firm have well-known brand names including Planters (nuts, oil), Fleischmann's (margarine, yeast, liquor), Royal (desserts), and Curtiss candies (Baby Ruth, Butterfingers). We are assuming that management wishes to know the average cost of capital which it will use in planning capital expenditures.

As discussed above, the required return on common stock is the most difficult value to estimate. The difficulties arise from trying to determine what shareholders are expecting with regard to the future performance of the firm. Since the firm's earnings and dividends have been growing fairly steadily since 1968 (in fact, dividends per share have risen every year for more than ten years), the constant growth model appears roughly appropriate. However, dividends have not grown as fast as earnings because an increased percentage of earnings has been invested. Suppose we assume that stockholders expect dividends to grow in the future at the same rate they have over the past six years, which is 4.7 percent per year. For 1975 let's assume $2 per share was expected since the firm paid a $0.50 dividend in the last quarter of 1974, which would imply an annual dividend of $2 if the quarterly rate was maintained. Applying Eq. (6-9), given a current stock price of $60,

$$k_s = \frac{D}{P} + g$$

$$= \frac{\$2}{\$60} + 0.047$$

$$= 8\%$$

A value of 8 percent for the shareholders' expected rate of return seems somewhat low, given that the bonds of Standard Brands yield over 9 percent and would be a safer investment.

Suppose that investor expectations as to future dividends for Standard Brands are based on past earnings growth rather than past dividend growth. This would be reasonable if investors expected earnings to continue to grow as they have in the past and expected that, on average, the firm maintains the current proportion of earnings paid out as dividends.

Using the historical earnings growth rate of 8.8 percent as an estimate of future dividend growth, we get

$$k_s = \frac{D}{P} + g$$

$$= \frac{\$2}{\$60} + 0.088$$

$$= 12.1\%$$

Exhibit 6-3. Cost of Capital Calculation for Standard Brands, Inc.

	Amount[a]	Proportion[b]	Rate, %	Prop. × Rate
Debt	$ 291	0.26	4.8[c]	1.25
Preferred stock	10	0.01	7.0	0.07
Common stock	833	0.73	12	8.76
Total	$1,134	1.00		10.08%

Average cost of capital $k_a = 10.08\%$

[a]These amounts are market values from Exhibit 6-2.

[b]Proportion is market value of financing type divided by total market value.

[c]Interest rate on debt is adjusted for tax rate of 48%. 9.2% (1−0.48) = 4.8%.

A value of approximately 12 percent for k_s appears more reasonable when compared with the 9 percent rate on bonds, and we will use 12 percent as our estimate of the required return on equity.

It should be apparent that estimating a required return on equity is not a cookbook procedure. The best one can hope for is to be able to devise a reasonably good approximation to the "real" value that cannot be directly observed.

Given the corporate income tax rate of 48 percent, we have all the information needed to calculate the average cost of capital for Standard Brands. The calculations are shown in Exhibit 6-3 and result in an estimated cost of capital of 10 percent (10.08 percent rounded off). This rate would be appropriate to evaluate investment opportunities available at the beginning of 1975.

SUMMARY

The average cost of capital for a firm is commonly used to evaluate investment projects. It is the minimum acceptable rate of return on new investments from the viewpoint of investors in the firm's securities. This cost of capital is suitable for investments with the same risks as past investments made by the firm, provided that the firm's financing policies do not change from what they have been in the past.

In order to assign a value to the average cost of capital, we must estimate the rates of return required by investors in the firm's securities (including all borrowings) and average those rates according to the market values of the various securities currently outstanding. The rates are determined as follows:

1. The debt rate is the average market interest rate on the firm's debt issues adjusted for the tax deductibility of interest. For bonds the yield to maturity is ordinarily used as the market rate.
2. The rate on preferred stock is the promised dividend payment on the preferred stock divided by the price of the stock.
3. The equity rate is the most difficult rate to estimate. The average historical rate of return earned by stockholders is sometimes used as an estimate of what stockholders currently require. If the firm seems to provide a constant growth in dividends, then the constant growth model may be appropriate. In this case, the equity rate is estimated as $k_s = D/P + g$, the expected dividend divided by the current price of the stock plus the expected growth rate of dividends. Another method is to base the estimated equity rate on the current interest rate of the firm's debt plus a premium for the added risk of the stock.

QUESTIONS

1. Why is the cost of capital the minimum acceptable rate of return on an investment?
2. Under what conditions is the firm's average cost of capital a valid criterion for new investment opportunities?
3. Why is it difficult to determine the rate of return required by investors in the firm's common stock?
4. Which method of calculating the rate on common stock would be most appropriate for the following firms:
   a) A profitable firm that has never paid a dividend but has had steady growth in earnings.
   b) An electric utility that has paid a dividend every year since 1895.
   c) A firm that had grown very rapidly until two years ago, when overcapacity problems in the industry produced severe price cutting in the firm's major product line. At the same time management decided to invest heavily in facilities to manufacture a new product. So far the manufacturing process has not worked properly. The firm lost $50 million last year, and the price of its common stock has dropped 80 percent in the past two years.
5. Is the cost of debt to the firm the debtholder's required rate of return? Why or why not?
6. If the firm has several different types of long-term debt outstanding, does it make any difference in principle if an average debt rate is calculated for use in computing the average cost of capital rather than treating each debt type separately with its own proportion and rate in

the cost of capital formula? Does it make any difference in practice?

7. Would you expect all the firms in a given industry to have approximately the same cost of capital? Why or why not?

8. Do you think that the cost of capital for a firm is fairly constant over time? Explain. What are the implications of your answer for business use of the cost of capital?

9. "Retained earnings should not be considered as 'costing' the firm anything. Therefore the average cost of capital should reflect only the use of common stock financing." Evaluate this argument.

10. How could one find an average cost of capital for a proprietorship or partnership. Can you think of any ways to do this? What problems are present for these firms that are not true of corporations?

PROJECT

Choose a business firm and estimate its average cost of capital as of some particular date. The following guides may be helpful in this project.

1. A large company will be easier to obtain data for than a small company; however, large companies are often more complicated to analyze.

2. Choose a date immediately following an available annual report for the company. The annual report will serve as a very important source of data on the firm's financial affairs.

3. Appendix A provides additional sources of data.

4. Avoid firms with bonds or preferred stock that are convertible into common stock. Convertible securities are difficult to analyze.

5. Many firms use large amounts of short-term debt, have long-term debt with interest rates that are tied to short-term interest rates, or have debt denominated in foreign currencies. Treat these items as was done for "other debt" in the Standard Brands example in the chapter.

6. Read the footnotes to the financial statements in the annual report. Leases are a form of debt. Their estimated value will be found in the footnotes.

PROBLEMS

1. The Ashland Mfg. Co. has the following bond issues outstanding:

	Senior bonds	Subordinated bonds
Market value	$16 million	$15 million
Maturity value	$20 million	$15 million
Yield to maturity	8%	9%
Coupon rate	7%	9%

a) What is the before-tax interest cost to the firm of each of the two types of debt issues?

b) What is the average rate on the bonds? [Ans.: 8.49 percent]

c) Assuming a 48 percent tax rate, what is the effective rate on the bonds? [Ans.: 4.41 percent]

2. Calculate the required rate of return (k) for common stock under the following situations:

a) Firm A has paid a $2 dividend for the past fifteen years and investors expect it to continue to do so in the future. Fifteen years ago firm A's stock sold at $20 a share, and the *Wall Street Journal* lists its current price at $20. [Ans.: 10 percent]

b) Firm B's dividends per share have grown at a constant rate of 5 percent a year. Investors expect a dividend of $1.50 next year. The current price of a share of the firm's stock is $20. [Ans.: 12.5 percent]

3. Calculate the rates to be used in an average cost of capital calculation for the following securities. Assume that they are issued by different firms and that the corporate income tax rate is 40 percent.

a) A seven-year (original maturity) note with a coupon interest rate of 7 percent paying $1,000 per note at maturity. The note matures in five years and has a current market price of $90 per $100 maturity value.

b) A bond issue is scheduled to mature in twenty years, bearing a coupon rate of 12 percent; however, the firm's management has announced plans to pay off the bonds one year from now after paying the interest due for the year. The bondholders would receive the maturity value at that time. The current price for the bonds as reported in the newspaper is $103.70.

c) A preferred stock pays $6.50 dividends per $100 par value. The current market price is $80.

d) The historical average rate of return earned by owners of the firm's common stock has been about 14 percent per year until very recently. The dividends of the firm have grown at an average rate of 10 percent per year over the same period. A major investment advisory service has issued a report that is somewhat critical of the firm's management and forecasts dividends and earnings to grow no faster than the overall growth rate in the general economy. The price of the firm's stock reacted sharply to the report, dropping from $60 per share to $30 per share. The long-run economic growth rate for the United States economy is generally thought to be 6 percent per year. The stock's dividends for next year are expected to be $2.40 per share.

4. Calculate the proportions to be used in calculating an average cost of capital for each of the following sets of data on different firms.

a)

Balance sheet data		Market value
Bonds	$10 million maturity value	$ 9.5 million
Preferred stock	$ 1 million par value	$ 1.0 million
Common stock	$ 8 million book value	$10.5 million

Bond price = $95 per $100 maturity value
Preferred stock price = $100 per $100 par value
Common stock price = $10.50 per share
(There are 1 million shares of common stock outstanding.)

b) There are two types of securities outstanding for the firm—bonds with a maturity value of $4 million and 200,000 shares of common stock. The current market price for the bonds is $127 per $100 maturity value, and the price of the stock is $25 per share.

c)

Balance sheet data	
Bonds (7% due 1992)	$10 million
Common stock (100,000 shares at $10 par value)	$ 1 million
Surplus	2.5 million
Retained earnings	6.0 million
Total Equity	$ 9.5 million

Market price for bonds = $90.00
Market price for stock = $160.00

d)

Balance sheet data	
Long-term debt	$5 million
Preferred stock ($100 par)	$1 million
Book value of common stock	$6 million

Other data	
Common stock	1.5 million shares outstanding; current price = $20 per share
Preferred stock	Current price = $80 per $100 par.
Long-term debt	These securities are not traded and no market prices are available. However, the debt is recently issued, and the interest rates being paid by the firm are approximately equal to current market rates.

5. The Kooky Cookie Company has had its problems in the past, but management currently expects the firm to be able to maintain a fairly steady growth rate of 8 percent per year in earnings and dividends. Kooky's common stock had been selling at a rather depressed price of $15 per share until the annual stockholders meeting, where management outlined its future investment and operating plans. The current price is now $25 per share. The $2.00 per share dividend that had been paid each year since 1969 is not expected to change next year, even though earnings will be higher because of the need to finance a complete modernization of the firm's bakery. Moreover in future years dividends will be increased as earnings rise. The annual meeting was rather lively as several major stockholders were very concerned about the company's prior performance. One stockholder noted that her 1967 investment in the company had provided a rate of return (given the price of $15 per share obtaining prior to the meeting) of only 4.25 percent. This, she caustically remarked, was much less than she would have earned in United States government bonds purchased at the same time. Further, she noted that she would have been better off being a bondholder of the company than a stockholder. The company's bonds are currently yielding 8 percent. What is your best estimate of the required rate of return on Kooky's common stock? (Note: There is no single exact answer to this problem.)

6. Sam and Fred are partners in Cozy Pines Resorts. The business presently consists of lakeshore property that has not been developed in any way. The partners have been offered $400,000 cash for the property which they believe is a fair price. However, the two partners are considering establishing a fishing-oriented resort which would require investment of $200,000 to build cabins, develop water supplies, provide sewage disposal, etc. They can borrow the money at an interest rate of 9 percent. The partners themselves feel that, given alternative investment opportunities available to them in the financial markets, they must expect to earn at least 14 percent before taxes on their investment in order for the venture to be worthwhile.

   a) What would be the amount of Sam's and Fred's investment in the venture assuming that they would be borrowing $200,000 to develop the property? [Ans.: $400,000]

   b) What is the minimum acceptable cash flow expected from the resort in order to provide the partners with an expected rate of return of 14 percent? (Ignore debt repayment and assume cash flows are level perpetuities.)

   c) What is the minimum acceptable rate of return on the venture given your answer to b. [Ans.: 12.3 percent]

   d) Calculate an average cost of capital and compare it to your answer for c.

7. The management of Glendale Dairies, Inc., is considering expanding their business early in 1980 to meet the demands of a growing popula-

tion in Glendale's market area. In order to evaluate the various alternative expansion plans, management wishes to estimate Glendale's current cost of capital. Various financial data for the firm are given below.

Balance sheet (000s)
(December 31, 1977)

Current assets	$1,000	Current liabilities	$ 500
Plant and equipment	4,000	Bonds ($100 par value)	2,000
Total assets	$5,000	Preferred stock	
		($100 par value)	1,000
		Common stock	
		(200,000 shares)	500
		Retained earnings	1,000
		Total liabilities	
		and equity	$5,000

Income statement (000s) (January 1, 1977– December 31, 1977)		Historical data—common stock		
		Earnings per share	Dividends per share	Avg. price per share
Sales	$6,000			
Cost of goods sold	4,300	1977 $1.50	$0.90	$14.00
Gross profit	$1,700	1976 1.52	0.90	13.75
Operating expenses	920	1975 1.35	0.75	15.00
Interest	80	1974 1.22	0.70	12.00
Taxable income	$ 700	1973 1.25	0.70	12.50
Taxes (50%)	350	1972 1.15	0.65	11.00
Net income	$ 350	1971 1.05	0.62	11.00
Preferred dividends	50	1970 0.96	0.58	10.00
Earnings to common	$ 300	1969 0.94	0.56	9.00
Dividends to common	$ 180			

Market data (January 15, 1978)

	Bonds	Preferred stock	Common stock
Price	$67	$55.50	$14.70
Yield[a]	8.5%	9.0%	6.1%

[a] Yield for bonds is "yield to maturity"; for preferred and common stocks, yield is dividend divided by price.

The firm's tax rate is 50 percent. Estimate Glendale's average cost of capital.

using the SML to estimate the rate on common stock[5]

If we can estimate the risk of the firm's stock and if we can specify the risk-return relationship in the securities market, we can calculate the rate of return required by investors in the stock. The model of the security market line (SML) explained in Appendix 5B provides both a precise definition of risk and a precise relationship between risk and return in the market. In this appendix we show how the SML can be used to estimate the rate of return on common stock. Standard Brands, Inc., stock will be used as an example for comparison with the solution in the chapter. The SML specifies the following relationship between a stock's rate of return (k_s) and its risk (Beta_s).

$$k_s = k_r + (k_m - k_r)\text{Beta}_s \tag{6-10}$$

Recall that k_r here is the riskless rate of interest and k_m is the expected rate of return on the portfolio of all securities in the market. Clearly, if we can estimate k_r, k_m, and Beta_s, we can calculate k_s.

ESTIMATING THE RISKLESS RATE

The riskless rate of interest is the easiest of the three basic values to estimate, but there are some problems. We normally identify the debt issues of the United States government as being free of risk, and certainly we expect the government to pay its obligations when they are due. However, there are many different United States government securities and their interest rates differ. (See the *Wall Street Journal* for a listing of United States government securities and their rates.) Which one should we use? The major differences in rates are due to differences in maturity. Generally, but not always, the interest rates on short-term securities (Treasury bills) are lower than the interest rates on long-term securities (notes and bonds). These differences can be large. On January 27, 1976, the *Wall Street Journal* reported yields on twenty-five-year bonds of slightly over 8 percent and yields on 30-day bills of 4.5 percent. Although there is some disagreement on this question, we suggest using long-term bond rates. Our purpose for estimating the rate of return on stock is to provide a standard for investments whose returns will generally stretch out many years into the future. We are, therefore, attempting to estimate a long-run cost of capital for the firm. Long-term bond rates reflect expectations of average future short-term interest rates and in that sense appear more

5. The reader is assumed to be familiar with Appendix 5B.

suitable than the short-term rates, which tend to vary considerably over time. In January 1975, which is the time setting of the Standard Brands example, short-term interest rates were about 5.6 percent and long-term bond rates were 7.8 percent. We will use the long-term bond rate of 7.8 percent as our estimate of k_r.

Developing estimates of the average rate of return on all securities in the market (k_m) is almost as difficult as estimating the rate of return on a particular security. After all, we cannot directly compute this number from observable data; we must infer it in some fashion. We note that either direct estimates of k_m or the difference between k_m and the riskless rate k_r will be sufficient. A possible procedure for estimating k_m directly is to use historical average rates of return on a large sample of securities, such as stocks and bonds listed on the New York Exchange. This procedure suffers from the same problems as using historical rates of return to estimate the rate for a single stock discussed on page 189. The problems of estimating either k_m or the difference ($k_m - k_r$) are substantial and involve both theoretical and statistical issues that are beyond the scope of this text. However, several studies using historical data suggest that the difference is typically about 5 percentage points.[6] We therefore suggest using this figure as a standard value in the estimating procedure. In January 1975, the riskless bond rate was about 7.8 percent; so k_m is estimated to be 12.8 percent at the time of the Standard Brands example.

ESTIMATING THE AVERAGE MARKET RATE

As indicated in Appendix 5B, Beta can be estimated using the historical relationship between the rate of return on the stock and the rate of return on the market. The procedure was illustrated there. One might well ask why using historical estimates of Beta shouldn't suffer from the same problems as using historical rates of return. The answer is that indeed similar problems are present; however, they are generally thought to be less serious when applied to estimates of Beta. First, there is theoretical work which indicates that the historical average rate of return can vary significantly from the "true" rate, yet an estimate of Beta made from past rates of return may be reasonably close to the "true" Beta.[7] Second, sev-

ESTIMATING BETA

6. "The Long Term Case for Stocks," *Fortune,* 90 (December 1974), pp. 97, 100. For a theoretical discussion and empirical evaluation of Beta, see M. C. Jensen, "Risk, the Pricing of Capital Assets, and the Evaluation of Investment Portfolios," *Journal of Business,* 42 (April 1969), pp. 167–247.

7. Jensen, op. cit.

eral empirical tests indicate that historical Betas tend to be more stable than average rates of return.[8] These results lend support to the use of historical Betas as estimates of the "true" Beta. For large firms whose risk has not changed significantly, historical values for Beta provide reasonable estimates.

We do not need to estimate Beta ourselves in order to estimate the rate on common stock for most large firms. Brokerage firms such as Merrill, Lynch, Pierce, Fenner, and Smith, Inc. and investment advisory services such as *Value Line Investment Survey* report Betas for many companies. Standard Brands' Beta has been estimated to be 0.80, and we will use this value in our calculation:[9]

$$\text{Estimated } k_s = k_r + (k_m - k_r)\text{Beta}_s$$

$$= 7.8\% + 5\% \ (0.8)$$

$$= 11.8\%$$

Thus we obtain an estimate of k_s for Standard Brands that is close to our earlier estimate of 12.1 percent even though that estimate was obtained by a very different method.

8. I. Friend and M. Blume, "Measurement of Portfolio Performance under Uncertainty," *American Economic Review*, 60 (September 1970), pp. 561–575.

9. *Value Line Investment Survey* (Dec. 12, 1975), p. 1501.

fundamentals of capital budgeting

Each year during the 1975 to 1985 decade, United States industry, as a whole, plans to spend $200 billion to $250 billion on new assets—plants, machines, tools, pollution control equipment, and transportation facilities, among other things. Unlike current assets, which are discussed in Chapter 14, these assets, called **capital assets,** are used by the company in the physical process of producing goods and services and are ordinarily used for a number of years. Because the dollar amounts involved are so large, businesses carefully plan and evaluate expenditures for capital assets. The plan for expenditures is called a **capital budget.** The process of determining both how much to spend on capital assets and which assets to acquire is called **capital budgeting.**

This chapter presents the basic concepts of capital budgeting. The budgeting procedure is first examined and then the techniques used to evaluate specific proposals are described. Several important issues, including inflation and capital rationing, are also discussed. The chapter ends with a look at the attitudes of business toward the various capital budgeting techniques.

THE CAPITAL BUDGETING PROCESS

Most firms prepare at least a short-run budget which indicates planned capital outlays for the current and immediately forthcoming periods. Many firms also prepare intermediate and long-term capital budgets which project capital requirements for three to five, and sometimes even ten, years into the future. Capital budgets are based on sales forecasts and on the anticipated plant and equipment needed to meet those expected sales.

The budgeting process begins when the firm's planning committee, often with the help of the company economist and sales department, estimates the future sales of the firm. This information is transmitted to the production department, which then provides an estimate of the plant and equipment requirements necessary to meet the anticipated production levels (which are based upon projected sales). This estimate may include various alternative methods of achieving planned output. These methods would then have to be compared and evaluated. The ultimate decision regarding capital expenditures is made by analyzing information from the production department in light of the anticipated cost of obtaining funds to undertake the investments (cost of capital).

In many cases, the centralized decision-making process just described is modified for small dollar-value capital expenditures. For example, division managers may be permitted to spend up to some given amount, say $50,000, for capital replacements and other outlays in a given year. All capital expenditures above that amount would require approval by central management.

Economic conditions are constantly changing, and as a consequence, even the best projections of future operations usually require revision over time. Capital budgeting is no exception. Investment plans are continually reformulated as new information regarding demand for the firm's products, changes in technology, and costs of production become available. Intermediate and long-term capital budgets are then revised accordingly. The new information not only provides a clue as to the appropriate level of future capital outlays, but also reflects upon past investment decisions. The wisdom or error of previous decisions is revealed by the success or failure of particular projects. Evaluation of current information on the progress and profitability of the firm's past investments is useful in several respects. It pinpoints sectors of the firm's activities that may warrant further financial commitments; or, on the other hand, it may call for retreat if a particular project becomes permanently unprofitable. The outcome of an investment also reflects upon the performance of those members of management associated with the project. Finally, past errors and successes may provide clues regarding the weaknesses and strengths of the capital budgeting process itself.

The remainder of this chapter examines alternative procedures for evaluating investment opportunities. These techniques relate to the capital budget in two ways. First, they set forth profitability criteria which investments must satisfy in order to be accepted. The criteria are used by firms to estimate the amount of funds that they can invest profitably. These estimated amounts are incorporated into the firm's intermediate or long-term capital budget. Since these figures are only predictions of future capital outlays, they will usually have to be revised as the actual investment date approaches. At this stage the second role of capital budgeting analysis comes into play. When the time arrives to determine the exact amount to invest and where, capital budgeting techniques such as present value and internal rate of return are used. As is explained next, the analysis of an investment first requires an estimation of its cash flows.

CASH FLOW FROM AN INVESTMENT Under each method of analysis described in this chapter, it is necessary to consider the costs and benefits of each investment opportunity. These methods for evaluating projects are based on the **cash flow** that results from each project. As we will see, a project should be undertaken only if its cash flow fulfills certain criteria.

What is cash flow, and why is cash flow the proper measure of a project's **Computing** costs and benefits? Cash flow is money paid or received by the firm as a **Cash Flow** result of undertaking the project. We can express cash flow for any period in terms of the relevant costs and benefits associated with an asset (or "project") for that period:

Net cash flow from the project = cash inflows − cash outflows

$$= \text{project revenues}$$

$$- \text{ expenses other than depreciation}$$

$$- \text{ capital expenditures}$$

$$- \text{ income taxes} \qquad (7\text{-}1)$$

where

Income taxes = tax rate × (project revenues

$$- \text{ project expenses other than depreciation}$$

$$- \text{ depreciation}) \qquad (7\text{-}1a)$$

The term in parentheses in Eq. (7-1a) is the computed taxable income from the project. Project revenues in Eq. (7-1) includes all inflows of cash to the firm due to acquisition of the asset, such as additional sales revenues or cash from eventually selling the asset (salvage value). Expenses other than depreciation include costs for labor, materials, and other outlays required by the use of the asset but do *not* include interest on firm debt.[1]

Depreciation affects the cash flow of Eq. (7-1) only through its impact on income taxes. Depreciation in Eq. (7-1) is not a cash expense (does not involve any expenditure of cash); it is simply a way to spread the cost of an asset (a capital expenditure) over the asset's life. From a cash flow standpoint, the capital expenditure is recorded as a cash outflow *when the*

---

1. Cash revenues and expenses are usually not equal to taxable revenues and tax-deductible expenses. However, in most cases the differences can be safely ignored, as is done here. Also, capital expenditures in Eq. (7-1) include investments in current assets, such as inventory, that are required by the project. This topic is discussed in detail in Chap. 14. The fundamental principle that is applicable here is that all cash flow effects must be taken into account.

asset is acquired and not over its useful life. This will be illustrated below in an example.

It is very important to note that taxes are computed as though the project were financed entirely with equity funds. Interest on debt is not included as an expense in determining taxable income. In other words, in computing aftertax cash flow, we are ignoring the method of financing the investment. Financing method is reflected in the cost of capital which takes account of the benefit derived from the tax deductibility of interest (see Chapter 6). As we will see later in the chapter, this cost of capital is used in evaluating the cash flow.

A method for determining the cash flow from an investment is to compare the firm's cash flow with and without that investment. The difference between the two is the additional cash flow due to the investment. To illustrate this method, assume that an investment costs $1,200, has a life of ten years, has an expected salvage value at the end of the ten years of $200, and is depreciated on a straight-line basis at $100 per year [($1,200 − $200)/10 years]. The corporate tax rate is 50 percent. At the time the asset is acquired, the net cash flow is simply the capital expenditure, which is an outlay (a negative cash flow) of $1,200. The computation shown in Exhibit 7-1 shows that the net cash flow for years 1 to 9 is $175. The net cash flow for year 10 is the $175 from using the asset during year 10 (computed as shown in Exhibit 7-1) *plus* the salvage value of $200 which is received for selling the asset at the end of year 10; this adds up to a year 10 net cash flow of $375 ($175 + $200). The asset cash flows are shown in Exhibit 7-2.

The approach for determining and analyzing the cash flow from an investment can be summarized in the following three steps:

1. Determine the change in the firm's cash flow from acquiring the new asset. This can be done by using the Exhibit 7-1 method of comparing the firm's cash flow with and without the asset. *All* changes in cash flow due to the investment must be taken into account, including any salvage value cash proceeds when the asset is sold.
2. Put the results of the step 1 computation in tabular form, showing the timing and amount of the cash flow (for example, as shown by Exhibit 7-2).
3. Analyze the cash flow using net present value or internal rate of return (these methods are described below) to determine whether the investment should be made.

It may still seem unclear as to why cash flow is the proper measure of the costs and benefits of a proposed investment. The answer is that cash flow represents the true inflow and outflow of purchasing power for the firm. When an asset is purchased, such purchasing power is sacrificed;

Exhibit 7-1. Determining the Annual Cash Flow on an Investment

	Firm's cash flow without the investment (1)		Firm's cash flow with the investment (2)		Added cash flow due to the investment (col. 2 − col. 1) (3)	
Annual revenues (R)		$2,000		$2,400		$400
Annual expenses other than depreciation (E)		1,500		1,650		150
Taxes:						
Revenues less expenses ($R − E$)	$500		$750		$250	
Less depreciation	200		300		100	
Taxable income (TI)	$300		$450		$150	
Tax (50% of TI)		150		225		75
Net cash flow ($R − E −$ tax)		$ 350		$ 525		$175

Assumptions:		Summary of above results:	
Life of asset	10 years	Revenues from the asset	$400
Price of asset	$1,200	Less:	
Tax rate	50%	Expenses other than depreciation	$150
		Taxes	75
Salvage value at			225
end of year 10	$200	Annual aftertax cash flow	$175

Exhibit 7-2. Net Cash Flow from the New Asset

Time	Net cash flow
Time 0 (when asset acquired)	−$1,200
Each year for year 1 to 9	$175
Year 10	$375

when a net cash flow is earned on the asset in later periods, purchasing power is received. The future cash flow from an asset is the money generated by the asset which is available for payment to the firm's stockholders and bondholders as dividends and interest to finance further investment. It is the stream of purchasing power provided by the asset and is therefore the measure of that asset's productivity.

Cash Flow and Uncertainty

Generally, future cash flows are uncertain, and only estimates of these flows are available for evaluating an investment proposal. The estimate that is often used is **expected cash flow,** which will be discussed in Chapter 8. In the present chapter, we assume that all investments have the same level of risk. Further, we assume that a numerical estimate can be made of the cash flow in each future year from any investment. The cash flow estimate is an "educated guess" based upon available information. It is ordinarily somewhere between the highest and lowest possible figures that can be expected, in other words, a middle estimate. In Chapter 8 we will be more precise. Since in this chapter all investments are assumed to be of identical risk, all will be evaluated using the same cost of capital, k. Rate k can be viewed as the minimum acceptable rate of return on the investment. In the examples of this chapter, k will be 10 percent.

EVALUATION TECHNIQUES

After the cash flows have been estimated, they must be evaluated to determine whether the investment should be undertaken. Several techniques are available to evaluate investment proposals. The chief ones are:

1. Present value
2. Internal rate of return (or simply rate of return)
3. Payback period
4. Accounting rate of return

A fifth approach which uses a profitability index will be discussed in the section on capital rationing.

Present Value

The time-value-of-money concept discussed in Chapter 4 can be used to evaluate the cash flows from an investment. The **present value** of a cash flow is what it is worth in today's dollars. Present value incorporates the time-value principle by **discounting** future dollars (computing their present value) using the appropriate discount rate (interest rate). In investment analysis, this discount rate is the cost of capital.

The present value rule states that an investment should be adopted only if the present value of the cash flow it generates in the future exceeds its cost, that is, if it has a positive **net present value (NPV).** The net present value of an asset equals

$$\text{NPV} = \begin{array}{c} \text{present value of} \\ \text{future cash flows} \end{array} - \text{initial cost} \tag{7-2}$$

$$= \frac{\text{CF}_1}{1 + k} + \frac{\text{CF}_2}{(1 + k)^2} + \cdots + \frac{\text{CF}_n}{(1 + k)^n} - I$$

$$= \text{CF}_1 \, (P/F, \, k, \, 1) + \text{CF}_2 \, (P/F, \, k, \, 2)$$

$$+ \cdots + \text{CF}_n \, (P/F, \, k, \, n) - I$$

where CF_1 is cash flow in period 1
CF_2 is cash flow in period 2, etc.
I is initial outlay or cost
k is cost of capital

The $(P/F, \, k, \, 1)$, $(P/F, \, k, \, 2)$, etc., terms are the present value factors discussed in Chapter 4.

If the future cash flow is a level annuity of CF per period for n periods (all cash flows are equal), then Eq. (7-2) becomes

$$\text{NPV (annuity)} = \frac{\text{CF}}{1 + k} + \frac{\text{CF}}{(1 + k)^2} + \cdots + \frac{\text{CF}}{(1 + k)^n} - I$$

$$= \text{CF} \, (P/A, \, k, \, n) - I \tag{7-3}$$

NPV is the net benefit that accrues to the firm from adopting the investment. A positive NPV means that the project yields a rate of return exceeding the cost of capital k. In this case, NPV is the total value in current dollars of the extraordinary return (the return above the cost of capital) earned by the investment. If a project's NPV $= 0$, it is just earning the cost of capital and is therefore just barely, or marginally, acceptable. If NPV is negative, less than the cost of capital is earned by the project; i.e., the project is not even earning the required rate of return, and it should therefore be rejected.

In Appendix 7A, it is shown that the net present value of an investment is equal to the benefit of the investment to shareholders and that therefore net present value is a valid guide to project selection.

The accept-reject decision Sometimes an investment decision involves the acceptance or rejection of a given opportunity and not the comparison of several alternatives. The present value method specifies that such an investment should be adopted if its NPV is greater than zero; if NPV = 0, it is a matter of indifference whether the project is accepted; and if NPV is less than zero, the project should be rejected.[2]

To illustrate the present value method, assume that a restaurant can buy a new sign which will increase net cash flow by attracting additional customers. The choice is either to buy the particular sign or to obtain no new sign at all. The sign costs $3,500, will last five years, and will increase

Cash flows from sign	
Initial outlay (*I*)	$3,500
Increase in annual cash flow for next 5 years	$1,000

net cash flow by an estimated $1,000 in each of the next five years. Using Eq. (7-3) and assuming a cost of capital k of 10 percent, the NPV equals

$$NPV = \frac{\$1,000}{1 + 0.10} + \frac{\$1,000}{(1 + 0.10)^2} + \cdots + \frac{\$1,000}{(1 + 0.10)^5} - \$3,500$$

$$= \$1,000 \ (P/A, \ 10\%, \ 5) - \$3,500$$

$$= \$1,000 \ (3.791) - \$3,500$$

$$= \$3,791 - \$3,500 = \$291$$

Since the NPV of $291 is positive, the sign should be purchased. The $3,791 is the value in today's dollars (the present value) of the future benefits from the asset, and the $3,500 is the cost in today's dollars; the difference is the net gain, $291.

Choices between alternatives Many, perhaps most, investment decisions involve a choice from among several mutually exclusive alternatives rather than the simple accept-reject decision of a single alternative. Two alternatives are mutually exclusive if adopting one means that the other will not be adopted (for example, to buy machine A or machine B or neither, but not both). The present value rule dictates that the alternative having the highest NPV is best and it is accepted if, and only if, its NPV is positive (indifferent if NPV = 0).

As an example, assume that a manufacturer is comparing two machines for its production line: the deluxe model which costs $3,000 and

2. As is explained later in this section, we are assuming that the firm can obtain additional funds for investment at the cost of capital. At the end of the chapter, capital rationing (limited funds available) is considered in detail.

will raise net estimated cash flow by $900 per year for the next five years, and the economy model, with a smaller capacity, which costs $2,000 and will raise net estimated cash flow by $610 per year for the next five years.

Cash flows of machine alternatives

	Deluxe machine	Economy machine
Initial outlay (I)	$3,000	$2,000
Increase in annual cash flow for next 5 years (CF)	$ 900	$ 610

Using Eq. (7-3), we can compute the NPV of each, assuming a cost of capital of 10 percent:

$$\text{NPV (deluxe model)} = \$900 \ (P/A, \ 10\%, \ 5) - \$3,000$$
$$= \$900 \ (3.791) - \$3,000$$
$$= \$412$$
$$\text{NPV (economy model)} = \$610 \ (P/A, \ 10\%, \ 5) - \$2,000$$
$$= \$610 \ (3.791) - \$2,000$$
$$= \$313$$

The deluxe model is superior, since its NPV of $412 exceeds the economy model's NPV of $313. Further, since the deluxe model has an NPV exceeding zero, it should be purchased.

The net present value method summarized   The net present value rule can be summarized as follows:

1. In an accept-reject decision, the investment is adopted if its NPV is positive. We are indifferent if its NPV = 0, and the investment is rejected if its NPV is negative.
2. In comparing mutually exclusive investment alternatives (at most, one alternative is to be accepted), we first determine which alternative has the highest NPV and reject all the other alternatives. We then accept the alternative with the highest NPV if its NPV exceeds zero. We are indifferent if its NPV = 0 and reject the alternative if its NPV is negative.

The above rules assume that the firm can obtain funds at the cost of capital (through borrowing, selling shares, etc.) as long as those funds can be profitably employed. Indeed, if this were not so, then "cost of capital" would have little meaning since "cost" means the price that must be paid to obtain something, in this case, capital or funds to finance investment. Later in this chapter, we will examine the case in which capital is limited or "rationed."

The Internal Rate of Return

We can look at the above capital budgeting problems in a somewhat different way. Instead of discounting the cash flows at the cost of capital to determine net present value, we can ask the following question: What rate of return does the project earn? If the rate of return exceeds the cost of capital k, it is a profitable project since the cost of capital is the minimum required rate of return. If the project's rate of return just equals k, it is only marginal (we are indifferent as to whether it is accepted). If the project's rate of return is less than the cost of capital, it should be rejected.

The rate of return concept   A project's rate of return is often referred to as its **internal rate of return** or IRR. Let's examine more closely what we mean by an investment's IRR. Assume a project requiring an initial outlay I and producing a stream of future net cash flows CF_1, CF_2, . . . , CF_n, over the coming n periods. When we say that the project's IRR is some amount r, we mean that if at time 0 (now) we were to put amount I into a fund actually earning rate of return r each period, we could withdraw from the fund amount CF_1 one period from now, amount CF_2 two periods from now, and so on including CF_n n periods from now and exactly exhaust the fund at the end of the n periods. It is similar to the idea developed in Chapter 4 of purchasing an annuity currently which pays a future income and provides a rate of return equal to the interest rate. Here, for an investment project, the price of the annuity is I, the income it provides is the CF_1, CF_2, . . . , CF_n stream, and the rate of return is r. To illustrate this concept, assume that project H costs $3,000 and generates cash flows of $2,400 in the first year and $1,440 in the second year. The cash flows are stated below.

Cash flows
of project H

$I = \$3,000$
$CF_1 = \$2,400$
$CF_2 = \$1,440$

The rate of return on the investment is 20 percent. As illustrated in Figure 7-1, if we deposit $3,000 at time 0 in a fund, we will have $3,600 in the fund at time 1 assuming a 20 percent rate of return earned during the first

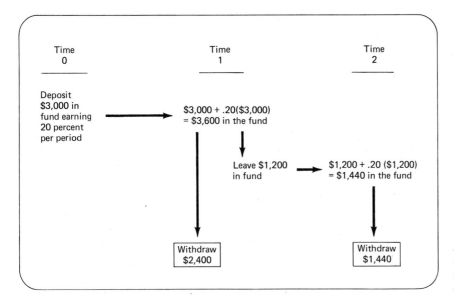

Figure 7-1. Internal rate of return is equivalent to interest earned on a deposit in a fund.

period. Since we want to produce a cash flow $CF_1 = \$2,400$, we withdraw $2,400 from the fund at time 1 and leave $1,200 in the fund. One period later, at time 2, the $1,200 has earned 20 percent and has therefore grown to $1,440 ($1,200 + 0.20 × $1,200), which we can now withdraw to produce our time 2 cash flow of $1,440.

A project with the cash flows $I = \$3,000$, $CF_1 = \$2,400$, and $CF_2 = \$1,440$ therefore implies that 20 percent per period is being earned on the $3,000 investment.

Determining the IRR In the above example we showed that the per period rate of return, or IRR, on project H is 20 percent. But, if we are given numerical figures for I and CF, how do we compute the IRR when it is unknown? *The IRR is that rate which discounts the project's cash flow to an NPV of zero.* Letting r signify the IRR, an investment's IRR is that rate r which satisfies the following relationship:

$$0 = \frac{CF_1}{1 + r} + \frac{CF_2}{(1 + r)^2} + \cdots + \frac{CF_n}{(1 + r)^n} - I$$

$$= CF_1 \, (P/F, \, r, \, 1) + CF_2 \, (P/F, \, r, \, 2) + \cdots$$

$$+ CF_n \, (P/F, \, r, \, n) - I \tag{7-4}$$

If the cash flow returns are a level annuity, that is, if $CF_1 = CF_2 = \cdots = CF_n = CF$, then Eq. (7-4) becomes

$$0 = \frac{CF}{1 + r} + \frac{CF}{(1 + r)^2} + \cdots + \frac{CF}{(1 + r)^n} - I$$

$$= CF \, (P/A, \, r, \, n) - I \tag{7-5}$$

The general procedure for computing an unknown rate that was described in Chapter 4 (page 100) is fully applicable here. The reader is encouraged to review that material.

We can see that $r = 20$ percent for project H discussed above since Eq. (7-4) is satisfied:

$$0 = \frac{\$2,400}{1.2} + \frac{\$1,440}{(1.2)^2} - \$3,000$$

$$= \$2,000 + \$1,000 - \$3,000$$

Notice that we can view the initial investment of $3,000 as made up of two parts:

A $2,000 amount which is the present value using a discount rate of 20 percent of the time 1 $2,400 cash flow; this $2,000 was invested for one period at 20 percent to produce the $2,400 at time 1.

A $1,000 amount which is the present value, using a discount rate of 20 percent of the time 2 $1,440 cash flow; this $1,000 was invested for two periods at 20 percent per period to produce the $1,440 at time 2.

The investment is therefore equivalent to putting the $3,000 into a fund earning 20 percent per period, with a $2,400 withdrawal (cash flow) at time 1 and a $1,440 withdrawal at time 2.[3]

In summary, to compute the IRR on an investment, we plug in I and the cash flows CF_1 to CF_n into (7-4) or (7-5) and then solve for r. Since (7-4) and (7-5) are simply present value equations with the present value equal to zero, in determining r we are determining that interest rate which would imply that the investment has a net present value of zero. Keep in mind that the interest rate we used in Eqs. (7-2) and (7-3) is k, the cost of capital, and this will equal r, the IRR, only if $r = k$, that is, only if the

---

3. In general, for

$$0 = \frac{CF_1}{1 + r} + \frac{CF_2}{(1 + r)^2} + \cdots + \frac{CF_n}{(1 + r)^n} - I$$

$$= Z_1 + Z_2 + \cdots + Z_n - I$$

where $Z_1 = CF_1/(1 + r)$, $Z_2 = CF_2/(1 + r)^2$, etc.

We can view I as made up of a set of smaller investments, Z_1 through Z_n, where Z_1 is invested for one period at rate r to produce $(1 + r) Z_1 = CF_1$, Z_2 is invested for two periods at rate r to produce $(1 + r)^2 Z_2 = CF_2$, etc.

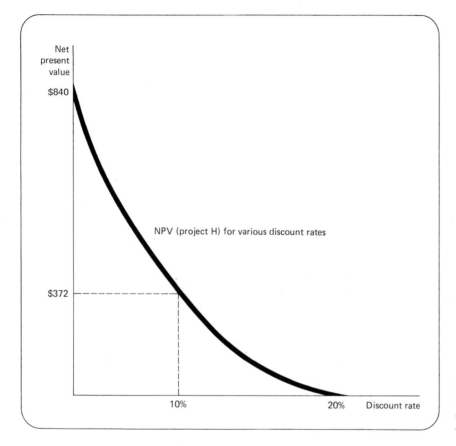

Figure 7-2. Deter-mining the IRR by examining NPV of cash flows for various discount rates.

project has an actual NPV equal to zero. (Remember in our discussion of present value that we said that if NPV = 0, the project is just earning the cost of capital k.) If NPV *exceeds* zero using cost of capital k, then ordi-narily r exceeds k, and the project is earning a rate of return that exceeds the cost of capital.[4]

In Figure 7-2 the relationships between NPV, k, and r are shown. At the cost of capital k of 10 percent, the NPV of project H equals

$$\text{NPV (project H)} = \frac{\$2,400}{1.1} + \frac{\$1,440}{(1.1)^2} - \$3,000$$

$$= \$2,182 + \$1,190 - \$3,000$$

$$= \$372$$

4. Actually, a positive NPV necessarily implies that the investment's rate of return exceeds the cost of capital only if the investment involves an initial outlay (cost) and produces a nonnegative cash flow return in future periods. This is the type of investment considered in the examples in this chapter.

The NPV (project H) schedule shows a NPV = $372 at a discount rate of 10 percent. Each point on the schedule shows the NPV of project H along the vertical axis for each discount rate shown along the horizontal axis. Notice that if the discount rate k were 20 percent, NPV (project H) = 0; therefore, internal rate of return r for project H is 20 percent, since r is that rate which sets the NPV equal to zero [see Eq. (7-4)]. In short, we can view the internal rate of return, r, as that cost of capital which would just make the project marginally acceptable (NPV = 0). Project H would be just marginally acceptable (NPV = 0) if the cost of capital k equalled 20 percent, and therefore its IRR is 20 percent; but since k equals 10 percent, project H earns more than the cost of capital (r exceeds k) and is quite profitable (it has a positive NPV).

The accept-reject decision The IRR method requires that if a particular investment is either to be accepted or rejected (and not to be compared with some alternative investment), it should be accepted if its IRR exceeds the cost of capital. The rationale is that if an investment earns more than the cost of the funds used to finance it, it should be adopted. We can apply the rule to the restaurant sign example used earlier. The sign costs $3,500 and produces a net cash flow of $1,000 in each of the next five years. Using Eq. (7-5) to determine r, the IRR, we solve the following:

$$\$1,000 \ (P/A, \ r, \ 5) = \$3,500$$

or

$$(P/A, \ r, \ 5) = 3.5$$

Using the tables, we find that r = 13.2 percent, that is, $(P/A, 13.2\%, 5)$ = 3.5.[5] The project returns 13.2 percent per year, and this exceeds the cost of capital k of 10 percent. Therefore, the sign should be purchased, a conclusion that is consistent with that reached earlier using net present value.

Choices between alternatives—the incremental approach The IRR method can be used to compare two or more alternative investments (mutually exclusive options; i.e., at most one alternative is to be accepted). However, it is somewhat more difficult to use than is the present value method in the same situation and must be applied rather carefully. The IRR procedure consists of first determining which alternative investment is the most profitable by applying the incremental approach (described below) and then determining whether that most profitable alternative is sufficiently profitable to adopt. The alternative is adopted only if its

5. Using interpolation (see Chap. 4), we find that $(P/A, 13.2\%, 5)$ = 3.5.

IRR exceeds the cost of capital. (It is shown in the next section that it is incorrect to simply select the investment with the higher IRR.)

To demonstrate the method, we can refer back to the example involving a comparison between the deluxe machine (alternative D) and the economy machine (alternative E). We assume as before that the cost of capital is 10 percent. The cash flows were as shown below:

| Alternative | Time | | | | | | IRR |
	0	1	2	3	4	5	
Deluxe machine (D)	−$3,000	$900	$900	$900	$900	$900	15.2%
Economy machine (E)	−$2,000	$610	$610	$610	$610	$610	16.0%

To compare alternatives D and E using the IRR method, we must first ask whether the additional (or incremental) investment of $1,000 in D as compared with E is justified. In other words, we look at the *difference* between D and E. The difference between the cash flows of the two alternatives is:

	0	1	2	3	4	5	IRR
D − E	−$1,000	$290	$290	$290	$290	$290	13.8%

If we pick D instead of E, an additional investment of $1,000 must be made and we would expect to receive an additional $290 per year for five years. The IRR on the additional investment is found to be 13.8 percent by using the IRR equation. If the firm's cost of capital k is less than 13.8 percent, then D is preferred over E; if k is greater than 13.8 percent, E is better than D. Since the cost of capital equals 10 percent (by assumption), D is preferred over E. If the cost of capital were 15 percent, then E would be chosen over D because the additional investment required by E does not provide a high enough rate of return.

The next step is to decide whether the better alternative, D, is sufficiently profitable to be acceptable. D is acceptable since its rate of return of 15.2 percent exceeds the cost of capital of 10 percent.

If we have more than two alternatives available, then we must pick the best one by making a series of comparisons. Suppose there are four alternatives, A, B, C, and D. We can start off with any two and find out which one is the better of the two by the procedure just illustrated. Suppose we look at A and B first and decide that A is better. Then we would want to compare A with C in the same way. Suppose again that A is more profitable. Finally we must compare A with D. Suppose D is better than A. By this process we could determine that D is the best of the four alternatives. Now we need only to decide whether D is worth undertaking at all by comparing its rate of return with the cost of capital as we did above; D should be adopted if, and only if, its rate of return exceeds the cost of capital.

The wrong way to choose between alternatives   A common error in using the IRR method to compare two alternatives is to select the one with the higher IRR. This is a very natural mistake and appears to many people to be a reasonable one in practice. We will show here why picking the alternative with the higher IRR is not in general a good idea.

Let us look at the example presented earlier of two alternatives, D and E. The required rate of return (cost of capital k) is assumed to be 10 percent and the following information has been determined.

	0	1	2	3	4	5	NPV	IRR
D	−$3,000	$900	$900	$900	$900	$900	$412	15.2%
E	−$2,000	$610	$610	$610	$610	$610	$313	16.0%
D − E	−$1,000	$290	$290	$290	$290	$290	$ 99	13.8%

Notice that the NPV of D is greater than the NPV of E, indicating that D is better. Also, the rate of return on the difference (D − E) is 13.8 percent, which is greater than 10 percent and therefore indicates that the extra investment in D is worthwhile. D rather than E should be accepted. This is so even though the rate of return of E, 16 percent, is greater than that for D of 15.2 percent. Picking the higher rate of return would suggest that E is better than D, which is not consistent with either the present value method or the IRR method as we have outlined it. Let's explore the problem a little further.

To many people it does not seem intuitively "right" to pass up a 16 percent rate of return in favor of a 15.2 percent rate of return. However, their intuition is wrong here. The 16 percent investment is *not* "passed up." Alternative D can be viewed as being a package of two investments E and (D − E) with the following characteristics.

	0	1	2	3	4	5	NPV	IRR
E	−$2,000	$610	$610	$610	$610	$610	$313	16.0%
D − E	−$1,000	$290	$290	$290	$290	$290	$ 99	13.8%
D	−$3,000	$900	$900	$900	$900	$900	$412	15.2%

Accepting D instead of E means taking on the investment package E and (D − E). E is an investment of $2,000 with a rate of return of 16 percent and (D − E) is an investment of $1,000 with a rate of return of 13.8 percent. The average rate of return on the total package [D = E + (D − E)] is 15.2 percent. Therefore, taking D over E means effectively investing in E plus another investment (D − E) which has a rate of return of 13.8 percent. If (D − E) is a good investment, which it is since 13.8 percent exceeds the cost of capital of 10 percent, you will want to take D in preference to E, since with D you in effect get investment E plus another good investment (D − E).

To further emphasize the error in simply choosing the investment with the higher IRR, assume two mutually exclusive investments, investment A involving an initial outlay of $1 and returning $10 one year hence (an IRR of 900 percent) and investment B involving an initial cost of $100,000 and returning $200,000 one year later (an IRR of 100 percent). If the cost of capital is 10 percent, the NPV(A) = $8.09 and the NPV(B) = $81,820. It should be clear that B is preferred to A even though A has the higher IRR. This is an extreme example used to highlight the need to use the incremental approach described above. Although actual situations are not so blatantly obvious, the same principle will still apply.

In the examples we just examined, the alternatives differed in the amount of initial investment; however, this is not the only situation in which simply picking the highest rate of return can lead to problems. Alternatives with the same initial investment but having unequal lives or just markedly different cash flow patterns over identical lives can also present this problem (see Appendix 7B). In general, therefore, picking the alternative with the highest rate of return can be incorrect. Instead, the incremental approach outlined here should be used.

IRR, present value, and reinvestment rate assumptions Although, as we just noted, it is ordinarily incorrect simply to pick the mutually exclusive investment with the highest IRR, there is a special case in which this general guideline does not apply and the mutually exclusive alternative with the highest IRR is best. In this case, the alternative with the highest IRR is the one that would also be chosen using the incremental IRR method or the present value method. The special case arises if the mutually exclusive investments require the same initial outlay and if the future cash flows from each investment can be reinvested by the firm in other projects which earn that investment's IRR until some particular future date, where that future date is the same for all the mutually exclusive projects. For example, mutually exclusive investments A and B might each involve an initial outlay of $1,000 in 1978; A has a three-year life and an internal rate of return of 20 percent, and all future cash flows generated by A will be reinvested by the firm in other projects to earn 20 percent per year (A's IRR) until 1985; and B has a four-year life and an internal rate of return of 30 percent, and all future cash flows will be reinvested to earn 30 percent per year until 1985. The rule that applies in this special case says that B is better than A because B has the higher IRR. B would also be chosen using the incremental rate of return and the present value methods. This special case is discussed in greater detail in Section 2 of Appendix 7B.

There is a broader issue than the specialized case just discussed above. This issue relates to how the rate of return that can be earned on *future* investments of the firm depends on which *current* investments are adopted. As explained in Section 1 of Appendix 7B, if the profitability of future investments (regardless of how profitable) does *not* depend on which current investments are adopted, then we can ignore the future investments in evaluating current projects. This was the assumption made above in explaining the present value and IRR methods, and both these methods are completely consistent and valid in this case. There are situations, however, in which investments lead to future profitable opportunities that would not be available to the firm if the investments had not been undertaken. For example, firms that established footholds in foreign countries in the 1950s often found that they had an advantageous position in those foreign markets in the 1960s and 1970s. If the choice of current investments affects the rate of return that can be earned on future investments, then in evaluating current projects it becomes necessary to analyze the cash flows from the current investments *and* also the cash flows from the future investment opportunities that depend on the current investments. Either the present value method or the IRR method can be used to analyze these present and future project cash flows. Both present value and IRR are appropriate for such an analysis whether it is assumed that the future investments earn a rate of return equal to the cost of capital, equal to each investment's IRR, or equal to any other rate, and whether the future investments are financed by reinvesting the future cash flows from current investments or are financed by any other source. The method of analyzing this type of problem is presented in detail in Section 3 of Appendix 7B.

IRR and present value compared   In most situations the internal rate of return method properly applied and present value provide the same choices. The IRR approach has the advantage of providing a rate of return that is easy to interpret and for that reason is particularly popular in industry. On the other hand, computing a rate of return is usually more difficult than computing a present value, although, with electronic calculators and computers readily available, this is not a serious drawback. In addition, the incremental IRR method, as we have seen, is conceptually more complex when choosing among alternatives. Most important, in some cases the cash flows imply more than one internal rate of return or no meaningful rate of return at all.[6] In these cases, the IRR method cannot be

6. Some cash flows imply more than one internal rate of return or only rates of return involving $\sqrt{-1}$ (imaginary numbers). In these cases the IRR method cannot be used. Such

used whereas present value can be. Finally, as is explained in the previous section and in Appendix 7B, even if special reinvestment rate assumptions are made regarding the current projects being evaluated, the present value method appropriately applied is the easiest method to use.

Overall, it is our judgment that present value is superior to internal rate of return as a capital budgeting approach. Any problem that can be treated with IRR can also be analyzed using present value, whereas the reverse is not the case. In Appendix 7A, it is shown that the gain to shareholders from an investment equals its net present value and the NPV is therefore a proper guide to selecting investments.[7]

The **payback period** is the length of time it takes to recover the initial investment on a project. For example, if a $1,000 investment returns an aftertax cash flow per year of $300, the payback period is $3\frac{1}{3}$ years ($1,000/$300). The payback period method dictates acceptance of a project only if the project has a payback period less than some level specified by management. In comparing two alternative options using this method, the one with the smaller payback period is preferred and is accepted if its payback period is less than the specified requirement.

The payback period approach has a number of problems. First, there is no consideration of returns after the required payback period. Assume that the firm has projects Q and R from which to choose and has set the required payback period at three years. Thus, only if the project recovers the entire investment within three years is the project acceptable. From Exhibit 7-3, we can see that the payback period of Q is two years and the payback period of R is 2.3 years. Both projects meet the three-year requirement, but Q is preferred since its payback period is less. However, notice that R returns a cash flow at time 3 of $1,000, whereas Q returns only $25 after its two-year payback period. These post-payback period returns are ignored in using the method since the standard is based entirely on the time required to recover capital. Beyond the payback period, returns are disregarded. Even though payback dictates the choice of Q, at a 10 percent cost of capital the present value of Q is − $138 and of R is

The Payback Period Method

---

problems will not arise if the cash flow involves an initial outflow (I_o) and positive cash flows thereafter. They can arise if some future cash flows are negative (cash outflows). For a complete discussion of these problems, see C. W. Haley and L. D. Schall, *The Theory of Financial Decisions* (New York: McGraw-Hill, 1973).

7. If we were to take into account flotation (sales) costs of issuing securities, investor costs in buying and selling securities, and personal tax effects, net present value has to be amended (so do IRR and other capital budgeting techniques). This topic is not appropriate for discussion here but has been explored in the financial literature. One proposed approach is the use of "adjusted present value"; see S. Myers, "Interaction of Investment and Financing Decisions," *Journal of Finance* (March 1974), pp. 1–25.

Exhibit 7-3. Payback Period Comparison

		Cash flows	
	Time	Q	R
Initial investment	0	−$1,000	−$1,000
Returns	1	200	600
	2	800	300
	3	25	1,000
Payback period		2 years	2.3 years
Net present value at cost of capital of 10 percent		−$138	$545

$545.[8] Present value, therefore, dictates the selection of R, the opposite result from that using payback. A primary reason for the different results for the two methods is that, in contrast to payback, present value does not ignore returns beyond the payback period.

Notice secondly that payback also ignores the pattern of returns within the payback period; i.e., the time value of money is not taken into accout. Assume that a choice is to be made between assets S and T described in Exhibit 7-4. S and T have a payback period of two years and are therefore equivalent on this basis. However, since we know that a dollar received sooner is better due to the time value of money, project T is the better investment as indicated by the greater net present value of T. Payback completely fails to account for the differences in the pattern of returns.

In spite of the flaws in the payback period method, it is still widely employed in industry. Three rationales have been offered in payback's defense. First, after the required payback period the uncertainty may be so great for some projects that requiring recovery of capital within that period is a justifiable means of avoiding undue risk. However, this argument does not confront the time-value-of-money problem within the payback period illustrated above for investments S and T (Exhibit 7-4). Furthermore, risk is rarely so great that returns beyond that period should be completely ignored. A second argument sometimes advanced in support of payback is that in practice it is generally used in combination with other criteria which do account for the time value of money and for the post-

---

8. It is easily shown that the IRR method using incremental analysis also dictates the choice of R.

Exhibit 7-4. Payback Period Comparison

		Cash flows	
	Time	S	T
Initial investment	0	−$500	−$500
Returns	1	100	400
	2	400	100
	3	500	500
Payback period		2 years	2 years
Net present value at a cost of capital of 10%[a]		$297	$322

[a]NPV(S) = 0.9091 ($100) + 0.8264 ($400) + 0.7513 ($500) − $500 = $297;
NPV(T) = 0.9091 ($400) + 0.8264 ($100) + 0.7513 ($500) − $500 = $322.

payback period returns. However, this is a roundabout way of saying that these two latter considerations must be taken into account. If this is so, why not employ the present value criterion in the first place? Furthermore, as explained in Chapter 8, if risk is in fact increasing over time, the discount rate used under the present value method can be adjusted to take this increasing risk into account.

The third, and probably weakest, argument used to defend payback is its simplicity. It certainly behooves a firm to use the best techniques available in appraising capital budgeting options. The expense of a more careful analysis is generally more than compensated for by preventing costly errors of choice in allocating funds. Further, with the availability of present value tables and computers, any computational advantages of payback have become negligible. Ease of use is not sufficient justification for employing payback, particularly in view of the importance of capital budgeting decisions.

In conclusion, payback has very little to recommend it and can be highly misleading. A comparison of available approaches clearly favors the present value or IRR method.

Accounting Rate of Return

The accounting rate of return (ARR) equals the average annual aftertax accounting profit generated by the investment divided by the cost of the investment. That is,

$$ARR = \frac{\text{average annual profit from investment}}{I} \tag{7-6}$$

where I is the investment's initial cost. ARR is a misleading measure of the benefits from an asset for two reasons: profit does not generally equal the asset's cash flow and may have a pattern very much different from that of cash flow and, second, the time value of money is ignored by the ARR method.[9]

To illustrate the ARR method, assume two assets, F and G, each of which requires an initial outlay I of $20,000. Each asset lasts for four years and is depreciated on a straight-line basis with zero salvage value; depreciation is therefore $5,000 per year on F or G. These data and the accounting profit for each asset are shown in Exhibit 7-5. If the cost of capital were 10 percent, asset F with a net present value of $16,902 would be preferred to asset G with a net present value of $15,109. But, using ARR, G is preferred to F since G's ARR of 35 percent exceeds F's ARR of 32.5 percent. Present value produces the correct results, and therefore ARR can lead to the wrong choices.

9. It is assumed in the table that aftertax profit equals cash flow less depreciation. This will be so if cash revenues R and cash expenses E are revenues and expenses for tax purposes; then cash flow $= R - E -$ taxes, and profit $= R - E -$ depreciation $-$ taxes $=$ cash flow $-$ depreciation. Also, the definition of the ARR stated in Eq. (7-6) is one of many alternative definitions that have been proposed; one of these alternatives uses $I/2$ in the denominator instead of I as in (7-6). All the commonly proposed ARR measures are inferior to present value as capital budgeting criteria because they do not evaluate cash flow or do not properly take into account the time value of money.

Exhibit 7-5. Comparison of Accounting Rate of Return (ARR) and Present Value

	Asset F		Asset G	
Year	Annual profit	Cash flow	Annual profit	Cash flow
1	$11,000	$16,000	$ 1,000	$ 6,000
2	11,000	16,000	1,000	6,000
3	2,000	7,000	1,000	6,000
4	2,000	7,000	25,000	30,000
Total	$26,000	$46,000	$28,000	$48,000
ARR[a]	32.5%		35%	
NPV		$17,808		$15,109

[a]ARR = (Total profit/4 years) ÷ $20,000.

This section considers four issues that commonly arise in analyzing capital expenditures: comparing investments with different lives, the treatment of the investment tax credit, incorporating inflation in the analysis, and the evaluation of projects that affect one another's cash flows.

SPECIAL PROBLEMS IN INVESTMENT ANALYSIS

Until now, in comparing mutually exclusive investments, we have assumed that the lives of the investments were the same. Often two or more options being compared do not have equal lives. Strictly speaking, to analyze such investments using present value or IRR, it is generally necessary to evaluate them for equal periods of time. To do this, we merely ask: "What would we do after the shorter-lived asset expires, if we were to obtain it instead of acquiring the longer-lived asset?" The examples below will illustrate the problem and its solution. We will then observe that in many cases, an approximation technique is adequate and that often we need not evaluate the investments for exactly equal periods of time.

Comparing Investments with Different Lives

Assume that a firm is comparing machines M_1 and M_2. M_1, which will last six years, costs \$1,000 at time 0 and will yield a net cash flow of \$400 per year. M_1, if purchased, will be replaced at time 6 by M_1', which will cost \$1,200 and will yield \$400 per year (from time 7 to time 12). M_2 will last for twelve years, will cost \$1,800 at time 0, and will yield \$400 per year for twelve years. The point to be made here is that the comparison should be between the NPV of M_1 and M_1' [signified NPV $(M_1 + M_1')$] and the NPV of M_2 [signified NPV (M_2)]. We can see from Exhibit 7-6 that this comparison leads us to choose M_1 now and to replace it with M_1' at time 6 rather than to obtain M_2 now, since NPV $(M_1 + M_1') = \$1,048$ and NPV $(M_2) = \$926$. It is improper to simply compare the NPV of M_1 (ignoring the replacement with M_1' at time 6) with the NPV of M_2. If we had done this, we would have chosen M_2 since NPV $(M_2) = \$926$ and NPV $(M_1) = \$742$.

In the above example, the two options [option $(M_1 + M_1')$ and option M_2] had identical time durations of twelve years. Often, to establish identical durations for options being compared, it is necessary to forecast replacements many years into the future.[10] In such cases, it is ordinarily

10. For example, if asset X and its future replacements each last ten years (replacement at time 10, time 20, etc.) and asset Y and each of its future replacements last thirteen years (replacement at time 13, time 26, etc.), we would have to analyze cash flows for the next 130 years (the shortest period ending when replacements of both X and Y also end). However, as noted below, adequate accuracy usually requires consideration of only a limited time period. Note also that this section assumes that investment (e.g., a replacement) in any particular time period does not depend on previous investment. Thus, in the above example, the NPV of any year 12 replacement does not depend on whether M_1 and M_1' or M_2 was used in the first twelve years. See Appendix 7B, Section 3, on analyzing investments which affect or depend on investment in other periods.

Exhibit 7-6. Comparison of Investments with Different Lives

Time	Cash flows		
	M_1	M_1'	M_2
Time 0 (cost)	−$1,000		−$1,800
Time 1–6 (returns per year)	400		400
Time 6 (cost)		−$1,200	
Time 7–12 (returns per year)		400	400

$$NPV(M_1) = -\$1,000 + \$400 \, (P/A, \ 10\%, \ 6)$$
$$= -\$1,000 + \$400 \, (4.355) = \underline{\$742}$$
$$NPV(M_1 + M_1') = \$400 \, (P/A, \ 10\%, \ 12)$$
$$- \$1,000 - \$1,200 \, (P/F, \ 10\%, \ 6)$$
$$= \$400 \, (6.814) - \$1,000$$
$$- \$1,200 \, (0.5645) = \underline{\$1,048}$$
$$NPV(M_2) = \$400 \, (P/A, \ 10\%, \ 12) - \$1,800$$
$$= \$400 \, (6.814) - \$1,800$$
$$= \underline{\$926}$$

Conclusion: Buy M_1 now and replace with M_1' at time 6 since NPV $(M_1 + M_1')$ exceeds NPV(M_2).

adequate to make the options only approximately, and not exactly, of the same duration.

For example, it would ordinarily be acceptable to compare the alternative of machines M_1 and M_1' (twelve-year total life) with the alternative involving M_2, even if M_2 had only an eleven- or even ten-year life; the discrepancy would be one or two years occurring a decade into the future. The importance of a time discrepancy between two investment alternatives is dependent upon three things:

1. *The shorter is the discrepancy, the less important it is.* Thus, we had to consider the replacement of M_1 with M_1' in the above example because a six-year discrepancy between M_1 and M_2 was too large to ignore.
2. *The further into the future is the life discrepancy, the less important it is.* For example, if we were considering alternative buildings for a vacant piece of land, we could ordinarily compare the NPV of a building with a forty-year life with the NPV of a building with a fifty-year life and ignore what each would be replaced with at the end of their lives. The ten-year discrepancy occurs forty to fifty years into the future and

can be ignored in most cases. The reason is that the NPV of cash flows occurring far in the future is usually very small.[11]

3. *The closer is the rate of return on future investments to the cost of capital, the less important are any time discrepancies.* This is because the NPV = 0 for any future investment which just earns the cost of capital. *If the NPV on a future investment is zero, then the time discrepancy can be ignored.* For example, assume that M_1' in the above example has the cash flows shown below instead of those shown in Exhibit 7-6.[12]

Time	Cash flow of M_1'
t_6 (cost)	−$1,200.00
t_7–t_{12} (returns per year)	$275.55

$$\text{NPV}(M_1') \text{ at time } 6 = \$275.55 \ (P/A, \ 10\%, \ 6) - \$1,200$$

$$= \$275.55 \ (4.355) - \$1,200$$

$$= \$1,200 - \$1,200 = 0$$

$\text{NPV}(M_1') = 0$; that is, *it adds nothing* to the NPV of M_1 and M_1' combined. We can just ignore M_1' and directly compare the six-year asset M_1 with the twelve-year asset M_2. Assuming that M_1 and M_2 have the cash flows and NPVs as shown in Exhibit 7-6 and M_1' has the cash flows and NPV shown above, the $\text{NPV}(M_1 + M_1') = \text{NPV}(M_1) = \$742$, since $\text{NPV}(M_1') = 0$. We choose M_2 since $\text{NPV}(M_2) = \$926$, which exceeds $\text{NPV}(M_1)$ of $742.

To summarize, to provide an exactly correct comparison between mutually exclusive options, the two alternatives must have equal lives. An alternative here refers to a particular course of action which ordinarily involves an investment now and may involve further investments (replacements) in the future. Often it is not practical or possible to establish equal lives for two alternatives. In this case, it is generally correct to ignore time discrepancies if they are small or if they occur far into the future or if the rates of return on investments subsequent to the ones being considered are close to the cost of capital (that is, if such future investments have small NPVs).

11. Even a very large net present value far into the future has a small value when discounted to the present using an economically realistic discount rate. For example, $1,000,000 at time 50 discounted to time 0 (now) has a value of $8,500 if the discount rate is 10 percent [$(P/F, \ 10\%, \ 50) = 0.0085$]. Of course, the larger is the future amount, the further into the future it must be for it to become insignificant when discounted to the present.

12. If M_1' cost $1,200 at time 6 and yields $275.55 per year for years 7 through 12, it has an IRR of exactly 10 percent [$(A/P, \ 10\%, \ 6) = 0.2296$]. At a cost of capital of 10 percent, the NPV of M_1' is zero at time 6, as is shown in the text computation below.

The above conclusions also apply if we are using the IRR approach in comparing alternatives. We must ordinarily use equal lives of the alternatives for an exactly correct answer. However, as with the present value method, this rule is subject to the above qualifications.

The Investment Tax Credit

To encourage investment by business, Congress has enacted the **investment tax credit.** It is effectively a gift by the federal government to the investing firm of part of the cost of a new asset and applies to all productive assets except real estate. To a very limited extent, it also applies to the purchase of used assets. The firm's tax bill is reduced by the amount of the tax credit which is generally equal to 7 percent of the cost of the asset.[13] To illustrate, assume a firm purchases an asset for $1,000 and plans to hold it for at least seven years. Assume that the firm has a taxable income of $200,000 from its other operations and pays $100,000 in income taxes on this income. The tax credit on the $1,000 investment is $70 (7 percent × $1,000). This credit is deducted from the taxes owed for the period; i.e., the firm's taxes become $99,930 ($100,000 − $70). Thus, the benefit is $70 in reduced tax expense. In effect, this means that the aftertax cost of the asset is only $930. That is, in purchasing the asset, the firm must invest $1,000 but gets $70 in a tax reduction from the government, the net outlay being $930. In computing the net present value of the asset, the initial investment I is $930. In computing the depreciation on the asset for tax purposes the entire $1,000 cost would nevertheless be the depreciation base.

In capital-intensive industries, e.g., oil, chemicals, automobile manufacturing, and especially public utilities, the investment tax credit can be a very significant factor. For example, the credit reduced Eastman Kodak's United States income taxes in 1974 by $15.4 million—and that's a sum of some consequence even to an industrial and financial colossus such as Kodak.

Inflation and Capital Budgeting

There was a time, not so long ago, when inflation was viewed by most Americans as a problem solely of South American banana republics and wartorn Europe. This illusion was perhaps permanently dispelled during the Vietnam and post-Vietnam era, as inflation assumed the archvillain's role in the United States economy. Economists are still befuddled in their search for an explanation for the unrelenting price spiral. Fortunately, the financial manager's task is enormously simpler than that of the macro-

13. The size of the credit varies depending upon the length of time the asset is held but equals 7 percent of the cost of the asset if it is held seven years or more. Also, for the period 1975 to 1980, the investment tax credit was raised to 10 percent.

economist. The manager merely wants to know how to incorporate inflation into the analysis of the firm's investment opportunities. The job is
surprisingly simple. The capital budgeting analyst should merely predict
the actual dollar cash flows that will occur, taking into account the inflationary trend. For example, if the firm sells product X and the aftertax
cash flow generated by sale of a single unit is expected to rise (due to inflation and any other factors) at the rate of 5 percent per year from the
current level of $1, then the aftertax cash flow to be discounted is $1 per
unit of product X sold this year, $1.05 per unit next year, $1.1025
(= 1.05 × $1.05) the year after next, and so forth to year 5, when the cash
flow will be $1.276 per unit. Thus, the firm should use its expectations
regarding inflation to estimate the actual dollar cash flows to be earned,
and then use those expected actual flows in the analysis. The inflationary
trend must be estimated, and usually this is done by selecting an estimate
made by leading economists or by professional forecasting groups such as
those associated with the Wharton School, UCLA, Chase Manhattan
Bank, and a number of private forecasting firms. These forecasts are
sometimes published in financial periodicals or are available for a fee from
the forecasters.

The appropriate discount rate to employ is still the market rate currently used by investors to discount cash flows of a similar risk. *Market
rates take into account inflationary expectations,* and a greater expected
rate of inflation will mean that investors will require a higher rate of
return. This is the reason that interest rates on bonds and the borrowing rate at banks (including the prime rate charged the banks' biggest
and least risky customers) increase as inflation accelerates. Figure 7-3 illustrates the similar historical patterns of the general price level and
market discount rates (an average of long-term bond rates in the figure).
The two trends show a marked upward direction during the inflationary
period of the late 1960s and the 1970s.

The essence of this approach is that the proper rate to apply in discounting a cash flow is the rate investors apply to cash flows of similar
risk. This rate will necessarily take into account inflationary trends. To illustrate the method, assume that a store is considering the purchase of a
display case for $1,500 which has an anticipated useful life of three years.
If there were no inflation, the added sales due to the display case would be
$2,500 per year, increased cost of goods sold would be $1,300, added nondepreciable expenses would be $200, and the rise in the firm's taxes
would equal $300. Thus, aftertax cash flow from the case would equal
$700 per year ($700 = $2,500 − $1,300 − $200 − $300) for three years.
However, with the expectation of continued inflation, the selling price of
the product and the magnitude of the costs will rise. Assume that the expected cash flows (taking into account inflationary expectations) are as
shown in Exhibit 7-7.

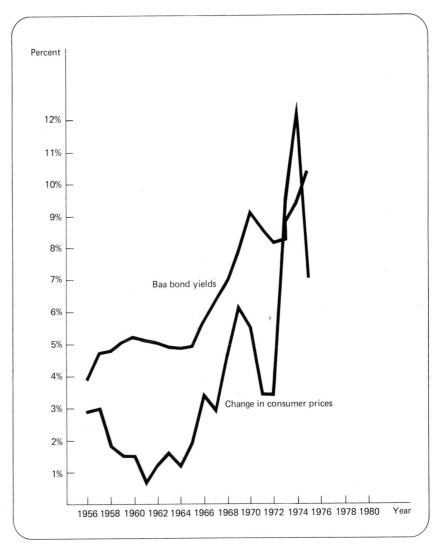

Figure 7-3. The behavior of market interest rates and changes in the general price level for goods and services. (Sources: U.S. Department of Labor, Bureau of Labor Statistics; Moody's Investors Service.)

Notice from the table that the impact of inflation on sales may differ from the impact on costs. Let the discount rate appropriate to the cash flow be 12 percent; that is, the rate of return required by investors for cash flows of similar risk is 12 percent. The net present value of the display case is the discounted value of the cash flows in Exhibit 7-7 less the $1,500 initial cost of the case; that is,

Exhibit 7-7. Cash Flows from the Investment with Inflation

	Year 1	Year 2	Year 3
Increase in sales	$2,700	$2,900	$3,200
Deduct:			
Increase in cost of goods sold	$1,400	$1,500	$1,600
Increase in other nondepreciation expenses	250	275	300
Increase in taxes	300	325	400
Total deductions	1,950	2,100	2,300
Change in firm's aftertax cash flow	$ 750	$ 800	$ 900

$$
\begin{aligned}
\text{NPV} &= \frac{\$750}{1.12} + \frac{\$800}{(1.12)^2} + \frac{\$900}{(1.12)^3} - \$1,500 \\
&= 0.8929(\$750) + 0.7972(\$800) + 0.7118(\$900) - \$1,500 \\
&= \$448
\end{aligned}
$$

Essentially it is the expected future dollar cash flows that are discounted, and it is the current market discount rate used by investors that is used for discounting. The cash flows are estimated so that they reflect anticipated inflationary trends, and the current discount rate allows for the inflationary expectations of investors.

Interrelated Investment Opportunities

Up to this point we have considered investment choices that either involved accepting or rejecting a particular project or involved a choice between two mutually exclusive options, e.g., whether the truck purchased would be a Ford or a Chevrolet. Frequently, however, two or more investments are being evaluated, any or all of which can be accepted and which affect one another's profitability. In this case, the decision involves selecting the set of investments having the highest net present value and accepting the set if its net present value is positive. To illustrate, assume that Blue Grass Realty owns two adjacent plots of land, plot 1 and plot 2. Intuitively we know that what is constructed on plot 1 may influence the profitability of what is constructed on plot 2. The two land uses are economically interdependent. Blue Grass has decided that its only options for plot 1 are to construct a rest home on plot 1 or leave it vacant; its only options for plot 2 are to construct an amusement park on plot 2 or leave it vacant. Its options are therefore to construct the rest home and not the amusement park, to construct the amusement park and not the rest home, to construct both, or to construct neither. Assume that to leave both plots vacant produces a zero cash flow and requires a zero investment. Also assume for simplicity that all options involve the same risk and the same cost of capital of 10 percent.[14] The costs and payoffs of each decision involving the construction of one or both of the amusement park and rest home are shown in Exhibit 7-8. It is not surprising that the total cash flow from both the amusement park and rest home together ($24,000) falls far short of even the rest home alone ($50,000 per year). The home would not be too restful (and patrons therefore few) with merry-go-round music and children's screams wafting through the air. The net present value of the rest home on plot 1, with plot 2 left vacant (no amusement park), is the highest of the three choices, and would be the option selected, since its present value of $200,000 is positive.

The above example suggests a general guideline for selecting investments from a set of interdependent options.[15] If we have any set of investments which have *interdependent* cash flows, e.g., investments A, B, and C, the following procedure is appropriate in determining the best course of action:

1. Determine the combinations of the interdependent options that are possible. For three interdependent options, A, B, and C, if none is mutually exclusive of any of the others (that is, all can be simultaneously adopted), then the possible combinations (which involve adopting at least one option) are:

   A but not B or C   B and C but not A
   B but not A or C   A and C but not B
   C but not A or B   A, B, and C together
   A and B but not C

2. Determine the investment required, the aftertax cash flows, and the net present values of each of the combinations of options identified in step 1 above (seven combinations in the above example of A, B, and C).

14. If different options involve different risk, then they will warrant different discount rates (costs of capital). For example, if the rest home were riskier than the amusement park, the former might warrant a 14 percent discount rate and the latter a 10 percent discount rate; and the two together might justify an 11 percent discount rate. The issue of differing risk is discussed in Chap. 8.

15. For a detailed analysis of cash flow interdependencies, see Haley and Schall, op. cit., chap. 3.

Exhibit 7-8. Interrelated Investment Opportunities

	Only amusement park	Only rest home	Amusement park and rest home
I_0	$100,000	$300,000	$400,000
Annual expected perpetual aftertax cash flow	$ 12,000	$ 50,000	$ 24,000
Net present value at 10%[a]	$ 20,000	$200,000	−$160,000

[a]NPV (only amusement park) = $12,000(10) − $100,000 = $20,000 where 10 is the 10% annuity present value factor for a perpetual annuity (see Appendix B); NPV (only rest home) = $50,000(10) − $300,000 = $200,000; NPV (amusement park and rest home) = $24,000(10) − $400,000 = −$160,000.

3. Choose the combination of options determined in step **2** above with the highest net present value. If that highest net present value is positive, adopt that combination of options; if not, reject that combination along with all the other combinations.

This procedure was followed in the amusement park–rest home example. In step **1**, we defined the combinations of options as the amusement park and not rest home, rest home and not amusement park, or both. In step **2**, we determined the initial outlay, cash flow, and net present values of each option (shown in Exhibit 7-8). In step **3**, we chose the rest home alternative since it had the highest net present value and that net present value was positive.

One might object at this point that all options of the firm are interdependent in some way. This would mean that an almost overwhelming task confronts the investment planner; i.e., every combination of investment opportunities would have to be analyzed rather than each option being examined individually. Fortunately, the problem is not as bad as that. Although strictly speaking all a firm's activities are somewhat dependent (i.e., affect one another's profitability), many options are approximately independent and can therefore be evaluated as separate projects. For example, if plots 1 and 2 of Blue Grass Realty were in different parts of the city, the land uses on each could be individually evaluated. In this case, the amusement park on plot 2 could be accepted or rejected and the rest home on plot 1 could be accepted or rejected without considering as a separate possibility the construction of both the amusement park and the rest home. Notice that if we had done this in the case of the adjacent (and therefore interdependent) plots described in Exhibit 7-8, we would have erroneously accepted the amusement park and the rest home, since each if done without the other has a positive net present value ($20,000 and $200,000, respectively). *With interdependencies that are significant we cannot consider each investment option individually.* This is so since the cash flow figures relating to the options as individual investments do not apply if more than one of the investments are undertaken. This is clearly illustrated in Exhibit 7-8, since the cash flow of the amusement park and rest home together ($24,000) is not equal to the cash flow of the amusement park alone ($12,000) plus the cash flow of the rest home alone ($50,000).

As a closing point, note that geographical separation between investments is not necessary to make the investments economically independent. For example, if placing a new roof on a firm's manufacturing plant does not affect the profitability of a decision to buy a new truck, then the roof and truck are independent. If the roof and truck were independent of all other investment options being considered, then the project evaluation procedure would involve evaluating the roof and truck separately. The roof would be built if, and only if, its net present value was positive, and the truck would be purchased if, and only if, its net present value was positive.

CAPITAL RATIONING

In certain cases, only limited funds may be available for investment and, at least in the short run, no additional capital may be obtainable from external sources. This might occur if the decision unit is not an entire firm but a division with a specific capital allocation for investment determined by the parent company. The problem is how the division manager should use the funds that are available. Capital constraints also characterize the situation confronted by government agencies which must allocate fixed appropriations among competing alternatives.[16]

16. If the reason that the firm cannot obtain capital at an acceptable rate (acceptable cost of capital) is that outsiders realistically view the firm's investment opportunities as unattractive, no capital rationing exists. This would simply be a case of a firm with investment opportunities that do not offer sufficient risk-return qualities to attract investors. Similarly, capital rationing does not exist just because credit is tight and funds in the economy are extremely expensive; the firm's resulting high cost of capital should nevertheless be used to evaluate current investments. If the company's investments do not provide a rate of return at least equal to this cost of capital (i.e., imply a positive NPV), they should be rejected since the firm can earn the cost of capital by simply investing (lending) its funds in the market. No investment that is inferior to such market opportunities should be accepted. On the other hand, capital rationing analysis would be appropriate if outsiders have an unrealistically pessimistic view of the firm's investment opportunities and consequently no external funds are available. The firm could use the normal rate of return in the economy on investments of the same risk class as the firm's (in the view of management) for evaluating investment proposals.

The present value approach to treating the capital constraint problem is to invest the funds that are available in that set of projects with the highest total net present value. That is, the goal is to maximize the net present value of the entire current investment.[17] For example, assume a fixed sum of $100,000 is available for an investment. Also, assume that the firm can invest in some combination of projects A through D. The data associated with each project are shown in Exhibit 7-9. Assume that A and B are mutually exclusive (cannot both be done), as would be so, for example, if A were a restaurant and B were a gas station on a given plot of land which only has room for one or the other. Also note that since we have only $100,000 to invest, we cannot do both C and D, nor can we do both A and D, because each combination involves an initial outlay of $110,000. Therefore, given the mutual exclusivity of A and B and the budget constraint of $100,000, the possible project combinations are A and C, B and C, and B and D. If B and C are done, there is $10,000 left over, since together they require only $90,000 of the $100,000 available. In Exhibit 7-10 the net present value of each feasible combination of projects is shown. The $60,000 net present value of the combination of A and C equals the net present value of A ($40,000) plus the net present value of C ($20,000), which were stated in Exhibit 7-9. The net present value of a

17. We are assuming in this discussion of capital rationing that the constraint on funds exists only in the current period and not in future periods. The same general concepts apply with multiperiod constraints, but the analysis is far more complex; an additional consideration that becomes important with multiperiod constraints is the rate at which funds can be reinvested by the firm in each period. For a proof of the validity of the method presented here, see Edwin Elton, "Capital Rationing and External Discount Rates," *Journal of Finance* (June 1970).

Exhibit 7-9. Net Present Values of the Firm's Investment Opportunities with Capital Rationing

Opportunity	Present value of future returns (1)	Initial outlay (2)	Net present value (col. 1 − col. 2) (3)
A	$90,000	$50,000	$40,000
B	50,000	40,000	10,000
C	70,000	50,000	20,000
D	65,000	60,000	5,000

Exhibit 7-10. Net Present Values of Alternative Firm Capital Outlays with Capital Rationing

Possible combinations of opportunities	Net present value of entire capital budget[a]
A and C	$60,000[b]
B and C	30,000[c]
B and D	15,000

[a] Computed by adding the net present values from Exhibit 7-9; for example, the net present value of A and C is $40,000 + $20,000, the sum of the net present values of A and C.

[b] A and C are the best combination.

[c] See text discussion and footnote 18 on why the unspent $10,000 is not added to the $30,000 in computing the net present value.

combination of B and C equals the sum of the net present values of B and C, and the net present value of the combination of projects B and D equals the sum of the net present values of B and D. Note that the $10,000 that is unspent if B and C are adopted has a *net* present value of zero since, if it is invested at the market rate, the benefits received will be worth $10,000, producing a net present value of zero.[18] Since the net present value of the combination of projects A and C is the greatest, as can be seen from Exhibit 7-10, this is the combination that should be selected.[19]

The above method for dealing with a capital constraint problem is valid, assuming that investors discount the returns from their investment. That is, if investors take into account the time value of money and discount streams in a fashion such as we described earlier, the method here is accurate. Thus, even if the firm or a division of the firm has a budget constraint, investors still want the cash flow generated by the investment to have the highest value possible. This value is determined by dis-

18. In order for an investment to have a positive NPV, the present value of the investment's future returns must exceed the investment's initial cost. The $10,000 invested at the going market rate of return will produce future benefits with a present value of $10,000, and therefore the investment has a zero *net* present value (i.e., a zero extraordinary return).

19. Dynamic programming can greatly facilitate the analysis of the combinations of investment opportunities. This problem is often referred to as the "knapsack problem"; see Harvey M. Wagner, *Principles of Operations Research,* 2d ed. (Englewood Cliffs, N.J.: Prentice-Hall, 1975).

counting the cash flow at the market interest rate appropriate to the riskiness of the cash flow.[20]

The above method is quite general and can be applied to investments even if they are interdependent (if they affect one another's cash flows or are mutually exclusive). However, if all the firm's investments are independent of one another (they do *not* affect one another's cash flows and are *not* mutually exclusive), then a simplification of the above procedure is possible. *The procedure is to rank the firm's investments by the ratio of the net present value per dollar of initial investment that they provide (NPV/I), and then select those investments with the highest NPV/I until the budget is exhausted.* NPV/I is referred to as the **profitability index.**[21] This procedure selects for adoption the combination of investments within the budget constraint which has the highest total net present value.

To illustrate, assume that the firm has up to $100,000 to invest and no more. Exhibit 7-11 indicates the firm's investment opportunities, their costs (I), NPVs, and profitability indices. The firm should invest its funds in projects A through F, a total outlay of $98,000. This leaves $2,000 ($100,000 budget limit minus $98,000 invested). The $2,000 is insufficient to accept either of the remaining opportunities with positive NPVs (G and H), and so the $2,000 can be held for future investment, be paid out in dividends, or be used to reduce company debt.

A problem may arise in using the above procedure which involves those investments that are just marginally acceptable (on the border between being accepted and rejected, for example, E, F, and G in Exhibit 7-11). The problem can arise if the projects that are accepted on the basis of highest profitability index do not fully exhaust the capital available. Thus, let the NPV of project G in Exhibit 7-11 equal $1,200 instead of $1,000; G's profitability index would become 0.24, still below the profitability index of project F. Using the above profitability index procedure, A through F would still be selected and G would be rejected. However, no-

20. For a complete discussion, see Elton, op. cit. Notice that the investments that make up the capital budget can differ in risk (for example, A, B, and C may be of different risk). As will be explained in Chap. 8, the cash flow from any combination of investments should be discounted at that rate appropriate to the riskiness of the total cash flow generated by that combination of investments. Thus, in the example, the cash flow from A and C might be discounted at 10 percent whereas the discount rate for the cash flow from B and C might be 12 percent. In this chapter we are assuming that all investments have the same risk and are therefore evaluated using the same cost of capital (discount rate).

21. The profitability index is also often defined as $(NPV + I)/I$ = (present value of benefits)/(initial outlay); this ratio is sometimes referred to as the benefit-cost ratio. Also, I is in some contexts defined as the present value of present and future capital outlays associated with the investment; for capital rationing in the current period, it is proper to define I as current capital outlays, as is done here. Multiperiod capital rationing is not examined here (see footnote 17).

Exhibit 7-11 Simplified Present Value Procedure for Capital Rationing

Project	Initial outlay (I)	NPV	Profitability index (NPV/I)
A	$50,000	$80,000	1.6
B	10,000	15,000	1.5
C	20,000	10,000	0.5
D	$98,000 { 15,000	6,000	0.4
E	2,000	800	0.4
F	1,000	300	0.3
G	5,000	1,000	0.2
H	3,000	300	0.1
I	4,000	0	0

tice that it would be more profitable (a higher total NPV for all projects combined) to select G and reject E and F since the NPV of G is now $1,100.[22] Therefore, the profitability index procedure is misleading in this case in selecting from among the marginal investments. The way to avoid an error of this type is simply to examine the investments close to the budget limit (the marginal investments) and make sure that an error is not being made.

It should be pointed out that it is infrequent that an inflexible budget constraint confronts a firm or even an operating division of a firm with subsidiaries. This is particularly true in the long run, that is, if sufficient time is available to inform sources of capital of the firm's profitable investment opportunities. A budget constraint means that only a limited quantity of capital is available *regardless of the profitability of the company's investments.* Such a limited capital situation can arise particularly for small businesses because of the inability of management to convince outside sources of capital of the attractiveness of the company's opportunities.[23] On the other hand, a large firm with profitable investments can usually either borrow additional funds or sell additional shares of stock to obtain the resources needed to make the investments. Of course, it will have to pay the going rates on the acquired funds, but this will be reflected

22. With E and F we have $2,000 left over. However, the *net* present value of any investment of that $2,000 will be zero; that is, the value of what is received on the investment of $2,000 will equal $2,000. Any investment outside the firm that earns just the normal rate of return has a zero *net* present value. All the investments with positive net present value should be included in the analysis of Exhibit 7-11 in determining the allocation of the $100,000.

23. See footnote 16.

in the cost of capital used to evaluate the investments. Similarly, if a division of a company has attractive projects, the division head can generally present his or her proposals to central management, which will allocate funds to the division if the investment proposals merit support.

INDUSTRY USE OF CAPITAL BUDGETING TECHNIQUES

Until the 1960s, only the largest firms in capital-intensive industries employed advanced capital budgeting tools (e.g., present value and internal rate of return). Other firms used simpler and less satisfactory techniques such as payback and accounting rate of return. Although the less accurate techniques are still widely employed, a majority of the largest 250 United States firms in terms of capital outlays use either the present value or internal rate of return for capital expenditure analysis. A survey by Klammer of large United States firms revealed that the use of the present value and IRR approaches has greatly increased since the 1950s.[24] By 1970, a significant majority of firms had at least one member of the company staff assigned to full-time capital budgeting. Not surprisingly, the companies using the more sophisticated capital budgeting methods were those with larger investment budgets, e.g., oil and chemical firms. The Klammer results, which are consistent with the findings of other surveys, demonstrate that companies will adopt improved methods of analysis if they produce earnings benefits. The benefits accrue because better choices are made in selecting projects and in determining the amount to be invested. There is a cost to employing superior techniques, however; since more information is required, computers may be needed to perform the analysis, and personnel with an understanding of these techniques must be found (and paid a salary commensurate with their talents). For these reasons, smaller as well as less capital-intensive firms have been slower to adopt the newer approaches. However, as the costs of obtaining information and employing computers decline, and as understanding of the approaches becomes more widespread, more firms will find it profitable to modernize their capital budgeting procedures.

EXAMPLE PROBLEMS
Asset Addition: Asset Reduces Costs

Assume that Streak Wholesalers is considering the acquisition of a delivery truck which will allow Streak to do its own shipping rather than purchase shipping services from another firm. The new asset, a truck, is not a substitute for an old one already in operation and is therefore defined here as an asset addition (rather than replacement) problem. Suppose that the

24. See Thomas Klammer, "Empirical Evidence of the Adoption of Sophisticated Capital Budgeting Techniques," *Journal of Business* (July 1972).

benefits from the truck would be a reduction in shipping costs. By reducing costs, the net cash flow of the firm as a whole is increased. The estimates of the costs and benefits associated with this investment decision
are shown in Exhibit 7-12. Notice that although the truck reduces annual
shipping costs by $15,000, additional expenses for a driver and for upkeep
of the truck are also taken into account. These expenses are $13,000 per
year, and therefore the return from acquiring the truck before taxes is
$2,000 per year. Taxes are then deducted in order to determine the af-
tertax benefit from making the new investment. Since the truck is a depre-

---

Exhibit 7-12. Asset Addition: Asset Reduces Costs

Truck purchase price: $7,200 (Truck will last 8 years with an $800 salvage value)

Returns per period for 8 years:

Reduction in shipping expenses		$15,000
Deduct: Salary for driver	$9,000	
Upkeep, gas, etc.	4,000	
Return before taxes		
($15,000 − $9,000 − $4,000)		$2,000

Taxes:

Pretax return		$ 2,000
Deduct: depreciation on truck[a]		800
Net taxable income		$ 1,200
Tax at 50% (0.50 × $1,200)		600
Increase in annual net cash flow ($2,000 − $600)		$1,400

Time	Cash flow
0 (cost)	−$7,200
1–7 (returns per year)	1,400
8 (return)	2,200[b]

Net present value at 10% (cost of capital):

$$\text{NPV} = \$1,400 \ (P/A, \ 10\%, \ 7) + \$2,200 \ (P/F, \ 10\%, \ 8) - \$7,200$$
$$= \$1,400 \ (4.868) + \$2,200 \ (0.4665) - \$7,200$$
$$= \$642$$

---

[a] Depreciation on a straight-line basis equals ($7,200 cost − $800 salvage value)/8 years = $800 per year.
[b] Aftertax cash flow from use + salvage value = $1,400 + $800 = $2,200.

ciable asset for tax purposes, depreciation must be deducted from the increased returns due to the truck in order to determine the part of the returns that is taxable; in the example, this taxable return is $1,200. Applying a tax rate of 50 percent and subtracting the resulting taxes of $600 produces a net cash return from the asset of $1,400 per year. As shown in Exhibit 7-12, the net present value of the project is $642 and therefore the project should be accepted. The truck would be a good investment.

Asset Addition: Asset Increases Sales

In the above example, it was assumed that the firm's sales were unaffected by the acquisition of the delivery truck. The benefits from the truck were a reduction in operating expenses. It is also possible that a new investment has an impact on the firm's sales as well as upon operating costs. For example, assume that a new machine, if purchased, will enable the firm to increase annual sales by $6,000, increase cost of goods sold by $2,500, and increase operating expenses by $500, producing a new rise in the firm's pretax cash flow of $3,000 annually ($6,000 − $2,500 − $500). Let the new machine cost $6,000 and have a five-year life with no salvage value. Using the same method as before, it is shown in Exhibit 7-13 that the change in aftertax cash flow is $2,100 per year. The net present value of the machine is $1,961, and it should therefore be purchased.

Replacement of an Existing Asset

Firms frequently consider the possibility of replacing assets currently in operation. Even if the old asset is economically productive, the new asset may be sufficiently more productive to warrant the replacement. In determining whether to replace, the crucial question is whether the added initial expenditure for the new asset (less salvage value of the old asset) is justified by the net aftertax increase in the firm's cash flow (aftertax cash flow from new asset minus aftertax cash flow from the asset being replaced). That is, are the incremental aftertax cash flow benefits from the changeover sufficient to warrant the initial investment required by the replacement?[25] An example will clarify the approach.

A new machine costing $29,000 can be acquired to replace a machine

25. The example presented below makes the simplifying assumption that the remaining life of the old asset currently being used by the firm equals the life of a new asset being considered as a replacement. This assumption, although unrealistic, allows us to present the basic approach to replacement problems. This approach is appropriate even when the lives of the old and new assets differ. However, if the remaining life of the old asset does not equal the life of the new asset, then we have to consider future replacements and we encounter the problems described earlier in comparing investments with unequal lives. This complicates the analysis but does not alter the basic method for computing or analyzing the cash flows.

Exhibit 7-13. Asset Addition: Asset Increases Sales

Machine purchase price: $6,000 (Machine will last 5 years with no salvage value)

Returns per period for 5 years:

Increase in sales	$6,000	
Deduct: Increases in cost of goods sold		
($2,500) and operating expenses ($500)	3,000	
Return before taxes ($6,000 – $3,000)		$3,000

Taxes:

Pretax return	$3,000	
Deduct: depreciation on machine[a]	1,200	
Net taxable income	$1,800	
Tax at 50% (0.50 × $1,800)		900
Increase in annual net cash flow ($3,000 – $900)		$2,100

Time	Cash flow
0 (cost)	–$6,000
1–5 (returns per year)	$2,100

Net present value at 10% (*cost of capital*):

$$\text{NPV} = \$2,100 \ (P/A, \ 10\%, \ 5) - \$6,000$$
$$= \$2,100 \ (3.791) - \$6,000$$
$$= \$1,961$$

[a] The machine has no salvage value, and therefore annual depreciation equals (machine's cost)/(machine's useful life) = $6,000/5 years = $1,200 per year.

presently in use ("old" machine); the old machine has a current salvage value of $3,000. Therefore, the net outlay required to acquire the new machine is $26,000, the amount to be paid for the new machine less the amount received for the old machine. The old machine could be maintained in service for six years and the new machine has a life of six years. The year 6 salvage value of the old machine will be zero and the year 6 salvage value of the new machine will be $5,000. As shown in Exhibit 7-14, the new machine will increase output and thereby raise sales by $1,500, will reduce nondepreciation production expenses by $7,000, and will consequently raise pretax net returns (sales − nondepreciation expenses) by $8,500. The $7,000 expense reduction equals the cost savings due to more

Exhibit 7-14. Replacement Problem

1. *Initial outlay:*

Price of new machine	$29,000
Salvage value of old machine	3,000
Net outlay for new machine	$26,000

2. *Firm's annual cash flow for the next six years (years 1 to 6) with old and new machine excluding year 6 salvage value of new machine*

Cash flow variable	With old machine (a)	With new machine (b)	Change due to new machine (col. b − col. a)
1. Sales	$100,000	$101,500	$1,500
2. Nondepreciation expenses	57,000	50,000	− 7,000
3. Sales − nondepreciation expenses [(1) − (2)]	43,000	51,500	8,500
4. Depreciation[a]	10,500	14,000	3,500
5. Taxable income [(3) − (4)]	32,500	37,500	5,000
6. Taxes [0.5 × (5)]	16,250	18,750	2,500
7. Net cash flow [(3) − (6)]	26,750	32,750	6,000

3. *Year 6 salvage value:*

Year 6 salvage value of new machine	$5,000
Year 6 salvage value of old machine	0
Added year 6 salvage value cash flow with new machine	$5,000

Time	Additional cash flow due to new machine
0 (cost)	−$26,000
1–5 (annual return)	6,000
6 (return)	11,000[b]

Net present value of replacement (at 10% cost of capital):

$$\text{NPV (replacement)} = \$6,000 \ (P/A, \ 10\%, \ 5)$$
$$+ \ \$11,000 \ (P/F, \ 10\%, \ 6) - \$26,000$$
$$= \$6,000 \ (3.791) + \$11,000 \ (0.5645)$$
$$- \$26,000 = \$2,956$$

[a] Depreciation on old machine = $500 per year; depreciation on new machine = $4,000 per year [($29,000 cost − $5,000 salvage value)/6-year life]; firm's depreciation on all *other* assets = $10,000 per year.

[b] $11,000 in year 6 = $6,000 per year from asset's use + $5,000 salvage value.

efficient production with the new machine less any increased expenses involved in producing the additional units sold. The firm's aftertax cash flow increases by $6,000 per year for the six years due to use of the new machine. In year 6, there is an added cash flow of $5,000 due to salvage of the new machine; the total cash flow increase in the sixth year due to the new machine is therefore $11,000 ($6,000 + $5,000).

As shown in Exhibit 7-14, the additional cash flows due to the replacement are an added outlay of $26,000 initially, an increase of $6,000 per year for the next five years, and an increase of $11,000 in the sixth year. The cash flow has a net present value of $2,956, and therefore the replacement should be made.

SUMMARY

The enormous cost of new capital equipment purchased each year by United States industry has motivated firms to carefully budget capital expenditures. Most firms prepare short-run budgets, and many companies plan capital outlays for the next three to five years. These budgets are estimates and are often revised as new information becomes available.

The additional aftertax cash flow generated by an investment is the relevant measure of the investment's productivity to the firm. The cash flow can then be evaluated using a capital budgeting technique such as present value, internal rate of return, payback, or benefit-cost. Using present value, a project should be accepted only if its net present value is positive. In comparing mutually exclusive investment alternatives (alternatives only one of which can be accepted), that with the highest net present value is the most profitable and should be adopted provided that its net present value is positive.

The internal rate of return (IRR) method specifies that only investments with an IRR greater than the cost of capital should be accepted. In comparing mutually exclusive options, the incremental method should be used. This method determines whether the additional cash flows of one alternative relative to another justify the former's acceptance. The IRR approach is often more cumbersome to use than is present value and in some cases is not applicable because of analytical problems. Present value is therefore recommended as the preferred evaluation technique.

The payback period method dictates acceptance of projects only if they return the cost of the investment within a specified period of time (the payback period). This method ignores the time value of money and does not take into account cash flows after the payback period. The accounting rate of return method requires that the investment with the highest accounting rate of return be adopted if the rate exceeds a specified level. As with payback, this method ignores the time value of money. Payback period and accounting rate of return are distinctly inferior to net present value and internal rate of return as capital budgeting criteria.

If investments being compared are not of the same life, then a completely correct analysis usually requires that future investments be taken into account. In many situations this is not necessary, however, and the net present values of the investments can be directly compared in the usual manner, or the incremental IRR method can be applied.

The investment tax credit allows a tax rebate when a new asset is acquired. For capital budgeting purposes, the tax rebate should be viewed as a reduction in the initial cost of the asset.

In the presence of inflation, the firm should still use the actual cash flows that are anticipated in computing NPV. Furthermore, the discount rate that is appropriate is, as in the case of no inflation, that rate used by investors to discount cash flows with a similar risk to the one being analyzed. This approach is valid, since the cash flow and the discount rate will both take the inflation into account and the investment's NPV will be its net benefit to the stockholders in terms of current dollars.

Investment opportunities may affect one another's cash flows if both are adopted, for example, a gas station and a restaurant next door to one another. In this case, the cash flows and net present values from undertaking each project alone and from undertaking them together must be computed. That combination of opportunities (an opportunity taken alone or with one or more of the interrelated opportunities) which produces the highest NPV is best and should be adopted if its NPV is positive.

A capital rationing problem exists if the firm does not have and cannot obtain (through borrowing or selling new shares) sufficient funds to adopt all projects with a positive NPV. In this case, the firm should adopt that set of investments not exceeding its budget constraint which has the highest total NPV. Under certain conditions, a shortcut analytic approach is applicable which specifies that the firm should adopt those investments with the highest profitability indices. A budget constraint generally does not exist for large firms. Such a constraint is ordinarily a short-run problem which may occur for small firms or for corporate divisions.

The use of sophisticated capital budgeting techniques has been primarily limited to large, capital-intensive firms. However, present value and IRR are rapidly gaining in acceptance and may eventually replace payback, accounting rate of return, and other less accurate methods.

QUESTIONS

1. What information is required to determine the cash flow from an investment opportunity?
2. Why do we use cash flow in evaluating an investment?
3. Depreciation is a noncash expense. Why, then, is it necessary to compute depreciation in order to perform a proper cash flow analysis?
4. What is an intuitive explanation of what an internal rate of return shows?

5. What are the advantages and disadvantages of the net present value method relative to the internal rate of return method?

6. The TOPCOA Industrial Corporation has been using the payback evaluation technique for a number of years. Recently, you have been hired by the firm as a financial analyst. Prepare a convincing memo to the vice-president for finance explaining your rationale for using another technique of investment evaluation. In your memo you want to be objective. Are there any situations in which the payback period method can be useful in capital budgeting analysis?

7. A recent graduate of the Wellduke Business School commented: "Capital budgeting is simple; just divide the investment's net income after taxes by the amount of the investment and compare this to the cost of financing the investment. If the return on investment is greater than the cost of financing, accept the investment." Comment critically.

8. Define the terms "cost of capital," "discount rate," and "minimum acceptable rate of return" and explain why they are equal to one another in project evaluation.

9. Strictly speaking, all activities of a firm are interdependent; that is, they affect one another's cash flows. Therefore any new investment in some way—directly or indirectly—affects the cash flows of every other investment the firm adopts. Since this is so, how can we justify ever evaluating a new investment by itself, i.e., without considering how it affects the cash flows of every other investment we are considering? What are the advantages and disadvantages of ignoring interdependencies?

10. Early in the chapter it was noted that intermediate- and long-term capital budgets are revised periodically. As a part of such a revision process, suppose a firm is reviewing the progress of a specific venture that has been in operation for five years. Outline the considerations that are relevant in performing the review process.

11. Assume that the federal government is considering the following four new policies to stimulate investment by private firms:

   a) Raise the investment tax credit on new assets from 7 percent to 12 percent.

   b) Allow firms to deduct 5 percent of the cost of new assets from their taxable income in the year the asset is acquired.

   c) Pay firms a cash subsidy of 5 percent of the cost of new assets in the year the asset is acquired.

   d) Allow firms to increase depreciation above what is currently allowed in the year an asset is acquired by 5 percent of the cost of the asset and to reduce future years' depreciation on the asset by 5 percent of the asset's cost; that is, to allow firms to accelerate depreciation by raising the current depreciation deduction by 5 percent of the asset's cost with an equal reduction in future depreciation.

Carefully compare these four policies in terms of the probable relative impact of each on a firm's level of investment.

Refer to library sources (e.g., the *Federal Reserve Bulletin*, the *Economic Report of the President*, the *Survey of Current Business*, etc.) and examine the past annual levels of investment, national income, federal income taxes, profits, and dividends in the United States. Try to find breakdowns of investment by industry or by sector of the economy. Also investigate forecasts of investment by industry, by sector, and for the entire United States economy.

PROJECT

1. The Rocky Mountain Glass Works has annual cash revenues of $400,000, annual cash expenses of $200,000, and annual depreciation of $60,000. These figures are expected to remain the same permanently, assuming that Rocky Mountain continues to have an outside firm do its packaging. If a packaging installation is purchased at a cost of $100,000, Rocky Mountain will be able to reduce delivery time to customers, and this will result in new business from customers who demand rapid delivery. The packaging system has a life of twenty years, with no salvage value, and will be depreciated on a straight-line basis. The new investment will increase the firm's annual cash revenues to $500,000, cash expenses to $260,000, and depreciation to $65,000; these increases will occur for the twenty-year life of the packaging installation. After the twenty years, the firm's cash flow will return to what it would be without the packaging system unless another system is then purchased. The firm's tax rate is 50 percent, both with and without the packaging system.

   PROBLEMS

   a) Set up a cash flow analysis table for this problem like Exhibit 7-1 in the text to determine the cash flow from the packaging system.

   b) Assuming that the appropriate discount rate on the investment is 10 percent, use net present value to determine whether the investment should be made. [Ans.: NPV = $91,565]

2. Crane Cork Corporation has just obtained a new cork cutter for $12,000. The future cash flow and profit generated by the cork cutter are:

Year	Cash flow	Profit
1	$6,000	$2,000
2	6,000	2,000
3	6,000	2,000

Compute the following for the cork cutter:

a) Internal rate of return [Ans.: IRR = 23 percent]

b) Net present value using a cost of capital of 12 percent [Ans.: $2,412]

c) Payback period [Ans.: two years]

d) Accounting rate of return [Ans.: $16\frac{2}{3}$ percent]

3. If the cash flow from the cork cutter in 2 could be kept fully invested until the end of year 3 at a rate of return of 20 percent per year, how much would the cork cutter cash flow accumulate to in year 3? [Ans.: $21,840]

4. Ben Endicott speculates in real estate and can buy a particular plot of vacant land for $50,000. He expects to be able to sell the land in one year for $60,000 (net of taxes). The land has no other cash flows. Ben's cost of capital is 15 percent. Determine whether Ben Endicott should purchase the land using both the net present value method and the IRR method.

5. Assume that the plot of land described in 4 will give Ben Endicott a return of $60,000 in *two* years. Using the information in 4, determine whether Ben should purchase the land using both the net present method and the IRR method.

6. Finsterwald Department Store can build a new sign for $13,500 which will increase its expected net cash flow by $2,000 per year (beginning one year hence) for the next twenty years by attracting additional customers. The sign has a zero expected salvage value. Finsterwald's cost of capital is 12 percent. Compute the sign's:

a) NPV

b) IRR

c) Payback period

7. Dimples Baby Products is deciding whether it should buy a new vegetable masher for manufacturing its product "Vegey Goo," a smooth, creamy, vegetable pablum for infants. The masher will cost $30,000 and will increase the firm's cash flow by $5,000 per year for the next fifteen years (assume that the first $5,000 occurs one year hence). At the end of the fifteen years it it expected that the masher can be sold for $4,000 (this is net of taxes). What is the masher's:

a) NPV using a cost of capital of 10 percent?

b) IRR?

c) Payback period?

8. Starbright Laundries is considering the purchase of new wash and dry equipment in order to expand its operations. Two types of options are available: a low-speed system with a $14,000 initial cost and a high-speed system with a $23,000 initial cost. Each system has a twenty-year life and no salvage value. The net cash flows associated with each investment are:

	Low-speed system	High-speed system
Initial cost	$14,000	$23,000
Annual cash flow for years 1 through 20	2,000	3,100

a) Analyze the above problem using the NPV method. Perform the analysis for each of the following costs of capital:
   1. 10 percent [Ans.: NPV (low-speed system) = $3,028; NPV (high-speed system) = $3,393]
   2. 12 percent
   3. 15 percent
   Compare your results for the three cases.
b) Analyze the problem using the IRR method, using each of the above costs of capital (10 percent, 12 percent, and 15 percent).

9. Hank Sykes and his wife, Hyacinth, have long dreamed of owning their own business. A recent inheritance has made realizing this dream possible. Cranberry farming has a particular attraction for the Sykes because Hank's family has for generations been in farming and both Hank and Hyacinth have very strong hands and arms (which will help in working the cranberry bog). The Sykes can acquire forty acres of cranberry bog land for $5,000 per acre. In addition to the bog land cost, a capital investment of $30,000 will be necessary to set up operations. The $30,000 in capital assets will be depreciated on a straight-line basis over fifteen years with zero salvage value. (Assume also a zero market value of the capital assets at the end of the fifteen years.) Each acre of land is expected to yield 150 barrels of cranberries per year, and berry prices are anticipated to remain at $15 per barrel indefinitely. Cash expenses will be 30 percent of the gross receipts from selling the cranberries. In addition, the Sykes will pay themselves total annual salaries of $25,000 ($12,500 each), which is what they would have to pay two other people to perform the work of operating the cranberry farm and exactly what the Sykes can earn in alternative employment. This $25,000 in salaries to the Sykes is to be deducted in computing company cash flow. The Sykes plan to sell the bog land in fifteen years, and they expect the land to increase in value at the rate of 3 percent per year over that time period. The tax rate applicable to all company income except the gain from selling the bog land is 30 percent; the tax rate on the gain from selling the bog is 15 percent. The appropriate discount rate on the firm's cash flows is 10 percent. Answer the following:

a) Why must the salaries of Hank and Hyacinth be included among company expenses in computing the firm's cash flow? Would the $25,000 in salaries have to be deducted as an expense if the Sykes decide not to pay themselves a salary?

b) Compute each year's net cash flow from the investment in the cranberry business.

c) Should Hank and Hyacinth invest in the cranberry bog?

10. The E. Z. Mann Electronics Company is considering a $12,000 outlay for a plant sound system designed to produce a more congenial working environment for those who work on a fairly tedious assembly line. Psychological experts are predicting such a system would increase work efficiency, which means it will reduce costs. In fact, over the fifteen-year life of the system, cost reductions are forecast at 2 percent of the current $240,000 per year to operate this line. The annual revenue of $1,260,000 and the other nondepreciation expenses of $900,000 will remain unaffected. The sound system will be depreciated to zero on a straight-line basis and will be added to a current depreciation allowance of $30,000 per year on existing plant and equipment. The firm's tax rate is 50 percent; however, a 5 percent tax credit is available on this investment. The cost of capital is 10 percent.

a) Set up a cash flow analysis table like Exhibit 7-1 for this problem.

b) Compute the net present value, internal rate of return, payback period, and accounting rate of return for this project. Should the project be adopted? [Partial ans.: NPV = $9,897]

11. Consider a variation in the opportunities described in 10. Because of increased efficiency E. Z. Mann can reduce the price of its product from $42 to $41. As a consequence of the price reduction, the number of units produced and sold will rise 5 percent from 30,000 to 31,500 units. Because of the increased efficiency on the assembly line, assembly costs will remain at $240,000. However, other nondepreciation expenses will increase from $900,000 to $927,000. Except for these variations, the figures of 10 still apply. Repeat parts a and b of 10. Should E. Z. Mann acquire the sound system but retain its old price ($42) and output level as in 10, or acquire the sound system and cut its price (to $41) and increase output as above, or not acquire the sound system and simply retain its old price ($42) and output?

12. Consider the following three projects, each of which has an investment cost of $90 and a life of three years.

	Net cash flow		
Year	A	B	C
1	$60	$20	$30
2	40	45	20
3	20	60	80

a) Which project is called for by the payback method?

b) Compute NPV for each project at discount rates of 0 percent, 5 percent, 10 percent, 15 percent, 20 percent, 30 percent, and plot the results (with NPV on the vertical axis). Which investment is superior for each of these discount rates?

c) Find the IRR of each project.

d) Note that IRR corresponds to the rate where the curve crosses the horizontal axis. From your plot, make some inference as to why two projects cannot be compared by comparing IRR.

13. Vertigo Optical Company is considering the replacement of a buffing machine. The existing machine is in good operating condition but is smaller than required if Vertigo is to expand its operations. The old machine has a current salvage value of $6,000, and a current book value of $5,000; the depreciation is at $500 per year (straight line) for tax purposes. The old machine will have a zero salvage value in ten years. The new machine will cost $25,000 and will be depreciated on a straight-line basis over ten years to a salvage value of $5,000. (Assume that $5,000 is also the expected market value if the machine is sold in ten years.) Vertigo expects that it will sell the old machine in ten years if it does not buy the new machine, and if it does buy the new machine it will retire the new machine in ten years and replace it with a more modern buffer. The new machine will allow Vertigo to expand current operations and thereby increase annual sales from $200,000 to $215,000, annual nondepreciation expenses from $120,000 to $130,000, and annual depreciation from $50,000 to $51,500. Vertigo's tax rate is 40 percent, and its cost of capital is 12 percent. Should Vertigo replace its existing buffer with the new buffer? Use an analysis similar to that shown in Exhibit 7-14. [Ans.: NPV (replacement) = $2,949; therefore Vertigo should replace the old machine with the new machine]

14. Milo Casing does a specialty retail business in chimes. He now has the opportunity to improve his business location by purchasing a double storefront in the heart of the business district. The purchase price is $120,000 (land $80,000 and building $40,000), and an additional $10,000 outlay will be necessary to remodel his store. The depreciation base for tax purposes is $50,000 ($40,000 for building plus $10,000 remodeling outlay), and the depreciation will be on a straight-

line basis over twenty-five years; that is, depreciation will be $2,000 per year. Milo plans to utilize only half of the available space for himself and will lease out, on a twenty-five-year lease, the other half of the space at a contracted rent of $4,000 per year. At the end of twenty-five years, the entire structure will be removed. (Assume that removal costs are negligible and can be ignored.) The value of the land at the end of the twenty-five years will be the same as it is now, $80,000.

Milo is at the end of the eighth year of a ten-year lease at his present location, but he can get out of the lease by paying a $1,000 penalty (tax deductible). His tax-deductible lease payments are $2,000 per year. At the end of the ten-year lease Milo can get a renewal for an additional twenty-five years at current terms ($2,000 per year).

Milo's annual revenues are $136,000, and his purchases are $70,000. These items will remain unchanged if he stays at his present location, but if he moves they will increase by 50 percent. His overhead and fixed expenses (including the lease payments of $2,000 and $200 depreciation of office furniture) are $6,000 and will also remain unchanged if he does not move. If he does move, these items will sum to $5,000 (and of course the rent portion will be zero). Assuming that Milo is in a 50 percent tax bracket and has a 10 percent cost of capital for discounting cash flows, and that the investment tax credit is not applicable, should Milo move to the new location?

15. Solve **14** but assume that the value of the land is increasing at 5 percent per year over the twenty-five-year holding period and that the new property will be sold by Milo at the end of the twenty-five years. Also assume a 25 percent tax rate on the gain from selling the property (since the building is completely depreciated at the end of the twenty-five years, the gain = property net sale price − $80,000, where $80,000 is the original price of the land). Assume no real estate brokerage costs in selling the property.

16. Louie DeFore Decorators needs a delivery truck and is evaluating the following two choices:

Choice A Buy a used Ford truck for $4,000. After four years sell the truck for $500 (net of taxes) and replace it with another used Ford truck which is expected to cost $6,000 and last six years with no salvage value.

Choice B Buy a new Chevrolet truck for $8,000. The Chevrolet will last for ten years and have an expected salvage value (net of taxes) of $1,000 at the end of the ten years.

The services provided by the Ford trucks and the Chevrolet truck are the same. Furthermore, it is clear that choice A and choice B have a positive NPV; the problem is to choose the better of the two alternatives.

If Louie DeFore Decorators has a 12 percent cost of capital, is choice A or choice B preferable? (Partial ans.: NPV (choice A) = $7,495)

17. Blain Corporation manufactures chemical products and is evaluating two new processes for producing a particular compound. Demand for the compound will be small during the next five years and will then increase. Process A requires equipment which is appropriate for small output levels; A will be replaced in five years with process B which will utilize equipment with an eighteen-year life. B is capable of meeting large output requirements. The alternative to using processes A and B is to install currently (time 0) process C, which employs equipment with an estimated life of twenty years. The costs of A, B and C are as shown in the table.

Time of outlay	Expected capital outlay for the process		
	A	B	C
Now (time 0)	$1 million		$2 million
Five years hence		$3.5 million	

The future annual net cash flows from each process are:

Time of cash flow (years)	Annual cash flow		
	A	B	C
1–5	$300,000		$250,000
6–20		$500,000	450,000
21–23		500,000	

The cost of capital is 12 percent. Answer the following:
a) Should the firm adopt A and B or adopt C? Justify your approach. (What about the three-year time discrepancy between the A-B combination and C?)
b) If the life of process C were only fifteen years instead of twenty years, would your approach to the problem be different? Explain.

18. A machine has an expected eight-year life and costs $20,000. The annual expected net cash flow from the machine is $5,000 for the first seven years and $9,000 in the eighth year. The asset will be depreciated on a straight-line basis over the eight-year life assuming a $4,000 salvage value. It is eligible for the 7 percent investment tax credit.
a) What will the firm charge off as depreciation expense on the machine each year?

b) If the cost of capital is 10 percent on the machine, what is the machine's NPV?

19. A particular home was worth $50,000 on January 1. The increase in the general level of prices (inflation) was 5 percent during the year from January 1 to December 31.

    a) If the real value of the house (value in terms of purchasing power) was the same on December 31 as on January 1, what was the dollar value of the house on December 31? [Ans.: $52,500]

    b) If the real value of the house was 4 percent greater on December 31 than it was on January 1, what was the dollar value of the house on December 31? [Ans.: $54,600]

20. Pinto Realty has just purchased a plot of vacant land for $100,000. The net cash flow from the property during the next four years will be zero. The best use of the land is simply to let it remain vacant for at least the next four years.

    a) If the property increases in value by 10 percent per year during the next four years, what is its value in four years? What pretax annual rate of return has Pinto Realty earned on the property during the four years?

    b) If after four years the property has increased in value by 10 percent per year during the past four years, is Pinto concerned about the inflation rate that has occurred during the four-year period? Why?

    c) Assume that, foreseeing no inflation, investors expect the property to increase in value at 10 percent per year over the next four years. If, on the other hand, investors were to expect an inflation rate of 5 percent per year, what value do you think they would expect the property to have in four years (assume as before that the current market value of the property is $100,000)? [Ans.: $177,960]

21. The Rainbow Paint and Dye Company wants to know whether to go ahead and market a promising new product, Formula Z paper dye. The firm is calculating on only a five-year basis because Formula Z will be phased out and replaced by a still more advanced dye process after five years. The table below indicates relevant projected cost

	1978	1979	1980	1981	1982
Revenues	$170,000	$230,000	$335,000	$290,000	$268,000
Depreciation expenses	20,000	20,000	20,000	20,000	20,000
Selling expenses	40,000	30,000	15,000	10,000	5,000
Production costs	107,000	138,000	202,000	174,000	161,000

and revenue data for each of the ensuing five years stated in *beginning of 1978 prices*.

Assume that the above flows occur at the *end* of the year (end of 1978, end of 1979, etc.). All of the above projections are at beginning of 1978 prices, i.e., they assume there will be no inflation after 1977. But in fact substantial inflation is expected. The projected inflation rate is 6 percent per year over the five-year period, and this rate is expected to apply uniformly to all prices (except depreciation). The 6 percent rate is the best estimate of top economists and is the forecast generally accepted by the public. All the cash flow items shown above (but not depreciation) are actually expected to be greater in proportion to the inflation rate; that is, the dollar amounts will be equal to those stated above in terms of purchasing power. Therefore, to compute the expected *dollar* cash flows, the data in the table (except depreciation) must be inflated by an inflation factor; for example, by (1.06) for the end of 1978 cash flows, by $(1.06)^2$ for the end of 1979 cash flows, etc.

The investment needed to initiate the Formula Z project is $180,000 at the *beginning* of 1978. At the end of 1982 all assets associated with the Formula Z project will be sold for $80,000 (in *beginning* 1978 prices). The firm's tax rate is 50 percent, and this tax rate is applicable to all net income and to any dollar gain on selling the assets at the end of 1982 (there is a gain if the asset is sold for a price that exceeds its end-of-1982 book value.) If the firm's current cost of capital is 16 percent, is this project worthwhile? In solving the problem keep in mind that actual dollar amounts should be used, *not* amounts stated in beginning of 1978 dollars.

22. Ready Chef Restaurants is considering three methods of stimulating business: a blitz advertising campaign (A), replacement of existing signs with new signs for all its restaurants (B), and the introduction of a delivery service which will require the purchase of a fleet of delivery trucks (C). The initial outlays for each alternative are:

Investment	Initial outlay
A Advertising campaign	$200,000
B Signs	300,000
C Delivery system	300,000

If A is done but B is not, A has an NPV (present value of added future cash flows less the $200,000 initial outlay) of $250,000. If B is done but A is not, B has an NPV of $90,000. The advertising draws customer attention to the signs. The NPV of doing both A and B is $400,000. The NPV of the delivery system, C, is $180,000. Its NPV is not dependent on whether A or B is adopted, and the NPV of A or B does not depend on whether C is adopted. Assuming that the firm has no budget constraint (can obtain funds at the cost of capital to finance any investment with a positive NPV), which of investments A, B, and C should Ready Chef adopt? [Ans.: Adopt A, B, and C]

23. Solve **22** assuming that the firm can invest only up to $500,000; that is, the firm has a $500,000 capital constraint. [Ans.: Adopt A and C]

24. The Impressive Paper Products Company currently manufactures paper napkins, towels, tissues, and bags. The company has been considering expanding its successful business. It is evaluating three options:

A Expand its paper bag line.

B Produce custom ordered and printed bags.

C Expand into a line of paper party accessories.

The returns from A, B, and C are as follows:

A The expansion of the paper bag line will require an initial investment in machinery of $100,000 and an additional initial outlay of $25,000 for plant improvements. The present value of the future cash flows generated by A is $210,000.

B Custom ordered and printed bags would call for a relatively small current investment of $30,000 for the purchase and installation of a printing press. The present value of the future cash flows from B is $80,000.

C To expand into a party accessories line will require a printing press somewhat more sophisticated than that needed for B. Also, new cutting and fabricating machinery will be needed. The required initial outlay is $200,000. The present value of the future cash flows from C is $330,000 assuming that A and B are not done.

If A and B (but not C) are both done, a more efficient higher capacity bag line will be justified. The total outlay for A and B together will be $190,000, but because of increased efficiency and lower operating costs the present value of the future cash flows generated by A and B together is $350,000.

If B and C (but not A) are done, the printing press used in the party accessories line will also be available for the custom printing of bags. This option would therefore eliminate all but $5,000 of the initial investment required for B. The initial outlay for B and C together is therefore $205,000. There are no other interdependencies between B and C.

If A and C (but not B) are done, there will be no interdependencies. The party accessory line will not compete with the bags for sales, and the production operations will be separate. The initial outlay for A and C together is therefore $325,000, and the present value of the future cash flows from A and C is $540,000.

If A, B, and C are all done, the advantages noted above from doing both A and B and from doing both B and C will still be available. However, the adoption of all three projects will require added plant space requiring an additional plant expansion cost of $120,000. If A, B, and C are done, the initial outlay will be $485,000, and the present value of future cash flows from A, B, and C will be $680,000.

Which options should Impressive Paper Products adopt?

25. The Panhandle Pot and Pan Corporation is considering a number of plant improvement investments and has allocated $315,000 to do the job. Under consideration are the following projects. Assume that the net annual cash inflows are all perpetuities.

Project	Outlay	Net annual inflows
A. Computerize stamping and assembly	$300,000	$36,000
B. Revamp assembly line	100,000	12,000
C. Increase warehouse space	100,000	8,500
D. Carpet executive suite	20,000	20,000 (better decisions)
E. Expand shipping dock	30,000	4,000

Not all these projects can be considered independently of one another. The following information may help clarify some of the relationships:

A and B are alternative (mutually exclusive) proposals for the same assembly line. The shipping dock expansion would take up the space which would be allocated for the stamping machine, and vice-versa.

If A is done, then the option of expanding the shipping dock (E) would cost only $10,000 because it could be done conveniently by the contractors on A.

If B is done, then $5,000 can be saved on the installation of the shipping dock (E). Also, under these circumstances there would be an increase in shipping efficiency, so that the shipping dock expansion would be worth $5,000 per year instead of $4,000.

All other combinations are mutually independent (do not affect one another's cash flows). The cost of capital is 10 percent. Which projects should be adopted?

26. The Omniburger Corporation, working against a self-imposed capital budgeting constraint of $350,000, is trying to decide which of a variety of new locations to open as a new outlet. The locations are such that

there is no market overlap between any two of them, and no combinations offer any extra economies over operating each location separately. The list of possible locations is presented below, along with the investments required and the net present value of the projected cash flows.

Location	Investment	NPV
12th Street	$ 50,000	$ 40,000
Wicker Way	120,000	90,000
Bonzo Island	160,000	100,000
College Place	110,000	150,000
Wattalia Avenue	90,000	100,000

How should Omniburger spend its $350,000?

27. Backrock Pillow Company has $1 million available for current investment. It has evaluated its options and has found that only four investments—A, B, C, and D—have positive net present values. A, B, C, and D are entirely independent of one another (the adoption of one investment does not affect the initial cost or future cash flows from any of the others). The data for these investments are:

Investment	Initial outlay	Present value of future cash flows from the investment
A	$400,000	$500,000
B	300,000	500,000
C	350,000	570,000
D	300,000	600,000

Which investments should the firm adopt?

28. Solve 27 but assume that A has a present value of future cash flows equal to $620,000 instead of $500,000.

29. The Heavenly Hills Shopping Center Association is an incorporated entity comprising the merchants in the center. As a corporation, the center has accumulated $275,000 in cash. The $275,000 is the maximum amount Heavenly Hills has available for investment. The center would like to begin a development on an adjacent vacant plot of land which it can buy for $120,000. On this land it can do one or more of the following.
A. Build a three-tier parking structure.
B. Build an ice-skating rink to be operated by the corporation.
C. Build and operate a movie theater.
D. Erect a fabulous sign advertising the shopping center.

The parking structure will cost $80,000 to build (in addition to the acquisition of the land for $120,000), and, by providing added customer convenience, is expected to yield an NPV of $40,000. The skating rink will cost $100,000 over and above the land acquisition, and will yield an NPV of $70,000. The theater will cost the value of the land plus $120,000 and will yield an NPV of $80,000. All NPVs are computed with the $120,000 cost of the land included in the initial outlay.

The land *can* accommodate both the skating rink and the same amount of parking space if the three-tier parking building and the rink are built as a single structure. The parking structure would cost only $60,000 to build over and above the cost of the rink, and the combination skating rink–parking building would yield an NPV of $270,000. The parking structure would provide needed parking for the rink. Similarly, the theater and parking structure could be done for a *total* of $150,000, excluding the land, yielding an NPV of $170,000. The rink and the theater would be infeasible because of insufficient parking. D may be done for $25,000, and no matter which of A, B, or C are done, D yields an NPV of $90,000 *if* the land has been acquired (i.e., not net of the $120,000 land cost); D would therefore not be done alone. Rank all the possible investment combinations and select the best combination which can be done for no more than $275,000.

why an investment's net present value equals its benefit to current stockholders

In calculating the net present value for project selection in the text of this chapter, we assumed that a project's NPV is the net gain to stockholders from the project. Criteria for investments under the NPV technique are:

1. If the firm can obtain funds (borrow funds or sell new shares) to finance profitable investments, for mutually exclusive investments, the one with the highest positive NPV should be adopted; and, in making accept-reject decisions, an investment should be adopted if and only if its NPV is positive.
2. If the firm faces a budget constraint, the set of projects with the highest positive total NPV should be adopted.

In this appendix, we will explain why the NPV of project cash flow equals the gain to current ("old") shareholders from that project. Current or old shareholders are those that own the firm when the investment decision is being made and does *not* include any new shareholders who buy additional shares of the company's stock which are sold to finance the investment. We will consider two kinds of financing of the investment: first, the use of idle cash (this is cash not held for productive purposes, such as paying bills or making change in a retail store), and second, the use of borrowing or selling new shares.

FINANCING WITH THE FIRM'S CASH

Idle cash is cash that has a value equal to its face value because it does not produce an above-average rate of return by serving the firm in a productive capacity. The cash has a value equal to its face amount *and is the property of stockholders*. If the cash is spent, it is therefore a sacrifice of that cash by the company's shareholders.

An investment paid for with idle cash is an exchange of cash in the amount I (amount of investment) for the newly acquired assets. The value of the cash given up is I; for example, an investment I of $100,000 of idle cash is a sacrifice by stockholders of the $100,000. The new asset obtained by investing I provides the firm with an added future cash flow. The net gain equals the present value of the returns from the investment less the cost of investment. That is, the net gain to stockholders equals

$$\begin{pmatrix} \text{Gain to} \\ \text{stockholders} \end{pmatrix} = \begin{pmatrix} \text{the present value of the} \\ \text{future cash flow from the} \\ \text{new assets acquired} \end{pmatrix} - \begin{pmatrix} \text{cash surrendered} \\ \text{in making the} \\ \text{investment} \end{pmatrix}$$

$$\left(\begin{array}{c}\text{Gain to}\\ \text{stockholders}\end{array}\right) = \frac{CF_1}{1 + k} + \frac{CF_2}{(1 + k)^2} + \cdot \cdot \cdot + \frac{CF_n}{(1 + k)^n} - I$$

$$= \text{NPV}$$

Terms $CF_1, CF_2, \ldots, CF_n$ are the cash flows from the project in period $1, 2, \ldots, n$; k is the discount rate; and I is the initial investment in the project (the cash expended on the project). The above relationship indicates that the net gain to shareholders is simply the NPV of the project. The net present value method is therefore appropriate if the investment is financed with idle cash.

FINANCING WITH FUNDS FROM BORROWING OR NEW STOCK

We wish to show that if the funds to finance new investment are acquired by selling *new* shares (in amount S^N) or through borrowing (selling new bonds in amount B^N), then the effect on the wealth of current shareholders (those owning the "old" stock) from the investment and its financing will equal the investment's NPV. This net wealth gain will be reflected in a rise in the market value of the firm's old shares by an amount equal to the project's NPV. Old shares refer to the stock outstanding *not* including the new shares issued (S^N). Management's objective is to select the set of investments which will maximize the value of the old shares since this will maximize the wealth of current shareholders. We will make the assumption that if an investment is profitable, the price of the company's stock will reflect that profitability.

To show that the effect on the value of the firm's *old shares* from a project is the project's NPV whether it is financed with new stock S^N, new bonds B^N, or a combination of the two, assume the following:

S = the market value of the old shares assuming the investment in a new project is made and is financed with some combination of new stock and new bonds

S' = the market value of the old shares assuming the investment is *not* made

B = the market value of the firm's old bonds (not including new bonds to finance the investment) if the investment is made

B' = the market value of the old bonds if the investment is *not* made

S^N = the market value of new shares sold to finance the investment

B^N = the market value of new bonds sold to finance the investment

V = the market value of the firm (value of all outstanding stocks and bonds) if the new investment is made

V' = the market value of the firm if the new investment is *not* made

New shares S^N and new bonds B^N are issued to finance investment and are not issued if there is no investment. Therefore, with investment of amount I financed with S^N and B^N we know that

$$S^N + B^N = I \tag{7-7}$$

For example, new investment of amount \$100,000 might be financed with \$40,000 of new stock and \$60,000 of new borrowing (bonds); thus, $I =$ \$100,000, $S^N =$ \$40,000, and $B^N =$ \$60,000.

Since, by definition, the value of the firm equals the value of all outstanding stocks and bonds, with the investment the firm's value is

$$V = \begin{pmatrix} \text{value of the} \\ \text{firm with the} \\ \text{investment} \end{pmatrix} = \begin{pmatrix} \text{value of all shares} \\ \text{outstanding with} \\ \text{the investment} \end{pmatrix} + \begin{pmatrix} \text{value of all bonds} \\ \text{outstanding with} \\ \text{the investment} \end{pmatrix}$$

$$= S + S^N + B + B^N \tag{7-8}$$

Furthermore, the value of the firm if the investment is *not* undertaken (signified by V') equals

$$V' = \begin{pmatrix} \text{value of the firm} \\ \text{without the investment} \end{pmatrix} = \begin{pmatrix} \text{value of all shares} \\ \text{outstanding without} \\ \text{the investment} \end{pmatrix}$$

$$+ \begin{pmatrix} \text{value of all bonds} \\ \text{outstanding without} \\ \text{the investment} \end{pmatrix} = S' + B' \tag{7-9}$$

We know that the change in the value of the old shares due to the investment equals $S - S'$, the value of the shares with the investment less the value without the investment. By rearranging (7-8) it is clear that $S = V - B - B^N - S^N$, and by rearranging (7-9) we know that $S' = V' - B'$; subtracting S' from S, the change in old share values is

$$S - S' = (V - B - B^N - S^N) - (V' - B')$$

$$= V - B - B^N - S^N - V' + B'$$

$$= V - V' - (S^N + B^N) - (B - B') \tag{7-10}$$

From Eq. (7-7) recall that $(S^N + B^N) = I$ and let $(B - B') = 0.$[26] Equation (7-10) becomes

26. The assumption that $B - B' = 0$ means that the new investment and its financing by selling additional shares or bonds does not affect the value of the *old* bonds. If the value of the old bonds were affected by a new investment—for example by reducing the likelihood of bankruptcy (thereby making the old bonds less risky and consequently more valuable)—then the value of the new investment to stockholders would equal the invest-

$$\begin{pmatrix} \text{Change in old share} \\ \text{value due to the} \\ \text{investment} \end{pmatrix} = S - S' = (V - V') - I \qquad (7\text{-}11)$$

The change in the firm's total value in Eq. (7-11), $V - V'$, is the additional value of the firm due to the investment. $V - V'$ is the present value of the future cash flow from the new assets. Since I is the current cost of the new assets, it follows that the right-hand side of Eq. (7-11) is the NPV of the new investment. Therefore, if investment is financed with funds from the sale of some combination of new stocks and bonds, the increase in the value of the old shares equals the net present value of the investment.

Exhibit 7-15.

	Without the investment	With the investment
1. Value of old shares	$500,000	$505,000
2. Value of old bonds	400,000	400,000
3. New stock sold for the investment	0	4,000
4. New bonds sold for the investment	0	6,000
5. Value of all stock outstanding [= (1) + (3)]	500,000	509,000
6. Value of all bonds outstanding [= (2) + (4)]	400,000	406,000
7. Value of firm (V) [= (5) + (6)]	900,000	915,000

Gain to old shareholders = rise in value of old shares = $505,000 − $500,000 = $5,000.
Net present value of the investment = (present value of future cash flows from the investment) − (cost of investment) = $(V - V') - I$ = ($915,000 − $900,000) − $10,000 = $5,000.

ment's net present value less the change in the value of the old bonds. The assumption made here that the old bonds do not change in value is made throughout this book and is generally made both in academic work and in actual business practice. This is because it not only simplifies the analysis but is ordinarily a realistic assumption. For a discussion of this point, see Haley and Schall, op. cit., chap. 12.

An example will help clarify the above concept. Assume that the firm is considering an investment outlay of $10,000 which would be financed with $6,000 from borrowing ($B^N = \$6,000$) and $4,000 from the sale of new stock ($S^N = \$4,000$). If the new investment *is not* adopted, the value of the currently outstanding stock would be $500,000 ($S' = \$500,000$) and the value of the currently outstanding bonds would be $400,000 ($B' = \$400,000$). The value of the firm (V') therefore would be $900,000. Assume that if the new investment *is* adopted, the value of the firm would be $915,000 ($V = \$915,000$), the present value of the additional aftertax cash flow to stockholders and bondholders from the new assets therefore being $15,000 (the rise in the value of the firm's total aftertax cash flow being $915,000 $-$ $900,000). The *net present value of the investment* is therefore $5,000, $15,000 less the cost of the assets of $10,000. *The increase in the value of the old shares* is consequently $5,000. The data associated with the problem are shown in Exhibit 7-15.

choices between mutually exclusive investments: internal rate of return versus present value

The three sections of this appendix cover the following:

1. The use of the present value and the internal rate of return methods in comparing mutually exclusive investments assuming either that future investment opportunities are not dependent on current investments or that all future investments will yield exactly the cost of capital. We show that the present value or the *incremental* IRR method must be used and that simply selecting the investment with the highest IRR is usually not the proper approach, i.e., can lead to adoption of the less profitable investment.

2. The special case mentioned on page 221 in which the best investment from among a set of mutually exclusive investments is the one with the highest IRR. In the discussion below, it is shown that the investment with the highest IRR is the best one as long as certain conditions hold. It is also the investment that would be chosen using the incremental IRR method or the present value method.

3. The general approach for analyzing investments when the firm's future investment opportunities *depend on which investments are currently adopted*. This approach is valid whether future reinvestment rates (the rates of return on future investments) are at the firm's cost of capital, at the current investments' IRRs, or at some other rate.

We assume throughout this appendix that the firm can obtain funds at the cost of capital. Capital rationing was considered in a separate section in the body of Chapter 7.

1. FUTURE INVESTMENTS INDEPENDENT OF CURRENT INVESTMENTS

It should be noted at the outset that if the profitability of future investment opportunities are not dependent on current investments, then it is correct to evaluate current investments using the present value and IRR techniques described in the text, with the incremental IRR approach applied if one is selecting from among mutually exclusive alternatives. This is true regardless of the rate of return that the firm expects to earn on future investments as long as those future investments do not depend on currently adopted projects. In this case, the *current* projects are accepted or rejected on the basis of the cash flows that they generate, and the *future* projects are accepted or rejected on the basis of the cash flows that they generate. Both present and future projects are evaluated using the firm's cost of capital, either as a discount rate or as a minimum acceptable rate of return.

A second important point is that, in evaluating current investments, we can ignore any future project that depends on current investments as long as that future project is expected to earn a rate of return not exceeding the firm's cost of capital. The reason that such future investments can be ignored is that all future projects earning less than the cost of capital will not be adopted, since they have a negative NPV (and so are irrelevant) and all future projects earning exactly the cost of capital have a zero net present value and therefore do not affect shareholder wealth (they are just marginally acceptable). In this situation, we can apply the present value and internal rate of return methods to the cash flows of current investments as explained in the text. In this section of Appendix 7B the use of the present value and incremental rate of return methods will be illustrated for the present case which allows us to ignore *future* investments. In this case it is ordinarily incorrect simply to select the mutually exclusive investment with the highest IRR. This is so even if the mutually exclusive investments have the same lives and require the same initial outlay. Either the incremental rate of return method or the present value method should be used.

To illustrate the principles involved, assume that the firm has two mutually exclusive investment opportunities, A and B, which each require an initial outlay now of $1,000. The cash flows from A and B are shown in Exhibit 7-16. Assume that the cost of capital is 10 percent. Observe that although the 30 percent internal rate of return of B, $r(B)$, exceeds $r(A) = 20$ percent, the net present value of A, NPV(A), of $283 ex-

Exhibit 7-16. Cash Flows from Mutually Exclusive Investments A and B

	A	B	A − B
Time:			
Now	−$1,000	−$1,000	$ 0
Year 1	50	1,200	−1,150
Year 2	100	100	0
Year 3	1,536	40	1,496
IRR(r)	20%	30%	14%[a]
NPV (at 10% rate)	$283	$204	$79
Conclusion: choose A since $283 exceeds $204.			

[a]The 14% rate is the IRR of the (A − B) cash flows; the added outlay of $1,150 in year 2 produces an added return of $1,496 in year 4, the rate of return being 14% per year. Since 14% exceeds the cost of capital rate of 10%, A is superior to B using the incremental IRR method [the (A − B) increment has an IRR that exceeds the cost of capital].

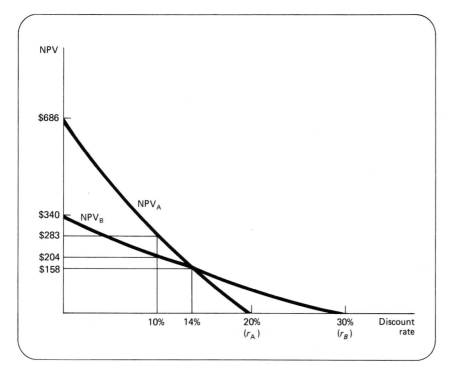

Figure 7-4. The NPV of investments A and B at different discount rates.

ceeds NPV(B) = $203. A is the superior investment. Also, notice that the incremental rate of return is 14 percent, which exceeds the cost of capital of 10 percent; therefore the incremental IRR method also correctly leads to a choice of A over B. Figure 7-4 shows the net present values of A and B for various discount rates. If the discount rate (cost of capital) is less than 14 percent, the NPV(A) exceeds NPV(B) (the case in the example where the cost of capital was assumed to be 10 percent); if the cost of capital were exactly 14 percent, NPV(A) = NPV(B) and we would be indifferent between A and B; and if the cost of capital were greater than 14 percent, NPV(B) would exceed NPV(A) and B would be preferred to A.

2. REINVESTMENT AT THE IRR FOR MUTUALLY EXCLUSIVE INVESTMENTS WITH THE SAME *I*

Assume that the firm is comparing two or more mutually exclusive investments and that conditions **a, b,** and **c** below apply to those investments:

a) All of the investments involve the same initial (current) dollar outlay.

b) Each investment provides the firm with the special opportunity to reinvest the investment's future cash flows at a rate of return equal to the investment's IRR.

c) The reinvestment opportunity described under **b** above lasts until T periods from the current investment (i.e., the funds can remain reinvested earning the internal rate of return until T periods hence), where T is the same for all the mutually exclusive opportunities being compared *and* T is no less than the life of the longest lived of the mutually exclusive investments (e.g., if the longest lived investment has a five-year life, T is no less than five years).

Conditions **a, b,** and **c** were noted in the text on page 221. If **a, b,** and **c** hold, then the mutually exclusive investment with the highest IRR is also that which provides the highest NPV and is the investment that would be chosen using the incremental rate of return method. We will use an example to show this.

Assume that investments C and D are being evaluated by the firm at time 0. The firm's cost of capital is 10 percent. C and D each require an initial outlay of $1,000 (condition **a**). The cash flows of C and D are shown in Exhibit 7-17. The IRR of C [signified $r(C)$] is 20 percent, and the future cash flows from C can be reinvested until time 5 at a rate of return of 20 percent per period; that is, by investing in C now, the firm obtains the opportunity to reinvest C's future cash flows in new projects which also earn 20 percent per period (until time 5). C is identical to A in Exhibit 7-16 except that we are now assuming that the future cash flows from A are reinvested at A's IRR. The IRR of D, $r(D)$, is 35 percent, and the future cash flows from D can be reinvested to earn 35 percent until time 5. Thus, condition **b** is satisfied. Note that T in condition **c** is equal to 5 in this example; therefore, condition **c** is satisfied since 5 is greater than the three-year life of project C, the longer-lived project. Since the firm's cost of capital is only 10 percent, we know that the firm will, if C is adopted, reinvest C's cash flow at the reinvestment opportunity rate of 20 percent and will, if D is adopted, reinvest D's cash flow at the reinvestment opportunity rate of 35 percent. Assuming such reinvestment, the firm will accumulate at time 5 the terminal amount $V_5(C) = \$2,488$ if C is adopted and amount $V_5(D) = \$4,484$ if D is adopted. $V_5(C) = \$2,488$ results by investing, at a rate of 20 percent per period, C's time 1 cash flow of $50 for four periods (to time 5), reinvesting C's time 2 cash flow of $50 for three periods, etc. $V_5(D) = \$4,484$ results by reinvesting at 35 percent per period D's time 1 cash flow of $1,350 for four periods to time 5. Notice that for any T in condition **c** (where T = 5 in the present example)

$$V_T = (1 + r)^T I = (F/P, r, T)I \qquad (7\text{-}12)$$

Equation (7-12) follows, since reinvesting all cash flows at the internal rate of return r is equivalent to simply investing I for T periods with all funds kept invested for the T periods earning rate r per period. This is like

Exhibit 7-17. Comparing Mutually Exclusive Investments with Cash Flows That Are Reinvested at the Internal Rate of Return

	C	D
Time:		
Now	−$1,000	−$1,000
Year 1	50	1,350
Year 2	50	0
Year 3	1,596	0
IRR(r)	20%	35%
NPV of above cash flows		
at 10% (ignoring reinvestment)	$286	$227
Year 5 terminal amount (V_5)	$2,488	$4,484
NPV of V_5 at 10%	$545	$1,784

Conclusion: Choose D since $1,784 exceeds $545.

putting I in a bank account earning r each period and leaving all interest in the account along with the principal until the end of the T periods.

The objective is to maximize the present value of the returns from the investment (using the cost of capital) and, using (7-12),

$$\text{NPV(C)} = \frac{V_5(C)}{(1 + k)^5} - I$$

$$= \frac{[1 + r(C)]^5 I}{(1 + k)^5} - I = \frac{(1.2)^5\ \$1,000}{(1.1)^5} - \$1,000$$

$$= \frac{\$2,488}{(1.1)^5} - \$1,000 = \$545 \qquad (7\text{-}13)$$

$$\text{NPV(D)} = \frac{V_5(D)}{(1 + k)^5} - I$$

$$= \frac{[1 + r(D)]^5 I}{(1 + k)^5} - I = \frac{(1.35)^5\ \$1,000}{(1.1)^5} - \$1,000$$

$$= \frac{\$4,484}{(1.1)^5} - \$1,000 = \$1,784 \qquad (7\text{-}14)$$

Notice from Eqs. (7-13) and (7-14) that as long as C and D involve the same I, T, and cost of capital k—which is the case here since I = $1,000, T = five years and k = 10 percent for both investments—the investment with the higher V_T is preferred. We can see from Eq. (7-12) that this is equivalent to choosing the investment with the higher internal rate of return.

Although simply selecting the alternative with the highest IRR is the easiest selection method under the present assumptions [(7-7), (7-8), (7-9) above], it should be clear that the net present value method leads to the correct choice. The procedure is simply to compute the terminal value, V_T, of each mutually exclusive investment and choose the investment with the highest terminal value since, with the same initial outlay and T for all the investments, highest terminal value also means highest NPV.

3. REINVESTMENT RATES IN GENERAL

In general, if future investment opportunities are affected by current investments, then those future opportunities must be taken into account in evaluating projects. All effects of current investments on the future cash flows must be taken into account, including future capital projects and returns from those projects. The net present value or incremental IRR methods can be applied in this case. It is not in general correct to choose the investment with the highest internal rate of return.

To illustrate the correct approach, assume that the firm is comparing mutually exclusive investments E and F which require current outlays of $2,000 and $5,000 in the current period. E has a life of two years (returns annual cash flows of $1,500 at the end of years 1 and 2), and the funds from E can be reinvested at a 20 percent rate of return until the end of year 4. E also provides the opportunity to invest an additional $1,000 at the end of the third year (three years hence) at 20 percent per year for one year. After year 4, investment E provides no special reinvestment opportunities, and all funds are withdrawn from E and its reinvestment projects at the end of year 4. Exhibit 7-18 describes these cash flows.

Investment F is a three-year project (returns annual cash flows of $2,500 from years 1 through 3) but provides no special reinvestment opportunities.

Do we choose E or F? *The preferred investment is that with the greater net present value of future cash flows, taking into account any reinvestment opportunities earning more than the cost of capital. The objective is to choose that investment plan which maximizes the net present value of cash flows.*

The net present value of E is computed by assuming that the $1,500 cash flows of years 1 and 2 are reinvested to earn 20 percent per year until the end of year 4; $1,000 is also invested at the end of year 3 until the end of year 4 at a rate of return of 20 percent. The total amount accumulated at the end of year 4 $[V_4(E)]$ is $5,952. The net present value of E is computed as follows:

Exhibit 7-18. Cash Flows from Investment E and Reinvestment

Time	Inflows (1)	Investment (2)	Net cash flow (col. 1 − col. 2) (3)	
Now		→ $2,000	−$2,000 ←	
Year 1	→ $1,500	→ 1,500	0	Net funds invested
Year 2	→ 1,500	→ 1,500	0	in project
Year 3		1,000	− 1,000 ←	
Year 4			→ 5,952 ←	Funds withdrawn from project at end of year 4 $[V_4(E)]$

$$\text{Amount accumulated at end of year 4 with E} = V_4(E)$$

$$= \$1,500(1.2)^3 + \$1,500(1.2)^2 + \$1,000(1.2)$$

$$= \$5,952$$

$$\text{Present value of new funds invested in E} = I(E) = \$2,000 + \frac{\$1,000}{(1.10)^3} = \$2,751$$

$$\text{Net present value of E [NPV(E)]} = \frac{V_4(E)}{(1.10)^4} - I(E)$$

$$= \frac{\$5,952}{(1.10)^4} - \$2,751 = \$1,314$$

For investment F, the net present value equals

$$NPV(F) = \frac{\$2,500}{1 + 0.10} + \frac{\$2,500}{(1.10)^2} + \frac{\$2,500}{(1.10)^3} - \$5,000$$

$$= \$2,500 \ (P/A, \ 10\%, \ 3) - \$5,000$$

$$= \$2,500(2.487) - \$5,000 = \$1,218$$

Since NPV(E) = $1,314 exceeds NPV(F) = $1,218, E is preferred; and since NPV(E) is positive, E should be adopted.

The Energy Crisis and Corporate Financial Planning

In the early 1960s, the oil producing nations got together and formed a cartel—a group of sellers who agree to act in collusion to control the price of their product. The cartel was named the Organization of Petroleum Exporting Countries—OPEC, for short. However, for a number of years OPEC's influence on oil prices was limited, since the supply-demand situation favored the buyers. Rising demand brought about a change in this situation in the early 1970s. Thus, when the Arab nations imposed their oil embargo after the outbreak of war with Israel in late 1973, the oil importing nations were more or less at the mercy of OPEC, which then proceeded to dictate increases in oil prices.

A strategy initiated by the Arabs, ostensibly to pressure the West into a pro-Arab stand in the Arab-Israeli dispute, became a permanent policy that enriched the OPEC countries at a steep price that was paid by virtually everyone else. This situation has meant a new economic burden on the United States, has created major dislocations in Europe and Japan, and has beggared underdeveloped countries whose resources can barely support the mounting fuel bills.

The radical increases in the cost of foreign crude oil had several major effects on the United States:

1. Americans were shocked into belatedly facing the harsh reality that conventional energy sources are limited.
2. Wealth was sharply redistributed in favor of the OPEC countries, with part of this bonanza to oil exporters being paid for by a greatly increased United States oil import bill.
3. A relative disadvantage was created for certain kinds of industries, particularly heavy users of energy such as airlines, aluminum and auto companies, and public utilities. Petroleum-dependent firms like producers of synthetic fibers and plastics (both of which require petroleum as an input) were hurt, too. The surge in energy costs also had negative implications for a variety of businesses related to travel—hotels and motels, amusement parks, auto rental firms, and manufacturers of private aircraft. On the other hand, substitutes for products high in energy consumption benefited—notably small cars, motorcycles, bicycles, and more efficient home appliances.
4. A new search was begun to expand known domestic energy reserves and to explore new energy sources.

United States congressional leaders, responding to the public outcry against the "obscene" profits of the oil companies in 1974, pushed through legislation which eliminated the oil depletion allowance for major oil companies and reduced other tax benefits for the industry. Petroleum firms will avoid further tax increases only if they undertake a massive investment program to help reduce United States dependence on foreign oil. Two issues are of interest here: the size and nature of the energy investments that will be undertaken and the method of financing those investments.

CAPITAL OUTLAYS: WHERE AND HOW MUCH

Energy demand in the United States is expected to grow from the mid-1970s to the mid-1980s at an annual rate of 4.5 percent. To meet this requirement and to replace existing obsolete equipment, total investment by the American energy industry will have to approximate $690 billion from 1971 to 1985, with $575 billion of the total in the petroleum and electricity generating sectors. This may be an underestimate, if Project Independence (discussed below) is fully pursued. Most capital expenditures by the petroleum industry will be for exploration and production, and outlays by the electric utilities will primarily be for new production plants.

The illustration shows the 1970 and 1980 estimated proportions of total energy use from various sources. Although nuclear power will grow dramatically in importance, petroleum and natural gas will retain their dominant position in 1980. The continued predominance of petroleum and gas will necessitate an enormous investment—around $250 billion be-

tween 1973 and 1985—by this sector. Even with expanding profits, funds to support capital outlays will have to come from new borrowing or the selling of additional shares. The extent to which external financing will be necessary will largely depend upon sales and profit margins. It has been estimated that between $28 and $73 billion in new borrowing and equity financing will probably be required over the years 1973 to 1985, the ultimate amount depending on the profitability of the firms in the energy sector during that period.

PROJECT FINANCING

In addition to the traditional financing methods such as selling new bonds and stock, a relatively new and imaginative financing technique has evolved, which is commonly referred to as **project financing.** This approach usually involves borrowing money to help finance an investment, with all the debt repayment to come from the revenues generated by that investment. The obligation to repay the borrowed

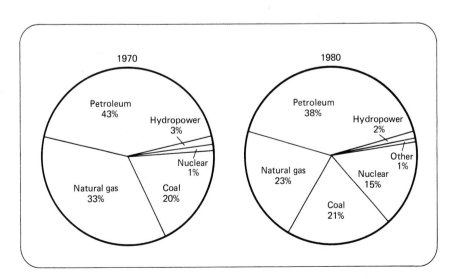

United States energy sources.

funds in this case rests entirely with the project and not with the company undertaking it. Another arrangement, common in the oil industry when a group, or "consortium," of companies is involved in a project, provides for an unconditional guarantee by each participant of all the debt obligations against the project. But regardless of who assumes the debt responsibility, project financing is an especially simple financing approach if several companies are involved in a single and very large investment.

Project financing is employed by utilities when the need arises to construct facilities beyond the financial capability of any one firm. It is also used by oil companies for tanker construction and for large pipeline projects—most notably the Alaska Pipeline, the most expensive facility ever built, where construction was financed by a consortium of seven companies.

Project financing by a group of companies can involve any of several binding agreements. The participating firms may set up a jointly owned subsidiary, which can then borrow or obtain added equity capital to acquire additional funds for the project. The firms can also form a joint venture, with each company investing a proportion of the necessary capital and thereafter sharing expenses and receiving an interest in the output. In the case of utilities, each firm can include its investment in its rate base for rate setting purposes.

An energy project may make use of a "take or pay" contract, under which each member of the investing group, or consortium, agrees to purchase a certain percentage of the output as well as to pay a like percentage of the project's expenses including debt repayment. A slight variation, called a "throughput and deficiency" contract is used in exploration and pipeline projects. It requires participants to pay their pro rata share of costs over and above those involved in construction of the facility should the project not pan out.

ALARMISM?

To those who waited in line for two hours to buy five gallons of gas during the 1973–1974 Arab oil embargo, and to the Japanese who watched their "miracle" of economic growth become past history, the so-called energy "crisis" is a very tangible fact of life. No one denies that a major shift in world income distribution has occurred in favor of oil producers. But in a sense the term "crisis" is a misnomer, because no actual disaster has so far arisen, nor does a disaster appear probable. Of course, if all the OPEC countries were to turn off the tap, the consequence would be economic catastrophe. But a total embargo by the OPEC would be an act of suicidal aggression, for the halt of oil export income would cripple the oil producers' economies and perhaps precipitate economic or even military reprisals. This reality has not been ignored by either side.

What then has happened? Three major consequences of the oil shortage are apparent. First, there is the redistribution of wealth in favor of the oil producers and to the detriment of the consumers—a very significant shift but not a cataclysmic one. The fuel is still flowing, albeit at a much higher price.

Second, the United States has made some effort under "Project Independence" to make this country energy independent by some time in the 1980s. (The original schedule was energy independence by 1980, a target that has since been declared impossible by both government officials and nongovernment energy experts.) The goals of Project Independence are to increase United States nuclear power generation five times, to double coal output, and to raise oil and natural gas production 50 percent (all from 1974 levels). Estimates of the investment needed to implement this plan range from $600 billion to $1,800 billion over the 1974–1984 period; this is equivalent to from two to six Apollo moon programs *each year* over that time span. On top of this are the ecological costs from strip mining and from processing plants that pollute the air. The states exposed to an environmental threat (and also benefiting from a stimulated economy) will be Colorado, North and South Dakota, Montana, Utah, and Wyoming. These states have 52 percent of the country's coal resources, 48 percent of its uranium, and large quantities of geothermal, petroleum, and natural gas reserves. Nuclear energy also is not free from the ecology-energy issue. Controversy over the safety of nuclear plants suggests the possibility that nuclear energy may not soon assume the major role that has generally been expected. It is not clear where the compromise between ecology and energy needs will be drawn, or indeed if the drive for energy independence, inspired by the 1973–1974 oil boycott, will lose its impetus as the memory of hardship fades.

A third outcome of the oil shortage has been the realization that similar shortages may arise in the future for other raw materials. The United States, for example, imports 100 percent of its natural rubber; over 90 percent of its manganese, cobalt, graphite, and chromium; and more than half of many other essential materials. Other developed countries are in the same or in an even more vulnerable position. Some economic Cassandras envisage a resource-starved industrialized world hocking much of its gross national product to pay for tiny rations of critical materials. It is more likely that, even if the other raw material producers follow the lead of the oil states and drive up their prices, the price increases will be tolerable, the strains will be absorbed by material users, and supplies will continue. Perhaps a political as well as an economic price will be exacted, but even here the threat of reprisals by the industrialized countries sets limits on the new terms.

In short, there appears to be virtually no likelihood that we will revert to a preindustrial state. Modern industries which depend upon imported raw materials will still obtain the needed supplies and will continue to operate. A boom for candles, horse-drawn surreys, and foot-warmers is not imminent. We are experiencing something witnessed many times in history—a shift of wealth and power among nations and, as always, the process is unpleasant for those at the losing end.

risk analysis
and capital budgeting

Although the cash flows from an investment can be estimated when the investment is made, the returns are not known until the cash flows actually occur. The uncertainty of the returns from the time funds are invested until management and investors know how much the project will earn is a primary determinant of a project's risk. The owners of a firm are ordinarily concerned with the riskiness of their stock, and management must therefore take risk into account in formulating investment policy.

You will recall that in Chapter 7 we assumed that all investments had equal risk and therefore were analyzed using the same minimum acceptable rate of return, or cost of capital. In this chapter we consider risk explicitly and describe how risk can be measured and then accounted for in making capital budgeting decisions. This chapter begins with a description of how probability distributions are used to compute expected cash flow and to estimate the uncertainty of the cash flow. We then examine the determinants of a project's risk and how risk is taken into account in evaluating the project. We also describe simulation and decision tree analysis, which are methods for analyzing available data in order to estimate a project's cash flows.

**PROBABILITY
DISTRIBUTIONS
AND CASH FLOW
ANALYSIS**

In Chapter 7 we analyzed the average or expected cash flows from an investment by using capital budgeting techniques, including present value and internal rate of return. Expected cash flow was defined as an "educated guess" of what the cash flow from the investment would be, this guess lying somewhere between the highest and lowest cash flow estimates for the project. In addition, we assumed that all projects were of identical risk and were financed in the same way and therefore justified the same cost of capital. We therefore ignored two important issues: how expected cash flow is computed and how risk is treated when it varies among investments. In this section we will see how expected cash flow is computed and how probability distributions are used to evaluate the uncertainty and risk of the cash flow. The next section explains how the risk of an individual project is determined.

**Expected
Cash Flow**

In analyzing an investment, some attempt must be made to estimate the project's future cash flows. If we consider some future year during the investment's life, it is ordinarily impossible to predict with certainty what the cash flow will be. Rather, there are several possible cash flows that might result, each with some likelihood of occurrence. A probability distribution shows the chance or probability that each possible cash flow level will occur. The concept of a probability distribution, its mean, and its standard deviation were discussed in Chapter 5 and the reader might review that material before proceeding here. In the present discussion we will apply the probability distribution concept to project evaluation and the computation of expected cash flow.

To illustrate the problem, assume that a new machine can be purchased for $2,500 and is expected to last for six years, at which time it will be junked with no salvage value. In each year of the asset's life, it is possible that the net cash flow will be $400, $600, or $800 (see Exhibit 8-1 and Figure 8-1). The uncertainty regarding each year's returns could be due to such things as year-to-year variations in sales or uncertainty regarding product pricing or the costs of production. A cash flow of $600 is viewed by management as more likely than $400 or $800. A probability or chance is assigned to the occurrence of each event, with a probability of $\frac{1}{2}$ assigned to $600, and $\frac{1}{4}$ to each of $400 and $800. (The total of all probabilities for a particular event must be 1 or 100 percent.) As explained in Chapter 5, the expected cash flow is a measure of the average level of cash return and equals the sum of each possible dollar return weighted by

Exhibit 8-1. Distribution of Project Cash Flow Returns in Each of the Six Years after the Initial Outlay

Cash flow (CF) per year (1)	Probability or chance the cash flow will actually occur (2)	Cash flow times probability (col. 1 × col. 2) (3)
$400	$\frac{1}{4}$	$100 ($= \frac{1}{4} \times$ $400)
600	$\frac{1}{2}$	300 ($= \frac{1}{2} \times$ $600)
800	$\frac{1}{4}$	200 ($= \frac{1}{4} \times$ $800)
Total	1	$600

Expected cash flow per year for years 1 through 6 (from col. 3 total)   = $ 600

Initial outlay on project   = $2,500

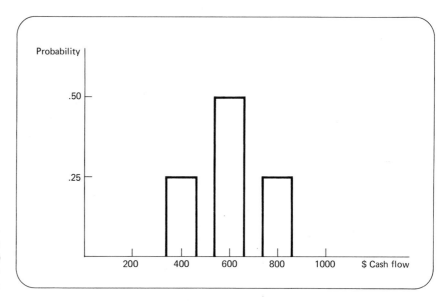

Figure 8-1. Symmetrical, discrete (finite number of outcomes) probability distribution.

the probability that the return will occur. The machine's expected cash flow equals

$$\text{Expected annual cash flow} = .25(\$400) + .5(\$600) + .25(\$800)$$

$$= \$600$$

The expected cash flow of $600 can be evaluated to compute the project's net present value or its internal rate of return. This is the procedure we used in Chapter 7. Therefore, assuming that the appropriate cost of capital for this project is 10 percent, we can compute the NPV and IRR as follows:

$$\text{NPV} = \$600(P/A, 10\%, 6) - \$2,500$$

$$= \$600(4.355) - \$2,500$$

$$= \$113.00$$

The IRR, r, satisfies the following equation:

$$0 = \$600(P/A, r, 6) - \$2,500$$

and $r = 11\frac{1}{2}$ percent since

$$0 = \$600(P/A, 11.5\%, 6) - \$2,500$$

The probability distribution in Figure 8-1 is referred to as a **discrete distribution** since it has only a finite number of outcomes ($400, $600, and $800). Instead of a finite set of possible outcomes, a cash flow distribution may indicate a continuous range of outcomes. For example, the distribution in Figure 8-2 implies a probability of $\frac{1}{4}$ that the cash flow will be between $300 and $500, a probability of $\frac{1}{2}$ that the cash flow will be between $500 and $700, and a probability of $\frac{1}{4}$ that the cash flow will be between $700 and $900. This type of distribution has an infinite number of outcomes (any outcome between $300 and $900 is possible) and is referred to as a **continuous distribution.**[1] Probability with a continuous distribution is measured by the *area* under the curve. For example, the area under the distribution from $300 to $500 is one-fourth of the total to reflect the probability of $\frac{1}{4}$ that the cash flow will be between $300 and $500. The total area under the distribution is 1. The expected value of a continuous distribution can be computed by integration, a technique we will not describe here. However, if the distribution is symmetrical, as is the one in Figure

1. Strictly speaking, any distribution of dollars will have a finite number of possible outcomes since the cash flows can vary in increments no smaller than $0.01. Therefore, the distribution in Figure 8-2 is only approximately continuous.

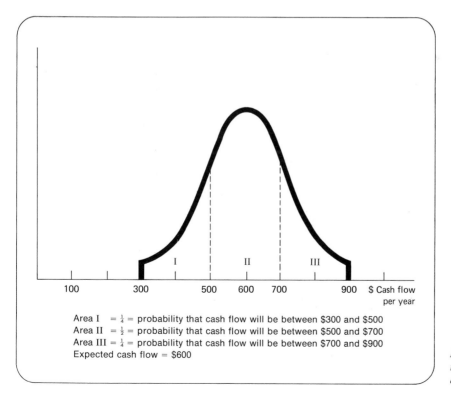

Area I $= \frac{1}{4} =$ probability that cash flow will be between $300 and $500
Area II $= \frac{1}{2} =$ probability that cash flow will be between $500 and $700
Area III $= \frac{1}{4} =$ probability that cash flow will be between $700 and $900
Expected cash flow = $600

Figure 8-2. Symmetrical, continuous probability distribution.

8-2, then the expected value is the middle of the range of possible outcomes; in the Figure 8-2 example, the expected value is $600, halfway between $300 and $900. The computation of NPV or IRR would proceed exactly as before. Thus, for an asset costing $2,500 with a net cash flow distribution as illustrated in Figure 8-2 for each of its six years of economic life, the NPV and internal rate of return computations would be just as they were above for the distribution in Exhibit 8-1 and Figure 8-1.

Cash Flow Uncertainty: Standard Deviation and Coefficient of Variation

The expected level of the cash flow indicates the average level but tells us nothing about the degree of uncertainty associated with the flow. The standard deviation and the coefficient of variation are measures of how dispersed or spread out the probability distribution is (that is, how uncertain we are about the flow). As is explained below, these two statistical indices are related to one another.[2]

Standard deviation   Recall from Chapter 5 that the standard deviation measures the likelihood that cash flow levels away from the expected value will be attained. The greater is the standard deviation of a probability distribution, the more spread out is the distribution.[3] For example, in Figure 8-3 cash flow distribution A is more spread out than cash flow distribution B, and therefore A has the greater standard deviation. Standard deviation is a number that describes the degree of uncertainty (or "spreadoutness") of a cash flow and is one measure of risk. If two cash flows have the same expected level (mean), the one that has the greater standard deviation has the higher degree of uncertainty.[4]

2. There are other characteristics of a probability distribution, for example, its skewness (degree of asymmetry), which we will not discuss here. Although these other statistical measures may be useful, most modern portfolio theory uses standard deviation or coefficient of variation as the measure of risk since they indicate at least a major part of the portfolio's risk.

3. To compute a standard deviation, assume that there are n possible levels of cash flow which are signified as CF^1, CF^2, . . . , CF^n; the mean of these cash flows equals CF. The probability of any CF^i is signified as P_i; for example, the probability of CF^3 is signified as P_3. The standard deviation equals

$$\sqrt{P_1(CF^1 - CF)^2 + P_2(CF^2 - CF)^2 + \cdots + P_n(CF^n - CF)^2} = \sqrt{\sum_{i=1}^{n} P_i(CF^i - CF)^2}$$

In the Exhibit 8-1 example, standard deviation equals $[(\frac{1}{4}(400 - 600)^2 + (\frac{1}{2}(600 - 600)^2 + \frac{1}{4}(800 - 600)^2]^{1/2} = [10,000 + 10,000]^{1/2} = \sqrt{20,000} = 141.4$. The *variance* is the square of the standard deviation and therefore equals 20,000. For further discussion of standard deviation and variance, see Chap. 5.

4. See the discussion below on the coefficient of variation for an explanation of why we cannot compare cash flows' standard deviations if their expected cash levels differ.

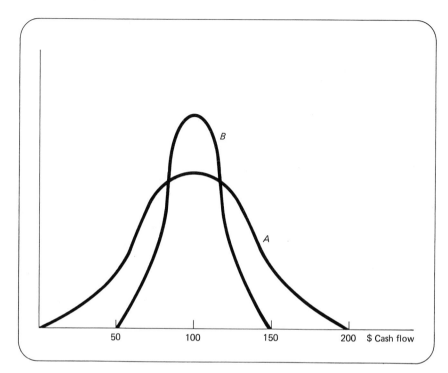

Figure 8-3. Symmetrical, continuous probability distribution with different standard deviations. The standard deviation of A *is greater than the standard deviation of* B.

Coefficient of variation   The standard deviation can be misleading in comparing the uncertainty of alternatives if they differ in size. For example, in Figure 8-4 we can compare the future annual cash flow of an oil drilling venture with the future annual cash flow of a large real estate complex. The oil project involves a $60,000 investment and will produce an annual return of nothing (dry hole), $10,000, or $20,000 with probabilities of $\frac{1}{4}$, $\frac{1}{2}$, and $\frac{1}{4}$, respectively.[5] The real estate development costs $60 million and is almost completely rented out under long-term leases to extremely large corporate tenants who are virtually certain to pay their rent; there is a small amount of office space yet to be rented. The real estate complex will return an annual cash flow of $9.98 million, $10 million, or $10.02 million with probabilities of $\frac{1}{4}$, $\frac{1}{2}$ and $\frac{1}{4}$, respectively. Can we conclude that because the standard deviation of the oil venture's cash flow ($7,071, shown below) is less than the standard deviation of the real estate project's cash flow ($14,142), the returns from the oil venture are more certain? The answer is no. The oil venture is the more uncertain because, *relative to the size or "scale" of cash flow,* the oil venture's cash flow has far greater

5. We are using discrete probability distributions (distributions with a finite number of possible outcomes, i.e., not continuous) simply because it helps in explaining the concepts. Ordinarily, continuous distributions are more realistic.

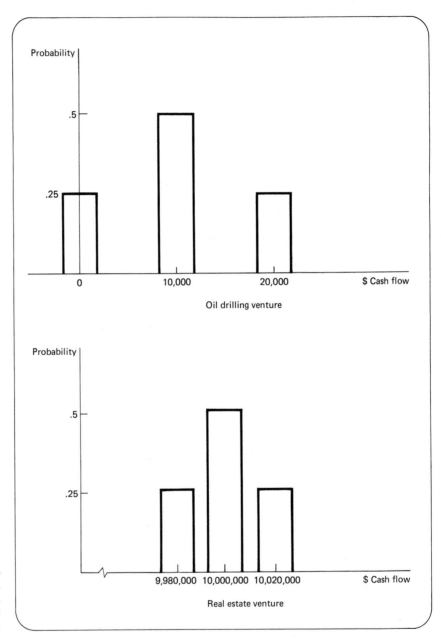

Figure 8-4. Cash flow probability distributions of oil drilling venture and real estate venture.

variation or uncertainty. To adjust for the scale problem, the standard deviation can be divided by the expected value to compute the coefficient of variation:

$$\text{Coefficient of variation} = \frac{\text{standard deviation}}{\text{expected cash flow}} \qquad (8\text{-}1)$$

The expected cash flow, standard deviation, and coefficient of variation for the oil and real estate ventures are shown below.[6]

	Oil venture	Real estate project
Expected cash flow	$10,000	$10,000,000
Standard deviation	$7,071	$14,142
Coefficient of variation	.707	.0014

A higher coefficient of variation implies greater uncertainty, and therefore the oil venture is more uncertain than the real estate development.

The significance of the coefficient of variation is clarified if we imagine owning one-thousandth of the real estate project, which would mean an expected cash flow on our share of $10,000 ($10,000,000/1,000). The probability distribution of our annual cash flow is shown in Figure 8-5. The cash flow has a standard deviation of approximately $14.[7] Compare this distribution with that of the oil project in Figure 8-4. It is clear that there is less uncertainty associated with our share of the real estate venture.

We can conclude at this point that the coefficient of variation is a better measure of the uncertainty of dollar returns than is the standard deviation. This is because the coefficient of variation adjusts for the size of the cash flow (adjusts for scale), whereas the standard deviation does not.[8] We will see in the next section that the coefficient of variation alone is not sufficient to determine risk. It is also important to consider how the cash flow varies with the economy, that is, the degree to which the cash flow moves up and down with general economic trends.

6. The coefficients of variation are computed using Eq. (8-1) and the definition of the standard deviation. The computations are:

$$\text{Coefficient of variation (oil venture)} = \frac{\sqrt{.25(10{,}000)^2 + .5(0)^2 + .25(10{,}000)^2}}{10{,}000} = .707$$

$$\text{Coefficient of variation (real estate venture)} = \frac{\sqrt{.25(20{,}000)^2 + .5(0)^2 + .25(20{,}000)^2}}{10{,}000{,}000} = .0014$$

7. Using the formula in footnote 3, the standard deviation of the cash flow provided by 1 percent ownership of the real estate venture equals

$$\text{Standard deviation} = \sqrt{.25(\$9{,}980 - \$10{,}000)^2 + .5(\$10{,}000 - \$10{,}000)^2 + .25(\$10{,}020 - \$10{,}000)^2}$$

$$= \sqrt{\$100 + \$100} = \$14.14$$

8. An alternative method of adjusting for scale is to use percentage rates of return as in Chap. 5 instead of the dollar cash flows. The standard deviation of the rate of return can then be used as a measure of uncertainty. This approach is not used here because it can introduce certain technical problems and because it is easier to directly evaluate the cash flows.

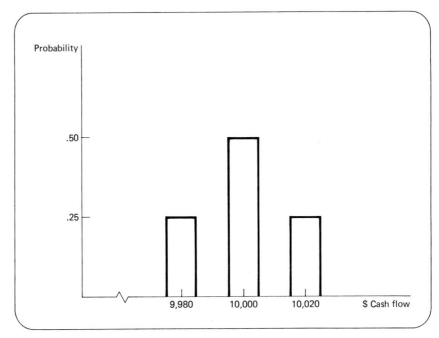

Figure 8-5. Probability distribution of returns from owning one-thousandth of a real estate development.

PROJECT RISK AND PROJECT EVALUATION

The Determinants of Project Risk

The stockholders of a firm ordinarily own many income-producing investments in addition to their stock, for example, stock in other companies, bonds, real estate, and savings accounts. The assets of a particular firm are owned by the stockholders, who view the firm's assets as part of a much larger portfolio of investments. As explained in Chapter 5, the risk of this portfolio is measured by the standard deviation (or coefficient of variation) of the portfolio's returns. In Chapter 5 in discussing risk and diversification we noted that the risk of a *single asset* depends on its impact on the overall risk of investors' portfolios (i.e., on the coefficient of variation of the portfolios' returns) and that this impact depends on two factors: the standard deviation (or coefficient of variation) of the asset's returns and, second, the correlation of the asset's returns with the returns from the other assets in the investors' portfolios. This correlation can be approximated by the correlation of the asset's returns with the economy.[9] Since a firm's project is one of the many assets in the stockholders' port-

9. The importance of the relationship between cash flow and the returns on other assets in the economy has been shown by several writers, including W. F. Sharpe, "Capital Asset Prices: A Theory of Market Equilibrium under Conditions of Risk," *Journal of Finance,* 19 (September 1964), pp. 425–442. The "economy" as used in the present discussion of capital budgeting refers to the returns from the economy as a whole not including the asset or project being analyzed.

folios, project risk depends on its cash flow coefficient of variation and cash flow correlation with the economy.

How do we put coefficient of variation and correlation with the economy together to determine a project's risk? The following general rules apply:

1. For any given coefficient of variation of a project's cash flow, the more closely the project's cash flow varies with the economy (i.e., the higher the correlation with the economy), the riskier is the project.

2. If the project's cash flow tends to move up and down with the general economy (positive correlation with the economy) or shows no tendency to move with or against the economy (zero correlation with the economy), the project is riskier the greater is the coefficient of variation of the project's cash flow.

3. If the project's cash flow tends to move in opposition to the economy (negative correlation with the economy), the project is *less* risky the greater is the coefficient of variation of the project's cash flow. A project with a cash flow that is negatively correlated with the economy has less risk than any project with a cash flow that is positively correlated with the economy.[10]

Point **1** is based on the idea that a firm's project is part of the stockholders' portfolios of other assets (including, as mentioned above, stock and bonds in other firms, real estate, etc.). To determine the riskiness of a project, we must therefore ask how investors determine the risk of an asset. The risk of an asset to investors depends on how it affects the risk of the investors' entire portfolios. These portfolios will ordinarily produce returns that vary rather closely with the economy. If a project's cash flow moves with the economy, it tends to move with the returns provided by other assets in the stockholders' portfolios (is positively correlated with the economy and with other assets in the portfolio). The stronger is this tendency to move together (the higher the correlation), the smaller is the portfolio risk reduction from diversification effects; that is, the project is more risky in the sense that it is less effective in reducing portfolio risk.[11] On the other hand, a low correlation with the economy means that the project's cash flow does not move closely with the income from other assets owned by stockholders and therefore the project is a good diversifying investment; that is, it tends to reduce portfolio risk for stockholders.

Point **2** implies that if the cash flows from two assets have positive and

10. Strictly speaking, these points under 3 hold only if the negative correlation is not extremely close to zero. For further details, see Appendix 8A-1.

11. Portfolio risk is measured by the coefficient of variation (or standard deviation) of the portfolios' returns. See Chap. 5.

identical correlations with the economy (roughly, this means they move up and down with the economy to the same degree), then the cash flow with the higher coefficient of variation, or uncertainty, is riskier. If a firm has several alternative investments the returns from which will tend to do well or poorly as the firm does well or poorly—and if the firm's returns tend to move up and down with the economy—then the implication of **2** is that we can compare the riskiness of the investments on the basis of their coefficients of variation.

Most asset returns have a positive correlation with the economy, and consequently **1** and **2** are by far more relevant than is **3** in actual business situations. Point **3** says that the wider are the swings (higher coefficient of variation), the better as long as they move contrary to the economy, i.e., contrary to the swings in the returns from the other assets making up the stockholders' portfolios. This is because the wider are the project's cash flow fluctuations, the more the cash flow will tend to smooth out (compensate for) the fluctuations in the cash flows from the other assets in the stockholders' portfolios.[12]

Exhibit 8-2 shows how rules **1, 2,** and **3** can be used to rank investments in terms of risk. The relative risk of investments B and C cannot be determined from the information provided because B has a higher coefficient of variation but C has a higher correlation with the economy. To ascertain which of B and C is riskier, we must know the relative weights of coefficient of variation and correlation with the economy in determining risk. Appendix 8A-3 shows how this can be done, and problem 8 at the end of this chapter involves the use of an equation which relates risk to coefficient of variation and correlation with the economy.

Appendix 8A-1 provides an illustration which indicates why rules **1, 2,** and **3** hold. Appendix 8A-2 includes an example similar to that in Exhibit 8-2 which further explores the problem of risk ranking using coefficient of variation and correlation with the economy. Appendix 8A-3 describes how the proper discount rate for a project can be determined using an equation which defines risk in terms of coefficient of variation and correlation with the economy.

We will now examine two methods for taking project risk into account once that risk has been estimated, that is, once we have an estimate of the project's coefficient of variation and correlation with the economy. The first method involves the use of **risk-adjusted discount rates** and the second, the uses of **certainty equivalents.**

12. It is assumed that a firm's project represents a small part of the investor's total portfolio of assets; that is, the project is assumed to not dominate the portfolio.
13. It should be repeated here that although it is the total income to stockholders from all the company's assets that determines the stock's value, the income from any individual project of the firm is a part of that firm's income and consequently is a component of the stockholders' total portfolio income. Therefore, the risk and value of the project must be assessed in light of what it adds to the shareholders' portfolios; and the market discount rate determined on the basis of investor portfolio decisions is the rate that is applicable

Exhibit 8-2. Ranking of Investments in Terms of Risk Using Coefficient of Variation and Correlation with the Economy

Investment	Cash flow's coefficient of variation	Rank by coefficient of variation	Cash flow's correlation with economy	Rank by correlation with economy	Rank by risk (highest risk has rank 1)
A	.9	1	.8	1	1
B	.7	2	.6	3	2 or 3
C	.6	3	.7	2	2 or 3
D	.4	4	.4	4	4
E	.3	5	−.2	6	6[a]
F	0	6	0	5	5

[a] E has the lowest risk because it is negatively correlated with the economy and all the other investments in the table are positively correlated with the economy; by rule 3 in the text above, any cash flow that is negatively correlated with the economy has a lower risk than a cash flow that is positively correlated with the economy. A, D, and F are easily ranked using rules 1 and 2 (see text) since they have the same relative ranking by coefficient of variation (rule 2) and by correlation with the economy (rule 1); this is not so for B and C (see text discussion).

Estimating the Project's Discount Rate

How do we estimate a project's minimum acceptable rate of return (MARR) or cost of capital? That is, what discount rate do we use in discounting a project's expected cash flow to compute its NPV or in comparing with the project's internal rate of return if the IRR method is used? In Chapter 7, it was assumed that any new investment did not affect the financial risk of the firm (did not affect the debt-equity ratio) and had the same business risk as the firm's other investments. As explained in Chapter 6, this meant that the cost of capital applicable to the firm as a whole was also applicable to the new investment. We used the firm's existing cost of capital for all new investment. In Chapter 6 the method for estimating the company's cost of capital was explained.

The firm's cost of capital applicable to the company's old assets cannot be used as the cost of capital for a new investment if the risk of the new investment differs from the risk of the old assets. Instead, the risk-adjusted discount rate appropriate to the project's level of risk should be used.[13] The proper cost of capital on the new project is that rate ordinarily

[13] Footnote 13 begins on page 288.

to the individual project. If cash flow benefits from the firm's diversification (see discussion later in the chapter) are negligible, an individual asset of the firm can be valued on the basis of the additional returns it generates for the firm using the *market* discount rate appropriate to those returns. For a detailed discussion and a proof of this point, see C. W. Haley and L. D. Schall, *The Theory of Financial Decisions* (New York: McGraw-Hill, 1973), chap. 12. Also see L. D. Schall, "Asset Valuation, Firm Investment and Firm Diversification," *Journal of Business* (January 1972), pp. 11–28; and S. C. Myers, "Procedures for Capital Budgeting Under Uncertainty," *Industrial Management Review* (Spring 1968), pp. 1–15.

earned on similar investments elsewhere in the economy; "similar" here means financed in a similar way and producing returns with a similar probability distribution, measured by coefficient of variation and correlation with the general economy.[14] The reasoning for this approach is as follows. The cost of capital, as you will recall from Chapters 6 and 7, is the minimum acceptable rate of return on an investment. The minimum acceptable rate or cost of capital on a project is clearly no less than that rate of return which the firm could earn by investing its money elsewhere in the economy in an investment producing cash flows with the same risk properties as those of the project. If the firm cannot earn as much on the project as it could earn elsewhere with the same risk, it should invest elsewhere before it adopts the project. Furthermore, the rate earned elsewhere on assets of similar risk as those of the project is that rate which satisfies investors, since if this were not true the price of such assets would fall. It is the rate which investors demand in providing capital to the firm for that type of investment since such a rate is available elsewhere in the economy on assets of similar risk. If the project earns more than the rate earned in the economy for that risk, the stockholders will be earning more than the going rate for that risk level and the value of the company's stock will rise. The conclusion is that the proper cost of capital, or minimum acceptable rate of return, on a new investment is the going rate in the economy on that risk class of investment.[15] Ordinarily, the going rate rises as risk rises. The more risky is a project, the higher is its cost of capital; that is, the discount rate is "adjusted" for risk by increasing it to compensate for greater risk. This is illustrated in Figure 8-6.[16]

To actually estimate the cost of capital is a difficult task. Chapter 6 outlines several methods. The basic procedure is to find a firm that has financing similar to that used for the project and has assets generating cash flows with a risk like that of the project [cash flow as defined by Eq. (6-1)].[17] The cost of capital of such a firm is then computed using the proce-

14. When we say the "rate ordinarily earned on similar investments," we mean the rate as defined by the aftertax weighted average cost of capital [as defined by Eq. (6-1)] on similar investments. Since this cost of capital depends upon the risk of the cash flow [cash flow as defined by Eq. (7-1)] and, second, on how the investment is financed (amounts of debt and equity financing), we must find investments elsewhere in the economy with similar cash flow risk and similar financing.

15. We are assuming here that asset prices at any point in time reflect prevailing knowledge, expectations, and investor preferences. This assumption appears to be substantiated by current research on the efficiency of capital markets.

16. The cost of capital is a linear function of risk, as illustrated in Figure 8-6, assuming the CAPM of Appendixes 5B and 6A. In general, the cost of capital increases with risk but not necessarily linearly.

17. The cash flow of Eq. (7-1) ignores the method of financing the investment. The cost of capital as computed in Chap. 6 depends on both the risk of the cash flow of Eq. (7-1) and the method of the firm's financing. Financing is important since the cost of capital is a weighted average of the cost rates (the k) of the various financing sources (debt, new shares, etc.).

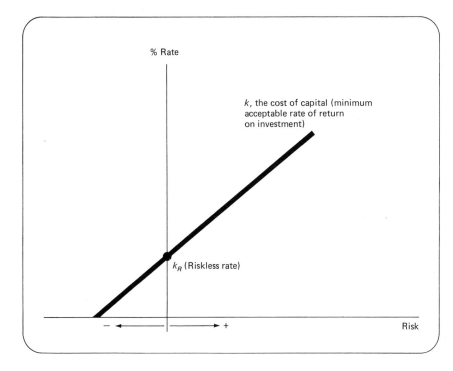

% Rate

k, the cost of capital (minimum acceptable rate of return on investment)

k_R (Riskless rate)

$-$ ← | → $+$

Risk

Figure 8-6. The relationship of the cost of capital to risk as measured by the cash flow's coefficient of variation and its correlation with the economy. Risk is defined here as negative if the correlation with the economy is negative, since in this case the asset actually offsets some of the variations of the other income produced by investors' portfolios. At zero risk (along the vertical axis), the cost of capital is k_R the riskless rate.

dures of Chapter 6. It may be difficult to find another company that exactly fits the financing and cash flow risk properties of the investments undertaken by our firm. If this is so, it may be necessary to estimate a range of cost of capital estimates for firms with similar financing and asset risk. Some point in the range can then be used as the firm's cost of capital on the investment being considered. For example, if the estimates vary from 10 to 14 percent, the firm might use 12 percent as the cost of capital on the new investment. A conservative policy would be to use the higher end of the estimated range, 13 or 14 percent in this example.

Discounting with varying risk over time If the riskiness of a cash flow differs between future periods, it might be appropriate to use a different discount rate or cost of capital for one future period than for another. For example, assume that at time 0 (now) we are evaluating project Q which costs $250 and which will yield an expected cash flow of $100 per year for the next four years. If we feel that the cash flow is riskier the further we look into the future (less certainty about the cash flow), we might want to use a higher rate to discount the expected cash flow of period 4 (CF_4) than to discount CF_3, a higher rate for CF_3 than for CF_2, and a higher rate for CF_2 than for CF_1. Let the rates for discounting CF_1, CF_2, CF_3, and CF_4 be 8, 9, 11, and 12 percent, respectively, where each CF is $100. The net present value of project Q then equals

$$\text{NPV (project Q)} = \frac{\$100}{1 + .08} + \frac{\$100}{(1 + .09)^2} + \frac{\$100}{(1 + .11)^3}$$

$$+ \frac{\$100}{(1 + .12)^4} - \$250$$

$$= \$64$$

If the expected cash flow were declining in risk over time instead of increasing, the discount rate used would be less for cash flows further into the future instead of greater as in the above example.[18]

Certainty Equivalent Approach

The certainty equivalent approach is an alternative to risk-adjusted discount rates for incorporating risk in capital budgeting analysis. This approach determines the riskless cash flow stream that is just as good as the risky cash flow anticipated from a project and then discounts that riskless stream at the riskless rate of interest to determine net present value.

To illustrate, assume that investment S is being evaluated and that it will require an initial $300 outlay (for simplicity, assume that this initial cost is known with certainty) and will generate an expected cash flow of $100 per year during the next two years and an expected cash flow of $200 in the third year. Assume that the cost of capital on the investment is 10 percent (risk-adjusted discount rate) and that the riskless rate of interest is 6 percent (rate of return earned in the economy on riskless assets). We could use the procedure described in Chapter 7 and simply compute the NPV of the asset using the 10 percent cost of capital. An alternative is to use the certainty equivalent approach which involves determining the riskless future stream of returns that investors would find equally desirable as the risky cash flow stream from the asset. Exhibit 8-3 is an example of such riskless amounts.[19] Thus, in this illustration, investors currently (when initial outlay of $300 is made) would be indifferent between receiving $96 one year hence for certain and owning the risky asset year 1 cash flow with expected dollar return of $100. That is, investors are indifferent between a sure thing of $96 received in year 1 and the cash flow

18. Robichek and Myers have shown that using the same discount rate for all periods actually implies a greater risk for the more future cash flows. If risk is the same for all future periods, then we must use a smaller discount rate for more future cash flows. See A. Robichek and S. C. Myers, *Optimal Financing Decisions* (Englewood Cliffs, N.J.: Prentice-Hall, 1965), pp. 79–86. Also see the discussion of certainty equivalents below and in Appendix 8B.

19. The numbers in col. 2 of Exhibit 8-3 are those, as shown below, which are consistent with a riskless interest rate of 6 percent and a risk-adjusted discount rate of 10 percent. In general, for investors who do not like uncertainty, we know that the numbers in col. 2 must be less than those in col. 1 for any cash inflows that are uncertain.

Exhibit 8-3. Certainty Equivalents for Asset S

Time (t)	Expected cash flow (1)	Riskless amount equivalent to risky flow (2)	Certainty equivalent factor a_t (col. 2 ÷ col. 1) (3)
Now	−$300	−$300	1.00
Year 1	100	96	.96
Year 2	100	93	.93
Year 3	200	178	.89

probability distribution with an expected level of $100. Similarly, investors would currently be just as happy to know that they will receive $93 for certain in year 2 as they would be to currently own the risky asset year 2 stream which has an expected payoff of $100 in year 2. And investors are currently indifferent between $178 to be received in year 3 and the asset's year 3 risky cash flow with mean $200. The reason investors are indifferent between the riskless stream and the risky stream with a higher expected level is that investors do not like risk. The asset provides an *expected* return of $100 in year 1, but the amount that actually will occur might be much less, for example, perhaps only $80 or even less; so, investors would be just as happy with $96 for sure.

Column 3 in Exhibit 8-3 shows the certainty equivalent factors, a_t, where the t subscript stands for the time period. Factor a_t states the amount of money received for certain in future period t that is just equivalent (just as good in the eyes of investors) to a period t cash flow probability distribution with $1 of expected return. Thus, investors are currently indifferent between $0.96 received for certain in year 1 and a year 1 cash flow probability distribution from project S with an expected level of $1. The lower is a_t, the less the year t risky cash flow is worth, i.e., the riskier it is perceived as being.[20] A lower a_t means that fewer dollars received for certain in year t are of equal value to the year t risky stream. In the example of Exhibit 8-3, we are assuming that investors view the stream as

20. Actually, a_t depends on both the perceived riskiness of the period t cash flow and how investors feel about incurring risk in period t. Therefore, a decline in a_t as t rises could occur because of increased risk or because of an increased dislike of risk, or both, as t increases. For simplicity we are assuming in the text discussion that the dislike of risk, or risk aversion, is the same for all t; given this assumption, a fall in a_t with greater t necessarily implies more risk as t rises, i.e., as we look further into the future.

more risky as they look further into the future; for this reason, a_t is decreasing as t increases, falling from $a_0 = 1$ down to $a_3 = .89$.

The above discussion implies that

$$\left(\begin{array}{l} \text{Risky period } t \text{ cash flow} \\ \text{with expected level CF}_t \end{array} \right) \text{ is equally desirable as}$$

$$\left(\begin{array}{l} a_t\text{CF}_t \text{ received for} \\ \text{certain in period } t \end{array} \right) \quad \text{(8-1)}$$

Equation (8-1) says that the present value to investors of the risky cash flow equals the present value of the equivalent riskless amount $a_t\text{CF}_t$. That is,

$$\left[\begin{array}{l} \text{Present value of the} \\ \text{risky cash flow} \\ \text{discounted at risk-} \\ \text{adjusted rate } k_t \end{array} \right] = \frac{\text{CF}_t}{(1+k_t)^t} = \frac{a_t\text{CF}_t}{(1+i)^t} = \left[\begin{array}{l} \text{present value of} \\ \text{the riskless amount} \\ \text{discounted at the} \\ \text{riskless rate } i \end{array} \right]$$

$$\text{(8-2)}$$

In (8-2), k_t is the risk-adjusted discount rate used to discount the period t expected cash flow, CF_t; i is the rate of return in the economy earned on riskless assets (the riskless rate of interest) and is therefore the rate used by investors to discount riskless amounts.[21] We use the riskless rate i in Eq. (8-2) to discount $a_t\text{CF}_t$ since $a_t\text{CF}_t$ is a riskless amount, i.e., is a riskless dollar amount that would be equally desirable as the risky cash flow from the asset.

In the Exhibit 8-3 example, $k_t = k = 10$ percent for all t. That is, the certainty equivalent factors a_t imply that investors view the cash flow risk as justifying a 10 percent risk-adjusted rate of return to discount the cash flow. To see this, let's use (8-2) and compute the net present value of the cash flows using the risk-adjusted discount rate method and the certainty equivalent method. Using a risk-adjusted discount rate of 10 percent, the NPV equals

$$\text{NPV} = \frac{\text{CF}_1}{1+k} + \frac{\text{CF}_2}{(1+k)^2} + \cdots + \frac{\text{CF}_n}{(1+k)^n} - I \quad \text{(8-3)}$$

$$= \frac{\$100}{1.10} + \frac{\$100}{(1.10)^2} + \frac{\$200}{(1.10)^3} - \$300$$

$$= \$91 + \$83 + \$150 - \$300 = \$24$$

21. In discussing certainty equivalents, we use i here and in Appendix 8B to signify the riskless rate solely for the purpose of notational clarity. Elsewhere in this chapter and in this book k_R is used to signify the riskless rate.

Using the certainty equivalent approach, with $i = 6$ percent, the net present value equals

$$\text{NPV} = \frac{a_1\text{CF}_1}{1 + i} + \frac{a_2\text{CF}_2}{(1 + i)^2} + \cdots + \frac{a_n\text{CF}_n}{(1 + i)^n} - I \qquad (8\text{-}4)$$

$$= \frac{(.96)\$100}{1.06} + \frac{(.93)\$100}{(1.06)^2} + \frac{(.89)\$200}{(1.06)^3} - \$300$$

$$= \$91 + \$83 + \$150 - \$300 = \$24$$

NPV in (8-3) and (8-4) must be equal since they are simply two different ways of computing the same value. We can use a risk-adjusted rate k which is greater than i, as in (8-3), or, instead, we can adjust the cash flows in the numerator to take care of risk and then discount the risk-adjusted cash flows at the riskless rate, as in (8-4). Both the risk-adjusted discount rate k and the certainty equivalent factors a_t are selected so as to correctly reflect the riskiness of the investment.

In Appendix 8B, the relationships between a_t, i, and k are examined in greater detail. An interesting conclusion is that using the same value for risk-adjusted discount rate k (e.g., 10 percent as in the above example) for all cash flows implies that the more future cash flows are riskier.[22]

The Firm's Diversification Benefits

When Safeco Insurance Company diversified into such areas as real estate development and computer services, one of its intentions was to enter new businesses that would provide additional earnings capable of offsetting fluctuations in the earnings from its existing insurance operations. Safeco's objective was to make its company income less erratic by diversifying into new ventures. Like Safeco, many companies have been attracted by the diversification concept. The conglomerate boom of the 1960s was based in part on the notion that by diversifying into many areas, the firm could reduce its overall risk. Indeed, the idea of not putting "all of one's eggs in one basket" has helped to spur a diversification trend that endures to the present.

We explained earlier that the portfolio diversification and risk consideration for stockholders is taken into account by the project cash flow's coefficient of variation and correlation with the economy. An implication of the *firm's* diversification idea is that we must *also* look at the effect of a

---

22. In the example, $k = 10$ percent and a_t declines from 1 to .89 in Exhibit 8-3. The decline in a_t means that the cash flow is riskier the further we look into the future; that is, the year 2 cash flow is riskier than the year 1 cash flow (since .93 is less than .96), etc. The use of $k = 10$ percent is consistent with this increasing risk since it produces the correct present value [in Eq. (8-2)] of $24.

project on the coefficient of variation of the firm's total cash flow. What additional benefits are produced by lowering the variability of the company's overall cash flow? The benefits that arise are a reduced probability of company bankruptcy and lower costs of financing and managing the firm. If firms could not become bankrupt, if there were no fees for conducting financial transactions (e.g., brokerage charges, flotation costs, and bank lending fees), and if there were no costs in supervising the firm's financial affairs (executive salaries, computer costs, etc.), then a project's coefficient of variation and correlation with the economy would be adequate indicators of a project's risk. However, with bankruptcy a possibility and with the above-mentioned other costs present, a project's impact on the firm's cash flow uncertainty becomes relevant in evaluating that project. The benefits from reducing the firm's cash flow uncertainty (the firm's coefficient of variation) are reduced likelihood of the firm's bankruptcy and lower costs of financing and managing the firm.[23] Let's examine these benefits a little further.

The benefits of the firm's diversification arise because a less variable cash flow often permits the company to avoid certain types of costs. One of these is the cost of bankruptcy. If the cash flow is relatively stable, there is less chance of bankruptcy and its associated costs (disruption of operations as creditors take over, legal and accounting fees, etc.). Also, a more predictable cash flow reduces the likelihood that an unexpected cash deficit will arise. A firm can either prepare for such a deficit by tying up capital in relatively low-return liquid assets such as time deposits and marketable securities (investments which provide a ready source of cash) or, when the need arises, obtain capital externally—by borrowing or selling new shares—which can involve significant costs (underwriting fees, finance charges, legal and accounting costs, etc.). A predictable cash flow obviates the need to maintain high liquidity or to turn frequently to outside sources for financing. It also reduces the resources that need be expended on cash management and financial planning, because these tasks are greatly simplified if cash flows are more predictable.

If an investment produces diversification benefits—i.e., produces the cost reductions mentioned above—these cost savings should be added to the cash flow associated with the project. These are cash flow benefits just as are any cost reduction gains provided by a new investment and

23. Some have argued that a firm's diversification assists investors by creating asset portfolios for the investors (stockholders), thereby eliminating the necessity for investors to do their own diversifying. This is a weak argument, since not only can investors do their own diversifying (and therefore will not significantly benefit if the firm does it for them) but there are mutual funds which perform the diversification function. Furthermore, a firm's diversification can actually be disadvantageous to investors since it can reduce the portfolio options that they have available. For example, if firm A buys firm B, then an investor can now no longer buy different proportions of firms A and B (for example, 10 percent of A and 15 percent of B) since the firms are now merged.

should be taken into account, at least informally. Bankruptcy costs are very hard to estimate and will consequently enter the analysis in a qualitative fashion; that is, projects which reduce bankruptcy risk will be favored, everything else equal. However, savings in terms of financing and financial management costs may be amenable to quantitative estimate and, when this is possible, can enter the cash flow analysis. For example, if these costs are reduced by an average of $20,000 per year for the duration of the investment, say ten years, then the $20,000 would be included in the stream of returns associated with the project.

What determines whether a new investment will produce diversification benefits? Such benefits occur if the variability of the firm's total cash flow is reduced by the investment. Diversification advantages are greater the less the new investment's returns vary in the same direction as do the returns from the firm's other assets, i.e., the lower is the correlation between the investment's cash flow and the firm's other cash flow.

To clarify the firm's diversification concept, assume a simple case in which the firm is considering investing in project A or project B. The economy has an equal probability of recession, normal business conditions, and boom. Project A's cash flow is positively correlated with the firm's other asset returns, which means that when one is high the other is high. This is shown in Exhibit 8-4. Thus, in a recession project A and the firm's other returns are both low, and in prosperity they are both high.

Exhibit 8-4. Positive Correlation (Project A) and Negative Correlation (Project B) between a Project's Cash Flows and the Firm's Other Cash Flows

	Business conditions	Probability	Project cash flow[a]	Other assets' total cash flow	Firm's total cash flow with project[a]
Project A (positive correlation)	Recession	$\frac{1}{3}$	$100	$500	$ 600
	Normal	$\frac{1}{3}$	150	650	800
	Prosperity	$\frac{1}{3}$	200	800	1,000
Project B (negative correlation)	Recession	$\frac{1}{3}$	200	500	700
	Normal	$\frac{1}{3}$	150	650	800
	Prosperity	$\frac{1}{3}$	100	800	900

[a] Project cash flow equals the increase in the firm's cash flow due to adopting the project, that is, equals the firm's total cash flow with the project less the other assets' total cash flow. The figures in the table do not include any resulting diversification benefits from the project; those dollar benefits must be added to the project cash flow column and to the firm's total cash flow with project column to get the amounts including diversification benefits (if any).

The fluctuations in the two therefore tend to reinforce one another. For example, when business is good, the firm generates $1,000, but when business is poor, the cash flow is only $600. On the other hand, project B's cash flow is negatively correlated with the firm's other asset returns, which means that the project generates returns that are relatively high when the firm's other assets produce returns that are low, and vice versa. This is shown in Exhibit 8-4. With recession, project B generates $200, whereas in boom periods it produces only $100. (Project B might be, for example, a credit analysis facility that saves more money in a recession by preventing extension of credit to customers who don't pay their bills.) But the other assets of the firm are more productive during prosperity than in recession. Thus, the result of adding project B is to reduce the firm's cash flow fluctuations because movements in B's cash flow tend to offset movements in the returns from the company's other assets. The firm's total cash flow is $700 in a recession and $900 if there is prosperity (a $200 range of variability) whereas without project B the firm's cash flow can vary from $500 to $800 (a $300 range). The firm's total cash flow is less variable with project B than with project A because in the former case the project's cash flow is negatively correlated with the firm's other cash flow.

In general, the lower is the correlation of a new asset's cash flow with the cash flow from the firm's other assets, the greater will be the diversification benefits from adding the new asset. Project B above is an extreme example involving a negative correlation. In fact, as long as the correlation is not $+1.0$, some diversification benefits can arise, the benefits becoming greater the closer is the correlation to -1.0. In practice, diversification benefits ordinarily arise with cash flows that are positively or zero correlated since negative correlation between investments is uncommon. The rarity of negative correlation is primarily due to the large influence that general economic trends have on the profitability of most investments.

How important are diversification effects in evaluating a project? The answer depends upon the firm. For some firms, diversification effects may be small. It may be that all prospective projects have cash flows that are highly (very positively) correlated with the firm's existing cash flow. This would be most likely if the new projects and the firm's current operations are in the same line of business activity—for example, if all are involved in producing a single product. In this case, if the firm does well, a given project will tend to generate greater returns than if the firm has poor overall performance; diversification effects are minor or do not arise at all. Further, in this situation, the greater is the new asset's cash flow variability (the higher its standard deviation and coefficient of variation), the greater will be the increase in the firm's total cash flow variability due to acquiring the new asset. That is, the greater the cash flow variability of the individual asset, the greater the increase in the firm's overall risk from adding that asset to the firm.[24]

For other firms, particularly those with many products or operating divisions, diversification benefits may be commonplace. Especially for large projects, including merger with or acquisition of another company, diversification advantages can be a primary consideration.

In the above discussion it was recommended that the cash flow diversification benefits generated by a project should be included with the rest of the cash flow produced by the investment in evaluating that project. However, diversification benefits are extremely difficult to estimate, and two alternative approaches are frequently used in practice. The first alternative is to make no attempt to estimate the cash flow diversification benefits but to lower the minimum acceptable rate of return on a project that is expected to produce the firm's diversification. That is, a project that creates diversification benefits is viewed as being less risky in the sense that it reduces the variability of the firm's total cash flow. Thus, for example, the risk-adjusted discount rate on an investment might be 12 percent ignoring diversification considerations but, because it significantly reduces the coefficient of variation of the firm's total cash flow, the risk-adjusted discount rate used to evaluate the project might be only 11 percent. The problem with this method is that it is difficult to determine how much the cost of capital on an investment should be adjusted to take into account diversification effects. Often, the cost of capital is simply adjusted downward a percentage or two with no formal attempt to estimate a precisely correct cost of capital adjustment.

A second alternative approach is less precise than including diversification benefits in the cash flows or adjusting the cost of capital. It is simply to informally favor a project if it provides diversification for the firm. Frequently, companies are selected in merger acquisitions because they are in a different line of business than the acquiring firm and therefore allow for diversification. Of course, there are advantages in addition to diversification benefits that can arise from merger, as is explained in Chapter 21.

---

24. The assumption here that greater cash flow variability means greater risk implies that we are assuming that the firm's cash flow is positively correlated with the economy, which is the usual situation; on this, see the earlier discussion in this chapter on the determinants of project risk. Also, it was assumed in Chap. 7 that the cash flows from all firm investments had the same coefficient of variation and were perfectly correlated with one another (all were high or low together). This implies that there were no diversification benefits from the firm's investment and that all had the same cost of capital.

COMPUTER SIMULATION: ESTIMATING AND EVALUATING CASH FLOWS

Estimating the impact of a project on the firm's cash flow can be a complex task, especially with large investments that affect many aspects of the company's operations. The cash flow impact of a project can be estimated using simulation. Simulation is the artificial duplication of a process, for example, the duplication, at an abstract and simplified level, of the operations of a firm. Simulation analysis can evaluate the effects of a particular policy or decision (such as purchasing a particular asset) on some measure of the firm's performance, for example, on the firm's cash flow. One result of the simulation study is an estimate of the probability distribution of the firm's additional cash flow resulting from the decision.

To illustrate, assume that the management of a multiplant firm wants to know the effect on the firm's cash flow of adding a manufacturing facility to produce a new product. Many changes in the firm's operations will occur which will ultimately be reflected in the firm's net cash flow. These changes might include:

1. Increase in the firm's revenue from sales of the new product. This will depend upon the sales price and quantity sold.
2. Funds might be borrowed to cover the initial cost of the plant. This will increase interest payments on debt in future periods and will thereby affect profits after taxes and interest.
3. Increased advertising and selling expenditures to promote the new product.
4. Increased outlay for labor, materials, power, etc. to produce the product.
5. Rise in managerial staff.
6. Increased bookkeeping and recording expenditures due to rise in overall activity described above.

It becomes immediately obvious that the problem of tracing all the effects through the firm and ultimately to profits is extremely complex. This is especially true since, in general, the various consequences of constructing the new plant are not known with certainty but each conforms to a probability distribution. Thus, the sales price, quantity to be sold, input prices, financing costs, and other quantities must each be represented by a *probability distribution rather than by a single number.* Furthermore, the network of interrelationships among the variables in the problem must be identified and then represented in the computer simulation program by mathematical equations. For example, equations might be included in the simulation to represent the relationship between physical inputs and output (manufacturing production function), and so on. The computer program includes these mathematical equations and the probability distributions for the uncertain variables (**stochastic variables**). The result is a mathematical model of how the investment project will affect the operations of the firm which is written into a computer program. The simulation model is meant to duplicate or simulate the series of events that would occur if the investment were undertaken. When the program is run, the magnitude of each stochastic variable is drawn from its probability distribution and a particular cash flow return is generated. This is done perhaps several hundred times by the computer in order to generate a probability distribution for the cash flow returns from the investment. The cash flow probability distribution is analyzed as described earlier, with the expected cash flow discounted to compute net present value (or used to compute internal rate of return). The riskiness of the cash flow is indicated by the cash flow probability distribution, and this risk evaluation is used as a basis in selecting the proper discount rate or cost of capital. Computer programs can also be designed to generate a probability distribution of rates of return on the investment. The simulation process is illustrated in Figure 8-7.

The use of simulation is currently restricted in most cases to analysis of large-scale investments by major firms. However, as computer services become less expensive and familiarity with simulation techniques increases, applications may come to include evaluation of smaller capital outlays by small as well as large companies. And although it may appear that estimating probability distributions is extremely difficult, and consequently only worthwhile for large projects, experience indicates that

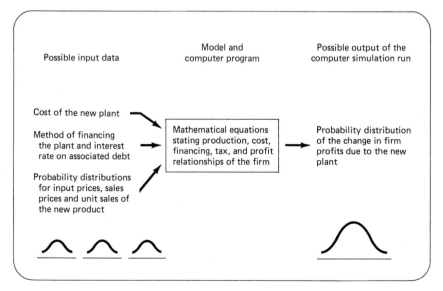

Figure 8-7. An example of the input and output for the simulation analysis of an investment.

acceptable estimates of probabilities can often be made by an experienced staff with only limited difficulty.[25] Furthermore, in a world of uncertainty, a range of estimates with probabilities is generally more realistic than a single estimate.

RISK EVALUATION AND DECISION TREE ANALYSIS

A frequent problem confronting management involves the choices between two or more actions, with uncertainty as to the exact consequences of each action. The diagrammatic layout of this problem is often referred to as a **decision tree** because it has the appearance of a tree with branches. The decision tree approach is a useful way of illustrating the alternatives confronting the firm and can assist a manager in "visualizing" the situation.

To illustrate a decision tree layout, assume that a firm is considering two options, only one of which will be adopted: alternative A to produce product A, and alternative B to produce product B. A will require a current outlay of $1,000,000, and B will require an outlay of $2,000,000. If A is adopted, there is a .3 probability of a future cash flow with a present value of $1,500,000 and a .7 probability of a future cash flow with a present value of $1,100,000. The probabilities that B will produce a future cash flow with a present value of $4,000,000, $2,500,000, and $1,000,000 are .2, .6, and .2, respectively. This situation is illustrated in Figure 8-8. The better choice is B since its NPV of $500,000 exceeds A's NPV of $220,000.

A particularly useful application of the decision tree format involves situations in which a decision at one point in time affects the firm's financial position and the decisions to be made at some later point. A technique referred to as **dynamic programming** can be applied in such a situation. Its advantage is that it can greatly reduce the number of steps to a solution by eliminating options that are clearly inferior to others at an early stage in the analysis. Rather than being required to consider every possible series of decisions which the firm might plan to adopt and then choosing the one with the highest NPV of expected cash flows, only certain series of decisions need be considered. Appendix 8C provides a simple sequential decision problem and the solution.

The dynamic programming technique is quite useful for relatively simple problems. However, if the number of alternative choices of action is very large or if the relationships are highly complex, the technique is not easily applied. As a result, dynamic programming has had only limited applications to actual business problems.

25. See David B. Hertz, "Risk Analysis in Capital Investment," *Harvard Business Review* (January–February 1964), pp. 95–106.

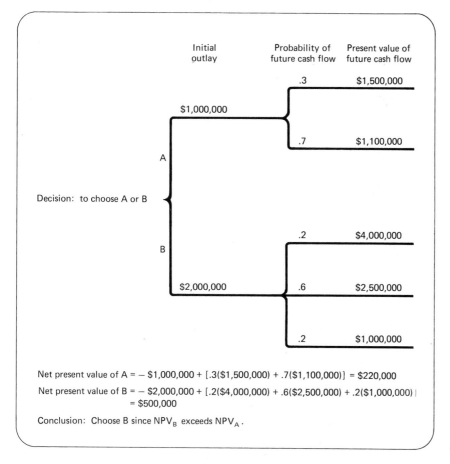

Net present value of A = − $1,000,000 + [.3($1,500,000) + .7($1,100,000)] = $220,000

Net present value of B = − $2,000,000 + [.2($4,000,000) + .6($2,500,000) + .2($1,000,000)]
= $500,000

Conclusion: Choose B since NPV$_B$ exceeds NPV$_A$.

Figure 8-8. Example of a decision tree.

SUMMARY

The cash flow generated by an investment can be represented by a probability or frequency distribution. The mean or average level of cash flow for each future period is computed by using the cash flow probability distribution for the period. The expected cash flow can be discounted to determine a net present value or can be analyzed in computing an internal rate of return. The cash flow distribution reflects the uncertainty of the project's cash flow, and this uncertainty is measured by the standard deviation and the coefficient of variation.

The risk of a project depends on its cash flow's coefficient of variation and correlation with the general economy (the degree to which the cash flow moves up and down with the economy). In evaluating a project, its risk can be taken into account by using a cost of capital (minimum acceptable rate of return) that is appropriate to that level of risk. Greater risk means a higher minimum acceptable rate of return. An alternative approach for incorporating risk into the evaluation process is to use certainty equivalents, which are riskless amounts that are viewed as equivalent to the risky cash flow generated by the project.

Computer simulation is an extremely useful tool for deriving a probability distribution of cash flows associated with a project. Decision tree analysis graphically represents the firm's options and the expected consequences of each option. It can be helpful in analyzing available alternatives.

QUESTIONS

1. Why is the standard deviation of an an investment's cash flow an inadequate measure of the investment's risk?

2. What are we assuming about investors in the firm when the correlation of a project's cash flow with the economy is used as one of the measures of the project's risk?

3. A firm has investments A, B, C, and D noted below. Rank them in terms of risk.

Investment	Cash flow coefficient of variation	Cash flow correlation with economy
A	.4	.5
B	.1	.2
C	.7	.5
D	.4	−.3

4. Assume that investments Q and R have cash flows with the following properties:

Investment	Cash flow coefficient of variation	Cash flow correlation with economy
Q	.4	.6
R	.7	.5

Is it possible without further information to rank Q and R in terms of risk? Why or why not? If not, what further information would you need?

5. Assume that a firm has raised $10 million by selling new shares and bonds to finance its entire current capital budget, which involves investing in many individual projects. What is the reasoning for using different costs of capital, i.e., different risk-adjusted discount rates, for investments of different risk if they are financed from the same $10 million source of funds?

6. If you are considering an investment in an apartment building and have estimated the expected future cash flows from the building, how might you go about estimating a proper risk-adjusted discount rate for the investment to determine the apartment's net present value?

7. What are the benefits to a firm from reducing the coefficient of variation of its total cash flow? In evaluating a particular project, what are the two methods of taking into account such diversification benefits to a firm that result from the project?

8. The expected return on insurance is negative in the sense that each dollar of premium paid to the insurance company produces less than $1 of expected proceeds from the insurance company. (If this were not so, insurance companies would go bankrupt since they must earn enough to cover their administrative costs and also produce a return to those investing capital in the insurance companies.) Why then do firms buy property insurance, and how does this relate to the discussion in this chapter?

9. Is it usually realistic to suppose that cash flows in year 2 are independent of those in year 1? If this is not assumed (that is, if we assume dependence), what happens to the number of possible outcomes which must be examined?

10. Discuss the practical limitations of:
    a) Performing computer simulations over more than a two or three year horizon period.
    b) Doing a decision tree analysis for more than a two or three year period.

Visit one or more large firms in your area and inquire about how the firms perform their capital budgeting analyses. Among the questions you might want to ask are:

PROJECT

1. How much does the firm spend each year on capital outlays?
2. What capital budgeting techniques are employed (present value, IRR, payback, accounting rate or return, etc.)?
3. If a cost of capital is used, how is the cost of capital determined and what is its numerical magnitude?
4. If cash flow is used in evaluating projects, how is it computed?
5. How is risk assessed for a particular investment, e.g., using probability distributions, subjective assessment without quantification, no assessment at all, etc.?
6. How is risk accounted for in analyzing investments, e.g., by using risk-adjusted discount rates, certainty equivalents, etc.?

PROBLEMS

1. Philos Libre is a rare book collector and in January he purchased a first edition of Timothy Crown's classic *Morning of Yesterday's Today,* for $300. Philos plans to sell the book in December at a book show and has assigned the following probability distribution to the book's sale price.

Price	Probability
$200	0.1
$300	0.2
$400	0.5
$600	0.2

   a) Graph the probability distribution of the book's December price.
   b) What is the expected price of the book in December? [Ans.: $400]
   c) What is the standard deviation and coefficient of variation of the book's price? [Ans.: $118; .295]

2. The probability distribution for the annual cash flow from a particular project is stated below.

Cash flow	Probability
$0 to $30	0.2
$30 to $60	0.6
$60 to $90	0.2

   a) Graph the probability distribution.
   b) What is the expected cash flow? [Ans.: $45]

3. Pathetic Props, Inc., manufactures specialty products for stage, motion picture, and television productions. The company has just signed a five-year contract with a small movie studio to produce whatever props are needed by the studio. The agreement specifies that Pathetic Props must immediately invest $25,000 in new production equipment to ensure its ability to fulfill the contract. For each of the next five years the net cash flows from sales under this contract and the associated probabilities are shown below.

Annual net cash flow	Probability
−$10,000	0.2
$0	0.2
$20,000	0.6

   Assume that the cost of capital on this project is 12 percent.
   a) What is the annual expected cash flow for the project?
   b) What is the standard deviation of the annual cash flow?

c) What is the coefficient of variation of the annual cash flow?

d) Should Pathetic Props have signed the contract?

4. Luke Taurus, a chemist for Jean Petit Snout, Inc., a small manufacturer of perfume, has just discovered a new fragrance that could be a sensation. Luke has tentatively named the fragrance "Here Lassie," because it evokes memories of the scent of his childhood dog, Chips. Luke has presented his discovery to the head of his department, and the department head feels that the best plan is to finish development of "Here Lassie," and then sell the formula to one of the major perfume companies. The current outlay to complete the development is $50,000. The project will require another $20,000 during the next year, and in two years the formula will be sold. The current $50,000 outlay and the coming year's $20,000 cash outlay (assume that this $20,000 occurs one period from now) *are known with certainty*. However, the price to be received for the formula is not known. The marketing manager of Jean Paul Snout believes that this project is an "all or nothing" venture. He feels that there is a 50 percent chance of total failure (zero cash flow in two years) and a 50 percent chance of tremendous success ($2 million cash flow in two years). This is shown below.

Year 2 (two years hence) cash flow	Probability
$0	0.5
$2 million	0.5

a) What is the expected cash flow for year 1 (one year hence) and year 2 (two years hence)?

b) What are the standard deviation and coefficient of variation of the year 1 and year 2 cash flows?

c) If the riskless rate of interest is 6 percent and the risk-adjusted discount rate on the year 2 expected cash flow is 15 percent, what is the NPV of the "Here Lassie" project?

5. The Turner-Buck Land Development Corporation believes in developing and disposing of its properties within a year of acquiring them. It is currently looking at a piece of land in a wilderness area which it can develop in one of two ways.

It can clear the land for a housing tract, install access roads, sewer lines, etc., and turn it over to a housing builder in the following year, or it can design a "Wilderness Tours" park and sell out within a year to Touring Lands Enterprises, a company specializing in recreation and entertainment—or to some comparable enterprise. During the year all of the risk involved in either choice will be assumed by Turner-Buck, and they will sell out at a price which will depend on conditions prevailing one year hence.

The tract development alternative requires an investment (including the land purchase) of $180,000, and the company has made optimistic, anticipated, and pessimistic estimates of the net cash flow accruing from the sale one year hence. The estimates are $260,000, $200,000, and $160,000, respectively. In addition, they have estimated the probabilities of these outcomes to be .3, .5, and .2, respectively.

The park development will require a total investment (including land) of only $94,000, and in this case the sale in one year will yield $120,000, $110,000, or $100,000, with probabilities .2, .6, and .2, respectively.

Both of these schemes are correlated with general economic conditions. The former is tied to the general housing market, and the latter will depend heavily on the willingness of individuals to make personal expenditures on recreation. Hence the housing project is estimated to have a correlation of .7 with the economy, and the park development a correlation of .4 with the economy. There are no internal diversification benefits to the firm. All the risk of these two investments is summarized by the coefficients of variation of the cash flows and their correlation with the economy.

a) Graph the probability distribution of the year-end cash flows for each of these two investments.
b) What is the expected cash flow for each investment?
c) For each investment find the standard deviation of the year-end cash flow and the coefficient of variation of each cash flow.
d) Which of the two investments is the more risky, or is this impossible to determine given the above information? In either case, explain.
e) If the risk-adjusted discount rate is 18 percent on the housing tract development and 12 percent on the wilderness park, which of these two investments should be chosen?

6. Mills Tooling has the following projects A through F. Rank them in terms of riskiness.

Project	Coefficient of variation	Correlation with the economy
A	.1	.3
B	.5	.6
C	.2	.4
D	.5	.4
E	1.8	.9
F	0	0

[Ans.: F, A, C, D, B, and E, with E the riskiest]

7. Napoleon Bakeries has investments A through F with the characteristics stated below. All cash flows are indicated by the figures in the
table. The risk of each project depends on its cash flow's coefficient
of variation and correlation with the economy.

Investment	Expected annual cash flow	Standard deviation of annual cash flow	Correlation of cash flow with the economy
A	$8,000	$2,000	.4
B	$10,000	$0	0
C	$9,000	$6,000	.6
D	$20,000	$10,000	−.2
E	$15,000	$3,000	.2
F	$10,000	$8,000	.5

a) Compute the coefficient of variation for each investment.
b) Rank the investments in terms of their coefficients of variation.
c) Rank the investments in terms of their correlations with the
economy.
d) How would you rank the investments in terms of risk? You may
wish to review the text discussion on the determinants of project
risk. You will find in solving this problem that the ranking by coefficient of variation will not be identical to the ranking by correlation with the economy; consequently you will not be able to determine relative risk in all cases. With such nonidentical rankings,
you need a specific equation which gives a numerical measure of
risk which is a function of the coefficient of variation and the correlation with the economy (see problem 8).

8. Figure 8-6 is deliberately vague about the exact way to measure risk.
Suppose we utilize the measure $\rho_i CV_i$ where ρ_i is the correlation coefficient between investment i and the economy and CV_i is investment
i's coefficient of variation. Therefore, the vertical axis of Figure 8-6 is
k_i, the risk-adjusted discount rate, and the horizontal axis is $\rho_i CV_i$,
the level of risk. Assume that the "price of risk" (which is the slope
of the line) is .1 and the rate of return required on a risk-free asset is 6
percent; thus, for each unit increase in risk ($\rho_i CV_i$) there is a 10 percent increase in k_i. Therefore, the discount rate for asset i is $k_i =$
$.06 + .1\rho_i CV_i$ (measured in decimals, e.g., $.08 = 8$ percent).

a) Draw a graph similar to Figure 8-6 showing the relationship
between k_i and risk (risk equal to $\rho_i CV_i$) that is implied by the information provided above.
b) Compute the risk-adjusted discount rates for Napoleon Bakeries'

investments A through F of problem 7. [Partial ans.: $k_A = 7$ percent]

c) Assume for simplicity that in the table of problem 7 the indicated expected annual cash flows for investments A, B, and C continue for ten years, with the first cash flow occurring one year hence. The initial outlay for investment A is $50,000, for B is $80,000, and for C is $40,000. A, B, and C are mutually exclusive. Using the net present value method, should Napoleon Bakeries adopt A, B, or C?

9. Parlor Games, Inc., is introducing a new game which, like the hula hoop of long ago, is expected to be a passing fad. The new game, called "Dish It Out," has an expected two-year life. The initial promotion and production outlays total $400,000. The expected cash flow in years 1 and 2 are $400,000 and $150,000 respectively. There is far greater uncertainty associated with the year 2 cash flow than there is with the year 1 cash flow, and therefore a discount rate of 20 percent is used on the year 2 flow whereas a 15 percent rate is used to discount the year 1 flow. Is the "Dish It Out" game a good investment for Parlor Games, Inc.? [Ans.: NPV = $51,993]

10. Cartwright Tools can obtain a distributorship in a new territory for $200,000. It is unsure about the profitability of the territory and has estimated the following expected cash flows and appropriate discount rates for each:

Time	Expected annual cash flow	Risk-adjusted discount rate
1	$20,000	10%
2	$30,000	12%
3 and thereafter	$40,000	15%

Cartwright management feels that a higher discount rate is appropriate for more future cash flows because of markedly increasing uncertainty about the more distant future.

What is the net present value of the distributorship?

11. If a project has an expected cash flow two years hence of $100, the riskless interest rate is 8 percent, and the certainty equivalent factor $a_2 = .94$, what would be the appropriate risk-adjusted discount rate for the investment? [Ans.: Risk-adjusted discount rate = 11.4 percent]

12. Chafe Lotions, Incorporated, produces hand and face lotions. It has just obtained a laboratory facility for $80,000. The facility will last for five years and has the expected cash flows shown on page 311:

Year	Expected cash flow	Certainty equivalent factor (a_t)
1	$20,000	.95
2	$40,000	.9
3	$40,000	.85
4	$40,000	.8
5	$50,000	.76

The riskless rate of interest is 6 percent. What is the facility's net present value?

13. Four Seas' Bounty Fish Packing, Inc., is evaluating a capital project which will require a current outlay of $400,000. The cash flows from the project will begin one year later and are stated below. The risk-free rate is 6 percent, and the risk-adjusted discount rate Four Seas has decided to use on the investment is 12 percent. Four Seas has also estimated the certainty equivalent factors for each year that are indicated below:

Year	Expected cash flow	Certainty equivalent factors (a_t)
1	$50,000	.912
2	$50,000	.880
3	$150,000	.695
4	$350,000	.880

a) Verify that the net present value is the same for this investment whether the firm uses the risk-adjusted discount rate of 12 percent or uses the certainty equivalent approach.

b) Is the above set of certainty equivalent factors equivalent to the 12 percent risk-adjusted discount rate? Why or why not? To answer this question, for *each* year (years 1 to 4) separately compute the risk-adjusted discount rate that would be appropriate for discounting that year's expected cash flow. To compute the risk-adjusted discount rate, use the certainty equivalent factors (a_t) shown above and the riskless rate.

c) Consider the alternative set of certainty equivalent factors a'_t shown on page 312 and determine the risk-adjusted discount rate that would be appropriate for discounting each year's expected cash flow. (This is done as in b above.)

Year	Expected cash flow	Alternative set of certainty equivalent factors (a_i)
1	$50,000	.946
2	$50,000	.896
3	$150,000	.848
4	$350,000	.802

d) What can you conclude from the results of **a, b,** and **c** above?

the determinants of project risk, risk ranking, and computing a risk-adjusted discount rate

This appendix explores the risk ranking of investments using the coefficient of variation and correlation with the economy. A simple numerical example will be used to illustrate rules **1, 2,** and **3** stated in the text discussion of the determinants of project risk. The rules are then applied in ranking a set of projects in terms of risk. The third section of the appendix shows how coefficient of variation and correlation with the economy can be used to compute a risk-adjusted discount rate if an equation to perform this computation is available. The equation we will use is that which is implied by the capital asset pricing model (CAPM) and which is used in practice.

1. THE DETERMINANTS OF PROJECT RISK

Rules **1, 2,** and **3** in the text section on the determinants of project risk will be restated below, with **3** in the text now stated in two parts as **3a** and **3b**.

1. For any given coefficient of variation of a project's cash flow, the more closely the project's cash flow varies with the economy (i.e., the higher the correlation with the economy), the riskier is the project.
2. If the project's cash flow tends to move up and down with the general economy (positive correlation with the economy), the project is riskier the greater is the coefficient of variation of the project's cash flow.
3. a) If the project's cash flow tends to move in opposition to the economy (negative correlation with the economy), the project is *less* risky the greater is the coefficient of variation of the project's cash flow.
   b) A project with a cash flow that is negatively correlated with the economy is less risky than any project with a cash flow that is positively correlated with the economy.[26]

In the illustrations below, the investments of the firm are viewed as part of the total portfolio of assets owned by stockholders in the firm. As

---

26. Actually, rules **3a** and **3b** hold for any project i only if $|\rho_i|$ (absolute value of ρ_i) is greater than $SD(CF_i)/SD(CF_E)$ where ρ_i is the correlation of project i's cash flow with the economy and where $SD(CF_i)$ and $SD(CF_E)$ are the standard deviation of the cash flow from the project and the standard deviation of the cash flow from the entire portfolio of other assets owned by investors in the firm. It is extremely likely that if ρ_i is negative it will satisfy the above condition (and rules **3a** and **3b** will hold) since $SD(CF_i)$ is generally much smaller than $SD(CF_E)$.

explained in Chapter 5, the risk of a single investment depends on how it affects the overall risk of investors' total portfolios. The risk of an investor's entire portfolio is measured by the coefficient of variation of the returns from the portfolio. To determine the risk of a project, we must ask how it affects the risk position of investors (stockholders) in the firm, and this depends on how the project alters the risk (coefficient of variation) of stockholders' portfolios. Rules **1** to **3b** indicate how the coefficient of variation and correlation with the economy of a project's cash flow determines how the project affects the risk of stockholders' portfolios. A project is considered riskier if it raises the coefficient of variation of the returns from the stockholders' entire portfolios of assets. The numerical illustration below shows how a project affects the risk of a stockholder's entire portfolio. We assume that stockholders are sufficiently well diversified that the returns from their portfolios of investments other than the projects we are analyzing (e.g., their real estate, other stocks and bonds, etc.) move up and down with the economy. This is consistent with current portfolio theory and is very useful in analyzing how rates of return in the asset markets arise.

The illustration below is extremely simple and is meant only to provide an intuitive understanding of the issues involved. In the example, the firm has investments G through N with the characteristics stated in Exhibit 8-5. E is the portfolio of investments held by an investor in the firm. The returns from portfolio E are assumed to move up and down with the

Exhibit 8-5. Cash Flows from the Firm's Projects

					Project				
	E	G	H	I	J	K	L	M	N
Business condition:[a]									
Boom	$1,200	$ 90	$ 40	$100	$100	$110	$160	$110	$160
Normal	1,000	100	100	90	40	90	40	100	100
Recession	800	110	160	110	160	100	100	90	40
Correlation with economy	1.0^b	−1.0	−1.0	−.5	−.5	+.5	+.5	+1.0	+1.0
Expected return	$1,000	$100	$100	$100	$100	$100	$100	$100	$100
Coefficient of variation	.16	.08	.49	.08	.49	.08	.49	.08	.49

[a] It is assumed that the probability is the same for boom, normal business, and recession (each has a probability of $\frac{1}{3}$).

[b] The correlation of any variable with itself is always +1.0.

economy, and therefore correlation of the firm's investment with E is the same as the correlation of the firm's investment with the economy. Let's see how each of rules **1, 2, 3a,** and **3b** is illustrated by the data in the table:

1. As shown in the upper half of Exhibit 8-5, investments G, I, K, and M each have a coefficient of variation of .08, but they have correlations with the economy of -1, $-.5$, $+.5$, and $+1$, respectively. What happens when E is combined with each of these assets? This is shown in Exhibit 8-6. E + G has a coefficient of variation of .141; E + I, E + K, and E + M have coefficients of variation of .145, .152, and .156, respectively. The risk of the portfolio of the project with E is greater (higher coefficient of variation of the combination) the higher is the correlation of the project with the economy. The same conclusion applies if comparing projects H, J, L, and N (each of which has a coefficient of variation of .49).

2. Compare project K and project L. K and L both have a correlation with the economy of $+.5$; L has the higher coefficient of variation and therefore, using rule 2, E + L is riskier than E + K. The same comparison can be made between projects M and N; N adds more risk because it has the higher coefficient of variation, and therefore E + N has a higher coefficient of variation than does E + M.

3a. Compare G and H. Both have a correlation of -1.0 with the economy, but H has the higher coefficient of variation. Combining E with H results in a portfolio (E + H) with lower risk than a portfolio combining E with G (E + G). This is because the wider swings in the returns from H are better at offsetting fluctuations in E than are the swings in the returns from G. H is therefore less risky than G in the sense that it results in a

Exhibit 8-6. Returns from Combinations of Investor's Portfolio E with the Firm's Projects

	Combination of E and projects							
	E + G	E + H	E + I	E + J	E + K	E + L	E + M	E + N
Business condition:[a]								
Boom	$1,290	$1,240	$1,300	$1,300	$1,310	$1,360	$1,310	$1,360
Normal	1,100	1,100	1,090	1,040	1,090	1,040	1,100	1,100
Recession	910	960	910	960	900	900	890	840
Expected return	$1,100	$1,100	$1,100	$1,100	$1,100	$1,100	$1,100	$1,100
Coefficient of variation	.141	.104	.145	.132	.152	.175	.156	.193

[a] It is assumed that the probability is the same for boom, normal business, and recession.

portfolio for investors with less risk. The same reasoning implies that J is less risky than I since E + J has a lower coefficient of variation than does E + I.

3b. Notice that if we combine E with any of the projects that is negatively correlated with the economy (G, H, I, or J), the resulting combination is less risky than a combination of E with any of the projects that is positively correlated with the economy (K, L, M, or N). Thus, the coefficient of variation of E + G, E + H, E + I, or E + J is less than the coefficient of variation of E + K, E + L, E + M, or E + N.

2. RISK RANKING USING COEFFICIENT OF VARIATION AND CORRELATION WITH THE ECONOMY

In the text a simple example was provided which showed how projects can be ranked in terms of risk by comparing their coefficients of variation and their correlations with the economy. Exhibit 8-7 provides a slightly more complex example.

The information in the exhibit is insufficient to determine whether T or U is the riskier project because T has the higher coefficient of variation but U has the higher correlation with the economy.

It is also impossible from the information provided to establish whether W or Y is the riskier investment. Y has the lower (more negative) correlation with the economy and by rule **1** above is therefore less risky on that basis; but W has the greater coefficient of variation, and by rule **3a**, an

Exhibit 8-7. Ranking of Investment in Terms of Risk Using Coefficient of Variation and Correlation with the Economy

Investment	Cash flow's coefficient of variation	Rank by coefficient of variation	Cash flow's correlation with economy	Rank by correlation with economy	Rank by risk (highest risk has rank 1)
Q	.9	1	.8	1 or 2	1
R	.8	2 or 3	.8	1 or 2	2
S	.8	2 or 3	.6	3	3
T	.6	4	.4	5	4 or 5
U	.5	5	.5	4	4 or 5
V	.3	6	.2	6	6
W	.2	7	−.3	8	8 or 9
X	.2	8	−.4	9 or 10	10
Y	.1	9	−.4	9 or 10	8 or 9
Z	0	10	0	7	7

investment that is negatively correlated with the economy is less risky the greater is its coefficient of variation, implying that W is less risky than Y. X is obviously the lowest in risk of all the investments since none of the projects has a lower correlation with the economy and X has as large a coefficient of variation as does W; therefore by rule **1** and by rule **3a,** no investment is less risky than is X.

In Exhibit 8-7, we found that some of the investments (*U* relative to *T,* and *W* relative to *Y*) could not be ranked in terms of risk because of conflicting rankings by coefficient of variation and by correlation with the economy. However, if we were to have available an equation which provides a single measure of risk in terms of coefficient of variation and correlation with the economy, then the investments could be ranked. The capital asset pricing model provides such a relationship. One way of mathematically representing risk using the CAPM is as follows:[27]

3. COMPUTING A RISK-ADJUSTED DISCOUNT RATE

$$\text{Risk of investment i} = q \cdot CV_i \cdot \rho_i \qquad (8\text{-}5)$$

where q is a number that evolves from the equilibrium model, CV_i is the coefficient of variation of the cash flow from asset i and ρ_i is the correlation of the cash flow from asset i with the economy (with the returns from all assets in the economy).[28] The risk-adjusted discount rate k_i that is appropriate to the investment equals[29]

$$k_i = \frac{1 + k_R}{1 - q \cdot CV_i \cdot \rho_i} - 1 \qquad (8\text{-}6)$$

27. Two more common measures of risk using the CAPM [both of which are consistent with Eq. (8-5)] are first, the covariance of the rate of return on an asset and the rate of return on all assets in the economy and, second, that covariance divided by the variance of the rate of return on all assets in the economy. The second definition is referred to as the asset's Beta. These measures of risk were discussed in Appendix 5B.

28. In Eqs. (8-5) and (8-6), $q = (k_E - k_R)/\sigma(r_E)$ where k_E is the expected rate of return on all assets in the economy, k_R is the riskless rate and $\sigma(r_E)$ is the standard deviation of the rate of return on all assets in the economy. Using this definition of q, Eq. (8-6) follows directly from the CAPM equilibrium valuation equation; for a proof of this, see C. W. Haley and L. D. Schall, *The Theory of Financial Decisions* (New York: McGraw-Hill, 1973), chap. 8, eq. (8-26), and related discussion (Haley and Schall use λ' instead of q). In Appendixes 5B and 6A we use k_M instead of k_E; they have identical meaning.

29. The capital asset pricing model defines "economy" as including the asset that is being analyzed whereas the rest of the discussion in this chapter defines economy as excluding the asset being analyzed. From a practical point of view, this definitional difference is of no importance since the project itself is likely to be of negligible significance in affecting the total economy. Using the CAPM definition of the economy, a project with a correlation with the economy of exactly zero ($\rho_i = 0$) will have a k_i in Eq. (8-6) equal to the riskless rate k_R.

Exhibit 8-8. Computing the Level of Risk and the Risk-Adjusted Discount Rates for Investments

Investment (1)	Cash flow's coefficient of variation (CV_i) (2)	Cash flow's correlation with economy (ρ_i) (3)	Risk $[= q \cdot CV_i \cdot \rho_i = .10 \times (2) \times (3)]$ (4)	Risk rank (highest risk first) (5)	Risk-adjusted discount rate k_i [see Eq. (8-6)] (6)
Q	.9	.8	.072	1	14.2%
R	.8	.8	.064	2	13.2
S	.8	.6	.048	3	11.3
T	.6	.4	.024	5	8.6
U	.5	.5	.025	4	8.7
V	.3	.2	.006	6	6.6
W	.2	−.3	−.006	9	5.4
X	.2	−.4	−.008	10	5.2
Y	.1	−.4	−.004	8	5.6
Z	0	0	.00	7	6.0

where k_R is the rate of return earned in the economy on riskless assets (the "riskless rate"). Notice in Eq. (8-6) that as CV_i or ρ_i increases, k_i also increases as long as the correlation with the economy ρ_i is positive (it can be shown that $q \cdot CV_i \cdot \rho_i$ cannot equal or exceed 1 as long as CV_i is finite).

In Exhibit 8-8, risk as measured by (8-5) and k_i as measured by (8-6) are computed for investments Q through Z of Exhibit 8-7. It is assumed in the computation that the riskless rate k_R is equal to 6 percent and $q = .10$. Since we now have an equation [Eq. (8-5)] that defines risk in terms of CV_i and ρ_i, the ambiguity that arose earlier concerning investments T, U, W, and Y no longer exists.

certainty equivalents and risk-adjusted discount rates

Using the text discussion of varying risk over time and varying discount rates, we can express net present value as

$$\text{NPV} = \frac{\text{CF}_1}{1 + k_1} + \frac{\text{CF}_2}{(1 + k_2)^2} + \cdot \cdot \cdot + \frac{\text{CF}_n}{(1 + k_n)^n} - I \qquad (8\text{-}7)$$

where k_t is the risk-adjusted discount rate for discounting the period t expected cash flow CF_t. We also know that, using certainty equivalents, NPV also equals

$$\text{NPV} = \frac{a_1\text{CF}_1}{1 + i} + \frac{a_2\text{CF}_2}{(1 + i)^2} + \cdot \cdot \cdot + \frac{a_n\text{CF}_n}{(1 + i)^n} - I \qquad (8\text{-}8)$$

The NPV's in (8-7) and (8-8) are equal, and so is each term in (8-7) equal to the corresponding certainty equivalent term in (8-8); that is

$$\frac{\text{CF}_t}{(1 + k_t)^t} = \frac{a_t\text{CF}_t}{(1 + i)^t} \qquad (8\text{-}9)$$

Equation (8-9) implies that

$$a_t = \frac{(1 + i)^t}{(1 + k_t)^t} = \left(\frac{1 + i}{1 + k_t}\right)^t \qquad (8\text{-}10)$$

Notice from (8-10) that if k_t is the same for all t, that is, if we use the same discount rate for all future period cash flows regardless of how far into the future the flows will occur, then a_t falls as t rises. For example, if $k = 10$ percent and $i = 6$ percent, then $a_1 = .96$, $a_2 = .93$, $a_3 = .89$ (these were the figures in the example in the text discussion of certainty equivalents). But with a_t falling as t gets bigger, we are saying that risk is becoming greater the further into the future cash flow occurs since, as explained in the text, a smaller a_t means that the cash flow is riskier (investors are willing to take a smaller certain amount for each dollar of expected cash flow). For any constant k ($k_t = k$ for all t) in (8-10), a_t must decline as t rises, implying that a constant k means rising risk. (See Figure 8-9.)

If we want to hold risk constant, that is, make a_t in (8-10) the same for all t, we must reduce k_t as t increases. For example, with $i = 6$ percent, if $a_t = .96$ for all t, then substituting these values into Eq. (8-10) and solving for k_t, we find that $k_1 = 10$ percent, $k_2 = 8.2$ percent, $k_3 = 7.4$ percent,

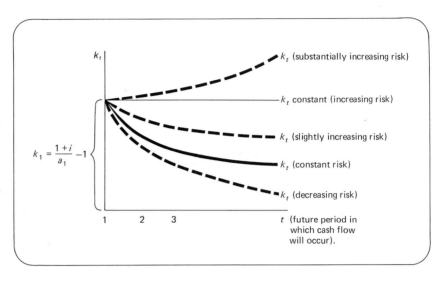

Figure 8-9. Behavior of k_t for different risk assumptions. If k_t falls less sharply (or is constant or rising) than the k_t (constant risk) schedule indicates, then risk is assumed to be rising; if k_t falls more sharply than the k_t (constant) schedule indicates, then risk is assumed to be falling.

etc. Holding risk constant as we look into the future means that we use a smaller and smaller k for cash flows further into the future in computing a present value in Eq. (8-7). This is illustrated in Figure 8-9.

decision tree illustration

To illustrate a decision tree analysis, assume that Bulaxy Corporation is about to introduce a new product but is uncertain whether the demand for the product will be high or low. It will immediately (at time 0) build a plant to produce the product and must decide whether the plant will be large or small. If a large plant is constructed, the firm will simply retain the large plant in future years regardless of demand. If a small plant is built at time 0, the firm can expand the plant one period later (at time 1) at an additional cost of $5 million. As we will see, such plant expansion will be justified only if demand is high. Let's look at the problem more closely to see how the decision tree layout in Figure 8-10 is helpful in deciding whether Bulaxy should currently build a large plant or a small plant.

We assume that the plant is built at time 0, cash flows occur between time 0 and time 1 (during period 1) from producing and selling the product, and, at time 1, the plant can be expanded if a small plant was constructed at time 0. After time 1, cash flows continue to be generated. By time 1, the permanent level of demand for the product (high or low) is known for certain; but at time 0, demand is uncertain, with a .6 probability that it will be high and a .4 probability that it will be low. The problem is to decide whether a small plant or a large plant should be constructed at time 0.

Notice that there are two points in time at which decisions can be made: now (time 0) and at time 1. A decision must be made at time 1 only if the firm builds a small plant at time 0 since a large plant initially built is simply retained thereafter whether demand is large or small. A solution procedure called "dynamic programming" involves looking at the most future decision first and then working back to the present to determine what should be done now (at time 0). To see how this procedure is applied, observe from Figure 8-10 that at time 1 there are two possible decision situations, both of which occur if a small plant was constructed at time 0 and both of which involve a choice between expanding the plant and keeping it small. One decision situation arises if demand is high and the other if demand is low. First assume that demand is high: the plant can be expanded at a cost of $5 million, and this produces a time 1 present value of future cash flows (i.e., cash flows *after* time 1 discounted to time 1) equal to $27 million; this implies a time 1 net present value of $22 million ($27 million − $5 million). If the plant is not expanded, the time 1 net present value of cash flows from time 1 and thereafter is $15 million. Expansion is better since its NPV of $22 million exceeds the no-expansion NPV of $15 million. *Therefore, if a small plant was built at time 0 and if demand turns out to be high, the firm should expand the plant at time 1;*

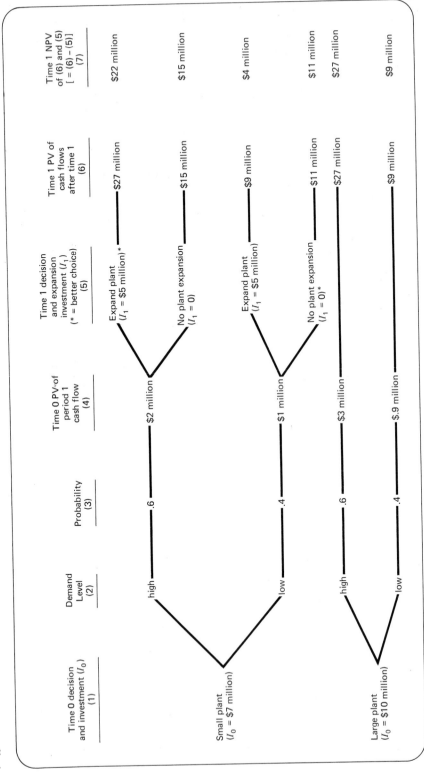

Figure 8-10. Decision tree.

and the time 1 NPV of cash flows from time 1 on is $22 million given such plant expansion.

Assume again that a small plant was built at time 0 but that demand turns out to be low. Expansion at time 1 means an outlay of $5 million and a time 1 present value of cash flows after time 1 of $9 million; this implies a time 1 NPV of $4 million ($9 million − $5 million). On the other hand, if the plant is not expanded at time 1, there is no expansion cost and the time 1 present value of cash flows after time 1 is $11 million; this implies a time 1 NPV of $11 million. Not expanding is better since its time 1 NPV is greater ($11 million exceeds $4 million). *Therefore, if a small plant was built at time 0 and demand turns out to be small, the firm should not expand the plant at time 1; and the time 1 NPV of cash flows from time 1 on is $11 million assuming no expansion.*

We can use the above analysis of the time 1 decision to determine the time 0 present value of the expected cash flows if we construct a small plant now. Assume a cost of capital of 10 percent for computing present values. From column 4 of Exhibit 8-9, the time 0 NPV if demand is high is $15 million and the NPV if demand is small is $4 million. *The NPV of expected cash flows if the small plant is built at time 0 is $10.6 million.*

Exhibit 8-9. Computation of the Net Present Value of Expected Cash Flows If a Small Plant Is Constructed at Time 0

Demand level (1)	Probability (2)	Best time 1 decision and investment (I_1) (3)	Time 0 NPV of cash flows from time 0 on[a] (4)	Probability × NPV (col. 2 × col. 4) (5)
High	.6	Expand plant (I_1 = $5 million)	$15 million	$ 9.0 million
Low	.4	Keep plant small (I_1 = 0)	$ 4 million	$ 1.6 million
Net present value of expected cash flows if a small plant is constructed at time 0 and the best decision is made at time 1				$10.6 million

[a] The NPV of cash flows from time 0 on are computed by discounting (using a discount rate of 10 percent) the relevant entry in col. 7 of Figure 8-10 to time 0, adding the result to col. 4 of Figure 8-10 and then subtracting the initial cost of the plant (I_0). Therefore, in col. 4 of Exhibit 8-9, $15 million = ($22 million/1.1) + $2 million − $7 million; and $4 million = ($11 million/1.1) + $1 million − $7 million.

Exhibit 8-10. Computation of the Net Present Value of Expected Cash Flows If a Large Plant Is Constructed at Time 0

Demand level (1)	Probability (2)	Time 0 NPV of cash flows from time 0 on[a] (3)	Probability × NPV (col. 2 × col. 3) (4)
High	.6	$17.5 million	$10.5 million
Low	.4	(0.9 million)	(0.36 million)
			$10.14 million

[a] The time 0 NPV of cash flows from time 0 on equals col. 4 of Figure 8-10 plus the discounted (to time 0, using a discount rate of 10 percent) value of col. 7 minus the $10 million cost of the large plant (I_0). Therefore, in col. 3 of Exhibit 8-10, $17.5 million = $3 million + ($27 million/1.1) − $10 million; and −$0.9 million = $0.9 million + ($9 million/1.1) − $10 million.

Now we must compute the NPV of the expected cash flows if the large plant is built. This computation is much easier than that for the small plant since there is no expansion decision at time 1. If the large plant is built at time 0, it is simply retained thereafter. Exhibit 8-10 shows the NPV computation for the large plant. *The NPV of expected cash flows if the large plant is constructed is $10.14 million.*

The NPV of the small plant ($10.6 million) is positive and exceeds the net present value of the large plant ($10.14 million), and therefore the small plant should be constructed.

Computers in Business

Norbert Wiener, the "father of cybernetics," once suggested that man had better beware of the vengeance of his multiplying flock of computer slaves. Someday, he said, computers might control the world, if not through their own conscious design, at least, like Mother Nature, as a dominant force upon which man critically depends. Other scientists have expressed similar fears. But the forces of economics have kept advances in computer technology moving apace at an accelerating speed. Computers now participate in virtually all aspects of productive activity, from supermarket checkout registers to medical diagnosis to cash flow simulation for corporate planning. It is a proven axiom that a computer will be introduced if it can improve upon old methods or provide a new service and do so profitably. This economic incentive has fueled the growth of the computer industry during the past quarter century.

A FAMILY TREE

Computers began as cumbersome, overheating crates of vacuum tubes, resembling Emperor Ming's control box in a 1930s Flash Gordon epic. Business began to use computers on a substantial scale in the mid-1950s, primarily for payroll, billing, and accounting applications. Largely unfounded fears arose within the ranks of labor of the coming of technological unemployment. As time passed, it became apparent that no such large-scale unemployment was to occur.

By 1958, the old vacuum tube machines were being replaced by a second generation of computers, which employed transistors and had a vastly increased logic and memory capacity. This second phase, which spanned approximately the years from 1958 to 1966, saw the widespread introduction of "computer software"—programs written for various special purposes, for example, sorting programs, input/output control systems, and compiler programs that translate information from user languages (e.g., FORTRAN and COBOL) to machine language. These computer systems made possible major innovations in such fields as credit cards, air travel, and securities trading.

From 1966 to 1974, a dramatic decline occurred in the costs of computers (cost per unit of service). The third generation computers introduced during this period utilized integrated circuits instead of transistors, an advance of the same magnitude as the earlier step from vacuum tubes to transistors. Perhaps the most important development was the massive use of remote terminals, which permitted geographically dispersed and distant users to communicate with a central computer. This significantly enhanced information access and reduced the time and other costs of computer utilization. This period also saw an increased centralization of the electronic data processing (EDP) function within the firm's organization. Even though a good deal of the decision making remained at the divisional level, divisional data became readily accessible to home office management, facilitating coordination and planning.

The fourth generation of computer systems was introduced around 1974. Improvements over earlier facilities have included greatly increased central data storage, the use of small satellite computers for specialized tasks, and the availability of computer programs with vastly enlarged computational and analytical capacity. Minicomputers (small computers selling for under $50,000) are becoming especially popular, allowing relatively small firms, or divisions of large firms, to have their own computers. One consequence of developments during this period has been a shift of the materials procurement, shipping, personnel administration, and cash management functions from the divisional level of the firm to the home office, largely because of the economies of scale in handling these tasks in one location. On the other hand, because of greater divisional access to current information and computer analytic facilities, tactical decision making has tended to move from headquarters out into the field. Moreover, the increased capacity of the computer has shifted managerial reliance from intuitive judgment to on-the-spot information and analysis provided by the computer. In one case, for example, the maximum loan a bank branch manager could make was quadrupled because of access to a central computer-based credit file.

The next, or fifth, generation of computers should appear around 1982. Although these systems do not yet exist, current trends foreshadow the kinds of innovations that will be involved. New hardware (the computer machinery) will be blended with software systems providing interactive communication (the user "talking" with—directly communicating with—the computer) and a variety of simulation options. (Simulation shows the consequences of a policy under given assumptions about the economic situation.) The manager will be provided with analytical tools of enormously expanded power and complexity, raising the level of decision making by allocating to the computer many routine evaluation tasks previously done by man. This will channel managerial effort to areas not amenable to computer analysis at an acceptable cost—for example, to those aspects of a problem that are unique to a particular situation or that involve interpersonal relations. The computer is not about to usurp management's role but rather will sharply redefine it.

THE WIDE, WIDE WORLD OF THE COMPUTER

The computer serves business in an amazingly broad variety of ways. The areas of application expand with each year's advances in technology. Computer use began in accounting, personnel, and payroll and has since spread to production, sales, financial analysis, and consumer service.

In autos, steel, and many other industries, computers control production at various stages and test products for defects. They also assist in market analysis and mailing list selection. *Playboy* magazine, for example, increased its normal direct-mail response rate of 1.7 percent to as high as 9.9 percent by computer selection of letter recipients, using information on the previous buying habits of consumers.

Innovative customer services now often rely directly on a computer facility. In Los Angeles, a major oil firm constructed five no-attendant gas stations which require the customer to put his credit card into a computer terminal. If the card is valid, the motorist pumps all the gas he needs. Electronic bartenders that automatically dispense liquor to customers are becoming common in bars and cocktail lounges. Many retail stores and some supermarket chains have installed computer-tied cash registers which automatically record the sale, the taxes collected, and the inventory change. The machines also check the validity of credit cards, saving merchants millions on fraud losses.

Investment analysis and financial transactions are more and more relying on the computer. Mutual and pension fund managers compute the rates of return on specific stocks and their portfolios; investment advisory services like Value Line analyze the historical trend in specific stocks and their price correlations with the stock market in general; "buy" and "sell" opportunities in the foreign currency and bond markets are detected using the computer. Kuhn Loeb, among other major investment banking houses, has programmed most of the widely traded debt securities. Each day, the computer generates a list of best buys. This kind of persistent and comprehensive search for bargains by many well-financed traders has made the bond market "nearly perfect," to quote a Kuhn Loeb vice-president.

A utilization of computers that was once considered science fiction but is now becoming a reality is one commonly referred to as electronics funds transfer system or EFTS. Its purpose is to transfer money quickly between persons and firms. Automated bank tellers (machines connected to computers) are now widely available which permit people to perform transactions involving their bank accounts without the aid of any bank personnel. Money can be withdrawn from accounts and can be instantaneously transferred from demand deposit accounts to savings accounts or vice-versa. In the future, people will even be able to direct the automated teller to pay their bills. It is likely that EFTS will allow a customer to purchase goods in a store without the use of cash or checks merely by directing a computer terminal in the store to transfer money out of his personal account and into the store's account.

Some companies are using simulation programs to predict earnings, the estimates being based on predictions of government fiscal and monetary policies and various business indicators. The use of computer simulation in capital budgeting and other financial planning areas has spread to most major industries.

The computer has even invaded the executive suite. The board room of Motorists Insurance Company, for example, is equipped with a computerized conference table console with electronic screens displaying data relevant to the topic under consideration. Each board member has an individual screen and can add lines or erase any part of the displayed images. According to users of the system, decision making has been enormously expedited by the computer's facilitating the flow of information to the executive and between executives.

GAMES PEOPLE PLAY— FRAUD AND THE COMPUTER

The computer is no exception to the axiom that great power for good is at the same time great power for evil. This has not been lost on those people whose imaginative moments are spent in plotting fraudulent schemes rather than in designing better mousetraps. It is no exaggeration to say that many computer cheating ploys have rivaled in ingenuity the cleverest applications of computer technology to what are normally regarded as productive purposes.

Some of the more recent cases of computer fraud include:

An $11,000 a year chief teller employed by the Union Dime Savings Bank in New York was charged with embezzling $1.5 million by allegedly robbing hundreds of accounts and then programming the computer to indicate that the accounts were in proper balance. The clerk allegedly used the embezzled funds to support a gambling habit that cost up to $30,000 in a single day.

A clerk at the Morgan Guaranty Trust Company, New York, was convicted of programming the company's computer to send $33,000 in dividend checks to the address of an accomplice and then to erase all records of the disbursements.

A thirty-year-old computer specialist employed by University Computing Company, Palo Alto, California, was convicted of stealing trade secrets worth approximately $15,000 from the memory bank of a competing company, Information Systems, Inc., of Oakland, California. The thief used a special identification code by telephone which allowed him access to Information Systems' data.

The above incidents are of miniscule importance when compared to the massive Equity Funding fraud. Using a computer, Equity Funding's life insurance subsidiary created approximately $2 billion (in face value) of phony life insurance policies on nonexisting persons. The policies were then sold to other life insurance companies for cash and the returns from these sales included in Equity Funding's growing reported earnings. The bogus assets Equity Funding created in this manner greatly exceeded the $75 million in total profits it reported over its entire thirteen-year history. The implication is that the company, which had been the darling of Wall Street for many years, may very well have always been a losing operation—a shocking revelation, particularly to those who had invested in the company on the basis of its 25 percent annual compound "earnings" growth record.

PANACEA?

The computer has not, and will not during the lifetimes of the readers of this book, solve all the decision maker's problems. Although many functions will be reallocated from man to machine, the computer's main impact will be a reallocation of functions between personnel and the creation of new functions necessary to maintain and improve upon existing systems. There will be problems along the way. Experience to date has been rocky: computers have often been installed where they were not needed because it was fashionable to have an in-house computer; software has frequently been inadequate to perform the prescribed job; labor unrest has occurred because of the threat of technological unemployment; and so on. But the road, although rough, clearly leads to wider use and greater sophistication, and the end is definitely not in sight. The trail has bends along with the rough spots and around them will be surprises—and, perhaps, a struggle to prevent Norbert Wiener's prophesy from coming true.

financing decisions and capital structure

The preceding discussion of capital budgeting showed how proposed investment opportunities are evaluated and combined into a capital expenditure program or planned capital budget. In this chapter we will examine the problems faced by a financial manager in deciding how to obtain the money needed to finance a given capital outlay. We will look at the four major financing sources used by firms—debt, preferred stock, common stock, and retained earnings—and examine the methods used to plan a complete financing program.

After describing each source of financing, we show how alternative financing plans are evaluated and their impact on the returns from investment and the risks to the firm and its owners. Then the problem of long-run policy as to financing sources is examined, and we discuss how the policy chosen affects the cost of capital used to evaluate investment opportunities. This chapter thus covers the basic financing decisions that must be made by the financial manager and the implications of those decisions for capital budgeting.

CHARACTERISTICS OF FINANCING METHODS

Debt, preferred stock, and common stock are alike in one essential feature. They are sources of money that are *external* to the firm and its operations, as opposed to retained earnings, which represent an *internal* source of funds. Provided that management can convince other people of the desirability of investing in or loaning money to the firm, there is virtually no limit to the amount of money that can be raised from external sources.[1] Retained earnings are internal to the firm, and the amount of money that the firm can raise by retaining earnings is strictly limited by the profits of the firm and the amount paid in dividends to its owners.

Common stock and retained earnings share an important feature. They are both sources of shareholders' equity, which is to say that they represent money contributed by the firm's owners rather than its creditors or preferred stockholders. The owners of the firm receive income only after all obligations due its creditors and preferred stockholders have been paid.

1. There is no practical limit to the amount of money the firm can raise as long as those with funds to invest in the firm (new stockholders or lenders) feel that the money will be invested in assets that provide an acceptable rate of return. However, the cost of financing may be quite high, particularly for small firms and firms with very risky investments.

Debt Financing

When a business firm raises money by borrowing, it must promise to repay the money borrowed (the principal) plus interest. These principal and interest payments are spelled out in the debt contract, which stipulates when and how much money must be paid by the firm. If the payments are not made on time and in the proper amount, the debtholders can take a variety of actions to force payment, depending on the terms of the debt agreement. They may take some of the firm's assets, cause management to be fired, or even force the firm to sell all its assets and thereby force it out of business. They can also legally prevent any payments being made to shareholders (owners) or preferred stockholders before the debtholders have been paid. The debtholders have priority over the other security holders in receiving money from the firm. A second important feature of debt financing is that the amount of money to be paid to the debtholders is limited to what has been specified in the debt agreement. For example, if the firm owes a bank $2 million, which is to be paid in one year with interest of $200,000, the bank must be paid $2.2 million, but only this amount.[2] Third, debt financing differs from the other sources in that interest payments are tax-deductible. As we noted in Chapter 6, the effective cost of debt financing is less than the interest rate paid to the debtholders due to the tax deductibility of the interest. (See Exhibit 6-1.)

Many different types of debt agreements are used by business firms, but for the purpose of this chapter these three characteristics—priority over other security holders, tax deductibility of interest, and limits on amount—are the most important. From the viewpoint of debtholders, the limitation on interest and principal payments to them also means that they are very concerned with the degree of certainty of these payments, as in the case of bonds discussed in Chapter 5. If the probability of not receiving the amounts promised is very high, lenders may not be willing to lend money to the firm at all. Even when the probability is moderate, the money may only be lent at a high rate of interest. This is so because the maximum amount the lender receives is the principal plus the interest rate in the debt agreement. The lender may receive much less and must therefore be compensated for this risk by a high interest rate. This suggests that businesses making investments with a high degree of risk may find it difficult and expensive to raise money through debt financing.

Preferred Stock Financing

Preferred stock has characteristics that are intermediate between debt and common stock. Preferred stock is similar to debt in that the payments to preferred stockholders, preferred dividends, are usually limited in

---

2. There may be additional charges if the firm fails to make the required payments, but these too would be specified in the debt agreement.

amount to a fixed dividend rate per share. However, a few preferred stocks are **participating,** which means that if the firm has high earnings and is able to pay high dividends to the common stockholders, preferred dividends will be increased. Preferred dividends have priority over common stock dividends. The preferred stockholders must be paid before common stock dividends can be paid; but if no common stock dividends are to be paid, preferred dividends need not necessarily be paid. Unlike debt interest, failure to pay preferred dividends does not expose the firm to the adverse consequences of failing to pay interest. Also, preferred stock rarely has a maturity; the face (par) value need never be repaid by the firm. Interest and principal payments to debtholders have priority over preferred dividends, and preferred dividends are *not* tax-deductible for the corporation.

The preferred stockholders are protected by several features commonly found in preferred stock agreements. The dividends are usually **cumulative,** which means that any dividends not paid when due remain as an obligation of the firm. No dividends to the common stockholders can be paid until all the preferred dividends which are owed to date have been paid. For example, if a firm fails to pay a $5 per share preferred dividend for four years in a row, a total of $20 (4 × $5) in back dividends plus the current dividend of $5 must be paid in year 5 before the firm can pay any dividends to common stockholders in year 5. Failure to pay preferred dividends for a specified number of years often permits the preferred stockholders to elect some of the firm's directors and to gain some control over the firm's policies. Finally, if the firm is liquidated, preferred stockholders have priority over the firm's owners. The face value of the preferred stock must be paid to its holders before the common stockholders can receive any proceeds from the sale of the firm's assets.

Common Stock Financing

A firm can raise money by issuing common stock and selling the shares to investors, who become owners if they were not already stockholders of the firm. Let us assume here that a firm raising money by issuing common stock is selling the stock to new investors as opposed to its existing owners ("old" owners).[3]

The sale of common stock divides the ownership of the firm into two parts—that part owned by the old owners and that part owned by the purchasers of the new stock. Suppose that 20,000 shares are held by the old owners and an additional 5,000 shares are sold. There would now be 25,000 shares outstanding. The original owners who had 100 percent of

3. As we will discuss in Chapter 10, this is not always true, but the assumption greatly simplifies the discussion without making any significant difference to the results.

the firm now have only 80 percent (20,000/25,000), and the new shareholders who bought 5,000 shares have 20 percent (5,000/25,000). If the firm now pays $100,000 in dividends, the money must be distributed equally among the shares. In this example, the old shareholders would be entitled to 80 percent of $100,000 while the new shareholders would be entitled to 20 percent of $100,000.

The amount of money raised by issuing a given number of new shares depends on what the new shareholders believe their proportionate interest in the firm is worth. Suppose that the total value of the firm's stock after financing (therefore, including the new shares) and investment has taken place is expected to be $1 million. The new shareholders would then be willing to pay 20 percent of $1 million, or $200,000, to the firm for 5,000 shares. This amounts to $40 per share ($200,000/5,000). In practice, management decides how much money is needed ($200,000), estimates the price that new investors will be willing to pay for the shares ($40), and from this information determines the number of shares that must be issued (5,000).

The shareholders as owners have voting rights through which they elect the firm's directors, who determine corporate policy and affect the shareholders' earnings. The new shareholders therefore acquire 20 percent of the voting power. In many cases firms are reluctant to sell common stock because the new shareholders may not agree with the policies followed by the management elected by the old shareholders. This is especially true of small businesses where the old shareholders usually are the firm's management. For example, the president of a small company who is also its largest shareholder might lose control of the business if he or she sold a large enough number of shares to other people. The new shareholders could then determine policy or even fire the president.

A major advantage of common stock financing over debt financing is the absence of any requirement to make payments to the shareholders. If the firm borrows money and then runs short of cash when a debt payment comes due, it may have to sell some of its assets to make the payment or even be forced out of business by the creditors. On the other hand, the firm does not have to pay dividends to its shareholders; and it never has to repay the money the new shareholders invested. The owners of common stock who wish to get back their original investment must either find someone to buy their stock or try to have the company liquidated. Common stock financing has only slight advantages over preferred stock financing in these respects since failure to pay a preferred dividend is not nearly so serious as failure to pay interest, and the money obtained from sale of preferred stock need never be repaid.

Retained Earnings   Retained earnings are the profits remaining in the firm after dividends are paid. As we indicated earlier, the major differences between retained earnings and the other three financing sources are that retained earnings are limited in the amount available but do not require the bringing in of "outsiders" (lenders or stockholders). However, financing with retained earnings reduces the dividends that can be paid to the firm's current owners. This means that the availability of retained earnings depends not only on the earnings of the firm, but also on the policies of the firm regarding dividend payments. We will discuss dividend policies in some detail in Chapter 10; for now, we will only note that firms generally try to avoid reducing their level of dividend payments even in the face of temporary reductions in earnings. This policy makes the amount of retained earnings (profits less dividends) available in any given year highly variable with profits. Therefore, the financial manager cannot rely on the availability of this source to finance investment.

Although it reduces the current money available for dividends, using retained earnings increases the future amount of money available for dividends to the current owners. The reason for this is that if the firm uses debt, it must pay the lenders interest in the future, thereby reducing the money available for future dividends; and if preferred stock is issued, preferred dividends must be paid in the future. If common stock financing is used, future dividends must be paid to the new shareholders as well as to the old ones. For example, if the new shareholders own 20 percent of the outstanding shares and the firm planned to pay $100,000 in dividends next year, the old shareholders would receive only 80 percent of $100,000, or $80,000. If retained earnings had been used instead of common stock financing, the original shareholders would have received the entire $100,000 next year in return for receiving lower dividends now. Of course, the basic reason for raising money by any method is to undertake investment projects that are expected to provide high enough returns to benefit current shareholders regardless of the financing method used.

It is also important to realize that the firm does not have to rely exclusively on the earnings retained from the current year's profits. Most managements forecast their investment needs several years into the future. Given this forecast, it is possible to begin to retain earnings and to invest in marketable securities or bank time deposits (which pay interest) prior to the use of the funds in acquiring productive assets.

Retained earnings substitute most directly as an alternative to common stock, since both represent investment by owners (old or new) of the firm. However, the use of common stock may present problems in maintaining control of the firm by the original shareholders. For this reason many small firms avoid common stock issues. Also the firm must pay various fees and costs to issue stock which are avoided when retained earnings are used (see Chapter 16).

At this point we have already begun to list some of the advantages and disadvantages of each source of financing. The basic characteristics of

Table 9-1. Characteristics of financing sources

Debt	Preferred stock	Common stock	Retained earnings
1. Firm must pay back money with interest.	1. Similar to debt in that preferred dividends are limited in amount to rate specified in agreement (like interest rate).	1. Money raised by selling ownership rights.	1. Lowers amount of money available for current dividends but can increase future dividends.
2. Interest rate is based on risk of principal and interest payments as perceived by lenders.	2. Dividends are not legally required, but no common dividends can be paid unless preferred dividends are paid; also usually cumulative, and passing dividend for a stated number of years may give preferred stockholders voting rights.	2. Value of stock is determined by investors.	2. Stockholders forgo dividend income, but they do not lose ownership rights as occurs if new common stock is issued.
3. Amount of money to be repaid is specified by debt contract.	3. No maturity but usually callable.	3. Dividends are not legally required.	3. Funds are internal— no need for external involvement.
4. Lenders can take action to get their money back.	4. No voting rights except as per (2) above.	4. Creates change in ownership.	4. Cost of issuing securities is avoided.
5. Lenders get preferred treatment in liquidation.	5. Preferred dividends are not tax-deductible.	5. Shareholders have voting rights.	
6. Interest payments are tax-deductible.		6. Common dividends are not tax-deductible.	

each one are summarized in Table 9-1. Let us examine more directly the considerations in choosing the means of financing investment.

ANALYZING EXTERNAL FINANCING METHODS

Financial managers base their financing decisions on the firm's forecasted capital budget. The period of time covered and the amount of care taken in developing this forecast will depend greatly on the size of the firm and its particular situation. A small firm whose present plans are only to acquire a new delivery truck may not do more than estimate when and at what price the truck is to be acquired. A large firm embarking on a major expansion program may forecast its financing needs for several years. For the purposes of this chapter, we will assume that the financial manager has undertaken this forecasting-planning process and has developed a clear picture of how much money is needed, at least during the next year, plus some idea of the likely financing requirements of the firm in the more distant future.[4] The manager knows what sources of financing are currently available and the prices, interest rates, and other characteristics of each source. A critical part of the financial manager's job is deciding on and arranging for external financing. We will discuss the problem of choosing among debt, preferred stock, and common stock first, assuming that external financing is needed. Later we will examine the use of retained earnings.

Impact on Shareholder Earnings

To see how the choice of financing affects the returns to current owners, let's look at an example. Auric Mining Company is planning the development of a mine and processing plant on land owned by the firm. At the present time this land is the firm's only asset. The development costs are $1 million to be paid in the first year. The expected cash flow before taxes from the operation is $480,000 per year. We will assume that all cash flow from the mine will be paid out in taxes, dividends, and interest and that the cash flow is expected to continue forever. The corporate tax rate is 50 percent and the aftertax cash flow is therefore $240,000, assuming, for simplicity, that no depreciation or depletion allowances are available. Suppose that the owners of Auric don't have any money of their own to finance this venture nor does the firm have any cash. The $1 million in development costs must be raised by borrowing the money, issuing preferred or common stock, or some combination of these methods. Let's look at common stock financing first so that we have a basis for the contrast with debt and preferred stock financing.

Common stock   If common stock is issued, the new stockholders will share in the future cash flows. Their share will depend on the percentage ownership they obtain in the firm in return for the $1 million they will be investing in it. The percentage ownership will be a bargain struck between the present owners, as represented by the firm's management, and the investors. In general, the investors will demand at least that the expected rate of return to them will equal the rate of return available in the financial markets on investments of comparable risk. As we know from Chapter 5, the relationship between risk and return in the financial markets is shown

---

4. Forecasting financial requirements is obviously an important problem for the manager, and methods for doing this are provided in Chapter 13.

by the security market line. If the financial manager acts in the best interests of the present owners of Auric, no greater rate of return should be provided than that minimum required. Suppose the required rate of return is 12 percent per year. Then to raise $1 million, stock investors must expect to receive 12 percent per year on $1 million, which is $120,000 per year on the average. The $120,000 represents 50 percent of the aftertax cash flow expected from the mine. Under these conditions, new shareholders must obtain 50 percent of the stock of the company in return for their investment of $1 million. The present owners will be left with the remaining 50 percent of the stock and an expected cash return of $120,000 per year. These values are shown in Exhibit 9-1.

Preferred stock   Preferred stock may be issued to finance the mine. The dividend rate that must be provided to preferred stockholders will reflect the risks borne by them. Since the preferred stock of a company is usually a less risky security than the common stock, let's assume that the required dividend rate is 10 percent. Preferred dividends on a $1 million preferred stock issue would therefore be $100,000, and the original owners would receive $140,000, as shown in Exhibit 9-1. Under this financing

Exhibit 9-1. The Impact of Debt and Stock Financing on Expected Income

	Common stock	Preferred stock	Debt
Before-tax cash flow	$480,000	$480,000	$480,000
Interest	0	0	(80,000)
Taxable income	$480,000	$480,000	$400,000
Taxes (at 50%)	(240,000)	(240,000)	(200,000)
Earnings after taxes	$240,000	$240,000	$200,000
Preferred dividends	0	100,000	0
Earnings to common	$240,000	$140,000	$200,000
Income to new stockholders	$120,000	0	0
Income to original owners	$120,000	$140,000	$200,000

Common stock financing:	$1 million raised from new stockholders, in return for 50% of the company's shares
Preferred stock financing:	$1 million raised from investors with a dividend rate of 10% per year
Debt financing:	$1 million raised from lenders with an interest rate of 8% per year

plan, the original owners will receive $20,000 more in dividends than if common stock is issued because the rate of return required by the preferred stockholders is less than that required by new investors in common stock.

Debt Suppose that the $1 million could be raised by borrowing the money at an interest rate of 8 percent per year. Lenders generally do not require as high an interest rate as stockholders because the risk is less. Interest would amount to 8 percent of the $1 million borrowed, or $80,000 per year. The aftertax cash flow available to the original owners would therefore be $200,000, as shown in Exhibit 9-1. The original owners would therefore expect to receive $80,000 per year more in income if debt financing were used instead of common stock ($200,000 − $120,000) and $60,000 more than if preferred were used ($200,000 − $140,000). These income differences are due to two factors. First, the interest rate on the debt (8 percent) is lower than the rate of return required by new shareholders (12 percent) or by preferred stockholders (10 percent). Of the $80,000 difference between debt and common stock, $40,000 is due to the difference in rates (4 percent of $1 million). Of the $60,000 difference between debt and preferred, $20,000 is due to the difference in rates (2 percent of $1 million). Second, the interest on the debt is tax-deductible, and this accounts for the remaining $40,000 for both common and preferred stock. When debt financing is used, we see from Exhibit 9-1 that the firm pays only $200,000 in taxes instead of the $240,000 in taxes paid with preferred and common stock financing. Therefore, the original owners benefit both from the lower interest rate on the debt and the tax deductibility of interest.

EBIT-EPS Analysis

An obvious question at this point in the analysis is what happens if the mine doesn't earn $480,000 before interest and taxes each year? We need to examine other levels of earnings. A common method used to evaluate the impact of financing decisions on shareholder income is to analyze the relationship between earnings before interest and taxes (EBIT) and earnings per share (EPS). Since the original stockholders will own the same number of shares regardless of the method of financing, EPS (earnings to common divided by the number of outstanding shares) is directly related to the income belonging to the original owners (EPS × number of original shares = original owners' income). The level of EBIT varies from year to year depending on how successful the firm's operations are. The analysis involves taking each financing method proposed and plotting on a graph the EPS that would result from a given value of EBIT. The relationship between EPS and EBIT for each financing method is a straight line. When the lines representing each method are plotted on the same graph, we can compare them. To see how this works, let's use the Auric Mining data in a general procedure. (In the Auric example, EBIT = before-tax cash flow.)

1. We need information on the existing financing (all common stock in this example) used by the firm and related data:
   a) The tax rate (50 percent)
   b) Interest per year on outstanding debt (none)
   c) Preferred dividends (none)
   d) Number of shares outstanding (50,000)
2. We need the terms of the alternative financing methods:
   a) Debt: interest on debt (8 percent on $1 million = $80,000)
   b) Preferred stock: preferred dividends (10 percent of $1 million = $100,000)
   c) Common stock: number of shares to be issued (50,000)[5]
3. Since the graphical relationship between EPS and EBIT for any given financing method is a straight line, only two points on the graph are needed to completely determine the line.[6] Therefore, given the above information in 2, we need to compute earnings per share at two different levels of earnings before interest and taxes for each financing method. Choice of the two EBIT values is not critical; however, they are usually chosen to be representative of levels of EBIT that the firm might have. Calculations of EPS at EBIT = $200,000 and EBIT = $600,000 are shown in Exhibit 9-2. The results of the calculations are plotted on a graph (Figure 9-1).

Figure 9-1 shows that at EBIT levels of over $160,000, the debt issue provides higher values for EPS than does common stock, whereas when EBIT is below $160,000 the common stock issue is better. This figure can be verified by calculation (recommended as an exercise). Debt provides higher EPS than preferred stock at all levels of EBIT. Preferred stock provides higher EPS than common at levels of EBIT greater than $400,000.

Suppose that the financial manager believes that it is unlikely that EBIT will be much below $160,000. Under these conditions he or she

---

5. Since new shareholders must own 50 percent of the firm according to the earlier analysis, they must acquire the same number of shares as held by the original owners. The 50,000 figure for the number of shares held by the original owners is simply assumed; from that assumption the number that must be issued follows.

6. The relationship between EPS and EBIT can be expressed as

$$EPS = \frac{(EBIT - interest)(1 - tax\ rate) - preferred\ dividends}{total\ number\ of\ shares\ outstanding}$$

The financing method chosen fixes the values for interest, the number of shares, and preferred dividends. So long as the tax rate is a constant, this relationship is a straight line.

Exhibit 9-2. Calculation of the Impact of Financing Methods on Earnings per Share

	Common stock		Preferred stock		Debt	
EBIT	$200,000	$600,000	$200,000	$600,000	$200,000	$600,000
Interest (old debt)	0	0	0	0	0	0
Interest (new debt)	0	0	0	0	(80,000)	(80,000)
Taxable income	$200,000	$600,000	$200,000	$600,000	$120,000	$520,000
Taxes	(100,000)	(300,000)	(100,000)	(300,000)	(60,000)	(260,000)
Earnings after taxes	$100,000	$300,000	$100,000	$300,000	$ 60,000	$260,000
Preferred dividends (old)	0	0	0	0	0	0
Preferred dividends (new)	0	0	100,000	100,000	0	0
Earnings to common (1)	$100,000	$300,000	$ 0	$200,000	$ 60,000	$260,000
Number of old shares	50,000	50,000	50,000	50,000	50,000	50,000
Number of new shares	50,000	50,000	0	0	0	0
Total common shares (2)	100,000	100,000	50,000	50,000	50,000	50,000
EPS[(1)/(2)]	$1.00	$3.00	$ 0	$4.00	$1.20	$5.20

probably would decide that debt financing is superior. On the other hand, if the financial manager felt that values of EBIT below $160,000 were quite possible, common stock might be better. In this example, there is no income advantage to preferred stock relative to debt.

Financial leverage   Figure 9-1 illustrates the concept of **financial leverage.**[7] Financial leverage refers to the response of shareholder income to changes in EBIT and is created by debt or preferred stock financing with fixed interest and dividend payments. If the firm is financed entirely with common stock, a given percentage change in EBIT results in the same percentage change in EPS. A 10 percent increase in EBIT results in a 10 percent increase in EPS. However, the use of debt or preferred stock financing increases the responsiveness of EPS to changes in EBIT. For example, when EBIT is $400,000, both common stock and preferred stock financing provide earnings of $2 per share (EPS = $2). A 50 percent increase in EBIT to $600,000 increases EPS with common stock financing to $3, a 50 percent increase also. If preferred stock is used, a 50 percent increase in EBIT leads to an EPS of $4, a 100 percent increase. Financial leverage works both ways, down as well as up. The percentage reduction

7. It is also referred to as "trading on equity." The British use the term "gearing."

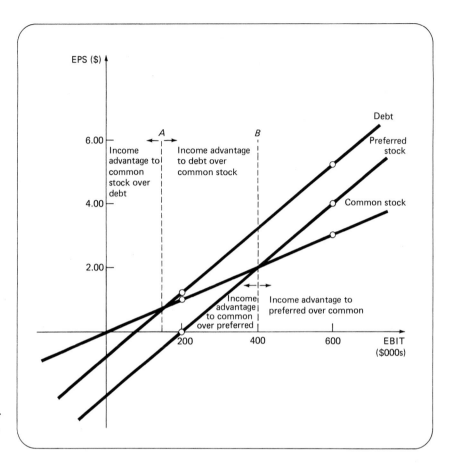

Figure 9-1. Impact of alternative financing methods on EPS.

in EPS is greater than a given percentage reduction in EBIT when debt or preferred stock financing is used. We will look more explicitly at the negative effects of leverage when we consider risk.

Businesses that have a lot of debt outstanding relative to their assets are often said to be "highly levered," since shareholder income tends to be more variable for such firms than for firms using less debt. A more precise measure of the degree of financial leverage than the proportion of debt used is the ratio of interest payments to EBIT (assuming no preferred stock is used).[8] Lenders and financial managers use this ratio (or its reciprocal) in evaluating the use of debt by the firm. Additional measures are discussed in Chapter 11.

8. The degree of financial leverage can be expressed more generally as a multiplier of the percentage change in EBIT; that is,

Percentage change in EPS = leverage multiplier × percentage change in EBIT

The leverage multiplier can be calculated from the following ratio:

Although debt and preferred stock financing provide income advantages over common stock if the firm does well, they increase the risk if it does not. The most risky financing is debt because interest and principal payments are contractual obligations of the firm. Preferred dividends need not be paid when earnings are poor, and the money raised from preferred stock financing need never be repaid. Since debt offers the greatest income advantage and the greatest risk, we will focus our discussion here on the choice of debt relative to common stock. We will consider preferred stock again in a later section.

Impact on Shareholder Risk

In Chapter 5 we discussed two types of risk to the owners of a firm, business risk and financial risk. Financial risk depends on the method of financing whereas business risk depends on the nature of the firm's operations. Business risk is directly related to the uncertainty as to the firm's ability to earn a satisfactory rate of return on its investments over the long run. It involves uncertainty as to the demand for the firm's products and the prices of the products. It is related to the degree of control the firm has over its costs, and how readily its assets can be converted into cash if the need arises. Business risk depends on the quality of the firm's management and the ability of management to react to unforeseen events. Fundamentally then, business risk involves uncertainty as to the long-run profitability of the firm (EBIT) and its investments and to the potential value of the firm in liquidation, if it cannot be operated at a profit.

If there were no business risks, the firm could finance as it pleased without affecting the risk to its owners and without paying a high interest rate. If the Auric Mining Company, its owners, and its creditors knew for sure that the mine would produce $480,000 per year forever, there would be absolutely no risk to the owners from borrowing $1 million at an interest rate of 8 percent per year since the $80,000 interest payments could always be paid from the earnings of the mine. If desired, the firm could be completely out of debt in a few years by paying the aftertax cash flow to the lenders until the $1 million debt was paid off. However, the returns from business investments are never certain. Let's look at Auric's financing problem when there is business risk in the mining investment.

To keep the problem simple and to isolate the source of risk, suppose that the costs of mining and the amount of product (gold) to be mined are

---

$$\text{Ratio} = \frac{\text{interest} + [\text{preferred dividends}/(1 - \text{tax rate})]}{\text{EBIT}}$$

Notice that this ratio equals interest/EBIT when there are no preferred dividends.

$$\text{Leverage multiplier} = \frac{1}{1 - \text{ratio}}$$

For example, with debt financing, interest is $80,000; at an EBIT of $400,000, the ratio equals .2, and the multiplier is 1.25. A 10 percent increase in EBIT from $400,000 will therefore increase EPS by 12.5 percent.

known for sure. However, the price is uncertain. There are three possible prices.[9] At the low price the mine will provide only $60,000 per year in before-tax cash flow net of the costs of mining the gold. At the middle price, the mine will provide $480,000 per year, and at the high price the mine will provide $600,000 per year. The probability of the high price is .35, the probability of the middle price is .55 and the probability of the low price is .10. The expected cash flow *before taxes* is therefore

$$\text{Expected cash flow} = .35(\$600,000) + .55(\$480,000)$$
$$+ .10(\$60,000)$$
$$= \$480,000$$

which is the same value for the before-tax cash flow used in Exhibit 9-1.

If high or middle prices are obtained, there is no problem with debt financing. We can see from Figure 9-1 that the income benefits of debt financing are substantial for EBIT of $480,000 and $600,000. However, there is a 10 percent chance that only $60,000 per year will be generated from the mine due to the low price of gold. If the firm must pay $80,000 in interest on the debt, sufficient money is not available from the mine's operations to meet this obligation. So what will happen? The answer in practice will depend on several things. Auric's owners might continue to operate the mine for a while, paying the $20,000 per year deficit ($80,000 − $60,000) out of their own pockets if they have hopes that prices will increase in the future. Failure to pay the interest would force the firm into bankruptcy and the mine would be sold for whatever it would bring. The lenders would have first claim on the proceeds from such a sale up to the $1 million principal amount of the debt. Under the circumstances of the example it is unlikely that the entire property could be sold for as much as $1 million, and so the lenders would take a loss and the owners would receive nothing.[10] In any case, the firm, its owners, and its creditors would be in trouble.

Also, the interest rate charged by lenders will be affected by the possibility that the mine will incur losses. If the entire $1 million is raised from debt and lenders require 8 percent on a safe loan, they will charge a higher rate on this loan; they may even not be willing to lend this amount of money.

9. A more realistic assumption which provides the same results is that the "prices" are average price levels for the product. It is not necessary to assume that the price of gold will be constant at, for example, $140 per ounce. The actual price could vary over time, say between $120 to $160, while averaging $140.

10. This assumes that Auric is a corporation and that the owners are not personally liable for the debt. Otherwise, the lenders would try to make up any losses by instituting legal action to claim personal assets of the owners.

In this simple example, the risk to the lender can be eliminated by the firm not borrowing so much money. Suppose only $750,000 is borrowed at 8 percent. The firm is then obligated to pay only 0.08($750,000) = $60,000 per year, which would be covered even in the worst case. Prudent financial managers would limit the amount borrowed to a level where they are confident that the interest can be paid from the firm's income. Exceeding this point subjects the firm and its owners to excessive risk and may also be costly due to higher interest rates being charged.

Using even limited amounts of debt is likely to increase the risk of losses for a firm. A more general situation is depicted in Figure 9-2. The curves in this figure were drawn assuming that the firm's earnings before interest and taxes is represented by the probability distribution shown by curve A. Curve A is also the income to all shareholders before taxes if no debt is issued. Curve B illustrates the effects of financing with some given amount of debt on shareholders' income before taxes. The fixed interest charges change curve A to curve B. Notice that the likelihood of the firm's incurring a loss has increased appreciably due to the use of debt. Generally the more debt that is used, the greater the risk of loss.

A third aspect to the risk of debt is its impact on the variability of shareholder income. From our discussion of financial leverage, we know that debt financing increases the responsiveness of earnings per share to changes in earnings before interest and taxes. Therefore, the use of debt (or preferred stock) amplifies the inherent variability of EBIT and increases the variability of shareholder income.

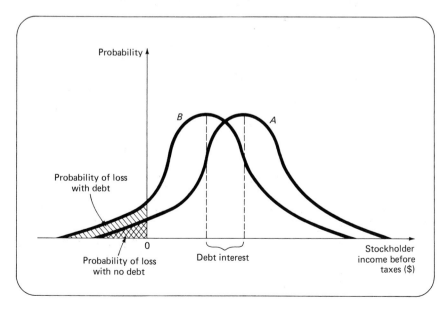

Figure 9-2. Effects of debt financing on stockholder income. Curve A shows EBIT for the firm, which equals stockholder income before taxes if the firm has no debt. Curve B shows stockholder income before taxes when debt is used. The fixed interest payment increases the probability of loss from that shown as the crosshatched area under A to that shown as the hatched area under B.

Exhibit 9-3. The Impact of Debt and Common Stock Financing on the Variability of Income

	Common stock		Debt	
	First year	Second year	First year	Second year
EBIT	$200,000	$180,000	$200,000	$180,000
Interest	0	0	(80,000)	(80,000)
Taxable income	$200,000	$180,000	$120,000	$100,000
Taxes (at 50%)	(100,000)	(90,000)	(60,000)	(50,000)
Net income	$100,000	$ 90,000	$ 60,000	$ 50,000
Income to original owners	$ 50,000	$ 45,000	$ 60,000	$ 50,000
Dollar change	−$5,000		−$10,000	
Percentage change	−10%		−17%	

For example, suppose that earnings before interest and taxes for the first year of Auric's operations are $200,000 and in the second year are $180,000, a decline of 10 percent. The effects of this decrease in EBIT on Auric's owners are shown in Exhibit 9-3 assuming that the entire investment of $1 million is being financed completely with either debt at an 8 percent interest rate or common stock. The decrease in income to the original owners is 17 percent with debt financing as compared with the 10 percent decrease with stock financing. With common stock financing all changes, positive or negative, in income are shared among all the shareholders, whereas with debt financing, the lenders receive a fixed interest payment and all changes are borne by the original owners.

CAPITAL STRUCTURE AND VALUE

From the preceding analysis we conclude that choice among alternative financing methods involves a trade off between risk and return. How is the financial manager to decide which method is best? We assume that the financial manager will make the decision that provides a maximum value for the firm's common stock. Therefore we must determine how that value is affected by the firm's financing. The term **capital structure** refers to the proportions of different types of financing used by the firm. Accordingly we are interested in how the firm's capital structure affects its value. In addition, we would like to know how capital structure and the choice of financing affect the firm's cost of capital. We know from

Chapter 6 that the cost of capital is closely linked to the value of the firm's securities; if we know how capital structure affects value, we will know how it affects the cost of capital. Since the cost of capital is a vital part of evaluating investment, the impact of financing decisions on the firm's value and cost of capital is an extremely important topic.

We will begin our analysis by looking at a highly simplified situation and then go on to consider the problem under more realistic assumptions. We focus here on the choice between debt and common stock to highlight the issues, although we will draw implications for preferred stock as well.

Suppose that a firm's securities (debt, preferred stock, and common stock) are issued and traded in a perfect capital market.[11] All investors in the market have the same probability distributions for the future returns from any securities or any investments undertaken by the firm. Assume also that there are no costs or penalties (such as legal fees and disruption of operations) incurred by the firm if it defaults on debt payments, although the debtholders may take over the firm. For now we assume that there are no corporate or personal income taxes. Under these conditions, how do financing decisions affect the value of a firm's common stock? Let's use the Auric Mining example to explore the problem.

The No-Tax Case

Recall that the expected income from the mine is $480,000 per year. As before, $1 million must be raised to undertake the investment. Our choice is between debt financing at an interest rate of 8 percent or common stock financing. Investors in common stock will require an expected rate of return of 12 percent. All income will be paid out as dividends and interest. No principal payments are required on the debt.

If common stock financing is used, the total market value of the outstanding stock will be the present value of the expected dividends to the stockholders. The expected dividends are a perpetual stream of $480,000 per year since there are no corporate income taxes. The value of the dividends is

$$\text{Market value} = \frac{\text{expected dividends}}{\text{required rate of return}} \qquad (9\text{-}1)$$

$$= \frac{\$480,000}{0.12}$$

$$= \$4 \text{ million}$$

11. In perfect capital markets, transactions (buying, selling, and issuing securities) are costless; investors have equal, costless access to information; and there are a large number of buyers and sellers of securities, no one of whom is able to affect market prices.

If the market value of all stock will be $4 million, 25 percent of the stock must be acquired by new stockholders to raise $1 million. Let's assume that the original owners will keep 75,000 shares, and 25,000 new shares will be sold, making total outstanding shares equal to 100,000.

$$\text{Price per share} = \frac{\text{market value}}{\text{number of shares}} \qquad (9\text{-}2)$$

$$= \frac{\$4 \text{ million}}{100,000}$$

$$= \$40$$

We can use the price per share of the common stock as a criterion for financing decisions in this instance.[12] We know that it will be $40 if common stock financing is used. The question now becomes: what will the stock price be if debt financing is used? If the price is greater than $40, we would prefer to use debt. If it is less than $40, we would prefer to use stock.

One way to approach the question is to examine the expected dividends that will be received by the owners if debt is used. Debt has an interest cost of 8 percent.

$$\begin{aligned}
\text{Expected income from mine} &= \$480,000/\text{year} \\
\text{Less interest on debt(8\% of \$1 million)} &= \$\ 80,000/\text{year} \\
\text{Net income} = \text{expected dividends} &= \$400,000/\text{year}
\end{aligned}$$

What will be the market value of $400,000 expected dividends per year? If the required rate of return remains at 12 percent, the market value would be [using Eq. (9-1)]

$$\text{Market value} = \frac{\$400,000}{0.12}$$

$$= \$3.33 \text{ million}$$

With only 75,000 shares outstanding (no new shares issued) the price per share would be

$$\text{Price} = \frac{\$3.33 \text{ million}}{75,000 \text{ shares}}$$

$$= \$44.44$$

---

12. In this example, there are no current dividends to old owners. If current dividend payments differ among financing methods (as is particularly true when retained earnings are used), current dividends plus stock price are an appropriate measure of owner benefits.

Therefore if stockholders' required rate of return is 12 percent, the price per share would be $44.44, which is higher than the $40 per share under common stock financing. However, is it reasonable for the required rate of return with debt financing to be the same rate as for stock financing? The answer is no, since we know that debt increases the stockholder's risk. The rate should be higher with debt financing, but how much higher?

At this point Professors Modigliani and Miller provide an answer.[13] The required rate of return on the common stock must be just high enough to make the stock worth $40. There is neither an advantage nor a disadvantage from debt financing in this situation. Appendix 9A contains a formal argument for this conclusion; however, the main point is that the value of the total project (or firm) does not depend on how it is financed. That is, if the risk of basic returns from the mine (which have an expected value of $480,000 per year) is such that a 12 percent rate of return is required by investors, the market value of those returns will be $4 million. If the total market value of Auric is $4 million and the value of the debt is $1 million, the stock value must be $3 million, and

$$\text{Price} = \frac{\$3 \text{ million}}{75,000 \text{ shares}}$$

$$= \$40$$

Dividing up the $480,000 of expected returns among different securities does not change the value of the total package. This conclusion applies to using preferred stock or any mixture of common stock, preferred stock, and debt. The total value must stay constant.

The cost of capital with no taxes The Modigliani-Miller conclusion has definite implications for the average cost of capital; namely, it is a constant value regardless of financing proportions. In our example the cost of capital is 12 percent. We can see this by using the constant value result. We know already that the cost of capital for the firm with all common stock financing is 12 percent. What about the cost of capital with debt financing?

With debt financing 25 percent of the market value of the firm will be debt ($1 million) and 75 percent stock ($3 million). The interest rate on debt is 8 percent. We need an estimate of k_s, the required rate on stock. We can get k_s from the prediction that the price of the stock must be $40. Given that the expected dividend per share is $5.33 per year ($400,000/75,000 shares), k_s is calculated as

13. F. Modigliani and M. H. Miller, "The Cost of Capital, Corporation Finance, and the Theory of Investment," *American Economic Review,* 48 (June 1958), pp. 261–297. Other theorists have reached the same conclusions using different models, but this paper is the classic on the subject.

$$k_s = \frac{\text{dividend}}{\text{price}}$$

$$= \frac{\$5.33}{\$40}$$

$$= 13.3\%$$

Using our cost of capital formula from Chapter 6 (tax rate is 0), the average cost of capital (k_A)

$$k_A = \text{debt rate} \times \text{proportion of debt} + \text{stock rate}$$
$$\times \text{proportion of stock}$$
$$= 8\%(.25) + 13.3\%(.75)$$
$$= 12\%$$

Notice that the required rate of return on stock has increased due to the use of debt. The general behavior of the average cost of capital k_A, the required rate of return on common stock, and the interest rate on debt for various proportions of debt is shown in Figure 9-3a. In it we also assume that as the amount of debt issued increases, so must the interest rate on debt. Figure 9-3b shows the corresponding impact of increasing use of debt on the market values of common stock, debt, and the total value of the firm (debt plus stock). In the Auric example, to achieve higher proportions of debt than 25 percent, the additional money borrowed beyond the $1 million required to develop the mine is assumed to be paid out to the stockholders either by purchasing their stock or as a "dividend" at the time the debt is issued.

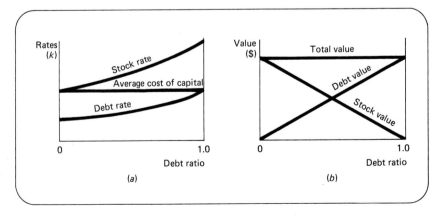

Figure 9-3. Modigliani-Miller results with no taxes. Debt rate shown is the rate expected to be earned by debtholders. Debt ratio = (debt value)/(total value).

Suppose that we now introduce corporate income taxes into the analysis while retaining the rest of our assumptions. If the corporate tax rate is 50 percent, only $240,000 in shareholder income is provided from the mine with common stock financing, as was shown in Exhibit 9-1. The market value of an expected dividend stream of $240,000 is $2 million given a required rate of return of 12 percent. Assuming that 100,000 shares will be outstanding after issuing new shares, half, or 50,000, must be sold to new investors to raise $1 million. The price per share will now be $20 ($2 million/100,000 shares). This lower value as compared with $40 per share for the no-tax case reflects the reduction in aftertax income due to payment of taxes.

The Effects of Corporate Income Taxes

The effect of debt financing is significantly different from the no-tax case. Since interest payments are tax-deductible, issuing $1 million in debt with interest payments of $80,000 required reduces the income to the shareholders to $200,000 (see Exhibit 9-1). The old owners have 50,000 shares, as no new shares are issued. The expected dividend per share with debt financing is $4 ($200,000/50,000 shares). Again we would like to know the price per share with debt financing. In the no-tax case we found that the required rate of return on stock, k_s, was 13.3 percent. We note that the financial leverage is the same in both cases. Our measure of financial leverage, interest/EBIT, is not affected by taxes.

$$\frac{\text{Interest}}{\text{EBIT}} = \frac{\$80,000}{\$480,000}$$

$$= 0.167$$

Furthermore, the analysis of this case by Modigliani and Miller indicates that k_s should be the same as in the no-tax case.[14] Using $k_s = 13.3$ percent,

$$\text{Price} = \frac{\$4.00}{0.133}$$

$$= \$30$$

A market price of $30 with debt financing is well above the $20 price achieved with common stock financing; therefore debt financing is better.

To understand why debt increases value, consider the total cash payments made to security holders. In the no-tax case the amount of money paid in dividends and interest is expected to be $480,000 per year regardless of the financing method used. With taxes, the total payments to security holders are less, and this is reflected in the total value of those pay-

14. F. Modigliani and M. H. Miller, "Taxes and the Cost of Capital: A Correction," *American Economic Review,* 53 (June 1963), pp. 433–443.

ments. When common stock is used, the total expected payments to security holders are $240,000 (all dividends). However, since interest payments are tax-deductible but dividends are not, debt financing increases the total outflow from the firm because the firm pays lower taxes. When $1 million in debt is issued, expected total payments to security holders rise to $280,000 ($200,000 dividends plus $80,000 interest) and taxes drop from $240,000 to $200,000. Compared with common stock financing, $40,000 more is expected to be paid to security holders and $40,000 less to the government. The value of the additional $40,000 is reflected in a higher price per share with debt financing.

We see that the existence of corporate taxes coupled with the tax deductibility of interest implies that debt financing is superior to common stock under rather stringent assumptions. What about financing with preferred stock? The answer is that preferred stock financing results in the same price per share as common stock financing. Therefore debt is superior to preferred stock as well. The reason is that preferred dividends are not tax-deductible; therefore an analysis of preferred stock relative to common stock is similar to the no-tax comparison between debt and common stock. Another point worth mentioning is the implications for small business finance. Although we won't analyze the problem in detail, we can indicate the general results. The advantage of debt financing results from a reduction in *corporate* income taxes. If a business is not paying corporate taxes,[15] then the no-tax case applies and there is no advantage to debt relative to any other method of obtaining money from external sources such as bringing in a new partner.

The cost of capital with taxes   Calculation of the cost of capital with taxes uses the procedure developed in Chapter 6. With all common stock financing, the cost of capital is 12 percent (100 percent stock × 12 percent required rate). To calculate the cost of capital with debt financing, we must first adjust the interest rate on debt for taxes.

$$\text{Effective rate} = (1 - \text{tax rate})(\text{interest rate})$$
$$= (1 - 0.5)(8\%)$$
$$= 4\%$$

The stock rate has already been determined to be 13.3 percent. We now need the proportions. The market value of the stock when debt financing is used will be the price per share of $30 times the number of outstanding shares (50,000), or $1.5 million. Since the market value of the debt is $1 million, the average cost of capital is calculated to be 9.6 percent.

15. The business may be a proprietorship, a partnership, or a small corporation which has elected to be taxed as a partnership. See Chapter 3.

	Market value	Proportion	Rate	Proportion × rate
Debt	$1.0 million	.40	4%	1.6%
Stock	$1.5 million	.60	13.3%	8.0%
Total	$2.5 million	1.0		9.6%

Therefore, the average cost of capital is less (9.6 percent) with debt financing than it is with common stock financing (12 percent). Thus, financing affects the cost of capital. Under the assumptions here the cost of capital declines with increased use of debt. The reduction in the cost of capital as debt increases is due to the tax deductibility of interest. The general behavior of the average cost of capital, the interest rate on debt, and the required return on stock are shown in Figure 9-4a. Figure 9-4b illustrates the behavior of the market values of the firm's securities. Both figures indicate the desirability of debt financing.

Capital Structure in Practice

The implication of the preceding analysis is that corporations should finance exclusively with debt. However, actual businesses do use other methods extensively, and we rarely see nonfinancial businesses with more than 60 percent of their assets financed with debt.[16] This divergence of observed practice from theory has prompted severe criticism of the realism of the assumptions made in deriving the above theory, in particular the assumption that no costs result from default on the firm's debt obligations. We examine the consequences of bankruptcy in Chapter 23; here we need only point out that a firm that defaults on its debt does face

16. Financial institutions such as banks usually have much higher financial leverage than business firms. They are able to do this in part due to their low business risk.

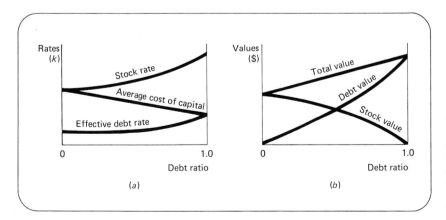

Figure 9-4. Modigliani-Miller results with corporate taxes. Effective debt rate = (1 − tax rate) × (expected rate on debt). Debt ratio = (debt value)/(total value).

serious costs. First, there is a host of legal and miscellaneous costs associated with the legal proceedings involved. Second, there is often serious disruption of the ongoing business activity of the firm. Third, even though the firm may not be able to raise enough money to meet its debt obligations, it may have profitable investment opportunities available. The firm is likely to be forced to forgo making these investments because it cannot finance them. This too is a cost of default. As the firm increases its financial leverage, the probability of default also increases. At some point the expected cost of default will be large enough to overcome the tax advantage of debt. At this point additional debt becomes undesirable relative to other sources.

One such source that we have yet to consider in detail is retained earnings. We compare retained earnings with external financing in the next section; however, here we might note that the tax advantage of debt relative to retained earnings is not as great as debt's advantage relative to common stock. This is due to the difference in taxation between capital gains and dividend income for individual investors. As we will see, many investors paying personal taxes will prefer internal financing to external, thereby lessening the advantage debt has due to its ability to reduce corporate taxes.

Other departures from the assumptions are also present. Lenders are reluctant to lend additional money to firms that are highly levered and may either not lend the money or charge a very high interest rate to compensate for their risk. Potential lenders and investors in the firm's securities may not agree with management's assessment of the future profitability of proposed new investments. They may be unwilling to commit large amounts of new money to a corporation that is already highly levered. This problem may be especially significant for firms with relatively high business risks. A summary of arguments against the Modigliani-Miller results is included in Appendix 9A. The general opinion of financial experts is that beyond some point, additional leverage reduces the value of the firm and increases its cost of capital.

Figure 9-5a illustrates current views on the impact of capital structure on the average cost of capital k_A, the required rate of return on stock, and the interest rate on debt. We show a range of capital structure policies (debt to total value ratios) over which the cost of capital is relatively constant. This is the optimal financing range for the firm. Beyond some point (R^*) the cost of capital is assumed to begin rising rapidly. This point is often called the firm's **debt capacity.** Figure 9-5b shows the corresponding values of the firm's securities. If the firm exceeds its debt capacity, its value falls sharply.

A precise determination of the optimal range or the debt capacity for a company is not currently feasible. Financial managers must formulate their own policies. One source of information is the behavior of the prices

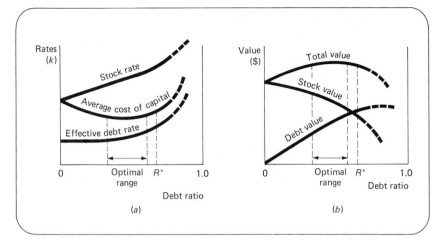

Figure 9-5. The effects of alternative debt ratios on the cost of capital and the value of the firm. Effective debt rate = (1 − tax rate) × (expected rate on debt). Debt ratio = (debt value)/(total value).

of the firm's securities. If the price of the firm's stock drops on announcement of a new financing program, this is an obvious sign that the planned financing will move the firm outside of the optimal range. Institutional lenders such as banks and insurance companies provide the financial manager with their views on the desirability of financing programs. If the firm must pay unusually high interest rates for its debt issues, this is a sign that debt capacity may be exceeded. A lowering of ratings on the firm's bonds by the bond-rating agencies is another sign. The firm's investment bankers, who are experts in the issuance of securities, are a major source of information and advice.

RETAINED EARNINGS AND INTERNAL FUNDS

Debt, preferred stock financing, and common stock financing force the financial manager to bargain with "outsiders." Lenders and investors must be convinced of the stability and profitability of the firm's present operations and of the desirability of new investment if they are to provide money at a reasonable cost to the firm and its present owners. The precise terms of these external financing sources will be determined by negotiations between management and the people providing the money. In any case the use of external financing reduces the future income available to the present owners. Financing investment by reducing cash and securities accumulated from the earnings of prior periods and by retaining cash generated from current operations does not present these difficulties. Instead the problem is to convince current shareholders (and perhaps current lenders) that the funds are best used for investment rather than for paying dividends or repaying debt before it is due. Usually this is an easier task because current shareholders and debtholders have already made a commitment to the future of the firm. Indeed, the firm has no legal obligation to pay debtholders prior to the scheduled principal and interest payments. The shareholders present a different problem, however.

The following type of problem has arisen for a large number of firms. Suppose the shareholders have become accustomed to receiving on average, about 50 percent of the profits as dividends. Profits and dividends have been growing at an average rate of 5 percent per year for several years. Management is about to embark on a major capital expenditure program which will probably continue for several years. New products will be manufactured and production facilities will be expanded. Management anticipates that these will be profitable investments to make, although only the current opportunities have been evaluated in detail. In any case some current decisions will commit the firm to investing large amounts of money for two or three years. Based on forecasts of current and future cash flows, a continuation of the 50 percent payout of dividends would imply substantial external financing, at least part of which would have to be in the form of common stock. The use of debt to cover all additional requirements would, in management's judgment, be unwise, as the required amounts would subject the firm to excessive risk. The debt capacity of the firm would soon be exceeded. Informal discussions with potential lenders have confirmed this judgment.

Given these circumstances, should management change the dividend policy of the firm to provide additional internal funds, plan to issue common stock as needed in the face of the uncertainties of future market conditions, try to borrow more money, or reduce investments? Notice that each of the above alternatives implies a cost to the current shareholders.

Foregoing profitable investments is not in the best interest of the stockholders unless there is no way to finance them at a reasonable cost. We have shown how the use of too much debt places the firm in a vulnerable position. Choosing to finance with debt causes the shareholders to bear both appreciable risk and a loss of income due to high interest rates. Therefore the source of the money must be either retained earnings (which implies lower dividend payments) or the sale of common stock. We feel, as do many financial theorists and managers, that usually the shareholders would be better off receiving lower dividends than having the firm issue common stock. This is so for several reasons.

1. If the firm retains earnings instead of paying higher dividends and issuing stock, the price per share of stock should be higher since earnings per share and future dividends per share will be higher if new stock is not issued. The shareholders could therefore get cash benefits from the investment by selling some of their stock. They would receive

capital gains on the stock rather than dividends, and a dollar of capital gains is worth more after personal taxes than is a dollar of dividends since capital gains are taxed at a lower rate than dividends. (We consider personal taxes in more depth in Chapter 10.)

2. There is a variety of costs (legal fees, commissions, etc.) associated with issuing common stock. These costs can amount to over 25 percent of the total dollars of stock issued.

3. Temporarily investing retained earnings in marketable securities for purposes of future investment increases both the safety of the firm and its financial flexibility. When the investment is to be made, the securities are liquidated and the proceeds used to finance the capital expenditure. On the other hand, if conditions change for the worse, sale of these securities brings cash quickly to meet debt payments, pay dividends, or pay expenses. Moreover, the existence of these funds does not preclude other financing if desirable. Their absence forces management to seek external sources to finance investment.

4. Sale of common stock may create control problems for the current owners of the firm.

Accordingly, we can see that there are sound reasons for preferring to finance investment through funds generated from operations and accumulated as marketable securities.

Despite the usual advantages to financing with retained earnings, this method of financing is not always possible or desirable. Shareholders may react very negatively to receiving lower dividend payments. It is one thing not to increase dividends as earnings rise and another to reduce them from prior levels. Shareholders may depend upon a given level of dividends, and reducing the dividends may force them to sell shares (and incur brokerage fees) to finance personal expenditures. The higher prices for the firm's stock due to the investment program may not be achieved immediately, and shareholders could be hurt under these conditions. Also, a reduction in dividends may actually cause temporary declines in the firm's stock. Investors may interpret the reduction of the dividend as evidence of weakness in the firm.

It may also be true that the amount of money available from not paying dividends would not be sufficient to avoid issuing some stock if the investment program is to be maintained. Under these conditions management is likely to be reluctant to risk even temporary declines in the stock price and may continue to pay dividends to support the price. Management will attempt to achieve a balance between the dividends paid and the increased number of shares needed to be sold. It should be clear that in effect some of the proceeds from the sale of common stock are being used to pay dividends any time a firm issues stock and also pays a dividend. This is not an uncommon occurrence.

THE IMPACT OF FINANCING ON INVESTMENT

The firm's average cost of capital is the standard by which investment projects having the same business risk as the firm are evaluated. We have seen that the magnitude of the cost of capital depends on the firm's capital structure. Therefore the impact of financing decisions on investment decisions is conveyed through the use of the cost of capital. However, there are situations where the procedures of Chapter 6 used to estimate the cost of capital will not provide an appropriate measure of the true value. We will consider two common problems here: (1) changing financing policies and (2) financing large capital budgets.

Changes in Financing Policy

Suppose that the financial manager has determined that the present capital structure of the firm is inappropriate. Economic conditions may have changed, or new management may have decided that past policies are not optimal. In any case, calculation of an average cost of capital using current proportions of outstanding securities will not reflect the proportions to be maintained in the future. In addition, the required rates of return on the securities are likely to change as capital structure changes. In theory, the solution is simple. A new capital structure for the firm is obtained by issuing new securities and retiring outstanding ones. For example, debt can be rapidly reduced by selling stock and using the proceeds to retire the debt. Once the new capital structure has been achieved, the market rates on the securities can be measured and a new cost of capital can be calculated using the new proportions.

In practice, major changes in capital structure are not often made rapidly. There are several types of costs and fees that would be incurred, such as cost of issuing new securities and penalties imposed on early retirement of debt. Instead, firms usually move gradually toward a new capital structure by disproportionate use of one financing source over another for several years. This procedure has the advantage of not only keeping costs down, but also permitting financial managers to assess the effects of the new policy, to "feel their way" toward the optimal range.

An operational solution to the problem of estimating the new cost of capital when changes are being made gradually is to use, not the current proportions of financing sources, but *the planned future proportions*. The rates used are those currently in effect. We assume here that the new policy has been announced to the market so that current rates on the firm's securities reflect the market's assessment of this new policy. The rates must be continually reevaluated as the actual capital structure changes, but this must be done in any case as capital market conditions change.[17]

---

17. The theoretical solution to this problem is complex, but the recommended solution serves as a reasonable approximation.

For example, if the financial manager believes that an appropriate capital structure for the firm is 30 percent debt, 10 percent preferred stock, and 60 percent common stock, then these are the proportions to be used in calculating the average cost of capital. The new capital structure policy is announced to the market, and new rates for the firm's securities are estimated based on the prices of outstanding securities after the announcement has been made. These rates are then used with the planned future proportions to calculate a new average cost of capital.

Financing Large Capital Budgets

The problem associated with the size of the capital budget can be most simply posed in terms of an example. Suppose that a firm with $10 million in assets is planning its capital expenditure program for the coming year. The financial manager has calculated the average cost of capital (using the procedure of Chapter 6) and has found it to be 12 percent. Would it make any difference if the capital expenditures for the year were $100 million or $1 million, given that all investments have positive net present values (all internal rates of return) greater than 12 percent? In most cases the answer would be yes.

If the firm were investing only $1 million, the money probably could come from internal funds and readily available debt (for example, a bank loan). If the firm is operating profitably and has not exceeded its debt capacity, neither lenders nor shareholders would be disturbed by a $1 million capital budget. However, suppose that the firm must raise $10 million, thereby doubling its assets in one year. In this case, new shares of common stock must be issued or substantial new debt acquired, or, more likely, both sources will be used. In any case, to raise this much new money compared with the past financing requirements of the firm is likely to cause lenders and stockholders to require a higher rate of return than in the past, thereby causing the true average cost of capital to be more than 12 percent.

There are several explanations why the cost of capital increases as the capital budget gets larger:

1. If the size of the capital budget is large relative to the size of the firm, external financing from new sources is probably needed. New investors, both stockholders and lenders, will be asked to provide the firm with the money needed to undertake the investment. New investors generally have a more pessimistic view of the firm's future than do ''old'' investors and will require a higher rate of return because of the greater risk.

2. Both old and new investors may be skeptical as to whether such large new investments have profit potential. They may be concerned that

management is being overly optimistic with respect to the proposed project.

3. Investors may also doubt the ability of management to control so much growth. That is, they may believe that the investments taken individually could be profitable, but will not be profitable if undertaken simultaneously. Many new people would have to be hired, trained, and organized; existing production processes may be disrupted; and so on. Therefore the investments will be viewed as being more risky.

4. The firm will incur issue costs if the volume of investment forces it to issue new securities (rather than use internal funds and direct loans from financial institutions). The issue costs associated with new common stock sales are especially significant.[18]

Figure 9-6 shows how the size of the capital budget affects the firm's average cost of capital. For small budgets the cost of capital for new financing is the same as the average cost of capital for the firm. As the amount invested and financed increases, the cost of capital for the new financing increases, causing the average cost of capital for the firm to rise. This means that the present average cost of capital is not a reliable standard for measuring the profitability of new investment when the volume of investment proposals is large relative to the present size of the firm. Basing investment decisions on the present cost of capital may cause so

18. However, once the capital budget is large enough to require common stock to be issued, there is an advantage to increasing the size of the issue because issue costs decrease as a percentage of the amount issued as the amount increases. See Chapter 16.

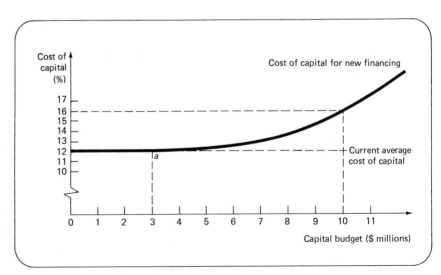

Figure 9-6. The impact of the size of the capital budget on the average cost of capital for the firm.

many investments to be included in the capital budget that the firm's average cost of capital rises, thereby making some of those investments unprofitable to undertake.

For example, suppose that the capital budget would be $10 million if 12 percent is used as the discount rate. That is, there are $10 million in new investments with a positive net present value using a discount rate of 12 percent. However, the $10 million could only be raised at a 16 percent cost of capital for new financing (new investors require a 16 percent rate of return). The correct cost of capital for $10 million in new investment is 16 percent, not the average cost of capital for the firm, which is less than 16 percent. However, if the cost of capital is 16 percent, many of the investments included in the capital budget when 12 percent was used will now be rejected. The internal rate of return on these rejected opportunities is greater than 12 percent but less than 16 percent. The total amount of planned expenditures might be significantly decreased, say to $3 million, if the minimum acceptable rate of return is set at 16 percent. But if the firm invests only $3 million, the cost of capital for new financing is likely to be less than 16 percent. In Figure 9-6, the cost of capital for $3 million is approximately 12 percent (point a). Now the firm may be undertaking too little investment, rejecting investments that offer rates of return less than 16 percent but greater than 12 percent.

The proper capital budget must be determined by finding that amount of expenditures having a cost of capital less than any projects included in the budget but with no profitable projects excluded. The problem is illustrated in Figure 9-7. The expected rate of return on the least profitable or marginal investment included in a given capital budget is plotted for different sizes of capital budget. This is the curve that falls as the amount invested increases. In other words, the firm has relatively few projects that have high expected rates of return but quite a few that have low expected rates of return. The cost of capital for new financing is the same curve depicted in Figure 9-6. Using a cost of capital of 16 percent will result in a capital budget of $3 million (point b), but a $3 million capital budget can be financed at a cost of capital of 12 percent (point a). In this hypothetical case the optimal capital budget has expenditures and required new financing of $7 million (point c). The minimum rate of return on any investment accepted and the cost of capital for new financing are both 13 percent.

In practice, financial managers do not have precise numbers that enable them to draw curves like those in Figure 9-7 and compute an exact answer. The cost of capital curve is especially hard to estimate, and more than two curves are required for investments that differ in risk. Instead, the financial manager evaluates the costs and difficulties involved in raising enough money to support the planned capital budget. If financing is a problem, those investments that were only marginally profitable when evaluated using the original estimate of the cost of capital are eliminated

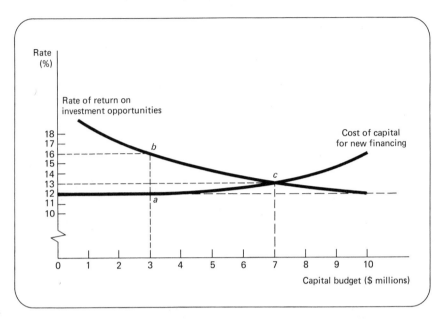

Figure 9-7. Rates of return and costs of capital for various investment and financing programs.

from the capital budget. A revised capital budget is developed and financing requirements are examined. This process is continued until management decides that the returns expected from the remaining projects in the capital budget are sufficient to justify the costs of financing them, and the budget is approved. In other words, the actual process produces results that come close to the ideal case shown in Figure 9-7.

SUMMARY   Business firms finance their investments from four major sources: debt, preferred stock, common stock, and retained earnings. The characteristics of each source are summarized in Table 9-1.

In developing a plan for financing the firm's capital budget, the financial manager must consider the risks and returns provided by alternative plans. Debt financing increases the financial leverage of the firm and, therefore, both the risk and the return. Debt financing amplifies the basic business risk of the firm. Financial risk is the increase in total risk caused by the use of debt. This is the risk borne by stockholders and the firm because of the requirements to pay the interest on and principal of the debt when they are due.

A theoretical analysis of the financing problem of business firms leads to the following conclusions:

1. Under idealized conditions with no corporate income taxes, there are no advantages or disadvantages to any given financing plan from the viewpoint of the firm's stockholders.

2. Under idealized conditions with corporate income taxes, debt financing provides an advantage over other financing sources because of the tax deductibility of interest.

3. In practice there exists an optimal range for the capital structure of the firm. If the firm exceeds its debt capacity, the value of the firm will decline and the cost of capital will increase.

Flexibility in future financing is provided by retaining earnings. Internal financing with retained earnings means that less dividends will be paid than would be the case with external financing (new stock or debt). Stockholders may be better off receiving lower current dividends for several reasons. First, the price of the firm's stock should increase, reflecting the additional money invested in the firm, and there are personal tax advantages to capital gains instead of dividends. Second, issue costs of common stock are avoided. Third, with internal financing present owners are better able to retain their control of the firm.

When a firm changes its financing policy, its cost of capital is likely to change. The average cost of capital should be calculated using the planned future proportions of the various financing sources and the current rates on its securities.

The cost of capital may be affected by the amount of financing required to support the planned capital budget. The capital budget may require revision to ensure that the returns expected from the least profitable investments being undertaken are sufficient to justify the costs of financing them.

QUESTIONS

1. Compare and contrast debt with preferred stock as alternative methods of financing.

2. What are the major differences between retained earnings and other sources of financing?

3. Financial institutions, such as banks, finance their assets with a very high percentage of debt (considering demand and savings deposits as forms of debt). How are they able to do this without exposing their stockholders to a great deal of risk?

4. Describe what happens if a firm finances investment by issuing common stock at an "unreasonably" low price because of unusual conditions in the security markets. How is this "bad" for the current owners of the firm?

5. From 1945 to 1965 the economy achieved high rates of growth, financial markets were relatively stable, and interest rates on long-term debt for major corporations did not vary much and were fairly low (3 to 4 percent). Profits also grew substantially during this period. What

types of financing do you think were most frequently used, say, in the early 1960s?

6. Regulated monopolies such as electric utilities and telephone companies use much more debt and preferred stock than do industrial corporations. Why do you think this is so?

7. If the corporate income tax were substantially reduced (say to a flat rate of 10 percent), how would the types of financing used by corporations be affected?

8. If dividends on common stock and preferred stock were tax-deductible expenses for the corporation, what would be the impact on the choice of financing?

9. Company A is in a high-risk business whereas company B is in a low-risk business. Sketch on one graph the behavior of the average cost of capital for each of the two firms as a function of the degree of leverage used under realistic assumptions as to the impact of leverage.

PROJECT   Estimate the relative proportions of debt, preferred stock, common stock, and retained earnings used as financing sources for each of the past ten years by nonfinancial corporations. Examine the level of long-term interest rates and the behavior of the stock market over the same period. Try to explain the variations in financing methods used over this period. See Appendix A for sources of this information.

PROBLEMS   1. The General Corporation currently has 880,000 shares of common stock outstanding. Management has developed a capital budget calling for total expenditures of $2.4 million in the next six months.
   a) If new stock can be issued at a price of $20 per share, how many shares must be issued to finance the entire capital budget from common stock?
   b) What will be the percentage of the firm's stock held by the new shareholders if shares are issued as in a? [Ans.: 12 percent]
   c) Last year General paid a dividend of $0.50 per share. Management plans to maintain this dividend rate. What were the total dividends paid by the firm last year? What will be the total dividends paid in the coming year if new shares are issued and the dividend rate is maintained? What percentage of the dividends paid in the coming year will be received by the new shareholders?

2. The financial manager of Organic Compost Company is considering issuing either debt or preferred stock to finance a new pulverizer facility

costing $1.5 million. The interest rate on debt will be 8 percent whereas the required dividend rate on preferred stock will be 8.8 percent. The firm's tax rate is 50 percent.

a) What annual interest payments will be required on the debt issue?

b) How much in additional earnings before interest and taxes must be generated from the new facility to cover interest on the debt?

c) What annual dividends will be required on the preferred stock issue?

d) How much in additional earnings before interest and taxes must be generated from the new facility to cover preferred dividends? [Ans.: $264,000]

3. The HTA Kite Company started in business five years ago manufacturing kites of unusual designs. The firm has grown rapidly and there are now 80,000 shares of common stock outstanding, largely owned by management. Last year's income statement is shown below. The chief designer of HTA Kite, L. Z. Byrd, has developed a new magnesium kite which he swears will fly in winds of 5 to 80 mph and will be practically indestructible. In order to manufacture this kite, new facilities will be required involving a total investment of $2 million. Two financing alternatives are being considered: issuing 40,000 shares of stock or borrowing the $2 million at an interest rate of 9 percent per year. Management has considered two possible future sales projections: a pessimistic projection of $1 million and an optimistic projection of $2 million, as shown in the table below.

a) Calculate the values needed to complete the table.

b) Develop an EBIT-EPS graph for the two alternatives.

c) Draft a statement to the chief executive officer explaining the advantages and disadvantages of the alternative financing methods as illustrated by the data in the table.

| | Last year actual | Next year projections | | | |
		Stock issue		Debt issue	
Sales	$1,000,000	$1,000,000	$2,000,000	$1,000,000	$2,000,000
Expenses	680,000	800,000	1,200,000		
Operating profit	$ 320,000				
Interest	0				
Taxable income	$ 320,000				
Taxes (50%)	160,000				
Earnings	$ 160,000	$ 100,000			$ 310,000
Earnings per share	$2.00	$0.83			$3.88

4. A movie theater is under construction. It will have a 500-seat capacity, and management plans to have 800 showings per year. The ticket price

will average $2.50 per person, and total annual operating expenses are almost certain to be $300,000. Management feels fairly confident that the theater will operate at 50 percent capacity on average. An optimistic estimate would be 70 percent, whereas a pessimistic estimate would be 30 percent. The cost of the new theater will be $900,000, of which $100,000 is available from internal funds. Three financing alternatives for the remaining $800,000 are being considered: using all common stock, raising $400,000 from a sale of common stock and $400,000 by borrowing money at an 8 percent annual rate, or borrowing $800,000 at a 10 percent annual rate. Assume common stock can be sold at a price of $100 per share, there is no existing debt or preferred stock outstanding, current shareholders own 10,000 shares of stock, and the income tax rate is 40 percent.

a) Develop an EBIT-EPS graph for the three financing alternatives.
b) At approximately what percentages of capacity do the alternatives provide the same EPS (comparing financing alternatives two at a time)?
c) Evaluate the three alternatives. Which one would you recommend? Is there any additional information that would be helpful in reaching a decision?

5. The Puget Power Company is an electric utility planning to build a new power generating plant of conventional design. The company has traditionally paid out all earnings to the stockholders as dividends and financed capital expenditures with new issues of common stock. There is no debt or preferred stock presently outstanding. Data on the company and the new power plant are shown below. Assume all earnings are expected to be level perpetuities.

Company data	Power plant
Earnings: $30 million Number of outstanding shares: 1.0 million	Initial outlay: $20 million Added annual earnings: $3 million

Management estimates the rate of return required by stockholders to be 10 percent per year and considers the power plant to have the same risk as existing assets.

a) *Assuming no taxes,* no costs to bankruptcy, and perfect capital markets, what will be the total market value of Puget Power if common stock is issued to finance the plant? [Ans.: $330 million]
b) Under the same assumptions as **a** what will be the total value (stock plus bonds) of the firm if $20 million in bonds at an interest rate of 6 percent are issued to finance the plant?
c) Given that bonds will be issued as in **b**, calculate the rate of return

required by the stockholders after the financing has occurred and the plant is built. [Ans.: 10.26 percent]

6. The Quasar Manufacturing Company has no outstanding debt or preferred stock. Management estimates that the required rate of return on Quasar common stock is currently 10 percent. The total market value of the stock is $40 million. An expansion program is planned that will involve $25 million in capital expenditures over the next three years. The estimated net present value of these investments is $10 million based on the current cost of capital of the firm. Therefore, assuming that only equity (common stock and retained earnings) is used to finance the expansion and that capital market rates do not change, the value of the firm's stock would be $75 million in three years.

Quasar's financial manager has suggested that debt be used to finance at least part of the $25 million. The following estimates have been developed:

Debt issued	Debt interest rate	Common stock value	Rate on stock	Value of Quasar securities	Average cost of capital
$ 0	—	$75 million	10%	$75 million	10%
$ 5 million	8%	$72.5 million	10.1%		
$10 million	8.2%	$70 million	10.1%		
$15 million	8.4%	$67 million	10.3%		
$20 million	8.6%	$63 million	10.5%		
$25 million	9%	$57 million	11.2%		

a) Determine the value of Quasar securities and the average cost of capital for each financing alternative given that Quasar's tax rate is 50 percent.

b) What financing plan would you recommend and why?

7. The AAA Corporation has the following investments available during the coming year:

Initial outlay	Expected rate of return
$ 100,000	30%
400,000	20%
200,000	15%
1,000,000	13%
800,000	12%
1,000,000	11%
2,000,000	10%
1,500,000	9%
Total $7,000,000	

The firm's average cost of capital was estimated at 9 percent. However the financial manager has determined that financing the entire budget of $7,000,000 would result in a higher average cost of capital for the firm. Only $2 million could be raised without increasing the cost of capital. The additional costs of raising more than $2 million are estimated to be as follows:

Additional financing	Cost of capital for additional financing
$2.0 million	9.5%
1.5 million	10 %
1.0 million	11 %
.5 million	12 %

What should the firm do?

8. Gregor Enzac, a recognized genius in the field of entomology, has established a new company called Enz, Inc. The company will produce insects for agricultural pest control and engage in research in this area. Gregor plans to raise $10 million to be used, primarily, to establish facilities for the production of a "super" ladybug species developed by him. Field trials of the ladybug have resulted in contracts estimated to provide $500,000 per year in pretax earnings (EBIT) once production is underway. Gregor and his associates have received 100,000 shares of Enz common stock in exchange for the rights to their research and for long-term contracts to work for the company. The problem Gregor faces is how to raise the $10 million in cash. Current interest rates are 6 percent on AAA corporate bonds and 9 percent on B rated bonds. The tax rate is 50 percent.

As financial advisor to Gregor and his associates, answer the following questions that they have asked:

a) "Since AAA bonds have a much lower interest rate than B bonds and interest on debt is tax-deductible, why shouldn't we issue $10 million of AAA bonds and not issue any more common stock?"

b) "Perhaps we should issue $5 million of debt and then raise the remaining $5 million through a preferred stock issue?"

c) "If we have to issue some common stock, what factors will determine how many shares must be issued and what price we will obtain?"

the Modigliani-Miller analysis of capital structure and value

As discussed in Chapter 9 above, Modigliani and Miller (MM) show that under idealized conditions in the capital markets and in the absence of taxes and bankruptcy costs, the value of a firm is unaffected by its financing. Both the total value of a firm's securities and its average cost of capital are independent of its capital structure. In this appendix we will provide an illustration of MM's analysis and present the major arguments against the applicability of their results.

THE MM ANALYSIS

Consider two firms which have identical business risks and (for ease of illustration) the same expected level of earnings before interest and taxes. We assume that all business risk is based on the probability distribution of EBIT and that these two firms have identical distributions. Leverage Inc. has $1 million of 8 percent bonds outstanding, and Equity Inc. has no debt. Data on the two firms are shown in Exhibit 9-4. The question at issue here is what the market value of Leverage's common stock and therefore its total value will be. If there is an advantage to debt financing, the total value of Leverage will be greater than that of Equity. If debt financing is undesirable, Leverage's value will be less than Equity's. We can solve the problem by examining the consequences of first assuming that debt reduces value and then assuming that it increases value. If we find that neither assumption is reasonable, then, logically, total value must be the same for the two firms. In addition, arguing the point in this way will be helpful in illustrating the underlying characteristics of the analysis.

Suppose that the total value for Leverage's securities is only $3.5 million compared with Equity's $4 million. Debt financing has reduced the value of Leverage. Its bonds are worth $1 million, and its stock is worth $2.5 million. Consider an investor who wishes to purchase the rights to an income stream with the risk of Equity. For an investment of $400,000, the investor could purchase 10 percent of Equity's stock and for this amount would have an expected income of 10 percent of Equity's income, or $48,000. The investor now considers investing in Leverage. The investor could purchase 10 percent of Leverage's bonds at a cost of $100,000, which would provide $8,000 interest and 10 percent of Leverage's stock at a cost of $250,000 with expected dividends of $40,000. The investor's total expected income from Leverage's securities would be $48,000, and *this*

Exhibit 9-4 Basic Data

	Leverage, Inc.	Equity, Inc.
EBIT	$480,000	$480,000
Interest	80,000	0
Dividends	$400,000	$480,000
Market value – bonds	$1 million	$ 0
Market value – stock	?	$4 million
Total market value	?	$4 million

income would have a probability distribution identical to that of the income from 10 percent of Equity's common stock. This is so because the investor would own a 10 percent share in Leverage's earnings before interest and taxes just as he or she would have from purchasing Equity's common stock. The data describing these alternative transactions are shown in Exhibit 9-5. But note that purchasing a 10 percent claim against Leverage's income would cost the investor a total of only $350,000. Obtaining the same expected income ($48,000) from Equity stock would

Exhibit 9-5. Assume Debt Lowers Value

Market value of Leverage's bonds	$1.0 million
Market value of Leverage's stock	2.5 million
Total market value of Leverage	$3.5 million

Equity's stock value = total value = $4 million
1. Purchase 10% of Equity's stock
      Purchase cost = $400,000
      Dividend income = $48,000/year
2. Purchase 10% of Leverage's stock and bonds

	Purchase cost	Income
Bonds	$100,000	$ 8,000/year
Stock	250,000	40,000/year
Total	$350,000	$48,000/year

Investors would prefer (2), investing in Leverage's stock and bonds.

cost the investor $400,000. If you were the investor, which choice would you make? Obviously you would prefer to buy Leverage's securities. In a perfect market, identical substitutes cannot sell at different prices. If all investors agree on the probability distributions of the two firms, their securities must sell at prices that provide the same returns. Either Equity's stock must sell for less than $4 million or Leverage's stock and bonds must sell for more than $3.5 million. *In any case the total value of Leverage's securities cannot be lower than the value of Equity's;* otherwise investors would all prefer to purchase a combination of stocks and bonds issued by Leverage rather than to purchase Equity's stock.

The result established by this example is that a firm using debt financing cannot lower its value below what it would have with all stock financing because investors can always undo the leverage by purchasing a combination of stocks and bonds issued by the firm. However, remember that we are assuming that the probability distribution of EBIT is not affected by financing.

What about the possibility that Leverage's value will be greater than Equity's? Suppose that Leverage's stock has a market value of $3.2 million and a total value of stock plus bonds of $4.2 million. A similar analysis can be performed in this case and the results are shown in Exhibit 9-6. Now investors desiring securities with the same risk as Equity's would purchase Equity's stock because they can get a better return than by purchasing 10 percent of Leverage's stock and bonds. However, what about

---

Exhibit 9-6. Assume Debt Increases Value

Market value of Leverage's bonds	$1.0 million
Market value of Leverage's stock	3.2 million
Total market value of Leverage	$4.2 million

1. Purchase 10% of Equity's stock

   Purchase cost   = $400,000
   Dividend income = $48,000/year

2. Purchase 10% of Leverage's stock and bonds

	Purchase cost	Income
Bonds	$100,000	$ 8,000/year
Stock	320,000	40,000/year
Total	$420,000	$48,000/year

Investors would prefer (1), investing in Equity's stock.

an investor who is willing to trade off some risk in order to achieve a higher rate of return on the investment? An investment of $400,000 in Leverage's stock will provide the investor with an expected return of $50,000 per year, or 12.5 percent ($50,000/$400,000), as compared with only $48,000 per year, or 12 percent, if $400,000 is invested in Equity's stock. Such an investor has another alternative, however. Under the assumptions of this analysis, the investor can borrow at the same interest rate that the company can by using stock as security for the loan. Suppose the investor takes $383,333, borrows an additional $100,000 at 8 percent, and purchases Equity stock with the total amount ($483,333). The results are shown in Exhibit 9-7. The investor's income is $50,000, the same as if the investor purchased Leverage's stock, and the out-of-pocket expense is only $383,333 instead of $400,000. Since investors would rather hold Equity's stock alone rather than a combination of Leverage's stock and bonds or they would prefer to borrow to invest in Equity's stock rather than hold Leverage's stock by itself, Leverage's stock value must be less than $3.2 million (or Equity's stock worth more than $4 million).

Suppose the market value of Leverage's stock and bonds is $4 million, made up of $3 million of stock value and $1 million of bond value. Equity's stock value and total value is $4 million. One final point is worth making. An investor seeking higher risk and return could invest in Leverage's stock or borrow to invest in Equity's stock. Is the risk and return from these two alternative strategies the same given the same dollar outlay by the investor? Exhibit 9-8 evaluates the returns achieved by the two strategies for three different levels of EBIT. Remember, Leverage and Equity are assumed to have identical probability distributions of

---

Exhibit 9-7. Using Personal Borrowing When Debt Is Assumed to Increase Value

1. Purchase 12.5% of Leverage's stock
   Purchase cost   = $400,000
   Dividend income = $50,000/year
2. Borrowing to invest in Equity's stock

	Purchase cost	Income
Stock	$483,333	$58,000
Borrowing	(100,000)	(8,000)
Net	$383,333	$50,000

Investors would prefer (2), borrowing to invest in Equity's stock.

EBIT (EBIT for the two firms have a correlation of 1.0). We see from Exhibit 9-8 that identical returns are achieved by the two investment alternatives; they have identical risks.

Therefore Leverage's total value cannot be greater than Equity's total value. Since we have also shown that Leverage's value cannot be less than Equity's value, the two must be equal.

MM used arguments similar to those above to examine the impact of corporate taxes. They found, as we discussed on page 349, that debt provides a benefit to the firm because of the tax deductibility of interest payments.

Leverage with Corporate Taxes

Exhibit 9-8. Assessing the Risk from Two Investment Strategies

	EBIT for leverage and equity		
	$80,000	$480,000	$600,000
Leverage interest	$80,000	$ 80,000	$ 80,000
Leverage dividends	0	400,000	520,000
Strategy A:			
Investor income	$ 0	$ 40,000	$ 52,000
Equity dividends	$80,000	$480,000	$600,000
Strategy B:			
Investor dividends	$ 8,000	$ 48,000	$ 60,000
Investor interest	(8,000)	(8,000)	(8,000)
Investor income	$ 0	$ 40,000	$ 52,000

Strategy A
    Investor purchases $300,000 of Leverage's stock, which has an aggregate market value of $3 million. Investor owns 10% of Leverage's stock.
                Out-of-pocket investment = $300,000
Strategy B
    Investor borrows $100,000 at 8% interest rate and buys $400,000 of Equity's stock, which has an aggregate market value of $4 million. Investor owns 10% of Equity's stock.
                Out-of-pocket investment = $300,000
Conclusion
    Both strategies provide the same income regardless of the level of EBIT for the firms; therefore the risk is the same for the two strategies.

The implication of their analysis in this case is that the value of the firm is maximized when its capital structure contains only debt. Although this extreme result is impractical because the Internal Revenue Service would never permit interest payments of this magnitude to be tax-deductible, the inference is that firms should use as much debt as they possibly can, subject only to the restrictions of the IRS and the willingness of creditors to lend to the firm. It is also quite clear that extensive use of debt financing would expose businesses to high probabilities of default; they would find it difficult to meet the promised payments of interest and principal.

The results of the MM analysis can be summarized as follows:

A. There is no benefit to debt financing other than the reduction in corporate income taxes due to the tax deductibility of debt interest.

B. There is no disadvantage or cost (other than interest) to debt financing.

Implications for financing   If a firm is not paying corporate income taxes, the financing decision is irrelevant. It doesn't matter one way or the other whether debt is used or not. A firm paying corporate taxes should maximize its use of debt. Debt is superior to any other financing source.

CRITICISMS OF THE MM ANALYSIS

There are three conditions which must be met in order to validate the MM analysis and produce the above results.

1. No costs are imposed on the firm when it defaults on debt payments or goes bankrupt.

2. Investors must be able to do their own borrowing, using "homemade leverage," if they desire higher returns (with higher risk) than the returns provided by debt-free or low-debt firms.

3. Investors must be able to undo the leverage achieved by a corporation by purchasing a proportionate share of all the outstanding claims against corporate income.

Critics of the MM position have focused their attack on the realism of these three conditions. We can separate these arguments into two groups. The first group of arguments is directed toward result **A**, that the only benefit from debt financing is due to the tax deductibility of interest. The second group of arguments is directed toward point **B**, that there is no disadvantage to debt even if used very heavily. We summarize the various arguments below.

Arguments Supporting Additional Benefits from Debt

1. The risk of leverage as perceived by an individual investor borrowing money is different from the investor's perception of the risk of leverage when the corporation borrows the money. Corporate leverage and homemade leverage are not perfect substitutes from the standpoint of the person doing the borrowing. Therefore, individuals will prefer that the corporation do the borrowing rather than themselves. One reason for this difference in risk is the limited liability of a corporate stockholder. If the corporation borrows and goes bankrupt, individuals lose at most their investment. If the individual borrows to finance stock purchases and the stock becomes worthless, the creditors can take other assets owned by the individual to pay off the debt.

2. The interest rate charged by lenders may be greater for an individual than for a corporation. Therefore, it will be cheaper from the viewpoint of the stockholders to have the corporation do the borrowing.

3. There are legal limitations inhibiting homemade leverage. Mutual funds and trust funds that invest heavily in common stock cannot borrow, and so these investors may prefer corporations with debt.

Arguments Implying a Disadvantage to Debt

1. The firm is likely to incur costs and suffer penalties if it does not meet its promised principal and interest payments. Legal expenses, disruption of operations, and loss of potentially profitable investment opportunities may result. As the amount of debt in the capital structure increases, so does the probability of incurring these costs. Consequently there are disadvantages to debt, and excessive use of debt may reduce the value of the firm. This is the most telling argument against result **B** above.

2. Investors seeking to undo excessive leverage will incur transaction costs (brokerage fees from buying and selling securities) that would otherwise not need to be paid. Therefore the securities of highly levered firms will sell at somewhat lower prices than MM would predict.

3. Much corporate debt is not marketable. It consists of loans made by banks and other financial institutions. Therefore, investors cannot undo excessive leverage because they cannot purchase a proportionate share of the outstanding claims (stock and debt) against the firm's income.

4. Many institutional investors such as banks and life insurance companies cannot purchase low-rated bonds such as those issued by a highly levered corporation. Therefore the interest rates on highly rated, "investment grade" bonds are significantly lower than those on more risky bonds.

SUMMARY   No amount of theoretical argument and criticism will ever settle the issue. The impact of leverage is primarily an empirical problem and must be ultimately dealt with through studies of firms' actual behavior. Unfortunately there are some serious difficulties in determining how much impact leverage has. For one thing, we rarely find firms of comparable business risk which have large differences in leverage. Whether this lack of difference in firms' financing policies is due to "herd instinct" or whether it reflects a common, correct determination of optimal capital structure on the part of the financial managers involved is not clear. The question of optimal capital structure remains a contentious issue in finance.

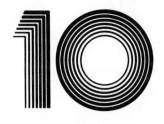

dividend policy and retained earnings

A corporation can use its earnings to pay dividends to its stockholders, or it can use the funds for other purposes, such as retirement of debt or financing new investments. Management must decide on the amount or proportion of earnings to pay out as dividends and the amount to retain for the internal operations of the firm. The more earnings that are used for dividends, the less that will be available for investment, which may mean that some investment will have to be financed with external funds (borrowing, sale of stock, etc.). An important point is that dividend policy and retained earnings financing of investments are interdependent. The long-run dividend policy of the corporation can affect its financing program and capital budget and is therefore an important consideration for the financial manager.

In the first section of this chapter, we will discuss the various factors which influence the firm's dividend policy. We then examine the alternative dividend policies actually adopted by business firms and explore the reasons that these policies are followed.

FACTORS AFFECTING THE DIVIDEND DECISION

The financial manager will take a variety of factors into account when establishing the level of current dividends or planning a long-term dividend policy.

Profitability of the Firm's Investment Opportunities

Clearly, if the company does not have a productive use for earnings (either to make long-term investment or to increase current assets) and does not wish to retire its debt, these earnings can be paid out in dividends. On the other hand, if profitable opportunities do exist, earnings can be used for their financing. A zero dividend payout is not uncommon for young, rapidly growing firms which have highly profitable uses for funds. Financing of investment from profits (internal financing) may be deemed preferable to paying larger dividends and financing investment externally by selling new stocks and bonds because of the preference of the firm's shareholders for capital gains income relative to dividend income. Furthermore, raising external capital involves transaction costs (for example, flotation costs), which are completely avoided by using internally generated funds from operations. Even if current projects are unattractive, when a profitable future investment is foreseen, it may be advisable to invest present earnings in liquid assets (for example, marketable securities) so that the funds will be available later to finance the investment.

Taxes

Shareholder taxes As was explained in Chapter 3, shareholders are subject to an ordinary income tax on dividends received from their investments and a capital gains tax on long-term capital gains (gains on assets held more than six months). The tax rate on capital gains is significantly less than that on dividends, implying that the tax system favors income earned as a capital gain.[1] Shareholder taxes encourage firms to finance investment internally from retained earnings and to keep dividends lower than they would if capital gains were not allowed a tax advantage. Why is this so? Each dollar that is *earned and retained* by the firm as cash or invested by the firm in a productive asset raises the value of the firm and, therefore, the value of the currently outstanding shares. Because the shares are a claim to the cash and other assets of the corporation, an increase in the value of the firm's cash or other assets provides an equal increase in the value of the shares.[2] The retained earnings thus raise the price of a share. *When the share is sold* by a stockholder, this price rise (gain) is taxed as a capital gain. If, on the other hand, the firm were not to retain the earnings but to pay them out in dividends, a tax on the dividend at the ordinary tax rate would be payable *immediately* by the stockholder. Thus, the return as a capital gain involves a lower tax rate and, in addition, permits the investors to postpone their tax payment until they sell the stock. Also note that stockholders who receive their share of corporate profits as capital gains and who want to receive cash in the current period can simply sell *some* of their shares to obtain the cash; stockholder income will then be in the form of a realized capital gain, which is taxed at a lower rate than would be the same amount of income received as dividends.

1. There is an exception to this. The tax law specifies that the first $100 of total dividends (dividends from all United States company stock owned), is tax-free. Therefore, those receiving very small dividend income ($100 or less) will prefer that income to an equal dollar amount of capital gain (which is taxable).

2. If the firm retains a dollar per share of earnings, the firm has the dollar and each share will consequently be worth approximately a dollar more than if the dollar per share were paid out as a dividend. The share is only worth *approximately* (rather than exactly) a dollar more if the dollar is retained because of the effects of taxes, transaction costs, and other factors which are ignored here for simplicity.

If the tax bias in favor of capital gains were eliminated and dividends and capital gains were taxed at the same rate and at the same time, retained earnings financing would lose its tax advantage for stockholders. A probable result would be higher dividends and greater use of external financing of investment by corporations.[3] This is so even though the problem is complicated by variations in tax brackets among individual stockholders, which imply differences in the impact of personal taxes on stockholder preferences between dividend and capital gain income. For those in very high brackets the relative advantage of capital gain income is greater. It must be kept in mind that at this point we are considering only personal tax effects; as we will see, some of the other factors (tax and nontax) influencing dividends may bias in favor of dividend income rather than capital gains.

Tax on excessive firm retentions Is a corporation able to pay out no dividends and permit its shareholders to earn all income in the form of capital gains? It can, *if* the funds that would have been paid in dividends are used to purchase productive assets by the firm and not merely retained in the form of cash and cash substitutes (stocks and bonds, Treasury bills, etc.). If the firm accumulates cash and cash substitutes beyond a limit deemed reasonable by the Internal Revenue Service in meeting the firm's liquidity needs, a special surtax will be imposed on the firm's improper accumulations. Although this penalty is unlikely to be imposed, it is an effective device in discouraging flagrant attempts by corporations to avoid paying dividends.

Corporate taxes From Chapter 9, recall that the tax deductibility of interest encourages the firm to use debt financing. This means that the firm will want to use some leverage and to finance some of its investments with debt. In the long run, the existence of the interest tax deductibility feature means a greater use of debt than would be the case if interest were not tax-deductible; that is, a larger proportion of the source of corporate capital will be debt and less will be equity (new stock and retained earnings). The implication is that more of the corporation's cash flow will be paid out as interest on debt and less will be paid out as dividends.

3. It is easily shown that if investors incur negligible brokerage fees in buying and selling securities and if information about a firm can be obtained by investors at a nominal cost, then the tax bias in favor of capital gains implies that firms will never finance an investment by selling new shares if the investment can be financed from retained earnings. That is, management will reduce dividends to provide funds for an investment before it will sell new shares to obtain the funds. On this see R. C. Stapleton, "Taxes, the Cost of Capital and the Theory of Investment," *The Economic Journal* (December 1972), pp. 1273–1292.

Legal Commitments and Requirements

Contractual restrictions   The contract between the firm and its creditors or between the firm and its preferred stockholders may include constraints on the firm's activities for protection of the lenders' or preferred stockholders' investment (see Chapter 19). Frequently, these protective covenants stipulate that dividends may be paid only out of profits earned in periods after the debt contract becomes effective. The firm also may be required to maintain a sufficient level of working capital or to restrict its investments. Preferred stock contracts, which provide for cumulative dividends to preferred stockholders, stipulate that there will be no dividend payment to common stockholders until current and all unpaid past preferred dividends have been paid.[4]

Statutory constraints on capital impairment   Most state laws provide that dividends may not exceed retained earnings (accumulated profits) plus paid-in surplus. That is, the firm may not pay dividends if the owners' equity (assets minus liabilities) is no greater than the total par value of all the firm's stock outstanding. This requirement is imposed to ensure that the assets of the firm exceed liabilities by a minimum cushion in order to protect the creditors. This cushion (the par value of the firm's stock) may be small in relation to the assets and liabilities of the firm, but nevertheless provides at least some safety margin to creditors. A second statutory limitation on dividends often applies if the firm is insolvent. Although the definition of insolvency varies, most states prohibit an insolvent firm from paying dividends.[5]

The Firm's Liquidity and Debt Needs

A firm will generally hold some liquid assets, such as cash and marketable securities, as a source of funds to meet unexpected cash requirements or to finance planned investments. The rate of return on such liquid assets, net of the costs of supervising them (for example, the costs of managing the portfolio of marketable securities), is generally low, and excessive accumulation of such assets is therefore unprofitable to the company. To eliminate such an excess, any extra cash and any proceeds from selling unnecessary securities can be paid out as a dividend. Conversely, a deficiency of liquid reserves may encourage the company to curtail dividends and to use earnings to establish the desired liquidity level.

Earnings also can be used for the retirement of some of the company's debt. Creditors may be demanding payment, or management may simply feel that the current degree of leverage exposes the firm to excessive financial risk.

4. See Chapter 19 on cumulative preferred dividends.

5. A firm is referred to as insolvent if the dollar level of its liabilities exceeds the value of its assets.

Costs of external financing and of dividend payments A firm may maintain a low dividend payout so that it can avoid external financing of its investments. The greater is the cost of obtaining external financing, the greater will be the incentive to finance internally from the firm's profits. The costs incurred in obtaining external capital include underwriting, brokerage commissions and fees, bank loan set-up costs, payments for legal and accounting services, and the expense of management's time in seeking and selecting the source of the outside capital. These costs are avoided by financing internally. Furthermore, the transaction costs involved in paying dividends (e.g., bookkeeping and postage costs) are also avoided if no dividends are paid. Consequently, from the standpoint of the firm, the out-of-pocket expenses of internal financing are always less than those for external financing.

Stockholder transaction costs Investors incur costs whenever they purchase a new asset such as a share of common stock or sell an asset that they already own. In the case of stock, this cost appears as a brokerage commission and as time spent by the shareholder in conducting the transaction.

If shareholders require income for current consumption or for investment in a different asset (for example, in the shares of another firm), the transaction costs to them will be less if they have dividend income than if they have to sell their shares in order to obtain the cash for consumption or for investment elsewhere. From a transaction-cost standpoint, therefore, those investors who need income to spend will prefer dividends to capital gains of the same amount (ignoring tax considerations). On the other hand, shareholders may prefer to keep their capital invested. If the firm pays them a dividend, they have to reinvest it themselves and pay the brokerage commissions involved in this investment. But, if the firm retains the dividend and invests it, shareholders will receive a capital gain which involves no transaction costs to them.[6] Therefore, in contrast to those who want cash and prefer dividends, investors who are net savers and who wish to keep their funds in the firm prefer income in the form of capital gains rather than in the form of dividends.

As a consequence of differing preferences between investors for capital gains and dividend income, firms that have a high dividend payout will tend to attract investors that require income for current consumption, and investors who prefer to keep their resources reinvested tend to prefer shares of companies which have low dividend payouts. This attraction of investors to firms with dividend policies that meet their consumption-investment preferences is referred to as the **clientele effect.** The clientele effect encourages corporations to maintain a stable, predict-

Firm and Stockholder Cost Considerations

6. See footnote 2, this chapter.

able dividend policy, because a radically different dividend payout may not appeal to most existing shareholders or potential investors. An unpredictable dividend policy will cause some stockholders to shift to other investments, and this shift means brokerage fees and perhaps the payment of a capital gains tax.

THE FIRM'S DIVIDEND POLICY

Two important dimensions of a firm's dividend policy are:

1. *Dividend stability:* whether dividends remain fixed or fluctuate from period to period
2. *Long-run dividend payout ratio:* the long-run average percentage of earnings paid out in dividends

Policy variables **1** and **2** are distinct from one another. Dividends can be stable or unstable whether the percentage of earnings paid out as dividends is high or low.

In examining the two above policy variables, we will be interested in the factors a firm must consider in determining its optimal policy and the empirical evidence concerning United States corporate behavior. The actual experience of corporations indicates which factors are most important.

Dividend Stability

Alternative policies and the evidence   Regardless of the policy determining the long-run dividend payout ratio, year-to-year fluctuations in dividends may follow any one of several guidelines:

1. *Stable dividend payout ratio.* This policy requires that the percentage of earnings paid out (dividend payout ratio = dividends ÷ earnings) each year is held stable. The result is dividends which fluctuate proportionately with earnings.
2. *Stable dollar dividend.* The dollar level of dividends is relatively stable from period to period or follows a steady upward or downward trend over time.
3. *Stable dollar dividend plus an "extra" dividend.* The company pays out a stable (in dollar level) regular dividend plus an added dividend at the end of particularly prosperous years.

Historical evidence suggests that whereas the first policy is rare, a stabilized dollar dividend is maintained by most major United States corporations. The third policy is practiced by a small minority, perhaps 10 percent, of large firms, with General Motors the most prominent example.

Figure 10-1 shows that earnings (net aftertax income) have historically been far more volatile than dividends, although both have experienced a general upward trend since the depths of the 1930s Depression. A classic study by John Lintner indicated that firms adjust their dollar dividends only gradually as earnings vary from year to year.[7] He also found a resistance on the part of corporations to reducing dividends below the amount paid in the previous period. Later studies by Brittain and by Fama and Babiak provided results generally consistent with those of Lintner.[8]

7. See John Lintner, "Distribution of Income of Corporations among Dividends, Retained Earnings, and Taxes," *American Economic Review,* 46 (May 1956), pp. 97–113.

8. See John A. Brittain, "The Tax Structure and Corporate Dividend Policy," *American Economic Review* (May 1964), pp. 272–87; Eugene F. Fama and Harvey Babiak, "Dividend Policy: An Empirical Analysis," *Journal of The American Statistical Association* (December 1968), pp. 1132–1161.

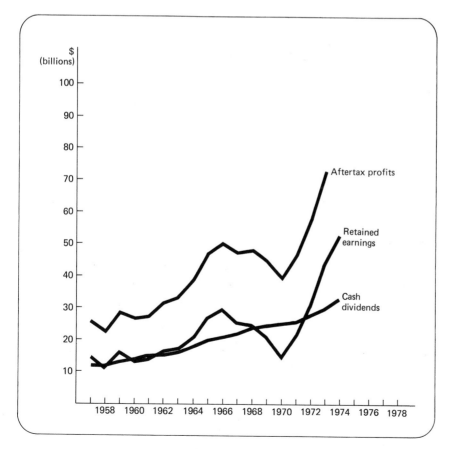

Figure 10-1. Aftertax profits, dividends, and retained earnings of United States corporations. (Source: U.S. Federal Reserve.)

An explanation of dividend stability   The ultimate criterion of company policy is whether or not it benefits shareholders. If a stable dollar dividend is to be justified, it must be shown that stockholders are thereby made better off. Several explanations for investor preferences for stable dollar dividends have been suggested.

First, investors may view dividends as a source of funds to meet their current living expenses. Such expenses are usually rather stable from period to period. Radical changes in dividend income will therefore necessitate either selling shares to obtain funds for living expenses, if dividends fall, or the reinvestment of some of the dividend income if dividends significantly rise. Selling shares or investing dividends involves brokerage fees and other expenses, including the time of the investor. These costs are avoided if the dividend stream is stable and predictable.

Second, the level of the current dividend payment is an effective means by which the corporation can convey information to the investing public on the *future* dividend-paying capacity (earning capacity) of the firm. If investors know that the firm will raise or lower dividends only if management foresees a permanent earnings increase or decrease, respectively, then the level of dividends informs investors about management's expectations concerning company earnings. A cut in dividends implies poor earnings expectations, no change implies earnings stability, and a dividend increase implies management's optimism about earnings. On the other hand, a company that pursues an erratic dividend payout policy is, in effect, not providing such information, thereby increasing the risk associated with the shares. Stability of dividends, where such dividends are based upon long-run earning power of the company, is therefore a means of reducing share riskiness and consequently increasing share value to investors. Of course, this rationale for stable dividends does not apply if information on management's assessment of earning power is available by means other than dividend policy. The actual world, however, involves significant costs of acquiring reliable information.

A third factor encouraging stable dividends is the requirement by many states that financial institutions, for example, mutual savings banks, insurance companies, and mutual funds, may invest in only those stocks with good dividend records. These financial intermediaries represent a significant force in the market, and their demand for the company's stock can have an enhancing effect on its price (and therefore on stockholder wealth). Also, federal laws covering pension plans encourage the purchase of stocks with high, stable dividends.

Long-Run Dividend Payout Ratio   The above discussion covered the first aspect of dividend policy, stability from year to year. The second aspect is the long-run average percentage of earnings that the firm pays out in dividends. The firm may plan a high or low long-run dividend payout ratio regardless of its policy toward period-to-period dividend stability. Thus, although most firms have relatively stable dollar dividends, firms differ in terms of their long-run payout ratios. There are two theories regarding long-run dividend payout policy that we will consider.

Two theories In our earlier discussion of the factors affecting the dividend decision, we identified two influences favoring the use of internal over external financing of investment. First, the personal tax bias toward capital gain income encourages firms to provide a higher fraction of returns in the form of capital gains and less as dividends than would be so if taxes were unbiased; to provide the capital gains, some or all of earnings are reinvested by the firm rather than distributed as dividends. A second encouragement to internal financing is the presence of dividend payment costs and of flotation costs in raising external funds. The implication of the internal financing advantage is that a firm will keep dividends low and use earnings to finance investment rather than pay large dividends and sell shares to finance investment. Firms with profitable uses for earnings will pay small or no dividends, and companies with poor investment opportunities will distribute a large fraction of earnings as dividends.

Two theories have been advanced regarding the significance of the advantage of internal relative to external financing. One school of thought argues that imperfections (tax biases, flotation costs, etc.) are important and that it is significantly less costly to finance internally than externally. An implication of this view is that more will be invested if internal funds are available than would be the case if funds for investment must be obtained by selling additional shares, a more costly source of financing. Furthermore, because there is an attempt to maintain a stable dividend, as we noted in the previous section, the level of investment might be affected if funds are required to meet dividend payments rather than to cover investment outlays. As is discussed in the next section, the **smoothed residual dividend policy** conforms to the imperfect markets view. It dictates that the firm should maintain a stable dollar dividend and set the dividend level so that equity investment (investment not financed by borrowing) is financed to the maximum degree possible with retained earnings rather than by selling new shares (since retained earnings financing is cheaper).

An alternative theory offered by the "perfect markets" school holds that the advantage of internal financing is negligible. Proponents of this theory maintain that the choice of investments is independent of dividend policy (that is, independent of whether financing is with retained earnings or with funds obtained by selling new shares). This would suggest that management views the costs of internal and external financing as equal. An even stronger assertion is made by some that investment policy and dividend policy are completely independent, which means that not only is investment unaffected by the source of equity funds (internal or external) but, also, the level of investment does not influence the size of the dividend.

As is often the case with economic phenomena, the evidence is not clear as to which theory is valid, although more evidence has been provided in support of the first hypothesis, which argues that imperfections are important. A recent study by E. F. Fama, which supports the perfect markets view, concludes that the evidence is insufficient to reject the notion that a firm's investment and dividend policies are independent.[9] The Fama results confront a significant body of contrary findings supporting the imperfect markets theory. Pye examined 330 United States firms and found that an abnormally low proportion of firms that issued new stock also paid dividends.[10] This suggests that firms tend to utilize retained earnings to finance investment before employing external stock financing. Similar conclusions were reached by Higgins, who found that, consistent with the residual payout policy, dividends vary positively with earnings and negatively with investment.[11] Dhrymes and Kurz found that a desire to maintain stable dividends may hamper investment by reducing internal funds available for capital expenditures. Furthermore, their results suggest that investment needs have an influence on dividends, with greater investment reducing the dividend payout, as predicted by a residual payout policy.[12] Baumol, Heim, Malkiel, and Quandt observed that the rate of return earned on internally financed investment was significantly lower than that earned on investment financed externally.[13] This is consistent with the view that more must be earned on externally funded capital outlays because external financing is more costly.

Residual dividend policy The most prominent dividend policy prescription to evolve from the theory that internal financing is cheaper than external financing is referred to as the **residual dividend policy.** As we noted, there is evidence that many companies follow this strategy. Before ex-

---

9. See E. F. Fama, "The Empirical Relationships between the Dividend and Investment Decisions of Firms," *American Economic Review,* 64 (June 1974), pp. 304–318.

10. See Gordon Pye, "Preferential Tax Treatment of Capital Gains, Optimal Dividend Policy, and Capital Budgeting," *Quarterly Journal of Economics* (July 1972), pp. 226–242.

11. See Robert C. Higgins, "The Corporate Dividend Saving Decision," *Journal of Financial and Quantitative Analysis* (March 1972), pp. 1527–1541.

12. See P. Dhrymes and M. Kurz, "Investment, Dividends, and External Finance Behavior of Firms," in R. Ferber (ed.), *Determinants of Investment Behavior* (New York: National Bureau of Economic Research, 1967).

13. See W. J. Baumol, P. Heim, B. G. Malkiel, and R.E. Quandt, "Earnings Retention, New Capital and the Growth of the Firm," *The Review of Economics and Statistics,* 52 (November 1970), pp. 345–355.

amining the major versions of the residual payout policy, let's examine the residual concept.

Funds for corporate investment are acquired from debt sources, re-tained earnings, and the sale of stock. We refer to investment funded by equity capital sources (retained earnings and stock sales) as **equity invest-ment.** In each period, management must determine the proportions of new investments to be supported by borrowed capital and by equity capital. Market interest rates and target debt levels set by management will deter-mine the relative proportions. The dividend *under a residual dividend pol-icy* equals the amount left over from earnings after *equity* investment. If equity investment equals earnings, no dividends are paid. If equity invest-ment is greater than earnings, then no dividends are paid and new shares are sold to cover any equity investment not covered by earnings. Finally, if equity investment is less than earnings, *all* such investment is covered from earnings (no new shares sold) and what is left over from earnings is paid out as a dividend. *Dividends are therefore merely a residual re-maining after all equity investment needs are fulfilled.* Notice carefully that a residual policy minimizes the use of external equity financing (sale of new shares) since, by this policy, equity investment has a higher-priority claim to earnings than do dividends.

Corporations have employed three general approaches in putting the residual dividend policy into practice. Before describing these ap-proaches, we will define the following variables:

D_t = dividend paid in year t

I_t^e = investment in year t that is financed from equity sources (retained earnings and stock sales)

E_t = earnings in year t

q_t = dividend payout ratio in year t where $q_t = \dfrac{D_t}{E_t}$

1. **Pure residual dividend policy.** Following this policy, the corporation will set the dividends paid each year as the amount of that year's earnings left after the year's equity investment is deducted. This can be expressed as

$$D_t = E_t - I_t^e$$

2. **Fixed dividend payout ratio.** Dividends set under this method are equal to a constant proportion (q_t) of yearly earnings. This can be expressed as

$$D_t = q_t \cdot E_t$$

If the percentage paid in dividends is 40 percent, for example, this would equal

$$D_t = q_t \cdot E_t = 0.4E_t$$

The percentage q_t is set so that, over the long run, dividends are equal to earnings minus equity investment.

3. **Smoothed residual dividend policy.** Under this method, yearly dividends are set at a constant dollar value. Dividends are set so that over the long run they will be equal to earnings minus equity investment. Exhibit 10-1 shows the dividend for five years paid out by a company using each of these methods. In the second method, the ratio (percent) used is 40 percent.

The pure residual dividend policy can produce highly volatile dividends, particularly if investment and earnings move in opposite directions from period to period (from years 2 to 3 and from years 3 to 4 in the Exhibit 10-1 example). The fixed dividend payout ratio residual dividend policy lets dividends fluctuate directly with earnings and will be as volatile as those earnings.

The smoothed residual dividend strategy generally produces the most stable dollar dividend. In a period in which earnings exceed dividends plus equity investment (years 1, 2, and 4 in Exhibit 10-1), the firm increases its holdings of liquid assets (cash and marketable securities). These holdings are used later for dividends and investment in periods in which dividends plus investment exceed earnings (years 3 and 5). Observe that

Exhibit 10-1. Earnings, Equity Investment, and Dividends of a Company Using a Residual Payout Policy

	Year					
	1	2	3	4	5	Total
Earnings E_t	$140	$180	$130	$200	$150	$800
Equity investment I_t^e	80	60	130	110	100	480
Pure residual dividend D_t	60	120	0	90	50	320
Fixed dividend payout ratio dividend D_t (ratio = .4)	56	72	52	80	60	320
Smoothed residual dividend D_t	50	60	60	70	80	320

the smoothed residual policy provides both a minimization of dependence on external financing of equity investment and the benefit of a stable dollar dividend.

Any residual dividend policy sets the long-run proportion of earnings paid out in dividends (the dividend payout ratio) on a residual basis. The residual dividend policy therefore refers to the second policy variable noted earlier, the first being dividend stability. The residual dividend policy was then divided into three types—pure residual policy, fixed dividend payout ratio residual policy, and smoothed residual policy. These three approaches are the same in terms of long-run dividend payout ratio since all are residual; but they differ in terms of the other policy variable, stability. A pure residual policy does not seek stability, whereas the fixed dividend payout ratio residual policy achieves stability in terms of the payout ratio and the smoothed residual dividend policy achieves stability in terms of the dollar level of dividends.

Generally, firms pay dividends once per quarter, i.e., four times per year. Normally, dividends are set at a level that the firm feels is sustainable even during the years of poor earnings. The firm projects its anticipated earnings and desired long-term payout ratio given the investment opportunities it anticipates and establishes a dividend payout rate that it feels it can maintain. This dividend, which is planned with the firm's long-run needs and earnings in mind, is referred to as the **regular dividend.** In addition, as noted earlier, some firms pay an **extra dividend** at the end of the year once the firm's earnings are known and investment needs have been determined.

The first step in the dividend payment procedure is the announcement by the board of directors of its decision to pay a specified dividend to shareholders of record at some particular future date. For example, the board of directors of Serrento Corporation announces on February 15, 1976, that dividends of 50 cents per share will be payable to all shareholders of record on March 15, 1976, payment being made on April 5, 1976. A shareholder of record on a given date is someone who is recorded on the company's books at the close of business on that record date as the owner of specific shares of stock. Thus, in the example, if Serrento Corporation were informed on March 15, or before, of a transfer of shares, the new owner (buyer) receives the dividend; if the corporation were notified of the sale on March 16 or thereafter, the old owner (seller) receives the dividend.

Since there is a lag of several days from the time a sale transaction takes place to the time the firm is informed of the transaction, a sale on say March 13 would not generally be recorded on the company's books

THE DIVIDEND PAYMENT PROCEDURE

until after the record date of March 15, i.e., the seller would still be entitled to the dividend. Recognizing this lag, the practice in the brokerage industry is that the right to the dividend goes with the stock up to, but not including, four business days before the record date; a buyer of the stock four business days before the record date or thereafter does not acquire the right to the dividend. The stock is referred to as ex-dividend four days before the record date or thereafter, since the stock no longer carries with it the right to the dividend. For example, assume that Bill Seller owns 100 shares of Serrento Corporation stock. There are five business days between Monday, March 8, 1976, and March 15, 1976. Therefore, if Bill Seller sells the stock on or before March 8, 1976, the purchaser, Alex Buyer, also acquires the right to the dividend; however, if Alex Buyer purchases the stock on March 9 or thereafter, the claim to the dividend remains with Mr. Seller, i.e., the stock is ex-dividend. The ex-dividend date is March 9.

The price of the firm's stock will reflect the fact that it has gone ex-dividend. Going ex-dividend will cause the price of the stock to fall by approximately the amount of the dividend. In our example, assuming no other cause for the stock price to change, a share of Serrento stock would sell for 50 cents per share (the amount of the dividend per share) less on March 9 than it did on March 8. For example, if Serrento stock sold for $30 per share on March 8, it would sell for approximately $29.50 per share on March 9. This is so since the buyer of the stock on March 8 is also entitled to the 50 cent dividend; a buyer on or after March 9 is not entitled to the dividend. The dividend checks would be mailed by Serrento Corporation on April 5, 1976, to shareholders of record on March 15, 1976.

Many firms allow stockholders to request that the firm not pay them the dividend but, instead, automatically reinvest it in the shares of the corporation. AT&T, Exxon, General Motors, and Uniroyal are among the numerous firms providing this option. The stockholder is still required to pay ordinary taxes on the dividend when it's payable, so there is no tax advantage. Automatic reinvestment can be beneficial to shareholders by providing a method to reinvest the dividend which is easier and less costly in terms of brokerage fees than would be reinvestment of a dividend by stockholders themselves.[14]

STOCK DIVIDENDS AND STOCK SPLITS

A stock dividend is a dividend payment in the form of additional shares of stock instead of cash. A stock split is essentially the same. When a stock splits, shareholders are given a larger number of shares for the old shares

14. See "Dividend Reinvestment Plans: Some Hidden Pluses," *Forbes* (Sept. 1, 1973), pp. 52, 54; R. H. Pettway and R. P. Malone, "Automatic Dividend Reinvestment Plans of Nonfinancial Corporations," *Financial Management* (Winter 1973), pp. 11–18.

they already own. In either case, each shareholder retains the same percentage of all outstanding stock as he or she had before the stock dividend or split.[15] Thus, for example, a 10 percent stock dividend would mean that each shareholder was given one share of stock for every ten shares already owned. Under a two-for-one stock split, each shareholder would be given one additional share of stock for every share already owned, thus doubling the number of shares owned by each stockholder.[16]

The effects of a stock dividend or a stock split can be summarized as follows:

1. There is no change in the firm's assets or liabilities or in shareholders' equity (assets less liabilities), and there is no change in the *total* market value of the firm's shares.
2. There is a fall in *per share* earnings, book value, and market price, and an offsetting rise in the number of shares held by each stockholder. Each stockholder, therefore, has no change in the total book value, total earnings, or total market value of all shares held since he or she owns the same percentage of the firm after the stock dividend as before.

A stock dividend or split does not change the assets of the firm, since nothing is received by the firm for new shares issued. The firm's debt is also unchanged by the stock dividend or split, since the debt is in no way involved. It follows that the total shareholders' equity (the firm's total assets less debt) is also unchanged. Since shareholders each retain their old percentage of the total shareholders' interest, each has the same claim to real assets after the stock dividend or split as before. The total value of a stockholder's shares will consequently be the same before and after the new shares are issued. The stockholders therefore do not gain or lose as a result of the new shares. An example will clarify this point.

Assume that the X. Y. Zoro Company (XYZ Co.) is planning a 25 percent stock dividend (one new share paid for each four already owned). The stock dividend will increase the number of shares outstanding from

15. There is a difference in the accounting procedure for treating stock dividends and stock splits. To record a stock dividend, the fair market value of the stock is transferred from the retained earnings account to the paid-in-capital account. In contrast, a stock split merely requires restating the par value of the stock; e.g., a two-for-one split of stock with an initial par value of $10 per share would only necessitate a change in the par of the common stock to $5 per share.

16. If a stockholder is entitled to a fraction of a share under a stock dividend or split, then the company will pay cash in place of the fractional share. For example, with a 2 percent stock dividend, a stockholder with ten shares is entitled to two-tenths of a share (2 percent × 10 shares). The firm would pay the stockholder two-tenths of the fair market value of a share in cash. If the market price per share were $20, the stockholder would receive $4 (0.2 × $20).

800,000 to 1 million. The firm's assets, the firm's debt, the stockholders' equity (assets minus debt), and the firm's income are left unchanged. Since the number of shares outstanding has increased, however, the *per share* book value, earnings, and market price decline. This is shown in Exhibit 10-2. Why has market price fallen in the same proportion as earnings and book value? Because a share of stock is nothing more than a claim on the assets and earnings of the firm; if the assets and earnings per share fall exactly by 20 percent, as is the case here, then it is reasonable for the share price to also fall by 20 percent. Notice that the shareholder is completely unaffected by the stock dividend. This is so because the fall in the figures per share in Exhibit 10-2 are exactly compensated for by the increase in the shareholder's number of shares owned. Consequently, the total book value, total earnings, and total market value of the shares the stockholder owns is the same after the stock dividend as before. To see this, assume a shareholder owned 100 shares of XYZ stock before the stock dividend and owns 125 shares after the stock dividend. The total book value of the shares owned *before* the stock dividend was $1,000 (100 shares owned × $10 per share); the total book value *after* the stock dividend of 25 shares is also $1,000 (125 shares owned × $8 per share). Total earnings on the shareholder's shares are also unchanged since earnings on the shares before the dividend were $200 (100 shares × $2 earnings per share) and earnings after the dividend are also $200 (125 shares × $1.60

Exhibit 10-2. The Effects of a Stock Dividend

	Total for firm before and after stock dividend	*Per share* figures before stock dividend (800,000 shares outstanding)[a]	*Per share* figures after stock dividend (1 million shares outstanding)[b]
Equity book value[c]	$ 8,000,000	$10	$ 8
Earnings[d]	$ 1,600,000	$ 2	$ 1.60
Market value of shares	$32,000,000	$40	$32

[a]This column is the total for the firm (col. 1) divided by 800,000.

[b]This column is the total for the firm (col. 1) divided by 1 million.

[c]Equity book value equals firm assets less liabilities as represented on the company balance sheet.

[d]Earnings equals net income to shareholders after taxes and after interest on debt.

earnings per share). Nor does the total market value of the shareholder's portfolio change; it was $4,000 (100 shares × $40 per share), and after the stock dividend it is still $4,000 (125 shares × $32 per share).

In short, all that has happened is that the firm has printed extra pieces of paper called additional shares and distributed them proportionally to all stockholders. The reason that the shareholder is unaffected in a real sense is that each shareholder still owns the same fraction of the firm's equity interest. Furthermore, the firm's equity interest does not change at all since the firm's total assets, debt, and earnings are unchanged. Therefore, no one benefits or loses from the stock dividend (or split).[17]

The New York Stock Exchange defines a stock split as a stock dividend that exceeds 25 percent (more than one share per four shares owned), and a stock dividend as a distribution of additional shares up to 25 percent of those outstanding. The distinction is arbitrary, and the principles described above apply fully to stock dividends and to stock splits.

Sometimes a firm *reduces* the number of shares outstanding by effecting a **reverse split.** Each shareholder is required to exchange with the corporation the shares owned for a smaller number of shares, e.g., to exchange each four shares owned for one share in return. This action frequently follows a decline in the price of the company's stock due to adverse earnings performance over several years. Colt Industries, Studebaker, and United Whelan are among corporations that have engaged in a reverse split after suffering financial difficulties and poor stock performance. Except for a possible minor benefit from having per share stock price in a popular price range, as with a stock split, a reverse split has no impact on the corporation's operations or on shareholder wealth. It is merely an exchange of claims (shares) with the same total value; for the stockholder, it is akin to receiving a $5 bill in exchange for five $1 bills.

Why do firms issue stock dividends or effect stock splits if there is no gain or loss involved? Even though the book value and claim on earnings are necessarily unaffected by the change in the number of shares, is it possible that market value will not fall exactly in proportion, thus leaving the shareholder better off? It has been argued that additional shares may benefit shareholders by reducing the stock's price range and thereby allowing investors to purchase round lots (multiples of 100 shares) rather than odd lots (less than 100 shares). The advantage here would be to reduce the brokerage fees since they are greater on odd lot purchases than on round lot purchases. This effect, however, is probably insignificant, since the brokerage fee differentials are not great. Empirical research suggests that any benefits that occur from stock dividends or stock splits are insignificant. The evidence indicates that share price benefits, when they

---

17. As is observed at the end of this section, there may be a minor change in the total value of the firm's shares because the per share stock price is in a more attractive price range.

occur, are due to earnings and associated cash dividend increases and not to stock dividends or splits.[18]

SUMMARY

The yearly earnings of a corporation can be paid out as dividends to stockholders or retained for internal purposes, e.g., financing new investment or retiring debt. The financial manager must *decide*. The level of dividends a firm chooses to pay is influenced by a variety of factors.

1. *Taxes*. Taxes on individual shareholders bias in favor of capital gains relative to dividends and therefore encourage the company to reinvest earnings rather than pay them out in dividends. Taxes on the firm's excess retentions of cash and cash substitutes encourage companies to pay dividends. Corporate income taxes, because of interest tax deductibility, favor the use of debt in financing investment; in the long run this reduces equity financing and reduces the firm's *total* dividends relative to what they would be if interest were not tax-deductible.

2. *Investment opportunities*. Exceptional investment opportunities will be an incentive to reinvest earnings rather than pay them out as dividends.

3. *Contractual restrictions*. Dividends may also be restricted by debt or preferred stock contracts and by state regulations prohibiting payment of dividends if stockholders' equity does not exceed the par or stated value of outstanding stock.

Some earnings may also be used to increase the firm's liquidity or to pay off debts rather than be payed out as dividends. The transaction costs in raising external funds and in paying dividends encourage the firm to finance investment with retained earnings and to therefore curtail dividends. Because of the transaction costs paid by stockholders in buying and selling shares, e.g., brokerage fees, stockholders prefer that dividends are stable and predictable rather than fluctuating. Investors differ regarding the proportions of their income that they prefer in dividends and in capital gains. A firm will therefore attract a "clientele" or type of investor preferring the company's particular dividend payout policy. This

18. Empirical studies suggest that stock dividends produce no benefits for stockholders, for example, see C. A. Barker, "Evaluation of Stock Dividends," *Harvard Business Review*, 36 (July–August 1958), pp. 99–114; E. Fama, L. Fisher, M. Jensen, and R. Roll, "The Adjustment of Stock Prices to New Information," *International Economic Review* (February 1969), pp. 1–21; J. A. Millar and B. D. Fielitz, "Stock Split and Stock-Dividend Decisions," *Financial Management* (Winter 1973), pp. 35–45.

clientele ordinarily wants the company to follow its established dividend policy and to maintain relatively stable (unerratic) dollar dividends (but perhaps with a growing trend). *A firm with profitable investment opportunities will generally find it advantageous to keep dividends low enough that investment can be financed from retained earnings rather than by selling new shares.*

Two important aspects of dividend policy are stability from period to period and the long-run proportion of earnings paid out in dividends. Dividend payments are relatively stable because investors prefer predictable and level rather than volatile dividend income.

Two theories have been formulated to explain corporate dividend policy. The perfect markets theory holds that the firm's dividend and investment policies are independent and that any advantage of internal over external financing of investment is negligible. The second theory, for which there is more current evidence, states that internal financing is appreciably cheaper and that firms will consequently use earnings for investment in profitable projects before those earnings are used for dividends. A particular dividend strategy conforming to this second theory is referred to as the smoothed residual dividend policy. Under this policy, there is an attempt to keep the dollar level of dividends equal to earnings less equity investment (investment that is not financed by borrowing). Additional shares are sold only if there is an unexpected shortage of cash to maintain a stable dividend and meet investment needs, as would be so, for example, if a very large project is undertaken which completely absorbs earnings and excess liquid reserves.

Stock dividends and stock splits merely involve the distribution of additional shares of stock to the firm's stockholders. Since stockholders retain their original fractions of the firm, they neither gain nor lose from the stock dividend or split. The possible exception to this is an advantage from reducing the price per share of stock; this permits investors to purchase shares in round lots (in multiples of 100 shares) which may involve slightly lower brokerage fees than purchases in an odd lot (less than 100 shares).

QUESTIONS

1. In what way are dividend policy and retention of earnings related to the financing of the firm's investments?
2. Investors presumably buy a firm's shares in order to receive a return on their investment. Further, it would seem that the more profitable are the firm's investments, the higher that return would be. Since the return to shareholders can take the form of dividends, why do we say that more profitable investment opportunities for the firm *lower* the firm's dividend payments?

3. It has been repeatedly stated that as long as a firm has a *productive use* for them, earnings should be retained. What do you think the term "productive use" means?

4. How can stockholder income tax considerations affect the dividend policy of firms?

5. It has been said that the tax deductibility of interest *lowers* a firm's total dividend payments. What is a rationale for this proposition?

6. Why might a firm borrow $100,000 and simultaneously pay a dividend of $100,000; that is, wouldn't it be wiser not to borrow and pay no dividend since there are transaction costs in borrowing (e.g., bond flotation costs) and in paying a dividend (accounting costs, postage, etc.)?

7. It is stated in the text that the personal income tax bias in favor of capital gains relative to dividend income leads firms to pay less dividends than they would pay if no such bias existed. In a particular year, in determining whether to change its level of dividends from the previous year, would you expect personal income taxes to be more of a consideration for the American Telephone & Telegraph Company, which has well over 3 million shareholders, or to Data I/O Corporation, which has only 7 shareholders? (Data I/O Corporation is a small company with $5 million in sales per year located in Issaquah, Washington and engaged in the computer business.)

8. What role do stockholder transaction costs play in determining corporate dividend policies?

9. What are the major factors that ordinarily would discourage a firm from issuing new shares to raise funds to pay higher dividends on existing shares? What might offset these factors and encourage a firm to sell shares and use some or all of the proceeds to pay dividends? Explain.

10. How can a stable dividend policy be said to reduce the riskiness associated with the shares on which the cash dividends are paid?

11. Discuss the essence of the "perfect markets" school of dividend policy.

12. If Poe Sleep Tablets declared a cash dividend on March 15, 1977, payable to all shareholders of record on April 15, 1977 and you bought the stock on April 13, 1977, were you a shareholder of record? In other words, would you be entitled to receive the cash dividend? If nothing else affected the price of Poe's stock and the company declared a $1 cash dividend, what would you expect the price of the stock to be when it went ex-dividend? Assume the stock was selling at $30 just prior to the ex-dividend date.

13. What particular advantage do *shareholders* have who own stock in a company which has a dividend policy that allows shareholders to

reinvest dividends automatically? What particular advantage is there *to a corporation* that allows automatic dividend reinvestment?

1. Find three stocks that have recently split and examine their price behavior before and after the splits.
2. Ascertain the dividend policy of a company in your area by talking with the firm's management. Inquire as to why the particular policy is followed and analyze the policy in light of the discussion of this chapter. Consider whether the policy is in the best interests of stockholders.

1. If Barton Manufacturing had 1977 earnings of $500,000, retained $200,000, and had 50,000 shares outstanding, what were the dividends per share? [Ans.: dividends = $6/share]
2. Karl Eigen owns 1,000 shares of Spencer Foods, which he bought in 1970 for $10 per share. The tax rate on Karl's dividend income is 50 percent, and the tax rate on long-term capital gains (gains on the sale of stock held more than 6 months) is 25 percent. In 1977, Karl received 50¢ per share in dividends from the Spencer Foods stock. Karl sold 500 shares of his Spencer stock during 1977 for $18 per share. Answer the following:
   a) What were Karl's dividends and realized capital gains in 1977 on the Spencer shares (realized capital gains equal gains on shares that are sold)? [Ans.: dividends = $500 and realized capital gains = $4,000]
   b) What taxes did Karl pay in 1977 on the Spencer stock? [Ans.: tax on dividends = $250; tax on realized capital gains = $1,000]
3. On January 1, 1974, Harry Fiord bought 100 shares of Kyro Plastics, Inc., (KP) for $8 per share and 100 shares of Childlike Toys, Inc., (CT) for $8 per share. The dividends and end-of-year share prices for KP and CT are shown in the table below for the years 1974 through 1977. Harry Fiord is in the 40 percent tax bracket, and this rate is applicable to all dividend income from KP and CT; the tax rate on any long-term capital gain (gain on stock held more than 6 months) is 20 percent. Solve the following:
   a) Compute the dividends Harry received during 1976 and compute the increase in the value of his KP and CT shares during 1976. What is the total return (dividend plus share value increase) for each stock?

b) Compute the taxes paid by Harry Fiord in 1976 on his KP and CT stock if he sold no shares in 1976.

c) Assume that Harry sells enough KP shares on December 31, 1976 to produce gross dollar proceeds (before tax) equal to the pretax 1976 dividends from CT (ignore brokerage commissions).

1. How many shares of KP must Harry sell?
2. What are the aftertax proceeds from the sale?

d) Assume that in addition to the transaction described in **c** above, Harry sells all remaining shares in KP and all 100 shares in CT on December 31, 1977 (ignore brokerage commissions on the stock sale). Determine the net cash flow after taxes received by Harry for 1974, 1975, 1976, and 1977 from dividends and sales of KP and CT stock.

1. Did Harry do better on his KP or CT shares? Explain.
2. Can we conclude that the firm that did not perform as well for Harry should have adopted the dividend policy of the other firm? Explain.
3. How would the presence of brokerage fees in selling shares affect your answer to 1?

Dividends and price per share of Kyro Plastics (KP) and Childlike Toys (CT) stock

	1974	1975	1976	1977
Kyro Plastics (KP)				
Dividends/share during year	$ 1	$ 1	$ 0	$ 1
Price per share on December 31 (ex-divided)	$ 8	$10	$12.50	$12.50
Childlike Toys (CT):				
Dividends/share during year	$ 1	$ 1	$ 2.50	$ 1
Price per share on December 31 (ex-dividend)	$ 8	$10	$10	$10

4. Akron Pipe Company had earnings of $1 million in 1976. Since 1960, earnings grew at a steady rate of 5 percent per year. Dividends in 1976 were $500,000. Earnings in 1977 were exceptionally high, $1,400,000, and investment was $800,000. It is expected that earnings will not stay at the higher level but will settle back down to the long-run 5 percent per year growth rate (expected 1978 earnings of around $1,100,000, etc.). What were dividends in 1977 assuming each of the following:

a) Akron follows a stable long-run dividend payout ratio of 40 percent.

b) Akron follows a stable dollar dividend payout policy.

c) Akron follows a pure residual dividend policy; assume that 20 percent of the 1977 investment was financed with debt.

d) 1977 investment was financed 60 percent with debt and 40 percent with retained earnings. All earnings not invested are paid out as dividends.

e) 1977 investment was financed 30 percent with debt, 30 percent with retained earnings, and 40 percent from the sale of new shares. All earnings not invested are paid out as dividends.

5. Bassett, Inc., has shares with a market value of $800,000 and debt of $200,000. Bassett's management is considering two dividend policy alternatives: I—to pay no dividends on existing shares; and II—to sell new shares which provide net (net of any flotation costs) proceeds to Bassett of $100,000 and then immediately pay the $100,000 proceeds to existing (not including new) stockholders.

a) Assume that the flotation costs in selling the new shares are zero.

1. Compare the total value of the firm's shares under policies I and II (value of existing shares under I compared with the value of the existing and new shares under II). [Ans.: the value of the shares under policies I and II is $800,000]

2. Compare the wealth position (dividends and value of shares owned) of existing shareholders under policies I and II.

3. What factors favor policy I? When might policy II be justified?

b) Assume that under policy II the new shares are sold for a price of $110,000 (assume this to be a fair price) and that flotation costs are $10,000; the $100,000 difference is received by Bassett and paid as a dividend. Answer questions 1, 2 and 3 under **a** above.

c) Compare the results under **a** and **b** above and observe how stock issuance flotation costs discourage the use of stock flotations simply to pay dividends.

6. The board of directors of Tilsdale Manufacturing Company is meeting to determine the dividend to be paid to common shareholders during the next year (1979). Tilsdale has profitable investment opportunities amounting to $1,500,000 and expects income after taxes to be $2,000,000, which can be retained or paid out as dividends. Tilsdale has a target book debt to book equity ratio of $33\frac{1}{3}$ percent and pursues a pure residual dividend policy. The firm's current (before the new investment) book debt to book equity ratio exactly equals its target of $33\frac{1}{3}$ percent. How much should Tilsdale pay out in dividends for the year? [Ans.: $875,000]

7. Assume that Tilsdale Manufacturing Company has, as in problem 6, $2,000,000 in expected 1979 aftertax earnings, $1,500,000 in investments and a firm target debt-equity ratio (using book values) of $33\frac{1}{3}$

percent. However, assume that because of past policies the company has the following balance sheet:

Balance sheet, December 31, 1978

Assets	$5,000,000	Debt	$1,625,000
		Equity	$3,375,000
			$5,000,000

If Tilsdale wishes to attain its target debt to equity ratio of $33\frac{1}{3}$ percent, how much should the firm pay out in dividends?

8. Consider the following projections for Stile Clothing Corporation:

Year	EBIT
1979	$225,000
1980	$245,000
1981	$270,000
1982	$300,000

Stile has (December 1978) total assets of $850,000, liabilities (all in the form of bonds paying a 6 percent coupon rate with eighteen years to maturity) of $340,000, and equity of $510,000. As Stile's financial manager, you are considering alternative future dividend policies in light of the fact that Stile is undergoing a $200,000 capital expansion program over the next four years. The expansion will take place at equal dollar costs in each of the next four years ($50,000 each year) and will be financed half with equity funds. The debt financing will be in the form of five-year $25,000 notes, with one note issued in each of the four years (1979 to 1982). Each note requires interest payments of 8 percent annually ($2,000 per year) with all the principal ($25,000) paid at the end of five years. Assume that Stile's tax rate is 48 percent.

a) What would be the dividend in each of the next four years under a pure residual dividend policy? [Partial ans.: 1979 dividend = $80,352]

b) Determine the dividend payout ratio and each year's total dividend payout assuming that Stile follows a long-run residual payout policy with a stable dividend payout ratio. Determine the dividend payout assuming that total equity investment plus dividends over the four years exactly equals total earnings over the four years. Cite any years in which new external financing might be required.

c) Suggest a schedule of dividends for the next four years assuming a smoothed residual dividend schedule. The total dividends plus equity investment over the four years need only approximate total earnings over the four years.

d) Having made the recommendations called for in **a**, **b**, and **c** above, you have noticed that the dividend growth under the expansion plan as it is now (given any one of the three policies in **a**, **b**, and **c**) would be much faster than Stile has had to date (approximately 13 percent under **a**, **b**, or **c** compared to 6 percent in the past) and you feel that Stile might not be able to maintain such a trend in the 1980s. The board of directors has decided that it does not want to convey the impression to investors that the rapid rate of dividend increase can be permanently sustained. Comment on the following courses of action that Stile might adopt to reduce dividend payments:

1. Retire some of the outstanding 6 percent bonds.
2. Finance the expansion plan completely with retained earnings.
3. Enlarge the expansion program and finance the added expansion with retained earnings.
4. Invest funds in excess of those required for a 6 percent to 8 percent dividend growth in liquid assets.
5. Adopt an alternative dividend policy (perhaps stable dollar dividend plus an "extra" dividend).

9. Wanda's Wonderful Insect Repellant, Inc., has declared a 25 percent stock dividend. Its shares are selling for $50 each. You own 40 shares.
   a) How many shares will you have after the stock dividend is paid?
   b) What would you expect the price of the shares to be after the stock dividend is paid?

10. On Tuesday, March 23, 1977 the directors of Hillsfield Tire and Rubber Co. declared a 2 percent stock dividend payable on May 5 to stockholders of record on April 9.
    a) On what day would you have had to buy stock in order to be a shareholder of record?
    b) At the time the company announced the stock dividend, it also announced that it will omit its 2.5¢ cash dividend, which it had paid in each of the four previous quarters. Furthermore, at the time the stock dividend and the cash dividend omission were announced, it was also pointed out that for the six years prior to March 1975, the company had paid 12.5¢ quarterly. What does this information suggest about Hillsfield?
    c) On April 3, the day on which the common stock went ex-dividend, the price per share of stock was $4.75. If all else remained the same between April 2 and April 3, what would you have expected the price of the stock to sell for on April 2? (Hint: Consider just the impact of the stock dividend. The market probably already anticipated the fact that the cash dividend would be eliminated.)

11. The Wynflight Aircraft Corporation has 2,500,000 shares of common

stock outstanding, and earnings per share amount to $1.00. Wynflight has a dividend payout ratio of 50 percent. The firm is considering a 4 for 1 stock split to lower the price of the common stock from $100 per share to a more attractive level. What will be the effect of the stock split on

a) EPS?
b) Dividends per share?
c) Price per share?
d) Market value of the firm?
e) The value of the holdings of Tom Jones, who currently owns 1,000 shares of Wynflight?

Inflation

"May you live in interesting times," is an ancient Chinese curse. One of the aspects of our times that contributes to its "interest" is inflation. Inflation is an increase in the general level of prices for goods and services. The reverse of inflation is deflation, a reduction in the general level of prices. For the past thirty years we have been experiencing some inflation almost continuously, and since 1965 it has become a serious problem for us. This essay is an overview of the consequences of inflation—how it is measured, why it creates problems for people, and how businesses and individuals react to it.

MEASURING INFLATION

Inflation is very difficult to measure accurately because prices of individual goods and services don't increase or decrease at the same time and by the same percentage amounts. The prices of some things (such as electronic calculators) are lower today than they were five years ago, even though the prices of most things have risen over this period. Also, people don't all buy the same things in the same relative proportions. If I drink tea and you don't, an increase in the price of tea is important to me, but you couldn't care less about it. Furthermore, even if we both drink tea, but you live in Boston while I live in Seattle, the price of tea may not be the same in both cities. The result is that a measure of inflation which is accurate for me may not be accurate for you. Despite all the problems involved we still would like to have some idea of what is happening to the prices of the goods and services consumed by people in general. Government statisticians collect data on the purchases of middle-income families. From this data they develop a profile of what the typical family spends its money on—the percentage of income spent on eggs, airplane tickets, and whatever. The statisticians then obtain sample prices of these goods and services each month and weight them by the proportions a typical family spends on them. The result is the **Consumer Price Index.** Changes in this index measure the changes in the general level of consumer prices in the economy and thus measure the degree of inflation or deflation occurring. The level of the index can be used to compare the level of prices at different points in time. An index of consumer prices since 1865 (the end of the Civil War) is shown in the illustration on page 402. The sharp increase in the price index reveals the severity of the inflation during the period 1965–1975.

THE FINANCIAL IMPACT OF INFLATION

Inflation has two major financial effects. It reduces the value of money and it increases risk. The risk effect was discussed in Chapter 5, here let's look at the impact of inflation on the value of money, and what individuals and businesses are doing to protect themselves against the reduction in the value of the dollar.

The basic impact of inflation is straightforward: A given amount of money will purchase less in the future than it does today. This means, for example, that people living on a fixed income of $500 per month will find it impossible to maintain their standard of living as time passes. Their money income stays the

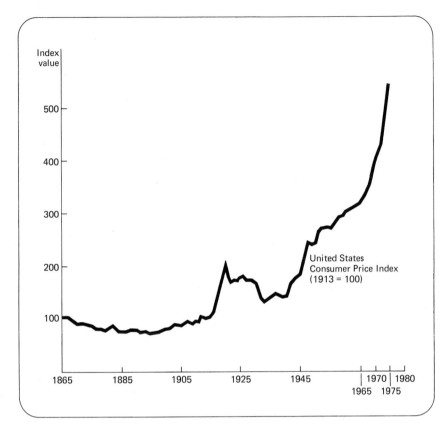

United States
Consumer Price Index
(1913 = 100)

United States Consumer Price Index (1913 = 100). (Sources: Federal Reserve Bank of New York and Bureau of Labor Statistics.)

same but they become poorer as the amounts of goods and services they can buy with their $500 monthly income declines. If prices are increasing at a rate of 10 percent per year, then peoples' incomes must increase at least 10 percent per year for them to stay even. A similar logic applies to investments. If the rate of inflation is 10 percent per year and the rate of return on the investment is 6 percent per year, you are actually earning a negative 4 percent per year on the investment in terms of your ability to purchase goods and services. To gain from the investment, you must earn more than the 10 percent per year inflation rate.

Individuals and businesses have been doing several things to protect themselves against inflation. Employees demand cost of living pay increases. Labor unions seek contracts with employers that provide inflation escalators. These escalators increase wages automatically if the Consumer Price Index or some other measure of inflation increases. For example, a contract might provide that an increase of 10 percent in the Consumer Price Index would result in a 10 percent increase in wage rates. The number of workers covered by major labor contracts with cost of living escalators increased from 2.8 million in 1970 to 5.9 million in 1975. Congress has also responded to pressures from retired people by including cost of living adjustments in social security payments and federal pensions.

Business firms are reluctant to enter into long-term fixed-price contracts to supply goods and services. Instead they will include some provision for increasing prices in the future depending on the degree of inflation. Similarly long-term leases for commercial real estate include escalators of various sorts so that lease payments will rise with inflation. Financial institutions are becoming more and more reluctant to make long-term loans at fixed interest rates. Major commercial banks now make long-term loans to business customers which have interest rates that change periodically to reflect the current interest rates in the economy. Since interest rates vary with the rate of inflation, such loan agreements help protect the banks. Variable-interest-rate home mortgages are also becoming more common. The interest rates on these mortgages are not fixed but vary according to the current level of interest rates on new mortgages.

Since inflation is an important factor in financial decisions, it is discussed in several places in this book. A guide to these discussions and the financial variable or decision affected by inflation is shown below.

Chapter	Page	The impact of inflation on
2	43	Interest rates
5	130	Risk
7	230	Business investment decisions
22	707	International exchange rates

FINANCIAL ANALYSIS AND WORKING CAPITAL MANAGEMENT

Part 3 covers some techniques of financial analysis, including the analysis of financial statements (Chapter 11), profit planning (Chapter 12), and forecasting methods (Chapter 13). These analytical methods use accounting data to evaluate a firm's current activities and to plan for the future. They are useful both to financial managers and to people outside the firm, such as investors in the firm's securities. The techniques are frequently used by lenders in determining whether to lend money to the firm.

Chapters 14 and 15 apply methods developed in earlier chapters to working capital management—the management of the firm's current assets and current liabilities. In Chapter 14 the basic investment concepts of Chapter 7 are modified to deal with the special characteristics of inventory, accounts receivable, cash, and securities—all of which constitute current assets of the firm. Chapter 15 shows how current asset decisions affect the method of financing. The major sources of short-term financing—trade credit, bank loans, and commercial paper—are discussed.

financial statement analysis

The body of information describing even the smallest firm is enormous, spanning the company's internal operations and its relations with the outside world. To be useful, this information must be organized into an understandable, coherent, and sufficiently limited set of data. Financial statement analysis can be very helpful in this respect because it highlights the company's weaknesses and strengths. Data from the financial statements can be used to quickly calculate and examine financial ratios and the flow of funds. Financial ratios efficiently provide a great deal of information regarding the company's condition. The value of a ratio compared with a target range of values serves as a meaningful indicator of the firm's financial health, as well as a means to detect imminent problem areas. The **funds flow statement** shows how a firm obtained and used the resources at its disposal during a time period. It can also pinpoint areas of mismanagement and potential danger. As with all shortcut methods of analysis, ratios and funds flow data must be used only in the light of other relevant facts.

We will primarily be concerned with two types of firm financial statements: the balance sheet and the income statement. The balance sheet states the company's assets, liabilities, and stockholders' equity (net worth) at a particular date, e.g., at December 31, 1978. The balance sheet of Macro Toy Company is shown in Exhibit 11-1. Asset values are usually shown at cost (what the company paid for the asset), and the stated liabilities indicate the amount owed. Stockholder's equity is simply the difference between assets and liabilities.

FINANCIAL STATEMENTS

The income statement reveals the performance of the company during a *particular period of time,* for example, for the year ended December 31, 1978. It shows the revenues from sales, and various costs, including interest on debt and taxes, which the company has incurred during the period. Macro Toy Company's income statement is presented in Exhibit 11-2.

There are two other frequently used financial reports, one dealing with retained earnings and the other with the source and use of company funds. The statement of retained earnings indicates the magnitude and causes of changes in the firm's retained earnings due to the year's activities. Retained earnings are the accumulated corporate profits which have been kept by the company over the years, that is, earnings not paid out in

Exhibit 11-1. Macro Toy Company Balance Sheet as of December 31, 1978

Assets		Liabilities	
Cash	$ 70,000	Accounts payable	$ 150,000
Marketable securities	30,000	Notes payable to bank (8%)	200,000
Accounts receivable, net	450,000	Accruals	20,000
Inventories	350,000	Federal income taxes payable	80,000
Total current assets	$ 900,000	Total current liabilities	$ 450,000
		Mortgage bonds (6%)	150,000
Gross plant and equipment	2,100,000	Debentures (7%)[a]	400,000
Allowance for depreciation	(500,000)	Total liabilities	$1,000,000
Net plant and equipment	$1,600,000	Stockholders' equity	
		Common stock	$ 500,000
		Retained earnings	1,000,000
		Stockholders' equity	$1,500,000
Total assets	$2,500,000	Liabilities plus equity	$2,500,000

[a]The annual sinking fund contribution is $25,000.

dividends, not used to purchase back the firm's shares (treasury stock), etc. The sources and uses of funds statement—which is discussed later in this chapter—shows where the company obtained funds during the year and how the funds were used. (Funds can be defined in several ways, but in this book the term refers to cash, that is, to dollars.)

RATIO ANALYSIS

Types of Ratios

The people whose job it is to analyze a firm's financial position will differ in the ratios they find useful. For example, short-term creditors are primarily interested in the firm's short-run performance and its holdings of liquid assets that can provide a ready source of cash to meet near-term company cash requirements. In addition to cash, such assets include marketable securities, accounts receivables, and inventories—all of which can be sold for cash or become cash through the normal course of business (as accounts receivable are paid by customers or inventories are marketed). Long-term creditors and stockholders, on the other hand, are concerned with the long-term as well as the short-term outlook. Management also uses ratios to gauge its own performance.

How to determine what ratio levels are considered satisfactory is dis-

Exhibit 11-2. Macro Toy Company Income Statement for Year Ended December 31, 1978

Net sales		$5,400,000
Cost of goods sold		4,400,000
Gross margin on sales		$1,000,000
Operating expenses		
Selling	$400,000	
General and administrative	130,000	
Lease payments	20,000	
Total operating expenses		550,000
Operating income		$ 450,000
Add: other revenues (interest on		
marketable securities plus royalties)		3,000
Operating income plus other revenues		$ 453,000
Less other expenses		
Interest on bank note	$ 16,000	
Interest on mortgage	9,000	
Interest on debentures	28,000	
Total interest		$ 53,000
Net income before taxes		$ 400,000
Federal income taxes (at 50%)		200,000
Net aftertax income available to		
common shareholders (net profit)		$ 200,000
Dividends		$ 30,000
Increase in retained earnings		$ 170,000

cussed later in this chapter. But first, using an example, we will define and compute the ratios that are especially useful in financial analysis. We will then explore how ratio analysis should be used in actual business applications and where the necessary information for computing ratios can be found.

Any given ratio reflects a particular aspect of a company. But usually that's not sufficient. That particular ratio and what it indicates must be viewed in the context of other ratios and other facts concerning the company. An historic illustration of this point is the case of Penn Central Corporation, which shortly before its collapse in 1970 had a seemingly safe ratio of debt to total assets. This created a false sense of security about the company which was not confined to small or naïve investors. Amazingly, the perilous condition of Penn Central was not recognized by a number of leading investment banking concerns and some of the nation's largest and most sophisticated financial institutions. Their error was a fail-

ure to perceive that the company's operations were generating insufficient cash flow and that its assets were highly illiquid (primarily real estate and railroad properties that could not readily be sold at a reasonable
price). The credit "crunch" of early 1970 made it impossible for Penn
Central to borrow enough to stave off a liquidity crisis, and bankruptcy
ensued. Thus, in this case, the relationship between debt and assets, iso-
lated from other considerations, was positively misleading.

Four types of ratios are used in analyzing the financial position of a
company.

1. **Liquidity ratios** indicate the company's capacity to meet short-run obligations.
2. **Leverage ratios** indicate the company's capacity to meet its long-term
   and short-term debt obligations.
3. **Activity ratios** indicate how effectively the company is using its total
   assets.
4. **Profitability ratios** indicate the net returns on sales and assets.

Each of these four types of ratios will be defined and examined within
the context of an example involving the Macro Toy Company.

Macro Toy Company manufactures games for children and adults. Relative to other firms in its industry, Macro is highly innovative and is
willing to take above-average risks in developing and marketing new
products. In addition to its regular line, the company produces a number
of expensive, special-order toys. Because of its innovativeness and
special-order service, the firm is somewhat more risky than the toy industry as a whole. Furthermore, the company recently discontinued production of an unprofitable product, resulting in significant unutilized
capacity at its plant.

Exhibits 11-1 and 11-2 show the balance sheet and income statement
of Macro for the year ended December 31, 1978. The ratios describing
Macro's financial condition were calculated from data in these two statements and are listed in column 5 of Table 11-1. Table 11-1 also shows
ratios in column 3 which are considered average for the toy industry; and
in column 4 it shows ratios which Macro must meet under current circumstances if it is to maintain its aggressive and innovative policies, and
yet remain financially healthy and attractive to investors and creditors.

Later in this chapter, we will demonstrate the methods used to determine the values of the ratios in column 4, which are considered financially
appropriate for Macro's particular situation.

Liquidity ratios   Liquidity ratios measure the firm's ability to fulfill
short-term commitments out of its liquid assets. These ratios particularly

Table 11-1.

Ratio (1)	Ratio formula (2)	Industry average (3)	Appropriate ratio level for Macro Toy Company (4)	Actual Macro Toy Company ratios (5)
Liquidity ratios				
Current	$\dfrac{\text{Current assets}}{\text{Current liabilities}}$	2.4	2.6	2.0
Quick	$\dfrac{\text{Current assets} - \text{inventory}}{\text{Current liabilities}}$	1.2	1.7	1.22
Leverage ratios				
Debt	$\dfrac{\text{Total debt}}{\text{Total assets}}$	.45	.4	.4
Times interest earned	$\dfrac{\text{Earnings before taxes} + \text{interest}}{\text{Interest charges}}$	6	6.5	8.55
Fixed-charges coverage	$\dfrac{\text{Income available for meeting fixed charges}}{\text{Fixed charges}}$	3.2	3.5	3.85
Activity ratios				
Inventory turnover	$\dfrac{\text{Cost of goods sold}}{\text{Average inventory}}$	5	9	11
Average collection period, days	$\dfrac{\text{Average accounts receivable}}{\text{Average sales per day}}$	56	46	30
Fixed-assets turnover	$\dfrac{\text{Sales}}{\text{Fixed assets}}$	11	10	3.375
Total assets turnover	$\dfrac{\text{Sales}}{\text{Total assets}}$	7	6.5	2.16
Profitability ratios				
Net operating margin, %	$\dfrac{\text{Operating income}}{\text{Sales}}$	5	6	8.33
Profit margin on sales, %	$\dfrac{\text{Net profit}}{\text{Sales}}$	2.6	3	3.7
Return on total assets, %	$\dfrac{\text{Net aftertax income} + \text{interest}}{\text{Total assets}}$	8	9	10.12
Return on net worth, %	$\dfrac{\text{Net profit}}{\text{Shareholders' equity}}$	9.5	11	13.33

interest the company's short-term creditors. Liquid assets include accounts receivable and other debts owed to the firm which will generate cash when those debts are paid in the near future. Also included are cash and such other assets as marketable securities and inventories, either of which can be sold to generate funds for meeting maturing short-run obligations. The current ratio and quick ratio are the two commonly used measures of liquidity.

Current ratio   The simplest measure of the firm's ability to raise funds to meet short-run obligations is the current ratio. It's the ratio of current assets to current liabilities. Current assets are viewed as relatively liquid, which means they can generate cash in a relatively short time period. Current liabilities are debts that will come due within a year. If the current ratio is too low, the firm may have difficulty in meeting short-run commitments as they mature. If the ratio is too high, the firm may have an excessive investment in current assets (relative to current liabilities). In the latter case, to reduce the current ratio, the component(s) of current assets that is too large should be reduced and the funds invested in more productive long-term assets, used to reduce debt, or paid out as dividends to the owners of the firm.

For Macro the current ratio equals

$$\text{Current ratio} = \frac{\text{current assets}}{\text{current liabilities}}$$

$$= \frac{\$900,000}{\$450,000}$$

$$= 2$$

Notice that "current assets" is an aggregate term. A poor current ratio may imply that only one or more of the specific current assets are at an undesirable level. Thus, a low current ratio could mean that cash, marketable securities, accounts receivable, or inventory should be increased. Similarly, a low current ratio may mean that one or more of the debts— accounts payable or notes payable, or accruals, or provisions for taxes—must be reduced.

We found that Macro's current ratio is 2. However, as indicated in Table 11-1, the acceptable current ratio for Macro is 2.6. Macro's position is somewhat precarious because there is inadequate coverage for current liabilities, considering the nature and risk of Macro's operations. It might seem that current assets equal to twice current liabilities should be sufficient. However, keep in mind that inventories are not extremely liquid, and, like marketable securities, can be subject to unpredictable market value fluctuations. Furthermore, there may be a delay in collecting accounts receivable. The firm could sell the accounts receivable to a factor (a firm specializing in the purchsse of accounts receivable from other companies). But, even if the receivables are sold, less than the $300,000 owed to Macro by its customers (see balance sheet, Exhibit 11-1) would be realized since the factor will demand a profit on the transaction. In short, Macro's current position should be improved and is a justifiable concern, both to management and to the firm's short-term creditors.

Quick ratio or acid test ratio   The quick, or acid test, ratio measures the firm's ability to meet short-term obligations from its most liquid assets. In this case, inventory is not included with other current assets because it is generally far less liquid than the other current assets. The quick ratio equals current assets, excluding inventory, divided by current liabilities. That is,

$$\text{Quick ratio} = \frac{\text{current assets} - \text{inventory}}{\text{current liabilities}}$$

$$= \frac{\$900,000 - \$350,000}{\$450,000}$$

$$= 1.22$$

The quick ratio for Macro reflects the same weak position reflected by the current ratio. Macro's quick ratio of 1.22 is significantly less than the acceptable level of 1.7 shown in column 4 of Table 11-1. The same reasons for concern that applied to the current ratio are relevant here.

Leverage ratios   Leverage ratios measure the extent of the firm's total debt burden. They reflect the company's ability to meet its short- *and* long-term debt obligations. The ratios are computed either by comparing fixed charges and earnings from the income statement or by relating the debt and equity (stockholders' investment) items from the balance sheet. These leverage ratios are important to creditors, since they reflect the capacity of the firm's revenues to support interest and other fixed charges, and whether there are sufficient assets to pay off the debt in the event of liquidation. Shareholders, too, are concerned with leverage, since interest payments are an expense to the firm that increases with greater debt. If borrowing and interest are excessive, the company can even experience bankruptcy.

The more predictable are the returns of the firm, the more debt will be acceptable, since the firm will be less likely to be surprised by circumstances that prevent fulfilling debt obligations. Utilities have historically had relatively stable incomes; they have also been among the industries with the heaviest debt. In contrast, furniture manufacturers and auto producers are cyclical businesses and normally include a far lower proportion of debt in their capital structures.

Recall that Macro is more speculative than most firms in its industry. Consequently, a more conservative level for the leverage ratios is warranted. For this reason, the three leverage ratio levels indicated in Table 11-1 that are appropriate for Macro (column 4) differ from those for the industry as a whole (column 3).

Debt to total assets ratio   This ratio equals total debt divided by total assets. That is, using the Exhibit 11-1 balance sheet data,

$$\text{Debt to total assets} = \frac{\text{total debt (= total liabilities)}}{\text{total assets}}$$

$$= \frac{\$1.0 \text{ million}}{\$2.5 \text{ million}}$$

$$= .4$$

The debt to total assets ratio is also referred to simply as the debt ratio. Generally, creditors prefer a low debt ratio since it implies a greater protection of their position. A higher debt ratio generally means that the firm must pay a higher interest rate on its borrowing; beyond some point, the firm will not be able to borrow at all.

Macro's debt ratio of .4 is satisfactory in that it is less than the maximum acceptable level of .45 for the firm indicated in Table 11-1. Recall that Macro's current ratio and quick ratio were too low. Since the firm's overall leverage is not excessive, it could reduce its current liabilities and keep total debt (long-term plus current liabilities) at a satisfactory level by borrowing long-term and using these funds to retire some of its short-term (current) obligations. Thus, Macro might borrow an additional $100,000 on a long-term basis (long-term debt rises from $550,000 to $650,000 in Exhibit 11-1) and use the money to pay off $100,000 in current liabilities (reducing current liabilities from $450,000 to $350,000). This would not affect the firm's debt ratio (total debt remains at $1,000,000), but by reducing current liabilities, it would be a means of establishing a more satisfactory relationship between current assets and current liabilities.

Times interest earned ratio   The times interest earned ratio equals earnings before interest and taxes (EBIT) divided by interest. In Exhibit 11-2, this equals net income before taxes plus interest all divided by interest:

$$\text{Times interest earned} = \frac{\text{EBIT}}{\text{interest charges}}$$

$$= \frac{\$400,000 + \$53,000}{\$53,000}$$

$$= 8.55$$

Times interest earned reflects the firm's ability to pay annual interest on its debt out of its earnings. Macro's times interest earned ratio of 8.55 means that Macro's earnings available to pay interest is 8.55 times the interest that must be paid; from Table 11-1, this is more than the appropriate level for Macro of 6.5. Creditors can feel highly confident that the debt interest will be paid, since interest is amply covered by EBIT. Notice that the numerator in the ratio, EBIT, is earnings *before* interest and taxes since all of EBIT is available for payment of interest. If interest equalled Macro's EBIT of $453,000, times interest earned would be 1; the company could just pay its interest and would pay no corporate income taxes since taxable income would be zero (earnings before interest and taxes − interest = taxable income, that is, $453,000 − $453,000 = 0). Keep in mind that EBIT fluctuates from year to year, and it may in the future fall far short of current EBIT. Therefore, a current times interest earned ratio greatly exceeding unity is desirable because it means that interest on currently outstanding debt will very likely be paid in coming years.

Fixed-charges coverage ratio The fixed-charges coverage ratio equals income available to meet fixed charges divided by fixed charges. Fixed charges include all fixed dollar outlays, including debt interest, sinking fund contribution, and lease payments. A fixed charge is a cash outflow that the firm cannot avoid without violating its contractual agreements. The firm periodically deposits money in a sinking fund which is eventually used to pay off the principal of the long-term debt for which the fund was set up (see Chapter 19 for details). Lease payments are made by Macro to lessors (owners) of equipment which is used by Macro in its operations. The fixed-charges coverage ratio therefore equals[1]

1. The bond agreement may require the firm to make periodic payments into a sinking fund which will eventually be used to retire the debt. If the sinking fund contribution is not made, the firm defaults. Sinking fund payments are not tax-deductible and therefore must be made from the firm's aftertax income. Notice that the fixed-charges coverage ratio is the number of dollars available from current operations to pay fixed charges divided by the amount that *must be* earned before taxes to assure the payment of fixed charges and also pay the firm's taxes. Fixed charges other than sinking fund payments are tax-deductible, and therefore to cover them the firm need only earn pretax amounts equal to those fixed charges. However, to cover the non-tax-deductible sinking fund contributions of $25,000, the firm must earn more than $25,000 in pretax returns. Thus, assuming a corporate tax rate of 50 percent,

$$\text{Pretax dollars needed to cover sinking fund} \times (1.0 - \text{tax rate}) = \text{sinking fund payment}$$

and, therefore,

$$\text{Pretax dollars needed to cover sinking fund} = \frac{\text{sinking fund payment}}{1.0 - \text{tax rate}}$$

$$= \frac{\$25,000}{1.0 - 0.5} = \frac{\$25,000}{0.5} = \$50,000$$

The firm needs $50,000 in pretax earnings to cover the $25,000 in sinking fund payments.

Fixed-charges coverage

$$= \frac{\text{income available for meeting fixed charges}}{\text{fixed charges}}$$

$$= \frac{\text{operating income} + \text{lease payments} + \text{other income}}{\text{interest} + \text{lease payments} + \text{before-tax sinking fund contribution}}$$

$$= \frac{\$450,000 + \$20,000 + \$3,000}{\$53,000 + \$20,000 + \$50,000} = \frac{\$473,000}{\$123,000}$$

$$= 3.85$$

The fixed-charges coverage ratio is significant since it indicates how much income there is to pay for all fixed charges. Macro's position is satisfactory since its actual ratio of 3.85 exceeds the minimum acceptable level of 3.5 for the firm, as shown in Table 11-1.

Activity ratios Activity ratios reflect the intensity with which the firm uses its assets in generating sales. These ratios indicate whether the firm's investments in current and long-term assets are too small or too large. If investment in an asset is too large, it could be that the funds tied up in that asset should be used for more immediate productive purposes. For example, the firm may have unused plant capacity which it could sell and then use the proceeds in some profitable way. If investment is too small, the firm may be providing poor service to customers or inefficiently producing its product. For example, the firm might benefit from an increase in inventories because current stocks are inadequate to efficiently service customers.

Most of the computations that follow use *the end-of-year asset* figures appearing on the balance sheet for Macro. Frequently, however, average levels for the year (e.g., the average of asset levels at the beginning of the year and at end of the year) are appropriate. In computing inventory turnover, the average inventory for the year will be computed and used to illustrate this approach. For the other ratios, it will be assumed that end-of-year asset figures are adequate approximations of the average levels for the year.

Inventory turnover Inventory turnover equals cost of goods sold divided by average inventory. Therefore, both balance sheet and income statement data must be used. Inventory may have changed significantly during a given year, and it is particularly important here to use a yearly average rather than the year-end inventory amount. For Macro, the beginning-of-the-year inventory is not shown on the balance sheet. But let's assume that beginning (January 1, 1978) inventory was $450,000; the balance sheet shows that the December 31, 1978 inventory is $350,000; therefore

$$\text{Average inventory for year} = \frac{\$450,000 + \$350,000}{2}$$

$$= \$400,000$$

and

$$\text{Inventory turnover} = \frac{\text{cost of goods sold}}{\text{average inventory}}$$

$$= \frac{\$4,400,000}{\$400,000}$$

$$= 11$$

Since inventories are valued in terms of their cost, cost of goods sold rather than sales was used in computing inventory turnover in our example. Although sales is a less accurate figure than cost of goods sold for calculating this ratio, sales figures are often used in practice. If inventory fluctuates seasonally, e.g., is high at the middle of the year but low at the beginning and end of the year, then it's somewhat more complicated to calculate the average. The point here is that an average must be used.

Inventory absorbs fluctuations in deliveries so as to avoid stockouts. A low inventory turnover implies a large investment in inventories relative to the amount needed to service sales. Excess inventory ties up resources unproductively. On the other hand, if the inventory turnover is too high, inventories are too small and it may be that the firm is constantly running short of inventory (out of stock), thereby losing customers. The objective is to maintain a level of inventory relative to sales that is not excessive but at the same time is sufficient to meet customer needs.

A substantial portion of Macro's business is special-order merchandise that is not inventoried, and consequently Macro's appropriate inventory turnover ratio is higher (since inventories are lower) than for the industry. However, Macro's inventory turnover of 11 is higher even than the level of 9 deemed appropriate for the firm (see Table 11-1) and may suggest that Macro is understocked with inventory. It may also be that inventories are being used with exceptional efficiency. Further investigation would be needed to provide the answer.

Average collection period   The average collection period is a measure of how long it takes from the time the sale is made to the time the cash is collected from the customer. To compute this figure, the average sales per day is determined by dividing the year's sales by 360. The average sales per day is then divided into year-end accounts receivable or into average accounts receivable for the year. Assume for simplicity that the level of accounts receivable has not varied significantly during the year and that year-end and average accounts receivable are therefore about the same.[2] Thus,

$$\text{Average sales per day} = \frac{\text{annual sales}}{360 \text{ days}}$$

$$= \frac{\$5,400,000}{360 \text{ days}}$$

$$= \$15,000/\text{day}$$

$$\text{Average collection period} = \frac{\text{accounts receivable}}{\text{average sales per day}}$$

$$= \frac{\$450,000}{\$15,000/\text{day}}$$

$$= 30 \text{ days}$$

The average collection period indicates the firm's efficiency in collecting on its sales. It may also reflect the firm's credit policy. If customers are given more time to pay without losing their cash discounts, then the collection period will generally be greater. A long collection period is not necessarily bad, since a stringent credit policy requiring customers to pay faster may lead to a reduction in sales. However, the longer time in collecting on sales from a lax credit policy is a cost to the firm, and it can only be justified if it produces greater sales. The sooner the firm receives the cash due on sales, the sooner it can put that money to work earning interest. That is, the cost of a long collection period is a return (interest) lost on these funds.

Given that the firm has a particular credit policy (i.e., requires payment by customers within a given time period), some acceptable average collection period is implied. If the collection period is too long, remedial measures must be implemented. The weakness may be slow billing procedures, ineffective incentives to get customers to pay on time, or poor selection of customers in extending credit. Macro's collection period of thirty days is well within the acceptable level for the firm of forty-six days (shown in Table 11-1).

2. If accounts receivable fluctuate significantly during the year, an average rather than year-end accounts receivable estimate would be preferable. Beginning- and end-of-year accounts receivable could be used, or, with seasonal variations in accounts receivable, a quarterly average (sum of end-of-quarter accounts receivable divided by 4) or a monthly average (sum of end-of-month accounts receivable divided by 12) might be used.

Fixed-assets turnover   This ratio is computed by dividing net sales by fixed assets (plant and equipment) and equals

$$\text{Fixed-assets turnover} = \frac{\text{sales}}{\text{fixed assets}}$$

$$= \frac{\$5,400,000}{\$1,600,000}$$

$$= 3.375$$

This ratio indicates how intensively the fixed assets of the firm are being used.[3] An inadequately low ratio implies excessive investment in plant and equipment relative to the value of the output being produced. In such a case, the firm would be better off to liquidate some of those fixed assets and invest the proceeds productively (or to pay off its debt, or to distribute the proceeds as dividends).[4]

Macro has an exceptionally low fixed-assets turnover of 3.375 relative to the proper level of 10 shown in Table 11-1. Recall that Macro's plant has significant unused capacity. The implication is that the firm would do better to move to smaller facilities unless it anticipates a significant increase in production and sales.

Total-assets turnover   Total-assets turnover equals sales divided by total assets; therefore,

$$\text{Total-assets turnover} = \frac{\text{sales}}{\text{total assets}}$$

$$= \frac{\$5,400,000}{\$2,500,000}$$

$$= 2.16$$

Total-assets turnover reflects how well the company's assets are being used to generate sales. Total-assets turnover for Macro is slightly below the industry average of 2.4. This is due to the excessive investment in fixed assets noted earlier. Recall also that the firm has an inadequate cur-

3. If fixed assets have changed significantly during the year, an average of the beginning- and end-of-year levels might be used instead of the end-of-year $1,600,000 (see the average inventory calculation for the inventory turnover ratio). Average assets would also be used in computing the total-assets turnover ratio and the return on total assets.

4. The use of a balance sheet (book) asset value (cost less accumulated depreciation) as a measure of the market liquidation value of the asset may be misleading, particularly if market values have changed since the asset was purchased by the firm. However, book magnitudes usually provide a useful, albeit rough, estimate of the company's situation.

rent ratio (current assets/current liabilities). Therefore, if it were to liquidate some of its fixed assets, such as plant and equipment, some of the
funds generated could be used to increase current assets (such as inventories) or to decrease current liabilities (for example, pay off the bank notes)
so as to raise the current ratio to an acceptable level.

Profitability ratios Profitability ratios measure the success of the firm in
earning a net return on sales or on investment. Since profit is the ultimate
objective of the firm, poor performance here indicates a basic failure
which, if not corrected over too long a time, would probably result in the
firm's going out of business.

Net operating margin The net operating margin equals net sales
minus the sum of cost of goods sold and operating expenses, all divided
by net sales. That is,

$$\text{Net operating margin} = \frac{\text{operating income}}{\text{sales}}$$

$$= \frac{\text{sales} - \text{cost of goods sold} - \text{total operating expenses}}{\text{sales}}$$

$$= \frac{\$5,400,000 - \$4,400,000 - \$550,000}{\$5,400,000}$$

$$= \frac{\$450,000}{\$5,400,000}$$

$$= 8.33\%$$

The net operating margin indicates the profitability of sales before
taxes and interest expense. Nonoperating revenues (for example, interest
on marketable securities and royalties) are not included in the returns,
and nonoperating expenses (such as interest) are not deducted. Nonoperating income and expense items are those not directly associated with
the production or sale of the firm's product (note that interest expense is a
financing cost and not a production cost). The purpose of this ratio is to
measure the effectiveness of production and *sales* of the company's product in generating pretax profits for the firm. The higher the net operating
margin the better. Macro's net operating margin of 8.33 percent is superior to the industry average of 5 percent.[5]

5. The net operating margin can be expressed as

$$\text{Net operating margin} = 1 - \text{operating ratio}$$

where the operating ratio is equal to (cost of goods sold + operating expenses)/sales.

Profit margin on sales   This ratio equals aftertax income divided by sales

$$\text{Net profits on sales} = \frac{\text{net profit}}{\text{sales}}$$

$$= \frac{\$200,000}{\$5,400,000}$$

$$= .037$$

By itself, profit margin on sales provides little useful information since it mixes the effectiveness of sales in producing profits (reflected by the net operating margin) with the effects of the method of financing on profits (since aftertax income is after deduction of interest on debt and of taxes, which are affected by interest). Macro's appropriate profit margin on sales shown in Table 11-1 is the level management seeks given its current debt level; it would be misleading to compare Macro's profit margin on sales with the profit margin of companies with different degrees of debt financing. In contrast, the net operating margin (operating income/sales) is useful since it reflects pricing policy relative to costs, a useful index for decision making.[6] Later in this chapter, we will see that net profit on sales is used, in combination with another ratio, to compute return on investment.

Return on total assets   This ratio equals net profit after taxes plus interest on debt, divided by total assets.

$$\text{Return on total assets} = \frac{\text{net aftertax income} + \text{interest}}{\text{total assets}}$$

$$= \frac{\$200,000 + \$53,000}{\$2.5 \text{ million}}$$

$$= 10.12\%$$

Return on total assets is the total after-corporate-tax return to shareholders and lenders on the total investment that they have in the firm. It is

6. The ratio of operating income to total assets could be used to measure the effectiveness of sales and pricing policies and of operations in generating income. This ratio is useful in gauging efficiency since it abstracts from financing effects (operating earnings are earnings before deductions for interest on debt and taxes). Notice that this ratio can be computed from ratios described in the text since

$$\frac{\text{Operating earnings}}{\text{Total assets}} = \frac{\text{operating income}}{\text{sales}} \times \frac{\text{sales}}{\text{total assets}}$$

$$= \text{net operating margin} \times \text{total-assets turnover}$$

the rate of return earned by the firm as a whole for all its investors, including lenders.[7] Macro's rate of return on total assets of 10.12 percent is significantly above the appropriate rate for the firm of 9% shown in Table 11-1. In an overall sense, Macro can therefore be viewed as a successful company.

Return on equity   This ratio equals the net profit of the corporation divided by the shareholders' equity.

$$\text{Return on equity} = \frac{\text{net profit}}{\text{shareholders' equity}}$$

$$= \frac{\$200,000}{\$1,500,000}$$

$$= 13.33\%$$

Management's objective is to generate the maximum return on shareholders' investment in the firm. Return on equity is therefore the best single measure of the company's success in fulfilling its goal. The various other ratios described above are meant to signal areas of weakness and strength in order that management can effectively supervise the firm. A satisfactory return on net worth is the signal that they have succeeded. Macro's return of 13.33 percent is well above the minimum desired level of 11 percent.

Use of Ratios: Macro Company Revisited   So far, we have defined thirteen ratios and briefly noted their significance. Does this mean that we can evaluate any company merely by plugging in the numbers and comparing the ratios with industry averages? Not so. Recall that as we calculated the various ratios for the Macro Toy Company, we compared them with ratios that Macro should meet (column 4, Table 11-1), not the average ratios for the *toy* industry (column 3). Let us now look at the reasons that the best ratios for Macro might not equal the industry average.

Firm standards versus industry averages   Companies that produce the same products generally confront similar problems. This would seem to imply that to evaluate a firm, it would be reasonable to compare that

7. To compute a completely accurate return on assets, interest paid on short-term debt as well as on long-term debt should be included in the return on capital. In practice, however, only interest on long-term debt is included. Ordinarily, interest on short-term debt is small relative to profit + long-term debt interest, and so the exclusion of short-term debt interest has only a minor distorting effect.

firm's ratios with the average ratio levels for companies in the same industry. This is valid in some cases, but it's only a rough approximation—sometimes very rough! There are at least two reasons that industry averages must be used cautiously.

First, as with individual firms, entire industries may be prosperous or sick. Using an industry standard to evaluate a firm implies that the industry performance is satisfactory on the average. However, this is not so for ailing industries (e.g., railroads). To make the judgment that an individual firm within the industry is healthy because it conforms to industry averages would be wrong in such cases. However, it would be fair to say that if a firm's ratios are as good as the industry's, it is likely that the firm's management is doing at least an average job in view of industrywide conditions, e.g., conditions relating to demand for the industry's products or supply of its inputs.

Second, and perhaps of greater importance, within an industry companies vary in size and the individual firm's products and services are not all exactly the same. This implies possible differences in risk and operating conditions. Therefore, the same ratio levels may not be appropriate for all companies in the industry. For example, some firms in the publishing industry may produce lower-risk technical and reference materials, whereas other firms publish higher-risk fiction and popular magazines. Riskiest of all is the underground press, which has had great successes, such as *The Village Voice* and *L. A. Free Press,* but many disasters, such as the *San Francisco Balloon* and *The Washington Rebel.*

Another thing to consider is that many firms straddle more than a single industry. To evaluate these firms properly, it is necessary to take into account the proportion of their activities in each industry. It may even be advisable to calculate separate sets of ratios for operations in each industry. For example, Gulf and Western's ratios probably show that its motion picture activities are highly successful (G & W produced *The Godfather*) but that its real estate activities may not be doing too well (glut of office space in major cities).

What standards should be used to establish the proper ratios for a particular firm? From the shareholders' standpoint, ratios should be at those levels which mean that the company will generate the best stream of net income over time—simply put, earnings per share with most desirable risk-return properties. Creditors seek assurance that their principal and interest on the debt will be paid, implying a preference on their part for the firm to be prosperous and for the liquidity and leverage ratios to be equal to or greater than some minimal safe level.

The inventory turnover ratio and operating ratio values should imply that the firm is maintaining and expanding sales and minimizing costs for any given level and quality of output. Excessive debt means an unacceptable likelihood of default on the debt, something that should be avoided since bankruptcy is disastrous to shareholders and to creditors. This risk is reflected in the liquidity and leverage ratios. The value of the profitability ratio should reflect an adequate return on investment given the risk of the company's activities. In any case, a firm's particular objectives and circumstances must be reflected in the ratio levels that are deemed appropriate for the company. Industry averages can, in most cases, offer no more than a general guide. The firm's ratios should coincide with the industry average ratios only if the firm's objective and circumstances are typical of the industry and the industry is made up of successful and well-managed companies.

In establishing the appropriate ratio levels for Macro Toy Company (column 4, Table 11-1), it was assumed that the industry ratio levels (column 3) were satisfactory for an average firm in the toy industry. That is, the industry is efficient and moderately prosperous and therefore provides a good average standard of performance. Macro Toy Company, however, is not representative since it has an exceptionally high volume of special-order sales and is relatively risky (greater uncertainty regarding future sales or costs, earnings, etc.). Because there is more than average risk, this firm should have a lower debt ratio and higher interest coverage, as well as a higher than normal profitability (to compensate for greater risk). This is reflected in the appropriate ratio values for Macro, which differ from the values of the ratios for the entire industry. Also, since Macro does many special-order projects, it will not require as large an inventory of finished products as competing companies with primarily mass production products. Therefore, Macro needs a higher inventory turnover ratio (a lower level of inventory relative to sales) than do its competitors in the industry.

Interrelationships of ratios Ratios must be evaluated together, not individually. For example, Macro Toy Company has a low current ratio (inadequate liquidity) but a better than adequate debt ratio, interest coverage, and profitability. The firm, therefore, is in a good position to seek additional long-term debt or equity financing if needed. As noted earlier, the current ratio could be improved (increased) by increasing long-term debt and using the proceeds to pay off short-term debt. Recall also that the firm has a high fixed-assets ratio, implying that some of the production facilities could be sold and the funds used to reduce current liabilities. Even if the firm does not reduce its current (short-term) liabilities, creditors can take note that the firm will be able to resort to long-term financing or sell its fixed assets to pay off short-term debts when they come due. Short-term creditors must be concerned not only with the current liquidity position of the firm, but also with its overall position. The current or quick ratios alone do not reveal the entire story. Indeed, another firm with an excellent current ratio but rapidly deteriorating overall position might offer a far greater risk to lenders or to suppliers that extend trade credit on a short-term basis. This is not to suggest, however, that the liquidity ratios are irrelevant. Higher liquidity ratios mean that the firm is better prepared to pay off debts that are coming due, without having to resort to long-term borrowing (which may be expensive or even impossible if the company is in financial distress).

Another striking example where additional information is needed to interpret a given ratio is the operating margin (operating earnings/sales). Knowing the value of the operating margin without knowing the volume of sales is not too helpful. The objective of the firm is to maximize the return on investment. The operating margin may be low relative to the industry average, but this may be because the firm has cut prices in order to increase total sales. The result may be that the firm's yield on investment is extremely high relative to the industry if its total sales are sufficiently great to compensate for a lower return per dollar of sales. To see this, observe that the operating income per dollar of assets (how well the assets are used in production and sales activities to generate income) equals

$$\frac{\text{Operating income}}{\text{Total assets}} = \frac{\text{operating income}}{\text{sales}} \times \frac{\text{sales}}{\text{total assets}}$$

$$= \text{operating margin} \times \text{assets turnover ratio}$$

That is, if the operating margin is low but the assets turnover ratio (sales/assets) is high, return on total assets may be high. A low operating margin due to a price cut policy which raises sales may consequently be a very profitable situation (high return on assets).

Similarly, the operating margin may be high but return on investment poor or lower than achievable. This is the case with Macro. The return on total assets, while more than acceptable, is not as high as it should be. This is because of the firm's excessive investment in fixed assets which are not being used to full capacity (low fixed-assets turnover). A reduction in fixed-assets investment or a rise in profitable sales, which were recommended earlier, would raise the return on investment.

Trends over time   Historical information can be useful in diagnosing a firm just as it is in medically diagnosing a patient. Whether the fever is rising or falling can be as important as its level. When a firm's weaknesses are revealed, the immediate reaction is to consider remedies. However, if trends indicate that the situation is improving, it may be that no remedy is warranted. Indeed, any attempts at improvement may have opposite consequences.

Time trends are important in another sense. Pricing and credit policies, production methods, and other areas of managerial control can be varied, all affecting the firm's performance. A survey of past policies and their effects on the firm, as reflected in such performance measures as the above ratios, can be a very helpful guide in formulating future policies.

An additional word of caution regarding the forecasting of future trends: historical data are suggestive, but not conclusive. A financial variable changing in one direction in the past may not continue to move in that direction in the future. Therefore, to determine if a variable is settling at some level or maintaining its trend, additional information regarding the company and the industry must be obtained.

Examining Macro's trends over time in Figure 11-1, notice that the liquidity ratios at the end of 1977 and 1978 are markedly below the levels of previous periods, implying that the current and quick ratios may be only temporarily depressed. Inadequate liquidity may, therefore, not reflect chronic mismanagement, but merely an extraordinary situation that will soon be corrected. However, the fact that the liquidity deficiency in 1978 is even greater than at the end of the previous year suggests that the problem should be investigated.

The debt ratio has not changed appreciably. From Figure 11-1, we see that sales have declined due to the discontinuation of an unprofitable line. This has increased profits per dollar of sales (increase in the operating margin) but has also created unused plant capacity and a resulting fall in assets turnover (sales/fixed assets and sales/total assets). The firm's profitability has increased, suggesting that the rise in the operating margin has more than compensated for the fall in sales. Of particular interest to the analyst would be projections of future sales. Additional information would be needed to formulate such a sales forecast.

DU PONT SYSTEM

Around World War I the Du Pont Company introduced a method of financial analysis which has won general recognition for its usefulness and has, in one form or another, been adopted by most major United States firms. Its purpose is to provide management with a measure of performance in the form of a return on investment, or ROI. Two common versions of ROI are profit to total assets, Eq. (11-1) below, and return on net worth, Eq. (11-2) below (this is the same return on net worth discussed earlier).

$$\text{ROI (total assets)} = \frac{\text{sales}}{\text{total assets}} \times \frac{\text{profit}}{\text{sales}} = \frac{\text{profit}}{\text{total assets}} \qquad (11\text{-}1)$$

$$\text{ROI (net worth)} = \frac{\text{sales}}{\text{total assets}} \times \frac{\text{total assets}}{\text{net worth}} \times \frac{\text{profit}}{\text{sales}}$$

$$= \frac{\text{profit}}{\text{net worth}} \qquad (11\text{-}2)$$

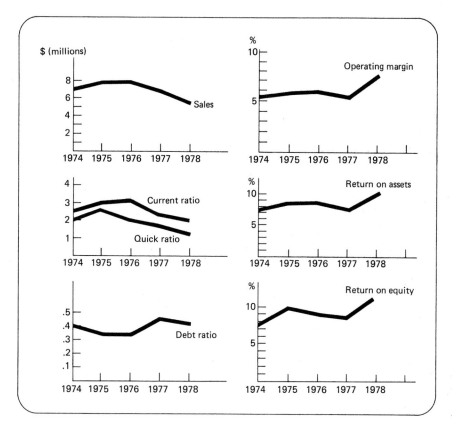

Figure 11-1. Time trends of the Macro Toy Company financial ratios.

The issues of interest here are: Which of the two above equations is more useful? How can the firm control its ROI if it is too low? And, perhaps most important, how good a measure of performance is ROI?

If a choice is to be made between the two ROI equations, the second should be selected. Profit is the return to those providing *equity* capital, that is, the return on net worth. The proper measure of return *on total assets* is *not* profit divided by total assets [Eq. (11-1)] but is profit *plus* interest on debt divided by total assets (this is the return on total assets ratio which was discussed earlier in this chapter). Although Eq. (11-1) is often used in practice, it is very misleading and can produce results at variance with Eq. (11-2) and with the return on total assets ratio described earlier. Indeed, it is easily shown that one company can have a greater return on net worth and a greater total return (profit + interest) on total assets than another firm but still have a lower ROI using Eq. (11-1) because the latter firm—the one with the higher ROI using (11-1)—has less debt.[8] Our conclusion is that if we want to measure return on total assets, we should use the (profit + interest)/total assets ratio previously described in this chapter. On the other hand, if we wish to use profits as the numerator in an ROI index of performance, then we are interested in return on net worth and we should use Eq. (11-2), which is also a valid measure of performance.

Can the firm raise its ROI by increasing its assets turnover (sales/total assets) or by increasing its margin on sales (profits/sales)?[9] Assets turnover is to a significant extent dependent on the company's line of business. Retailers such as grocery stores and automobile dealers, generally have a high assets turnover, whereas utilities, real estate-based service companies (such as hotels) and the capital intensive manufacturers ordinarily have relatively low assets turnovers. Assets turnover tends to decline as the period of time required for the company to produce the product increases and as the proportion of costs going into physical plant increases. Table 11-2 presents ratios for several industries. Assets turnover can be increased by the more efficient use of available assets and the elimination of any excess capacity (unused plant). However, there is ordinarily an upper limit on assets turnover that is determined by the nature of the business.

Profit margin on sales is highly sensitive to pricing policy (which is influenced by competitive conditions), cost control, and the level of sales. Because of the existence of fixed costs—for example, depreciation on plant—the company will earn no profit at all unless sales reach a certain level.[10] Firms that keep per unit costs down and keep sales up are those

8. For example, assume that firm A has profits of $1.1 million, assets of $10 million, and no debt; so, ROI (total assets), ROI (net worth), and return on total assets are 11 percent. Compare this to firm B which has profits of $1 million, assets of $10 million, and debt of $4 million and pays $400,000 per year in interest; firm B has an ROI (total assets) of 10 percent (less than firm A's) but has a higher ROI (net worth) ($1 million/$6 million = $16\frac{2}{3}$ percent), and a higher return on total assets [($1 million + $400,000)/$10 million = 14 percent] than does firm A. Therefore, using ROI (total assets) firm A is outperforming firm B; but using ROI (net worth) and return on total assets, firm B is outperforming firm A.

9. As is clear from Eq. (11-2), ROI (net worth) is also dependent upon the ratio of total assets to net worth. This ratio can be expressed in terms of the firm's debt to net worth ratio (using book values, that is, values from the financial statements) since we know from a balance sheet that total assets equal firm debt plus net worth. Therefore,

$$\frac{\text{Total assets}}{\text{Net worth}} = \frac{\text{debt} + \text{net worth}}{\text{net worth}}$$

$$= \frac{\text{debt}}{\text{net worth}} + 1$$

10. By definition, fixed costs do not vary with the level of output, and if output is very small, the sales revenues less variable costs (costs that do vary with output, such as labor and materials) may not be sufficient to cover the fixed costs. On this, see the discussion of costs and of operating leverage in Chap. 12.

Table 11-2. Ratios for various industries

Industry	Sales / Total assets	Sales / Net worth	Profit[a] / Sales	Profit[a] / Net worth	Debt / Net worth
Grocery and meat retailers	5.84	15.0	1.4%	20.3%	1.5
Auto retailers— new and used	4.59	14.4	1.5%	21.6%	2.1
Motels, hotels, and tourist courts	.71	1.7	6.7%	11.4%	3.7
Water utilities	.22	.5	18.2%	9.1%	1.5
Detective agencies	3.43	7.3	2.8%	20.4%	3.8
Aircraft manufacturers	1.36	4.3	4.7%	20.2%	1.6

[a] Before-tax profit.
Source: Robert Morris Associates.

with high sales profitability and usually high ROIs. Profit on sales generally varies more within a given industry than does assets turnover.

Regardless of the ROI measure that is used [Eq. (11-1), Eq. (11-2), or return on total assets described earlier in the chapter], ROI is only a very rough measure of performance. Only under very unusual circumstances will the actual rate of return being earned on the firm's assets equal the computed ROI. This is due to the definition of ROI, which uses accounting profits rather than cash flow and uses accounting depreciation in computing profits and net assets. Accounting depreciation is generally not equal to actual depreciation, and therefore profits and asset values are distorted. In spite of these deficiencies, it is true that ROI and the real rate of return tend to move together; a high ROI over several accounting periods ordinarily means a high real rate of return, and therefore, ROI is a rough index of performance. It can be used in comparing the relative performance of different firms or of divisions within a firm.

Since the mid-1960s, ROI has been the target of criticism as a basis of performance measurement. The central issue is that ROI is not a very accurate index of true rate of return earned on the company's assets. Although ROI is likely to survive for some time, it is also likely that the ROI concept will eventually be significantly altered or abandoned in favor of more useful measures of performance.

Data for computing the ratios of particular firms can be obtained from the annual and interim financial reports of the firm and from investment advisory services such as Moody's, Standard & Poor's, and Value Line. Brokerage houses, particularly those with large research departments, distribute financial information on all companies listed on the national ex-

SOURCES OF INFORMATION ON FIRM AND INDUSTRY RATIOS

changes and on some of the larger firms traded in the over-the-counter market. Data can also be obtained from the firm directly. However, company officials may be reluctant to provide a great deal of help for fear of violating Securities and Exchange Commission "inside information" regulations or of disclosing information valuable to competitors.

There are several sources of information on the various sectors of the economy (e.g., manufacturing, retailing, wholesaling, etc.) and on particular industries. Some of these sources are noted below.

Dun & Bradstreet   Dun & Bradstreet annually publishes key business ratios, including fourteen key ratios for firms in 125 types of retailing, wholesaling, manufacturing, and construction. A large sample of data is used in computing each of the ratios, and values are provided for the upper quartile (top fourth), median, and lowest quartile (bottom fourth).

Robert Morris Associates   In its annual statement studies, this association of bank loan officials provides ratio data on 156 lines of business activity. Eleven ratios are provided for each line with the information derived from the financial statements of firms which the banks deal with. A breakdown is provided showing the relationship of the ratio levels to firm size, although the companies in the samples tend in general to be among the larger United States firms.

Trade associations   Many trade associations compile data on financial ratios for various industries. Examples are the National Retail Furniture Association and the National Hardware Association.

Government agencies   The Federal Trade Commission and the Securities and Exchange Commission jointly publish the *Quarterly Financial Report for Manufacturing Corporations,* which provides income statement and balance sheet data based upon a wide sample of manufacturing corporations. The data analysis is presented by industry groups and by firm asset size. The United States Department of Commerce and the Small Business Administration frequently publish studies covering large and small businesses, often including information on the standard financial ratios.

Other sources   In its semiannual publication, *The Barometer of Small Business,* the Accounting Corporation of America provides income statement and balance sheet data for companies grouped by sales volume and by geographic region. The National Cash Register Company publishes information on expense percentages for firms in fifty-seven lines of business activity. The First National Bank of Chicago publishes semiannual data on a sample of finance companies.

Ratios are a shortcut method of conveying certain crucial facts about a firm's operations and financial situation. Admittedly, the same information could be conveyed (but often less efficiently) without the computation of ratios, and even when ratios are used, they should be supplemented with additional data. The analyst will be interested in absolute magnitudes, such as dollar sales and dollar value of assets, as well as relative magnitudes, such as assets turnover (dollars of sales/value of assets).

When creditors provide funds to a firm, their primary interest is the future capacity of that company to repay the debt. This is true of short-term and long-term lenders. Before extending a loan, banks and other financial institutions generally apply ratio analysis to a prospective borrower's financial statements. The results of the analysis can be a determining factor in whether or not the loan is made. Ratio analysis is also among the tools used by Moody's and Standard & Poor's in rating the bonds of corporations.

Short-term creditors will be particularly concerned with the firm's liquidity ratios, since the existing or near-term current assets are generally used to liquidate short-term debts. The overall condition of the firm, however, is also important, because the general financial health of a firm reflects its ability to repay even short-term debt. A company borrowing funds may have a strong current assets position, but that can disintegrate rapidly if the company is losing money on its operations or is in the process of reducing its current assets through capital investment or distributions to the owners or other creditors. On the other hand, even if the firm's current liquidity position is weak, if its long-run financial strength seems assured, short-term creditors can feel somewhat reassured by the knowledge that they will very likely be repaid because the company can borrow funds from long-term sources. Therefore, the long-run outlook for the firm is relevant to short-term lenders to the extent that it affects the borrower's capacity to obtain additional outside financing as a means of repaying short-term debts.

Clearly, long-term lenders are interested in the current and future prosperity and financial strength of the firm. These lenders are concerned with any financial ratio which reflects the ability of the firm to meet long-run debt requirements. Long-term lenders will be concerned with the liquidity ratios both as a measure of the firm's policy and ability with respect to liquidating short-term debt. The leverage ratios particularly interest lenders because they reflect how much the company is presently in debt. Only in exceptional situations would the lender examine activity ratios, since for most lending purposes the profitability ratios offer a sufficiently good measure of the firm's operating effectiveness.

In evaluating the firm as an investment prospect, security analysts frequently examine the financial ratios. The analyst is interested in the desir-

THE PURPOSES OF RATIO ANALYSIS

ability of the firm's stocks and bonds as an investment and in any information reflecting upon the firm's operating efficiency and financial strength. For regulated industries—e.g., utilities, airlines, and railroads—financial ratios will be of interest to government agencies, both for the purpose of appraising the financial health of the regulated firm and for rate setting (setting the prices the firms may charge customers).

The management of a firm is concerned with all aspects of its operations and its relations with creditors, investors, and the government. The firm's ability to fulfill commitments to creditors (liquidity and leverage ratios) and to minimize costs (activity and profitability ratios) determines whether it will meet its ultimate objective of providing shareholders with a maximum return (reflected in the profitability ratios). Financial ratio analysis is therefore not just a device for outsiders. It is also useful as a managerial tool.

FUNDS FLOW ANALYSIS

The determination of the sources of cash flowing into the firm and the uses of that cash by the firm is referred to as funds flow analysis.[11] Funds flow analysis provides a comprehensive view of a firm's receipts and outlays. It is particularly useful for monitoring how well a firm realizes its established plans for obtaining funds (from its sales as well as its lenders and investors) and for using those funds. Lenders are particularly interested in a sources and uses statement because it provides an excellent overview of what transpired during the year and whether financial events occurred as planned earlier.

Fund (cash) sources and uses are associated with specific types of changes:

Sources of funds involve:

1. A decrease in assets (other than cash), or
2. An increase in liabilities, or
3. An increase in owner's equity (from a rise in paid-in capital or in retained earnings)

Uses of funds involve:

1. An increase in assets (other than cash), or
2. A decrease in liabilities, or

11. Funds are defined here as cash. Funds flow analysis could also examine changes in the firm's net quick assets or net working capital, in which case funds would be defined as quick assets or working capital, respectively. On this, see most intermediate accounting texts, such as Walter B. Meigs, Charles E. Johnson, Thomas F. Keller, and A. N. Mosich, *Intermediate Accounting*, 3d ed. (New York: McGraw-Hill, 1974).

3. A decrease in owner's equity (from a decrease in paid-in capital or in retained earnings)

Sources of generating cash are selling assets (decrease in assets), borrowing money (increase in liabilities), issuing and selling new shares (an increase in paid-in capital), or retaining net income earned rather than paying it out in dividends (an increase in retained earnings).

These funds would then be used in the following ways: to purchase assets (an increase in assets), to retire debt (a decrease in liabilities), to retire common or preferred stock by purchasing it or calling it in (decrease in paid-in capital and perhaps retained earnings), or a loss (negative income) incurred by the firm (a decrease in retained earnings).[12]

An example will help to clarify the concept of sources and uses of funds. Exhibit 11-3 shows the balance sheet figures for the Macro Toy

---

12. A company is said to "call" its preferred stock or bonds when it exercises its right to buy back the security from the preferred stockholder or bondholder at a price specified in the initial preferred stock or bond contract (for details, see Chap. 19).

Exhibit 11-3. Macro Toy Company Comparative Balance Sheets and Sources and Uses of Funds Statement (In Thousands of Dollars)

	Dec. 31, 1977	Dec. 31, 1978	Sources	Uses
Assets				
Cash	$ 100	$ 70	$ 30	
Marketable securities	20	30		$ 10
Net accounts receivable	600	450	150	
Inventories	280	350		70
Gross fixed assets	1,750	2,100		350
Allowance for depreciation	(400)	(500)	100	
Total assets	$2,350	$2,500		
Liabilities and owners' equity				
Accounts payable	$ 160	$ 150		10
Notes payable	200	200		
Accruals	15	20	5	
Federal income taxes payable	65	80	15	
Mortgage bonds	200	150		50
Debentures	400	400		
Common stock paid-in capital	480	500	20	
Retained earnings	830	1,000	170	
Liabilities and owners' equity	$2,350	$2,500	$490	$490

Company for the periods ending December 31, 1977, and December 31, 1978, and the differences between them are either sources or uses of funds. Notice that a decrease in assets is a source of funds, and an increase in assets is a use of funds. Increases in liabilities and owners' equity accounts are sources of funds and decreases are uses of funds. Exhibit 11-4 summarizes the transactions generating funds and their uses.

As we will see in Chapter 13, which examines financial budgeting and forecasting, planning requires a forecast of future sales, capital transactions, and applications of funds in purchasing assets and retiring liabilities. Data based upon forecasts can be used to prepare a projected or pro forma sources and uses statement. A pro forma statement is, in effect, a plan of action based on expected future cash inflows and outflows associated with production, sales, and existing contractual obligations. This statement summarizes a firm's expected financial activities for a specified time period. It is useful both as a planning tool for management and as an indication to creditors of the firm's future capacity to meet its debt obligations.

Exhibit 11-4. Macro Toy Company Statement of Sources and Uses of Funds, 1978
(In Thousands of Dollars)

	Sources of funds	
Assets	⎡*Decrease in cash*	$ 30
	│ Decrease in accounts receivable	150
	⎣ Increase in allowance for depreciation	100
Liabilities	⎡ Increase in accruals	5
	⎣ Increase in income taxes payable	15
Owners' equity	⎡ Sale of additional common stock	20
	⎣ Increase in retained earnings	170
		$490

	Uses of funds	
Assets	⎡ Purchase of marketable securities	$ 10
	│ Increase in inventories	70
	⎣ Increase in gross fixed assets	350
Liabilities	⎡ Decrease in accounts payable	10
	⎣ Decrease in mortgage	50
		$490

Ratios provide the analyst with a set of summary measures of the firm's debt burden, operating efficiency, and profitability. There are four types of financial ratios:

Liquidity ratios indicate the firm's ability to fulfill short-run commitments.
Leverage ratios indicate the firm's debt burden.
Activity ratios indicate how effectively a firm uses assets.
Profitability ratios indicate the net returns on sales and assets.

The ratios are computed from data in a firm's balance sheet and income statement and then compared with levels considered desirable for the firm. In determining what ratio levels would be desirable for a particular company, the average ratios for that company's industry are a helpful guide, recognizing that adjustments should be made to fit the firm's special circumstances. For example, if the company is riskier than the industry average, it may warrant a higher liquidity and a lower debt ratio. Interrelationships between ratios should be examined since each ratio reflects only one aspect of the company. Weakness in one area may be compensated for by strength in another. Changes in ratios over time should be examined, since this information may reveal whether a problem is being solved or new remedies are needed. Deteriorating ratios may also signal difficulties not yet present but looming over the horizon.

Data on individual firms, industries, and sectors of the economy are available from a variety of sources. These sources include the company being analyzed, private data collection services and financial institutions, trade associations, and government agencies.

Ratios can be helpful to the firm's short- and long-term creditors, to investors and investment analysts, to government agencies, and to the firm's management. Regardless of the user's purpose, however, ratios provide only a partial description of a firm and should be used in combination with other available information.

Funds flow analysis identifies all sources and uses of cash by the firm during the year. The sources and uses statement can be useful to management and to creditors, since it offers a comprehensive view of company activities.

SUMMARY

QUESTIONS

1. It is said that a balance sheet measures stocks and an income statement measures flows. Explain.
2. Sam Swift has a strategy for making a killing in the stock market. He plans to buy the shares of the companies with the lowest share

market price relative to share book value (book value per share = common stockholders' equity/number of common shares outstanding). Appraise this strategy.

3. What is a shortcoming of the current ratio as an indicator of the firm's ability to meet short-term obligations?

4. The greater the firm's current assets, the more capable is a firm in meeting its current liabilities. Why then would a stockholder ordinarily prefer to see the firm with a current ratio of 3 than a current ratio of 10?

5. Sartre Meditation, Inc., is a nationwide chain of transcendental meditation training studios. Except for its small home office in Faroot, New York, Sartre rents all its studios under long-term leases; on the average, the leases currently have eight years to expiration. In computing all its financial ratios, neither the leased assets' values nor the lease obligations are included on the balance sheet; however, lease rentals are included as expenses on the income statement. Sartre owns its small home office building, and there is an outstanding mortgage on the building, which is the firm's only interest-bearing debt. The entire building is occupied by Sartre employees and no space is rented to outside tenants. Seventy-five percent of Sartre's noninterest expenses are in wages to transcendental meditation experts, with most of the remaining twenty-five percent going for rent on the studios and advertising; depreciation on the home office building is negligible relative to total expenses.

Sartre is generally viewed as being in a very risky type of business.

Harding Poker Chips and Playing Cards, Incorporated, has been in business since 1920 and has well-established, stable markets for its products and highly predictable costs. The firm's new manufacturing facility in Cleveland, Ohio, is its main fixed asset. Harding leases no assets but does have some long-term bonds outstanding.

Assume that Sartre and Harding are both expertly managed and each firm has financial ratios that are appropriate to its line of business. With no further information, what would you expect regarding the relative magnitudes of the ratios stated below for Sartre and Harding (for example, which firm has the larger debt ratio, etc.). Explain your choice.

a) Debt ratio
b) Times interest earned
c) Fixed-charges coverage
d) Inventory turnover
e) Fixed-assets turnover
f) Total-assets turnover
g) Return on total assets
h) Return on net worth

6. Is it possible for a firm to have a consistently high profit margin on sales and yet be unable to meet its debt obligations?

7. Why is it important to analyze the trends in financial ratios as well as their levels at a particular point in time?

8. Sonny Smiles owns a surfboard manufacturing company, Surf, Inc., and is seeking additional capital from the bank for expansion. Sonny tells William Folde, the bank loan officer and Sonny's golf chum, "My firm is a winner and expansion is clearly justified. Why, over the past three years the profit on sales has averaged 1.3 times the industry average and the profit on total assets has averaged 1.1 times the industry level." Evaluate Sonny Smiles' argument.

9. What types of ratios would the following investors be particularly interested in? Explain.
   a) Banks specializing in short-term loans to commercial enterprises
   b) Pension funds wishing to purchase shares of common stock for their portfolios
   c) Individuals purchasing twenty-year bonds
   d) A firm's management

10. Why is depreciation considered a source of funds?

11. In analyzing a firm's balance sheets for December 31, 1978 and December 31, 1979, state whether each of the following is a source or a use of cash:
   a) Purchase of a new machine for $300,000
   b) $500,000 received from sale of land
   c) Sale of 2,000 shares of common stock for $25 per share
   d) Issuance of $2,500,000 in twenty-year bonds
   e) Repurchase of 3,000 shares of common stock
   f) Decrease of $5,000 in the allowance for depreciation
   g) Income after taxes of $20,000
   h) Dividend payment of 50¢ per share on 100,000 shares outstanding
   i) Decrease in accounts receivable resulting from a get tough policy toward customers
   j) Change in inventory from $250,000 in 1975 to $340,000 in 1976

First refer to *Dun's Review* or to the Robert Morris Associates' *Statement* and examine the financial ratios of different industries. Try to account for the differences. Then obtain the financial statements of two firms in different industries and compare their ratios with the industry averages. Try to account for the differences between your firms and the averages for their industries.

PROJECT

PROBLEMS 1. The 1978 balance sheet and income statement for HOC, Inc., are given below. Compute the financial ratios for HOC and compare them with the standards given. Evaluate HOC's performance using the standards.

HOC, Inc., balance sheet, December 31, 1978

Assets	
Cash	$ 45,000
Marketable securities	30,000
Accounts receivable, net	280,000
Inventories	600,000
Gross plant and equipment	900,000
Allowance for depreciation	(217,000)
	$1,638,000

Liabilities and equity	
Accounts payable	$ 200,000
Notes payable (6%)	250,000
Accruals	48,000
Long-term debt (9%)	290,000
Common stock	400,000
Retained earnings	450,000
	$1,638,000

HOC, Inc., income statement for year ended December 31, 1978

Net sales		$1,600,000
Cost of goods sold		1,300,000
Gross margin on sales		$ 300,000
Operating expenses		
Selling	$110,000	
General and administrative	75,000	
Total operating expenses		$ 185,000
Operating income		$ 115,000
Other revenues		25,000
Gross income		$ 140,000
Less		
Interest on long term debt	$ 26,100	
Interest on notes payable	15,000	
Total interest		$ 41,100
Income before taxes		$ 98,900
Federal income taxes (50%)		49,450
Income after taxes		$ 49,450

	HOC	Standard for comparison
Current ratio	_____	2
Quick ratio	_____	1
Debt ratio	_____	.50
Times interest earned	_____	3
Fixed-charges coverage	_____	2.8
Inventory turnover*	_____	2.1
Average collection period*	_____	60 days
Fixed-assets turnover	_____	2.5
Total-assets turnover	_____	1
Net operating margin	_____	6.8%
Profit margin on sales	_____	2.8%
Return on total assets	_____	5.6%
Return on net worth	_____	6%

* Based on balance sheet and income statement figures.

2. The Sasquatch Salmon Cannery Company purchases salmon from local fishermen to can and then to sell to retail outlets in the Pacific Northwest. A large portion of Sasquatch's assets is in inventories of canned fish. The firm's busiest period is during the spring and fall salmon runs. To finance increased working capital needed during these two periods, Sasquatch obtains loans from the Puget County National Bank. In the beginning of January 1978 Sandra Mass, financial vice-president and treasurer of Sasquatch, began analyzing the firm's latest ratios in preparation for negotiating the loan with the bank. She became alarmed about the apparent deteriorating condition of the firm. She was especially concerned about undertaking action to bring the ratios in line with the 1975 ratios, which she felt were appropriate for the firm. Below are the ratios for Sasquatch Salmon as of December 31 for the years 1975 through 1977. Assume that, during the 1975 to 1977 period, sales remained approximately constant.

	1975	1976	1977
Current ratio	2.00	2.50	2.60
Quick ratio	1.30	.90	.60
Debt ratio	.50	.50	.50
Inventory turnover	13	9	4
Average collection period (days)	30	35	40
Fixed-assets turnover	6	6	6
Total-assets turnover	4	3	2
Net operating margin	.08	.07	.05
Profit margin on sales	.05	.04	.02
Return on total assets	.10	.08	.06
Return on net worth	.12	.06	.04

a) Using the 1975 ratio levels as the standard of comparison, what ratios appear to have deteriorated by 1977?

b) What might explain the ratio deterioration and what action might Sasquatch undertake to bring the ratios back in line?

3. The Tahoma Tin Can Company, Incorporated, manufactures tin cans for sale to vegetable and soft drink canneries throughout Washington State. Tahoma currently has $1 million in total assets, $300,000 in debt, and $700,000 in common stock and retained earnings. The 1977 income statement for Tahoma is shown below.

Tahoma Tin Can Company, Inc., income statement for year ended December 31, 1977

Net sales		$3,500,000
Cost of goods sold		2,450,000
Gross margin on sales		$1,050,000
Operating expenses		
Selling	$500,000	
General and administrative	320,000	
Lease payments	20,000	
Total operating expenses		$ 840,000
Operating income		$ 210,000
Less interest on debt		30,000
Net income before taxes		$ 180,000
Federal income taxes (50%)		90,000
Net income after taxes		$ 90,000
Dividends		40,000
Increase in retained earnings		$ 50,000

Tahoma management believes that sales revenues will increase by $500,000 in 1978 if the firm expands its total assets to $1,500,000. Management feels that if it finances the expansion using $450,000 in additional debt and the 1977 increase in retained earnings, its profitability ratios will rise substantially. Tahoma makes an annual sinking fund payment of $10,000 per year on its long-term debt. With the additional debt the sinking fund payment will rise to $15,000 per year. The pro forma (forecasted) income statement below reflects management's expectations for the firm's performance if the expansion is undertaken.

Tahoma Tin Can Company, Inc., pro forma income statement for year ended December 31, 1978

Net sales		$4,000,000
Cost of goods sold		2,740,000
Gross margin on sales		$1,260,000
Operating expenses		
Selling	$550,000	
General and administrative	330,000	
Lease payments	20,000	
Total operating expenses		$ 900,000
Operating income		$ 360,000
Less interest on debt		75,000
Net income before taxes		$ 285,000
Federal income taxes (50%)		142,500
Net income after taxes		$ 142,500

a) If Tahoma undertakes the expansion and increases its debt ratio to 50 percent, what will its times interest earned and fixed-charges coverage ratios be?

b) Will the firm's profitability ratios increase as a result of the expansion?

4. Neologism Services, Inc., assists in the design, development, and manufacture of new products for test marketing. Neologism is staffed with highly trained personnel from various fields including chemistry, engineering, and physics. Although Neologism's sales have increased each year from 1974 to 1977, profits have remained very low. Furthermore, future sales for 1978 and beyond are highly uncertain because of the entry of new competition into the field. In comparison with other companies in the same industry, Neologism is smaller, less well-established, and consequently a riskier enterprise. However, except for Neologism's greater sales uncertainty, Neologism is very similar to other companies in the industry (i.e., in terms of personnel, types of products and methods of production). The industry is growing steadily and is comprised mostly of competitive, well-managed firms.

a) Compute the key ratios for Neologism for the years 1974 through 1977. (See tables on pages 442–443.)

b) Graph the trends in each of the ratios.

c) Comment on any strengths or weaknesses you found in **a** and **b**.

d) What changes do you recommend to improve Neologism's condition?

Neologism Services, Inc., comparative balance sheets
(All Figures in $000's and Rounded to Nearest $000)

	1974	1975	1976	1977
		Assets		
Current assets				
Cash	$ 11	$ 13	$ 17	$ 23
Securities	6	4	5	3
Accounts receivable, net[a]	12	14	18	20
Inventories[a]	69	78	91	100
Total current assets	$ 98	$109	$131	$146
Fixed assets				
Gross plant and equipment	$520	$575	$651	$722
Reserve for depreciation	(69)	(82)	(92)	(120)
Net plant and equipment	$451	$493	$559	$602
Total assets	$549	$602	$690	$748
		Liabilities		
Current liabilities				
Accounts payable	$ 12	$ 17	$ 24	$ 28
Accrued wages & salaries	6	7	11	14
Taxes payable	8	11	15	19
Bank loan (9.5%)	3	4	3	6
Total current liabilities	$ 29	$ 39	$ 53	$ 67
Long-term liabilities				
Mortgage (7.5%, 20 yr.)[b]	$115	$104	$ 92	$ 79
Debentures (9.0%)	50	50	50	50
Subordinated bonds (8%)	100	150	230	280
Total long-term liabilities	$265	$304	$372	$409
Total liabilities	$294	$343	$425	$476
		Stockholders' equity		
Common stock ($10 par)	$120	$120	$120	$120
Additional paid-in capital	18	18	18	18
Retained earnings	117	121	127	134
Total stockholders' equity	$255	$259	$265	$272
Total liabilities and stockholders' equity	$549	$602	$690	$748

[a] Accounts receivable at end of 1973 were $12,000. Total inventory at end of 1973 was $58,000.
[b] 1974 payment: $19,620; $10,236 principal, $9,384 interest
   1975 payment: $19,620; $11,052 principal, $8,568 interest
   1976 payment: $19,620; $11,832 principal, $7,788 interest
   1977 payment: $19,620; $12,719 principal, $6,901 interest
   1978 payment: $19,620; $13,672 principal, $5,948 interest
[c] Only interest payments are made yearly until 1985, when the debt matures and the principal is repaid.

Neologism Services, Inc., comparative income statements
(All Figures in $000's & Rounded)

	1974	1975	1976	1977
Net sales	$711	$715	$821	$890
Cost of goods sold	573	569	660	712
Gross margin on sales	$138	$146	$161	$178
Operating expenses:				
Selling	22	25	29	34
General and administrative	45	48	52	57
Lease payments	15	15	15	15
Total operating expenses	$ 82	$ 88	$ 96	$106
Operating income	$ 56	$ 58	$ 65	$ 72
Other revenues:				
Income from securities	$ 2	$ 1	$ 0	$ 1
Royalties	3	1	2	2
Total other revenues	$ 5	$ 2	$ 2	$ 3
Gross income	$ 61	$ 60	$ 67	$ 75
Other expenses:				
Interest on bank loan	$ 0	$ 0	$ 0	$ 0
Interest on mortgage	9	9	8	7
Interest on debentures	5	5	5	5
Interest on subordinated bonds	8	12	18	22
Research	25	26	24	27
Total other expenses	$ 47	$ 52	$ 55	$ 61
Net income before taxes	$ 14	$ 8	$ 12	$ 14
Federal income taxes (at 50%)	7	4	6	7
Net income available to shareholders	$ 7	$ 4	$ 6	$ 7
Dividends	$ 0	$ 0	$ 0	$ 0
Increase in retained earnings	7	4	6	7

1977 Industry ratios

Ratio	Industry 1977 level
Current ratio	2.00
Quick ratio	.50
Debt ratio	.40
Times interest earned	6.48
Fixed-charges coverage	1.50
Inventory turnover	7.25
Average collection period (days)	7.5
Fixed-assets turnover	2.7
Total-assets turnover	1.8
Net operating margin	9%
Profit margin on sales	4%
Return on total assets	9%
Return on net worth	11%

5. The Hogness family owns land on which natural spring water flows. The family is considering building a brewery on the land to take advantage of the natural resources. Since industry standards often provide an indication of what a firm's balance sheet will look like, the Hogness family has obtained the industry ratios for the brewing industry to prepare a balance sheet. Using the ratios given, complete the balance sheet below assuming that income after taxes will be $100,000. Round your figures to the nearest $1,000; ratios below are rounded.

Current ratio: 2.6
Collection period: sixteen days
Inventory turnover: sixteen times (based on sales)
Current debt to net worth: 20 percent
Total debt to net worth: 100 percent
Return to net worth: 10 percent
Profit margin on sales: 4.75 percent

Hogness Brewing Company balance sheet for year ended December 31, 1978

Cash	_____	Accounts payable	_____
Accounts receivable	_____	Long-term debt	_____
Inventory	_____	Total debt	_____
Total current assets	_____	Net worth	_____
Fixed assets	_____		
Total assets	_____	Total liabilities and net worth	_____

6. The 1977 and 1978 balance sheets for Kline Furniture, Incorporated, are given below. Indicate whether each balance sheet change is a source or a use.

Kline Furniture, Inc., comparative balance sheets
(In thousands of dollars)

	Dec. 31, 1977	Dec. 31, 1978	Source	Use
Assets				
Cash	$ 100	$ 400	_____	_____
Marketable securities	200	500	_____	_____
Net accounts receivable	500	400	_____	_____
Inventories	600		_____	_____
Gross fixed assets	2,800	2,500	_____	_____
Allowance for				
depreciation	(600)	(500)	_____	_____
Total assets	$3,600	$4,000		
Liabilities and owners'				
equity				
Accounts payable	$ 00	$ 500	_____	_____
Notes payable	500	300	_____	_____
Accruals	200	500	_____	_____
Long-term debt	1,300	900	_____	_____
Common stock	400	600	_____	_____
Retained earnings	900	1,200	_____	_____
Total liabilities				
and owners' equity	$3,600	$4,000		

a) Prepare a sources and uses of funds statement for Kline Furniture, Inc.
b) Assume that Kline Furniture, Inc., had income after taxes of $2,000,000 in 1978. Explain the change in retained earnings shown above from $900,000 to $1,200,000.
c) What transaction or transactions could account for the change in gross fixed assets and in the allowance for depreciation.

break-even analysis and the measurement of leverage

The level and riskiness of a company's profits are of primary concern to its stockholders and determine the value of the company's shares. This chapter is concerned with the firm's underlying cost factors that affect profits. Break-even analysis, the first topic to be discussed, examines the relationship between output, profits, and costs. It also considers pricing and cost structure changes which can contribute to greater profitability. The tools we will introduce would be useful in analyzing the profitability, for example, of an airliner or movie theater with periods of only half capacity operation or of a real estate complex with a fluctuating vacancy rate. The latter half of the chapter discusses leverage, which is the existence of fixed costs (costs that do not vary with output) among the company's costs. **Operating leverage** is due to the existence of fixed production costs, whereas **financial leverage** is due to the presence of fixed financing costs (interest). As we will see, both operating leverage and financial leverage are major determinants of the level and variability of company profits.

BREAK-EVEN ANALYSIS

Like ratio and funds flow analysis, break-even analysis is used to examine and compare financial data. Break-even analysis deals with the relationship of profits to all costs, both direct and indirect, to pricing policy, and to volume of output. A knowledge of this relationship enables a financial manager to maximize profits by specifying production methods, pricing, and output volume.

Break-even analysis is primarily concerned with:

1. How profit varies with changes in sales volume (if cost structure and output prices are unchanged)
2. How profit varies with changes in costs and prices

From an examination of the relationship between costs, prices, and profit, the financial manager gains insight about the business risk of the firm.

Profit is net income to shareholders and equals revenues from sales less all costs, including depreciation, interest on debt, and taxes, as well as labor, materials, advertising, and other current expenses. By comparing the profits from different levels of output, under different cost and price structures, the financial manager can guide the firm in the selection of the best strategies for investment (which products to produce and how) and for marketing (lower sales price versus increased advertising, for example).

We will first discuss the nature of production costs and then proceed to break-even analysis.

Fixed costs are expenditures of a company that *do not vary as output changes*. The cost of office and factory space and equipment, the cost of an executive staff to oversee operations and a production staff to supervise the manufacturing process, real estate property taxes, etc.—all are fixed costs.

    Variable costs are expenditures of a company that *vary with the level of output*. Variable costs include production materials, direct labor, power for production equipment, shipping services, and office materials used directly for purchasing and billing.

    Some costs may be classified as variable or fixed depending upon any of the following:

Fixed and Variable Costs

1. The magnitude of the change in output
2. The amount of time required to change the cost
3. The length of time the change in output is expected to last

If the expenditure varies with output, the cost is variable; if it does not, the cost is fixed. Let's consider each of these cases.

    1. Some costs will be fixed in the long and short run, but only for certain ranges of output. For example, a machine may have a production capacity of 50,000 units annually and be the most economical machine to use for any output between 30,000 and 50,000 units. Over the range of 30,000 to 50,000 units, machine cost is fixed; that is, the same machine is used and neither more nor fewer machines are employed. Outside the 30,000-to-50,000 range, machine cost may be variable. Thus, a rise above 50,000 units annually will necessitate additional machinery; machine cost will therefore vary if output rises above the 50,000-unit level.

    2. There are some cases in which costs can be varied if enough time is available but are fixed (cannot be varied) in the short run. For example, a new manufacturing plant may take three years to construct. Existing plant capacity may be 100,000 units of output annually, with production above 70,000 units requiring much higher labor costs due to round-the-clock operation and overtime pay for workers. The company experiences an increase in annual product demand from 55,000 to 95,000 units. In the short run (less than three years), the size of plant used for production cannot

change; production plant cost (depreciation, property taxes, etc.) is fixed over the three-year period, even though output has risen from 55,000 to 95,000 units. In the long run (more than three years), the company will expand its plant capacity so as to produce the 95,000 units more economically; in the long run, plant costs are variable.

3. Some changes in output can result in fixed or variable costs. For example, if a decrease in output is considered temporary (perhaps less than one year), a company may be reluctant to reduce its executive staff or certain segments of its production staff. The cost of their salaries is considered fixed. However, if the downturn is permanent, the firm may decide to reduce its staff or liquidate its plant and equipment. These costs are then variable because they change with output. Similarly, the machine discussed in (1) above may be the most economical means of producing 30,000 to 50,000 units annually; but, if yearly output were to fall permanently below 30,000 units, a smaller machine might be warranted. In the long run, machine cost would be variable for output declines to below 30,000 units annually.

To determine whether the firm will operate at a profit or a loss or just break even, the financial manager must examine the fixed and variable costs of the company and compare them with income from sales. Break-even analysis can be applied for short-run changes in output, in which case some costs are fixed due to the time considerations in (2) and (3), or for long-run changes, in which case such costs are variable. In the discussion below, we will assume that output variations are short run and some costs are fixed, either because they can't be changed in the short run [as in (2)] or because it isn't profitable to change them simply to respond to temporary changes in output [as in (3)].

The costs considered in our discussion of break-even analysis which will be fixed and variable are:

Fixed costs:
　　Depreciation on plant and equipment
　　Minimum maintenance costs on plant and equipment
　　Salaries and wages of executive and research staff
　　Rentals on long-term lease agreements
　　Office expenses
　　Advertising expenses (if not dependent on output)
　　Interest on debt
Variable costs:
　　Direct labor wages
　　Materials costs
　　Sales commissions and salaries

To illustrate the cost relationships, assume that Arcan Corporation has the fixed costs and variable costs listed in Exhibit 12-1.

Exhibit 12-1. Costs of Arcan Corporation

Fixed costs:	
Depreciation	$100,000
Plant maintenance	15,000
Executive salaries	40,000
Rentals	8,000
Office expense	12,000
Advertising	5,000
Interest on debt	20,000
Total	$200,000
Variable costs per unit of output:	
Labor	$ 3.00
Materials	5.00
Sales commissions	2.00
Total	$10.00

Arcan's fixed costs are $200,000; whatever output during the year may be, these costs are unaffected. For each unit of output, the firm must incur an additional $10 of cost; i.e., variable cost is $10 per unit. Arcan's total variable cost depends on the level of output. Exhibit 12-2 shows the costs and sales revenues for Arcan at various output levels. Figure 12-1 illustrates these data. The diagonal total cost line in Figure 12-1 shows the total costs (fixed plus variable) for each level of output. This line corresponds to the total cost column in Exhibit 12-2. (See pages 449–450.)

Measuring Profitability

To calculate profitability using break-even analysis, revenue from sales must be compared with costs. Assume that Arcan sells its output at a price of $15 per unit. Total sales, costs, and profit for each level of output are shown in Figure 12-1 and stated in Exhibit 12-2.

At what level of output should the firm operate for maximum profitability, and at what level must it operate in order to just "break even," that is, earn zero profit? In answer to the first part, the firm will generally be somewhat uncertain as to the ultimate demand for its product. From Figure 12-1 and Exhibit 12-2, we can see that profit increases as the number of units sold increases, assuming the unit variable cost of $10 and sales price of $15. Therefore, Arcan Corporation will seek to maximize its sales. But sales depend as much upon customer demand for the product as upon the willingness of a firm to sell the product. The firm may not be able to sell as much as it is capable of producing. Future demand is generally uncertain and subject only to an estimate.

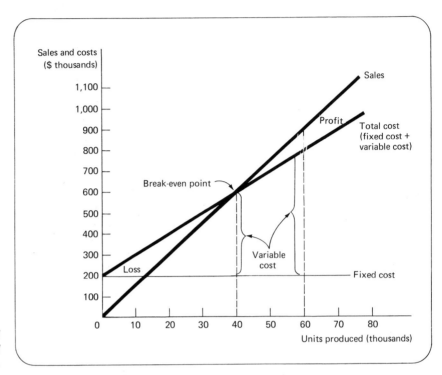

Figure 12-1. Cost and sales relationships and the break-even point.

What sales are necessary for Arcan to break even? We can see from Exhibit 12-2 that profits are zero at sales of 40,000 units. This break-even point of 40,000 units is also illustrated in Figure 12-1 by the intersection of the total cost and sales curves. Sales below 40,000 units imply losses, and sales above 40,000 units involve profits.

We can analyze the above problem algebraically, but before doing so we might ask ourselves exactly what is being assumed about the relationship of costs and revenues to sales. We are assuming that certain costs are fixed (at $200,000) over the range of output being considered, that variable costs per unit ($10) are constant over the range of output, and that sales price per unit ($15) is fixed. Later in the chapter we will consider variations in sales price and the effect on the analysis if variable costs per unit change as output changes.

Determining the Break-even Point   We can solve for the break-even point by trial and error (just by scanning the numbers in Exhibit 12-2 or by examining Figure 12-1) or algebraically. The following variables are needed for an algebraic solution:

Exhibit 12-2. Arcan Corporation Cost and Profit Schedule

Units sold x	Total fixed cost F	Total variable cost vx	Total cost $F + vx$	Sales px	Profit[a] (loss) (sales − total cost)
0	$200,000	$ 0	$200,000	$ 0	$(200,000)
10,000	200,000	100,000	300,000	150,000	(150,000)
20,000	200,000	200,000	400,000	300,000	(100,000)
30,000	200,000	300,000	500,000	450,000	(50,000)
40,000	200,000	400,000	600,000	600,000	0
50,000	200,000	500,000	700,000	750,000	50,000
60,000	200,000	600,000	800,000	900,000	100,000
70,000	200,000	700,000	900,000	1,050,000	150,000

Unit selling price $p = \$15.00$
Fixed costs $F = \$200,000$
Unit variable cost $v = \$10.00$
Total cost $F + vx = \$200,000 + \$10x$
Break-even point $= 40,000$ units

[a] Before-tax profit.

x = number of units sold
F = fixed costs = $200,000
v = variable cost per unit = $10
p = sales price per unit = $15
x_b = level of x at the break-even point (break-even x)

We know that

$$\text{Profit} = \text{total sales} - \text{total costs}$$

$$= px - (vx + F)$$

$$= px - vx - F$$

$$= x(p - v) - F \qquad (12\text{-}1)$$

At the break-even point, profit is zero. Therefore, to solve for the break-even output x_b, set profit above equal to zero and solve. Thus, using (12-1), at the break-even point

$$x_b(p - v) - F = 0$$

$$x_b = \frac{F}{p - v} \qquad (12\text{-}2)$$

and, therefore

$$\text{Break-even } x = x_b = \frac{F}{p - v} = \frac{\$200{,}000}{\$15 - \$10} = 40{,}000 \text{ units}$$

Notice that 40,000 units is the same as the value determined by examining Exhibit 12-2 and Figure 12-1.

What if we want the break-even level of dollar sales? This is just the sales price p times the break-even point in units (x_b). That is,

$$\text{Break-even dollar sales} = px_b = p \left(\frac{F}{p - v} \right)$$

$$= \$15 \left(\frac{\$200{,}000}{\$15 - \$10} \right) = \$600{,}000$$

From Exhibit 12-2 we see that the dollars of sales at the break-even point of 40,000 units are in fact $600,000. This is also shown in Figure 12-1.

The quantity $(p - v)$ in Eqs. (12-1) and (12-2) is called the **contribution margin.** The contribution margin equals the increase in profits from an additional unit sold. From Eq. (12-2) we can see that the break-even output x_b is simply fixed costs divided by the contribution margin.

Sales Price and Cost Changes

Break-even analysis can be useful in analyzing policies which affect sales (e.g., changing sales price) or which affect the level of fixed or variable costs. For example, by lowering its sales price, the company may be able to increase total sales. A lower sales price implies a fall in the slope (decrease in steepness) of the total sales schedule. Although profit per unit of sales decreases, total sales and profits may actually rise. This is illustrated in Figure 12-2. If the decrease in sales price from p_1 to p_2 produces an increase in units sold from q_1 to q_2, then profits will increase.

Alternative marketing strategies can be compared using the profit analysis. The firm might be comparing a new long-term advertising campaign with the alternative of a price reduction in order to increase sales. If the advertising campaign adds amount A to fixed costs, then we could compare the relative benefits of the lower prices with the benefits of the advertising. In Figure 12-3 we see that adoption of the advertising campaign raises sales to q_2 (assuming that unit sales price remains at p_1). Advertising increases profits by more than the increase due to the lower sales

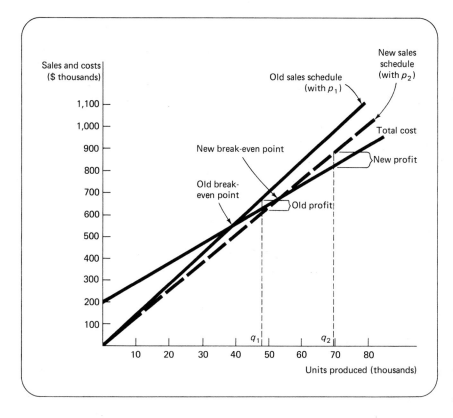

Figure 12-2. Effects of a change in sales price.

price strategy in Figure 12-2. This firm will therefore seek to increase sales and profits by advertising rather than by lowering its sales price.

Nonlinear Break-even Analysis

In the previous discussion it was assumed that costs increased linearly with output: each added unit required the same additional variable cost outlay. Although this may be valid for some ranges of output, it is not likely to hold over the entire range for an actual firm. Thus, the variable cost of the twenty thousandth unit may be higher or lower than the variable cost of the ten thousandth unit. In Figure 12-4 the cost of an additional unit of output (unit variable cost) is assumed to decrease and then to increase as production increases. Since profit equals sales minus total cost, at point q^* the firm's profits are maximized (maximum vertical distance between sales and total cost).[1] Notice that there are two break-even points q_b and q_b'. All sales between q_b and q_b' produce profits. Notice that

1. At q^*, the *slope* of the total cost schedule equals the slope of the sales schedule, implying that the price of output equals the variable cost (marginal cost) of the q^*th unit of output.

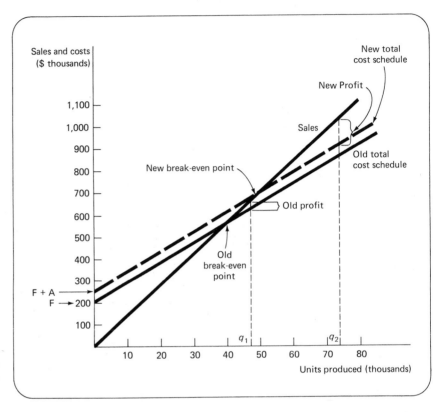

Figure 12-3. Effects of a change in fixed costs.

even if customers demand more than q^* units, the firm will not produce them, since beyond q^* profits are decreasing, that is, profits are greater by selling only q^* units.[2]

Where will the firm operate? As with linear costs, demand for the firm's product is uncertain, and therefore so is the level of sales and production. The firm will not be willing to maintain production and sales of above q^* since profits are decreasing above that level of output. As long as sales are between q_b and q^*, the firm will earn a profit. If sales happen to fall below q_b, we can see from Figure 12-4 that the firm will suffer a loss. If this continues, the firm will eventually go out of business. An essential point here is that the exact level of sales is generally unpredictable. The figures only tell us what profits will be for each level of sales. This also was true with linear costs. The analysis using nonlinear costs is essentially very similar to that using linear costs.

2. The firm may in the short run produce more than q^* as a service to customers so that their patronage will not be lost. However, as long as costs and product price do not change (i.e., as long as the sales and cost schedules in Figure 12-4 remain valid), the firm will not produce beyond q^* in the long run since q^* maximizes profit.

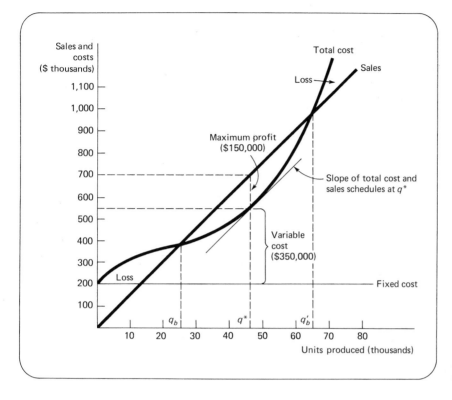

Figure 12-4. Nonlinear costs.

Limitations of Break-even Analysis

Even with the introduction of nonlinear costs, break-even analysis has serious limitations. As we noted earlier, the distinction between fixed and variable costs depends upon several assumptions, including the output range that is relevant and the time period involved. A change in assumptions may necessitate an entirely new analysis (new set of numbers and diagrams). Furthermore, the fixed and variable costs and the price at which the product is to be sold are assumed to be known at each level of output. In real situations, however there is often uncertainty as to what costs and price will be for any particular output level. If this uncertainty is incorporated into the break-even framework, the analysis may become unwieldy and another approach may be required. Simplicity is both the virtue and weakness of break-even analysis. Although it can be helpful as a rough guide to decision making, it generally falls far short of being a complete planning tool.

THE CONCEPT OF LEVERAGE

Leverage is the existence of fixed costs among a firm's costs. It is useful to categorize leverage as operating and financial. Operating leverage depends on the company's operating fixed costs (fixed costs other than interest on debt), such as administrative costs, depreciation, advertising expenditures, and property taxes. Financial leverage, which was examined in Chapter 9, depends upon debt interest, a financial fixed cost. We will see that operating and financial leverage can be joined together to provide a measure of total or "combined" leverage. Before proceeding, assume the following definitions:

$$F_o = \text{operating fixed costs}$$
$$\text{(administrative costs, depreciation, etc.)}$$
$$F_f = \text{financial fixed costs (interest on debt)}$$
$$F = \text{total fixed costs} = F_o + F_f$$
$$\text{EBIT} = \text{earnings before interest and taxes} = px - vx - F_o$$
$$= x(p - v) - F_o$$

Operating Leverage

Operating leverage arises when there are fixed operating costs in the firm's cost structure. With positive (i.e., nonzero) fixed operating costs, a change of 1 percent in sales produces more than a 1 percent change in EBIT. A measure of this effect is referred to as the degree of operating leverage and it equals

Degree of operating leverage = DOL

$$= \frac{\text{percentage change in EBIT}}{\text{percentage change in units sold}}$$

and this can be shown to equal[3]

$$\text{DOL} = \frac{x(p - v)}{x(p - v) - F_o} \tag{12-3}$$

where x is the output level at which DOL is computed, and p, v, and F_o are unit sales price, unit variable cost, and operating fixed costs, respec-

---

3. Equation (12-3) for DOL is derived as follows:

$$\text{EBIT} = x(p - v) - F_o$$

$$\Delta\text{EBIT} = \Delta x(p - v) \text{ since } p, v, \text{ and } F_o \text{ do not change } (\Delta \text{ means "change in")}$$

$$\frac{\Delta\text{EBIT}}{\text{EBIT}} = \frac{\Delta x(p - v)}{x(p - v) - F_o}$$

$$\frac{\Delta\text{EBIT/EBIT}}{\Delta x/x} = \frac{\Delta x(p - v)/[x(p - v) - F_o]}{\Delta x/x} = \frac{\Delta x(p - v)}{x(p - v) - F_o} \cdot \frac{x}{\Delta x}$$

$$= \frac{x(p - v)}{x(p - v) - F_o} = \text{DOL}$$

tively. It is important to keep in mind that operating fixed costs F_o for computing DOL *exclude* interest on firm debt as an expense.

The greater is a firm's DOL, the more its EBIT will vary with respect to sales fluctuations. We can see from the formula that the firm's cost structure (fixed and variable costs) will determine its DOL for any given sales price p. In Exhibit 12-3, two firms with different cost structures are compared. Clear Glassworks has lower fixed costs and higher per unit variable costs than Strand Paper. Both firms charge $10 ($p$) for each unit sold. Notice that at an output of 50,000 units, both firms have the same profits ($60,000). However, as sales fluctuate, the EBIT of Clear Glassworks fluctuates far less than the EBIT of Strand Paper. Strand Paper has a higher DOL. We can see this by computing the DOL for each firm at an x of 50,000 units.

DOL of Clear Glassworks at an output of 50,000 units

$$= \frac{x(p-v)}{x(p-v)-F_o} = \frac{50,000(\$10-\$7)}{50,000(\$10-\$7)-\$90,000} = 2\tfrac{1}{2}$$

Exhibit 12-3. Cost and Profit Schedules for Clear Glassworks and Strand Paper Company

Clear Glassworks				Strand Paper Company			
Units sold x	Sales px	Total cost	Profit (sales − total cost)	Units sold x	Sales px	Total cost	Profit (sales − total cost)
10,000	$100,000	$160,000	$(60,000)	10,000	$100,000	$240,000	$(140,000)
20,000	200,000	230,000	(30,000)	20,000	200,000	290,000	(90,000)
30,000	300,000	300,000	0	30,000	300,000	340,000	(40,000)
40,000	400,000	370,000	30,000	40,000	400,000	390,000	10,000
50,000	500,000	440,000	60,000	50,000	500,000	440,000	60,000
60,000	600,000	510,000	90,000	60,000	600,000	490,000	110,000
70,000	700,000	580,000	120,000	70,000	700,000	540,000	160,000
80,000	800,000	650,000	150,000	80,000	800,000	590,000	210,000

Unit selling price $p = \$10$
Fixed costs $F = \$90,000$
Unit variable cost $v = \$7$
Total variable cost $vx = \$7x$
Total cost $F + vx = \$90,000 + \$7x$
Break-even point = 30,000 units

Unit selling price $p = \$10$
Fixed costs $F = \$190,000$
Unit variable cost $v = \$5$
Total variable cost $vx = \$5x$
Total cost $F + vx = \$190,000 + \$5x$
Break-even point = 38,000 units

DOL of Strand Paper Co. at an output of 50,000 units

$$= \frac{50,000(\$10 - \$5)}{50,000(\$10 - \$5) - \$190,000} = 4\tfrac{1}{6}$$

The above computations indicate that a 1 percent change in sales will produce a $2\tfrac{1}{2}$ percent change in profits for Clear Glassworks and a $4\tfrac{1}{6}$ percent change in profits for Strand Paper. The profits of the firm with the higher DOL (Strand) show a greater variation with a change in sales. From Exhibit 12-3, you can see that an increase in Strand's sales from 50,000 units to 60,000 units (a 20 percent rise) will raise profits from $60,000 to $110,000, an $83\tfrac{1}{3}$ percent rise ($4\tfrac{1}{6}$ times the 20 percent sales rise). The same 20 percent increase in unit sales for Clear Glassworks will increase profits from $60,000 to $90,000, only a 50 percent rise ($2\tfrac{1}{2}$ times the 20 percent increase in sales). Notice from the table that a fall in sales below 50,000 units causes a greater percentage decline in Strand's profits than in Clear Glassworks' profits. A high DOL means exceptionally large profits if sales are great and exceptionally large losses if sales are depressed. DOL is therefore a measure of firm risk. A high DOL indicates a high risk (a high variability of EBIT if sales vary), as in the case of Strand Paper.

The DOL is also important in production planning. For example, the company may have the opportunity to change its cost structure by introducing labor-saving machinery and thereby increasing fixed capital costs and reducing variable labor costs. This rise in fixed costs and decline in variable costs will increase DOL. In this case, a financial manager would want to evaluate the probability that sales will be high so that the firm can enjoy the increased earnings of increased DOL—or that sales will be low, in which case the higher fixed costs and higher leverage would be disadvantageous. The greater the likelihood of high sales, the more attractive will be the shift to a higher DOL (higher fixed cost and lower variable cost) method of production.

Operating leverage is often incorrectly used as a synonym for "business risk." Business risk refers to the uncertainty or variability of the firm's EBIT. A company with a highly unpredictable EBIT is regarded as having high business risk. It is true that the greater is the DOL, the more sensitive is EBIT to a given change in unit sales and that, everything else being equal, a higher DOL means higher business risk. But risk also depends on two other factors: the variability of the firm's sales and the variability of the company's cost and price structures. Let's examine these two other factors.

Assume first that output price and the company's cost structure are known (p, F_o, and v are known, as was the case in our computation of DOL). The DOL indicates how EBIT will change with sales; but, to evaluate the variability of EBIT (the company's risk), we must also know something about the variability of sales. A company with large fixed and low variable costs—for example, a utility or an office building—will have a large DOL, but it may have extremely stable revenues and consequently a stable EBIT and low risk. Conversely, a firm with low fixed costs and high variable costs, and therefore a low DOL, may have very unpredictable sales and a highly unpredictable or variable EBIT—for example, a construction firm with most of its costs being wages, material purchases, and equipment rentals.

EBIT can vary not only because sales fluctuate but also because of changes in the company's output price and unit costs, i.e., changes in p, F_o, and v. Indeed, unit sales might remain fixed while EBIT gyrates wildly because of cost or price variations. Notice also that with price and costs uncertain, DOL is uncertain, since DOL is defined in terms of p, F_o, and v. In such cases, the use of DOL in evaluating business risk is somewhat limited.

The main point here is that DOL is only one measure that can be useful in some situations for determining the behavior of EBIT. The analysis must also examine sales variability and, in many instances, must take into account uncertainty regarding output price and cost structure.

Financial Leverage

Recall from Chapter 9 that financial leverage arises when a company borrows (a firm with no debt has no financial leverage). To illustrate the impact of debt on earnings per share, assume that $500,000 is required to set up the operations of Clear Glassworks. Three financing options are described in Exhibit 12-4 and the impact on earnings is shown in Exhibit 12-5: case A, all equity financing (stockholders' investment $500,000); case B, $400,000 of equity and $100,000 of debt financing; and case C, $300,000 of equity and $200,000 of debt financing. The interest rate on all debt is 10 percent.

Exhibit 12-4. Three Alternative Financing Plans for Clear Glassworks

Case	Total financing	Debt proportion, %	Dollars of debt (10% interest rate)	Dollars of equity	Number of shares outstanding
A	$500,000	0	$ 0	$500,000	5,000
B	$500,000	20	$100,000	$400,000	4,000
C	$500,000	40	$200,000	$300,000	3,000

Exhibit 12-5. Illustration of Financial Leverage — Clear Glassworks

Units sold	EBIT[a]	Interest[b] on debt	Taxes[c]	Net earnings (loss) (EBIT − interest − taxes)	Earnings per share (aftertax profit/no. of shares)[d]	Rate of return on equity, %[e]
A. No debt; equity investment = $500,000 (5,000 shares at $100 per share)						
10,000	($60,000)	0	$(30,000)[f]	$(30,000)	$(6.00)	− 6
20,000	(30,000)	0	(15,000)[f]	(15,000)	(3.00)	− 3
30,000	0	0	0	0	0	0
40,000	30,000	0	15,000	15,000	3.00	3
50,000	60,000	0	30,000	30,000	6.00	6
60,000	90,000	0	45,000	45,000	9.00	9
70,000	120,000	0	60,000	60,000	12.00	12
80,000	150,000	0	75,000	75,000	15.00	15
90,000	180,000	0	90,000	90,000	18.00	18
B. Debt = $100,000; equity investment = $400,000 (4,000 shares at $100 per share)						
10,000	$(60,000)	$10,000	$(35,000)[f]	$(35,000)	$(8.75)	− 8¾
20,000	(30,000)	10,000	(20,000)[f]	(20,000)	(5.00)	− 5
30,000	0	10,000	(5,000)[f]	(5,000)	(1.25)	− 1¼
40,000	30,000	10,000	10,000	10,000	2.50	2½
50,000	60,000	10,000	25,000	25,000	6.25	6¼
60,000	90,000	10,000	40,000	40,000	10.00	10
70,000	120,000	10,000	55,000	55,000	13.75	13¾
80,000	150,000	10,000	70,000	70,000	17.50	17½
90,000	180,000	10,000	85,000	85,000	21.25	21¼
C. Debt = $200,000; equity investment = $300,000 (3,000 shares at $100 per share)						
10,000	$(60,000)	$20,000	$(40,000)[f]	$(40,000)	$(13.33)	−13⅓
20,000	(30,000)	20,000	(25,000)[f]	(25,000)	(8.33)	− 8⅓
30,000	0	20,000	(10,000)[f]	(10,000)	(3.33)	− 3⅓
40,000	30,000	20,000	5,000	5,000	1.67	1⅔
50,000	60,000	20,000	20,000	20,000	6.67	6⅔
60,000	90,000	20,000	35,000	35,000	11.67	11⅔
70,000	120,000	20,000	50,000	50,000	16.67	16⅔
80,000	150,000	20,000	65,000	65,000	21.67	21⅔
90,000	180,000	20,000	80,000	80,000	26.67	26⅔

[a] See Exhibit 12-3 for the computation of EBIT for Clear Glassworks.
[b] Interest rate on debt is 10%, interest on debt = 0.10 × debt.
[c] The tax rate is assumed to equal 50%; taxes = 0.50 × (EBIT − interest on debt).
[d] It is assumed that there are 5,000, 4,000, and 3,000 shares of stock outstanding in cases A, B, and C, respectively. Earnings per share equal aftertax earnings of the firm divided by the number of shares outstanding.
[e] Rate of return on equity = (net earnings)/(equity investment) = (earnings per share)/$100, where $100 = price per share.
[f] A negative tax means a tax credit due to a negative taxable income [negative (EBIT − interest on debt)]

The degree of financial leverage is a measure of the extent of the company's borrowing and is represented by the following formula:

$$\text{Degree of financial leverage} = \text{DFL} = \frac{\text{percentage change in EPS}}{\text{percentage change in EBIT}}$$

which equals

$$\text{DFL} = \frac{\text{EBIT}}{\text{EBIT} - F_f} \qquad (12\text{-}4)$$

where, as before, F_f is interest on debt (fixed financial costs) and EPS refers to aftertax earnings per share.[4] Using the data in Exhibit 12-5, DFL at 50,000 units for cases A, B, and C equals:

$$\text{Case A: DFL} = \frac{\$60,000}{\$60,000 - 0} = 1.0$$

$$\text{Case B: DFL} = \frac{\$60,000}{\$60,000 - \$10,000} = 1.2$$

$$\text{Case C: DFL} = \frac{\$60,000}{\$60,000 - \$20,000} = 1.5$$

Therefore, a 1 percent change in EBIT produces a 1 percent change in EPS if Clear Glassworks has no debt, a 1.2 percent change in EPS with

4. Equation (12-4) for DFL can be derived as follows:

$$\text{EPS} = \frac{(1 - T)(\text{EBIT} - F_f)}{n} \qquad (a)$$

where T = corporate tax rate
F_f = interest on debt
n = number of shares

The change in EPS due to a change in EBIT equals

$$\Delta\text{EPS} = \frac{(1 - T)\,\Delta\text{EBIT}}{n} \qquad (b)$$

since T, F_f, and n are constants (do not change as EBIT changes). Therefore, the percentage change in EPS equals

$$\frac{\Delta\text{EPS}}{\text{EPS}} = \frac{[(1 - T)\,\Delta\text{EBIT}]/n}{[(1 - T)(\text{EBIT} - F_f)]/n} = \frac{\Delta\text{EBIT}}{\text{EBIT} - F_f} \qquad (c)$$

The degree of financial leverage equals the percentage change in EPS divided by the percentage change in EBIT which using (c) equals

$$\text{DFL} = \frac{\Delta\text{EPS}/\text{EPS}}{\Delta\text{EBIT}/\text{EBIT}} = \frac{\Delta\text{EBIT}/(\text{EBIT} - F_f)}{\Delta\text{EBIT}/\text{EBIT}}$$

$$= \frac{\text{EBIT}}{\text{EBIT} - F_f}$$

$100,000 in debt, and a 1.5 percent change in EPS with $200,000 in debt. Notice from Exhibit 12-5 that *the greater is the leverage, the wider are fluctuations in the return on equity*. This is illustrated in Figure 12-5, where rate of return on equity for each level of EBIT is graphed for funding plans A, B, and C; the steeper the schedule, the greater the change in earnings for a unit change in EBIT.

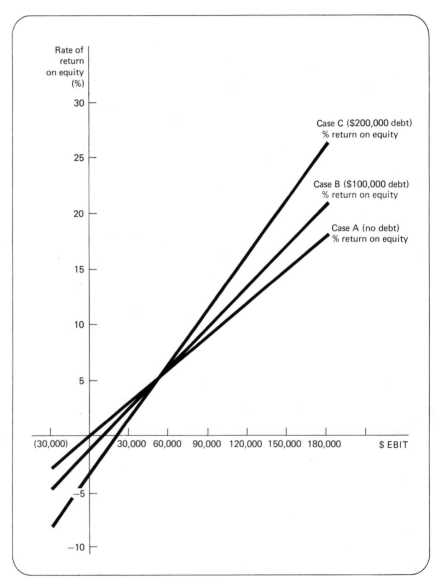

Figure 12-5. Variability of the rate of return on equity increases with greater leverage.

Combined leverage is the measure of the total leverage due to both operating and financial fixed costs. It is easily computed using the DOL and DFL formulas. The degree of combined leverage equals

Combined Leverage

$$\text{Degree of combined leverage} = \text{DCL} = \frac{\text{percentage change in EPS}}{\text{percentage change in sales}}$$

which equals[5]

$$\text{DCL} = \frac{x(p - v)}{x(p - v) - F} \qquad (12\text{-}5)$$

where, as before, $F = F_o + F_f =$ total (operating plus financial) fixed costs. For Clear Glassworks, at an output of 50,000 units ($x = 50,000$) and debt of $100,000,

$$\text{DCL} = \frac{50,000(\$10 - \$7)}{50,000(\$10 - \$7) - (\$90,000 + \$10,000)} = \frac{\$150,000}{\$50,000} = 3.0$$

where, $F = F_o + F_f = \$90,000 + \$10,000$. At an output of 50,000 units, each 1 percent variation in sales will cause a 3 percent change in EPS. In Exhibit 12-5, a 10 percent rise in sales to 55,000 units will increase earnings from $6.25 to $8.125 (a 30 percent increase in EPS) since

$$\text{EPS}_{55,000 \text{ units}} = \text{EPS}_{50,000} + \text{EPS}_{50,000} \times (\% \text{ change in EPS})$$

$$= \text{EPS}_{50,000} + \text{EPS}_{50,000} \times (\text{DCL} \times \% \text{ change in sales})$$

$$= \text{EPS}_{50,000} + \text{EPS}_{50,000}(3.0 \times 10\%)$$

$$= \$6.25 + \$6.25(30\%) = \$8.125$$

5. Equation (12-5) for DCL can be derived by observing that DCL = DFL × DOL; that is,

$$\text{DOL} \times \text{DFL} = \frac{\text{percentage change in EPS}}{\text{percentage change in EBIT}} \times \frac{\text{percentage change in EBIT}}{\text{percentage change in sales}}$$

$$= \frac{\text{percentage change in EPS}}{\text{percentage change in sales}} = \text{DCL}$$

Therefore, using Eqs. (12-3) and (12-4),

$$\text{DCL} = \text{DOL} \times \text{DFL} = \frac{x(p - v)}{x(p - v) - F_o} \times \frac{\text{EBIT}}{\text{EBIT} - F_f} \qquad (a)$$

But, EBIT $= x(p - v) - F_o$, and substituting this into (a) (and noting that $F_o + F_f = F$),

$$\text{DCL} = \frac{x(p - v)}{x(p - v) - F_o} \times \frac{x(p - v) - F_o}{x(p - v) - F_o - F_f} = \frac{x(p - v)}{x(p - v) - F}$$

which is DCL in Eq. (12-5) in the text.

A greater DOL or DFL will raise DCL. DCL is a measure of the overall riskiness or uncertainty associated with stockholders' earnings which arises because of operating and financial leverage.

SUMMARY

Break-even analysis is largely concerned with the effects of changes in the firm's sales volume, or in cost and price structure, on company profits. An important aspect of cost structure is the relationship between fixed and variable costs. Fixed costs do not vary with output changes, whereas variable costs do vary with output. Some costs can be classified as fixed or variable, depending upon the assumptions of the analysis. Break-even analysis can be used to examine the effect of changes in sales price and cost structure on firm profitability. Although linear costs are often assumed in break-even analysis, nonlinear costs as well as variable price can also be assumed. The technique can therefore be adapted to realistic assumptions and often serves as a useful tool in financial planning. However, break-even analysis can become unwieldy if many policy alternatives are being compared. It is therefore generally used in combination with other analytical approaches.

Operating leverage is created by the presence of fixed operating costs, such as depreciation or property taxes. The greater are fixed costs relative to variable operating costs, the more variable will be earnings before interest and taxes (EBIT) and the higher will be the firm's degree of operating leverage (DOL). Operating leverage is not the only cause of fluctuations in EBIT, since EBIT can also change with variations in the company's cost structure (level of fixed or per unit variable cost) or sales price.

Financial leverage occurs when the company borrows money. The greater is the firm's debt, the greater will net aftertax earnings per share change due to a given change in EBIT. The degree of financial leverage (DFL) increases directly with greater firm's borrowing. The degree of combined leverage (DCL) indicates the percentage change in net aftertax earnings due to a 1 percent change in sales. DCL rises as operating leverage and financial leverage rise and is therefore a measure of the impact of operating and financial fixed costs on the variability of net earnings.

QUESTIONS

1. Define and give examples of fixed costs and variable costs.
2. Explain how the following may change the classification of a cost into the fixed or variable class:
   a) The magnitude of a change in output
   b) The amount of time required to change the cost
   c) The length of time the change in output is expected to last

3. Explain what is meant by "contribution margin."

4. In each of the following situations explain what happens to the break-even point in units:
   a) The selling price increases and all other variables remain unchanged.
   b) The fixed cost increases and all other variables remain unchanged.
   c) The variable cost increases and all other variables remain unchanged.

5. Abbot Company has a degree of operating leverage (DOL) of .8 and Baker, Inc., has a DOL of 1.5. Neither firm has any debt. Define DOL and explain whether we can infer that Baker is riskier than Abbott.

6. In the text it is said that DOL and business risk are often incorrectly used as synonyms. Explain why such usage is incorrect and point out the differences between DOL and business risk.

7. Define the degree of financial leverage (DFL) and explain why it is a measure of risk.

8. Define the degree of combined leverage (DCL) and explain how DCL depends on operating and financial leverage.

PROJECT

Obtain the financial statements of two companies in different industries and compare the firms in terms of the relationship between fixed costs, variable costs, and sales. Assume that the sales price and variable cost per unit of output of one of the companies is the same for all levels of production and compute the company's break-even level of sales, its degree of financial leverage, its degree of operating leverage, and its degree of combined leverage. Hint: To compute break-even dollar sales, note that:

$$\text{Break-even dollar sales} = px_b = p\left[\frac{F}{p-v}\right] = \left[\frac{F}{1-\dfrac{vx}{px}}\right] = \left[\frac{F}{1-\dfrac{\text{variable costs}}{\text{sales}}}\right]$$

PROBLEMS

1. A manufacturing company is selling its product at a price of $40 per unit. Fixed costs amount to $250,000. Variable cost per unit is $15.
   a) Calculate the firm's break-even point in number of units.
   b) Calculate the firm's break-even point in dollar sales.
   c) What is the company's profit if 25,000 units are sold?

2. Mickey Krock and his wife, Sola, have decided to start a pottery business which they will call Krock Pottery. Sola will manage the business so Krock Pottery will not have to hire a manager for $15,000 per year. Instead of working the pottery business, Mickey will contribute the

$16,000 to finance the enterprise and will keep his current job as a clown for Percey-Gercy Circus. Krock Pottery will manufacture pottery sets which Krock will sell for $40 per set. Krock Pottery will sign a five-year, $300 per month lease to obtain space for the company. The $16,000 Mickey is investing in the company will pay for equipment and initial materials and supplies. The minimum expenditures for equipment maintenance, power, and telephone will be $100 per month. Depreciation on the equipment is $1,200 per year. The only other costs of production are labor, materials, and other minor outlays; these costs vary directly with output and equal $15 per pottery set.

a) What are Krock Pottery's annual total fixed costs and per unit variable cost? (Hint: Sola will manage the company full time regardless of output.)

b) What is Krock Pottery's break-even point in units and in dollar sales?

c) What are profits at 1,200 units?

d) What is the contribution margin?

e) Assume that Krock Pottery is selling 1,200 units per year and has the costs and unit sales price of **a** through **d** above. The company has the opportunity to add a new machine that greatly lowers labor costs; the machine will increase annual fixed costs to $22,000 but will lower per unit variable costs to $8. If Krock maintains its sales price at $40 and output at 1,200 units, will adding the new machine increase profits?

f) Assume that Krock Pottery is selling 1,200 units and has the costs and sales price indicated in **a** through **d** above. The company can lower the sales price to $35 per unit and thereby raise sales to 1,500 units. Would the sales price reduction increase Krock Pottery's profits?

3. During the year 1977 Synthia Paints sold $500,000 worth of paint, which is its only product. The paint is sold in 1-gallon cans at $25 a can. During the same year the company's total fixed costs amounted to $150,000, and the total variable cost on the units sold amounted to $300,000.

a) What was the company's profit in 1977?

b) How many cans of paint must the company sell to just break even?

c) For 1978, the company expects a 10 percent increase in fixed costs because of an increase in property taxes.

    1. What is the new break-even point in units (cans) if the price cannot be increased above $25?

    2. By how much should the price per can be increased in order for the company to make the same profit as in 1977 assuming that sales and variable costs remain unchanged and assuming that the number of cans sold does not change?

3. The production manager now believes that productivity could be improved by using the existing equipment and personnel more efficiently, thereby reducing variable cost per unit. Assuming that the selling price remains at $25 per can, what reduction in the variable cost would result in the same break-even point as in 1977?

4. The Neptune Company sells marine equipment. In 1977 the company had $300,000 earnings before interest and taxes. On January 1, 1977 the company borrowed $300,000 at a rate of interest of 10 percent. The company had no previous debt and its profits are taxed at 50 percent.

   a) What was the degree of financial leverage prior to 1977?
   b) What is the 1977 degree of financial leverage using the actual 1977 earnings figures?
   c) What would have been the change in EPS (in percent) if EBIT had been 50 percent higher?
   d) What percentage increase in EBIT would bring about a 10 percent increase in EPS?
   e) In 1977 the company sold 12,500 items at $60 per item. The fixed operating cost was $300,000, and the total variable operating cost was $150,000. What was the degree of combined leverage using the actual 1977 earnings figures?
   f) Suppose the 1977 EPS is $2.00. What would EPS be if sales increased by 10 percent?
   g) Compute DOL and check the relation DCL = DOL × DFL using the results of b and e.

5. The Pluto Company has just recovered from a severe slump in business and has projected sales at $1,200,000 for next year. Based on the existing production equipment, total fixed operating costs and total variable operating costs are expected to be $600,000 and $300,000, respectively, so that the EBIT will be $300,000. The selling price per item produced is $50. The firm has a $500,000 five-year note outstanding on which it pays interest of 12 percent. Pluto plans to pay off the five-year note with funds borrowed at a lower interest rate. The production manager has suggested the modernization of the old equipment. This would result in a 10 percent increase in fixed operating costs and a 20 percent decrease in per unit variable operating costs.

   The general manager agrees with the modernization plan as long as the firm's risk, as measured by the DCL, does not change. This could be made possible by the refunding of the outstanding five-year note. Pluto will borrow $500,000 from the bank in order to pay off the note. How much lower must the interest rate on the new $500,000 loan be for the modernization plan to become acceptable in the eyes of the manager? Assume that sales price and sales will be unaffected by the cost changes. (Hint: DCL = DFL × DOL)

financial forecasting and planning

In Chapters 11 and 12 we discussed financial analyses that are based on past and current financial performance. Although these techniques are helpful in judging what the future performance of the firm may be, they were not forecasts of future performance. To increase the profitability of the firm, the financial manager must be able to anticipate its future needs for cash. Financial forecasting allows the financial manager to make educated guesses about the future financial condition of the firm. From these forecasts he or she can then plan the financing of the firm and arrange for external sources, such as debt and stock, if they are needed. The financial manager also develops budgets which indicate, as time passes, whether the forecasts are proving to be accurate. In this chapter we will look at the problem of forecasting future cash requirements and the general financial condition of the firm. We will then show how these forecasts are used to develop plans and budgets.

Forecasts are important for several reasons:

1. Cash forecasts show when and how much new financing will be needed, given current operating and investment decisions.
2. The data obtained from forecasts provide a basis for the decisions regarding cash management and investment in marketable securities. This is discussed in Chapter 14.
3. Budgets prepared from forecasts provide a way to maintain control over the firm's financial affairs and a signal of changing conditions which are reflected in the cash flows of the firm. (For example, if cash were expected to increase by $100,000 in June and the increase turned out to be only $50,000, the financial manager would want to know what happened.)
4. Lenders such as commercial banks are favorably impressed by careful financial planning, especially on the part of small businesses where such planning is frequently not done.

In general, forecasting permits the financial manager to be more effective in monitoring the firm's financial affairs, in controlling and investing cash, and in developing financing. These activities increase profits and reduce risk and are therefore vital to the continuing success of the firm.

Forecasts of the total financial condition of the firm are normally developed from forecasts of individual financial variables. For example, to develop a balance sheet for some future period, it is necessary to forecast accounts receivable and inventory. The forecasts of the individual accounts are combined into a forecast of the complete balance sheet. In this section we will look at several approaches to forecasting single financial variables. In the next section we will show how the forecasts of single variables can be combined into an integrated forecast of the financial condition of the firm.

FORECASTING SINGLE FINANCIAL VARIABLES

Most forecasts combine objective analysis of historical data with the subjective insights of the forecaster. In the descriptions of trend, ratio, and statistical forecasting methods that follow, we focus on the objective analytical techniques. When we show how the forecasts of single variables are combined into a forecast of the firm's cash flows, income statement, and balance sheet, examples of objective forecasts modified by management to reflect its judgment will be presented.

Trend forecasts rely solely on historical information about the variable being forecast. The most elementary trend forecast is to predict "no change" from the current value of the variable when information available suggests that there will be no change. For example, if management does not plan to issue or retire any common stock, it would forecast "no change" in common stock outstanding. "No change" forecasts are also used when there is a complete lack of information as to the extent and direction of any change which may occur, in other words, when the current value is the only information available.

Trend Forecasts

More commonly, trend forecasts are based on past trends and seasonality. For example, if sales have grown at an average rate of 8 percent per year, then a forecast for next year's sales might be 8 percent above current levels. Past seasonal patterns are also considered. If sales in December are typically 15 percent of annual sales, then it would seem reasonable that sales for next December might be 15 percent of forecast sales for the year.

All trend forecasts are essentially a projection of recent historical values for the variable into the future. A basic technique used in analyzing the past history of a variable is to plot the values over time. For example, suppose we wish to forecast the level of inventory next month (month 13). The history of inventory levels over the past twelve months is illustrated in Figure 13-1. Based on this history we would forecast inventory in month 13 to be I^*. There are statistical techniques available for performing such projections mechanically; their use is covered in statistics courses.

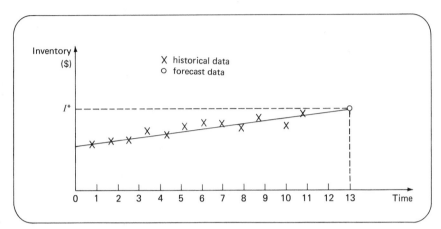

Figure 13-1. A trend forecast of inventory.

Forecasting Based on Relationships between Variables

Trend forecasts are useful, but they do not take into account what else is expected to happen in the firm or the economy. For example, suppose government and private economists are forecasting that a recession will occur next year. If you were forecasting sales of General Motors cars, you might want to forecast lower sales regardless of recent car sales trends, because car sales are affected by general economic conditions. Similarly, if you were forecasting income statement accounts such as cost of goods sold and earnings before interest and taxes, you would want the forecasts for each account to be consistent with forecasted sales. In developing forecasts of single financial variables, the financial manager will want to be sure the forecasts are consistent with each other. Forecasts of one variable are frequently based on a forecast for another variable, which we refer to as the **base variable.**

The levels of assets, liabilities, income, and expenses are known to be related to sales volume. The most obvious examples are the income and expense accounts; however, assets such as accounts receivable are also related to sales. Other things being equal, an increase in sales will almost surely result in an increase in the level of accounts receivable.[1] Therefore, given a forecast for sales, it is often useful to forecast accounts receivable (or collections) based on past relationships with sales. For example, suppose that the average collection period of the firm is thirty days. This means that there are about thirty days' worth of sales in accounts receivable. A forecast of accounts receivable for the end of December would equal the sales forecast for December.

1. Of course if the increase in sales were confined to customers who pay cash, then an increase in accounts receivable would not occur.

Using ratios in forecasting The simplest relationship between two variables is the ratio of the two. Gross margin is a ratio of gross profit to sales. Ratios, such as those discussed in Chapter 11, can be used in forecasting as follows:

1. The ratio itself is forecast or estimated using historical data. Frequently the average value of the ratio over the past year or two is used, although sometimes a trend forecast with adjustments for seasonality is made. For example, if the firm's gross margin has averaged 30 percent in the past, it might be forecast to remain at 30 percent.
2. The base variable is forecast (sales). The base variable here is the denominator of the ratio. In many cases someone else's forecast of the base variable is used. For example, the marketing manager may provide the financial manager with a sales forecast.
3. The individual financial variable is forecast as

$$\text{Variable} = \text{ratio} \times \text{base variable}$$

For example, if sales for next year are forecast to be $10 million and the gross margin is forecast to be 30 percent,

$$\text{Gross profit} = \text{gross margin} \times \text{sales}$$
$$= 0.30 \times \$10 \text{ million}$$
$$= \$3 \text{ million}$$

Sales are the most common base variable in forecasts using ratios since most of the financial variables of the firm are related to sales, at least in the long run. A forecast of sales is often used to provide long-term forecasts for variables that are not directly related to sales in the short run. Plant and equipment would not be likely to vary with sales on a month-to-month basis. However, a forecast of plant and equipment needed by the firm five years from now might be based on the past average ratio of these assets to sales. Accounts payable (and payments to suppliers) are primarily related to purchases. In the short run, purchases may differ appreciably from sales levels. In the short run, therefore, a forecast of accounts payable should be based on expected purchases. In the long run, however, purchases and sales are apt to move together in a fairly stable relationship since goods must be purchased before they can be sold. Therefore, a forecast of sales serves indirectly as a forecast of purchases, and consequently the average ratio of accounts payable to sales can be used as a reasonable basis for a long-range forecast of accounts payable given the sales forecast.

Although sales are the most common base for forecasts using ratios, the general method may be applied using other bases. For example, inventory, wages, or electricity costs might be more related to production levels than to sales. Given a forecast of production, the historical ratio of wages to production might then be used to forecast future wage payments. Similarly, if the ratio of accounts payable to inventory tends to be a constant ratio, a forecast of inventory could serve as a base to forecast accounts payable.

Graphical and statistical methods   Suppose that it is now 1978 and we wish to forecast inventory levels over the next five years, 1979 to 1983. Either trend or ratio methods may be used; however, there are more accurate alternatives. One of the less complicated of these alternatives is to examine the past relationship between inventory and sales as illustrated in Figure 13-2. Each point on the graph represents the particular values of inventory and sales for a given year.

There is a general tendency for higher sales to require higher inventories. Suppose we fit a straight line to these as indicated in Figure 13-2. The line may be drawn by hand or it may be estimated using statistical methods. The line shows the average past relationship between inventory and sales. If the points lie on a line through the origin (sales and inventory equal to zero), a fixed ratio between sales and inventory would be indicated. Since they do not, the ratio method will not provide accurate forecasts in this case.[2] Given the sales forecast for 1979, inventory for 1979 is forecast as shown. Similarly the 1983 sales forecast is used to provide an inventory forecast for 1983.

This approach is quite general because it can be based on the relationship between any two items of interest. For example, accounts payable could be related to inventory just as inventory was related to sales in the above case. A forecast of inventory could then be used in conjunction with the line relating accounts payable to inventory to forecast accounts payable.

More elaborate techniques are also available. Statistical techniques can be used to fit a straight line to the data rather than drawing it by hand.

---

2. The equation for the line is

$$I = a + bS$$

where I is inventory, S is sales, and a and b are constants. The ratio of inventory to sales is

$$\frac{I}{S} = \frac{a + bS}{S} = \frac{a}{S} + b$$

Therefore the ratio is not constant with respect to sales levels unless a is zero. If a is greater than zero, the higher the sales, the smaller is the ratio of inventory to sales.

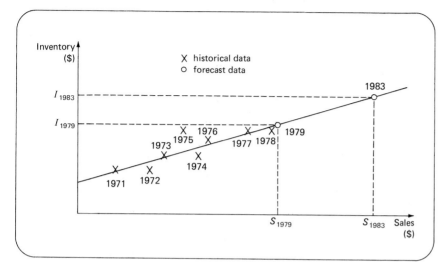

Figure 13-2. Forecasting inventory using historical relationships with sales.

It is possible to fit curved lines rather than straight lines if a curved line describes the relationship better. It is also possible to use more than one variable to forecast another. For example, inventory could be related to both the level of sales and the change in sales from the prior period, or it could be related to sales and production. A major advantage of statistical methods is that they provide measures of how well the fitted relationship matches the actual data. Such methods are generally covered in statistics courses.

Problems in Forecasting

The forecasting methods we discussed are "scientific" in the sense that two people applying the same method to generate a forecast should arrive at the same result. Repeatable results, however, do not guarantee accurate forecasts. As we noted earlier, good forecasting relies on a subjective assessment of the firm's performance combined with an objective analysis of the data. Therefore a financial manager should approach a forecast by considering the choice of methods available, using the ones which are judged to provide the most reliable results, and deciding whether mechanical methods alone will be accurate. A financial manager, for example, may want to forecast earnings by multiplying the sales forecast by the expected profit margin. The profit margin can be based on historical patterns, but it might be better to consider the firm's future outlook for prices and costs. If the firm has just undertaken a major cost reduction program, it would not seem reasonable to use historical profit margins as a basis for forecasting future profits. Management can also utilize the judgment of economists as to the future prospects of the industry and the economy. If the economy is headed for inflation, then the forecast of sales and prices should take that information into account. Here, the judgment of the financial manager may be much more accurate than mechanical calculation methods.

FINANCIAL FORECASTING

So far we have discussed forecasting as if we were solely concerned with the future value of a particular financial variable. However, financial managers usually are more interested in forecasting the total picture. They will use one of the more comprehensive financial forecasting methods—the **cash flow method** or the **balance sheet method.** Both of these approaches forecast the cash position of the firm and make use of single-variable forecasts.

The cash flow method forecasts the cash available to, or needed by, the firm by focusing on the payments and receipts of cash over time. The balance sheet method forecasts the balance sheet accounts of the firm and also the firm's cash position. Since there are differences in the information provided by each method, a comprehensive financial forecast requires the use of both. Both start with a sales forecast, and both require a forecast of the firm's income statements. Generally someone other than the financial manager (such as the marketing manager) is responsible for forecasting sales. Similarly, for manufacturing firms, production schedules are also normally provided by someone else (such as the production manager).

The sales forecast is the backbone of a comprehensive financial forecast because many of the other variables are related to sales. A production schedule, for example, cannot be developed in the absence of a forecast for sales. Any of the methods of forecasting single variables may be used in developing the sales forecast; however, it is important that the financial manager be aware of how the forecast has been developed. In particular the sales forecast used for financial forecasting should be the best estimate available and not a sales target or goal developed to motivate sales personnel. Careful attention must be paid to competitive conditions within the firm's industry, the outlook for the general economy, and any other factors (such as technological changes in other, competing industries) which may have a significant impact on the firm's future sales.

Income Statement Forecasts

We used simple income statement forecasts in Chapter 9 in order to examine the impact of alternative financing methods on the firm's profits. Income statement forecasts are widely used in financial planning since an important consideration in any financial decision is the impact of the decision on the firm's profits. The critical variable in any income statement forecast is the sales forecast. The financial manager usually takes the sales forecast provided by the marketing manager and uses it as the base variable in forecasting the variable costs of the goods and services sold. The financial manager will also forecast other income (for example, interest income on securities investment), operating expenses, interest on debt, depreciation, and any other expenses that may be incurred during the forecast period. Given all income and expense items, the financial manager can calculate income taxes owed to the government and arrive at a forecast of net income (profits) for the firm.

Interest costs on outstanding debt and interest income on present securities investment can be forecast accurately since the financial manager knows the interest rates on debt and securities. However, interest costs of new debt and interest income on new securities cannot be forecast accurately until a cash flow or balance sheet forecast has been made. The amount of new borrowing and the cash available for investment are important results from the forecast. Yet neither a cash flow forecast nor a balance sheet forecast can be completed without having an income statement forecast. Fortunately, these interest items are rarely large relative to other financial variables. Therefore standard procedure is either to ignore the interest on new debt and new securities investment or to use a "no change" forecast from the previous year. Once a preliminary estimate of borrowings and securities investment has been made, the forecast can be revised to reflect these items more accurately. This is part of the planning and budgeting process discussed later in the chapter.

We will show an example of an income statement forecast in conjunction with the example of a cash flow forecast in the next section.

Cash Flow Forecasts

To develop a cash flow forecast for the firm, the financial manager must estimate the cash receipts and payments of the firm over the forecast period. The primary sources of cash receipts are cash sales and collections of accounts receivable. Other cash receipts may result from the sale of assets, the maturing of securities investments, and the proceeds from issuing debt or common stock. Cash payments are made for a wide variety of purposes. They include salaries and wages paid by the firm to its employees, payments to suppliers of goods and services, government taxes, dividends, scheduled payments of principal and interest to lenders, and plant and equipment expenditures. Cash flow forecasts are most often used for monthly plans although they may be made for longer or shorter periods of time.

Large firms often make daily forecasts for the coming month, monthly forecasts for the coming year, quarterly forecasts for the next year or two, and annual forecasts for several more years. This type of forecasting permits the financial manager to plan the firm's financing requirements several years into the future while focusing on short-run needs which can be forecast relatively more accurately and which require current decisions.

An example Suppose that the financial manager of the Snip Tool Company wishes to forecast monthly cash flows for the fiscal year beginning October 1, 1978. Snip manufactures a complete line of lawn and garden tools. Its sales are highly seasonal since half of the sales of Snip's products are made in only four months (February through May). As is common for firms with seasonal sales, Snip's fiscal year does not coincide with the calendar year.[3] Snip's financial statements for the year ending September 30, 1978, are shown in Exhibit 13-1.

The marketing manager estimates sales for next year to be $6 million, with monthly sales as shown in Exhibit 13-2. In forecasting monthly collections, the financial manager must consider the past payment habits of the firm's customers as well as the terms of sale. Snip asks its customers to pay within thirty days, but in the spring months many customers delay payment due to their cash flow problems. Accordingly, the financial manager uses the historical monthly relationship between collections and sales to forecast collections, as shown in Exhibit 13-2. For the first three months, sales made in one month are forecast to be collected in the next month. Then, as indicated in the table, collections begin to slow down in relation to sales. In August the firm's customers begin paying when due again.

Despite the high degree of seasonality of sales, Snip's production is maintained at an even rate throughout the year. This enables the firm to stabilize its manpower requirements and achieve significant economies in production costs. In the past Snip's material costs have been about 50 percent of sales and labor costs have been about 30 percent of sales. The financial manager expects these historical relationships to hold for 1979 as well. The production manager has indicated that normal (level) production schedules will be followed for 1979 and no changes in year-end (September 30) inventories are planned. Since 1979 sales are forecast to be $6,000,000, Snip's labor expenses for 1979 will be forecast as 0.30($6,000,000) = $1,800,000 and materials expenses will be forecast as 0.50($6,000,000) = $3,000,000. Since no change in materials inventory is planned, purchases of materials for the year will equal materials expenses, $3,000,000. With level production schedules, these forecasts imply that purchase of material will be about $250,000 per month ($3,000,000/12) and labor expenses will be about $150,000 per month

---

3. Fiscal years are established for convenience in preparing annual accounting statements. Seasonal firms often pick a time when they are not busy to begin their fiscal year. For example, department stores commonly start their fiscal year on February 1 because their inventories and sales are low then.

Exhibit 13-1. Snip Tool Company Financial Statements for the Fiscal Year Ending Sept. 30, 1978
(Dollar Figures in Thousands)

Balance sheet
Sept. 30, 1978

Cash	$ 100	Accounts payable	$ 160
Securities	150	Accrued expenses	90
Accounts receivable	180	Mortgage (current)	50
Inventory	620	Current liabilities	$ 300
Current assets	$1,050	Mortgage (8%)	600
Plant and		Common stock	2,000
equipment (net)	3,000	Retained earnings	1,200
Other assets	50	Total	$4,100
Total	$4,100		

Income statement
Oct. 1, 1977, to Sept. 30, 1978

Net sales	$5,500
Cost of goods sold[a]	4,550
Gross profit	$ 950
Operating expenses	330
Operating profit	$ 620
Other income	10
Less interest on debt	(70)
Profit before taxes	$ 560
Federal income taxes	270
Net profit	$ 290
Dividends	120
Additions to retained earnings	$ 170

[a] Includes depreciation of $150, labor expenses of $1,650, and materials expenses of $2,750.

($1,800,000/12). By a similar analysis, operating expenses are forecast to be $360,000 for 1979, or $30,000 per month. Labor and operating expenses are paid in cash monthly; however, purchases are not cash payments. The cash outflow occurs when payment is made to suppliers. Snip normally has thirty days to pay for its purchases and pays on time. Any materials bought by Snip will be paid for in the month following their purchase. Note that at the end of September 1978 (Exhibit 13-1), Snip owed

Exhibit 13-2. Snip Tool Company Forecasts of Sales, Collections, and Accounts Receivable

Month	Sales	Collections	Accounts receivable (end of month)
October 1978	$200,000	$180,000[a]	$200,000
November	200,000	200,000	200,000
December	400,000	200,000	400,000
January 1979	400,000	300,000[b]	500,000
February	600,000	300,000[c]	800,000
March	800,000	500,000	1,100,000
April	900,000	700,000	1,300,000
May	900,000	850,000	1,350,000
June	500,000	900,000	950,000
July	500,000	700,000	750,000
August	400,000	750,000	400,000
September	200,000	400,000	200,000
Total	$6,000,000	$5,980,000	

[a] September 1978 accounts receivable assumed collected in October.

[b] December sales not fully collected in January.

[c] Half of the sales made in January will not be collected until March. This collection pattern is assumed to continue through July.

$160,000 to its suppliers (accounts payable). Therefore, in October 1978 Snip will be paying $160,000 to them.

Other cash flows which must be forecast include income tax payments, investment expenditures on plant and equipment, interest and principal payments on debt, other income from investments in securities and new financing. Expenditures on plant and equipment are usually planned well in advance. Snip currently plans to build a new warehouse whose total cost will be $100,000, with $50,000 being spent in October and $50,000 in November. In addition, replacement and upgrading of the firm's production facilities will require $30,000 per month for the next ten months beginning in October. Therefore, monthly plant and equipment expenditures will be $80,000 for October and November and $30,000 for December through July. Income taxes will be paid as equal installments in December, April, June, and September based on the income forecast for the year. An income statement forecast is needed to estimate income taxes. This must be done before the cash flow forecast can be completed.

A forecast of Snip's monthly income statements is shown in Exhibit 13-3. Using the sales forecast of Exhibit 13-1, Snip's financial manager estimates cost of goods sold as 80 percent of sales (30 percent labor plus 50 percent materials) plus depreciation expense. Depreciation expense is forecast based on the depreciation schedules for existing assets plus the depreciation that will be taken on depreciable assets acquired during the year. This is estimated to be $160,000. The expense is prorated against the sales in each month. The easiest method to do this is to take the percentage of depreciation for the year ($160,000) to sales for the year ($6,000,000):

$$\text{Annual percentage} = \frac{\$160,000}{\$6,000,000} = 2.7\%$$

Then add this to the estimated labor and materials percentage (80 percent) to get cost of goods sold as a percentage of sales (82.7 percent). So

Exhibit 13-3. Snip Tool Company Forecast Income Statements, October 1978 to September 1979
(Dollar Figures in Thousands)

	Oct.	Nov.	Dec.	Jan.	Feb.	Mar.	April	May	June	July	Aug.	Sept.	Total[a]
Sales	$200	$200	$400	$400	$600	$800	$900	$900	$500	$500	$400	$200	$6,000
Cost of goods sold[b]	165	165	331	331	496	661	744	744	413	413	331	165	4,960
Gross profit	$ 35	$ 35	$ 69	$ 69	$104	$139	$156	$156	$ 87	$ 87	$ 69	$ 35	$1,040
Operating expenses	30	30	30	30	30	30	30	30	30	30	30	30	360
Operating profit	$ 5	$ 5	$ 39	$ 39	$ 74	$109	$126	$126	$ 57	$ 57	$ 39	$ 5	$ 680
Less interest on debt[c]	5	5	5	5	5	5	5	5	5	5	5	5	60
Profit before taxes	$ 0	$ 0	$ 34	$ 34	$ 69	$104	$121	$121	$ 52	$ 52	$ 34	$ 0	$ 620
Federal income taxes[d]	0	0	17	17	35	52	60	60	26	26	17	0	310
Net profit	$ 0	$ 0	$ 17	$ 17	$ 34	$ 52	$ 61	$ 61	$ 26	$ 26	$ 17	$ 0	$ 310
Dividends[e]			30			30			30			30	120
Additions to retained earnings	0	0	(13)	17	34	22	61	61	(4)	26	17	(30)	190

[a] Totals may not agree with sums of rows due to rounding.

[b] Including depreciation of $160 for the year, $150 as per 1978, plus $10 additional for new assets.

[c] Net of other income; same as 1978, preliminary assumption.

[d] 50% tax rate used.

[e] Planned for 1979, same as 1978.

monthly cost of goods sold is forecast as 82.7 percent of monthly sales. Other expenses, such as electricity, which are included in cost of goods sold but which are forecast separately (not in relation to sales) can be treated similarly to depreciation and added into the cost of goods sold percentage.

The other items on the income statement which are forecasts (rather than calculations) are operating expenses and interest on debt discussed above. A line for dividends is included. Dividends are forecast based on the dividend policy set by management. Dividend payments will depend in part on the forecast of net income for the year and also on financing requirements. Therefore, dividends, like interest, are a preliminary estimate. Interest payments are forecast as "no change" from the prior year as per the discussion in the section on income statement forecasts. Having calculated income taxes, which is the reason the income statement forecast is necessary for a cash flow forecast, let us examine the cash flow forecast for Snip.

Monthly cash flow forecasts are shown in Exhibit 13-4. The forecasts are based on the assumptions in the text and the income statement forecasts. The bottom row of Exhibit 13-4, "Cumulative funds required," provides the information of most interest to the financial manager. This figure shows the total amount of money that must be available from financing sources outside of the firm in each month. We have assumed that the financial manager will maintain average minimum cash balances of $100,000 (no change from September 30, 1978) and that securities will be sold before any borrowing is done. The forecasts of cumulative funds required indicate that the financial manager must begin to arrange for financing immediately because $90,000 will be required by the end of October. At the peak, in February, the firm must have $1,078,000 from some source available to support its operations. However, by August the firm will be able to repay all outside financing and will have $223,000 available for investment in securities or for other purposes. These extra funds will not be available for long since only $120,000 will remain by the end of September 1979.

Although the issues involved in determining minimum cash balances, investing in securities, and financing seasonal operations will be examined in Chapters 14 and 15, this example shows the value of the cash flow forecast for Snip's financial manager. Having projected the cash needed and available for 1978 and 1979, the manager is in a good position to arrange for financing and to develop an accurate plan or budget for the period. Snip's financial manager relied on knowledge of past performance in making many of the original assumptions. The payment habits of customers and estimates of labor and material costs as a percentage of sales were all based on historical information. Current plans for investment in plant and equipment also were used. A forecast of the cash flows

Exhibit 13-4. Snip Tool Company Preliminary Cash Flow Forecast, October 1978 to September 1979 (Dollar Figures in Thousands)

	Oct.	Nov.	Dec.	Jan.	Feb.	Mar.	April	May	June	July	Aug.	Sept.
Operating cash receipts												
Collections of accounts receivable	$180	$200	$200	$300	$300	$500	$700	$850	$900	$700	$750	$400
Operating cash payments												
Payments to suppliers	160	250	250	250	250	250	250	250	250	250	250	250
Wages-production	150	150	150	150	150	150	150	150	150	150	150	150
Operating expenses	30	30	30	30	30	30	30	30	30	30	30	30
Total	$340	$430	$430	$430	$430	$430	$430	$430	$430	$430	$430	$430
Net operating cash flow	$(160)	$(230)	$(230)	$(130)	$(130)	$ 70	$270	$420	$470	$270	$320	$ (30)
Other cash inflows (outflows)												
Plant and equipment expense	(80)	(80)	(30)	(30)	(30)	(30)	(30)	(30)	(30)	(30)		
Mortgage payments and other interest[a]				(51)						(49)	(10)	
Federal income tax[b]			(17)				(104)		(146)			(43)
Dividends[c]			(30)			(30)			(30)			(30)
Net cash inflow (outflow)	$(240)	$(310)	$(307)	$(211)	$(160)	$ 10	$136	$390	$264	$191	$310	$(103)
Cash available—securities	150											
Funds required (available)	$ 90	$310	$307	$211	$160	$(10)	$(136)	$(390)	$(264)	$(191)	$(310)	$103
Cumulative funds required (available)	90	400	707	918	1,078	1,068	932	542	278	87	(223)	(120)

[a] Principal $25 every six months; Interest 8% per annum paid every six months on outstanding balance plus additional $10 interest payment in August (see footnote *c*, Exhibit 13-3).

[b] Due December, April, July, and September. See Exhibit 13-3 for estimates.

[c] Planned, same as 1978.

for an entire fiscal year provides the Snip Tool Company with a consistent projection of its needs and financial expectations for the coming year.

Balance Sheet Forecasts

Forecasted or **pro forma**[4] **balance sheets** can be used to provide estimates of funds required and available just as the cash flow forecast does. Therefore, a balance sheet forecast can serve as an alternative to a cash flow forecast. Long-term forecasts (over one year) are often made using only pro forma balance sheets and income statements; however, for short-term

4. Forecasted income statements are also called pro forma income statements.

forecasts, such as the Snip example, a balance sheet forecast serves only as supplementary data and utilizes figures from the cash flow forecast so that the two forecasts are consistent. Accordingly, the procedure used to forecast the balance sheet depends on whether a cash flow forecast has been made. We will first show how a pro forma balance sheet is developed based on a cash flow forecast using the Snip Tool Company example. Then we will discuss the forecasting problem when only pro forma balance sheets and income statements are desired.

Supplemental balance sheet forecasts　Given income statement and cash flow forecasts covering a period of time, developing a pro forma balance sheet for the end of the period is primarily a problem of computation rather than forecasting. A supplemental balance sheet must be based on the assumptions and estimates used to forecast the income statement and cash flows of the firm; otherwise the balance sheet would not be consistent with the other forecasts. The general procedure used to forecast balance sheet accounts is as follows:

$$\begin{array}{cccc} \text{Ending balance} & = \text{beginning balance} & + \text{ flows in} & - \text{ flows out} \\ \text{(forecast)} & \text{(known)} & \text{(forecast)} & \text{(forecast)} \end{array}$$

The financial manager takes the current value of the account (beginning balance) and adds the net change in the account derived from the income statement and cash flow forecast (flows in − flows out) to arrive at the forecast value for the end of the period (ending balance). For example, accounts receivable is forecast as:

$$\begin{array}{ccccc} \text{Ending} & & \text{beginning} & \text{sales on} & \text{collections} \\ \text{accounts} & = & \text{accounts} & + & \text{credit} & - & \text{during} \\ \text{receivable} & & \text{receivable} & \text{during period} & \text{period} \end{array}$$

Notice that the figure for sales comes from the income statement forecast and the figure for collections comes from the cash flow forecast so that the ending balance of accounts receivable is derived from these forecasts.

Suppose that Snip's financial manager wishes to forecast two supplemental balance sheets—the balance sheet for February 28, 1979, because that is when the need for financing is the greatest, and the balance sheet for September 30, 1979, because that is the end of the forecast period. In practice, these are the two most common times to forecast a supplemental balance sheet, although a complete set of monthly balance sheets is sometimes developed.

Snip's two pro forma balance sheets and the assumptions used to generate them are shown in Exhibit 13-5. If all calculations are performed correctly and are consistent with the forecasts of the income statement and cash flow, the balance sheet will balance as it does here.

Exhibit 13-5. Snip Tool Company Balance Sheet Forecasts
(Dollar Figures in Thousands)

	Feb. 28, 1979	Sept. 30, 1979	Assumptions
Cash and *funds available*	$ 100	$ 220	$100 minimum plus funds available from Exhibit 13-4.
Accounts receivable	800	200	From Exhibit 13-2.
Inventory	1,200	620	See example *a* below.
Current assets	$2,100	$1,040	
Plant and equipment (net)	3,183	3,240	See example *b* below.
Other assets	50	50	Same as Sept. 30, 1978.
Total	$5,333	$4,330	
Funds required	$1,078	$ 0	From Exhibit 13-4.
Accounts payable	$ 250	$ 250	From text.
Taxes payable	52	0	From Exhibit 13-3 and payment schedule.
Accrued expenses	90	90	Same as Sept. 30, 1978.
Mortgage (current)	50	50	Repayment schedule (Exhibit 13-4).
Current liabilities	$ 442	$ 390	
Mortgage (8%)	575	550	Repayment schedule (Exhibit 13-4).
Common stock	2,000	2,000	Same as Sept. 30, 1978.
Retained earnings	1,238	1,390	Sept. 30, 1978 value plus additions
Total	$5,333	$4,330	from Exhibit 13-3.

Example *a*:

Beginning inventory	(Sept. 30, 1978)	$ 620	(Sept. 30, 1978)	$ 620
Plus production	(Oct.–Feb.)	2,067	(Oct.–Sept.)	4,960
Less cost of goods sold	(Oct.–Feb.)	1,487	(Oct.–Sept.)	4,960
Ending balance	(Feb. 28, 1979)	$1,200	(Sept. 30, 1979)	$ 620

Example *b*:

Beginning net plant and equipment	(Sept. 30, 1978)	$3,000	(Sept. 30, 1978)	$3,000
Plus additions to plant and equipment	(Oct.–Feb.)	250	(Oct.–Sept.)	400
Less depreciation ($13.33/month)	(Oct.–Feb.)	67	(Oct.–Sept.)	160
Net plant and equipment	(Feb. 28, 1979)	$3,183	(Sept. 30, 1979)	$3,240

The balance sheets show the amounts of assets and liabilities of the firm and permit the financial manager to see the relationships between them. These data can be analyzed using the procedures of Chapters 11 and 12. In addition, lenders usually require supplemental balance sheets for the time when the need for funds is maximum.

Primary balance sheet forecasts Pro forma balance sheets may also be the primary method of forecasting funds required and available; a cash flow forecast will not be made. This is most often used in long-range forecasting and planning. A general procedure for three- to five-year forecasts is presented below:

1. Annual income statements are forecast. Included is a preliminary estimate of dividend payments.
2. Individual balance sheet accounts are forecast using one of the single-variable methods.
3. The retained-earnings account is forecast using the income statement forecast of additions to retained earnings (net income less dividends) and the beginning balance in the account.
4. The balance sheet is balanced by "plugging in" additional cash or funds required as needed. That is, all assets and liabilities (including equity accounts) are forecast by whatever method the financial manager considers to be the most accurate. But total assets must equal total liabilities plus equity. If the sum of all assets forecast is less than the sum of liabilities plus equity, then the firm must have additional assets, funds available, so that balance is achieved. Similarly, if the sum of liabilities plus equity is less than the asset total, additional liabilities, funds required, must be obtained.

As an example of the balancing procedure, look at the Snip forecast in Exhibit 13-5. On the balance sheet for February 28, 1979, suppose that all assets and liabilities have been forecast except "Funds required." There must be an additional liability of $1,078,000 so that the balance sheet balances. This number could be calculated as:

$$\text{Funds required} = \text{total assets} - (\text{liabilities} + \text{equity})$$
$$= \$5,333 - (\$442 + \$575 + \$3,238)$$
$$= \$5,333 - \$4,255$$
$$= \$1,078$$

Similarly, the balance sheet for September 30, 1979, must have an "extra" $120,000 on the asset side (added into the cash balance) to be in balance.

FINANCIAL PLANS AND BUDGETS Financial managers forecast in order to plan and use forecasts to indicate whether or not their plans for the future are consistent with the goals of the firm. Forecasts therefore are a major part of the planning process.

Management uses forecasts to anticipate problems so that action may be taken to alleviate them. Promotional campaigns may be developed to increase sales. Equipment may be purchased to reduce the costs of production or to increase the productive capacity of the firm. Such decisions affect the financial aspects of the firm's operations and must be planned well in advance of their implementation. Once management has determined a plan of action for the future, these plans are incorporated into a written **financial budget.** A financial budget is a formal statement of expected values of the financial variables of the firm over a future period. There may be a number of separate budgets for the various activities of the firm showing in detail management's plans for the future. For example, the capital budget would indicate expenditures on the capital projects planned over the budget period. The budget for operating expenses would be broken down by expense categories. The separate, detailed budgets are summarized in a cash budget that shows the various cash flows of the firm similar in form to the cash flow forecast shown in Exhibit 13-4. However, a cash budget would include the sources for financing planned in the future and the use of funds available.

There are two general approaches to developing a financial budget for the total firm—**top-down** and **bottom-up.** Top-down planning begins with a set of overall goals for the firm for the planning period. Then the activities which must take place in order to reach those goals are developed. This approach is most commonly used in long-range planning. Suppose, for example, that management establishes a goal of increasing earnings per share at an average rate of 10 percent per year over the next five years. Management then must determine the revenues that must be obtained in order to reach that goal. These revenue goals are then considered for their implications with respect to the assets required to achieve them, the production requirements, financing requirements, and so forth. The result of this approach is an overall plan or budget for the firm which is consistent with the goal established.

The bottom-up approach begins with estimates of the component activities of the firm. Each product line sold by the firm or each division might be forecast individually. Budgets are established for each area and then added together to provide a total financial plan for the firm. This approach is more like the forecasting procedure discussed earlier in which forecasts of single financial variables are combined into an integrated forecast of cash flows, income statements, and balance sheets.

In large firms both approaches are often used. Management may develop a general plan based on goals it has established. Forecasts of the firm's activities are then made, added together, and compared with the general plan. This dual procedure provides information on aspects of the firm's operations which must be given more attention. Also it tells management whether the original goals are realistic.

Once the budgets have been established, they may then be used as a means of controlling the firm's operations. Lower-level management personnel can be provided with budgets for their own areas of responsibility and can be asked to operate within the confines of their budget. Budgets used in this way make it more likely that the firm's actual operations will approximate the overall plan.

If actual results deviate appreciably from the budgeted values, management investigates the reasons for the deviations. Depending on the reasons, either the budget will be revised to reflect changing conditions in the firm's environment or action will be taken to bring the firm's operations back into line with the plan.

The planning and budget process in large corporations usually involves a department whose sole activity is planning, and the process is more complicated than we have indicated here. In small firms, planning is usually limited to a forecast of cash flows and financial statements for the coming year and a preliminary plan for financing.

SUMMARY

Forecasting and planning the future financial condition of the firm are an important part of financial management. There are several basic techniques for forecasting single financial variables. These methods are:

1. The use of historical trends for the variable to forecast future values.
2. The use of the ratio of two variables to forecast one given a forecast of the other.
3. The application of statistical methods to historical data to determine the relationship between one or more variables; then one variable can be forecast using forecasts of the others.
4. The application of judgment and subjective evaluation of the future.

The forecasts of individual financial variables can then be combined to develop complete forecasts of the firm's financial position over time. There are two general approaches which may be used. The cash flow method focuses directly on movements of cash into and out of the firm. The balance sheet method relies on forecasts of individual balance sheet accounts. Income statement forecasts are used with both approaches. Each forecast provides somewhat different information about the financial condition of the firm over time, and both may be calculated if the financial manager wishes to have a complete forecast of the financial aspects of the firm's operations.

Forecasts are used as part of the planning and budgeting process of the firm. Budgets are formal plans used as an aid to controlling the firm's operations. Two approaches to planning are in common use. The top-down approach begins with some general goals for the firm for the planning period, and then the activities necessary to achieve these goals are estimated. The bottom-up approach starts with estimates for the separate parts of the firm. These separate plans or budgets are then combined to provide a total plan. Often both approaches are used to ensure consistency of separate budgets with the general goals established by management. The budgets for individual departments or operating units of the firm enable a firm's management to control its operations.

QUESTIONS

1. Why is forecasting an important part of the financial manager's job?
2. How do "trend" forecasts differ from "ratio" forecasts?
3. Under what circumstances would a "no change" forecast be best?
4. What is a "base variable"? What's the most common base variable in financial forecasting, and why is it used so often?
5. A scientific forecasting method provides the same results when used by different people. Does this mean that scientific methods provide the best forecasts?
6. What are pro forma financial statements?
7. What are the principal operating sources of cash receipts for a business firm?
8. There are two general approaches to forecasting a firm's balance sheet at a given future date. What are the two approaches, and under what circumstances is each one used?
9. Describe the two planning procedures discussed in the chapter.

PROJECT

Obtain the annual reports for at least the past two years of a company (may be assigned by your instructor). Using data from the earlier financial statements, forecast the balance sheet and income statement for the year of the most recent annual report that you obtained. Assume that you have accurately forecasted the sales volume for the most recent year; that is, use the year's actual sales as a base variable. Compare your forecasts of all the data other than sales with the actual results. Try to determine why any major errors (greater than 5 percent) occurred.

PROBLEMS

1. Operating expenses for a company have increased an average of 5 percent per year for the past five years. Last year operating expenses amounted to $100,000. Forecast operating expenses for next year using a trend forecast. [Ans.: $105,000]

2. The cost of goods sold for a retailer has averaged 60 percent of sales for the past three years. Sales are forecast to be $800,000. Forecast cost of goods sold using the ratio method. [Ans.: $480,000]

3. The Crispy Cookie Company has the following history of sales as of 1978

Year	1977	1976	1975	1974	1973	1972	1971	1970
Sales (millions)	$14.2	$14.0	$13.8	$13.0	$12.5	$12.2	$11.0	$10.0

a) Comparing 1977 sales with 1970 sales, calculate the average annual percentage increases over the seven-year period. Forecast 1978 sales using this figure. [Ans.: $15.05 million]

b) Apply a graphical approach to forecasting 1978 sales by fitting a straight line to the data from 1970 to 1977.

c) From an inspection of the data, is there any other forecast that you feel might be better than the forecasts in **a** and **b**?

4. The financial manager of the AIR Company has found from experience that the collections of accounts receivable in a given month can be estimated as being 10 percent of the current month's sales plus 70 percent of the previous month's sales plus 20 percent of the sales made two months ago. For example, a forecast of August collections would equal 10 percent of August sales + 70 percent of July sales + 20 percent of June sales.

At the beginning of January, a sales forecast for the year is as follows:

Month	Sales (thousands)	Month	Sales (thousands)
January	$100	July	$180
February	$100	August	$150
March	$120	September	$100
April	$140	October	$80
May	$200	November	$70
June	$200	December	$70

Last November sales were $50,000, and last December sales were $60,000. Accounts receivable as of December 31 are $64,000.

Using the above data, forecast monthly collections and end-of-month accounts receivable balances for January through December.

5. As of January 1978, Super Star, Inc., had recorded the following sales and average inventory:

Year	Sales ($000)	Average inventory ($000)
1970	400	200
1971	500	200
1972	600	280
1973	650	250
1974	700	300
1975	900	340
1976	900	405
1977	1,000	370

The financial manager would like to know what the average level of inventory is likely to be in 1979. Sales of $1,400,000 have been forecast for that year.

a) Obtain forecasts of 1979 inventory in the following ways:
   1. Use the ratio of inventory to sales estimated over the last two years of data.
   2. Use a "trend" approach.
   3. Use a simple graphical method to estimate the relationship between inventory and sales.

b) Compare the three forecasts obtained in **a** and discuss their validity.

6. Last year's income statement for Perfect Pulley Company is shown below. Sales for next year are expected to be $500,000. Interest expense is expected to stay the same. The corporate income tax rate is 22 percent on the first $25,000 of income and 48 percent on income over $25,000. The other income statement items are expected to maintain their past relationship to sales. Forecast next year's income statement using these assumptions.

	Last year	Next year (forecast)
Sales	$400,000	$500,000
Cost of goods sold	240,000	_____
Gross income	$160,000	
Operating expenses	40,000	
Interest expense	2,000	
Profit before taxes	$118,000	_____
Income taxes	50,140	
Profit after taxes	$ 67,860	_____

7. An analyst working under you has prepared the partially completed balance sheet forecast shown below. He doesn't know what to do next. Can you complete the forecast for him? The cash balance must be no less than $50,000.

Assets		Liabilities and equity	
		Financing required	
Cash		Accounts payable	$100,000
Accounts receivable	$200,000	Other liabilities	50,000
Inventory	300,000	Current liabilities	
Current assets		Long-term debt	$250,000
Fixed assets	$600,000	Stockholders' equity	800,000
Total assets		Total liabilities and equity	

8. The analyst of problem 7 has just entered your office looking very upset. He informs you that he forgot that additional capital investments had been planned which would result in a forecast value of $800,000 for fixed assets instead of the $600,000 shown above. Revise the forecast balance sheet to reflect the new information. How much new financing will be needed? [Ans.: $150,000]

9. Develop a pro forma balance sheet in the following form for the end of year 3 given the data below:

Assets		Liabilities and equity	
Cash	_____	Financing required	_____
Accounts receivable	_____	Accounts payable	_____
Inventory	_____	Long-term debt	_____
Fixed assets	_____	Common stock	_____
Total	_____	Retained earnings	_____
		Total	_____

Year	1	2	3
Sales forecast	$1,000,000	$1,100,000	$1,200,000

Minimum cash balance = 3% of annual sales

Accounts receivable = 10% of annual sales

Inventory = $100,000 + 5% of annual sales

Fixed assets = $400,000 (current value, no additions planned)

Accounts payable = 50% of inventory

Long-term debt = $300,000 less $30,000 per year principal repayment

Common stock = $200,000 (current value, no issues planned)

Retained earnings = $150,000 (current value) + annual additions

Net income per year = 4% of annual sales

Dividends per year = 50% of net income

10. The Pickett Bandage Company's balance sheet as of December 31, 1976 is shown below (amounts are in thousands of dollars):

Cash*	80
Accounts receivable*	600
Inventories*	1,600
Current assets	2,280
Plant and equipment*	800
Other assets	200
Total	3,280
Accounts payable*	400
Accrued expenses*	200
Short-term loans	500
Current liabilities	1,100
Bonds	600
Common stock and surplus	1,300
Retained earnings	280
	3,280

In 1976 the company had sales of $4 million. The ratios of the asterisked accounts to sales have been quite stable during the past few years and are expected to remain so in the future. The ratio of net income to sales has been 1.5 percent for the last three years. Other accounts are not related to sales in the short run. No dividends will be paid next year.

Prepare a balance sheet forecast for December 31, 1977 based on the assumption that 1977 sales will be $5 million and determine whether the firm will need to obtain additional financing. Assume that short-term loans will be used for any financing required.

11. The Cheapo Import Company must pay cash on receipt of the goods it imports. For competitive reasons, the company extends ninety days of credit to its customers. Indeed, the average customer pays ninety days after the time the goods are sold. Fortunately, Cheapo does not have to maintain any inventory. All goods are shipped to customers immediately upon their receipt by Cheapo, since orders for goods are taken while they are in transit. Many times Cheapo will not purchase

goods unless customers for them are known in advance. Other than the costs of goods sold (Cheapo's purchase prices), the firm's operating expenses do not vary much from month to month. These expenses are expected to average $50,000 per month during the coming year, including estimated interest expenses.

Shown below are Cheapo's current balance sheet, a forecasted income statement for the coming year, and a forecast for sales (shipments) by months.

Income taxes at a 50 percent rate are paid quarterly (April, July, October, January) based on income in the preceding quarter (ending March 31, June 30, September 30, and December 31, respectively). Dividend payments of $40,000 per quarter are planned for January, April, July, and October. Make any additional assumptions as needed provided that they are consistent with the above information.

a) Forecast income statements and cash flows for each quarter of the coming year.

b) Forecast the end-of-quarter balance sheets for the coming four quarters using the forecasts from a.

Cheapo Imports financial data

Assets		Liabilities and equity	
Cash	$ 50,000	Notes payable—bank	$ 300,000
Accounts receivable	910,000	Taxes payable	100,000
Fixed assets	40,000	Stockholders' equity	600,000
Total	$1,000,000	Total	$1,000,000

Pro forma income statement			Month	Sales (= shipments)
Sales	$3,600,000			
Cost of goods sold	2,400,000	actual	November	$300,000
Gross profit	$1,200,000		December	200,000
Operating expenses	600,000	forecast	January	100,000
Income before taxes	$ 600,000		February	150,000
Taxes (50%)	300,000		March	200,000
Net income	$ 300,000		April	400,000
			May	500,000
			June	300,000
			July	100,000
			August	100,000
			September	400,000
			October	600,000
			November	450,000
			December	300,000

12. In order to ease the financing burden faced by the Cheapo Import Company of problem 11, Cheapo's financial manager, Francis Matz, is proposing a change in the credit terms provided to customers. Instead of extending ninety days of credit, Francis wants the company to extend only sixty days. Since other firms are also being more stringent, Francis believes that Cheapo's sales will not be affected by this change. Francis is also proposing that an increased dividend be paid to the firm's stockholders, $60,000 per quarter instead of $40,000.

a) Prepare *monthly* cash flow forecasts for the Cheapo Import Company assuming that all customers will pay sixty days after sale of the goods and that the higher dividend will be paid. (You will need a quarterly income statement forecast to do this. The income statement forecasts from problem 11 can be used here.)

b) Using the forecasts from **a**, prepare end-of-quarter balance sheet forecasts for the coming four quarters.

c) Rework the cash flow forecast from **a** assuming that the original planned dividends of $40,000 per quarter are maintained. Adjustments need only be made to the summary figures.

d) If you have a solution to problem 11, compare and contrast the financing requirements in **c** above with those from problem 11. Notice that the only difference in assumptions between these two forecasts is the change in credit terms provided to Cheapo's customers.

13. The Neptune Company manufactures depth sounders for fishing boats. In early January, Neptune's financial manager, Hector Alvarez, is in the process of developing a monthly cash flow forecast for 1980. The following information is available.

Month	Sales forecast ($000's)
January	50
February	70
March	200
April	500
May	900
June	600
July	300
August	200
September	80
October	60
November	30
December	10
Total sales forecast	3,000

Sales in November and December 1979 were $40,000 and $20,000, respectively. The depth sounders are sold to retailers who generally buy on credit. It is estimated that 10 percent of sales are for cash, 70 percent are collected in the month following sales, and 20 percent are collected in the second month following sales. Even though sales are quite seasonal, production is maintained at an even rate throughout the year. No changes in year-end (December) inventories are planned.

Hector has observed the following historical relationships over the past several years:

$$\text{Cost of raw material} = 50\% \text{ of sales}$$

$$\text{Cost of labor} = 30\% \text{ of sales}$$

These relationships are expected to hold during the coming year as well. The raw materials will be purchased evenly over the year in relation to production needs. Payments for raw materials are made during the month following purchase. Labor costs and operating expenses are paid in the month incurred. Total operating expenses are forecast to be $240,000 for the year and, like raw materials and labor, will not vary appreciably from month to month. Total depreciation for the year is expected to be $120,000 and is included in the cost of goods sold.

The company is constructing a new laboratory and will make two $20,000 progress payments, one in May and one in September. Other expenditures on plant and equipment are forecast to be $30,000 per month from April to September. Neptune has an outstanding mortgage, which requires principal payments of $50,000 in June and in December. Interest expenses for the year are estimated to average $9,000 per month. The Neptune Company will continue to pay $10,000 per quarter in dividends in March, June, September, and December as they did for the last two years. A minimum cash balance of $75,000 is required.Quarterly income taxes are due in April, June, September, and December. Neptune pays taxes each quarter based on its estimated total taxes for the year.

Given this information, do the following:

a) Develop monthly income statement and cash flow forecasts for the coming year.
b) Forecast Neptune's balance sheets for the month in which the maximum amount of financing is needed as determined in **a** and for December.

Neptune Company financial statements for the fiscal year ending December 31, 1979

Balance sheet
(Dollar figures in thousands)

Cash	$ 75	Accounts payable	$ 140
Securities	100	Accrued expenses	30
Accounts receivable	150	Mortgage (current portion)	100
Inventory	800	Current liabilities	$ 270
Current assets	$1,125	Mortgage	1,400
Plant and equipment (net)	5,000	Common stock	3,000
Other assets	45	Retained earnings	1,500
Total	$6,170	Total	$6,170

Income statement
January 1, 1979 to December 31, 1979
(Dollar figures in thousands)

Net sales	$2,700
Cost of goods sold[a]	2,268
Gross profit	$ 432
Operating expenses	220
Operating profit	$ 212
Other income	2
Less interest on debt	(74)
Profit before taxes	$ 140
Federal income taxes[b]	70
Net profit	$ 70

[a] Includes materials expenses of $1,350, labor expenses of $810, and depreciation of $108.
[b] 50 percent tax rate.

current asset management

The four major types of current assets are cash, securities, accounts receivable, and inventory. The basic principles of asset investment discussed in Chapters 7 and 8 apply to these assets, as well as to long-term assets such as plant and equipment. However, each type of current asset has unique characteristics which the financial manager must consider in deciding how much money should be invested in that particular asset. In this chapter we describe the four types of current assets and examine the decisions which determine the level of investment in each.

Managing current assets requires more attention than managing plant and equipment expenditures. The financial manager cannot simply decide that the inventory investment, for example, should be $1 million and stop there. The level of investment in each current asset varies from day to day, and the financial manager must continuously monitor these assets to ensure that desired levels are being maintained. In most cases the desired level is, itself, a changing quantity. For example, the desired level of inventory for the Snip Tool Company of Chapter 13 at the end of February 1979, when its sales are very high, would not be the same as the desired level at the end of September 1979, when its sales are very low (see Exhibit 13-5).

Since the amount of money invested in current assets can change rapidly, so does the financing required. Mismanagement of current assets can be costly. Too large an investment in current assets means tying up capital that can be more productively used elsewhere (or it means added interest costs if the firm has borrowed to finance the investment in current assets). Excess investment may also expose the firm to undue risk if inventory cannot be sold or accounts receivable cannot be collected. On the other hand, too little investment also can be expensive. For example, insufficient inventory may mean that sales are lost since the goods that a customer wants to buy are not available. The result is that financial managers spend a large percentage of their time managing current assets because these assets vary quickly and a lack of attention paid to them may result in appreciably lower profits for the firm.

We begin with a discussion of the general rules that apply to investment in any current asset. Then we discuss each asset separately, first inventory, next accounts receivable, and then cash and securities. Three aspects of each asset will be examined:

1. The basic characteristics of the asset and how it is used by firms

2. The benefits and costs associated with the level of investment in the asset

3. The risks involved in investing in the asset

A final section of the chapter discusses the relationship between current asset investment and long-term investment decisions.

PRINCIPLES OF CURRENT ASSET INVESTMENT

The same general rules developed for the firm's investment decisions in Chapters 7 and 8 apply to current assets with some modifications that reflect their unique characteristics. First, although the amount of investment in any current asset ordinarily varies from day to day, the average amount or level over a period of time is used in current asset analysis. Using an average greatly simplifies planning. Second, both the dollar level of investment and the type of current assets held are important decision variables. Think of the inventory of a dealer in construction equipment. The dealer must decide how many bulldozers to keep in stock, as well as whether to stock bulldozers or dump trucks. From the viewpoint of the financial manager all the decisions as to particular items add up to an average level of inventory for a given item, and these averages for all items add up to the total average inventory investment of the firm. The result is that there is a very large number of alternative levels of investment in each type of current asset. Therefore, in principle, current asset investment is a problem of evaluating a large number of mutually exclusive investment opportunities.

Solution of this problem by the methods presented in Chapter 7 requires that:

1. The financial manager estimate the costs and benefits from each alternative.

2. The net present value be calculated for each alternative given the cost of capital for the degree of risk involved.

3. That alternative with the highest net present value be chosen.

However, the net present value approach is not used in practice. There are too many alternatives that must be evaluated, and they must be regularly reevaluated since the most profitable level of investment depends on the sales volume of the firm, which is continually changing. Procedures to handle the computational requirements exist, but differ for each asset. Net present values also are somewhat difficult to calculate and interpret for current assets.

So, instead of net present values, an alternative equivalent method is used: maximize average net profit with the cost of capital treated as an annual dollar cost. Let us explore this further.

Net Profit and Net Present Value

Suppose we are investing $1,000 and will continue to receive $100 per year so long as we keep the $1,000 invested. At any time we can choose to withdraw our $1,000 and the annual cash flow of $100 stops. This type of investment is described as being **reversible** since the transaction can be "reversed"; we can get the amount of the investment back if we want to. A savings account is a reversible investment. Current assets are usually evaluated as reversible investments.

One characteristic of reversible investments is that net present values are difficult to interpret. How would you calculate the present value of the above investment given a cost of capital of 8 percent?

$$\text{NPV} = -\$1,000 + \frac{\$100}{1.08} + \frac{\$100}{(1.08)^2} + \cdots + \frac{\$100}{(1.08)^n} + \frac{\$1,000}{(1.08)^n}$$

$$= -\$1,000 + \$100(P/A, \ 8\%, \ n) + \$1,000(P/F, \ 8\%, \ n)$$

The above NPV is the present value of the net gain, or profit, from the investment. But there is a problem as to what time period n to use. The net present value depends on the time period you choose. However, the nice thing about reversible investments is that *when* the investment period ends is generally not important. To see this, let's calculate the annuity that has a present value equal to the net present value computed above. This annuity is the average net profit per period from the investment.

$$\text{Net profit} = \text{annuity} = \text{NPV}(A/P, \ 8\%, \ n)$$

$$= [-\$1,000 + \$100(P/A, \ 8\%, \ n)$$

$$+ \ \$1,000(P/F, \ 8\%, \ n)](A/P, \ 8\%, \ n)$$

$$= \$100(P/A, \ 8\%, \ n)(A/P, \ 8\%, \ n)$$

$$- \ [\$1,000 - \$1,000(P/F, \ 8\%, \ n)](A/P, \ 8\%, \ n)$$

But, $(P/A, \ 8\%, \ n) = 1/(A/P, \ 8\%, \ n)$, so

$$\text{Net profit} = \$100 - \$1,000[1 - (P/F, \ 8\%, \ n)](A/P, \ 8\%, \ n)$$

The first term in the above equation is the annual cash flow of $100. The second term is the annual dollar cost of the investment of $1,000, and this amounts to 8 percent of $1,000 regardless of the number of periods n of the investment.[1]

Therefore,

$$\text{Net profit} = \$100 - 0.08 \ (\$1,000)$$
$$= \$100 - \$80$$
$$= \$20$$

The $80 is the annual dollar cost of the $1,000 investment at an 8 percent cost of capital, and the annual net profit of $20 does not depend on when the investment is reversed. The result is that we can use net profit per period as a criterion for choosing among alternative reversible investments and that investment with the highest value of net profit per period is also the investment with the highest net present value. Investments with positive NPVs have positive net profits; investments with zero NPVs have zero net profits; and investments with negative NPVs have negative net profits.

Many inventory decisions are made on the basis of minimizing cost. The same procedure as above is valid here. Instead of minimizing the net present value of costs, it is easier to minimize total annual cost where the annual capital cost of the investment is the cost of capital rate times the amount invested. We will discuss this further in the next section which deals specifically with inventory.

Stating our results more generally, if the cost of capital is k percent,

$$\text{Net profit} = (1 - \text{tax rate}) \times (\text{annual cash revenues}$$
$$- \text{ annual cash costs}) - k(\text{investment}) \qquad (14\text{-}1)$$
$$\text{Total cost} = (1 - \text{tax rate}) \times (\text{annual cash costs})$$
$$+ \ k(\text{investment}) \qquad (14\text{-}2)$$

In the analysis below we will treat current asset investments as reversible and therefore select policies which maximize net profit or minimize total cost. The choice between a profit or cost approach depends on the particular problem being analyzed.

---

1. The annual dollar cost for any reversible investment is the cost of capital k times the amount of the investment. We can show this mathematically by expressing the interest rate factors in their algebraic form from Appendix 4A.

$$[1 - (P/F, k, n)](A/P, k, n) = [1 - (1 + k)^{-n}] \left[\frac{k}{1 - (1 + k)^{-n}} \right] = k$$

INVENTORY   Managing the level of investment in inventory is like maintaining the level of water in a bathtub with an open drain. The water is flowing out continuously. If water is let in too slowly, the tub is soon empty. If water is let in too fast, the tub overflows. Like the water in the tub, the particular items in inventory keep changing, but the level may stay the same. The basic financial problems are to determine the proper level of investment in inventory and to decide how much inventory must be acquired during each period to maintain that level. Let's examine the various types of inventory to see how each kind is used.

Types of Inventory   Business firms keep inventories for many different purposes. Firms that operate equipment often maintain inventories of spare parts so that breakdowns can be quickly repaired. All firms must have some inventories of office supplies such as paper, pencils, and pens. The three most important types of inventories for most business firms are raw materials, work-in-process, and finished goods. Raw materials consist of goods purchased from another firm which are used to manufacture a product. Work-in-process inventory contains partially completed goods in process of production. Finished goods are goods ready for sale. The classification of a particular item depends on the kind of business being discussed. For a coal mining firm, coal is finished goods. For a steel mill, coal is raw materials, as it will be used in the production of steel. Similarly, steel is finished goods for a steel mill, but raw materials for an automobile manufacturer. Once goods have been produced in a form suitable for the consumer (automobiles, refrigerators, furniture, canned food, etc.), they are classified as finished goods. For example, an automobile dealer purchases automobiles from the factory; therefore in a sense they might be considered raw materials for the dealer. However, since the dealer sells a car essentially as it is to the consumer, the stock of automobiles is considered finished goods.

The inventory of a manufacturing firm contains all three major types. Wholesalers, retailers, and other firms involved in the distribution of goods from the manufacturer to the ultimate consumer hold finished goods that have been purchased from another firm. Firms which sell services rather than products rarely have any of these three, only supplies and perhaps spare parts. Airlines, bus companies, and railroads are firms whose inventories are primarily spare parts. The level of investment in inventory differs greatly for firms in different industries. Table 14-1 shows inventory as a percentage of assets for different types of firms. The figures shown are industry averages. You might speculate on why firms in some lines of business invest in more inventory than others.

Table 14-1. Average inventory investment for selected businesses

	Inventory/Assets, %
Manufacturers	
Aircraft	48.0
Apparel	35.0
Drugs	21.0
Lumber	19.0
Petroleum refining	7.0
Wholesalers	
Footwear	51.0
Drugs	45.0
Lumber	30.0
Petroleum products	15.0
Retailers	
Shoes	64.0
Drugs	58.0
Department stores	45.0
Lumber	37.0
Gasoline stations	7.0
Miscellaneous	
Soft drink bottlers	13.0
Laundry and dry cleaners	10.0
TV stations	0.1

Sources: Robert Morris Associates and Federal Trade Commission. Data as of Dec. 31, 1973.

The Basic Inventory Decision

Although the benefits, costs, and risks vary for every kind of inventory, all inventories have two characteristics in common: (1) costs must be incurred to acquire inventory and (2) there are costs to holding inventory. Let's analyze this basic case before considering other aspects of inventory investment.

Inventory is constantly being used up. This is true regardless of the type of inventory. Raw materials and work-in-process inventories are being used in production. Finished goods are being sold. Spare parts are replacing worn-out parts. The rate at which the inventory is being used up is called the **usage** or **sales rate,** depending on the type of inventory. We can express this rate as S units of goods per year. For example, a steel mill may be using 10 million tons of coal per year. A grocery store may be selling 50,000 cans of chicken soup per year. To replace the inventory that is being used up, **orders** must be made. An order may be placed with a supplier (coal mine) or within the production facility of the firm. The person managing the finished goods inventory of a steel mill places an order for more steel bars with the production manager of the mill. An order is for some quantity Q.

If the usage rate is constant, orders are made at even intervals for the same amount each time, and inventory goes to zero just before an order is received. In this case the number of units in inventory will be as shown in Figure 14-1. For example, suppose that the usage rate is 1,200 units per year (100 per month) and orders of 100 units are placed every month. When an order is received, there will be $Q = 100$ units in stock. The amount in stock will be reduced, on average, 100 units/30 days = $3\frac{1}{3}$ units each day, and at the end of the month inventory will be zero.

The average number of units in stock will be $Q/2$. The average level of investment in this item will be the cash outlay required to acquire each unit (C) times the average number of units.

$$\text{Average investment} = \frac{CQ}{2} \qquad (14\text{-}3)$$

If the cost per unit is $20, average investment in this item will be $20($^{100}/_2$) = $1,000.

From the viewpoint of the person managing the inventory, the basic decisions are how much to order, Q, and when to place the order. From the viewpoint of the financial manager, the decision is what level of investment should be made, $CQ/2$. Regardless of who makes the decision, there are four important types of costs that will be incurred: acquisition costs, order costs, holding costs, and the cost of funds.

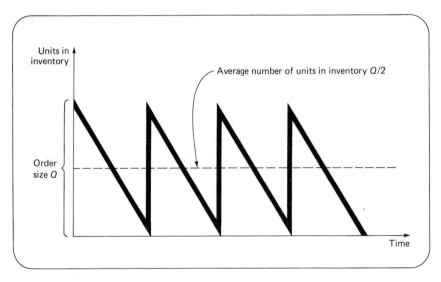

Figure 14-1. Inventory levels over time when usage rate is constant.

Acquisition costs and quantity discounts Acquisition costs are the cash costs per period of acquiring inventory (either making goods or buying them). These costs can be calculated as the cash outlay per unit C times the usage rate S,

$$\text{Acquisition cost} = CS \qquad (14\text{-}4)$$

For purchased goods, C is the purchase price; for manufactured goods, C is the cash cost per unit produced. Determining C for manufactured goods is a difficult problem in cost accounting, so we shall use purchased goods in our examples to keep the variables in the problem clearly defined.

If neither the usage rate S nor the cash outlay per unit C is affected by the order quantity or investment decision, the level of acquisition costs will not affect the decision regarding the level of Q. That is, if acquisition cost is a constant value regardless of the inventory decision, this cost can be ignored in making the decision. Appendix 14A presents the solution to the inventory decision when acquisition cost is constant. Here let's consider the more complicated and realistic case of varying acquisition cost caused by quantity discounts on purchased goods.

A **quantity discount** is a reduction in price for ordering more than a minimum quantity of goods at a time. Quantity discounts are usually expressed as a percentage reduction in list price. For example, a discount of 10 percent on orders of 500 units or more for an item with a $20 list price means that the unit price will be $18 ($20 − 0.10 × $20) if the firm orders at least 500 units at a time. Often discounts are available at several levels of order quantity. For example:

Discount, %	Amount ordered (Q)	Price (C)
0	1–99	$20.00
5	100–499	19.00
10	500–999	18.00
15	1,000 and over	17.50

Quantity discounts are normally given to reflect the savings in costs to the supplier from filling large orders. Special, temporary discounts are also occasionally offered when a supplier is overstocked on an item and wishes to reduce inventory quickly.

The effect of a quantity discount is that acquisition cost depends on the quantity ordered Q since the cash outlay per unit C varies with Q. Remember that in analyzing the basic decision we are assuming that the usage rate S is constant. To calculate acquisition cost, we must specify a value for Q. If Q is fifty units, we see from the table above that $C = \$20$

and with a usage rate $S = 1,200$ units per year it follows from Eq. (14-4) that

$$\text{Acquisition cost} = \$20 \times 1,200$$
$$= \$24,000 \text{ per year}$$

If $Q = 500$, $C = \$18$, and

$$\text{Acquisition cost} = \$18 \times 1,200$$
$$= \$21,600 \text{ per year}$$

Order costs Order costs are the costs which vary with the *number* of orders. In the basic model we assume that every time an order is made, a fixed dollar cost is incurred. For inventories such as work-in-process and manufacturers' finished goods, order costs include any costs of setting up equipment to produce the item. For these inventories the term ''set-up costs'' is used. Typical types of order and set-up costs are shown in Table 14-2.

The dollar cost of orders in a period depends on how many orders are made in the period and the cost per order. The number of orders per period is

$$\text{Number of orders per period} = \frac{\text{usage rate}}{\text{quantity per order}}$$

$$= \frac{S}{Q} \qquad (14\text{-}5)$$

With a usage rate of 1,200 units per year, if each order is for 10 units, 120 orders must be made per year. However, if 100 units are ordered at a time, only twelve orders per year must be made.

Define the cost per order for a given inventory item as f. The order cost per period for the item is

Table 14-2. Typical costs of ordering and holding inventory

Order and set-up costs	Holding costs
Transportation costs	Storage costs
Clerical costs of making orders	Fire insurance
Costs of placing goods in storage	Property taxes
Downtime on equipment	Spoilage and deterioration

Order cost = cost per order × number of orders

$$= f \frac{S}{Q}$$

$$= \frac{fS}{Q} \tag{14-6}$$

For example, if the cost per order f is \$25 and twelve orders are made per year ($Q = 100$, $S = 1,200$), the annual order cost for the item will be

Annual order cost = \$25 × 12

= \$300

Holding costs Holding costs are costs due to holding (owning) inventory. Typical kinds of holding costs are shown in Table 14-2. Generally holding cost is calculated as a percentage of the average dollar investment in inventory. The financial manager determines the holding cost rate h by adding up the cost rates for the various kinds of holding costs. For example, suppose the following costs are estimated:

Storage costs = 2.5% per year per dollar of inventory
Property taxes = 1.0% per year per dollar of inventory
Other miscellaneous costs = 0.5% per year per dollar of inventory
Holding cost rate h = 4.0% per year per dollar of inventory

The holding cost per period is the rate h times average investment in inventory [defined by Eq. (14-3)].

Holding cost = holding cost rate × average inventory investment

$$= h \frac{CQ}{2}$$

$$= \frac{hCQ}{2} \tag{14-7}$$

If 100 units are ordered each time ($Q = 100$) with a price of \$19 per unit ($C = \$19$), average investment will be \$950 (\$19 × $^{100}/_2$). With a 4 percent annual holding cost rate,

Annual holding cost = 0.04 × \$950

= \$38

Cost of funds The cost of funds describes the cost measured as the cost of capital rate times the average level of investment. This cost reflects the minimum dollar return required on the money tied up in inventory. As we discussed earlier in the chapter, a reversible investment can be evaluated on the basis of total costs [Eq. (14-2)] including the cost of funds defined here. The cost of capital k which applies to investment in inventory may differ for items according to the risk of investing in them. The risks in inventory investment are discussed in the next section. For now we will take the cost of capital as given for the item in question.

$$\text{Cost of funds} = \text{cost of capital} \times \text{average inventory investment}$$

$$= k\,\frac{CQ}{2}$$

$$= \frac{kCQ}{2} \tag{14-8}$$

Given a cost of capital k of 10 percent per year and an average investment of $950 ($C = \$19$, $Q = 100$),

$$\text{Cost of funds} = 0.10 \times \$950$$

$$= \$95$$

Total cost   The total cost of inventory for the basic model can now be expressed by plugging the cost elements we have developed thus far into the general total cost equation [Eq. (14-2)]:

$$\text{Total cost} = (1 - \text{tax rate}) \times (\text{acquisition cost} + \text{order cost}$$

$$+ \text{holding cost}) + \text{cost of funds}$$

$$= (1 - \tau) \times \left(CS + \frac{fS}{Q} + \frac{hCQ}{2}\right) + \frac{kCQ}{2} \tag{14-9}$$

where τ is the tax rate. The cost of funds is not multiplied by $1 - \tau$ since k is an aftertax cost of capital. The decision variable in this equation is Q, the quantity ordered. Alternatively, we could express the total cost equation as

$$\text{Total cost} = (1 - \tau) \times \left(CS + \frac{fCS}{2I} + hI\right) + kI \tag{14-10}$$

where I is the average level of investment ($I = CQ/2$). Regardless of which way the equation is written or whether Q or I is considered to be the decision variable, we wish to minimize total cost. This can be accomplished by calculating total cost for different values of Q (or I) given values for all the other variables in Eq. (14-9) [or (14-10)] and plotting the results.

Exhibit 14-1. Total Cost Calculated for Various Order Quantities

Total cost $= (1 - \text{tax rate}) \times (\text{acquisition cost} + \text{order cost} + \text{holding cost})$
$+ \text{cost of funds}$

Quantity Q	Acquisition cost CS	Order cost $\dfrac{fS}{Q}$	Holding cost $\dfrac{hCQ}{2}$	Cost of funds $\dfrac{kCQ}{2}$	Total cost
50	$24,000	$600	$ 20	$ 50	$12,850
100	22,800	300	38	95	12,130
120	22,800	250	46	114	12,120
200	22,800	150	76	190	12,160
300	22,800	100	114	285	12,250
400	22,800	75	152	380	12,350
500	21,600	60	180	450	11,810
800	21,600	38	288	720	12,120
1,000	21,000	30	350	875	11,990
1,200	21,000	25	420	1,050	12,200

Assumptions	*Quantity discount schedule*	
	Quantity (Q)	Price (C)
Usage rate $S = 1,200$ units per year	1–99	$20.00
Cost per order $f = \$25$ per order	100–499	$19.00
Holding cost rate $h = 4\%$ per year	500–999	$18.00
Cost of capital $k = 10\%$ per year	1,000 and over	$17.50
Tax rate $\tau = 48\%$		

Exhibit 14-1 shows several such calculations using the example data, and Figure 14-2 is a graph of total cost as the quantity ordered increases. The "jumps" in the curve reflect the quantity discounts provided at quantities of 100, 500, and 1,000 units ordered. As can be seen both from Exhibit 14-1 and Figure 14-2, total cost is minimized at $Q = 500$ units, which means that average inventory investment in this item is

$$I = \frac{CQ}{2}$$

$$= \frac{\$18 \times 500}{2}$$

$$= \$4,500$$

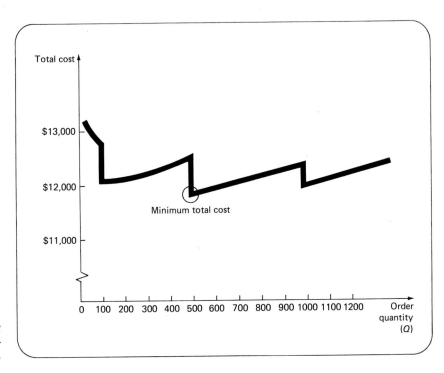

Figure 14-2. Total cost of inventory as a function of order quantity.

The basic inventory decision is to find the order size or average level of investment that produces a minimum total cost. Small, frequent orders allow a low level of investment which has low holding cost and cost of funds, but frequent orders are expensive because of order costs and because quantity discounts may not be available. Large, infrequent orders keep order costs down and may provide quantity discounts but cause high holding cost and cost of funds. The best inventory decision is the one which balances all types of costs so that total cost is minimized.

Benefits from Inventory Investment

An alternative way to think of the basic inventory decision is that increasing investment in inventory provides benefits from a reduction in order costs and from the possibility of quantity discounts. This benefit is offset by the increase in holding costs and the requirement that inventory investment provide a satisfactory rate of return, the cost of capital k. Now let's look at some other benefits from inventory investment which are not directly related to order quantity.

Avoiding stockouts In our development of the basic model we implicitly assumed that the usage rate was known precisely and that we knew exactly when an order would be received once it was placed. These assumptions are not usually valid in practice. Suppose the firm tried to use the solution developed above. The average usage rate is 1,200 units per year or 100 units per month. Every five months an order will be placed for 500 units. If it takes a month between the time an order is placed and the time it is received, an order must be placed when the inventory reaches 100 units, which is one month's supply. What happens if the demand for the item is greater than 100 units in the month before the order is received or if the order takes forty-five days to arrive? The firm will not have enough units in stock to satisfy the demand. This is called a **stockout.**

Stockouts are expensive. If the inventory item is finished goods, the customer may buy the goods from someone else; therefore, the profits on the sale will be lost. Even if the customer is willing to wait until the goods arrive, some goodwill is lost. If a firm is often not able to supply goods when customers want them, its reputation suffers and it will lose business—more business than just the orders that were not filled for lack of inventory.

Stockouts of raw materials or work-in-process can cause the production process to stop. This will be expensive because employees will be paid for time not spent in producing goods or, if they are temporarily laid off, the firm will be assessed higher unemployment taxes. Some production processes are so expensive to shut down that management will go to great lengths to avoid running out of raw materials. There exists a company whose business is flying parts to automobile assembly plants so that they won't have to shut down when they run out of a critical item. The cost to the automobile manufacturer of having parts flown in by private jet planes can be several times the cost of the parts themselves. However, paying the high cost of transportation is preferable to shutting down an entire plant.

Stockouts of spare parts can also stop production of the goods or services of the firm. A transportation company which cannot meet its schedules because its equipment is out of service loses both revenues and customer goodwill.

To avoid stockouts, firms maintain **safety stocks** of inventory. Safety stock is the minimum level of inventory desired for an item given the expected usage rate and the expected time to receive an order. If an order is placed when the inventory reaches 150 units instead of 100 units, the additional 50 units constitute the safety stock. The manager expects to have fifty units in stock when the new order arrives. The safety stock protects the firm from stockouts due to unanticipated demand for the item or to slow deliveries. Increasing the amount of inventory held as safety stock reduces the chances of a stockout and therefore reduces stockout costs over the long run. The level of inventory investment is, however, increased by the amount of the safety stock.

The best level of safety stock for a given item depends on how much a stockout costs and on the variability of usage rates and delivery times. If the usage rate and the delivery time can be forecast with a high degree of accuracy and if the cost of a stockout is estimated to be small, then little or no safety stock will be needed. If the circumstances are not so favorable, then a significant investment in safety stock will be desirable.

A simple solution to the problem is to examine the costs associated with a given level of investment in safety stock.

$$\text{Safety stock costs} = (1 - \text{tax rate}) \times (\text{expected stockout cost}$$
$$+ \text{holding costs}) + \text{cost of funds} \quad (14\text{-}11)$$

Holding cost can be calculated as the holding cost rate times the dollar investment in safety stock. Cost of funds is the cost of capital times safety stock investment. Expected stockout cost must be estimated at various levels of investment. Given the cost estimates, we wish to find that level of investment which minimizes total cost. Exhibit 14-2 illustrates a solution to the problem given the assumptions shown. Minimum cost is achieved at 100 units of safety stock and an investment of $1,800.

A complete solution to the problem of determining the proper level of safety stock for an item is complex and beyond the scope of this text. For example, the frequency of orders affects the number of stockouts. Since some costs, such as loss of customer goodwill, are very difficult to estimate accurately, safety stocks are typically established by rules of thumb and managerial judgment. Depending on the type of inventory, avoiding stockouts is important to production or marketing management. The financial manager's role in the decision is often that of reminding other members of management that money invested in inventory should earn at least the cost of capital. Therefore, total avoidance of stockouts by maintaining large safety stocks may not be the best solution.

Marketing benefits   So far we have discussed the benefits and costs of investing in individual inventory items. We have not considered the decision as to what items to stock. Generally the wider is the variety of items stocked, the higher the inventory investment will be. What benefits are derived from stocking many types of inventory?

Most items in raw materials and work-in-process inventories of manufacturing firms are necessary in that production cannot proceed without them. The decision as to what items produced by the manufacturer will be kept in finished goods inventories depends on the frequency of customer orders for the item, the time required to produce it, how important rapid delivery times are to customers, and the costs of carrying the item in stock. However, the demand for an item may depend on whether it is normally available. This problem is similar to the problem of determining the proper level of safety stocks. In both cases the sales and profits forgone as a result of not having an item in stock must be evaluated.

Exhibit 14-2. Total Cost of Safety Stock Investment

Total cost = (1 − tax rate) × (expected stockout cost + holding cost) + cost of funds

Investment Cu	Expected stockout cost sN	Holding cost hCu	Cost of funds kCu	Total cost
$ 0	$2,000	$ 0	$ 0	$1,040
450	1,200	18	45	680
900	800	36	90	525
1,800	400	72	180	425
3,600	0	144	360	435

Assumptions

Investment Cu = cash outlay per unit C × number of units of safety stock u
Cash outlay per unit $C = \$18$
Holding cost hCu = holding cost rate h × investment Cu
Holding cost rate $h = 4\%$ per year
Cost of funds kCu = cost of capital k × investment Cu
Cost of capital $k = 10\%$ per year
Tax rate $\tau = 48\%$
Expected stockout cost sN = stockout cost per stockout s × number of stockouts per year N
Stockout cost per stockout $s = \$40$

Stockout estimates

Safety stock u, units	Number of stockouts per year N
0	50
25	30
50	20
100	10
200	0

A further consideration is the extent to which having a more complete inventory in terms of the number of items stocked increases sales of all items. Most customers purchase more than one item at a time. A manufacturer who stocks a complete line of products is likely to obtain more business on each item than one who stocks only the items in greatest demand.

The decision as to which items to stock is of particular importance to distribution firms such as retailers and wholesalers, since their business is based on the availability of goods to meet their customers' demands. Inventory decisions are therefore very much related to the marketing approach used by the firm.

For example, Levitz Furniture Corporation virtually revolutionized furniture retailing by its marketing strategies which included maintaining an unusually large variety of furniture in stock. As a result, inventory investment for Levitz was over 50 percent of total assets as compared with the industry average of 36 percent in 1974.

Although the financial manager's role in these decisions is usually secondary, financial considerations can be very important. For example, in 1975 top management of Sears, Roebuck and Company sent a directive to store managers to reduce their inventories by 5 percent. Individual store managers were permitted to decide just how this was to be accomplished. The decision to reduce inventories was made because Sears was having to borrow at high interest rates and management wished to reduce total borrowing.

Inflation and inventory speculation During periods of inflation when the prices of purchased items are rising rapidly, firms have an incentive to invest more heavily in inventory than is indicated by the minimum cost calculation. If management believes the price of an item will increase by 10 percent in the next month, substantially more of that item may be ordered than normal. **Inventory speculation** is the term used to describe this extra investment.

The financial manager must keep speculative investment in inventory within prudent limits, since it can be both expensive and risky if carried to extremes. During inflationary periods, interest rates are usually high and so the cost of capital is high. An unusually large inventory may require the firm to rent additional storage space as well as to incur all the normal holding costs. There is always the possibility that demand for the item will fall and the firm will be stuck with a large inventory for a long time. This possibility raises the problem of risk in inventory investment. The risks are not inconsequential, so let's look at them.

Risks in Inventory Investment

The main risk in inventory investment is that the market value of inventory may fall below what the firm paid for it, thereby causing inventory losses. The sources of market value risk depend on the type of inventory. Purchased inventory of manufactured goods is subject to losses due to changes in technology. Such changes may sharply reduce final prices of the goods when they are sold or may even make the goods unsalable. This risk is, of course, most acute in products embodying a high degree of technological sophistication, for example, electronic parts. Distributors of electronic calculators experienced this problem in the early 1970s as prices dropped over 50 percent in less than a year. In some cases the current retail price was less than the price charged by the manufacturer a few months earlier. Essentially, firms shouldn't have a lot of buggy whips in stock when buggies are becoming obsolete.

There are also substantial risks in inventories of goods dependent on current styles. The clothing industry is particularly susceptible to the risk of changing consumer tastes. A merchant with a large stock of bell-bottom pants is in trouble when straight legs become the fashion.

Agricultural commodities are a type of inventory subject to risks due to unpredictable changes in production and demand. A bumper crop of a commodity like corn or, better yet, cocoa, can send prices plummeting. Of course, there is also the potential for shortages in these commodities, which cause rapid price rises.

All inventories are exposed to losses due to spoilage, shrinkage, theft, or other risks of this sort. Insurance is available to cover many of these risks and, if purchased, is one of the costs of holding inventory. Also, poor inventory control and storage systems can "lose" inventory. That is, inventory may still exist in the storeroom, but if it cannot be found when desired by a customer, the firm doesn't profit from its investment.

The financial manager must be aware of the degree of risk involved in the firm's investment in inventories. The manager must take those risks into account in evaluating the appropriate level of inventory investment. This can be done either by including the relatively predictable losses as part of the holding costs or by applying a higher cost of capital to those items which are subject to greater risks.

MANAGING ACCOUNTS RECEIVABLE

Accounts receivable is the total of all credit extended by a firm to its customers; therefore this balance sheet account represents unpaid bills owed to the firm. From the viewpoint of the financial manager the dollar amount of accounts receivable can be divided into two parts. One part represents the cash outlays made by the firm in providing the goods that have been sold. The other part is the difference between the cash outlays and the prices of the goods. The cash outlay portion is the actual investment by the firm in accounts receivable; the remainder represents accounting entries. The nature of accounts receivable is illustrated by the following example.

Suppose a wholesaler of automobile parts buys mufflers from the manufacturer at a price of $20 each. The wholesaler has invested $20 in each muffler in inventory plus cash expenses associated with inventory investment (holding costs and order costs) of $1 per muffler on average. The cash outlay per muffler is $21. The firm sells ten mufflers to a garage for $26 each on credit. It costs the wholesaler $5 cash expenses to sell and deliver the ten mufflers. The cash outlay by the firm is now $215 for the ten mufflers, $200 initial cost plus $10 inventory expense plus $5 selling and delivery expense. The garage owes the wholesaler $260 for the ten mufflers. This is an account receivable. The cash investment (out-of-pocket costs) in this account is $215 and the remaining $45 represents accounting profits. What has happened is a transformation of real assets, mufflers owned by the wholesaler, into a financial asset, money owed by the garage to the wholesaler.

What if the garage never pays for the mufflers? The wholesaler will lose the $215 it has spent in acquiring, holding, and selling the goods, nothing more. The $215 therefore measures the investment made by the wholesaler in this account.

The basic decision to be made regarding accounts receivable is how much credit to extend to a given customer and on what terms. However, the financial manager sets policies that have a great deal to do with this decision, and it is these policies that we will examine. Let us begin with an analysis of credit extension to a single customer and then see how general credit policies affect this decision and therefore the total investment in accounts receivable.

The Credit Decision

Business firms extend credit to three groups of customers—other business firms, individual consumers, and governmental units. Some firms sell and extend credit only to other firms and to governmental units (for example, a defense contractor may extend credit to the government). This is particularly true of manufacturers. Other firms, primarily retailers, sell exclusively to individuals. A few firms sell to both types of customers. For example, automobile dealers will sell the same parts to individuals that they sell to service stations, although the prices to each type of customer are usually different. We will confine our analysis to firms selling either to other businesses or to individuals. Governmental units are similar enough to business firms to require no special treatment in an introductory discussion.

Consumer credit Businesses selling goods to individual consumers normally provide some sort of credit terms for purchases. The major exceptions are the supermarkets. However, most small merchants do not provide this credit directly themselves; they accept **credit cards.** Sales made with credit cards do not create accounts receivable for the merchant; the bank or whoever issued the card (American Express, Master Charge, Diners Club, etc.) pays the merchant when it is notified of the charge. The issuer of the credit card has the accounts receivable. Large merchants (department stores, Sears, etc.) usually extend credit directly to the consumer. Sales made on credit by these merchants do create accounts receivable for them. Automobile and appliance dealers who extend long-term consumer credit in the form of installment contracts frequently sell the contracts to a financial institution, such as a commercial bank, instead of holding them.

Consumer credit decisions and indeed all credit decisions are based primarily on the creditor's assessment of the customer's likelihood of payment. Setting a maximum on the amount of credit offered to a customer limits the exposure of the firm to the risk that he or she doesn't pay. In deciding to provide credit to a customer, the credit manager must evaluate the chances of nonpayment and estimate the benefits of extending credit. The benefits result from making sales which would otherwise be lost to competitors or would not be made because the customer cannot afford to pay cash for the goods. In addition, consumer credit extending beyond thirty days usually carries with it an interest charge.

Risk assessment is a quantitative analysis of the likelihood that an individual won't pay for goods purchased on credit and assists the credit manager in deciding whether credit should be extended to a particular customer. Consumers applying for credit supply information about themselves that the firm evaluates. The firm may also seek information about customers from a credit bureau. Credit bureaus gather information on the credit history of people and sell it to businesses extending credit. Obviously, people who have failed to pay their bills in the past are viewed as greater credit risks than those who have an unblemished credit record. The information supplied by the individual and the credit bureau is evaluated in terms of the firm's experience with customers having similar characteristics. For example, firms have found that people who own their own home are more likely to pay their bills than those who rent. On the basis of this evidence renters would be looked upon less favorably than home owners when they apply for credit. The types of information asked for may include employment history, income, home ownership, checking and saving accounts, other assets, outstanding debts, etc. The extent of the information asked for depends on the size of the typical credit purchases at the firm. If a large amount of credit is being extended, more information will be requested.

The end result of this risk assessment is the classification of a credit customer into one of a set of **risk classes.** Large firms may use computerized statistical methods. An example classification scheme is shown in Table 14-3.

The general credit policy of the firm will specify which classes of customers will be extended credit. Since the considerations of general credit policy are similar for both business customers and consumers, we will discuss them together after we look at the credit decision for business customers.

Business credit The majority of the sales by one business firm to another are made on **open account.** That is, the buyer is not required to pay for the

Table 14-3. Risk classification

Class	Average loss ratio, %
1	Negligible
2	0.5
3	1.0
4	4.0
5	10.0
6	25.0
7	50.0

goods immediately on receiving them and does not sign a formal debt contract. The buyer is asked to pay for the goods within a specified period, typically thirty days. The seller may also offer a discount or reduction in the cost of the goods if payment is made sooner. For example, the buyer might get 1 percent off the amount of the invoice if payment is made within ten days. The **credit terms** of the seller involve the specification of the type of account (open account or some other arrangement), the credit period (when payment is due), the size of the discount, and a discount period. A description of various credit terms is provided in Chapter 15 (see Table 15-1). In addition, the seller usually sets a limit on how much credit will be extended to a particular customer. Once the customer has reached the limit, no further sales on credit are made until some of the amount owed is paid off.

Generally, the basic credit terms of a company selling in a particular market are competitively determined in the market. The firms in a given line of business usually have very similar credit terms, and the credit terms of a firm will apply to all its customers. Credit terms are not normally varied from customer to customer. This is true of consumer credit as well. The decisions regarding a particular customer are whether or not to extend credit at all and what the maximum amount extended should be.

In making the decision to extend credit to a particular firm, the credit manager will seek information about its financial condition and past history. The primary source of information is credit agencies, such as Dun and Bradstreet, which provide credit ratings and credit reports on firms throughout the country. From this information the credit manager will attempt to determine the degree of risk involved in extending credit to the customer. In other words, the credit manager tries to estimate how likely it is that the firm will pay its bills. If the amount of credit involved is large, and if a cursory investigation suggests that the financial condition of the firm is weak, the credit manager may seek additional information by requesting financial statements from the firm. Techniques such as ratio analysis are often used to evaluate the financial condition of the firm. However, even if there is a significant chance of loss present, the credit manager must also consider the potential profits to be gained from selling to the customer. If the credit manager turns down the request for credit, the customer is likely to buy from someone else. A firm that has no bad debt losses is likely to be turning away many customers to whom it would be profitable to extend credit. Once a customer has been identified as being risky, the limits on credit become important. By restricting the amount of credit extended to a customer with financial problems, the potential loss is reduced.

The techniques developed to classify consumers as to credit risk are not easily applied to business firms. Assessing the risk of extending credit to a business firm is much more of an art than a science, and experienced credit managers tend to rely heavily on their assessment of the "moral character" of the firm's owners and managers as it relates to their tendency to pay their creditors. However, if the credit manager has not had past dealings with the people requesting credit, he or she must rely on financial data and on the firm's past record with respect to other creditors.

Credit Policy

Decisions regarding extension of credit to particular customers of the firm are based in part on general credit policy. If the firm has a policy of being fairly restrictive as to its credit terms and the customers to whom it will extend credit, it will have a lower investment in accounts receivable, lower bad debt losses, and very likely lower sales volume. Conversely, as the firm provides easier credit terms and sells on credit to poorer credit risks, its sales will rise but so too will its bad debt losses and level of accounts receivable.

Alternative credit policies can be evaluated by the net profit approach [Eq. (14.1)] outlined earlier in the chapter. The financial manager must estimate the cash revenues (collections of accounts receivable plus cash sales) the firm will obtain from each credit policy. Cash expenses and the amount of investment are also estimated for each credit policy. Given these estimates plus the cost of capital k and the firm's tax rate τ,

$$\text{Net profit} = (1 - \tau)(\text{cash revenues} - \text{cash expenses})$$
$$- k(\text{investment}) \qquad (14\text{-}12)$$

The credit policy that provides the highest net profit should be established. To see how an evaluation of net profit is done, let's look at an example.

Suppose the financial manager is considering the adoption of five different credit policies, A through E. To determine which of these policies should be pursued, we first need to know the impact on accounts receivable, revenues, and expenses. Exhibit 14-3 displays values for these variables. No accounts receivable are shown for policy A. Credit policy A is selling for cash only. Naturally there are no bad debt losses with this policy. Policy B provides credit for low-risk customers who will pay on time. There are no bad debt losses for policy B, but there are some accounts receivable equal to fifteen days of sales. Policy C involves selling on credit to more risky customers; and occasionally the firm will have bad debt losses. Also, these customers will take longer on average to pay for the goods sold to them on credit. Policies D and E involve selling to even more risky customers on longer credit terms. Of course, the advantage of providing credit is the increase in the sales (revenues) for the firm. In order to evaluate these alternative policies, we need to know the net revenues after taxes from the sales volume achieved. The aftertax revenues provided by each credit policy are shown in column 7 of Exhibit 14-3.

As we discussed in connection with inventory policy, a decision on the level of investment in an asset requires us to consider the amount of investment. Exhibit 14-4 shows the investment required for each credit policy. The key figures are in column 3—"Total investment"; however, these

Exhibit 14-3. The Impact of Alternative Credit Policies on Revenues and Expenses

Credit policy	Annual revenues (1)	Accounts receivable (2)	Acquisition cost of goods sold (3)	Bad debt losses (4)	Operating cost (5)	Net revenues before taxes (6)	Net revenues after taxes (7)
A	$ 60,000	$ 0	$ 42,000	$ 0	$12,000	$ 6,000	$ 3,120
B	120,000	5,000	84,000	0	21,000	15,000	7,800
C	150,000	12,500	105,000	300	25,000	19,700	10,244
D	170,000	21,000	119,000	1,300	28,500	21,200	11,024
E	180,000	30,000	126,000	2,500	30,000	21,500	11,180

Assumptions and definitions

Acquisition cost per unit sold = 70% of selling price

Net revenues = annual revenues − acquisition cost − operating cost − bad debt losses

Aftertax revenues = $(1 - \tau)$ net revenues

Tax rate $\tau = 48\%$

Operating costs = holding and order costs of inventory plus sales commissions, collection expenses, and other costs of accounts receivable

Exhibit 14-4. Investment for Alternative Credit Policies

Credit policy	Cash investment in accounts receivable (1)	Investment in inventory (2)	Total investment [(1) + (2)] (3)
A	$ 0	$ 7,000	$ 7,000
B	4,000	14,000	18,000
C	10,000	17,500	27,500
D	16,800	19,800	36,600
E	24,000	21,000	45,000

figures are simply the sum of the data in columns 1 and 2. Note first that the values for "Cash investment in accounts receivable," column 1, are not the same values as shown for accounts receivable in Exhibit 14-3. The figures in column 1 of Exhibit 14-4 are 80 percent of the corresponding figures for accounts receivable in Exhibit 14-3. The remaining 20 percent is accounting profit. As we discussed at the beginning of the section on accounts receivable, cash investment is less than the value of accounts receivable on the firm's financial statements. The 80 percent figure reflects acquisition costs plus costs in stocking and selling the goods.

Another important aspect of Exhibit 14-4 is the inclusion of inventory investment. Note that increasing sales are assumed to require additional inventory. We have assumed that the firm would maintain sixty days' worth of sales invested in inventory. We have also assumed that the costs of goods in inventory equals their acquisition cost. Two questions might occur to you. First, why are we including inventory in a credit policy analysis? Second, if it is proper to do it here, why didn't we include accounts receivable in the inventory example earlier in this chapter? Taking the second question first, we assumed that usage (sales) rates were constant in our numerical examples. Therefore, accounts receivable were unaffected by the inventory decisions examined. The reason for including inventory here is that, whenever there is a choice among alternative policies causing differences in the sales volume of the firm, the impact on the investment in all current assets of the firm must be considered. This is so regardless of the nature of the decisions being made—whether they involve new production methods, marketing strategies, personnel policies, or whatever. An exception to this would be firms that do not carry inventory, such as firms selling services. Unless the firm sells services for cash, an increase in sales will almost always require an increase in accounts receivable and inventory.[2] This added investment in the firm must be evaluated by the financial manager.

A general procedure for dealing with such problems is to determine the optimal inventory investment for each credit policy given the sales (usage rate) estimated for each policy and then, given the amount of inventory to be held, to proceed with the analysis as shown in this section. In other words, each inventory level shown in column 2 of Exhibit 14-4 can be viewed as having been determined by an analysis similar to that performed earlier. Since the amount of inventory investment differs for each credit policy, that investment must be included in the analysis.

The remaining factor in the equation for net profit [Eq. (14-12)] is the cost of capital k. Suppose that $k = 10$ percent; then net profit can be calculated as shown in Exhibit 14-5. We see that a maximum net profit of $7,494 is achieved with credit policy C. This leaves us with the question of how risky is investment in accounts receivable.

Risk in Accounts Receivable

Accounts receivable is generally considered a relatively low-risk asset. The basic risk is due to the possibility that the firm will not be able to col-

2. Even a service firm selling for cash might wish to increase its holdings of cash and securities if volume increases substantially. We will discuss this in more detail in the next section of this chapter.

Exhibit 14-5. Net Profit for Alternative Credit Policies

Credit policy	Net revenues after taxes[a] (1)	Total investment[b] (2)	Cost of funds (3)	Net profit (4)
A	$ 3,120	$ 7,000	$ 700	$2,420
B	7,800	18,000	1,800	6,000
C	10,244	27,500	2,750	7,494
D	11,024	36,600	3,660	7,364
E	11,180	45,000	4,500	6,680

Net profit = net revenues after taxes − cost of funds
Cost of funds = cost of capital k × total investment
Cost of capital $k = 10\%$

[a] From col. 7, Exhibit 14-3.
[b] From col. 3, Exhibit 14-4.

lect all that is owed to it by its customers. Under normal circumstances the total bad debt losses a firm will experience can be forecast with reasonable accuracy, especially if the firm sells to a large number of customers and does not change its credit policies. These "normal" losses can be considered purely a cost of extending credit. The real risk arises from the possibility that a significant number of the firm's customers may suddenly get into financial difficulties. For example, suppose an appliance dealer is located near a large industrial plant and 90 percent of its accounts receivable represent credit sales to the plant's employees. If, for some reason, the plant shuts down for an extended period of time, the dealer is likely to be unable to collect a large portion of the accounts receivable. There are companies which provide insurance against unusual losses (credit insurance), and this is one way to reduce the risk. In most cases, accounts receivable is not a particularly risky asset.

MANAGING LIQUID ASSETS AND CASH FLOW

The liquid assets of a firm are currency, demand deposits in commercial banks, and marketable securities. There are a number of reasons for firms to hold such assets, and we will discuss them in this section. In addition we will look at the flow of cash through the firm and discuss ways in which the cash flow can be managed efficiently. Let's begin by examining the liquid assets held by business firms.

The vast majority of payments and receipts of business firms involve checks drawn on demand deposits at commercial banks.[3] Most businesses pay their employees and suppliers with checks, and their customers pay them in the same way. Relatively few transactions involve the use of currency, and these are primarily retail sales. We will use the term "cash" to refer to both currency and demand deposits. Cash is one of the two types of liquid assets we will be discussing. The second type of liquid asset is marketable securities. There is a variety of such securities held by firms, including securities issued by the U.S. Treasury, commercial paper, certificates of deposit, and the tax-exempt securities issued by state and local governments. These are all money market securities which were discussed in Chapter 2.

Why Do Firms Hold Cash?

Business firms hold cash balances for basically the same reasons individuals do—to have funds available to meet checks drawn on their accounts.

3. In the future many of these transactions will probably be made electronically. Even now some firms and government agencies pay their employees by delivering a magnetic tape to a central processing facility which automatically transfers funds from the firm's demand account to the accounts of each employee. In some parts of the country, individuals can pay bills by telephoning into a bank's computer and instructing the computer to transfer funds from their accounts to the account of the business to which they owe money.

However, the cash balance needed depends not only on the withdrawals from the account but also on the deposits of checks received. If you know that every day you will be depositing $100 and that $100 of your checks will be withdrawn, you might think that the average balance could be zero. However, this isn't so. When you deposit a check, the bank will not let you withdraw funds until the check has been "cleared"—in other words, until the funds have been withdrawn from the account on which the check was drawn. Normally the funds will be available within three days. Therefore you would need to have three days' worth of deposits in your account in order to have funds available to pay your checks. In this example, your bank balance (total value of checks deposited less total withdrawals) would have to be $300 for this reason.

However, deposits and withdrawals are usually made at irregular intervals. One day you might deposit nothing and the next day $300. The checks you have written are likely to arrive at your bank at unpredictable times. Therefore you must keep higher average balances in order to ensure that funds will be available at all times.[4] As a consequence, cash balances must be maintained to permit the normal transactions of the business. This is sometimes referred to as the **transactions motive** for holding cash.

There are other reasons for holding cash balances that relate to the banking relationships of the business. Commercial banks have historically wanted firms to maintain demand deposits as a means of paying the bank for some of the services it provides instead of charging fees for them. Such services include not only the processing of the firm's checks, but also purchasing securities for the firm and providing credit information on new customers of the firm.

For most large firms the requirements of their banks are a major factor determining the average cash balances held. These firms have ready access to bank credit and can borrow money quickly if needed. Funds available in excess of normal cash requirements are usually invested in securities to provide a return. Aggressive financial managers try to keep cash balances to the barest minimum sufficient to meet transaction requirements.

Investment in Securities Firms invest in securities for two basic reasons—they are seeking control of another company by buying its common stock or they have excess funds that they wish to invest temporarily. The acquisition of other companies is discussed in Chapter 21; we will concentrate here on the concept

---

4. An alternative is to have an overdraft privilege. This is a service provided by the bank which automatically lends you the money to cover checks exceeding your available balance. Of course, interest is charged for this service.

of excess funds. The real question is, "Why does the firm ever have excess funds to invest?" There are a number of situations in which investing in securities is an appropriate action for financial managers.

Firms with seasonal sales patterns usually have periods of one or more months during which they have excess funds. This usually occurs in the months immediately after the peak sales period. At this time inventory and accounts receivable reach their low point of the year. Even though the firm may be borrowing heavily to finance seasonal buildups of inventories and accounts receivable, it will typically be able to pay off the debt and have funds available for investment at some times during the year. An example of a firm with this pattern is Snip Tool Company in Chapter 13. Firms in industries where sales vary substantially over the business cycle often have excess funds during recessions for reasons similar to those for seasonal firms. If management expects sales to increase as the economy comes out of the recession, it will maintain excess funds expecting to use them later to finance the additional inventories and accounts receivable needed to support expanding sales.

Some firms try to maintain a semipermanent "ready reserve" of liquid assets to ensure that funds will be available to meet unexpected needs for cash. This reason for holding excess funds is sometimes called the **precautionary motive.** The practice of maintaining precautionary balances is characteristic of conservative financial managers.[5] Most firms that can afford to do this have ready access to bank credit which serves as an alternative source of funds in emergencies and therefore makes precautionary balances somewhat unnecessary. An exception might be small firms operating in highly risky lines of business. For these firms a ready reserve could prove highly desirable.

Another reason for holding excess funds is to meet a large planned payment of cash in the near future. Firms will accumulate liquid assets in order to meet taxes, dividends, or payments on long-term debt. A similar situation arises when the firm has raised long-term capital to invest in a new plant. Such financing is often arranged in advance of the actual need for funds, and the proceeds from the sale of the firm's securities will be temporarily invested in other securities prior to paying for the plant.

In cases such as these, most financial managers will invest in money market securities, often planned so that the securities will mature just before the cash is needed. In the case of precautionary balances, the funds at maturity will be reinvested. The main advantage of money market securities is that they may be sold very quickly with little chance of loss due to changes in interest rates.

5. There is a motive for holding liquid assets called the **speculative motive** which is not so important for business firms. This motive refers to holding cash and short-term securities in order to speculate on a possible decline in interest rates. This would *not* be typical of a conservative financial manager.

There are other situations in which firms will accumulate excess funds and invest them over longer periods of time. These usually involve the long-run planned expansion of the firm and a desire on the part of the financial manager to finance anticipated needs with internally generated funds rather than issuing new debt or stock. Also, funds may be accumulated to retire an issue of long-term debt either prior to or at maturity. In such situations the funds may be invested in long-term debt securities or even common stock.

The decisions as to specific investments in securities depend greatly on conditions in the securities markets and the circumstances of the firm. The financial managers of large corporations have become very astute in their management of cash and securities. Let us now look at the process of managing the cash flow through the firm.

Managing Cash Flows

Almost everyone who has a checking account probably does some management of his or her cash flow. The purpose of cash flow management is to maximize funds available for investment and consumption. Efficient cash management also permits a given cash balance to support a higher volume of transactions. Business firms are looking for investable funds, while consumers are usually trying to obtain as high a volume of purchases as possible. In both cases the principles involved are the same—speed up the movement of cash into the bank account and slow down the movement out.

The individual's strategy for efficient cash flow management is relatively simple. Checks are deposited as soon as possible and bill payments are delayed as long as possible without incurring a finance charge. Credit cards and charge accounts are particularly useful in this respect since the time between purchase and payment can run as long as several months in some instances. Both business firms and consumers essentially attempt to do the same things—to minimize the time they are providing someone else with free credit and to maximize their own free credit.[6]

Businesses attempt to speed up their cash receipts by several different methods. They often offer cash discounts to customers who pay promptly. Firms try to reduce the time that elapses between the moment a check is mailed to the firm and the time the funds are available to the firm. One method of reducing the time involves establishing a Post Office box in an area where there are many customers. A local bank picks up the checks and deposits them in the firm's account with that bank. After the

---

6. Most of the consumers' "free credit" comes from banks and business firms. The free credit of business firms comes largely from other business firms. Since all are trying to do the best they can, it is no wonder that the income velocity (GNP/money supply) of money keeps increasing. The banks, by the way, are in the middle of this battle, and some bankers feel that they are getting the worst of it.

checks have cleared, the funds are available to the firm. This is called a "lock box" system. Reductions in time of two or three days are possible with such systems. If checks are being received at a rate of $100,000 per day, reduction of three days effectively frees $300,000 of cash for use by the firm. Perhaps the most important thing a firm can do is simply to make sure all checks received are deposited immediately. Large firms which may have accounts with many banks also need to be careful to maintain close watch over balances in each account so that excess cash does not build up. Any cash not needed in an account can be invested to earn interest.

Careful control of disbursements is the other aspect of efficient cash management. Small firms often delay making payments when due in order to wait until sufficient cash has come in to cover the payments. All firms seek to maintain close control over disbursements to avoid early payments whenever possible.

Efficient cash management is more difficult for large national firms which have many local facilities paying bills, a number of bank accounts, and customers all over the country. Firms with international operations have even greater problems. However, the sums of money involved are generally large enough to justify the use of specialists to keep close watch over cash flows. A one-day speedup in receipts or a one day slowdown in disbursements may not be terribly important to a firm with cash flows of $1,000 per day. For a firm with cash flows of $1 million per day, a one-day speedup means that $1 million in additional funds is available. At 6 percent interest, which is typical of many short-term investments, $1 million provides $60,000 per year, which will easily cover a full-time specialist whose job is to synchronize the firm's cash flows.

We have seen that current asset investment is an important problem for most firms. From our analysis of inventory, accounts receivable, and cash we know that the amount of investment is closely related to the firm's sales volume. The implication of this is that a firm investing in plant and equipment to increase sales volume must also plan for an increase in current asset investment. Indeed, increases in current assets must be included in the total investment when the decision to expand is being made. For example, a firm considering investing $1 million in a plant to manufacture snowshoes must also estimate the amount of inventory (raw materials, work-in-process, and finished goods) that will be needed to operate the plant efficiently. If the snowshoes are sold on credit, there will be investment in accounts receivable. Higher cash balances will have to be maintained at the firm's banks because of the increase in transactions that the firm will have. The total increase in current assets required might well

CURRENT ASSET INVESTMENT AND FIRM EXPANSION

be as great as the plant investment itself. In other words, instead of looking at a $1 million investment, the financial manager must consider the total investment to be $2 million: $1 million in plant and $1 million in current assets.

How is the financial manager to determine the amount of current assets needed? In principle each asset must be analyzed to determine the proper level of investment based on the sales volume forecast for the plant. In practice this is too time-consuming for the degree of accuracy possible. Instead, the manager will use approximations based on the forecasting techniques discussed in Chapter 13.

In addition to including current assets as part of initial investment, any anticipated changes in the level of investment over the life of the project must be included. Additions to current assets due to forecasted increases in sales volume reduce net cash flow in the period when the increase occurs. Reductions in current assets increase net cash flow. At the end of the investment period, current assets due to the project will fall to zero and the reduction in current asset investment is part of the salvage value of the total project.

SUMMARY

This chapter described the problems of determining the level of investment in current assets. Investment in current assets differs from fixed-assets investment because the amount may vary substantially over short periods of time and the investment is reversible. For these reasons net profit or total cost is used to evaluate alternative average levels of investment.

Decisions regarding manufacturing inventory are complicated by the nature of the manufacturing process, which varies from industry to industry. The general considerations regarding raw materials and finished goods inventories are, however, similar in many respects to those regarding the finished goods inventories of retailers and wholesalers. The factors influencing the decision to invest in inventory include costs of holding inventory, costs of ordering new stock, availability of quantity discounts, and the costs of stockouts. A safety stock of inventory is often carried to reduce the chances of stockouts. There are risks to carrying inventory due to the possibilities of variation in the market value of the goods held and possible deterioration, theft, or spoilage. In addition, the benefits from increased investment are uncertain. The minimum acceptable rate of return or cost of capital for inventory investment should reflect the risk as well as the basic time value of money.

The level of accounts receivable depends primarily on the sales volume of the firm and its credit policy. The basic decisions are whether or not to extend credit to a given customer and the maximum amount of credit to be provided. The general credit policy of the firm provides a basis for these decisions and affects the sales volume of the firm. Restrictive credit policies reduce bad debt losses and the amount of investment in accounts receivable relative to sales. However, restrictive policies also limit sales. An evaluation of alternative credit policies must consider the impact of additional sales volume on the investment in inventory as well as on accounts receivable.

The management of cash and marketable securities involves four considerations: (1) the minimum cash balance, (2) the amount of excess funds to be invested in marketable securities, (3) the particular securities to be purchased, and (4) efficient management of the firm's cash flow.

Any decision which affects sales volume also affects the level of investment in current assets. Inclusion of added investment requirements for current assets is particularly important in capital investment decisions.

QUESTIONS

1. What is a "reversible" investment and why is reversibility an important characteristic for analyzing current asset investments?

2. How do the concepts of "net profit" and "total cost" as used in this chapter differ from the normal accounting concepts of profit (net income) and cost?

3. How would the following developments affect the level of investment in inventory by a firm? Specify which types of inventory costs have changed (if any) and whether the costs have increased or decreased.
   a) Faster and cheaper transportation of goods.
   b) Using an existing computer to generate purchase orders.
   c) Expectations of greater future inflation.
   d) Changing from English measures (pounds, inches) to metric measures (kilograms, centimeters). Discuss both the short-run and the long-run impact.
   e) Increasing the number of models in a product line.
   f) An increase in the price per unit of purchased goods.

4. Would you expect the cost of capital for investment in an inventory of diamonds to be higher, lower, or the same as the cost of capital for investment in an inventory of diamond rings? Why?

5. In what sense does "safety stock" provide "safety" to a firm? Is there such a thing as being "too safe"?

6. There is potential conflict in inventory decisions between the views of the financial manager and the marketing manager. Why? Why would there be a possible conflict between the financial manager and the production manager regarding inventory?

7. What are the major costs and benefits in establishing a severe credit policy as compared with a more lenient credit policy?

8. In the past four years, the Z Company has not experienced a bad debt loss in its accounts receivable. Sales and profits have increased an average of 4 percent in this period. Evaluate the performance of the Z Company's credit manager.

9. How would you adjust the credit policy of your firm in the following situations? Be as specific as you can.
   a) You are trying to attract customers in a wider geographic market.
   b) Your customers are paying, on average, thirty days after payment is due.
   c) You are asked to manufacture a custom product for a small firm and you are unsure of its financial condition.

10. If accounts receivable are $200,000 as of the end of the year for the Abacus Company, is the firm's investment in accounts receivable $200,000? Why or why not?

11. Does the credit policy of a firm affect its cost of capital for investment in accounts receivable? In what ways?

12. The marketing manager of your firm has suggested installing an electronic communications network connecting all the firm's plants and offices around the country. As financial manager would you find such a network useful in managing the firm's cash position? What kinds of information would you want and how would you use it?

13. Suppose you are considering various alternative means of investing $10 million which will be needed in thirty days to pay federal income taxes. What alternatives would you consider? (A review of Chapter 2 may be helpful here.)

14. A representative of Big City National Bank is trying to obtain your firm's demand deposit account. As part of the bank's sales pitch, a "lock box" system is being heavily promoted. How interested would you be in this system if you were the financial manager of the following businesses:
   a) A nationwide chain of self-service laundromats
   b) An auto parts wholesaler selling primarily to service stations in the Kansas City metropolitan area
   c) A manufacturer of speaker cabinets made on custom order selling to hi-fi dealers on the West Coast
   d) A mail-order retail clothing business that provides its customers with fifteen days inspection of the merchandise before they have to pay

15. Within the past fifteen years or so retail merchants who provide charge accounts, gasoline companies with credit cards, and similar businesses have shifted from billing all customers at the end of each

month to "cycle billing." With cycle billing, customers are billed throughout the month. For example, customers whose last names begin with "A" may be billed on the first day of the month, those with last names beginning with "L" in the middle of the month, and those with last names beginning with "Z" at the end of the month. Any given customer is billed at the same time each month.

a) As a customer of a firm who has just switched over, would it matter to you? Would it make any difference if your personal income is received weekly rather than monthly when considering the impact of the change in billing?

b) Discuss the advantages and disadvantages of this system to the business firms. Consider the impact on accounts receivable, cash flows, and any costs involved.

16. "Beth, we have just received an offer from Ace Packing Company. They are willing to sell us 10,000 cases of candied kumquats at a price of $40 per case. At current prices of $50 per case, the savings amount to $100,000. I think we should take them up on it. I know that we normally sell only 1,000 cases per year, but we could use this as one of our 'Super Specials,' and I'm sure we can move the merchandise within a reasonable period of time. Can we do it? They want an answer within twenty-four hours. Otherwise they'll go to High Roller Stores, our biggest competitor. Let me know if you need any additional information."

This phone call from Fred Mayer, vice-president for marketing for Save Lots Discount Stores (SLDS), left Elizabeth Morgan, vice-president for finance, with a sticky problem. She knew that Fred was always on the look-out for good deals that could be used as promotional features and that the use of "Super Specials" was a major factor in the continued growth in sales and profits for the firm; but this offer sounded peculiar.

You are a senior financial analyst at SLDS under the direct supervision of Ms. Morgan. You have been assigned the task of analyzing the proposal. How would you go about this? What information would you need to know and where would you go to get it? Outline a general plan of attack on the problem including all relevant factors that must be considered.

PROJECTS

1. Interview the manager of a small local business and find out how current assets are managed. What kinds of decisions are made regarding inventory, accounts receivable, and liquid assets? Does the manager try to minimize cash balances by investing in securities or interest-bearing deposits? What constraints are placed on demand deposit bal-

ances by the firm's bank? (*Note:* This project could be done by teams rather than individuals.)

2. Suppose you are an assistant to the manager of a small business. The firm has $100,000 cash which will not be needed in its operations for six months. Using the *Wall Street Journal* or other sources, develop a recommendation to the manager concerning how the money should be invested. You may wish to review Chapter 2 for a discussion of various types of securities available. Include in your recommendation an estimate of the earnings to be achieved and discuss any risks your investment strategy entails.

PROBLEMS

1. Perform the indicated calculations using a cost of capital of 10 percent per year and an income tax rate of 50 percent:
   a) Net profit for a reversible investment of $2,000 providing $1,200 in additional annual cash revenues and $400 in additional annual cash expenses. [Ans.: $200]
   b) Total cost for a reversible investment of $1,500 with annual cash costs of $600. This is one of several alternative investments all of which provide the same level of annual revenues. [Ans.: $450]
   c) Calculate the net present value for the investment in **a** assuming that funds are withdrawn (investment is reversed) in five years time. Check your calculation by using two equivalent procedures.
   d) Calculate the present value of costs for the investment in **b** assuming that funds are withdrawn in ten years time. Check your calculation by using two equivalent procedures.

2. The manager of a garden products store is evaluating two alternative levels of investment in lawn fertilizer inventory, A or B. Relevant data for the two alternatives are shown below

	A	B
Average dollar investment	$1,000	$2,000
Monthly cash revenues	$600	$800
Monthly cash costs	$200	$390

The cost of capital for this investment is 12 percent per year or 1 percent per month. The income tax rate is 50 percent. In six months time inventories of this item will be reduced to zero at the end of the season. The manager expects to realize the amount invested at that time.
   a) Calculate the monthly net profit (as defined in this chapter) for the two alternatives. [Ans.: A = $190; B = $185]
   b) Calculate the net present value for the two alternatives. [Ans.: A = $1,101; B = $1,072]

c) Which alternative is best? Does it matter whether net profit or net present value is used to decide on the alternative?

3. A building supply store sells on average twenty-five pipe valves per month. Valves are currently ordered in lots of fifty at a time, and the cost per valve is $3.

a) What is the store's average investment in pipe valves assuming no safety stock is maintained? [Ans.: $75]

b) If it costs $5.00 to place an order of valves, what are the annual order costs? [Ans.: $30]

c) Suppose holding costs average $0.06 per dollar invested per year. What are the annual holding costs of valves? [Ans.: $4.50]

d) Given a cost of capital of 10 percent per year for inventory investment, what is the annual cost of funds invested in inventory? [Ans.: $7.50]

e) Given a tax rate of 50 percent, what is the total cost of this inventory policy excluding acquisition costs? [Ans.: $24.75]

4. Using the data of problem 3, calculate the total costs (excluding acquisition costs) for the following order quantities: 75 valves per order, 100 valves per order, and 150 valves per order.

a) Which order quantity provides minimum total costs? Assume that the price per valve is $3 regardless of the amount ordered.

b) Would inclusion of acquisition costs affect your decision in this case? Why or why not?

5. Suppose the valve supplier of problem 3 offers the following quantity discounts from the base price of $3 per valve.

Valves per order	0–99	100–199	200 or more
Discount from base price	0%	5%	10%

What inventory policy minimizes total cost? (Assume valve orders are in multiples of twenty-five.)

6. Northwest Fabricators manufactures extruded aluminum products. The company has a standard line of extrusions and does custom work. The sales manager of Northwest has been concerned about losing sales of the standard lines because of the low levels of inventory the firm carries. An analysis of losses due to stockouts carried out by a task force set up to investigate the problem suggests the following relationship between average minimum inventory levels and stockout losses:

Average safety stock investment	$100,000	$150,000	$200,000	$250,000
Annual stockout losses	$50,000	$20,000	$6,000	0

Holding costs for this type of inventory average 4 percent per year per dollar of inventory. The firm's tax rate is 50 percent, and management estimates the cost of capital applicable to this type of investment to be 8 percent.

As financial manager of Northwest Fabricators, what level of safety stock would you recommend?

7. A gasoline service station has a moderate volume of muffler replacement work. Current policy is not to stock mufflers but rather to have an attendant drive to a parts store and pick up mufflers when needed. The store manager estimates that the cost of this policy is $400 per year (before taxes). The parts supplier is willing to make free deliveries if the station orders at least twenty mufflers at a time. However, given the large number of different mufflers used in automobiles, the station manager has been unwilling to stock any mufflers because the investment and space required to carry all the various types of mufflers would be prohibitive given the number used each year. You have been hired as a station attendant and have noticed that three types of mufflers are called for much more frequently than the rest. Half the trips made are to pick up these three types. Therefore about half the annual cost of picking up mufflers would be eliminated if the three types were stocked and ordered in lots of twenty or more.

Space is available to stock up to twenty-five mufflers without any problems. Estimated costs of holding inventory are 5 percent per year, and the station manager feels that a 12 percent cost of capital is appropriate. The tax rate is 40 percent, and the cost of the three high-volume mufflers is $15 apiece. Since there are three types involved, a new order must be placed whenever one of the three is out of stock. The minimum stock when an order is placed is expected to average four mufflers.

Should the station manager order twenty mufflers at a time and therefore invest in an inventory of mufflers?

8. A distributor of industrial cleaning products has outstanding accounts receivable of $140,000. The out-of-pocket costs in acquiring, holding, and selling these products amount to 90 percent of the selling price. What is the actual dollar investment in accounts receivable for this firm? [Ans.: $126,000]

9. A wallpaper manufacturer has a line of designer wall coverings. The direct manufacturing cost of this product averages 30 percent of the selling price. Shipping, handling, and sales related expenses are 10 percent of the selling price. Dealers purchasing the wall coverings from the manufacturer are supposed to pay for all orders during a given month twelve days after the end of the month. However, many of the dealers are somewhat late. On average, accounts are paid sixty

days after a sale is made. The firm's sales of this product are currently $25,000 per month.

What is the firm's current dollar investment in accounts receivable?

10. Stivers Associates is a consulting firm specializing in office layout and design. Amos Stivers handles the firm's financial affairs and he also specializes in color coordination. The firm bills its clients at the end of an assignment on terms net 30; that is, the customer is supposed to pay within thirty days after the billing date. Lately Amos has been alarmed about a buildup in accounts receivable and the pressure placed on the firm's cash position caused by the resulting slowdown in collections. He is also concerned about the bad debt losses the firm has experienced. After analyzing the situation with some care, Amos was able to classify the firm's clients into two groups, normal risk and high risk. Data for the two classes of clients is shown below:

	Annual revenues	Annual operating costs	Annual bad debt losses	Current accounts receivable
Normal risk	$120,000	$ 60,000	$ 1,000	$10,000
High risk	60,000	40,000	10,000	15,000
Total	$180,000	$100,000	$11,000	$25,000

The marginal tax rate of the firm's partners is 50 percent, and they feel that a 15 percent cost of capital would be appropriate in assessing the desirability of extending credit to high-risk clients. The dollar investment in accounts receivable is difficult to evaluate because the major investment is in time spent by the partners on the client's problems; however, for purposes of analysis Amos decided to consider the foregone revenues from the investment of time as being part of the dollar outlay in the accounts receivable. The level of $15,000 in accounts receivable of high-risk clients is, therefore, estimated to reflect $12,000 in dollar investment.

Should Stivers Associates stop extending credit to high-risk clients, assuming that this business would be lost entirely if such a policy were implemented? Base your decision on the "net profit" from accepting high-risk clients. [Ans.: Net profit = $3,200]

11. The High Value Hardware Company operates a chain of retail hardware stores in the Midwest. The firm's financial manager, Tony Verazo, is investigating the impact of establishing a new credit policy for the firm. For many years High Value extended credit only to a select number of customers who were known personally by the managers of their stores. In an effort to increase sales and to compete more

effectively, management changed their policy two years ago to one of extending thirty days of credit to anyone who asked for it. This policy proved successful in increasing sales but also caused a tremendous increase in accounts receivable and bad debt losses. Tony thought that by being somewhat more selective in extending credit and by adding an interest charge to accounts more than thirty days overdue, most of the benefits of the wide-open policy might be retained while reducing costs. The following estimates were requested by Tony from the marketing staff and are based on an analysis of customer accounts (dollar figures are in thousands):

Credit policy	Annual sales	Cost of goods sold	Operating costs	Average inventory	Accounts receivable
Restrictive	$40,000	$24,000	$10,000	$6,000	$1,000
Selective	$50,000	$30,000	$12,500	$7,000	$6,000
Wide open	$55,000	$33,000	$13,500	$7,500	$8,000

(*Note:* Operating costs include bad debt losses.)

Tony estimated that the interest charge on accounts extending past thirty days under the selective policy would provide an income of $300,000 per year in addition to the sales revenues shown above for this policy. He was also aware that the actual dollar investment in accounts receivable would be somewhat less than the book figures shown, but he wasn't sure how this should be handled. He did know that the firm's accountants estimated that 20¢ out of every dollar of sales went to costs associated with handling, storing, and selling goods. This figure included, however, salaries of some store personnel that do not vary appreciably with sales volume. About 8¢ out of the 20¢ fell into this category.

Another thorny issue was the question of what cost of capital should apply. Senior management of High Value had differences of opinion on this topic. The chief executive officer leaned toward application of the company's average cost of capital (currently estimated to be 12 percent) to investments in inventory and accounts receivable on the grounds that such investments constituted the majority of the assets of the firm. The marketing manager thought this was too high for such relatively secure assets as accounts receivable and pointed out that the major increase in investment was in this asset. He recommended that a rate of 9 percent apply. Tony thought both positions had merit and in the case of the restrictive and selective policies a rate of 9 percent would indeed be appropriate. However, he thought the firm's average cost of capital, 12 percent, should be used to evaluate the wide-open policy, because the risks of this policy more closely approximated the overall risk of the firm.

Evaluate the three credit policies and develop a recommendation as to which one should be implemented. Use a tax rate of 50 percent.

12. The Olé Enchilada Company is franchiser of a national chain of fast food restaurants. The company sells a variety of supplies to its franchises, and its cash receipts average $600,000 per day. Based on an analysis of the payments received, Olé's management estimates that it takes seven days on average between the time a check is mailed to the firm and the time the money is actually available for use.

a) How much money is being tied up by the seven-day delay? [Ans.: $4,200,000]

b) Suppose that the delay could be reduced to five days. How much additional money would be available for other uses?

c) The company's bank has indicated that by introducing special handling of the checks and going to a lock box system the delay could be reduced from seven days to three days. In order to do this, however, the bank says that Olé must increase its deposits by $800,000; that is, the firm's average balance must increase by that amount. In addition the firm would incur a variety of additional costs amounting to $60,000 per year. The financial manager of Olé plans to invest the money freed by the new cash management system into marketable securities yielding 6 percent per year. Is the new system worth implementing?

the economic order quantity model

In Chapter 14 we showed how to find the order quantity that minimizes the total cost of inventory investment. The solution method was to calculate total cost [Eq. (14-9)] for different order quantities and find the minimum either numerically or by examining a graph. The total cost equation is

$$\text{Total cost} = (1 - \text{tax rate}) \times (\text{acquisition cost} + \text{order cost}$$
$$+ \text{holding cost}) + \text{cost of funds}$$
$$= (1 - \tau) \left(CS + \frac{fS}{Q} + \frac{hCQ}{2} \right) + \frac{kCQ}{2} \qquad (14\text{-}9)$$

Suppose that acquisition cost does not vary with order quantity in this equation. Acquisition cost is therefore constant, insofar as the decision regarding Q is concerned, and will not affect the decision. All variables except Q in Eq. (14-9) are assumed to be constants unaffected by the value of Q. Under these conditions, we can derive a formula for the value of Q that minimizes total cost, Q^*. We wish to minimize the total cost function

$$\text{Total cost} = \text{TC} = (1 - \tau) \left(CS + \frac{fS}{Q} + \frac{hCQ}{2} \right) + \frac{kCQ}{2}$$

To do this, calculate the derivative of the total cost function with respect to Q, the decision variable in this case, and solve for the value of Q that will make the derivative equal to zero (this value of Q is Q^*).

$$\frac{d(\text{TC})}{dQ} = (1 - \tau) \left(\frac{hC}{2} - \frac{fS}{Q^2} \right) + \frac{kC}{2}$$

$$(1 - \tau) \left(\frac{hC}{2} - \frac{fS}{(Q^*)^2} \right) + \frac{kC}{2} = 0$$

$$(Q^*)^2 \left(\frac{hC}{2} + \frac{kC}{2(1 - \tau)} \right) - fS = 0$$

Let $k' = \dfrac{k}{1 - \tau}$

$$(Q^*)^2 = \frac{2fS}{C(h + k')}$$

$$Q^* = \sqrt{\frac{2fS}{C(h + k')}} \qquad (14\text{-}13)$$

where $k' = k/(1 - \tau)$. The variable k' can be interpreted as a "before-tax cost of capital" and is used to simplify the formula.

The value of Q that minimizes total cost, Q^*, is often called the **economic order quantity,** and Eq. (14-13) is widely used as the basis for inventory management. Besides the convenience of having a simple way to calculate Q^*, the formula is also useful because it indicates how Q^* and therefore the average investment in inventory $CQ^*/2$ is affected by the variables in it. In particular we can see that as usage rates (sales rates) S increase, the economic order quantity Q^* and the average investment in inventory also increase. However, the increase in investment is not directly proportional to S, but rather proportional to $\sqrt{S}$. Suppose we rewrite Eq. (14.13) in terms of the average level of inventory investment I and rearrange terms

$$\begin{aligned} I &= \frac{CQ^*}{2} \\[2mm] &= \frac{C}{2}\sqrt{\frac{2fS}{C(h + k')}} \\[2mm] &= \left[\sqrt{\frac{fC}{2(h + k')}}\right]\sqrt{S} \qquad (14\text{-}14) \end{aligned}$$

The variables inside the brackets are all cost factors and usually don't change very much. The usage rate S is subject to change. From the formula it is clear that an increase in usage rate with no change in costs will increase average inventory investment in proportion to the square root of S which is less than S.

Electronic Banking

The future is now. After a decade of discussion the application of computers and electronic communication devices is starting to change the basic means by which individuals, governmental units, and business firms transfer money. There are advantages to everyone in the changes that are taking place, but there is also much controversy. What is happening, and why is so much fuss being made over it?

The controversy comes from the realization by the management of financial institutions around the country that electronic banking may be a determining factor in how the vast consumer financial market is divided up. Individual consumers hold over $800 billion in deposits and have over $200 billion in loans, excluding home mortgages. The firms that get there "fustest with the mostest" are likely to have the best chances to gain the lion's share of this market. The battle is pitting large commercial banks against small commercial banks, commercial banks against savings and loan associations and mutual savings banks, retail firms such as Sears, Roebuck and Penney's against financial institutions, and the credit card companies such as American Express against everyone. The hottest battlefields are presently the courts, the United States Congress, state legislatures, and the agencies that regulate financial institutions. However, the fight is also going on in the consumer marketplace itself as the parties involved begin to offer electronic banking services to the consumer.

ELECTRONIC BANKING SERVICES

Electronic banking services mean increased convenience for the customer. The primary ele-
ment is a plastic card with a magnetic strip on the back. A shove of the card into a machine permits the person who owns the card to withdraw cash from his or her bank account (checking or savings), transfer money from one account to the other, borrow money, and pay off a loan. In many places this can be done at any time during the day or night, seven days a week. The machine may be imbedded in the outside wall of a conventional bank office or found in a shopping center mall, an airline terminal, a supermarket, or an employee cafeteria. As the services expand nationally, a Californian visiting Washington, D.C., will be able to undertake many of the same sorts of transactions 3,000 miles away from home.

Other electronic banking services include automatic deposit of payroll, dividend, and social security payments. The money is directly deposited into the person's bank account with no action on the recipient's part. Retail purchases may be paid for by electronic transfers from the purchaser's account to the retailer's account or through a loan extended electronically. Some transactions may be made over the telephone from the person's own home.

The result for the consumer is a reduction in the costs (including time) of making a variety of financial transactions. Electronic banking makes it easier for people to obtain cash, make payments, and deposit money at any time of day and at many physical locations.

IMPACT ON FINANCIAL INSTITUTIONS

The most contentious aspects of electronic banking are the elimination of traditional barriers to competition among financial institutions and the increased competition from non-financial corporations.

One impact, therefore, is increased competition that may imply lower prices for financial services. In addition, electronic banking facilities are expensive to establish. These expenses plus lower prices would appear to imply lower profits for financial institutions. However, the cost per financial transaction is expected to drop dramatically as the volume of electronically processed transactions increases. It is also much cheaper to install an automatic teller ($40,000) than a new branch ($200,000). The result is that smaller accounts become more desirable (profitable). The net impact on profits is not clear at the present time. The potential for increased competition in the provision for financial services is quite clear, however.

Electronic banking should significantly affect a major barrier to competition for consumer accounts due to laws restricting depository financial institutions from establishing branches outside a limited geographic area. Banks headquartered in one state cannot build branches in other states and therefore have not been able to compete effectively in those other states for consumer accounts. In many states, especially in the South and Midwest, banks are limited to operating from a single office. These geographic limits on branching have not prevented banks around the country from competing for large corporate accounts, partly because corporations conduct much of their business by telephone, and partly because the loans and deposits of these customers are large enough to pay for the banks to send people to the corporation offices when personal contact is needed. Consumers and small businesses call on the banker. Therefore, those banks with nearby offices attract these smaller consumer and business customers more readily than banks with offices that are far away. Electronic banking reduces the need for small customers to come to the bank. Therefore, the geographic location of bank branches becomes less important in the customer's decision on where to bank.

Another barrier to competition is the restriction of checking accounts to commercial banks. Since other types of financial institutions have been restricted in their ability to offer checking accounts, commercial banks have had an advantage in competing for all types of customers. Electronic banking is breaking down this barrier by making it possible to transfer money out of savings accounts to pay bills and to obtain cash easily from savings accounts. Savings accounts, which are offered by many different financial institutions, are able to be used much like checking accounts with electronic banking. Therefore, the thrift institutions (savings and loan associations, mutual savings banks, and credit unions) are becoming more competitive in this area.

One of the biggest questions is the extent to which nonfinancial corporations will begin to compete directly with financial institutions. More people use Sears, Roebuck credit cards than BankAmericards and Master Charge cards combined. Sears already provides some financial services through its insurance subsidiary (Allstate). Major retailers such as Sears are currently converting to electronic cash registers to aid in managing their inventory. If retailers should start offering electronic financial services at the point of sale using their credit cards, financial institutions will face strong rivals in the market.

The existence of so much present and prospective competition means that many cost savings provided by electronic banking will be passed on, at least in part, to customers. Those firms that invest heavily in electronic banking may not reap extraordinary profits. However, those that wait too long before investing are apt to find themselves losing a substantial portion of the consumer market.

IMPLICATIONS FOR BUSINESS FIRMS

So far we have been discussing electronic banking as if its impact were confined to consumers and firms providing financial services. This is not strictly true, since there are some implications for business firms. Retailers are substantially reducing their losses from bad checks by utilizing check guarantee systems offered by many banks. When a customer writes a check to the retailer in payment for goods or for cash, the retailer can electronically verify that the check is good provided the customer has a card issued by the bank. The bank will guarantee all checks which have been verified; thus the retailer is not exposed to the possibility of losing money from accepting a bad check. The use of electronic means to pay bills will reduce the time needed for collections, thereby reducing accounts receivable and freeing cash for use elsewhere in the business.

Firms that pay their employees by direct deposit will gain reductions in the cost of processing payrolls. However, they will also have to have the money on deposit when payment is made and can no longer rely on some employees taking a few days to cash their payroll checks.

Overall, the major benefits of electronic banking will go to consumers and to the firms that offer the most effective electronic banking services. One thing is clear. Barring the imposition of stringent controls by the government, the market for consumer financial services will be in a state of flux for years to come.

short-term financing

Once the financial manager has planned investment in current assets and forecast funds required by the firm over the coming year, he or she must arrange for financing. The general principles of financing decisions were examined in Chapter 9. After deciding on the combination of debt and equity sources to be used, the financial manager must decide on the particular types of debt financing. Short-term borrowing is typically used to finance temporary investments in current assets. In this chapter we will discuss the principles used by the financial manager in deciding how much and what types of short-term financing to obtain.

Our discussion will be divided into three parts:

1. Some general principles that are useful in selecting methods of short-term financing will be examined. We will also consider decisions as to whether to use long-term or short-term financing. Here short term will mean one year or less.
2. The characteristics of major sources of short-term financing, such as bank loans, will be presented. We will evaluate the advantages and disadvantages of each source of credit and analyze the real cost of each credit source to the borrower.
3. Finally, the pledging of inventory and accounts receivable to lenders as security for short-term credit will be examined. We will describe the types of secured debt agreements used by businesses for short-term financing.

PRINCIPLES OF SHORT-TERM FINANCING

The Matching Principle

The matching principle, one of the oldest principles in finance, can be stated as follows:

Finance short-term needs with short-term sources, and finance long-term needs with long-term sources.

The idea expressed in this principle is to "match" the maturity of the source of funds to the length of time the funds are needed.

The underlying logic is that in the long run the firm will be exposed to less risk and lower financing costs if the principle is followed. If the firm finances long-term needs with short-term borrowing, it will have to refinance (reborrow) its short-term debts as they become due, thereby exposing the firm to added transaction costs (accounting and legal costs, fixed borrowing fees by lenders, etc.) and to the risk that new borrowing will be available only at higher interest rates. If the firm finances short-term needs with long-term sources, there will be times when there are excess funds which may have to be invested in low-yielding securities.

To see how the matching principle is applied, let us examine a graph of the total assets of the firm over time. For simplicity we will break the assets into only two types, current assets and fixed assets. Current assets include cash, marketable securities, accounts receivable, and inventory; fixed assets are long-term assets such as plant and equipment. In Figure 15-1 the fixed assets are shown increasing at a steady rate, as we are assuming a growing firm. Current assets are added to fixed assets to arrive at total assets. The matching principle states that the fixed assets of the firm should be financed with long-term sources (long-term debt plus equity); but what about current assets? Notice that in Figure 15-1 current assets have their ups and downs over time but they, too, are increasing on average. To see this more clearly, we can look at just the current assets over time in Figure 15-2. We have divided the current assets held by the firm into two types: temporary working capital and permanent working capital. Permanent working capital is the minimum investment in current assets which management has determined as being appropriate to support the current sales of the firm.

The point here is that the matching principle also calls for financing of permanent working capital by long-term sources. Only the temporary

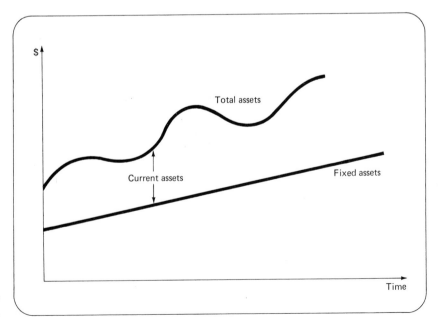

Figure 15-1. The firm's assets over time.

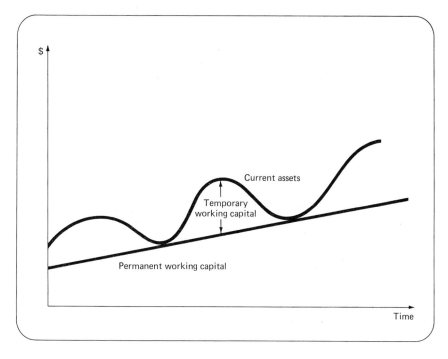

Figure 15-2. The firm's current assets over time.

working capital investment would be financed with short-term sources.[1] The matching principle is not always followed by financial managers; however, let us take the principle as a given rule of thumb and discuss some of the factors which affect the choice among the various sources of short-term financing.

In choosing a source of short-term financing, the financial manager will be concerned with the following five aspects of each financing arrangement.

1. *Cost:* Generally the financial manager will seek to minimize the cost of financing, which usually can be expressed as an annual interest rate. Therefore, the financing source with the lowest interest rate will be chosen. However, there are other factors which may be important in particular situations.

2. *Impact on credit rating:* Use of some sources may affect the firm's credit rating more than use of others. A poor credit rating limits the availability, and increases the cost, of additional financing.

---

1. This does not mean that current liabilities will be zero at the low point of the year. There are always some current liability accounts with nonzero values. Such accounts as taxes payable, salaries and wages payable, and current maturities of long-term debt are generally not zero.

3. *Reliability:* Some sources are more reliable than others in that funds are more likely to be available when they are needed.

4. *Restrictions:* Some creditors are more apt to impose restrictions on the firm than others. Restrictions might include dollar limits on dividends, management salaries, and capital expenditures.

5. *Flexibility:* Some sources are more flexible than others in that the firm can increase or decrease the amount of funds provided very easily.

All these factors must usually be considered before making the decision as to the sources of financing.

MAJOR SOURCES OF SHORT-TERM FINANCING

The three primary sources of short-term financing for business firms are, in descending order of importance, trade credit, loans from commercial banks, and commercial paper. Both trade credit and commercial paper are unsecured forms of credit, whereas banks make both secured and unsecured loans. A secured loan is one for which the borrower pledges specific assets as security for the loan. Automobile loans and home mortgages are secured consumer loans. Business firms usually pledge accounts receivable or inventory as security for short-term loans. In this section we will consider only unsecured types of credit from the three major sources; secured financing arrangements are covered later in the chapter.

Trade Credit

Trade credit for a business firm is equivalent to a charge account for a consumer. When a firm (the purchaser) buys goods from another firm (the supplier), it normally does not have to pay for those goods immediately. During the period of time before payment becomes due, the purchaser has a debt outstanding to the supplier. This debt is recorded on the purchaser's balance sheet as a liability, **accounts payable.** The corresponding account for the supplier is, of course, accounts receivable, which was discussed in Chapter 14. Normal business transactions therefore provide the firm with a source of short-term financing, trade credit, because of the time between delivery and payment. The amount of financing depends on the volume of purchases and when the purchases are paid for. For example, suppose the firm purchases $1,000 per day from its suppliers and pays thirty days after receiving the goods. The firm would have $30 \times \$1,000 = \$30,000$ of accounts payable or trade credit outstanding at all times.

An attractive feature of trade credit as a financing source is that it responds readily to an increase in the firm's purchases such as might occur during a seasonal buildup of inventory. If purchases double to $2,000 per day, accounts payable will double to $30 \times \$2,000 = \$60,000$, assuming the firm continues to pay on a thirty-day schedule.

The cost to the firm for utilizing this financing source depends on several factors, one of which is the credit terms granted by the firm's suppliers. Table 15-1 shows the different terms under which goods are sold. These terms vary considerably according to the industry involved. As we indicated in our discussion of accounts receivable, credit terms tend to be fairly similar within a given industry. However, some suppliers may provide more lenient terms than others. If the quality, price, and service provided by the more lenient firms are not inferior to those provided by others, purchasing from those suppliers *may* be to our advantage. Why isn't it *surely* to our advantage?

The answer depends on the nature of the credit terms offered and our alternatives. Suppose two suppliers of comparable products offer the following ordinary credit terms. Supplier A sells on terms 2/10, net 30, and supplier B sells on terms 2/10, net 60 (see Table 15-1). Since B offers better terms than A, you might think that it is clearly better to buy from B. However, the cash discounts offered by both are the same, 2 percent if the account is paid within ten days.

Suppose you are considering purchasing from B and waiting for sixty days before making payment. The cost of forgoing a cash discount (that is, of paying after the ten-day discount period) can be expressed as an annual interest rate as follows:

1. Dollar cost of forgoing discount = discount × price

$$\left\{ \begin{array}{c} \text{Dollars of financing received if} \\ \text{discount not taken} \end{array} \right\} = (100 - \text{discount}) \times \text{price}$$

$$\text{Rate per period} = \frac{\text{dollar cost}}{\text{dollars of financing}}$$

$$= \frac{\text{discount} \times \text{price}}{(100 - \text{discount}) \times \text{price}}$$

$$= \frac{\text{discount}}{(100 - \text{discount})}$$

2. Financing period = payment period − discount period

$$\text{Number of periods per year} = \frac{\text{days per year}}{\text{financing period}}$$

$$= \frac{365}{\text{payment period} - \text{discount period}}$$

Table 15-1. Terms of sale

Terms	Definition	Use
CBD	Cash before delivery: goods must be paid for before shipment is made.	High-risk customers
COD	Cash on delivery: goods are shipped to customer, who must pay the shipper before taking possession.	High-risk customers or those for whom credit information is lacking.
SDBL	Sight draft—bill of lading attached: when goods are shipped, a draft for the purchase price plus a bill of lading (shipping document) is sent to firm's bank for payment. Firm must pay for goods in order to obtain bill of lading needed to get goods from shipper.	Automobile manufacturers, meat packers, and fruit and vegetable canners are typical sellers. Sometimes used by others when large shipments are made.
Net cash (net 7 days; net 10 days; bill to bill)	Goods must be paid for in 7 or 10 days depending on industry. Bill to bill terms require payment on previous delivery when a new one is made.	Retail store purchases of tobacco, produce, fresh meat, and dairy products.
Ordinary terms (2/10, net 30; 2/10, net 60; 1/15, net 30; net 30, etc.)	Terms of 2/10, net 30 provide a discount of 2% if payment is made within 10 days of the invoice date; otherwise payment is due in 30 days.	Many lines of business. Most common trade credit terms.
Monthly billing (2/10, EOM, net 30; 2/10, prox., net 30; 8/10, EOM)	A single payment for all purchases made before the 25th of one month is made in the next month. A cash discount for payment within the first 10 days (2/10) may be quoted. EOM stands for "end of month"; "prox." is an abbreviation of *proximo,* Latin word meaning "next."	Apparel trades, lumber, books, and other lines of business where several orders may be placed during a given month by the purchasing firm.
Seasonal dating (net 30, January 1; net 30, October 1; 2/10, net 30, January 1)	Payment for all goods shipped prior to the indicated date (January 1) is due according to the rest of the terms (net 30; 2/10, net 30).	Businesses with distinct seasons, such as toys, Christmas cards, and school textbooks.

Table 15-1. (*Continued*)

Terms	Definition	Use
Consignment	Payment for goods is made after they are sold by purchasing firm. Title to the goods remains with original supplier until sale by purchasing firm.	May be used in any business but commonly for rack jobbers in supermarkets, magazines, and photographic supplies.

3. Annual interest rate = rate per period × number of periods per year

$$= \frac{discount}{100 - discount} \times \frac{365}{payment\ period - discount\ period} \quad (15\text{-}1)$$

In the example above the discount is 2 percent, the payment period is sixty days, and the discount period is ten days. Therefore the annual interest rate is

$$Annual\ interest\ rate = \frac{2}{100 - 2} \times \frac{365}{60 - 10}$$

$$= 0.0204 \times 7.3$$

$$= 0.1489\ or\ approximately\ 15\%$$

The reasoning behind this formula is that if you do not pay within ten days, you must pay 100 percent of the invoice price of the goods. If you do pay within ten days, you will only pay 98 percent (100 − 2) of the invoice price. The first ten days (discount period) do not cost you anything. The amount of financing you are really getting after ten days is therefore 98 percent of the invoice price, but you are incurring a dollar cost of 2 percent of the price for the privilege of delaying payment. The ratio 2/(100 − 2) expresses the basic interest cost of forgoing the discount for the period involved. If you pay sixty days (payment period) after receiving the goods, you have really gotten only an additional fifty days (payment period − discount period) of credit. You are therefore paying 0.0204 or 2.04 percent for fifty days of credit. At an annual rate this amounts to 365/50 × 0.0204 = 15 percent per year.

If you were to buy from supplier A and pay thirty days later, it would cost you 37 percent [2/(100 − 2) × 365/(30 − 10) = 0.37]. By this measure B is still a better deal.[2] However, do you really want to pay 15 per-

2. If payment to A were delayed for sixty days, the interest cost would be the same as for B. However, now the account is overdue and this may cause problems in the future as discussed below.

cent for short-term financing from supplier B? If you have cash available or can borrow from the bank at 8 percent, you would probably rather take the cash discount no matter which supplier you buy from. Therefore it might not make any difference to you, since both suppliers offer the same discount. If A provided better service, you might prefer A in this case.

Using Eq. (15-1) to compute the annual interest rate enables the financial manager to determine the cost of forgoing cash discounts. This cost is the basic interest cost of trade credit financing. There are other factors which are also important in assessing the desirability and possibilities of using this source of short-term financing.

The dollar volume of a firm's purchases determines the amount of trade credit financing available to it. This type of financing arises only from the firm's not paying immediately for its purchases. As such it is flexible and very convenient, but rather limited in amount. Trade credit does not provide a direct source of cash to pay other bills. Purchases provide goods, not cash. Moreover, a firm that persistently does not pay its bills when due is apt to develop a poor credit rating. Suppliers may become reluctant to provide credit, requiring the firm to purchase on COD or even CBD terms (see Table 15-1). This can present problems for the firm in several ways.

First, the firm may not be able to find alternative sources of credit (for example, a bank loan). In this case the amount of inventory which the firm can carry may be severely limited, and therefore its sales and profits will fall. Second, the loss of trade credit imposes a cost on the firm that is not inconsequential. Suppose that the Tight Company is purchasing on terms of net 30 (no cash discount) and is delaying payment for sixty days. If purchases are $1,000 per day, the firm would have $60,000 of accounts payable. If Tight paid within thirty days, it would have accounts payable of $30,000. However, delaying payment to sixty days gives Tight a poor credit rating, and suppliers may start requiring the firm to pay cash for goods ordered. Its accounts payable would then shrink to zero. Suppose Tight can borrow from the bank at a rate of 7 percent. If the firm pays its suppliers on time (within thirty days), it will have $30,000 of free credit from suppliers and $30,000 of bank credit at 7 percent. If instead, Tight delays payment to sixty days, it may be required to borrow the entire $60,000 at 7 percent. By paying on time, the firm would be paying 7 percent on $30,000 and 0 percent on $30,000 for an average rate of $3\frac{1}{2}$ percent on its short-term financing of $60,000. On the other hand, by delaying payment, Tight would end up paying 7 percent on $60,000. The interest cost of delaying payment is twice the cost of paying on time, and the firm acquires a bad credit reputation in addition.

Moreover, COD terms impose costs of their own on the firm. Fees are charged by the shipper to collect payment, and cash discounts are not offered to COD customers. Of course, if alternative sources of credit are very expensive and if suppliers are relatively forgiving, it may be desirable to "stretch the payables" (as paying late is called). Occasionally delaying payment or paying only a few days later can be done without disturbing suppliers. However, this practice can be expensive for the firm if carried to extremes.

Bank Loans

The second major source of short-term financing for business firms is loans from commercial banks. Short-term commercial bank loans are generally made in the form of a **note**—a written and signed statement in which the borrower agrees to repay the loan when it is due and to pay interest. Notes may be payable on demand by the bank (demand notes), or payable in thirty days, ninety days, or one year (thirty-day notes, ninety-day notes, etc.). This is in contrast with trade credit, where the only evidence the supplier has of money owed is the purchase request and the invoice. In this section we will discuss some general characteristics of unsecured bank loans. Secured loans are described in more detail in the next section.

Seasonal loans Seasonal loans have traditionally been the basic type of credit provided by banks to business firms. Such loans are called **self-liquidating** as they are used to finance temporary increases in inventory and accounts receivable, which are soon converted into cash to repay the loan. For example, textbook publishers have a well-defined pattern of seasonal borrowings. Their borrowings begin in February, as inventory accumulates and books are shipped out to the schools and bookstores, and reach their peak in September/October, at which time payments start pouring in. The majority of seasonal loans are unsecured, although in recent years an increasing number of them have involved collateral. A typical seasonal loan is based on a line of credit previously requested by the firm and approved by the bank.

A **line of credit** is an informal agreement by the bank to lend up to a stated maximum amount to the firm. The bank does not have a legal commitment to supply the funds when the firm requests them, but banks tend to feel a moral obligation to do so. The procedure works as follows for a firm which has been a regular customer of the bank. At the low point of the season, the financial manager estimates funds required for the coming year and then asks the bank for a line of credit equal to the maximum expected need for funds. Let's assume it is $100,000. Usually the firm will provide the bank with its most current financial statements and may include forecasted financial statements to support its request. If everything looks reasonable to the bank, one of its officers will write a letter to the firm indicating the amount of the line, the interest rate, and usually a statement that the firm should be "out of the bank" (not borrowing) for at least one or two months during the year. This latter provision is intended to ensure that the loan is really a short-term seasonal loan and does not involve permanent financing. The firm will then borrow money as it needs it in the form of thirty- or ninety-day notes, where the total outstanding cannot exceed the credit line.[3]

There is another type of credit arrangement, similar to a line of credit, called **revolving credit.** In this case, the bank makes a legal commitment to extend credit up to the maximum. Revolving credit agreements usually involve both seasonal and longer-term financing and extend over several years. The bank may require a fee based on the unused portion of the credit. For example, if the maximum is $500,000 and the firm is currently borrowing $300,000, a fee such as 0.5 percent per year might be charged on the $200,000 not being used in addition to the interest on the $300,000 borrowed. Since revolving credit agreements are most often longer term in nature, they will be discussed again in Chapter 16.

Bankers consider seasonal lines of credit to be one of the most desirable types of loans for them to make. The interest rates are often lower on this type of loan than on any other that might be requested by a given firm. However, banks usually require that a firm borrowing under a line of credit maintain a minimum average demand deposit with the bank. This amount is called a **compensating balance** and is expressed as a percentage of the loan. For example, a compensating-balance requirement of 15 percent means that if the firm is borrowing $100,000, its minimum average checking account at the bank must be $15,000. In addition, there may be a compensating-balance requirement on the unused portion of the credit line. This is invariably a lower percentage than that for the borrowed portion. For example, if the credit line of this borrower were $150,000, then the compensating balance on the unused portion might be 8 percent. When the firm is borrowing $100,000, $50,000 of the credit is unused and an additional $4,000 (0.08 × $50,000) balance in the firm's bank account would have to be maintained. The total compensating balance would therefore be $15,000 (15 percent of $100,000) on the borrowed portion and $4,000 (8 percent of $50,000) on the unused portion for a total of $19,000.

What is the impact of compensating-balance requirements on the cost of the loans? The answer depends on what the average balances of the firm would normally be. If the firm would normally maintain $10,000 average balances, in order to have $19,000 in its account an additional $9,000 must be borrowed merely to meet the requirement. Suppose the interest rate on the $100,000 borrowed is 7 percent. The firm really only

---

3. In Europe such lines are often executed by the firm's simply writing checks on its account. If there are insufficient funds in the account to cover the checks, the bank will honor the overdraft and create a loan. This arrangement is more flexible since the firm isn't confined to borrowing money over an entire thirty-day period if it only needs the funds for fifteen days. We may see this type of loan available to business firms in the United States in the next few years. Some banks already offer overdraft loans to customers.

has use of $91,000 since $9,000 of the total borrowed must be kept in the bank to meet the compensating-balance requirement. The firm would be paying $7,000 (0.07 × $100,000) per year to get $91,000, and therefore the effective rate of interest would be $7,000/$91,000 = 7.7 percent. On the other hand, if the firm were planning to keep $20,000 in its account for transaction purposes, the required compensating balance of $19,000 would not affect the cost of the loan.

Interim financing   Short-term bank loans are often used for the initial financing of construction by contractors or of plant and equipment investment by business firms where the ultimate financing will be long term in nature. This use of short-term loans is called **interim financing** (bridge financing), as the loans are intended to cover the funds needs in the interim before the long-term money is made available (bridge the gap between need and availability of long-term financing). Such loans are found most frequently when money is being spent over several months in the construction of apartment houses, shopping centers, or industrial plants. Real estate developers may obtain a commitment from a long-term lender such as an insurance company to provide funds when a project is completed and the bank supplies funds during the period of construction. Manufacturers may use this type of loan prior to issuing long-term securities to finance a new plant. The alternative procedure for these firms would be to issue the securities in advance of their need for funds and invest the proceeds in marketable securities.

   A rather unusual example of interim financing was provided by Control Data Corporation (CDC) during the 1960s. As CDC's need for funds was increasing rapidly over time, the firm was frequently issuing long-term securities. However, CDC would first utilize its bank credit lines until the maximum credit allowed by its banks was reached. Then CDC would issue long-term debt or equity securities and pay off the banks. The line of credit would once again be available to borrow against as additional financing became necessary.

Interest rates on bank loans   The interest rates on business loans are determined through personal negotiations between the banker and the borrower. Generally all loan rates are scaled upward from the bank's **prime rate,** the lowest rate of interest on short-term loans charged to businesses with the highest credit rating. Figure 15-3 shows the prime rate compared with the interest rate on commercial paper for the past few years.

   The prime rate moves in jumps although changes have become much more frequent since 1970. The prime rate at large banks throughout the country was $4\frac{1}{2}$ percent from August 1960 to December 1965. In 1975 it changed twenty-one times and ranged from 7.0 to 10.5 percent. Some of the large banks since 1971 have begun to set their prime rates using a for-

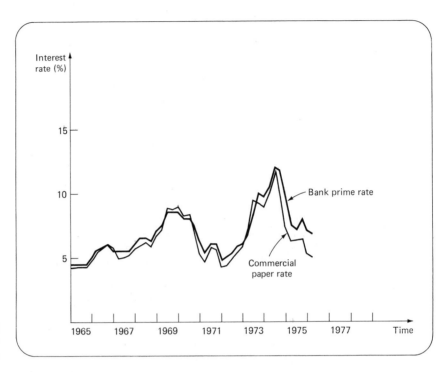

Figure 15-3. Bank prime rates and commercial paper rates.

mula based on the rates prevalent on short-term marketable securities, especially commercial paper. Generally, the riskier the borrower, the higher is the interest rate on the loan. However, bankers have traditionally been unwilling to make loans with high risks. Instead they have tended to refuse to make loans to high-risk borrowers, forcing them to find other sources of credit.

There are two different ways by which the interest on a loan may be paid. The true rate depends on the method used. **Ordinary interest** is paid at the maturity of the note. If you borrow $10,000 at 8 percent per year and repay the loan with interest at the end of one year, you will pay $800 in interest at that time. The true interest rate is 8 percent. However, interest may also be paid (as determined by the bank) by **discounting** the note. This procedure involves deducting the interest from the face value of the note initially. For example, suppose a firm borrows $10,000 on a discount basis for one year at a stated rate of 8 percent per year. The firm would receive only $10,000 − $800 = $9,200, the loan amount less the $800 interest. At the end of the year, the firm would pay $10,000. The true interest rate here is determined by dividing the interest by the amount actually received; that is, the rate would be $800/$9,200 = 8.7 percent. If the loan is discounted, the true interest rate is therefore higher than the stated rate.

Commercial paper is a type of short-term marketable security sold by business firms to investors—usually other firms, small banks, and other financial institutions. It is an unsecured debt of the firm issuing the paper and usually has a maturity of 270 days or less to avoid the registration requirements of the Securities and Exchange Commission (see Chapter 16). Most commercial paper is issued by financial institutions (finance companies and bank holding companies); however, large nonfinancial businesses are also important users of this method of short-term financing. Just prior to the Penn Central bankruptcy in 1970, medium-sized corporations had also begun to issue commercial paper in significant quantities. One of the problems of Penn Central was that it had $80 million in commercial paper coming due which it could not repay or refinance. Only three weeks prior to the company's filing for bankruptcy its commercial paper had been considered to be of very low risk. After the Penn Central defaulted on its commercial paper, investors became very cautious and have been reluctant to purchase any commercial paper not issued by companies of the highest financial reputation. The market has recovered somewhat, but only those firms with excellent credit ratings and which need $10 million or more can easily find dealers to sell the paper for them.

A few large finance companies sell their paper directly to investors using their own salespeople who call on potential buyers. However, most issues of commercial paper are marketed through dealers who do the actual selling to investors. The main advantage of commercial paper over short-term bank loans is the cost. The interest rate for "prime"-rated (low-risk) issues of commercial paper is normally lower than the prime rate charged by commercial banks.[4] Moreover, there are no compensating-balance requirements. Most issuers find it desirable (or even necessary) to have lines of credit with commercial banks to backstop their issues of commercial paper. This is to provide protection to the firm in the event that it has financial problems when it has to repay commercial paper that is coming due. The commercial paper market is highly impersonal, and investors are understandably reluctant to purchase the issues of shaky firms. Commercial banks, however, are generally more willing to stand by a customer who gets into difficulty and not require payment when the loan is due. This is one of the major advantages of bank loans as compared with commercial paper.

Commercial Paper

Firms whose credit ratings are not sufficiently high to qualify them for unsecured loans are often required to pledge a portion of their assets to the lender as security for a loan. The pledged assets are called **collat-**

SECURED BORROWING

4. An exception occurred during 1973 when banks were under political pressure to keep bank interest rates from rising too rapidly in the face of strong credit demand.

eral for the loan. The advantage to the lender is that if the firm is liquidated, the lender has first claim against the assets pledged as security. This means that the lender is provided additional protection against loss (in addition to a general claim against the firm's assets) if the firm gets into trouble. We will discuss the problems associated with financial distress and bankruptcy in Chapter 23; however, it should be clear that the lender is usually the party that requires security. Since there are costs involved in establishing and maintaining the security, it is rare that a firm which could borrow on an unsecured basis would elect to pledge assets to secure the loan.

There are several sources for secured short-term loans, with commercial banks, finance companies, and factors being the most important. The most common business assets pledged as security are accounts receivable and inventory. We will look at the use of these two assets separately as financing arrangements differ more by the asset pledged than by the particular lender providing the money.

Accounts Receivable as Collateral

Accounts receivable represent money owed to a business by the individuals or firms to which it has extended credit. Ordinarily, as we discussed in Chapter 14, accounts receivable represent a fairly safe asset for a firm to hold. They usually serve as excellent collateral for loans for the same reasons. In order for a lender whose loan is fully secured by accounts receivable to take a loss, not only must the firm fail but also the money owed to the firm must be uncollectible. From the lender's point of view, however, this does not mean that there is little or no risk in loans secured by accounts receivable. For one thing, the goods sold by the firm may be returned by the purchaser for various reasons, perhaps because they are defective. This would reduce the amount that could be collected. Also, there is the possibility that the firm may falsify records to show nonexistent accounts, as occurred in the Equity Funding scandal (see page 328). For these and other reasons lenders are not likely to loan the full amount of accounts receivable pledged when collateral is deemed necessary.

There are two common approaches to using accounts receivable as collateral. The simpler approach, which is less costly but also involves some risk for the lender, is to lend money using all the firm's accounts receivable as collateral. This is called a **general lien** on accounts receivable. The lender may be willing, for example, to loan up to 75 percent of outstanding accounts receivable as part of a secured credit line. The firm is obligated to tell the lender on a regular basis the amount of accounts receivable outstanding. The firm can borrow, as with any credit line, up to the agreed maximum amount.

Another approach is for the borrower to present invoices to the lender as collateral in sufficient amount to cover the amount of the loan; however, the lender may reject some of the accounts as being too risky. In other words, lenders can select the accounts on which they are willing to base loans. In such cases, since lenders have some control over the quality of the collateral, they will be willing to loan on a higher percentage of the face value, sometimes 90 percent or more.

As we said, the cost of such arrangements is usually high. The borrower has the costs and problems associated with presenting accounts to the lender, and the lender has the costs involved in keeping track of the accounts pledged. For this reason lenders charge an additional fee to cover costs for secured loans. Finance companies make such loans and will usually charge higher rates than a bank since they are frequently lending to firms which cannot qualify for bank credit even on a secured basis.

Factoring Instead of pledging accounts receivable for a loan, some firms sell their accounts receivable to a **factor.** The sale of accounts receivable is called **factoring.** Factors may be specialized financial institutions or even bank subsidiaries. Historically, factoring has been most common in the textile industry although other types of firms also utilize factors. The typical factoring arrangement is more than just a way to raise money; it usually includes services. The factor may provide credit analysis of the customers and collection of payments due, thereby relieving the firm of most if not all of the expense of maintaining a credit department. The factor may also provide temporary unsecured financing to the firm in addition to the funds furnished by sale of the accounts receivable. While factoring is generally considered an expensive method of financing, these additional advantages may make it the preferred method of short-term financing.

Credit cards The widespread use of bank credit cards has virtually revolutionized the financing of accounts receivable at the retail level. Major retailers have for many years provided charge accounts for their customers. With the introduction of bank credit cards, smaller retailers can provide equivalent services to customers holding such cards. From the customer's point of view, acceptance of his or her card by a retailer is roughly equivalent to the extension of credit by the retailer. The retailer is paid immediately by the bank upon submission of the credit invoice; thus the retailer has no investment in accounts receivable.

For this service the retailer pays the bank a percentage (for example 3 percent) of the invoiced amount. The arrangement has many of the same characteristics as a complete factoring agreement. The bank does all the credit analysis on the customer and provides immediate funds just as a factor does. The two major differences between a credit card agreement and factoring are, first, that credit card customers are consumers whereas the customers of a firm factoring its accounts receivable are other businesses and, second, that a credit card customer does not usually perceive the retailer as extending credit whereas the customer of the factoring firm does. This loss of customer identification with the retailer (the customer does not have a charge account at the particular store) is one of the reasons that many large retailers have been reluctant to abandon use of their own charge account systems.

Inventory as Collateral

Many types of inventory are easily sold and serve as fairly good security for short-term loans, whereas other types of inventory are valueless as collateral from a lender's point of view. The major consideration in the suitability of inventory as a means of securing a loan is the marketability of the inventory. Work-in-process inventories (goods still in the manufacturing process) are almost never considered suitable, since such partially completed products are difficult to sell. Many raw materials such as grain, primary metals, and industrial chemicals are good collateral since a ready market exists for them. Manufacturer's finished goods inventories and retail inventories may or may not be good collateral depending on the nature of the goods. New cars, appliances, paper, and lumber are usable as collateral. Women's clothing, perishable goods, and specialized equipment are not very usable. If an inventory is suitable collateral, the lender will advance some percentage of the total value. The more stable is the market value of the inventory, the higher the percentage will be. For example, commodities such as cocoa, which are subject to wide price variations, would have a lower percentage than wheat, which generally does not vary as much in price.

There are several ways in which a lender can gain a secured interest in inventory. Since each of the methods have somewhat different implications for the cost and flexibility of the financing arrangement, we will consider them separately.

General lien Just as was true of accounts receivable, the lender can obtain a lien against all or part of the firm's inventory, whatever the specific items may be. This type of arrangement is very easy to set up, but it doesn't provide much security since there is no telling what the inventory will be like in the event of the firm's liquidation. Since the lender cannot maintain good control over the quality of the collateral, the amount loaned as a percentage of the inventory's value is likely to be small, unless collateral is not a significant element in the credit decision of the lender. The interest rate may also be somewhat higher for this type of inventory loan.

Floor planning   Floor planning is a type of security arrangement often used in financing automobile dealers, farm and industrial equipment dealers, and sellers of consumer durable goods. Under this type of agreement the goods are specifically identified by the serial numbers of the items in stock. When an item is sold, the proceeds are supposed to be given to the lender in repayment of the loan against that item. As new inventory is purchased, the borrower signs a form describing the items purchased and specifying the terms of the agreement. The lender then pays the supplier for the goods. Periodically a representative of the lender checks out the current inventory of the dealer to make sure that all items covered by the floor plan are still in stock.

Floor plan agreements are fairly inexpensive to administer and provide all the flexibility most borrowers require. The security from the lenders' point of view is good provided that the merchandise has not been sold without the lender's being notified. Unfortunately this happens often enough to mean that lenders cannot consider such plans totally secure.

The lender may be a bank, a finance company, or even the manufacturer of the product. Manufacturers engaging in this type of arrangement usually do so in order to encourage their dealers to carry a complete line of goods to boost sales. When such financing is available from the manufacturer, it often carries lower interest rates than the dealer would be able to get from a normal lender.

Warehousing arrangements   Under warehousing arrangements a third party controls the borrower's access to the goods held as security. Since this party must be paid for its services, this is a relatively expensive procedure. There are two basic types—**field warehouses** and **public warehouses.** In field warehousing arrangements, the warehousing company establishes an area on the borrower's premises as a field warehouse. The company is supposed to maintain strict control over the inventory so that the lender should be able to find out at all times exactly what inventory is there. The borrower has ready access to the goods since they are stored on the borrower's property; however, they must be accounted for continuously. Even with the degree of control afforded by this type of arrangement there have been cases of fraud. The most spectacular case was the Allied Salad Oil scandal of 1963, which caused over $100 million of losses to the lenders involved. Money was lent on salad oil supposedly stored in a field warehouse (large tanks). The tanks turned out to contain water with a little oil floating on top.

Even tighter control over the inventory used as security is provided by public warehouses. In this case the inventory is held in a physical location apart from the borrower's place of business and under control of the warehousing company. The major disadvantage of this type of security arrangement is the cost to the borrower of obtaining the goods for use or for sale. Goods may be moved out of the warehouse only with the consent of the lender. Of course the warehousing company must also be paid for its services. This is the most expensive form of security arrangement.

SUMMARY   The matching principle is often used to govern decisions as to the amount of short-term financing used by a firm. The matching principle states that the maturity of the source of funds is matched to the length of time the funds will be needed. Short-term needs for funds should be financed with short-term sources. Short-term loans are used to finance the temporary working capital investment of a firm with seasonal sales.

The factors that affect the types of short-term financing chosen are interest cost, impact on credit rating, reliability, restrictions, and flexibility. The credit rating of the firm affects the availability of financing and the terms of financing.

Trade credit (accounts payable) is a very important source of credit to small firms and is used to some extent by all firms. Credit terms vary considerably from industry to industry. The amount of trade credit available to the firm depends on its volume of purchases as well as its credit rating. A major advantage of trade credit as a source of financing is that it increases as the firm's activity increases. The cost of using trade credit is the amount of any discounts forgone so long as the firm pays its bills when they are due. Delaying payment past the due date, while often done, tends to have an adverse impact on the firm's credit rating and may result in suppliers refusing to provide credit.

Loans from commercial banks are a major source of short-term credit to businesses. Compensating balances are often required by banks. A compensating balance is an amount which the firm must maintain in its checking account with the bank and is stated as a percentage of the credit line. The interest rate charged on a bank loan depends on the credit standing of the firm and the level of short-term interest rates in the economy. The lowest rate charged by banks is called the prime rate. Banks sometimes deduct the interest from the principal of the loan in advance. This increases the effective rate of interest.

Commercial paper is a short-term debt security issued by large firms and financial institutions. While the interest cost of commercial paper is usually lower than the rates charged by banks, if the firm becomes unprofitable, it may have trouble refinancing its commercial paper issues.

Lenders such as commercial banks may require firms whose credit rating is weak to pledge assets as security for a loan. Accounts receivable and inventory are often used as collateral. Accounts receivable are usually the best collateral since the risk to the lender is less with these assets. There are several methods used by lenders to obtain a security interest in accounts receivable. Generally the more control the lender has over the pledged accounts, the less risk there is to the lender but the cost of administering the loan is greater. Lenders frequently require a fee in addition to the interest charge to compensate them for the costs of administration. Factoring is the sale of accounts receivable, but may also involve other services. Credit cards reduce or eliminate the need of retailers to provide credit to their customers. The credit card company provides the credit, and the merchant is paid immediately on presentation of an invoice.

Inventory may also be pledged as security for a loan. The suitability of inventory as collateral depends on its marketability and the predictability of its price if it is sold. Floor planning, field warehousing, and public warehousing are methods used by lenders to keep track of inventory used as collateral.

QUESTIONS

1. The two partners of Smith and Hodgekins Enterprises recently had the following discussion:
   Smith: "Next period we expect our working capital needs to be $300,000—$250,000 of permanent working capital and $50,000 to meet the temporary increase in sales. In view of these asset requirements, I suggest we obtain a long-term bank loan."
   Hodgekins: "On the contrary, since working capital is current assets, the $300,000 should be financed with a short-term bank loan." Can you help Smith and Hodgekins?
2. "The objective of a financial manager is to minimize the cost of financing when seeking short-term funds." Comment on this statement considering other aspects that may affect the choice of short-term financing arrangements.
3. Rank the three major sources of short-term financing in terms of availability to the following types of business:
   a) A large manufacturer with a high credit rating
   b) A medium-sized manufacturer with a good credit rating
   c) A small retailer with a fair credit rating
4. What is the basic cost of trade credit and why is it a cost?
5. What determines the amount of trade credit to a firm?
6. "The cost of incurring a bad trade credit reputation is simply the cost of obtaining financing from other sources." Do you agree? Why or why not?
7. Distinguish between a line of credit and revolving credit from the viewpoints of the lender and the borrower.

8. Which types of short-term financing would you expect to be used by the following firms:
   a) A small open air market selling fresh sea foods and eggs
   b) A woman's apparel shop specializing in clothing for taller women
   c) A large metropolitan department store
   d) A dealer selling new and used cars
   e) A contractor constructing the coolers for nuclear reactors
   f) A finance company with branch offices nationwide.
   g) A partnership selling and servicing Whirlpool appliances

9. An article in the *Harvard Business Review* (1972) reported that the CIT Corporation, a consumer and business finance company, uses primarily commercial paper to meet its short-term financing requirements. Why do you think CIT uses commercial paper rather than bank loans?

10. Why are accounts receivable generally considered a better source of collateral than inventories?

11. Given that the following firms use secured financing arrangements, would they be more likely to be pledging inventory, accounts receivable, or both as collateral? Why?
    a) A company manufacturing custom electronic equipment for major aerospace firms
    b) A wholesale lumber dealer
    c) A retail appliance (refrigerators, etc.) store
    d) A children's clothing manufacturer

12. Distinguish between the following types of secured financial arrangements in terms of benefits and costs to the borrower:
    a) Factoring
    b) General lien
    c) Floor planning
    d) Warehousing arrangements

PROJECT Obtain a recent annual report for a nonfinancial business. Analyze the sources of short-term financing currently used by the firm. Have the amount or composition of short-term financing sources changed from the previous year? Estimate their costs to the extent possible. Does the firm appear to be applying the matching principle or not? Be sure to read the footnotes to the balance sheet, where much of the detail on financing will be found.

561

(Note: For ease of calculation in all the problems below, assume that a year has 360 days in it.)

1. As financial manager for Polaris Electronics, you have completed the two-year cash flow forecast shown below. All cash inflows and outflows have been forecast, given the minimum cash balance of the firm, except for any new financing required and temporary investments in securities. Cash discounts are assumed to be taken when available. (Dollar figures are in millions.)

Quarter	1	2	3	4	5	6	7	8
Cash inflow (outflow)	$2.2	($6.5)	($4.0)	$1.3	$5.0	($2.0)	$1.5	$0.5
Cumulative inflow (outflow)	$2.2	($4.3)	($8.3)	($7.0)	($2.0)	($4.0)	($2.5)	($2.0)

a) How much "permanent" financing appears to be needed by this firm?

b) Given your answer from **a**, what is the maximum "temporary" financing required and when does it occur? [Ans.: $6.3 million in quarter 3]

2. As Polaris Electronics' financial manager (problem 1), you must develop a financial plan for the firm.

a) Evaluate the following alternative financing proposals submitted by your staff. Which ones are consistent with the matching principle? Might any fail to meet the financing needs of the firm? Are any particularly unsuited for the firm in other ways?

   1. Obtain a line of credit for $3.0 million and issue $6.0 million of long-term debt in quarter 2.
   2. Plan to issue ninety-day commercial paper as needed.
   3. Obtain a two-year revolving credit agreement with a limit of $9.0 million.
   4. Obtain a line of credit for $6.5 million and issue $2.0 million in long-term debt in quarter 2.
   5. Issue $2.0 million of common stock in quarter 2 and use trade credit as needed.
   6. Plan to finance with ninety-day bank loans as needed.

b) Trace the implications of financing alternatives 1, 4, and 6, assuming the following:

   1. Interest rate on long-term debt will be 9 percent.
   2. Interest rate on line of credit will be 8 percent.

   3. Interest rate on temporary investments will be 6 percent.
You should determine the actual loans and investments that will be outstanding in each quarter and the total cost of the two financing plans over the two-year period treating the interest received on securities as an offset to interest expenses on debt. Rank the three alternatives with respect to interest cost and with respect to financing risks. What do you observe?

3. Ace Novelty purchases $250 per day from suppliers whose terms are net/30.
  a) If Ace pays its bills on time, what will its accounts payable balance be? [Ans.: $7500]
  b) Suppose sales (and purchases) increase 20 percent over previous levels, what will the new accounts payable balance be? [Ans.: $9,000]
  c) At the new level of purchases in **b,** how much additional financing could Ace obtain by paying, on average, 15 days late? [Ans.: $4,500]

4. Kay's Bookstore is a small proprietorship located in an urban shopping center. The terms on purchases of books from a central wholesaler are 3/15, net 30. How much would it cost Kay's to forgo the discount and pay in 30 days rather than 15 days? [Ans.: 74.2 percent per year]

5. Suppose that Kay's Bookstore can purchase from either of two wholesalers. The first wholesaler offers terms given in problem 4 above while the second offers a trade discount of 2/10, net 60. Kay's can borrow from a bank at 12 percent per year interest cost. What are your recommendations?

6. Firstline State Bank has granted Camino Yacht Company Incorporated a line of credit for $350,000, under the stipulation that Camino maintain a 15 percent compensating balance in its account with the bank on any loans outstanding and a 10 percent compensating balance for the unborrowed portion of the credit line. Firstline also charges Camino an interest rate of 9 percent for funds borrowed.
  a) If Camino borrows $200,000 on the line of credit, what is the dollar amount that must be maintained in Firstline as a compensating balance? [Ans.: $45,000]
  b) What is the effective interest rate on Camino's borrowings of $200,000 assuming the firm would normally only keep $15,000 in the account? [Ans.: 10.6% per year]

7. Bank A offers a one-year loan at an interest rate of 9 percent per year, where the interest is paid at the end of the year when the loan matures. Bank B offers to loan at a stated rate of 8.5 percent per year but deducts the interest at the beginning of the year. Which bank offers the lower cost financing?

8. The E. Fenton Company, Inc., requires additional short-term financing of $10.0 million. It has excellent relationships with its bank and its suppliers and a high credit rating in general. The company maintains normal deposit balances of $500,000. The following alternatives are available:

1. Trade credit. Fenton's purchases average $200,000 per day on terms of 1/10, net 30; the firm presently pays within 10 days.
2. An 8 percent loan from the bank which will require 15 percent in compensating balances to be held on deposit with the bank.
3. Commercial paper bearing a 7.75 percent interest rate. In order to issue the paper, the firm must maintain backup lines of credit with a bank. The bank will charge an annual fee of 0.5 percent of the credit line and require the firm to maintain 10 percent of the line as deposits at the bank.

Evaluate each of these three alternatives. Which one would you recommend?

SOURCES OF LONG-TERM CAPITAL

Part 4 discusses the alternative sources of long-term capital available to the firm. Chapter 9 provided general guidelines for selecting the best combination of capital sources. Chapters 16 through 20, which comprise Part 4, explain the procedures used in raising money and provide a detailed description of each type of security that may be issued by corporations.

Chapter 16 explains how capital is raised through direct arrangements with financial institutions such as banks or insurance companies, or by selling securities to the public. Chapter 17 describes various forms of leasing arrangements, indicates why leasing may have advantages over purchasing, and explains how the financial manager decides whether to lease or purchase a particular asset. Chapters 18, 19, and 20 describe the major types of securities a company can issue: common stock, debt, preferred stock, convertibles, and warrants. The rights and privileges of security holders and the associated obligations of the firm are important considerations in choosing which kinds of securities should be issued.

When a business firm needs money to pay for new assets or to pay off debt obligations that are coming due, the financial manager must choose a source for the money. In Chapter 9 we examined the problem of choosing among debt, preferred stock, common stock, and retained earnings. In Chapter 15 the nature and use of short-term debt sources were presented. We are now going to look at some more technical aspects of the decision and the process by which firms actually raise money. Our discussion focuses on debt issues with maturities of more than one year and on stock issues.

For example, suppose that as the financial manager of a business you have decided that the firm should borrow $10 million—what happens next? What decisions should be made and whom should you talk to about providing this money? The answers to these questions are the subjects of this chapter.

There are two related decisions to be made once the firm has determined the amount of financing needed and the type of financing to be used (debt, common stock, or some other type). The financial manager must choose between public or private financing, and then the maturity of any debt to be issued must be fixed. A **public security issue** is sold to individual and institutional investors. The actual selling is usually handled by an investment banker, who buys the securities from the firm and sells them to investors. If a **private security issue** is chosen, the firm approaches one investor or a small number of investors directly and sells the securities to them. This process is also called private placement. Usually the investors in a private issue are financial institutions such as commercial banks and insurance companies.[1] While a number of factors influence the choice between public and private financing, the major considerations are the

GENERAL DECISIONS IN RAISING FUNDS

---

1. The terms "issuing securities" or "securities issues" as used in practice generally connote public issues of debt and stock. In the interests of simplicity in our discussion we employ these terms in their broader sense of the agreements between a firm and the people or firms which have supplied money to it. Similarly the term "investor" tends to be associated with a person or firm who either purchases public issues of debt and stock or owns common stock. It normally does not apply to financial institutions making direct loans to a business firm. We use "investor" in its broader sense of one who has invested money in the firm or owns its securities, regardless of the nature of the investor.

size and type of financing needed. Common and preferred stocks are usually sold as public issues, whereas debt is issued publicly and privately. Large issues of long-term debt (over $10 million and over ten years) are more often public issues, whereas smaller and shorter-term debt issues are more often private ones. There will be more on these points later.

Once the financial manager has decided that debt with a maturity greater than one year is appropriate, the particular maturity must still be chosen. Is it to be two years or forty years? The traditional answer to this question is the same "matching principle" discussed in Chapter 15, namely, that the maturity of the debt should match the period of time for which the money will be needed. While this principle makes much sense when applied to the question of short-term versus long-term financing, it is not nearly so helpful in the decision as to whether debt with a maturity of five years or a maturity of fifteen years should be used. Traditionally, maturity of debt is determined by the economic life of assets acquired with the money raised. There is an implicit assumption that the use of any debt is temporary in that once the "need" has passed the debt will be retired. However, as we have seen in Chapter 9, many firms will plan to maintain debt as a normal part of their outstanding securities. This means that as old debt issues mature, they will be repaid with new debt issues, not by selling assets or drawing down cash balances. Determining debt maturity for these firms is largely a decision as to how often the firm wishes to refinance its debt. We will return to this problem at the end of the chapter after some of the factors which influence the decision have been discussed.

A comment on nomenclature is appropriate here. In the financial world, "short-term" generally refers to debt with maturity of less than one year. This usage is quite common. The words used to describe longer-term financing arrangements are not so well-defined. Many people use "intermediate-term" to refer to maturities of over one year but less than ten years and reserve "long-term" for maturities over ten years. However, "long-term" may also be used to describe maturities in excess of five years. The five- to ten-year area is therefore somewhat fuzzy. To one person a $7\frac{1}{2}$-year loan may be intermediate term and to someone else it may be long-term. In this text we will not attempt any special definition, but rather use "long-term" rather loosely to refer to any debt issue with a maturity in excess of one to two years. We will not distinguish "intermediate-term" from "long-term" because for our purposes the distinction is not very meaningful.[2]

_____

2. There is a variety of historical reasons for making such distinctions. For example, people would consider intermediate-term debt as temporary, whereas long-term debt would be considered permanent. Moreover, certain types of debt issues tend to have intermediate-term maturities (term loans), whereas others tend to have long-term ma-

Let us turn now to the procedure involved in making a public issue of securities.

**PUBLIC
SECURITIES
ISSUES AND
INVESTMENT
BANKING**

Most companies making a public issue of debt or stock use the services of an investment banker, who does the actual selling of the securities. In some situations, firms do try to sell the securities to the investors themselves. This is called a **direct securities issue** and, for nonfinancial corporations, is largely confined to common stock. In this section we will examine the function of investment bankers. Direct issues of common stock are covered in Chapter 18.

Firms use investment bankers to sell securities to investors because it is cheaper and easier than doing it themselves. Investment bankers specialize in selling new securities issues. They are familiar with the desires of investors as to the type and features of securities and are organized to contact potential buyers. They normally earn their money on the difference between the price at which they acquire the securities from the firm and the price at which the securities are sold to investors. Let us look at a typical public issue and the procedure that is followed.

Most public issues are sold through **negotiated underwritings.** In this process a firm chooses an investment banker, negotiates the price and conditions of the issue, and sells it to the banker. Underwriting is the process whereby the investment banker purchases the issue from the firm at a given price and then sells it as best it can. In an underwritten issue, the investment banker bears the risk that it will not sell well. In contrast, the firm is guaranteed a fixed price. Alternative procedures are also possible.

Some firms, primarily railroads and public utilities, use **competitive bidding** rather than negotiation both to pick the investment banker and to determine the price of the issue. In a competitive bidding situation, the firm announces that it wishes to issue securities and invites bids from investment bankers. Often on large issues several investment bankers join together in a **syndicate** and submit a single bid for the group. The firm specifies the type of security and any conditions or features that it has. The investment bankers then submit bids on the price (or interest rate) for the issue, and the best bid is awarded the issue.

Regardless of whether the investment banker is chosen by negotiation or bidding, the banker acts as an underwriter in both cases. Another approach is for the firm to ask an investment banker to sell its securities on a **best efforts** or **agency** basis. In this case the investment banker is not

---

turities (bonds). Modern financial managers do not appear to be concerned with whether a given debt issue is intermediate or long term, but rather with the particular characteristics of alternative issues. Maturity is one such characteristic.

acting as an underwriter, but merely sells the securities for a commission. This procedure is used either by very large firms, which are confident that their securities will sell fairly easily or (much more frequently) by very small firms, when the investment banker feels the risks of an unsuccessful issue are too high. Table 16-1 provides information on the relative amounts of securities issued through investment bankers. Notice that 94 percent of the dollar volume of all issues is underwritten, but common stock is often issued on an agency basis (11 percent) or direct (11 percent).

Preliminary Discussions A typical security issue begins with discussions by the firm's financial manager with one or more investment bankers. Large firms often establish continuing relationships with an investment banker which may last for many years. At this stage the investment banker can provide helpful advice to the firm, especially regarding investors' reactions to debt policy, the possible features or conditions of a debt issue, and an estimate of the price or interest rate that investors will require. The financial manager will usually ask for a written proposal as to what the security issue might be, and when discussions are carried out with more than one banker, the proposals provide a basis for choosing among them. The investment banker chosen in this process is called the **originating house.** For large issues, other investment bankers may be brought in to form the underwriting syndicate. The originating house will normally serve as the manager of the syndicate and underwrite the largest portion of the issue.

The fees paid to the investment banker for undertaking the issue can be divided into two parts—underwriting commissions and sales commissions. As their names imply, the underwriting commission is the portion that represents the payment for risk bearing and the sales commission represents the payment for doing the actual selling of the securities. The

Table 16-1. Corporate securities issues by method of issue, November 1974 to November 1975
(Dollar figures in millions)

	Underwritten		Agency basis		Direct		Total	
	Amount	Percent[a]	Amount	Percent[a]	Amount	Percent[a]	Amount	Percent[a]
Bonds and notes	$30,500	97	$ 344	1	$ 728	2	$31,572	100
Preferred stock	$ 2,830	99	0	—	$ 16	1	$ 2,846	100
Common stock	$ 5,700	78	$ 834	11	$ 752	11	$ 7,286	100
Total issues	$39,030	94	$1,178	3	$1,496	3	$41,704	100

[a] Percentages are based on row totals.
Source: *Statistical Bulletin,* Securities and Exchange Commission.

Table 16-2. Costs of issuing corporate securities[a]
(Cost expressed as a percentage of issue amount)

Size of issue ($ millions)	Debt, %	Preferred stock, %	Common stock, %
$0–$0.49	12.0	14.5	23.0
$0.5–$0.99	11.5	12.2	18.4
$1–$1.9	8.3	8.1	13.4
$2–$4.9	6.0	5.2	10.8
$5–$9.9	3.5	3.5	7.9
$10–$19.9	1.9	1.3	6.3
$20–$49.9	1.5	1.4	5.9
$50 and over	1.2	1.4	4.5

[a] Data are for 1969 except for issues of debt and preferred stock of less than $5 million, for which averages for issues from 1961 to 1969 are used.
Source: Investment Bankers Association.

manager of a syndicate is compensated for this job out of the underwriting commission, and the remaining part (after expenses are deducted) is paid to the members of the syndicate in proportion to their original share of the underwriting. Sales commissions are paid based on the actual sales of the syndicate members.

The division of the fees is not too important to the firm issuing the securities; it is the total amount that is most relevant. Table 16-2 provides some data on the costs of issuing securities through negotiated underwriting. Notice that issue costs as a percentage of the proceeds decline rapidly until the issue size reaches about $10 million. Also note that the underwriting commission for common stock is higher than the commission for bonds. The difference is due to the greater price fluctuation of common stock and hence the greater risk borne by the underwriter.

Once agreement has been reached between the investment banker and the issuing firm, an investigation and evaluation of the firm will be made. If new plant and equipment are going to be acquired through the proceeds of the issue, engineering firms may be hired to analyze the technical aspects of the assets. An accounting firm may be called in to audit the firm's accounts.

A major portion of the preissue activity of the investment banker consists of meeting the requirements imposed by the state and federal agencies regulating new issues. Most of these requirements involve the disclosure of information regarding the company's operations and financial condition, the ownership of outstanding securities by officers and

Setting Up the Issue

directors of the firm, and any legal problems the firm may be having. The regulatory authorities are especially concerned that the relevant facts about the company are fully disclosed and that incorrect information is not given to potential investors. The purpose of this regulation is, therefore, to protect the purchasers of the securities from basing their decision to buy on erroneous information and to provide sufficient, accurate information that a thoughtful decision can be made.

The final price or interest rate to the firm is not usually set until after the registration procedure has been completed. If the firm is issuing bonds and already has outstanding bonds which are being traded in the bond market, the interest rate will be set slightly higher than the current rate in the market. Similarly, if the firm is issuing stock and its stock is currently traded in the stock market, the price that the firm will receive will be somewhat lower than the market price at the end of registration. In both cases, how much different the terms of the issue will be from the market rate or price will depend on how stable the market has been recently and is a matter for negotiation between management and the investment banker. The problem facing a firm that has never had a public issue of the security in question is more difficult.

If the firm is issuing bonds and there are no publicly traded bonds outstanding, management and the investment banker must decide on what the proper interest rate should be. They will rely primarily on comparisons with other firms which do have outstanding bonds. In addition they may ask for the bonds to be rated by one of the firms which provide such services (as was discussed in Chapter 5, page 142). If management and the investment banker know that the bonds will be rated A, for example, then they will use the current interest rate on A-rated bonds as a basis for determining the rate on the issue. The rating firms charge a fee for this service which is part of the cost of issuing the bonds. Rating increases the marketability of a bond issue, since the existence of a rating reduces the amount of work needed by investors to decide whether they wish to buy the issue. For this reason most public issues are rated, regardless of whether the firm has currently outstanding bonds or not.

Pricing a New Issue of Common Stock

A firm making its first public issue of common stock is said to be **going public.** Prior to going public the firm would have only a few shareholders, who purchased their stock directly from the firm or who were the founders of the firm and their families. Now, either the firm needs more equity capital than can be provided by retained earnings or the original owners wish to sell a part of their interest in the firm to others. Going public almost always substantially increases the number of shareholders in the firm. There is no established market price for such firms, and an estimate must be made by the firm's management and the investment banker as to the market value of all the firm's shares once the stock is issued. Once the total market value has been estimated, the estimated price per share is simply the market value divided by the total number of outstanding shares. For example, suppose that the market value of the firm is estimated to be $1 million and there will be 200,000 shares outstanding after issue. Then the estimated price per share is

$$\text{Price} = \frac{\$1,000,000}{200,000 \text{ shares}} = \$5 \text{ per share}$$

Here we are not concerned about the number of *new* shares to be issued, only the total number that will be outstanding after issue. The problem then is to estimate the market value of the common stock.

The basic principles required to estimate the value of common stock were presented in Chapter 5. There we developed the idea that the value of an asset was the present value of the income produced from it. From the viewpoint of the owners of a firm's common stock, the relevant income is the dividend stream paid by the firm. There are two practical problems that complicate the direct application of this principle to estimate the market value of a firm. First, it is difficult to estimate what investors might forecast the long-run dividend stream to be. Second, as we know from Chapter 6, it is difficult to estimate the required rate of return on common stock if the stock does not already have a market price. Depending on the history and future prospects of the firm, an assessment of its market value may or may not be possible through a straightforward application of the basic principle. Let us first examine a situation where it is a reasonable approach.

The constant growth model Suppose that the net income and dividends of the firm have risen at a fairly regular rate over the past several years, say 7 percent per year. Neither management nor the investment banker has any reason to believe that the future performance of the firm will differ much from the past. If the two parties believe that investors will evaluate the firm in a similar manner, the constant-dividend growth model used in Chapters 5 and 6 would be appropriate. The value of the firm V can be estimated using the relationship

$$V = \frac{D}{k - g} \tag{16-1}$$

where D = expected dividend payment next year to all shareholders
$\quad\quad k$ = rate of return required by investors
$\quad\quad g$ = long-run dividend growth rate

Let us suppose that the firm expects to earn $100,000 and pay $40,000 in dividends next year. Given a growth rate of 7 percent, the only other factor is k. In Chapter 6 we discussed the problem of estimating k. Indeed, we used the above model in a situation where we knew the current price of the firm's shares. Since the value of the shares is what we are trying to estimate here, we need an alternative approach to estimating the required rate of return. There are several ways to develop an estimate. Management and the investment banker may have some idea of the required rate of return based on their knowledge of the securities market and the firm. The rates of return on shares of other companies which are similar to this firm and whose stocks are traded in the market may be used to get some idea of the "going rate." Adding a 4 percent to 6 percent premium to current long-term interest rates on corporate bonds is another possibility. Let us suppose that, based on one of these procedures, the required rate of return is estimated to be 11 percent. We now have sufficient information to use the formula above to estimate the total market value of the firm.

$$V = \frac{\$40,000}{0.11 - 0.07}$$

$$= \frac{\$40,000}{0.04}$$

$$= \$1,000,000$$

Unfortunately, the constant growth model using historical growth rates is not often applicable. Most firms going public do not have a record of stable growth in income and dividends. Many of them have never paid any dividends and do not plan to do so for some time due to their need for money to finance investments. Also, investors are unlikely to use historical growth rates for the firm blindly in their assessment of its future potential. If the firm has grown much more rapidly than the economy or its industry in the past, investors will probably not expect such high rates of growth to continue indefinitely. In these cases an alternative approach may be used.

Comparative price-earnings ratios Perhaps the most popular method of all for pricing stock is the use of comparative price-earning ratios. The ratio of market price to earnings per share P/E can be used to compare stock prices of firms. To use P/E as a valuation method, the ratios are computed for several firms similar to our firm which have publicly traded stock. In addition, the P/E ratios for other firms which have recently gone public are examined. The financial conditions, growth prospects, management ability, and any other information deemed potentially relevant of these other firms are compared with the same attributes of our firm. From this examination a subjective judgment is made as to what might be an appropriate P/E for the firm. The most important factor which affects the value used is expected future growth in earnings. The resulting ratio multiplied by current net income provides an estimate of the market value of the firm.

$$V = P/E \times \text{net income} \qquad (16\text{-}2)$$

Once we have the total market value V, it is a simple matter to estimate the price as outlined earlier.

The P/E method is simply a systematic way to estimate the value of the firm using as much information as possible. However, a large amount of judgment necessarily enters into the process. This is not bad, but it does mean that management and the investment banker may well reach different estimates even though they have the same basic data. The two parties will then have to discuss the question until they either agree on a proper price or terminate the deal. If too high a price is set, the underwriter will lose money. If too low a price is set, the current owners of the firm will not receive full value on the sale. Ultimately, the market will determine the actual value when the stock is sold and will reveal whose price estimate was the more accurate. However, prior to sale, the issue price is purely the result of a bargaining process.

Advantages of Underwriting

The investment banker provides a variety of services including counseling on the type and terms of the securities to be issued and maintaining a market for common stock after issue. For small companies going public, this latter service can be quite valuable, as it provides the old shareholders with an opportunity to sell some of their stock more easily than before. A public issue of common stock handled by an investment banker also reduces the chances of the original owners losing control of the company to outsiders. The stock will be sold to many investors rather than to only a few, making it less likely that the new shareholders will be able to agree that current management should be replaced. This is an important consideration for firms which are controlled by a few people and yet need substantial new equity to finance investments. Finally, there is the advantage of knowing exactly how much money will be raised and at what cost. The firm receives the money when the underwriter pays for the entire issue. The alternative is to have the sale of the securities occur over a period of time with varying prices (or interest rates) depending on the reaction of investors and changing economic conditions. In an underwritten issue the investment banker bears these risks.

Regulation of Public Issues

Public securities issues must comply with a variety of state and federal regulations. In 1911, the Kansas state legislature passed one of the first laws regulating securities issues. A member of the legislature remarked at that time that the new law would prevent sellers of securities from promising the "blue sky" to unsophisticated investors. As a result such state regulations are called **blue sky laws.** Generally state requirements impose some minimum standards for disclosure of the business and financial affairs of the issuing firm and regulate the activities of investment bankers and securities broker-dealers. The laws in some states set limits on the percentage of the issue that can be paid in compensation to the investment banker.

The principal federal laws in this area are the Securities and Exchange Acts of 1933 and 1934. The 1934 act established the Securities and Exchange Commission (SEC) as the primary federal regulatory agency responsible for securities issues and trading. The 1933 act was specifically directed toward regulation of new securities issues. The major result of this law was to force firms issuing securities to the public to disclose fully any information relevant to an investor in the new security being offered. Before a security can be issued, the firm must file a registration statement containing this information which must be approved by the SEC before the securities can be issued. The registration process may take two to four months to complete. In addition, copies of a condensed version of the registration statement must be available to prospective investors before they purchase the securities. This package of information is called a **prospectus.**

For purposes of SEC regulation a public issue is one which will be sold to more than approximately twenty-five investors; however, not all public issues need be registered with the SEC. The major exceptions are:

1. Small issues, less than $500,000 in amount
2. Issues limited to purchase by citizens of a single state
3. Debt issues with maturities of less than 270 days (commercial paper is in this category)
4. Firms in industries already regulated by another federal agency (railroads are regulated by the Interstate Commerce Commission)

From an investor's viewpoint it is important to remember that the SEC *does not* prevent firms from issuing trashy securities. Stock may be greatly overpriced, or debt may have too low an interest rate for the risk involved. The firm may even be doing illegal things such as paying bribes to foreign government officials as in the corporate bribery scandals of 1975. The firm may be unprofitable and close to bankruptcy. All the SEC requires is that complete and accurate information be disclosed. It is up to the individual investor to sort out the trash.

The distinguishing differences between public and private issues include the number of buyers of the securities and the extent of contact between the firm issuing the securities and the buyers. In a public issue many investors will purchase the securities, whereas a private issue will involve only a few investors. A firm making a public issue will not normally have any contact with the investors prior to their becoming stockholders or bondholders of the firm. In a private issue, the firm will be discussing the terms of the issue directly with prospective purchasers.

Common stock and preferred stock are much less likely to be privately placed than is debt. The Securities and Exchange Commission reported that only 3 percent of the common stock and 10 percent of the preferred stock issued in 1975 were privately placed. On the other hand, 23 percent of bonds issued were privately placed in 1975, and firms used many private sources of long-term debt other than just bonds (commercial bank term loans, for example). In some years, such as 1966, over 50 percent of all bonds issued are privately placed; however, recent heavy demands for debt financing have forced businesses to rely more on public issues. Let's consider the factors that influence the choice between the two methods to see why these things are so.

PRIVATE PLACEMENT

Public versus Private Issues

Private issues have some definite advantages over public ones. For one thing the firm is spared the time, trouble, and expense of having to register the issue with regulatory authorities and comply with their requirements. Moreover, since the main requirements of public issues involve disclosure of information about the company, many firms dislike the idea of having to "tell all" to their employees, their competitors, and the general public. Privately placed debt issues provide advantages if the firm gets into difficulties later on. The firm can discuss the problem directly with the lender and make modifications in the debt agreement. For example, a scheduled loan payment might be delayed or refinancing arranged with the same lender (usually at a higher interest rate). This is much more difficult to do when there are many holders of a public debt issue.

However, private issues have some disadvantages. First, the investor-lender may monitor the operations of the firm much more carefully than the purchaser of a public issue. In the case of common stock financing, the investor or investor group is more likely to try to gain control of the firm. Second, the interest rate paid on debt issues is likely to be higher and the price of common stock issues lower if they are private placements. Therefore, the advantage of lower issue costs for private issues may be partially or completely offset by the higher rate of return required by a private investor. This is especially true for large issues because issue costs tend to be relatively smaller for them (see Table 16-2). Third, it is more difficult to finance large amounts privately than it is to make a public issue. The result is that large securities issues tend to be public issues, whereas smaller issues tend to be private.

The feature which distinguishes different private placements is not *what* securities are issued, but *who* provides the money. Therefore we will look at some of the major private sources of intermediate- and long-term financing.

Commercial Banks   Business firms acquire money from commercial banks through two long-term debt arrangements—mortgages and term loans. A mortgage is a loan secured by real estate—land and buildings—which is repaid in periodic installments.[3] Mortgage loans to business firms are similar to mortgage loans to individuals except that the maturity of the loan is usually less for business mortgages. Mortgage loans to people buying a house to live in (**residential mortgages**) usually are repaid over a period of twenty to thirty years. Business mortgages (usually called **commercial mortgages**) normally do not extend past twenty years and may be repaid over only ten years. Residential mortgages almost always require equal monthly payments, whereas commercial mortgages sometimes are repaid quarterly.

Term loans may or may not be secured by assets of the firm. Payment schedules are highly variable but do not extend beyond ten years. A typical term loan would be paid off in quarterly installments over a period of three to five years. Term loans differ from mortgage loans in that the principal payments are usually the same each quarter (or month), whereas the interest payments are based on the outstanding balance of the loan. A mortgage normally involves the same amount of cash payment each period. For example, suppose that a firm could borrow $100,000 for ten years using either a mortgage or a term loan with quarterly payments required. The interest rate on both loans is 8 percent per year, or 2 percent per quarter. The mortgage loan would require a payment each quarter, for forty quarters, of $3,656 calculated as

$$A = \$100,000 \ (A/P, \ 2\%, \ 40)$$

$$= \$3,656$$

The term loan would require a principal payment of $100,000/40 = $2,500 per quarter plus interest on the outstanding balance. In the first quarter the interest would be $100,000 \times 0.02 = $2,000$, and so the total payment would be $2,000 + $2,500 = $4,500$ in the first quarter. However, in the last quarter the loan is outstanding, the interest payment would be $2,500 \times 0.02 = 50 for a total payment of $2,550. Therefore, a term loan

---

3. The term "mortgage" has a particular legal definition. Our use includes other types of loans secured by real estate (e.g., deeds of trust) as well.

of the same maturity as a mortgage would involve higher initial cash payments than the mortgage and lower payments later on.

There are some other features of term loans which are important. They will often carry **restrictive provisions** or constraints on the firm. For example, the loan agreement may require that the firm not pay any dividends in excess of earnings for the year or that the firm maintain net working capital equal to a fixed percentage of long-term debt. The majority of term loans made by banks are now **variable rate** loans. That is, the interest rate in effect each quarter may vary over the life of the loan. The rate is usually expressed as a fixed percentage over the current prime rate of the bank. For example, the agreement might read that the rate will be "1 percent over prime." If the current prime rate were 9 percent, the current interest rate on the loan would be 10 percent. A quarterly interest payment would then be calculated as $2\frac{1}{2}$ percent (10 percent/4) of the outstanding balance. If in the next quarter the prime rate dropped to 7 percent, then the interest rate would be 8 percent and the quarterly interest payment would be determined as 2 percent (8 percent/4) of the balance owed on the loan.

The rise of variable rate loans has concerned financial managers of business firms. They now often attempt to negotiate a ceiling on the average interest rate over the period of the loan. Such a ceiling is called a **cap.** A loan agreement might specify a cap of, say, 8 percent. This means that if interest rates rise and stay over 8 percent for a long time, future interest payments made by the firm will be reduced so that the 8 percent cap is not exceeded. This does not mean that the rate in any given period cannot exceed 8 percent, only that the average interest rate paid on the loan must not be greater than 8 percent.

Revolving credits, as we mentioned in Chapter 15, are a type of term loan. Although the loans are usually made in the form of ninety-day notes, the bank has made a formal commitment to the borrower to continue lending up to the maximum amount stated in the revolving credit agreement until the end of the agreement. Three years is a typical period for such an agreement to run. So long as the borrower abides by the terms of the loan (restrictive provisions, etc.), the bank is legally obligated to continue lending. Therefore when the ninety-day note is due, the borrower may reduce the amount borrowed for the next ninety days, renew the note, or increase it to the maximum at the borrower's option. Often, at the end of the revolving credit agreement, there is a provision that the loan may be converted into an ordinary term loan with a regular repayment schedule. Revolving credits are becoming quite common because of the flexibility they provide to the borrower. The interest rates change every ninety days as in other variable rate term loans.

A recent innovation in bank term loans is the **bullet** loan. This is a loan which has a single principal payment at maturity. Interest payments would usually be made quarterly. The maturities of bullet loans are usually from five to ten years. For example, a firm might borrow $100,000 for seven years. It would pay interest each quarter on the $100,000, usually with a variable rate. At the end of seven years the entire $100,000 would be due. Bullet loans can ordinarily be repaid in whole or in part prior to maturity without penalty. They therefore provide financial managers with a great deal of flexibility. Since most banks do not like to make bullet loans, they are difficult to get when loan demand is strong.

Insurance Companies

Life insurance companies are normally another important source of long-term debt financing for business firms. Term loans and bonds with maturities of over ten years are the types of financing available. Besides the longer maturities, insurance company term loans differ from bank term loans in that a penalty is often assessed for payments made ahead of schedule. In addition, these loans usually carry a provision prohibiting the firm from prepaying by refinancing the loan in order to gain a lower interest rate. The loans are made at a fixed rate of interest and the insurance company does not want the firm to be able to repay the loan early by issuing new debt at a lower rate, because the insurance company would then only be able to invest the money at the lower rates. Since banks generally prefer shorter maturities than insurance companies, it is quite common for a bank and an insurance company to participate in the same loan. In a fifteen-year term loan, the principal payments made in the first seven years might go to the bank whereas the payments made in the last eight years would go to the insurance company. Of course, the interest would be paid on the balance owed to each party and the interest rate may differ on the two portions, with the rate paid to the bank often being lower than the rate paid to the insurance company.

One of the most interesting term loans ever made was a $250 million term loan by Prudential Insurance Company to Chrysler Corporation in 1954. The maturity of the loan was 100 years, with the entire balance due in 2054. Chrysler "took down" the loan in four annual installments of $62.5 million each so that the full amount was not borrowed until 1958. There was a provision in the loan agreement that after 1964 either party could convert the loan into a twenty-year term loan to be repaid annually. The interest rate on the original loan was $3\frac{3}{4}$ percent; however, the rate would drop to $3\frac{1}{2}$ percent if the twenty-year option were taken. Needless to say, with much higher interest rates prevailing in 1964, the insurance company took the option as soon as it could and Chrysler had to begin paying off the loan.

Government Financing

The federal government provides financing to business firms in several ways, although much of it is short term. Some government financing does extend longer than one year. Advance payments on defense contracts are frequently made. For items with long lead times in development and production, these payments amount to intermediate-term financing. In 1973, Congress passed laws specifically guaranteeing loans made by commercial banks to the Lockheed Aircraft Corporation. This was done to prevent the company from going bankrupt. Congress has also been providing money to the bankrupt Penn Central Railroad to keep it in operation.

The Small Business Administration (SBA) has the authority to make loans to small business in general and has special provisions for low-income and other economically disadvantaged persons. The SBA also may guarantee up to 90 percent of a loan made by a private lender (e.g., a bank) to a qualified borrower. The maximum amount of money either guaranteed or lent by the SBA to a firm is $350,000, and maturities do not extend past fifteen years. They are ordinarily repaid in monthly installments. Generally, the SBA prefers to guarantee a loan rather than to lend the money directly. Also, neither direct loans nor guarantees will be made unless the firm is unable to get loans on reasonable terms from private sources. Interest rates on SBA or SBA-guaranteed loans are usually below the rates on normal loans made by financial institutions.

Another source of financing that has been a topic of considerable debate is provided by local governments—**industrial revenue bonds.** Industrial revenue bonds are issued by a city or county to build a plant which is then leased to a business firm. The interest on such bonds is exempt from federal income tax, and the bonds therefore have a relatively low interest rate. The lease payments made by the firm are used to pay off the bonds. The bonds themselves are issued through investment bankers who acquire the issue through competitive bidding. The business firm negotiates with the local officials on the lease payments and conditions for the use of the plant. The tax exemption of bond issues greater than $5 million was eliminated in 1968, but smaller issues are still popular. The purpose of this type of financing is to attract business firms to an area by providing them with low-cost facilities. From the viewpoint of the financial manager this is a cheap way to finance a plant. The U.S. Treasury, however, feels that this method of financing encourages the issuance of too many securities with tax-exempt interest. That is why the tax exemption of large issues was stopped.

Small business investment companies Small business investment companies (SBICs) are private firms licensed under the Small Business Investment Act of 1958 and organized to provide long-term debt and equity financing to small businesses. The owners of an SBIC are generally required to contribute at least $300,000 in equity capital. The SBIC can then borrow from the SBA, at low interest rates, an amount up to a specified multiple of its capital account (the multiple is between 2 and 3, depending upon the size of the capital account).

The SBIC may use its capital only to finance small businesses. A small business is defined in this context as one with average aftertax income of less than $250,000 per year, assets of less than $5 million, and a net worth of less than $2½ million. The SBIC may either lend the funds or purchase common stock of the small business. Stock accounts for slightly over half of the financing provided by SBICs. Frequently, the SBIC will purchase convertible debentures (unsecured bonds that can be converted into common stock). The SBIC may not place more than 20 percent of its capital account in any single business.

SBICs receive very generous federal tax treatment. Any dividends received from its investments are exempt from the corporate income tax. A loss on its investments is treated by the firm as an ordinary loss (deductible from operating income) rather than as a capital loss. Furthermore, in determining their personal income taxes, the owners of the SBIC may deduct a loss on their investment in the SBIC as a deduction from ordinary income rather than as a capital loss.

In spite of the considerable government incentives to SBICs, they have had only varying success. The history of the SBICs suggests that finding good small business opportunities has generally been quite difficult and costly. Many of the investments made have been to firms which are close to the upper limit of the size requirement for a "small business." The number of SBICs in existence has varied considerably. There was a major shakeout in the industry during the 1960s and early 1970s when many of the newly established SBICs found out that tax advantages do not compensate for a lack of profitable investment opportunities. In 1968 there were 542 SBICs licensed by the SBA, and by 1973 the number had declined to 385. There was a substantial increase in 1974 back up to 443 by December 31, 1974, but of these, only 265 were actually operating.[4]

Other Sources of Financing In addition to those above, there are many corporations, partnerships, and individuals who provide financing for business firms. One type of financial institution, leasing companies, is discussed in the next chapter. Business finance companies provide one- to ten-year loans on purchases of equipment. The manufacturers of large, expensive equipment often offer long-term financing to purchasers. There are many venture capital firms and individuals who are willing to provide equity money to promising companies. The more organized groups (including many SBICs) often provide management consulting to a business in which they have invested money.

Many people argue that small businesses have more difficulty in obtaining long-term financing than large businesses. It is certainly true that smaller firms must often pay a high price for the money they raise, for a

4. Source: Annual reports of the Small Business Administration.

variety of reasons. However, there is usually no shortage of money for those willing and able to pay the price.

SUMMARY

Firms can raise money by offering intermediate- and long-term securities which can be issued publicly or placed privately.

Investment bankers are the middlemen who sell the firm's securities to the public. Investment bankers provide several services including advice on the terms of an issue, underwriting, and selling the securities to investors. The underwriting service transfers the risk that the securities will not be purchased at their offering price from the firm to the investment banker. The banker buys the securities from the firm at one price and sells them to the public at a higher price. The difference between the two prices is the compensation to the investment banker.

In the negotiations between the firm and the investment banker, setting an appropriate price for the securities is a critical problem. For debt issues, a rating is usually obtained from the rating agencies and the interest rate is based on the rates available in the market for debt with the same rating. Pricing a new issue of common stock is especially difficult. Several approaches are used, but the most popular involves estimating an appropriate price-earnings ratio for the stock.

An alternative to a public issue of securities is private placement. In this procedure, the firm may directly negotiate with a few investors or lenders or it may employ the services of an investment banker to act as the firm's representative in the negotiations. The major advantages of private issues of securities are the lower issue costs and the elimination of delays due to registration requirements on public issues. The terms of private debt issues are also more easily modified later on. In recent years there has been an increase in the private placement of common stock although debt issues still are the more likely candidates for this approach.

Commercial banks and life insurance companies are the major financial institutions offering long-term funds directly to businesses. Commercial banks offer term loans and mortgages, and life insurance companies offer term loans and bonds. Other sources include federal agencies, local governments, finance companies, SBICs, and wealthy individuals.

QUESTIONS

1. How does a public securities issue differ from a private securities issue?
2. What factors will be considered by the financial manager in choosing between a public issue of common stock and a private issue of common stock?

3. Which of the following firms would be more likely to use private placement instead of a public issue? Why? All the firms wish to issue long-term debt.
   a) A local shoe store.
   b) A medium-sized ($20 million annual sales) electronics manufacturer.
   c) An electric utility company serving customers in three states.
   d) A large electronics manufacturer whose research staff has made a major technological breakthrough. Financing is needed to exploit this new technology as rapidly as possible.

4. What are the distinctive characteristics of an underwritten securities issue as compared with other methods of raising money?

5. Why would a corporation use negotiated underwriting rather than obtaining competitive bids?

6. How is an investment banker compensated for services provided to the corporation?

7. What services are performed by an investment banker in a negotiated underwriting?

8. "Large, well-known corporations have no real need for the services of an investment banker. There is little done by the investment banker that cannot be done by the financial staff of the corporation." Evaluate this statement.

9. How does a revolving credit arrangement differ from a line of credit?

10. In recent years many large corporations have made public issues of five-year maturity notes. These notes pay fixed interest to the purchaser, and the principal value is paid in full at maturity. Speculate on why corporations might choose to issue such notes rather than obtaining term loans of the same maturity.

11. In what ways do governments aid businesses in obtaining financing?

12. Suppose you are managing an SBIC. What kinds of businesses would you be interested in financing through common stock purchases?

PROJECT Obtain the prospectus for a recent security issue (may be provided by instructor). Review the prospectus in general. What types of information does it contain? Determine the following:

1. The issuing firm and the investment banking firm.
2. The type of security and the terms (price or interest rate of the issue).
3. What type of issue is it (negotiated, etc.)?
4. How much is the issue costing the firm?
5. How much is the investment banking firm getting paid?

1. Using the data in Table 16-2, estimate the dollar costs that would be incurred by a firm for issuing the following securities:
   a) $4 million in debt
   b) $8 million in debt
   c) $15 million in debt
   d) $4 million in common stock
   e) $8 million in common stock

2. If the total market value of common stock is estimated to be $4.0 million, at what price should the stock sell if 200,000 shares will be outstanding after going public? What would the price be if 400,000 shares were to be outstanding? [Ans.: $20; $10]

3. Management feels that a desirable price for the firm's first public stock issue would be $25 per share. There are presently 50,000 shares outstanding (privately held), and the total market value of the firm's equity is estimated to be $2.5 million after issue. How many new shares should be issued to obtain the price desired by management? [Ans.: 50,000 shares]

4. A firm is planning a public issue of stock. Price-earnings ratios for other firms in the same industry average fifteen times earnings. The firm's earnings are $2.0 million and 1 million shares will be outstanding after issuing the stock. What is a likely issue price per share?

5. The financial manager of a firm planning to go public estimates that investors will require an expected rate of return on the stock between 10 percent and 12 percent. Earnings and dividends are each expected to grow at an average rate between 4 percent and 8 percent per year over the long run. Management plans to pay $400,000 in dividends next year. What is the range of possible current market values for the common stock of this firm?

6. As financial manager of Apex Manufacturing you have estimated that you will need to raise $10 million in long-term debt over the next two years. You have decided to evaluate the three alternatives shown below on the bases of net cost to the firm (ignoring timing of the costs over the two years) and risk. What are the costs and risks of the alternatives? Assume $5 million is needed this year (now) and $5 million is needed next year (12 months from now). Which would you recommend?
   a) Issue $10 million in long-term debt this year at an interest rate of 8 percent. Issue costs will be $350,000. The excess funds will be invested in a one-year Treasury bill yielding 5 percent.
   b) Issue $5 million in long-term debt this year and $5 million next year. Issue costs are expected to be $250,000 for each issue. The interest rate on the debt issued this year will be 8 percent. You expect interest rates to be stable over the next eighteen months and therefore you expect to be able to issue debt next year at 8 percent.

c) Borrow $5 million in short-term debt this year at an interest rate of 7 percent and issue $10 million in long-term debt next year and use $5 million of the proceeds to repay the short-term debt. There are no issue costs on the short-term debt; the cost of issuing the long-term debt is expected to be $350,000. The interest rate on the debt issue next year is expected to be 8 percent.

7. The Glitter Mining Company is planning its first public issue of common stock. The firm's mineral reserves are substantial, enough to last for 100 years if mined at current rates. Average prices for gold, silver, and the six other minerals produced by Glitter have increased at an average rate of 8 percent per year for the past ten years. The increasing prices have been reflected in a comparable growth in earnings and dividends. The firm will pay a $2.00 per share dividend next year from earnings of $2.50 per share, based on the total number of shares to be outstanding after the issue. H. F. Arden and Company, an investment banking firm, has proposed to Glitter's management that stock be issued at a price of $25 per share.

a) What is the price-earnings ratio that Arden is applying to the firm?

b) What required rate of return is implied by the price of $25 if investors' expectations of the future are consistent with the history of the firm? [Ans.: 16 percent]

c) As financial manager, you believe that investors may be somewhat more pessimistic than past history would indicate. You consider 6 percent to be a conservative estimate of the long-term growth potential of the firm. Furthermore you have carefully estimated the rates of return required by investors in stocks issued by other mining companies. These seem to range between 10 percent and 14 percent. What range of issue prices for the common stock would you feel is appropriate for Glitter given this set of estimates?

d) Price-earnings ratios of other mining companies range from 9 to 15. What range of stock prices for Glitter is implied by these P/E ratios?

e) Given your analysis in a through d, how would you respond to Arden's proposal?

Venture Capital

Invest $100,000 and get back $5 million three years later? Sounds great—where do you sign up? Invest $100,000 and get back not one thin dime? Find some other pigeon. Both these results, however, are possibilities in the great financial game of venture capital investment. Venture capital is money invested in a small, usually new business by people who usually have no interest in managing the firm, although some will provide advice. The venture capitalist normally receives common stock in return for the money invested. The hope and expectation of the venture capitalist is that the business will turn out to be very profitable. If this occurs, the stock will be worth much more than its initial cost. Unfortunately, many new businesses never become profitable. Indeed, a large percentage fail after a few years and the stockholders receive little or nothing.

WHO ARE THE VENTURE CAPITALISTS?

Venture capital comes from a surprisingly wide variety of sources. The traditional suppliers of this type of financing for new businesses are wealthy individuals. These people frequently form partnerships or corporations which then invest money in several new businesses. Hopefully, the winners will more than compensate for the losers and the investors will end up obtaining significantly higher average rates of return than would be obtained from more conventional investments. Also, the returns from venture capital investments are capital gains and therefore are subject to a lower tax rate than dividends and interest. If you are in the 70 percent tax bracket, you are not very interested

in dividends. Lately, however, other people have been getting into the act.

Investment bankers establish venture capital sections to nurture small, growing firms. When these firms grow large enough to go to the market with public issues of stocks and bonds, the investment bankers who helped them grow expect to handle the issues. Of course, earning high returns on their investment is not irrelevant to these investment banking firms.

Many commercial banks, such as Bank of America, First National of Boston, and First National of Chicago, have established small business investment companies (SBICs) to provide venture capital. Again there are two reasons for the bank's interest. One is profit, and the other is to be better able to attract and service business customers of the bank. Some small acorns grow into mighty oaks, and the bank that aided the process can expect to retain the banking business of the firm as it grows.

A relatively new group of venture capitalists consists of large corporations such as General Electric, Sun Oil, Ford Motor Company, and Du Pont. Ford and Du Pont dropped out of the game after some dismal experiences, but many others are still going. The corporations are attracted in part because of the prospects of higher returns on their venture capital investments than on conventional investments in their business. However, the corporations also hope to gain access at an early stage to new ideas and technology that will benefit other aspects of their operations.

Venture capitalists, therefore, come in all shapes and sizes. They may be SBICs owned by a bank, by an insurance company, by a few individuals, or by publicly held companies with their own traded common stock. They may be investors in a limited partnership organized around a talented person who acts as the general partner. About the only thing they have in common is their interest in finding new firms that need money and that have good prospects.

WHAT KIND OF VENTURES ATTRACT CAPITAL?

The classic recipient of venture capital is a person with limited financial resources, with an idea for a new product involving high technology, and with business sense (or teamed with someone who has business sense). However, almost any type of business can attract venture capital provided there are reasonable prospects of future profits. *Patient Care,* a magazine for doctors, was launched with the support of American Research and Development Corporation, one of the largest and most successful venture capital firms. The company that introduced Minute Maid frozen orange juice was helped by J. H. Whitney and Company, a highly successful partnership. Indeed, Whitney suggested bringing in Bing Crosby to promote the product.

There are definite advantages to being located in an area where there are a large number of venture capital firms. The Boston and San Francisco metropolitan areas are hot spots of venture capital activity. There are both a large number of venture capital firms and a large number of businesses started with the aid of venture capitalists in these two areas. New York, Massachusetts, California, Illinois (Chicago area), and Texas are the top states in number of venture capital firms. Location is important to the business seeking venture capital because the venture capital firms like to keep fairly close watch over the businesses they in-

vest in, and they also provide management advice and guidance to the businesses.

Perhaps the most critical feature of a business seeking venture capital is the people involved. Whenever the heads of successful venture capital firms are asked what they look for in a potential investment, they respond "creative," or "talented," or "high quality" management. People rank first and ideas second.

A GREAT MAN

When General Georges Doriot retired at age seventy-two in 1972, he left a legacy few people will equal. Born in France, he came to the United States in 1921 and served during World War II as deputy director of research and development in the Defense Department. He was a professor and assistant dean at the Harvard Business School at the time of his retirement. In 1946 he was hired as president of American Research and Development Corporation (ARDC), then just established as an investment company. General Doriot was to make ARDC a prototype for publicly held venture capital firms. From an original base of $19 million in capital, ARDC financed approximately 100 firms in its twenty-six-year history and produced profits in excess of $400 million.

General Doriot's assignment, as he saw it, was to "seek out creative men with the vision of things to be done. Help breathe life into new ideas and processes and products with capital—and with more than capital—with sensitive appreciation for creative drive."[1] He was not particularly pleased with the changes in the venture capital industry following the introduction of small business investment corporations in 1959. He viewed many of the new firms that were established as being primarily speculative ventures rather than constructive

1. ARDC Annual Reports

agents in the formation and development of new businesses.

ARDC owed much of its success to General Doriot. When he retired, no suitable replacement could be found. In 1972 the firm ended its existence as an independent venture capital operation and merged with Textron, Inc., a $26 billion (1975 sales) conglomerate. It continues to operate as a subsidiary of Textron, enabling the parent to be in at the beginning of new technological developments. Thus both ARDC and General Doriot have passed from the business scene together, marking the end of an era in venture capital activity.

leasing

Virtually any asset that can be purchased can also be leased. Most people are familiar with a residential apartment lease, in which a renter acquires the right to inhabit the apartment in return for monthly rental payments. Any lease is a contract between the owner of an asset, called the **lessor,** and another party, called the **lessee,** who makes periodic payments to the owner for the *right* to use the asset. From the introduction of leasing by Phoenician shipowners 3,000 years ago until the mid-1960s, only a few types of assets could be leased and the volume of lease transactions was not very large compared with the volume of purchases. However, in recent years leasing has grown dramatically, and by the mid-1970s the value of capital equipment leased in the United States approached the $100 billion level. This compared with barely $20 billion at the end of the 1960s. In addition to the well-established leasing operations in computers, office equipment, transportation equipment (railroad cars, autos, aircraft, ships), and machinery, leasing arrangements now extend to such areas as shipping containers, nuclear fuel cores, medical equipment, and pollution control devices. Approximately one-fifth of all new equipment in the United States is leased. A striking example is Anaconda Aluminum's reduction mill near Sebree, Kentucky, which is entirely leased; $110,000,000 of the mill's $138,000,000 initial construction cost is in equipment. That single plant represents approximately 3 percent of the entire United States aluminum production capacity. Even the United States Navy began leasing ships in 1971 when Congress failed to appropriate funds for the purchase of needed fuel tankers. Leasing, indeed, has come of age.

WHO PROVIDES LEASES?

As we noted, at least two parties are involved in any leasing agreement—the lessor, who owns the asset, and the lessee, who acquires the right to use the asset for a fee (rental payment to the lessor). In a **leveraged lease,** there is also a lender (for example, an insurance company), from whom the lessor borrows the capital to purchase the asset. In other leasing situations, a **lease packager** or an investment bank may arrange the lease agreement for a fee without participating directly as a lessor, lessee, or lender. The types of firms that are active as lessors and lease packagers are listed in Table 17-1. By mid-1976, several firms each had equipment

Table 17-1. Lessors and lease packagers

Type of lessor	Specific firms engaged in leasing
Lease packager	U.S. Leasing International
	ITEL Leasing
Investment banker	Solomon Brothers
	Dillon Read
	Kidder, Peabody
	Morgan Stanley
	Lehman Corporation
Finance company	General Electric Credit
	Commercial Credit
	C.I.T. Financial
	Bankers Leasing
	Leasco
Commercial bank	Citicorp
	First Chicago Leasing
	Manufacturers Hanover Leasing
	Union Bank
	Security Pacific
Industrial company	General American Transportation
	Greyhound Leasing and Financial
	Trans Union
	Ford Motor Credit
	Chrysler Financial

under lease or had arranged the leasing of equipment with an original cost of over $2 billion.

TYPES OF LEASES

Operating Lease

An **operating lease** is a lease that is cancellable by the lessee or the lessor upon due notice to the other party. This type of lease is therefore an arrangement of indefinite duration. Vehicles, computers, copiers, amusement equipment, display fixtures, and furniture are among the assets commonly acquired on an operating lease basis.

Financial Lease

A **financial lease** is a commitment by the lessor and lessee, under which the lessee makes lease payments over a specified period of time in exchange for the use of the leased asset. The lease can be canceled only if the lessor and lessee agree to the cancellation. If the asset is equipment, the lease duration will generally equal at least half of the expected useful life of the asset. Real estate leases often extend for twenty or more years, but may nevertheless encompass only a small fraction of the structure's expected life. Maintenance or other services are not generally provided by the lessor under a financial lease although this is subject to the particular arrangement.

Assets that are frequently subject to a financial lease include real estate, office equipment, medical equipment, railroad cars, airplanes, and construction equipment. If the leased asset is real estate, the lessor may be an individual property owner or a business firm, frequently an insurance company. An equipment lessor is commonly a finance or leasing company or a commercial bank. A common procedure for leasing equipment is for the lessee firm to determine the equipment it wishes to lease and to settle upon a purchase price with the manufacturer. The firm will then find a leasing company or bank, which will purchase the asset and lease it to the firm for a specified rental providing an adequate return on the lessor's investment.

A financial lease will ordinarily provide a means for the lessee to continue possession of the property after the expiration of the initial lease. This may be allowed for under a renewal option which permits the lessee to obtain a new lease at a specified rental after the initial lease expires. The lease may also contain a purchase option which gives the lessee the right to buy the asset for a particular price at the lease's expiration.

The lease payment is a fixed obligation of the lessee and, as with debt interest, failure to make the rental payments can result in insolvency and bankruptcy court action. Although the lessor's claim against the lessee in the event of bankruptcy is usually somewhat less stringent than that of most creditors, it does provide for repossession of the leased asset and at least partial payment to the lessor of lease rentals applicable to the remaining term of the lease. Perhaps more relevant is that, for the going concern, leases involve a fixed charge like interest, and therefore fluctuations in firm income are absorbed by the lessee. In other words, a financial lease, like debt, involves the benefits and dangers of leverage.

Sale and Leaseback   A firm may sell an asset it already owns to another party and then lease it back from the buyer. In this way the firm can obtain cash (proceeds from the sale) and still have use of the asset. Similarly, if the firm wants to lease an asset it does not own, it can purchase it, sell it to another party, and then lease it back. Either of these arrangements is called a **sale and lease-back.** Financial leases (rather than operating leases) are almost always used in sale and leaseback arrangements. Whether the firm directly leases an asset or negotiates a sale and leaseback, the firm's ultimate position is one of a lessee making rental payments and without an ownership claim to the asset. As explained earlier, the financial lease will ordinarily provide for an option either to renew or to purchase the asset at the end of the lease term.

As with a direct financial lease, the buyer and lessor under a sale and leaseback agreement will frequently be an insurance company if the asset is real estate, or it will be a leasing firm, finance company, or commercial bank if the asset is equipment. The lease provisions are the same as those described for financial leases in general.

A **maintenance lease** requires the lessor to provide maintenance services for the lessee. Maintenance leases are ordinarily short-term, or operating (see above), leases and are often used in leasing autos, copiers, computers, and other types of technical equipment which require expert technicians for maintenance. The lessee ultimately pays for the maintenance services, since the lease rental is higher than it would be if no such services were provided. A lease which does not provide for maintenance is sometimes referred to as a **nonmaintenance lease.**

Maintenance Lease

A **leveraged lease,** or **third-party lease,** is one that involves a third party, who is a lender, in addition to the lessor and lessee. Under this arrangement, the lessor borrows funds from the lender to acquire the asset. The lessor leases the asset in the usual manner to a user, or lessee.

A variation of the leveraged lease, one which frequently includes a commercial bank as the lessor, involves the establishment of a **trust** (in effect, a subsidiary company) which acquires the asset to be leased. The trust obtains the funds to purchase the asset by selling an **equity** (ownership) **interest** in the trust to the lessor bank and selling **mortgage bonds** to other investors. These bonds are usually guaranteed by the lessee (that is, the lessee pays them off if the trust defaults on the bonds).[1] The periodic lease payments go to the trust, which uses them to pay off the bonds. Whatever is left over after making the bond payments is income to the ownership (lessor) interest in the trust.[2] A leveraged lease employing a trust can be advantageous since it allows the lessor company to borrow some of the funds through the trust (by issuing the mortgage bonds) to cover the asset's cost, while at the same time limiting the lessor's liability on the bonds (since the lessee guarantees the bonds).

Table 17-2 summarizes the characteristics of the major types of leases.

Leveraged Lease

---

1. This means that if the trust defaults on the bonds, the bondholders can take possession of the trust's assets (including the leased assets), and if the assets are not worth enough to repay what is owed on the bonds, the lessee must pay what is still owed. The lessor (commercial bank) is not liable on the bonds.
2. Income from the trust is allocated to the lessor in computing corporate income taxes. The taxable trust income to the commercial bank lessor is the rental payments less interest deduction on the mortgage bonds less depreciation on the asset.

Table 17-2. Types of leases

Type of lease	Parties involved	Duration	Does lessor maintain asset?
Operating lease	Lessor and lessee	Short term	Often yes
Financial lease	Lessor and lessee	Long term	Generally no
Sale and leaseback	Lessor (buyer) and lessee (seller)	Long term	Generally no
Maintenance lease	Lessor and lessee	Generally short term	Yes
Leveraged lease	Lessor, lender, and lessee	Long term	Generally no

LEASE OR BUY ANALYSIS

Back in Chapter 7 it was explained that the net benefit to the firm from acquiring an asset through purchase is measured by its net present value. The asset should be purchased only if the net present value is positive. Leasing provides an alternative way for a firm to have use of a new asset. To determine whether leasing or buying an asset is more beneficial, the net present value of the asset's cash flows to the lessee firm under the lease agreement must be computed and compared with the net present value with purchase of the asset. The option (lease or purchase) with the greater net present value is preferred and the asset is acquired if, and only if, that preferred option has a *positive* net present value. The analysis proceeds in the following steps:[3]

1. Compute the net present value of the asset's cash flows if the asset is purchased [signified NPV(purchase)]; this step is *identical to* that described in Chapters 7 and 8 (since Chapters 7 and 8 were concerned with the evaluation of an asset purchase).

2. Compute the net present value of the cash flows generated for the firm by the asset if it is leased [signified NPV(lease)].

3. Compare NPV(purchase) with NPV(lease). The option—purchase or lease—with the higher NPV is superior, and the other option should be rejected. The superior option should be adopted if, and only if, its NPV is positive.

3. The analytical procedure presented here is shown to be valid, and many other procedures shown to be incorrect, in L. D. Schall, "The Lease or Buy and Asset Acquisition Decisions," *Journal of Finance* (September 1974). The approach shown here is slightly different from that in the Schall paper in that *in computing taxes* Schall deducts interest on any debt used to finance an asset purchase; Schall then uses a pretax, rather than aftertax, cost of debt capital. The method here and the Schall method are otherwise the same and are fully consistent with one another.

The remainder of this section illustrates how the above analysis is performed.[4]

With purchase of the asset, the firm assumes all the risk and benefits associated with ownership, including the salvage value (the sale value of the asset when the firm no longer has use for it). It also incurs all the costs of maintaining the asset, e.g., upkeep expenses and property taxes. If the firm borrows to finance the asset, it will pay interest and principal on that debt. All maintenance expenses, debt interest, and depreciation on the asset are tax-deductible. With a lease, on the other hand, the firm receives the benefits from using the asset but has no claim to its residual sales value (salvage value), since this is reserved for the asset's owner. The lessee firm must make lease payments and may also be required to cover some or all of the maintenance expenses on the asset. Lease payments and all expenses associated with the asset are tax-deductible for the lessee. The lessee cannot deduct depreciation on the asset, since this is a tax deduction for the lessor (owner).

The cash flow from purchasing the asset is computed in the manner described in Chapter 7. This cash flow in year t, CF(purchase)$_t$, equals

$$\left\{ \begin{array}{c} \text{Cash flow in year } t \\ \text{with purchase of asset} \end{array} \right\} = \text{CF(purchase)}_t$$

$$= \text{revenues}_t - \text{expenses}_t - \text{capital expenditures}_t - \text{taxes}_t$$

$$= \text{revenues}_t - \text{expenses}_t - \text{capital expenditures}_t$$

$$- \tau(\text{revenues}_t - \text{expenses}_t - \text{depreciation}_t) \qquad (17\text{-}1)$$

where τ is the corporate tax rate. Equation (17-1) is identical to Eq. (7-1). "Capital expenditures" in Eq. (17-1) represent any capital outlays (cash outlays) during the life of the asset necessary to maintain the asset (e.g., a new roof or lighting fixture if the purchased asset were a manufacturing plant). If the asset is sold (e.g., near the end of its useful life), there is a cash inflow equal to the net aftertax proceeds from selling the asset, and this is reflected in Eq. (17-1) as a negative capital expenditure (i.e., is a positive cash flow). The example in Exhibit 17-1 on page 598 illustrates

---

4. The lease or buy decision is often posed as a choice between leasing the asset or purchasing it using *all* debt financing. However, in actual situations, this is frequently not the relevant problem since a purchase may involve equity as well as debt financing; for example, the asset may be purchased with 20 percent of the purchase price covered by cash and 80 percent by borrowed funds. The approach presented here does not assume 100 percent debt financing and permits us to assume whatever is realistic with regard to the source of the funds used for a purchase.

how salvage value is treated.[5] As explained in Chapter 7, in (17-1) interest on debt is not included in expenses. $CF(purchase)_t$ is discounted using the firm's cost of capital if the purchase is financed in the same way (same proportions of debt and equity financing) and is of the same risk as the company's other assets. On the other hand, the cost of capital will differ from that used on the firm's other assets if its financing or risk differs from that of the firm's other assets. The method for determining the cost of capital in this latter case is described in Chapter 8. The analysis of an asset purchase here is therefore identical to the analysis described in Chapters 7 and 8. Once we have estimated the cost of capital, k, we compute the net present value with purchase, which equals

$$NPV(purchase) = \frac{CF(purchase)_1}{1 + k} + \frac{CF(purchase)_2}{(1 + k)^2}$$

$$+ \cdots + \frac{CF(purchase)_n}{(1 + k)^n} - I$$

$CF(purchase)_n$ includes the net aftertax salvage value of the asset assuming it is sold in year n. I is the initial cost of the asset.

With leasing, the cash flow in year t from the asset, $CF(lease)_t$, equals

$$\left\{ \begin{array}{c} \text{Cash flow in year } t \\ \text{with leasing of} \\ \text{the asset} \end{array} \right\} = CF(lease)_t$$

$$= revenues_t - expenses_t - \text{lease rental}_t - taxes_t$$

$$= revenues_t - expenses_t - \text{lease rental}_t - \tau(revenues_t$$

$$- expenses_t - \text{lease rental}_t)$$

The expression in parentheses is the taxable income from the asset if it is leased. All the $CF(lease)_t$ returns from the asset go to the company's stockholders [since there is no debt used to finance the asset and $CF(lease)_t$ is net of the lease rental payments]. The appropriate discount rate for $CF(lease)_t$ is a rate which reflects the riskiness of $CF(lease)_t$. This lease cash flow is likely to be riskier than $CF(purchase)_t$ since $CF(purchase)_t$ is the total aftertax stream to equity *and* to any debt used to purchase the asset, whereas $CF(lease)_t$ is the net cash flow over and above the amount payable to the lessor; that is, $CF(lease)_t$ is an equity cash flow

5. To illustrate how salvage value is included in Eq. (17-1), if, using the Exhibit 17-1 example, a firm purchases an asset and, after five years, sells it for $500, the year 5 capital expenditure on the asset is −$500; in Eq. (17-1) cash flow = revenues$_5$ − expenses$_5$ − capital expenditures$_5$ − taxes$_5$ = $1,500 − $700 − (−$500) − $1,100 (see Exhibit 17-1 for these data).

after meeting the fixed charge in the form of the lease payment. The rate k_L for discounting CF(lease)$_t$ may approximate the firm's equity rate k_S (the rate used to discount the firm's equity cash flow, as described in Chapter 6). The net present value of the lease cash flow equals

$$\text{NPV(lease)} = \frac{\text{CF(lease)}_1}{1 + k_L} + \frac{\text{CF(lease)}_2}{(1 + k_L)^2} + \cdots + \frac{\text{CF(lease)}_n}{(1 + k_L)^n}$$

Leasing is preferred if NPV(lease) exceeds NPV(purchase), and purchase is preferred if NPV(purchase) exceeds NPV(lease). The preferred choice, lease or purchase, is accepted only if its NPV is positive. For example, if NPV(lease) = $2,000 and NPV(purchase) = $1,000, lease is preferred since NPV(lease) exceeds NPV(purchase); and the asset should be leased since NPV(lease) is positive. However, if NPV(lease) = −$1,000 and NPV(purchase) = −$1,500, lease is preferred over purchase (it's less bad), but leasing is rejected along with purchase since NPV(lease) is negative. In this situation, acquiring the asset by lease or by purchase is unprofitable.

A numerical illustration will help to clarify these equations. Assume that the firm can purchase, for $2,500, an asset with a useful life (to the firm) of five years. The asset will be sold after five years for a salvage value of $500 and depreciation for tax purposes is to be on a straight-line basis, that is, $400 per year for five years [($2,500 − $500)/5 years].[6] Purchase and use of the asset will increase the firm's expected revenues by $1,500 per year and will raise its expected operating expenses (not including depreciation or debt interest) by $700 per year. The corporate income tax rate is 50 percent. Assume that the cost of capital on the asset is 10 percent. As shown in Exhibit 17-1, NPV(purchase) = $85.

The firm can also lease the asset for a yearly rental of $650. With the lease, the increase in expected revenues from using the asset is $1,500 (as with purchase) and the increase in the firm's expected nondepreciation expenses is $600 (this differs from the $700 increase in expenses with pur-

6. In the example, there is no tax on the sale of the asset at the end of year 5 since it is sold for its book value of $500. If the asset were sold for more or less than its book value, then the cash flow would be net of the tax affect. For example, if the asset were sold for $700 [producing a gain of $200 (sale price − book value)] and the tax rate on the gain were 50 percent, then the cash flow from the sale would be (sale proceeds − tax on the sale proceeds) = $700 − tax rate × gain = $700 − 0.5($200) = $600; the $600 amount would be included in the cash flow analysis as an aftertax inflow for year 5. If the asset were, for example, sold for $400 (loss = $100), the aftertax cash flow would be $400 + 0.5($100) = $450, where there is a $50 tax benefit from deducting the loss from taxable income. Note: Under the Federal Income Tax Code, most gains (if the asset is sold for no more than its original cost) and losses on non-real estate assets used in a trade or business are treated as ordinary gains and losses (not capital gains and losses) and are therefore subject to the ordinary, not capital gain, tax rate.

Exhibit 17-1. Computation of the Net Present Value of Purchasing the Asset

Year (1)	Revenues (2)	Non-depreciation expenses (3)	Depre-ciation (4)	Taxes {0.50 [(2) − (3) − (4)]} (5)	Salvage value (6)	Net cash flow [(2) − (3) − (5) + (6)] (7)	10% Present value factor (8)	Present value of net cash flow[a] [(7) × (8)] (9)
1	$1,500	$700	$400	$200	$ 0	$ 600	0.9091	$ 545
2	1,500	700	400	200	0	600	0.8264	496
3	1,500	700	400	200	0	600	0.7513	451
4	1,500	700	400	200	0	600	0.6830	410
5	1,500	700	400	200	500	1,100	0.6209	683
								$2,585

NPV(purchase) = present value of future cash flows − cost of asset = $2,585 − $2,500 = $85

[a] Figures are rounded.

chase since it is assumed that $100 of the asset's maintenance expenses will be covered by the lessor). The discount rate to be used in discounting the expected net cash flow from leasing the asset is 12 percent. Exhibit 17-2 shows the lease computations. Since NPV(leasing) = $451, and, as shown in the table, NPV(purchase) = $85, the asset should be leased.

OTHER CONSIDERATIONS

There are several considerations in addition to the basic cash flow analysis presented above that may be important in choosing between lease and purchase of an asset. Sometimes these factors are misunderstood and improperly used to justify a lease or purchase decision. Each consideration is discussed below, with particular attention directed to the type of situation in which it is actually relevant.

Availability of Cash

It is sometimes argued that leasing rather than buying imposes less of a current cash drain on the firm, thus freeing capital that can be used for other productive purposes. This argument is valid only if the firm can lease the asset but cannot borrow to buy the asset (and cannot buy the asset on an installment payment basis, which is in effect a borrowing

Exhibit 17-2. Computation of the Net Present Value of Leasing the Asset

Year (1)	Revenues (2)	Nondepreciation expenses other than lease payments (3)	Rental payment (4)	Taxes {0.5 [(2) − (3) − (4)]} (5)	Net cash flow [(2) − (3) − (4) − (5)] (6)	12% present value factor (7)	Present value of net cash flow[a] [(6) × (7)] (8)
1	$1,500	$600	$650	$125	$125	0.8929	$112
2	1,500	600	650	125	125	0.7972	100
3	1,500	600	650	125	125	0.7118	89
4	1,500	600	650	125	125	0.6355	79
5	1,500	600	650	125	125	0.5674	71
							$451

NPV (lease) = present value of net cash flows with leasing = $451

[a] Figures are rounded.

arrangement). This is not ordinarily the situation faced by a firm. If the firm can purchase the asset using borrowed funds, there is no net cash outlay, since the funds borrowed can equal the price paid for the asset. With leasing or a purchase using debt, therefore, the firm has the asset for its use and a fixed commitment to make future payments (to a lessor or to a lender). Thus, in most situations, the firm can conserve cash even if it purchases the asset.

Effect on the Firm's Borrowing Capacity

Lenders (as well as shareholders) pay serious attention to the company's ability to meet its debt obligations. Too much debt will restrict the firm's capacity to borrow further. What of leasing? Is leasing somehow a method of obtaining assets on credit without the penalty of a reduced capacity to incur additional debt? Clearly, a lease imposes a fixed charge on the firm and poses a similar threat to the firm's solvency as does debt (lease-holders can demand payment just as creditors can). At issue here is whether lenders view the lease in this regard or merely ignore outstanding leases in computing fixed charges of the firm. It would appear that, until recently, leases were not properly acknowledged in evaluating the firm's degree of financial leverage. Obtaining assets by leasing rather than borrowing and purchase, therefore, had less of an effect in reducing the firm's ability to incur additional debt. To illustrate, assume a firm with $10 million in assets, $5 million in liabilities, and $5 million in owners' equity (common stock). If the firm were to add $5 million in new assets under a lease and not reveal this on the balance sheet, its new balance sheet would appear no different than before the asset acquisition (case A in Exhibit 17-3). If the assets were obtained with debt financing, however, debt and assets would rise by $5 million as indicated by case B in Exhibit 17-3. The debt-equity ratio (which is one way to indicate the firm's debt burden) as computed from the balance sheet figures is higher in case B than in case A.

Leases have recently come to be treated as similar to debt and are now taken into account in appraising the firm's financial structure. Partially due to pressure for improved disclosure by the Securities and Exchange Commission and by The American Institute of Certified Public Accountants, financial statements now disclose, at least in a footnote, the assets held under a lease and the associated rental payment obligation. Some financial statements go so far as to list the leased assets and the present value of the future lease payments directly on the balance sheet. This is illustrated in case C in Exhibit 17-3. The disclosure illustrated by case C is

Exhibit 17-3. Alternative Methods of Disclosure by a Lessee of Existing Lease Commitments (Dollar Figures in Millions)

Case A: No disclosure of added $5 million in assets acquired by lease		Case B: Disclosure of added $5 million in assets if acquired with debt funds		Case C: Disclosure of added $5 million in assets acquired by lease	
Assets	$10	Assets	$15	Assets (owned)	$10
Liabilities		Liabilities		Assets under	
(bonds)	5	(bonds)	10	lease	5
Owners' equity	5	Owners' equity	5	Liabilities:	
Debt-equity		Debt-equity		Bonds	5
ratio = $5/$5 = 1		ratio = $10/$5 = 2		Discounted	
				(present value)	
				of lease rental	
				payments	5
				Owners' equity	5
				Ratio of (debt + lease obligation) to equity = $10/$5 = 2	

clearly a better reflection of the firm's actual financial position than are the presentations in cases A and B.

Although a lease commitment is very similar to debt and will be regarded as such by outsiders, it may involve less binding restrictions (see discussion of next section) than some forms of debt. For example, whereas a lease may be subordinate to any future borrowing by the company, debt incurred to purchase an asset will frequently require all future debt to assume a subordinated position (future debt is paid last). This means that leasing an asset may have a less constraining effect on the firm's future borrowing capacity than would the purchase of the asset with borrowed funds. Of course, this advantage will not exist if the lease agreement stipulates that new debt is to be subordinated to the lease. Notice, also, that even if the lease does not require subordination, the lessor will demand a higher rate of return (to compensate for the higher risk) than will a lender who does require subordination. The financial manager must decide if the advantage of maintaining borrowing capacity using a lease is worth the added rental payment.

Avoidance of Restrictions on the Firm

Lenders frequently impose restrictions on the firm with the idea of improving the firm's capacity to pay off the loan. Examples are limits on dividends, subordination clauses, and restrictions on new investment or sales of firm property. This is discussed in regard to bank term loans in Chapter 16 and also in Chapter 19. Lease agreements may also include such constraints, but they are less frequent and are usually less restrictive. However, in contrast with debt, a lease agreement may involve constraints on the use of the leased property, for example, how many hours per week a machine may be used. These restrictions are meant to protect the asset (since it is still owned by the lessor) rather than to enhance the lessee's rental paying ability.

Observe that burdensome debt restrictions protect the lender and consequently reduce the risk, thereby reducing the interest the lender will demand on the debt. If a lessor does not require similar restrictions on the firm, the risk to the lessor will be greater than on debt and, to compensate for this, the lease rentals will imply a higher rate of return to the lessor than to a lender. The recurring theme applies once again. The marketplace rarely provides something for nothing. The benefit to the lessee firm of no restrictions on its operations is reflected in higher lease payments. Whether the lack of restriction is worth the added cost will depend upon the particular situation.

Shifting of Risk of Obsolescence

Can the lessee escape the risk associated with the possibility that the asset will become obsolete? With an operating lease the lease can be terminated at the will of the lessee firm when it chooses: even with a financial lease, the lease term can be sufficiently short (e.g., 50 percent of the asset's expected economic life) that the lessee can avoid being compelled to hold an obsolete asset. But here again the rental price on the asset will mirror the costs borne by the lessor. To be willing to assume the obsolescence risk, i.e., the risk that the asset may become worthless because it is obsolete, the lessor will require a higher rental than if such risk were assumed by the lessee. In effect then, the lessee ends up paying for the obsolescence risk.[7] But, what if the lessor is better able than the user (lessee) to find an economic use for a somewhat outdated asset? This might occur because of the lessor's access to many potential users of the asset. Under these conditions, the economic cost of obsolescence is less under leasing than under purchase by the user. This economic advantage will be at least partially passed on to the lessee (in the form of lower lease payments) as lessors compete for customers in a competitive market. In this case, the customer (lessee) firm can gain by leasing since the overall economic obsolescence risk is lower than if the lessee were to buy.

Tax Considerations

Only the owner of an asset can use depreciation as a tax-deductible expense or take the investment tax credit. The tax benefits are therefore directly available to the firm if it purchases the asset. However, since a *lessor* can also take the tax credit and use accelerated depreciation and *will in a competitive market pass at least some of this benefit on to the lessee in the form of lower rental charges,* we cannot assume that these tax advantages constitute a bias in favor of purchase relative to lease. Indeed, these tax benefits to the lessor may make leasing cheaper than purchase for the lessee.

In short, tax factors encourage that choice between leasing and purchase which minimizes the total taxes associated with the asset's use and ownership (ownership by the user with purchase or by the lessor with lease). Whether lease or purchase is preferred on the basis of tax considerations depends on such factors as the lessor's and lessee's tax brackets, the method of depreciating the asset (straight line, sum of the years digits, etc.), and the degree to which the asset is debt financed by its owner (the user under purchase or the lessor under a lease). These factors vary from case to case and the impact of taxes will therefore depend on the particular situation.

7. Even if the lessee pays the lessor for assuming the obsolescence risk, there may be an advantage for the lessee in this arrangement in that the lease rental payments are predictable (since they are specified in the lease contract), whereas the future impact of obsolescence on the value of the asset is uncertain. Therefore, the lessee is in a more predictable position by leasing rather than by buying. But, again, it should be emphasized that the lessee pays a higher rental to the lessor for having the latter assume the less predictable position. Whether the asset user is willing to pay the extra amount to a lessor in order to shift the uncertainty to the lessor (rather than for the user to buy the asset) will depend upon the particular circumstances.

There is sometimes a temptation for the seller and the buyer of an asset to disguise a sale as a lease if a lease minimizes the total taxes paid by the two parties. The Internal Revenue Service is aware of this ruse and requires that certain conditions be met which indicate a lease is indeed a lease and not a sale. The essential requirement is that the lease payments must realistically reflect *rental* value and must not include an amount which implies that the user is purchasing an ownership interest in the asset. For example, assume an asset costing $10,000 were "leased" for ten years and the "rental" payments were $3,500 per year for the first four years and $200 per year for years five through ten. This would generally *not* qualify as a lease but would be deemed a sale for tax purposes, since the payments imply that the user is really purchasing an ownership interest in the asset during the first four years, the last six "lease" payments being nominal. Only if it could be proved that the asset's value did in fact fall to nearly nothing after four years would the contract be considered a lease by the Internal Revenue Service.

Salvage Value

The owner of the asset receives salvage value (residual value), but the higher the expected salvage value the lower the lease rentals need be in order that the lessor firm earn a satisfactory return on its investment. The anticipated salvage value is therefore reflected in the lease payments required on an asset, and there is no implied gain to a firm from owning relative to leasing. Indeed, if the lessor firm is more capable of finding productive economic employment of the asset after it is used by the lessee, the salvage value will be greater for a lessor than for a user-lessee. This economic advantage would make leasing more economical than purchase by the user-firm. On the other hand, if the user anticipates that the asset will have a higher future value than others (lessors) expect—as might occur, for example, if the asset were real estate—then the firm might wish to purchase. This is a gamble on the part of the firm's management that its expectations are more likely to be fulfilled than those of the lessor. This gamble might be justified if the firm has superior information or greater skill in evaluating information. In some cases this may be so. However, knowledge tends to circulate throughout the economy. What is thought to be secret or superior information may in fact be known to many others, including the seller or lessor of the asset. This would imply that what appears to be a bargain because of "superior information," may, in fact, involve a rental that fully takes into account the relevant facts, in which case there may be no bargain at all.

An interesting example that illustrates, in the extreme, how important residual or salvage value can be in some cases involves Gulf Oil's lease of a property in West Texas. In 1925, Gulf negotiated a fifty-year lease of the Waddell Ranch oil properties owned by wildcatter W. H. McFadden. Because oil output during the fifty-year lease duration was unexpectedly restricted by the Texas Railway Commission (which sets oil extraction rates in Texas), much of the oil remained in the ground when the lease expired in 1975. Gulf Oil foresaw this during the late 1960s and sued to have the lease extended. It was several years before the court decision was rendered, but finally the Texas Supreme Court ruled against Gulf, declaring that the lease specified fifty years and the unexpected intervention of the Texas Railway Commission did not alter that fact. The stock of Southland Realty Company, the owner of Waddell Ranch, rose sharply after the court decision.

SUMMARY

Under a lease arrangement, the user of an asset (the lessee) pays the owner (the lessor) a rental per period for the usage right. Several types of leases are available. An operating lease is one which is cancellable at any time (but with due notice) by the lessee, whereas a financial lease involves a mutual commitment by the lessee and lessor for a stipulated minimum period of time. A maintenance lease obligates the lessor to provide asset maintenance services. A sale and leaseback contract provides for the sale of the asset by the user, who then leases it back from the purchaser. The owner of the asset realizes the cash market value of the asset immediately. Real estate is the most common type of property covered by sale and leaseback contracts.

The purchase and lease alternatives for acquiring an asset can be evaluated by comparing their cash flows. The alternative with the higher net present value of cash flows is preferred and is adopted if its net present value is positive.

In some situations leasing is preferred to purchase of an asset because it may:

1. Impose less of a current cash drain on the firm than would purchase (if the firm cannot borrow a large part of the asset's cost were it to be purchased)
2. Have less effect in reducing the firm's future borrowing capacity than would purchase
3. Impose fewer restrictions on the firm than would debt incurred to purchase the asset
4. Reduce the risk of obsolescence for the firm relative to purchase and ownership of the asset
5. Provide tax advantages relative to purchase

In many cases, few or even none of the above advantages exists with leasing, and consequently purchase is preferable.

1. Describe the major difference between an operating lease and a financial lease.
2. Explain why a leased asset is evaluated in essentially the same way as one which is purchased outright.
3. How is the discount rate used to evaluate a lease determined? Explain fully.
4. "The neat part about leasing is that there is less cash drain on a company than if it buys the asset outright." Evaluate this statement.
5. "Leasing is a good deal because it does not add debt to the capital structure. Therefore, by leasing a firm can borrow more money and gain access to more assets." Evaluate this statement.
6. What rationale, if any, can be given for the procedure of listing the leased assets and the present value of lease payments on the balance sheet?
7. Restrictive provisions are commonly found in debt contracts but not in lease arrangements. Furthermore, the return required by lessors is usually greater than that required by creditors. Reconcile these facts.
8. "Leases should be preferred over ownership when there is a high risk of obsolescence. In this way the firm avoids the risk." Evaluate the statement.
9. "The trouble with leasing from the lessee's standpoint is that the lessor gets the advantage of taking depreciation for tax purposes, not the lessee." Evaluate this statement.
10. Explain the role that salvage value plays in leasing.
11. Describe in words the proper way to evaluate a lease.

1. Select a major asset used by one or more firms in your area and find out how you would negotiate the lease and the purchase of the asset.
2. Select several assets that can be purchased and can be leased and determine whether purchasing or leasing is preferable. Assume first a 48 percent tax rate and then a lower tax rate, say 30 percent. Do the analyses assuming first that the asset is entirely equity financed, then assuming that some significant portion (e.g., 50 percent) is debt financed), and, finally, assuming that the asset is entirely debt financed. The interest rate on the debt that you assume may affect your results.

1. Corinthian Nurseries is in the process of evaluating the purchase or lease of new greenhouse equipment. The estimated increase in annual revenues is $2,500, and the estimated increase in operating expense is

$1,000, regardless of whether the asset is purchased outright or leased from the manufacturer. The equipment costs $5,000 to purchase and has an estimated life of five years, at the end of which time it can be sold for $1,000. If the asset is leased, the annual payments come to $1,200, payable at the end of each year. The company plans to depreciate its new equipment on a straight-line basis with a salvage value of $1,000. The financial manager has decided that the proper rate with which to evaluate the leased equipment is 10 percent; for the purchased equipment, it is 8 percent. The firm's tax rate is 40 percent. What should the company do: purchase or lease? Show all calculations. [Ans.: NPV (purchase) = $552; NPV (lease) = $683]

2. You are the financial manager of a manufacturing firm considering leasing a small computer to use for inventory control and billing. The computerized system is expected to produce significant annual savings over the present manual system, which is slow and inaccurate. The lease payments would be $25,000 per year for four years of a maintenance lease, with the lease payment due at the end of each year. Your company would have to hire an operator at a salary of $12,000 per year and pay for electricity, heating, and air conditioning (for the machine and the room where it will be operated) at an estimated cost of $3,000 per year. If taxes are 40 percent and the discount rate for the cash flow from leasing (k_L) is 12 percent, what annual savings must the computer produce to justify the lease? (Assume that the computer cannot be purchased.)

3. As the financial manager of Mort's Sports, Inc. you must determine whether to lease new display cases or to buy them. The new cases will replace existing old-fashioned ones which, although usable, are not very attractive and have no significant market value. The new cases will raise before-tax net cash flow by $5,000 per year before deducting an additional $100 per year upkeep expense on the new cases and before deducting any lease payments if the new cases are leased. If you buy the new cases, you must make a cash outlay of $20,000. The display cases are estimated to last fifteen years, at the end of which time you think you can sell them for $2,000. However, the manufacturer will lease the same display cases for a period of fifteen years at the yearly rental rate of $3,500 a year for the first nine years and $2,800 a year thereafter. The lease payments are due at the end of each year. You estimate the new cases will require an additional $100 a year for maintenance and upkeep (above the upkeep costs of the existing old-fashioned cases), regardless of whether you buy or rent them. Your firm depreciates all such assets on a straight-line basis and is in the 40 percent tax bracket. The old cases are no longer being depreciated for tax purposes, and the new cases would be depreciated over fifteen years to a salvage value of $2,000. You estimate that the riskiness of

the purchase and lease cash flows are equal, both requiring a 12 percent discount rate. What should you do? Show all calculations.

4. As a real estate developer in Corntown, Indiana, you have just been approached by a representative of Enchilada International (EI), a worldwide fast-food chain, about putting a "Bill's Beer and Crackers Pub" on Main Street in Corntown. EI has purchased a suitable site for $15,000, will erect the pub at a cost to them of $30,000, and wants to sell the building and land to you for $50,000. You will then, under the terms of a fifteen-year financial lease, lease the property to EI for $8,500 per year. EI will pay all costs in maintaining the pub, but you pay property taxes of $1,000 annually and retain ownership of the land at the end of the fifteen years (at which time EI will demolish the building and the land is expected to be worth $45,000). You plan to sell the land at the end of the fifteen years and expect to net (after taxes) $40,000 from the land sale. Your accountant has informed you that you can straight-line depreciate the building to a zero salvage value. You may place a $30,000 current value on the building for depreciation purposes. Your tax rate is 40 percent. If you plan to finance with your own equity (i.e., you have the $50,000 available without borrowing) and want at least a 10 percent aftertax rate of return, should you accept EI's offer?

5. At the recent board of directors meeting of Tell-It-Like-It-Is Corporation, one of the directors argued that the company would be better off if it leased assets rather than bought them with borrowed money. He commented, "After all, ya won't have a balance sheet showing debt on it. And that's good, 'cause we can borrow later on if we want to." Another director pointed out that lease payments are viewed as the equivalent to fixed charges on debt and that no one would be fooled by the lease versus debt issue. A third director thought the company would have to capitalize the leases in order to depict the true nature of the balance sheet.

If the firm has $10 million in assets before acquiring new assets, show what the balance sheet would look like under each of the proposed systems if the firm were to lease the assets or buy them with borrowed money. The cost of the assets to be acquired is $1 million. The firm can borrow the money to finance them at the market rate of 8 percent a year for twenty years. The annual lease payments, if the assets are leased, will be $160,000 for the twenty-year period. The company currently has a book debt-equity ratio of $\frac{3}{7}$.

common stock

In Parts 2 and 3 we examined and analyzed the problems that a financial manager must deal with in order to maximize the firm's profits. In choosing among investment opportunities, obtaining funds to finance investments, and planning a long-term investment program, the financial manager, we have noted, is serving the interests of the firm's owners, or *stockholders*. In the first part of this chapter, we will look more closely at the rights and privileges of the stockholders in order to get a better idea of the importance of these rights and privileges both to stockholders and to the corporate planner.

Actually, we have already discussed many features of common stock. In Chapters 1 and 2, we defined the stockholders as the firm's owners and explained the institutions in the financial system through which stocks and other securities are traded. In Chapter 9, the financial manager's role in providing funds for new investments was analyzed, and common stock was identified as an important source of funds for the corporation. What we have not yet looked at are the rights and privileges of owning shares of stock, that is, what a firm guarantees to its shareholders, or owners, when it makes a common stock offering. In the first part of this chapter we will evaluate this issue—from the viewpoint of the shareholder—and round out our knowledge of common stock. Following that, we will consider some additional problems and decisions that confront management.

Before proceeding, we should point out that management, as well as shareholders, is concerned with what potential investors in the company want in terms of the rights and privileges they receive by buying the firm's stock. This is so for two reasons. First, management represents shareholders and must be sensitive to their rights if shareholder interests are to be effectively served. Second, the firm may wish to issue additional shares to raise new capital, and the more attractive is the stock, the easier it is to sell (or, equivalently, the higher the price for which it can be sold). Of course, management does not want to "give away the store" and will stipulate provisions in any new security (e.g., stock) agreement that also protects existing stockholders. But the common stock must have sufficiently attractive features to appeal to new stockholders. In raising new capital, whether the firm issues stock or any of the various other types of securities which we will discuss in Chapters 19 and 20, the sale essentially involves bargaining between management (i.e., the existing stockholders represented by management) and the new investors. The securities issued carry provisions that are meant to appeal to new investors while not giving away too much. Obviously it behooves management to understand what the new investors want in return for the funds they are investing in the company.

RIGHTS AND PRIVILEGES OF STOCKHOLDERS

Income

The rights of shareholders to the firm's income can be referred to as **residual;** i.e., shareholders receive what is left over after all other investors in the firm have been paid. For example, if income before taxes and interest on debt is $100,000, and if interest on debt is $60,000, stockholders receive before-tax earnings in the current period of $40,000 ($100,000 − $60,000 = $40,000). On the other hand, if interest on debt is $120,000, stockholders incur a loss of $20,000 in the current period ($100,000 − $120,000 = − $20,000). Of course, if losses are great enough, the firm may suffer bankruptcy and even the bondholders may not receive all that is due to them; in this case, stockholders would lose their entire investment. But notice that being in a residual position also has its advantages. If the firm were to earn $500,000 during the current period, bondholders would still receive only their fixed interest, say $60,000, and stockholders would receive $440,000. Along with the greater risk of a residual interest goes the chance of a greater reward. This is the concept of financial leverage, which was discussed in Chapters 9 and 12.

The income to stockholders may be retained by the firm or be paid out in the form of dividends. Dividends are paid after they are declared by the board of directors. In most cases, the firm's income exceeds the payment of dividends and some of the period's aftertax income is retained by the firm. As a consequence of the retention, there is an increase in the value of the firm's shares. For example, if the firm earns $200,000 during the year and pays dividends of $120,000, the value of the firm's shares will rise by $80,000 ($200,000 − $120,000 = $80,000).[1] The shareholders have therefore received benefits in two forms: first, in the form of dividends of $120,000, and secondly, in the form of an increase in the value of their shares (a capital gain).[2] Companies that reinvest a large fraction of their

---

1. In reality, share prices will probably not rise by exactly $80,000. This is so because of differential taxes on capital gains and dividends. Furthermore, note that when it is stated here that share values will rise by $80,000, this means that the retained earnings will have an upward effect on share prices of $80,000. Factors other than current retained earnings (e.g., general stock price trends, expectations about the firm's future earnings) may also be affecting share values, causing them to rise by more or less than $80,000.

2. An increase in the price of a stockholder's shares is referred to as a capital gain whether or not the shares are sold by the stockholder. The capital gain is referred to as **realized** if the shares are sold for cash (the gain is realized in the form of cash).

earnings will have low dividend payments relative to earnings but will have higher than average share value increases each year; that is, more income to shareholders will be in the form of capital gains.

Control Stockholders control the firm through their right to elect the board of directors of the corporation. The board of directors, in turn, appoints the members of the management who supervise the daily operations of the company. Although, in theory, the stockholders directly control the firm by electing directors who then appoint the officers of the corporation, in practice this control is somewhat limited. Most often, management selects the board of directors. At the time of the election, management will send stockholders proxy statements requesting that the shareholders assign to management the right to vote their stock. Of course, shareholders may give their proxies to some outside dissident group if they so choose; however, this is the exception rather than the rule. Stockholders who neither appear at the stockholders meeting nor give their proxies to someone else to vote do not exercise their right to vote, and those who do vote consequently elect the new board of directors. Shareholders usually sign and return the proxies they have received from existing management or simply fail to exercise their vote. Only a small fraction of stockholders attend most annual meetings. As a result, management usually retains control of the corporation and chooses the board of directors.[3] Effective control of a corporation, therefore, generally does not require even 50 percent ownership of the outstanding common stock. The inertia or apathy of many shareholders often ensures that a minority position retains control of the firm. Successful takeover by an outsider group is usually possible only after existing management has mismanaged the corporation for an extended period of time, which is usually indicated by a long period of declining earnings or losses by the corporation. A more detailed description of the voting process is presented later in this chapter.

Some firms have more than one class of common stock outstanding, one of which does not carry the voting privilege. For example, the class A common stock may have the right to vote, whereas the class B common stock may not. The nonvoting stock may or may not provide an identical claim to dividends, income, and assets as the voting shares. Even if the different classes of stock differ only in voting rights, the nonvoting shares

3. Rebelling against the annual stockholders meeting as a waste of time and money, J. B. Fuqua, chairman of Fuqua Industries, polled his stockholders on their reaction to the idea of discontinuing such meetings. He received 99 percent support. Although Delaware law would have allowed discontinuing the annual meetings, they are required by the New York Stock Exchange for all listed firms. So the meetings continue even though no more than a dozen of the Fuqua shareholders (out of 18,000) generally attend. See *Business Week* (April 7, 1973), p. 33.

usually have a slightly lower market value since the voting privilege is a valuable right.

The **preemptive right** is the right of existing stockholders to maintain their share of the ownership of the corporation by purchasing any new shares issued by the corporation. For example, if the corporation has outstanding 100,000 shares of common tock and plans to issue 50,000 new shares, a stockholder owning 100 of the 100,000 outstanding shares (0.1 percent) will have the right to purchase 50 of the 50,000 new shares (0.1 percent) before those new shares are offered to anyone else. The preemptive right is provided under common law. However, some states deny the preemptive right by statute unless it is specifically included in the corporate charter; in other states, the preemptive right exists unless denied under the corporate charter.

Stockholders' Preemptive Rights

The preemptive right is an important protection of the shareholders' ownership position. When this right is not provided, management can issue stock to individuals favorably inclined to management and thereby retain its position of control. Of even greater importance is the protection afforded stockholders against dilution of their financial interest in the firm. *If additional shares are sold to new stockholders at a price below the stock's current market price, owners of the old shares will suffer a fall in the market value of their holdings.* For example, assume a firm with 100,000 shares of common stock but no bonds outstanding and a market value of $10 per share; the market value of the firm is therefore $1 million (100,000 × $10). The firm is to issue 50,000 new shares at $4 per share, thereby raising $200,000 of new capital. After issuance of the new stock, the value of the firm is approximately $1,200,000 ($1,000,000 + $200,000 raised by issuing new stock) and there are 150,000 shares outstanding. The market value per share of the stock is equal to $8 ($1,200,000 divided by 150,000 shares = $8) instead of the preissuance price of $10. The original stockholders lose $2 per share of stock owned. The preemptive right ensures that current stockholders get the first chance to buy any new shares at $4 per share. The procedure by which stockholders exercise the preemptive right is discussed in detail below in the section on stock rights.

If the firm issues securities which are convertible into common stock, existing shareholders are generally permitted under the preemptive right the opportunity to purchase these convertible securities before they are offered to outsiders. On the other hand, if new stock is issued in exchange for property, the preemptive right does not apply. Furthermore, stockholders may vote to waive the preemptive right upon management's request if the existence of preemptive rights is considered a hindrance to issuing new shares.

Stockholders' Right to Inspect the Firm's Books

A stockholder has the right to obtain information from management regarding the firm's operations. However, this right is not unlimited, and is only effective to the extent that the release of such information will not injure the competitive position of the firm. This limitation is imposed in order to protect other stockholders. A stockholder who feels that management is withholding information that would expose malfeasance or gross negligence in managing the company may take the case to the courts. This is an example of the general rule that management's control is protected unless a determined (and often very expensive) effort is undertaken to reduce or eliminate that control.

Claim on Assets under Bankruptcy

As in the case of income, the position of stockholders with regard to the firm's assets is also residual. Other claimants, e.g., creditors and preferred stockholders, have prior claim on the company's assets, and are paid out of the firm's assets before stockholders receive anything. If the firm fails to make required interest and principal payments to creditors, control of the firm may shift from shareholders to creditors. The firm's assets may be sold and the creditors paid off, or the firm may continue to be operated under court supervision until creditor claims have been met.

Right to Transfer Shares

In the discussion of business organizations in Chapter 3 we noted that one advantage of the corporation is the ease with which a shareholder may transfer his or her ownership claim to another investor. No permission is required from management or from other stockholders if a particular shareholder wishes to sell his or her shares. Furthermore, in contrast to single proprietorships or partnerships, the corporation continues to exist regardless of any changes in ownership due to transfers of stock by shareholders. A shareholder may directly sell his or her stock to another party merely by signing that stock (on the back of the certificate) over to the buyer. If the stock is publicly traded, the shareholder may also transfer the stock through a broker. The purchaser of the stock (or the broker) sends the stock certificate, which has been transferred to the purchaser, to a transfer agent representing the corporation. The transfer agent then issues a new certificate under the name of the purchaser so that the new owner may be listed on the firm's books as the owner of record. The new shareholder is now entitled to receive dividends on the shares and has all the rights and privileges associated with stock ownership.

Limited Liability

A particularly attractive feature of the corporation, from the standpoint of the shareholder, is the separation of the shareholder from the liabilities of the company. Because the corporation is a distinct entity under the law, a stockholder is in no way liable for the debts incurred by the corporation, just as the corporation is not liable for the personal debts of its shareholders. The owner of a single proprietorship, on the other hand, would be personally liable for debts owed by the business.

This corporate shield between the stockholder and the firm's creditors, however, is not impenetrable in all cases. If the corporation is used by its stockholders for illegal or morally reprehensible purposes, the stockholders may become liable for the *corporation's acts*. However, for large corporations, this qualification is of less significance, and shareholders are generally protected from liability for the firm's debts.

We noted earlier that one of the rights of stockholders is to elect the board of directors of the corporation. Although the shareholders are the owners of the corporation, their participation in the management of the firm is limited to selecting the firm's board of directors and to voting on certain types of corporate actions (e.g., on merger decisions or on adopting bylaws to the corporate charter). Furthermore, stockholders may exercise these rights only at legal corporate meetings.

Two types of voting systems are in general use—majority rule and cumulative voting.

STOCKHOLDER VOTING

Unless otherwise provided by statute or under the corporate charter, the will of the majority of those voting is effective in electing the board of directors. Each share entitles its owner to one vote; an owner of 100 shares has 100 votes. Each position on the board of directors is voted on individually. Therefore, if six positions were to be filled, an owner of 100 shares would cast 100 votes for a candidate for position 1, 100 votes for a candidate for position 2, etc. Thus, if the firm has 100,000 shares outstanding, a group with 50,001 shares acting together could elect the candidate it prefers for each position on the board of directors. Any individual or group owning a majority of the firm's shares can choose the entire board and prevent election of any directors by the minority. It is for this reason that an alternative voting system has evolved, one which gives the minority a greater opportunity for representation on the board. This system is cumulative voting.

Majority Rule Voting

Under cumulative voting each shareholder receives a number of votes equal to the number of his or her shares times the number of directors to be elected. For example, if six directors were to be elected, a shareholder with 100 shares would have 600 votes. All the shareholder's votes may be

Cumulative Voting

applied in support of one candidate or they may be spread over a number of candidates. With six directors to be elected, a shareholder with 600 votes could cast all 600 votes for a given candidate, or, say, 400 votes for one candidate and 200 for a second candidate, or 100 votes in favor of each of six candidates, etc. Under both the majority rule and cumulative voting systems, those candidates receiving the most votes are the ones elected to the board of directors. If six positions on the board were to be filled, and there were twelve candidates for the board, those six candidates with the most votes would win the election. However, whereas under the majority rule system a majority is able to elect all members of the board, under cumulative voting a significant minority is assured of at least some representation on the board, if it properly distributes its votes among the candidates.

An example may help to illustrate the differences between the majority rule and cumulative voting systems. Assume that a firm has five directors to be elected and twelve candidates are seeking election. Assume further that the firm has a total of 10,000 shares outstanding. Since there are five directorship openings, each share of stock is entitled to five votes under the cumulative voting method; an owner of 100 shares therefore has 500 votes. An owner of 100 shares could distribute all 500 votes in any manner between the twelve candidates, e.g., 50 votes for each of candidates 1 through 10, or all 500 votes for candidate 1, etc.

The number of shares that must be controlled in order to guarantee the election of a particular number of directors can be calculated by the following formula:

Number of shares needed to elect desired number of directors

$$= \frac{[\text{number of firm shares outstanding}] \times [\text{number of directors stockholders desire to elect}]}{\text{total number of directors to be elected} + 1} + 1 \quad (18\text{-}1)$$

Using this equation in the above example, in order for a group of shareholders to be sure of being able to elect one director it would have to have 1,667 shares,[4] since

$$\frac{10,000 \times 1}{5 + 1} + 1 = 1,667\tfrac{2}{3} \text{ or } 1,667$$

If the group were to vote its 1,667 shares for one candidate (e.g., for candidate 6), then the group would be assured of electing that candidate regardless of how the majority group (which owns the remaining 8,333 shares) were to cast its votes. In order to elect two directors, the minor-

4. Fractions are dropped in the equation.

Exhibit 18-1. Comparison of Majority Rule and Cumulative Voting Systems

Candidate	Majority rule		Cumulative voting	
	Votes	Election results	Votes	Election results
1	6,666	Elected	6,667	Elected
2	6,666	Elected	6,667	Elected
3	6,666	Elected	6,667	Elected
4	6,666	Elected	6,665	Not elected
5	6,666	Elected	6,664	Not elected
6	3,334	Not elected	8,335	Elected
7	3,334	Not elected	8,335	Elected
8	3,334	Not elected	0	Not elected
9	3,334	Not elected	0	Not elected
10	3,334	Not elected	0	Not elected
11	0	Not elected	0	Not elected
12	0	Not elected	0	Not elected

Note: The majority group casts all its votes for candidates 1 through 5; the votes for the other candidates are cast by the minority group.

ity group would have to have 3,334 shares.[5] With 3,334 shares, the minority group would have 16,670 (5 × 3,334) votes. If it were to cast exactly half its votes for candidate 6 and half of its votes for candidate 7, it would be assured of electing these two candidates regardless of how the majority voted (the majority would own the remaining 6,666 shares and therefore have 5 × 6,666, or 33,330, votes).[6] Exhibit 18-1 illustrates this situation for the majority rule and cumulative voting systems. We assume that the majority group prefers candidates 1 through 5 and that the minority group prefers candidates 6 through 10. Under the majority rule system, the majority with 6,666 shares would be able to elect all five directors.

5. Using the formula $[(10,000 \times 2) / (5 + 1)] + 1 = 3,334\frac{1}{3}$, that is, 3,334 shares by rounding off the fraction.

6. If we wished to know how many directors we could elect with a given number of shares owned, rearranging the terms in the equation we find that

$$\frac{\text{Number of directors that can}}{\text{be elected with shares owned}} = \frac{[\text{number of shares owned} - 1]}{\text{total number of shares outstanding}} \times [\text{total number of directors to be elected} + 1]$$

A stockholder owning 4,000 of the 10,000 shares outstanding could therefore elect two directors since

$$\frac{(4,000 - 1) \times (5 + 1)}{10,000} = 2.4 \text{ or 2 directors}$$

**ISSUING NEW
SHARES**

We noted in Chapters 9 and 16 that in order to obtain capital to finance company operations the firm may issue new shares of stock. In this section we will examine how the firm records the stock issuance on its books and how **par value** is distinguished from a stock's market value. We will then look at the use of stock rights and its implications for the company's stockholders.

**Recording a Stock
Issue**

When a company issues new shares, it ordinarily receives, in payment, cash from the investors buying those shares. To show how this is recorded by the firm, assume that Infotex, Inc., has issued 1 million new shares of stock at $11 per share (the price paid by those buying the stock) and that the flotation costs (fees to investment bankers) are $1 million. The net proceeds to Infotex from the sale are $10 million. On its books, Infotex records the sale by increasing both cash and stockholders' equity by $10 million. If the stock has a par value (explained below) of, say, $5 per share, the $10 million increase in stockholders' equity is made up of a $5 million rise in each of par value and paid-in surplus on the balance sheet. Paid-in surplus is the amount above par value received by a corporation for shares it sells to investors. Exhibit 18-2 illustrates the balance sheet changes for Infotex from the stock sale assuming that the stock has a par value of $5 per share.

Par value is a per share amount assigned to the corporation's stock by the board of directors. The assignment of a par value to stock is meant to protect creditors, since the law in many states requires that the corporation shall not make payments to stockholders which reduce the shareholders' equity below that total par of outstanding shares.[7] For example, Infotex cannot reduce stockholders' equity below $20 million after the new shares are issued since this is the total par value of the company's stock (see Exhibit 18-2).

State law may not require that a par value be set for stock. However, in this case the board of directors is required to assign a **stated value** per share which is equivalent to a par value. The firm is not permitted to make payments to shareholders which reduce owners' equity below the firm's stated capital (stated value per share times the number of shares outstanding).

A distinction should be made between par or stated value and the market value of the shares when issued. Generally, the firm will issue new shares at a price significantly above par or stated value. Except for the restriction placed upon payments to shareholders described above, it is the market price of the shares upon issue (the amount received by the firm for issuing the stock, ignoring flotation costs) which is of economic signifi-

---

7. Shareholders' equity (or the firm's net worth) consists of paid-in capital (what stockholders paid the firm in purchasing the shares) plus retained earnings. This is equal to the firm's assets minus liabilities.

Exhibit 18-2. Recording the Issuance of New Shares by Infotex, Inc.

	Balance sheet		Change in balance sheet figures
	Before new shares are issued	After new shares are issued	
Assets			
Cash	$ 5,000,000	$15,000,000	$10,000,000
Other assets	60,000,000	60,000,000	0
Total assets	$65,000,000	$75,000,000	$10,000,000
Liabilities and owners' equity			
Liabilities	$30,000,000	$30,000,000	
Owners' equity:			
Par value	15,000,000	20,000,000	$ 5,000,000
Paid-in surplus	10,000,000	15,000,000	5,000,000
Retained earnings	10,000,000	10,000,000	0
Total liabilities and owners' equity	$65,000,000	$75,000,000	$10,000,000

cance to shareholders and management. It is this market price that new investors are willing to pay for the firm's shares, and it is this price that these investors place upon the stock as the measure of its true worth. Moreover, it is this issue price that management feels is a fair payment in exchange for the ownership interest in the firm being purchased by the new stockholders. Generally, it will be market price and not par or stated value that will be of interest in analyzing the financial decisions of the firm.

Rights Offerings

Earlier in the chapter we explained that preemptive rights protect the shareholder's position in the firm. If preemptive rights exist, the corporation must issue **rights** (technically called stock subscription warrants) to existing stockholders when the firm is raising capital through the sale of new shares of common stock. A right is an option to purchase stock at the issue price of the new shares. One right is issued for each share of currently outstanding common stock; however, the number of rights needed to purchase a new share depends on the terms of the rights offering. Let's examine how the financial manager plans the rights offering (for example, the number of rights per new share and the price of the new shares) so as to best serve the company's shareholders.

Planning the rights offering   An example will help to clarify the issues involved. Assume that Crown, Inc., is considering a rights offering and that the relevant data are as follows:

Shares outstanding	1,000,000
Market price per share	$25
Total value of shares outstanding	
(1,000,000 shares × $25)	$25,000,000
Funds to be raised	$5,000,000

In order to ensure that all rights are exercised, the firm will set the subscription price for the new shares at a level somewhat below the market price of $25. If the exercise price were set near $25, say $24, a small decline in the stock's market price (e.g., to $23) would prevent any rights from being exercised (since no one would pay $24 for a share selling in the market at $23). Therefore, Crown's manager sets the subscription price for new shares at $20. Since the firm plans to raise $5 million in new funds and will receive $20 per new share, it follows that

$$\text{Number of new shares} = \frac{\text{funds to be raised}}{\text{subscription price per new share}}$$

$$= \frac{\$5,000,000}{\$20 \text{ per new share}} = 250,000 \text{ new shares}$$

We know that one right is issued on each of the 1 million original shares. Since the firm wishes to sell only 250,000 new shares, if all rights are to be surrendered in obtaining new shares, the firm must require that four rights be surrendered for each new share purchased. That is,

$$\frac{\text{Number of rights}}{\text{(to buy a new share)}} = \frac{\text{number of rights issued}}{\text{number of new shares}}$$

$$= \frac{1,000,000 \text{ rights}}{250,000 \text{ new shares}} = 4 \text{ rights per new share}$$

Therefore, a stockholder must surrender four rights plus pay the subscription price of $20 to obtain one new share.

Effects of a Rights Offering   The effect of a rights offering on the price of the firm's stock is stated in Exhibit 18-3 and illustrated in Figure 18-1. Crown, Inc., announces the rights offering on March 15. The announcement indicates that the rights will be issued on June 15 to all shareholders of record on May 15 (re-

Exhibit 18-3. Price per Share before and after the Rights Offering

A. Value of firm's shares before rights offering	$25,000,000
B. Number of shares outstanding before offering	1,000,000
C. Value per share before rights offering [A/B]	$25
D. Cash proceeds from rights offering added to firm's assets	$5,000,000
E. Value of firm's shares after rights offering [A + D]	$30,000,000
F. Number of shares outstanding after offering	1,250,000
G. Value per share after rights offering [E/F]	$24

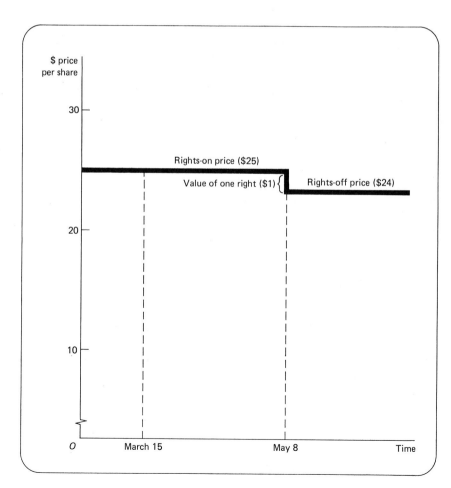

Figure 18-1. Price per share with a rights offering announced on March 15. The last day that the stock sells rights-on (sells at $25) is May 8; on May 9, the stock sells rights-off (sells at $24).

corded in the company's books on May 15 as shareholders). However, keep in mind that there is a delay between the time a stock sale transaction takes place and the time the transaction is recorded on the books of the corporation. Anyone owning the stock on May 8 (five business days before May 15) will still be the stockholder of record on May 15 and will be entitled to the rights. Therefore, a buyer of the firm's stock on or before May 8 will buy the stock **rights-on** and will receive the rights; a buyer on May 9 or thereafter will not receive the rights and will buy the stock **rights-off** or **ex-rights**. Since each share of stock entitles the owner to one right, *the rights-on price of a share is equal to the rights-off price plus the value of a right.* In the example, the value of a right is $1 (the computation is explained below). This is illustrated in Figure 18-1.

What is the market value of a right and the impact on the shareholder of the rights offering? We can calculate the value of a right, using the equations given below. The right has a value because of the opportunity it provides to purchase the firm's shares at less than the stock's market value. Observe that the value of a new share received upon exercising the right will take into account that

1. There are 25 percent more shares outstanding after the new stock issue than before the issue.
2. The firm receives $5 million from selling the new shares.

As shown in Exhibit 18-3, before the rights offering, the value of each share of stock was $25. If we assume that the added $5 million received for the firm raises the total value of the shareholders' interest by $5 million, then the value of all the firm's stock will increase from $25 million to $30 million. Since the rights offering raises the number of shares to 1,250,000, the new price per share will be $24 ($30 million divided by 1,250,000 shares = $24). Notice that the new share value we are referring to here is the market value of a share *after* the new shares are issued; we noted earlier that this new share value is referred to as the rights-off (or ex-rights) share price.

Now let us determine the value of a right. It takes four rights plus $20 to buy a new share with a value of $24. What are the four rights worth? The answer: $4, since with four rights a buyer of a new share saves $4 (i.e., only pays $20 for a share worth $24); one right is therefore worth $1. We consequently have a formula for determining the value of a right:[8]

---

8. The value of a right can also be expressed in terms of the rights-on value of the stock:

$$\text{Value of one right} = \frac{(\text{market price of one share rights-on}) - (\text{subscription price})}{(\text{number of rights required to purchase one share}) + 1}$$

$$= \frac{\$25 - \$20}{4 + 1} = \$1$$

See the text discussion of rights-on value.

$$\frac{\text{Value of}}{\text{one right}} = \frac{\left(\begin{array}{c}\text{market price of one} \\ \text{share rights-off}\end{array}\right) - (\text{subscription price})}{\begin{array}{c}\text{number of rights required to} \\ \text{obtain one new share}\end{array}}$$

$$= \frac{\$24 - \$20}{4} = \$1$$

Notice that in Figure 18-1, as a share of stock goes from rights-on to rights-off status on May 9, the value of the share falls by the $1 value of the right.

Value of a rights offering to shareholders Clearly, stockholders will not simply let their rights expire without selling or exercising them. By exercising rights, stockholders can acquire shares at a price ($20 in the example) less than each share's market value ($24). By exercising rights, stockholders can make a $4 profit per share by buying the stock at $20 and selling each share for $24. Or stockholders can simply sell their rights for $4 (see above discussion). Does this imply that a rights offering makes the shareholder richer? The answer is no. It is easy to show that the rights offering makes the shareholder neither better off nor worse off *as long as the rights do not expire without being exercised or sold.* In fact, the shareholder can always sell the appropriate number of his or her rights and use the proceeds to exercise the remaining rights and be exactly in the same position as before the rights offering. By way of illustration, assume in the example above that investor George Goodwin owns 600 shares of Crown, Inc., stock before the rights offering. The value of his portfolio before the rights offering is $15,000 (600 shares × $25 per share = $15,000). Since Goodwin owns 600 shares, he receives 600 rights. Assume that Goodwin sells 500 of his rights for $500. He has 100 rights remaining and can purchase twenty-five new shares (four rights per new share are required) for $20 each (subscription price); the total cash outlay for the twenty-five new shares is $500 (25 × $20). The $500 used to purchase the new shares is exactly the proceeds he received from selling 500 rights. Goodwin now has a total of 625 shares, each worth $24 (rights-off value); just as before the rights offering, his portfolio is worth $15,000 (625 shares × $24).[9]

9. The sale of 500 rights and exercise of 100 rights (purchase of twenty-five new shares with a cash payment plus four rights per new share) reduces the stockholder's percentage ownership of the firm from 0.6 percent (600 shares owned/100,000 shares originally outstanding) to 0.5 percent (625 shares/125,000 shares outstanding after the rights offering). However, the value of the firm's shares has increased from $25 million to $30 million because of the $5 million raised by the firm under the rights offering. The shareholder's portfolio therefore does not change in value (0.006 × $25,000,000 = 0.005 × $30,000,000).

Of course, if Goodwin wishes to reduce the value of his holdings in the firm, he can sell all his rights and keep the cash or invest it elsewhere. On the other hand, if he feels that the firm is a particularly good investment, he might increase his investment in the firm by exercising all his rights.[10] Given the above relationships, he will not be provided with any improved selling or buying opportunities in the firm's stock merely as a result of the rights offering.

The point of the above example is that the rights offering itself does not produce any costs or benefits for shareholders. If the firm were to invest the new funds in an exceptionally profitable venture (earning more than the firm's cost of capital), shareholders would benefit. However, the benefit in this case is due to the profitability of the investment and not to the rights offering. The resulting price behavior of the stock after the offering will depend upon the impact of the investment on the future earnings of the firm.

It was pointed out earlier that the preemptive right of shareholders protects current shareholders from a dilution of their investment and control. It does this by preventing management from selling new shares to outsiders for less than their true worth.[11] However, even without the preemptive right the firm could avoid a dilution of shareholders' investment merely by placing a price on new shares sufficiently *high to reflect their true worth*. Outsiders buying the new stock would pay for what they get and the old shareholders need suffer in no way.[12] Therefore, as long as management is in fact attempting to serve the interests of shareholders and sells new shares for their true value, the preemptive right is not necessary. The right exists *as a protection to shareholders in those instances in which management is not acting in good faith.*

Advantages of rights offerings In addition to ensuring that the position of current shareholders is not jeopardized, external equity financing via a rights offering has certain advantages. Rights offerings are generally much

---

10. If Goodwin exercises all his rights (sells none of them), he must invest an additional $3,000 ($3,000 = 150 shares × $20/share) but will continue to own 0.6 percent of the firm's shares (600 shares out of 100,000 before the rights offering and 750 shares out of 125,000 after the offering). The value of Goodwin's portfolio of shares rises from $15,000 (600 shares × $25 per share) to $18,000 (750 shares × $24 per share), an increase of $3,000, which is exactly the additional amount invested in the firm. There is therefore no net gain for the investor.

11. In the example, if the firm had simply sold new shares to outside investors for $20 per share without issuing rights to old shareholders, old shareholders would have suffered a loss of $1 per share owned (since the stock price fell from $25 to $24 per share).

12. The sale of shares by the firm to new investors is equivalent to the stockholders' selling part of their ownership in the firm (like bringing in new partners), with the cash from the stock sale remaining in the firm.

less expensive in terms of brokerage and underwriting fees than is a public sale of stock. This is a real saving to the firm, and therefore to the firm's owners, its shareholders. Since the shares in a rights offering are sold directly to investors who have a favorable view of the firm's prospects (since they are willingly the firm's current shareholders), the rights method is a particularly low-cost means of offering the new shares to a receptive market. A public offering is a much more costly and indirect means of reaching the potential buyers. With a rights offering, however, even if some of the existing shareholders sell their rights, a large percentage of them generally exercise the rights and obtain additional shares of the firm. The costs of issuance to the firm under a rights offering may be less than half the flotation costs involved in a public issue.

Rights also provide shareholders with the opportunity to borrow a high proportion of their investment in the new shares. The margin requirement for purchasing shares under a rights offering is generally much less stringent than the requirement for purchasing other listed shares.[13] For example, whereas an investor might be allowed to borrow only up to 50 percent of the funds used to buy other listed shares, 70 percent might be allowed for purchasing shares under a rights offering. This provides the investor with a wider range of risk-return alternatives in building a portfolio.

REPURCHASING STOCK

Corporations sometimes repurchase some of their own shares from stockholders; e.g., Allied Chemical may buy back some Allied Chemical stock from its own shareholders. Stock purchased by the issuing firm is referred to as **treasury stock.** These shares have not been retired but are held by the firm for possible resale or for use as payment, for example, in buying another company. Treasury stock carries no stockholder privileges; thus it receives no dividends and does not have the voting right. If treasury stock is resold, it is again outstanding (is no longer treasury stock) and carries with it the same rights and privileges associated with the other outstanding common stock of the firm. A sale of treasury stock is essentially the same as the sale of any other stock issued by the company.

It is important to understand that treasury stock is not an asset of the firm. The firm is a bundle of real assets (plant and equipment, current assets, goodwill) against which claims in the form of stocks and bonds are issued. If the firm owns a share of its own stock, it in a sense owns a claim against itself (like owing yourself money). To see this, merely imagine

---

13. The Federal Reserve Board sets a limit on the percentage of the purchase price of a listed stock that one can finance with borrowing. Buying with funds that are in part or wholly borrowed is known as buying **on margin.**

that the firm holds some treasury stock and then destroys that stock (say, burns the certificates). Has the firm lost anything in the process? No, except the paper certificates that have been destroyed.[14] One must be very careful to contrast this situation with securities of *other* firms held by the firm. If the firm owns securities issued by another company, these securities are assets since they are claims against the real assets of the other company. Firms quite frequently own the stocks and bonds of other enterprises, and these securities are generally and properly regarded as assets.

Management's duty is to serve all shareholders of the firm and to provide all shareholders with adequate information regarding the firm's future prospects. It would be inconsistent with this principle for management to use inside information—e.g., regarding a secret and particularly profitable investment opportunity—to buy the firm's stock when its market price is unreasonably depressed. Assuming management's assessment is correct, the effect of such a purchase would be a gain to shareholders who do not sell their shares at the expense of those shareholders who do sell their stock to the company. This exploitation of the selling stockholders would not only be unconscionable, it would also be of questionable legality. On the other hand, if a treasury stock purchase is not based upon inside information, but upon management's assessment of publicly revealed information concerning the company, the stock repurchase would not be morally or legally tainted. However, it would be a gamble on the part of management and the nonselling shareholders that management is more astute than the selling shareholders in evaluating the company's prospects. In spite of the intuitive appeal of such a presumption, the record suggests that management is often overly optimistic.[15] An extreme example of this was a tender offer, made in January 1973 by Macmillan Inc., to repurchase 1.2 million shares of its own stock, then trading at around $11.50, for $13 per share. Nearly 3.9 million shares were tendered by stockholders (meaning that out of every 100 shares tendered, only 31 were bought by the company and the remaining 69 were returned to the stockholder). Macmillan stock then went into a prolonged and steep decline which carried its price all the way down to around $3. As of mid-1976, it was still selling below $7. This was clearly a case in which management erred in its evaluation of the company's prospects and the

---

14. In effect, by burning the stock certificates, the corporation has eliminated a claim it owed against itself; i.e., it has destroyed an asset and an identical liability.

15. The evidence indicates that the prices of shares of firms that have repurchased stock do not outperform share prices in general. This implies that managements have not been notably skillful in buying their stock back at "bargain prices." See, for example, *Forbes* (April 15, 1973), p. 60; *Business Week* (May 5, 1973), p. 70; *Wall Street Journal* (May 22, 1973), p. 1.

general trend in stock prices, and the purchase of company stock was injurious to nonselling stockholders.

There are, of course, valid reasons that might encourage a firm to purchase its own shares. In order to raise its debt-equity ratio to a higher level (i.e., to increase financial leverage), the firm could sell bonds and simultaneously purchase its common stock with the proceeds from the bond sale. If the firm has excess cash and already has bonds outstanding, a purchase of its shares on the open market will also increase the firm's ratio of debt to equity by lowering the investment that stockholders have retained in the firm; this same effect can be achieved if a firm with outstanding debt pays dividends. Whenever a firm makes payments to its shareholders—whether through treasury stock purchases or dividends—it is reducing the investment that shareholders have left in the firm and is thereby reducing stockholders' equity.

Another reason that the firm may purchase treasury shares is to block a takeover bid by an outside group. Management may believe that the outside purchaser will operate the company in a manner injurious to its remaining shareholders. Thus, for example, if the outsider were offering $40 per share to existing shareholders for their stock, the firm might make a counterbid of $45 per share. The firm might also wish to purchase its own shares from a minority group of shareholders who are unhappy with an existing management which has the support of a majority of shareholders. The majority may be optimistic about the firm's prospects and wish to expand its share of the company. This will in effect be achieved if the firm purchases the minority group's shares.

Purchasing its own shares in the open market is not always a good policy. For example, it is ordinarily unwise for a company to acquire its own shares for use in stock option plans (to sell to its employees) or for acquiring other firms (the stock can be used as payment for the purchased company). If the firm requires shares for these or any other purpose, it can usually just issue new shares. An increase in the number of shares outstanding is generally a simple procedure and involves smaller transaction costs (e.g., brokerage fees) than those incurred in purchasing shares on the open market. Moreover, open market purchases of company stock are subject to a number of burdensome restrictions imposed by the SEC.

Treasury stock purchases have a tax advantage for the shareholder as compared with dividend payments. Dividends are taxed on an ordinary tax basis, whereas any gain realized from *selling shares back to the corporation* is taxed as a capital gain. For example, if Alice Brown holds $1,000 of firm's stock for which she paid $500, a sale of that stock to the firm for $1,000 produces a gain of $500, taxable as a capital gain. If, however, that $1,000 were received as a dividend, the entire $1,000 would be taxed as ordinary income at a tax rate greater than the capital gains tax rate. If the capital gains rate were 20 percent and the ordinary rate 40 percent for Brown, she would pay $100 in capital gains tax on sale of her stock to the firm [0.20 × $500 (capital gain) = $100]; she would pay $400 in taxes on the dividend [0.40 × 1,000 (dividends) = $400]. It should be noted, however, that under existing federal income tax regulations, if the firm makes frequent treasury stock purchases, the gain earned on selling shares back to the corporation ($500 in the example) would have to be treated by the shareholder as a dividend and not as an ordinary sale of stock subject to the capital gains tax.

THE LISTING OF STOCK

A corporation is referred to as **closely held** if it has relatively few shareholders. An existing group of shareholders may wish to keep the company closely held in order to maintain privacy or to retain full control over operations (and not be answerable to a dissident group of stockholders). However, if a firm has 500 or more shareholders and total assets in excess of $1 million (both conditions must apply), it must publicly disclose its financial position by filing an annual statement with the SEC.[16]

The shares of a **publicly held** corporation are owned by the general public. These shares are traded publicly in the over-the-counter market or on one of the thirteen organized exchanges in the United States. From the standpoint of the firm, it is debatable whether a listing provides significant gains. As was explained in Chapter 2, both over-the-counter and listed stock transactions usually involve brokers who act as intermediaries between buyers and sellers of the stock. SEC regulations are essentially the same for listed and unlisted companies. One might expect a benefit from listing since some financial institutions are permitted (under state laws) to own only listed stocks, and since listed securities enjoy somewhat greater publicity (e.g., trading volume in the stock and price quotations are published in more newspapers if the stock is listed). However, it is not clear from the empirical evidence that the market price of a company's stock is enhanced merely because it is listed on an exchange.[17]

If a firm does wish to list its stock, it is required to file papers with the exchange and with the SEC. The various exchanges have minimum listing requirements pertaining to assets, earnings, number of shares outstanding, and number of shareholders. The SEC regulations include the requirement that the firm publish both quarterly earnings reports and annual overall financial statements.

16. If the company has securities that are convertible to stock, owners of the convertible securities are added to the number of shareholders to determine whether the minimum of 500 shareholders is met (e.g., 400 stockholders and 100 owners of bonds convertible into stock would satisfy the requirement).

17. See J. C. Van Horne, "New Listings and Their Price Behavior," *Journal of Finance* (September 1970), pp. 783–794.

Ownership of the firm's common stock entitles the stockholders to the following:

SUMMARY

To receive the residual portion (after other investors, e.g., creditors, are paid) of the firm's income

To elect the board of directors

In most cases, to purchase any new firm shares before they are sold to outsiders (preemptive right)

To inspect the company's books

To transfer their shares

To be immune from liability to the corporation's creditors

To own a residual claim to the firm's assets in the event of liquidation

The election of the board of directors may be conducted under the majority rule or cumulative voting procedures. Under the majority rule, ownership of a majority of the shares ensures the power to elect the entire board, whereas under the cumulative voting method votes are distributed so that a significant minority is assured of representation on the board.

The firm's decision with regard to the timing and size of a new stock issue will depend upon the productivity of the funds to the firm and the cost of the funds. When any new shares are issued for sale, the existence of the stockholders' preemptive right gives stockholders the opportunity to buy the new shares before they are offered to outsiders. For each share of stock already owned, the shareholder receives one right.

The stockholder can exercise the rights and buy additional shares of stock by surrendering the rights and paying a stipulated price for each new share purchased. The rights can also be sold to someone else who may then exercise them. The existence of the preemptive right and the use of rights in offering new shares have two principal advantages. First, the right protects the shareholder against management's issuing new stock to outsiders at a price below its reasonable value. Second, in terms of flotation costs, the use of rights is a more economical method than a public offering.

The corporation may repurchase some of its own shares from stockholders. Such shares are referred to as treasury stock. The company may purchase its stock to raise the firm's debt-equity ratio (since the purchase reduces the stockholder investment in the company), to distribute the firm's excess cash to stockholders, to block an outsider takeover bid, or to buy out dissident stockholders.

A publicly held corporation—that is, one which is owned by many stockholders—may have its stock traded on the over-the-counter market or on an organized exchange. Securities traded on an exchange are referred to as listed. Listing of a stock requires fulfillment of both exchange and SEC requirements.

QUESTIONS

1. Itemize the rights of common stockholders. For each right you itemize, indicate whether it invariably attaches to common stock or its inclusion depends upon the terms of the stock offering, which vary from one stock to another.

2. "As an investor in a firm's common stock, I am really only interested in one thing, namely, that I get a rate of return consistent with the level of risk I assume. The management of a company cannot do anything more for me than that, so all this business about the rights and privileges of stockholders mentioned at the very beginning of the chapter is just so much baloney." Evaluate this statement.

3. "If an unprofitable company wishes to issue additional shares, no matter what provisions the shares contain in the contract, the shares are not likely to have much value." Comment on the validity of this statement.

4. If a firm were reasonably profitable and the provisions protecting common stockholders were broad, what would you expect to happen to the firm's cost of equity capital if it chose to sell additional shares? Explain fully.

5. Explain the advantages of having a residual claim on the income of the firm.

6. If a firm earns $200,000 and retains half of it, how much would you expect the value of its shares to increase assuming there are no other influences except earnings retention on the value of the shares.

7. What is a proxy statement?

8. American Telephone & Telegraph Company has over three million shareholders, no one of whom owns more than one-tenth of one percent of the total of roughly 560 million shares outstanding. Of what value do you think the voting "privilege" is to each of these shareholders? Explain fully.

9. Data I/O Corporation, a closely held computer manufacturing firm located in Issaquah, Washington, has fifteen shareholders. The company is incorporated in the state of Washington, and the one shareholder who owns more than 51 percent of the voting shares controls the firm. Of what value is the voting right in this case? Explain fully.

10. Of what value is the preemptive right provision in common shareholder agreements?

11. Differentiate between majority rule voting and cumulative voting.

12. What relationship, if any, exists between par value and market value? Explain fully.

13. If Brook Paper Products, Inc., announces on April 13, 1976 that it plans to sell new stock to shareholders of record as of May 13, 1976 and you hold the stock as of May 6, 1976, are you a shareholder of record?

14. "Rights offerings are a good deal because they let a person buy shares below the current market value." Comment on the validity of this statement.

15. When a firm buys back some of its own shares from stockholders it pays money for those shares (treasury stock). Yet, we say that the treasury stock is not a real asset of the firm (the treasury stock could be destroyed with no loss) since it is simply a claim of the firm against itself. Why would the firm pay money for treasury stock if it is not an asset? Aren't remaining stockholders (those who haven't sold their shares to the company) worse off as a result of the treasury stock purchase? Explain.

PROJECTS

1. Obtain from your state's secretary of state (or other appropriate official) information on the requirements for forming a corporation in your state and the rights and privileges of stockholders. Compare the provisions of your state law with those outlined in this chapter.

2. Obtain from a local stock brokerage firm or from financial publications (e.g., *Barron's*) data on a recent rights offering. Observe the behavior of the stock's price as the stock goes from a rights-on to a rights-off basis.

PROBLEMS

1. The Drummand Bugle Corp. manufactures brass musical instruments. It has outstanding $5,000,000 in 6 percent long-term bonds (thirty-years maturity) and 200,000 shares of common stock (with a current market value of $25 per share). Drummand pays taxes at the rate of 50 percent. Show the earnings per share for this corporation if earnings before interest and taxes are $1,200,000; $600,000; and $200,000. In the last case, explain how the bond obligation is paid.

2. Straight Arrow, Inc., is having an election of directors. There are eight directors to be elected. If there are 100,000 shares outstanding, how many shares are needed to ensure the ability to elect one director if Straight Arrow uses a) majority rule voting and b) cumulative voting. How many shares are needed to elect two directors under each method?

3. The Isoquant Corporation is chartered with majority rule voting provisions in its procedure for electing the ten-member board of directors. Two slates of directors are running for election this year. Slate A is preferred by 800 of the 2,000 stockholders, who happen to hold 620,000 of the 1 million outstanding shares. Slate B is preferred by 1,200 shareholders, holding 380,000 shares.

a) How many votes are cast in all, assuming all votes are cast?

b) Which is the minority slate?

c) Can any of the minority slate be elected?

d) Show how votes will be cast for each position.

4. Suppose the Isoquant Corp. in problem 3 has instead a cumulative voting rule, and the above-described contest for the board of directors takes place.

a) How many minority members can now be elected?

b) Show how the votes are cast for each position to achieve the result in **a**.

5. Below is the balance sheet of Moonlight Cheese, Inc., before it issued 100,000 shares of new common stock at a price of $21 each. The underwriting fees aggregated 5 percent of the total sale. Show the net effect on the company's balance sheet of the sale of the new stock.

Assets	
Cash	$ 2,000,000
Other assets	48,000,000
Total	$50,000,000
Liabilities and owners' equity	
Liabilities	$25,000,000
Owners' equity:	
Common stock ($5)	1,000,000
Paid-in surplus	5,000,000
Retained earnings	19,000,000
Total	$50,000,000

6. If Green Belt Nurseries, Inc., issues 100,000 new shares of common stock to existing shareholders at a price of $25 a share, what would you expect the price of the common shares to be if it was $30 a share before the issue? There are currently 400,000 shares outstanding. Show all calculations.

7. Brown Trucking, Inc., plans to sell 250,000 shares of new stock to existing shareholders. It has 1 million shares outstanding. The selling price will be $25. The current market price of the outstanding shares is $30.

a) How many rights are needed to buy one new share?

b) What is the value of each right?

8. You own 100 shares of Tamaroon, Inc. The company decides to offer new shares to existing shareholders at the rate of one new share for each ten shares held. The current market price per share is $50. The subscription price is $45. What is the value of the right before the ex-rights date?

9. The Common Divisor Corporation has 1 million shares of stock outstanding and intends to raise more equity capital by issuing an additional 200,000 shares. To ensure that the issue will be bought, Common Divisor is pricing the offering at $35, while the current market price is $43. Lotta Rice currently holds 220 shares. In the following, ignore all brokerage or underwriting costs.

a) What will the market value of a share of stock be after the stock issue, assuming the value is affected only by the conditions of the issue?

b) Assuming Common Divisor awards one right per share, how many rights in addition to $35 will be required to purchase a share of stock?

c) How many shares is Lotta entitled to buy at $35?

d) If Lotta decides not to buy any new shares, what can she sell her rights for?

e) Verify that Lotta's net gain (or loss) is zero, whether she exercises her rights or sells them.

f) How should Lotta dispose of her rights in such a way as to end up with exactly the same *value* in Common Divisor stock as she had before the rights offering?

10. The Surf-It Beach Products Corporation announced on August 2 a rights offering of 20,000 new shares at a subscription price of $35. The rights offering is for shareholders of record as of October 20, and the rights are to be issued on November 20. A buyer of the stock on or before October 13 is entitled to the rights, whereas a buyer on October 14 or thereafter is not (stock goes "ex-rights" on October 14, five *business days* before October 20). Three rights are required to purchase one new share and one right will be issued for each share outstanding on October 20. The market price of Surf-It as of August 2 is $41. Assume there are no changes in the market value of the stock except those due to the rights offering.

a) What is the value of one right?

b) Can you infer how many shares are outstanding on October 20?

c) Trace the market price of a share of Surf-It from August 2 to November 20.

long-term debt and preferred stock

Long-term debt and preferred stock are often referred to as **fixed-income securities** because the firm promises the security owner a fixed annual income (fixed interest on the debt or fixed dividends on the preferred stock). We see from Table 19-1 that long-term debt and preferred stock are important sources of capital. It is therefore essential that the financial manager understand fully the nature of the obligations they impose on the company. It is equally important to investors that they understand what they are entitled to through ownership of the company's securities. Investors must decide whether they are receiving rights to income that are adequate to compensate them for the funds they are providing to the corporation. The reader may wish to review the discussion in the introduction to Chapter 18, which points out that the financial manager must know what types of securities investors want. This is crucial if the firm is to raise capital from investors in the most advantageous way.

LONG-TERM DEBT

Debt is usually referred to as long term if the term of the loan is at least ten years. Although there are many forms of long-term debt, depending on the provisions in each debt contract, all debtholders are guaranteed a prior claim over stockholders to the firm's income. That is, *creditors receive what is contractually promised to them before stockholders receive anything*.

The use of debt by a firm is motivated by two factors. First, as explained in Chapter 9, there is a tax advantage since interest on debt is tax-deductible by the corporation whereas dividend payments and retained earnings of shareholders are not. This means that for most corporations the aftertax cost of capital on debt is lower than on equity, at least up to some level of borrowing. In most cases, therefore, a corporation will have some debt in its capital structure. Secondly, even if the corporate tax did not favor debt as it does, the firm would probably employ some degree of financial leverage (borrowing), since some investors prefer the type of low-risk income provided by debt and others prefer the higher-risk returns from shares of a levered firm. By so providing returns that have the risk-return properties that investors desire, it is easier for the firm to obtain capital.

When the corporation borrows funds on a long-term basis, it issues a long-term promissory note, called a **bond,** to the lender. The contract

Table 19-1. New issues of securities by United States corporations (in millions)[a]

	Common stock	Preferred stock	Bonds	Total
1960	1,664	409	8,081	10,154
1961	3,294	450	9,420	13,165
1962	1,314	422	8,969	10,705
1963	1,022	342	10,856	12,211
1964	2,679	412	10,865	13,957
1965	1,547	725	13,720	15,992
1966	1,939	574	15,561	18,074
1967	1,959	885	21,954	24,798
1968	3,946	637	17,383	21,966
1969	7,714	682	18,347	26,744
1970	7,240	1,390	30,315	38,945
1971	9,291	3,670	32,123	45,090
1972	9,694	3,367	28,896	41,957
1973	7,642	3,337	21,049	32,025
1974	3,994	2,253	32,066	38,311
1975	7,420	3,458	42,761	53,638

[a] Gross proceeds (offering price times number of units sold).
Source: *Federal Reserve Bulletin.*

between the corporation and lender is referred to as the **bond indenture.** The indenture ordinarily specifies that the creditor will receive regular interest payments, usually semiannually, during the term of the debt and then receive the **face value** or **maturity value** of the bond at the date of maturity. For example, a twenty-year, $1,000 bond promising a **coupon rate** of 6 percent per year sold on January 1, 1977, will pay $60 per year (0.06 × $1,000) until January 1, 1997; the $60 annual interest will commonly be paid in two $30 semiannual installments. On the maturity date, January 1, 1997, the corporation will also pay the lender the bond's maturity value of $1,000.

Let's now look at how the market value of a bond is computed and then at some of the important provisions in a bond contract.

The Value of a Bond

What is the *market value* of the twenty-year, $1,000 bond described above, which was issued on January 1, 1977? That is, what value do investors place on this bond in the bond market? The market value equals the discounted value (present value) of the dollar payments promised to the bondholder using the market interest rate to discount those payments. The market interest rate is the rate of return required by investors on the bond and was referred to in Chapter 5 as the *yield to maturity* on the bond. If the annual market interest rate on comparable securities were 6 percent, then you will recall from Chapter 5 that the market value of the bond would be[1]

$$V = \frac{\$60}{1.06} + \frac{\$60}{(1.06)^2} + \cdots + \frac{\$60}{(1.06)^{20}} + \frac{\$1,000}{(1.06)^{20}} = \$1,000$$

In this example, the bond has a market value equal to its face value of $1,000.

A bond generally does not sell for its face value. The bond could sell for more or for less than $1,000, depending upon the market interest rate used to discount the payments received by the bondholder. Recall that the coupon rate is only a way of computing the dollars the firm will pay on the bond each year in coupon payments, $60 in the above example. To determine the value that the bond payments would have to someone seeking an 8 percent return on investment, we find the present value of the coupon and maturity payments at 8 percent:[2]

$$V = \frac{\$60}{1.08} + \frac{\$60}{(1.08)^2} + \cdots + \frac{\$60}{(1.08)^{20}} + \frac{\$1,000}{(1.08)^{20}} = \$804$$

If an investor were to purchase the bond for $804 and hold it for twenty years, the return on this investment would be 8 percent per year. Therefore, if investors demand an 8 percent rate of return on the firm's bonds, the firm's bonds will sell for $804 (since $804 is the price investors will pay for the bond). Notice that the coupon of $60 per year is only part of the net return to the bond investor. The rest of the return is in the form of a capital gain, this capital gain equaling $196—the $1,000 received by the bondholder in 1997 less the $804 paid in 1977. This difference between maturity value and 1977 market value, which equals $196 in the example, is called the **discount** on the bond. Thus, if the firm were to sell its bonds initially for $804, it would be selling them at a discount of $196.

The bond may also sell at a **premium.** If investors are satisfied with a 4 percent return on their investment, the value of the bond to them is then equal to[3]

$$V = \frac{\$60}{1.04} + \frac{\$60}{(1.04)^2} + \cdots + \frac{\$60}{(1.04)^{20}} + \frac{\$1,000}{(1.04)^{20}} = \$1,272$$

Investors are willing to pay $1,272 for a promised return of $60 per year for twenty years, plus $1,000 in twenty years. By doing so, they will earn

1. Using the factors of Chap. 4, $V = \$60(P/A, \ 6\%, \ 20) + \$1,000(P/F, \ 6\%, \ 20) = \$60(11.4699) + \$1,000(0.3118) = \$1,000.$
2. Using the factors of Chap. 4, $V = \$60(P/A, \ 8\%, \ 20) + \$1,000(P/F, \ 8\%, \ 20) = \$60(9.8182) + \$1,000(0.2146) = \$804.$
3. Using the factors of Chap. 4, $V = \$60(P/A, \ 4\%, \ 20) + \$1,000(P/F, \ 4\%, \ 20) = \$60(13.5903) + \$1,000(0.4564) = \$1,272.$

exactly a 4 percent return on their investment of $1,272 (assuming that the firm does not violate the bond contract). If the firm were to issue the bond for $1,272, it would be issuing the bond at a premium of $272($1,272 − $1.000).

The real interest rate (market rate) that investors demand and earn on a bond was referred to above as the yield to maturity. The yield to maturity was 8 percent in the case of the bond selling at a discount, and was 4 percent in the case of the bond selling at a premium.[4] The **coupon rate** was 6 percent in both cases, and is important only in that it is used to compute the coupon (interest) payable in dollars each period to the bondholder. The coupon rate should not be confused with the real interest rate or yield. If the bond sells at neither a discount nor a premium, then it has a present value equal to its face value, and its coupon rate and yield to maturity are equal. In the example, if the bond has a present value of $1,000, its yield to maturity and coupon rate are both 6 percent. The relationship between the coupon rate, market rate, and bond discount or premium is shown in Figure 19-1. If the market rate is less than the coupon rate, the bond sells at premium, and if the market rate exceeds the coupon rate, the bond sells at a discount.[5]

4. Notice that the yield to maturity is similar to the internal rate of return discussed in Chap. 7. The yield to maturity is the rate of return earned on the bond *assuming that the firm does not default* (default means that promised payments are not met) since the interest and face value payments that are discontinued are those promised by the firm. As explained in Chap. 5, if there is a chance of default, the expected dollar return for each year can be determined and these returns can be discounted at the expected rate of return demanded by investors to compute the bond's value. With default risk, the expected dollar return in each year is less than the promised dollar return, and therefore the expected rate of return is less than the yield to maturity. Therefore, in order to value a bond, we can use the yield to maturity demanded by investors to discount the promised stream of payments (coupon plus face value at maturity); or we can use the expected rate of return to discount the expected payments. The discounted values will be the same with either approach, since both discounted values equal the market value of the bond.

5. For simplicity, we are assuming in the computation that interest is paid once per year and is discounted at the annual rate. Since the interest is actually paid semiannually, another approach often used in practice involves discounting each semiannual interest payment using a six-month rate of $k/2$, where k is the *annual* nominal interest rate and $k/2$ is the rate that applies to each six-month time interval. To illustrate, if the bond in the text example has a yield to maturity k equal to 8 percent, then the value of the bond equals

$$V = \frac{\$30}{1 + k/2} + \frac{\$30}{(1 + k/2)^2} + \cdots + \frac{\$30}{(1 + k/2)^{40}} + \frac{\$1,000}{(1 + k/2)^{40}}$$

$$= \frac{\$30}{1 + 0.04} + \frac{\$30}{(1 + 0.04)^2} + \cdots + \frac{\$30}{(1 + 0.04)^{40}} + \frac{\$1,000}{(1.04)^{40}}$$

$$= \$30(P/A, 4\%, 40) + \$1,000(P/F, 4\%, 40)$$

$$= \$30(19.793) + \$1,000(0.2083) = \$802$$

In the remainder of this chapter we will simply compute values by discounting the annual interest payments at the annual interest rate.

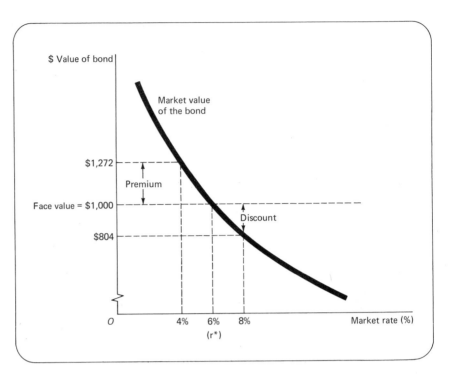

Figure 19-1. The relationship between the bond's market price, the coupon rate, and the market interest rate. Coupon rate = r* (r* = 6 percent in the example). If the market interest rate is less than r*, then the bond sells above face value and at a premium. If the market interest rate is greater than the coupon rate, the bond sells for less than face value and at a discount.

Income Priority

Creditors are in a preferred position relative to stockholders with regard to corporate income—that is, they receive what is promised to them before the stockholders receive anything. A bondholder is promised a payment each year (coupon rate × face value of bond), plus a payment at the end of the life of the bond (maturity or face value). Whatever is left after these payments is available to shareholders. For example, assume that the firm has stock and bonds outstanding and that the bonds are promised $80,000 per year in coupon interest payments. The income to shareholders is shown for three cases in Exhibit 19-1. Notice that the bondholders always receive their $80,000 payment as long as the firm has the resources to make the payment. In case 3, the firm is incurring a current loss, but it still pays the coupon payment of $80,000. Shareholders receive what is left over after taxes and interest ($60,000, $10,000, and a loss of $10,000, in cases 1, 2, and 3, respectively).

Provisions of the Bond Contract

General provisions Bonds may be secured or unsecured. Unsecured bonds, called **debentures,** are issued against the general credit of the corporation, whereas secured bonds are backed by a pledge of specific assets. This section discusses general provisions which apply to both kinds of bonds. The particular properties of unsecured and secured bonds are examined later.

Exhibit 19-1.

	Case 1	Case 2	Case 3
Earnings (sales minus operating costs) before interest and taxes (EBIT)	$200,000	$100,000	$60,000
Interest payable on bonds	(80,000)	(80,000)	(80,000)
Earnings before taxes (EBT)	$120,000	$ 20,000	($20,000)
Taxes (0.50 × EBT)	(60,000)	(10,000)	10,000[a]
Net aftertax earnings	$ 60,000	$ 10,000	($10,000)

[a] If a firm incurs a loss (negative EBT), then it may receive a rebate on past taxes paid equal to the tax rate times the loss, in this case equal to 0.50 times the $20,000 loss; this reduces the loss by the amount of the rebate. Such a rebate is available as long as the firm has profits in the previous three years against which losses have not already been taken (carried back). Losses in a period can also be carried forward for five years.

Before examining the provisions, it is worth noting that a provision in the bond agreement which protects the bondholders generally means greater constraints or obligations for the firm. The provision makes the bonds more attractive to lenders and therefore facilitates borrowing—that is, it means the firm can borrow at a lower interest rate than without such a provision. The added constraint is the price the firm pays for this borrowing advantage. Whether a particular provision is included in a bond contract will therefore depend on the company's situation (which determines how burdensome the provision is) and on the attitudes of lenders (how much they value the provision).

Terms and enforcement of the bond agreement The bond contract or indenture specifies the various terms agreed upon by the corporation and bondholders. The indenture stipulates the payments to be made by the corporation to the bondholders, the identity of any property that is pledged, the call provisions, and any restrictions on the firm's financial activities required to protect the interest of the bondholders. These additional restrictions are referred to as **protective covenants.** They relate to the right of the firm to pay dividends, to the need to maintain a given level of working capital, and to any other requirements needed to ensure the capacity of the firm to meet its debt obligations. Such restrictions represent an important protection to bondholders.

A **trustee,** most frequently a commercial bank, is assigned to represent the bondholders by ensuring that the bond contract meets legal requirements and that the corporation fulfills the terms of the debt contract once the bonds are issued. If the corporation fails to meet its interest or principal obligations, it is said to be in **default.** It is the responsibility of the trustee to act promptly to protect the bondholders if the firm is in default. Bond issues in excess of $1 million and registered with the Securities and Exchange Commission are subject to the Trust Indenture Act of 1939. This federal act provides that the indenture terms must be clear and not deceptive and that the trustee act strictly in behalf of the interests of the bondholders.

Call provision The call provision in the bond agreement provides that the firm can repurchase ("call") the bonds after they are issued at some stipulated call price, which is generally above the face value of the bonds. The difference between the **call price** and the bond's face value is referred to as the **call premium.** For example, if a $1,000 (face value), thirty-year, $7\frac{1}{2}$ percent bond can be called by the firm for $1,075, the call premium is $75 ($1,075 − $1,000). The premium is frequently equal to one year's coupon payment ($75 on a $7\frac{1}{2}$ percent, $1,000 bond). Sometimes the call premium is one that declines over time: it might be $75 the first year the bonds are outstanding, $72.50 the second year, and so on, the premium declining by $2.50 per year for thirty years to zero at the maturity date.

Investors would prefer that there be no call provision, since it means that the firm can force them to sell back their bonds at a particular price. For example, assume that a $1,000, 8 percent, twenty-year bond is issued on January 1, 1977, at par (that is, for $1,000) and has a call provision that allows the firm to repurchase the bond at any time for $1,050. The investor pays $1,000 for the bond and, if the firm does not call the bond, will receive an interest of $80 per year for twenty years, plus $1,000 at the end of that period. Assume that interest rates in the market fall to 6 percent because of a change in economic conditions after the bond is issued and the firm decides to call the bond on January 1, 1979. The corporation will probably wish to call the bond in this case, since it can now borrow at 6 percent instead of 8 percent. Is the investor worse off than if the firm could not call the bond? The answer is clearly yes. If there were no call option, the value of the bond (using a 6 percent discount rate) would be $1,217—the present value of $80 per year for eighteen years (January 1979 to January 1997) plus the present value of the $1,000 face value received in eighteen years.[6] However, the firm pays the bondholder only $1,050 (the call price) for the bond. To compensate the bondholder for the call provision disadvantage, bonds with such a provision generally pay a somewhat higher coupon rate. Thus, if the $1,000 bond issued at par in this case did *not* have a call provision, it might have had a coupon rate of only 7 percent instead of 8 percent; i.e., the promised coupon payment per year would have been only $70 instead of $80.

---

6. Using the factors of Chap. 4, the value of the bond = $V = \$80(P/A, 6\%, 18) + \$1,000(P/F, 6\%, 18) = \$80(10.828) + \$1000(0.3503) = \$1,217$.

Sinking fund provision The bond agreement may include a sinking fund provision which requires the corporation to retire a given number of the bonds in certain specified years. The stipulated means of retirement may be by calling the bonds or by purchasing them in the open market. For example, if the firm issued $10 million of twenty-year bonds on January 1, 1980, it might agree to retire 5 percent of the bonds ($500,000 of par value) in each year beginning in 1981. Sinking fund provisions vary significantly and may require that only some or all the bonds are retired before maturity. The sinking fund retirements may not begin immediately, but may commence several years after original issuance of the bonds. For example, for the twenty-year bonds issued on January 1, 1980, the indenture might require the retirement of 5 percent of the bonds in the years 1990 to 1999, with the reamining bonds retired at maturity on January 1, 2000.

The funds for retirement are transferred to a trustee, who then proceeds to call the bonds or purchase them in the market (depending upon the agreement). The regular retirement of bonds under a sinking fund agreement reduces the outstanding bonds of the firm. This retirement procedure is a benefit to remaining bondholders since the reduction in debt outstanding due to sinking fund retirements reduces the risk of the remaining debt by diminishing the amount of the firm's debt still outstanding.

Other provisions Bondholders will prefer constraints on management's discretionary powers if the constraints increase the likelihood that the firm will meet its bond commitments. A bond indenture might include a restriction on the dividends the firm may pay to its shareholders; or the firm may be required to maintain a minimum current ratio or level of net working capital. A limitation on the amount of further debt that the firm may incur is very common. Particularly in the case of small firms, the bond agreement may also include restrictions on the corporate officers' salaries or on firm investments. Some bonds are convertible into common stock at the option of the holder; convertible bonds are discussed in Chapter 20.

Unsecured bonds

Nature of bondholder's claim Unsecured bonds, or debentures, are backed by the general credit of the corporation—that is, by all the firm's assets which are not pledged as security on secured debt. These bonds are therefore not secured by any specific property. Large corporations with excellent credit standing—e.g., AT&T, General Motors, and Sears, Roebuck—are those most likely to issue debentures instead of secured bonds. The type of assets owned by the firm also affects the choice between issuing secured or unsecured debt. Whereas a railroad with large fixed assets may find it advantageous to issue secured bonds, a firm with liquid or intangible assets, as for example, a publishing company (whose assets may largely be in the form of copyrights and goodwill), will generally have to resort to unsecured debt.

Bond indentures will frequently include a **negative pledge clause,** stipulating that no new debt will be issued by the firm which takes priority over the debentures in their claim to the firm's assets. This may apply to assets acquired in the future as well as to those already owned by the firm. Thus, if the firm were later to pledge any of its assets to secure new debt, the debenture holders would have to be given equal security.

Subordinated debentures   One issue of debt is subordinated to another if it has a lower priority claim to the firm's assets in the event of bankruptcy. The indenture clearly specifies whether the debentures are subordinated and which debt has the preferred position relative to the debentures. Debentures are often subordinated to bank loans and other short-term debt. Subordinated debt allows the firm to increase its borrowing without jeopardizing the security position of senior debt. Thus the firm can obtain senior loans at a relatively low interest cost by specifying that any further debt will assume a subordinate position.

To illustrate the effect of subordination on the payment to creditors in the case of liquidation, assume a firm with the balance sheet before liquidation as shown in Exhibit 19-2. The senior debtholders must be paid before the subordinated debtholders receive anything. The other debt, however, receives the same amount whether there is subordination or not, that is, other debt is not involved in the subordination provision. In Exhibit 19-3 the payments to creditors are indicated for the case in which $600 is realized on the liquidation of the firm's assets and for the case in which $900 is realized.

Exhibit 19-2. Balance Sheet

Total assets		$1,800
Liabilities and net worth:		
Senior debt	$600	
Subordinated debt	300	
Other debt	100	
Total liabilities		$1,000
Stockholders' equity (net worth)		800
Liabilities and net worth		$1,800

Exhibit 19-3. Payment to Creditors under Bankruptcy

	Amount of claim	If $600 realized on asset liquidation		If $900 realized on asset liquidation	
		Payment without sub-ordination	Payment with sub-ordination	Payment without sub-ordination	Payment with sub-ordination
Senior debt	$600	$360	$540	$540	$600
Subordinated debt	300	180	0	270	210
Other debt	100	60	60	90	90
Common stock	800	0	0	0	0

Assume, first, that $600 is received by the firm for the liquidated assets. Without subordination, since a total of $1,000 is owed to all creditors but $600 is realized on the asset liquidation, all creditors receive 60 percent of what is owed to them ($600/$1,000). With subordination, the other debt receives the same amount as without subordination, since the subordination does not affect the payment to the other debt. However, under the subordination agreement, the senior debt receives all of what is left until it is fully paid; i.e., the subordinated debt receives nothing until the senior debt is entirely paid. Since the senior debt claim is $600 and $540 is left over after paying the other debt, the remaining $540 goes in payment to the senior debt.

Similar reasoning applies if $900 is realized on the asset liquidation. The other debt receives $90 with or without subordination; $810 is left over ($900 − $90). First the senior debt of $600 is entirely paid off; then the remaining $210 is paid to the subordinated debt.

The general rules for the two cases illustrated in Exhibit 19-3 are as follows:

Without subordination
 Each debt claim receives

$$\frac{\text{Amount realized on asset liquidation}}{\text{Amount owed to all debt}} \times \text{amount of debt claim}$$

Common stock receives what remains after all debt claims are paid.

With subordination

Other debt receives same amount as without subordination (see above). Senior debt receives what it would receive without subordination, plus all of what remains (except for the amount due to other debt) until the senior claim is paid. Subordinated debt receives the remainder until fully paid. Common stock receives what remains after all debt claims are paid.

Income bonds   Income bonds are a form of unsecured debt that requires payment of interest only to the extent that it is earned by the firm. For example, if the annual interest on the bonds is $100,000 and the firm earns only $50,000 (before interest and taxes), the company has to pay only $50,000 interest on the income bonds. If the firm had earned $150,000, $100,000 in interest would be paid on the income bonds.

Income bonds are frequently used by companies whose capacity to meet interest payments is questionable, e.g., after corporate reorganizations (see Chapter 23). Income bonds may also be used by successful firms as a substitute for preferred stock. The advantage of income bonds is the same as that of other bonds—interest is tax-deductible whereas preferred stock dividends are not. The advantages of preferred stock are that the stock never need be retired (whereas all corporate bonds must have a maturity date for the interest to be tax-deductible) and that preferred dividends need not be paid even if earned in a given year.

Income bond indenture provisions vary. Interest payments are sometimes cumulative; that is, if not paid in a given period, they must be paid in future periods if earned by the firm. Sinking fund provisions are common, and some income bonds are convertible into common stock.

Secured debt

Nature of claim   The distinguishing feature of a secured bond is that particular corporation assets are specified in the bond indenture as security on the debt. In the event of bankruptcy, the secured bondholder has first claim to the assets securing those bonds. A **mortgage** is used to pledge real property (land or buildings), and a **chattel mortgage** is used to pledge personal property (property that is not real property).

Priority of debt   A given secured bond issue may have a senior claim to specific assets, in which case the bonds would be referred to as **first mortgage bonds.** The claim to the assets may be subordinate to that of other creditors, in which case the bonds carry a junior mortgage on the property and would be referred to as second mortgage bonds or third mortgage bonds, etc. This situation is analogous to the familiar first, second, and third mortgages on residential real estate.

The mortgage contract may have a **closed-end provision,** which prohibits the firm from issuing further debt *of the same priority* against the same property. For example, if the firm has $5 million of first mortgage bonds covered by a mortgage on $10 million worth of property, a closed-end provision would prevent the firm from issuing further first mortgage bonds on the property, but it may allow the issuance of second mortgage bonds on that property. If the mortgage were an **open-end mortgage,** the firm would be allowed to issue further first mortgage bonds against the property. Clearly, first mortgage bonds under a closed-end mortgage contract are less risky for investors than under an open-end mortgage contract. Thus, in the above example, if the $5 million in bonds were secured by a closed-end first mortgage, and the firm were to issue additional bonds worth $1 million, the new bonds would be subordinated to the $5 million of first mortgage bonds. In this case, if the firm in liquidation were to realize $5 million on the assets, the first mortgage bonds would be fully paid and the second mortgage bonds would receive nothing. Under an open-end first mortgage contract, however, the additional $1 million of new bonds have equal priority with the initial $5 million of bonds; with $5 million realized on the liquidation of the assets, all bondholders would receive $83\frac{1}{3}$ cents on each dollar of debt ($5 million realized on assets/$6 million of debt). The bond contract may also provide for a **limited open-end mortgage,** which allows the issuance of further first mortgage bonds up to a given limit. In the above example, the limited open-end mortgage might allow the issuance of an additional $2 million of first mortgage bonds beyond the initial bond issue of $5 million.

Property securing the debt A mortgage may relate to specific land and buildings or may be a **blanket mortgage** covering all the real property owned by the corporation. Instead of a mortgage (which is a security interest in real property), the firm may use personal property as collateral on the bonds. If equipment is used, bonds are referred to as **equipment trust certificates.** This type of security has been used frequently by railroads. Sometimes securities or inventory or other intangible assets (e.g., patents) are used as collateral, in which case the debt securities issued by the corporation would be referred to as **collateral trust bonds.**

To strengthen the security position of the bondholders, the bond indenture may include an **after-acquired property clause.** This provides that any property acquired by the firm in the future will also serve as collateral for the bonds. In addition to the after-acquired property clause, the bond contract may permit the firm to issue additional debt secured by the same property as the bonds so long as any new debt does not exceed a specified limit.

An illustration of a mortgage bond is provided by Inland Steel's first mortgage $8\frac{7}{8}$ bonds, maturing on April 15, 1999. The bonds can be called on or before March 31, 1975, at a price depending upon the call date. The properties securing the bonds are the following:

1. The Indiana Harbor Works and certain parcels of land in East Chicago, Indiana
2. Certain iron ore properties in Michigan and Minnesota
3. The coal properties of the company in Jefferson County, Illinois
4. Approximately 400 acres of vacant land in Porter County, Indiana

The mortgage is open-ended, with the indenture permitting the issuance of additional debt under the mortgage so long as interest is adequately covered by the firm's income.

The Advantages of Long-Term Debt

Bonds offer the attraction to investors of providing a fixed stream of returns with a relatively high degree of safety. On the other hand, bondholders do not share in any exceptional profitability which the firm may achieve. Furthermore, bondholders generally do not have the right to vote. Bonds are therefore meant to appeal to investors willing to sacrifice the chance of extraordinary gain for safety of return.

The company must weigh several advantages and disadvantages of raising additional capital by issuing debt rather than by selling new shares of common or preferred stock. As explained in Chapters 3 and 9, since interest is tax-deductible whereas payments to other security holders are not, the aftertax cost of debt capital is lower, at least up to some level of borrowing. Even with this tax advantage, however, the firm will limit its borrowing so as to avoid increasing the possibility of bankruptcy. Shareholders also benefit from the fact that the bondholders do not participate in any extraordinary profits and do not enjoy the voting privilege. Offsetting these advantages is the added risk to the firm of incurring the fixed debt commitment. Except for income bonds (see above discussion), periodic coupon payments must be met or the firm will be in default. Furthermore, in the case of bonds (including income bonds) the firm must retire the bonds at maturity by paying their face value. These fixed commitments on the debt must be met regardless of the corporation's profitability. In addition, as we noted earlier, many bond indentures include restrictions on the firm's operations, e.g., on working capital and dividend payments. In short, the greater safety provided to bondholders implies greater risk to shareholders.

Conditions in the securities markets may influence the choice between new debt and new equity financing. Bond prices and stock prices sometimes move in opposite directions, or in the same direction but to a different degree. The market price reflects what the firm will receive on any new securities it issues. If external capital is to be secured, the firm will tend to find it advantageous to issue bonds if bond prices are relatively high (interest rate low) and share prices low and to issue stock when stock prices are relatively inflated and bond prices are low (interest rates high).

The firm's choice of capital structure will depend largely upon the predictability of its earnings. Firms with relatively stable and predictable profits can borrow extensively with a high degree of confidence that the debt obligations will be met. The advantage of interest tax deductibility can be fully exploited in this situation. On the other hand, firms with unpredictable and volatile earnings will make less use of debt, since default is more likely. This greater probability of default will mean that the firm must pay a higher rate of interest on its debt. Furthermore, shareholders will be averse to excessive borrowing by the firm, since the danger of bankruptcy is undesirable to them just as it is to bondholders.

Preferred stock is an intermediate form of financing between debt and common stock, since it has some of the properties of each. Preferred stockholders have a prior claim relative to common stockholders to the firm's income after interest and taxes and to the firm's assets in the event of bankruptcy. Preferred stock is subordinate to all debt with regard to earnings and assets. Preferred shareholders generally have voting privileges on certain matters, e.g., on the issuance of new debt by the firm. The firm need not pay dividends on preferred stock if it so chooses, so long as it also fails to pay common stock dividends. Therefore, the existence of preferred stock does not increase the probability of firm bankruptcy. Indeed, any added capital provided by the issuance of preferred stock reduces the likelihood of bankruptcy by increasing the firm's capital.

PREFERRED STOCK

Dividend payments

Par value   Preferred share dividends are generally stated as a percentage of par; e.g., a dividend of 8 percent of par on preferred shares with a par of $100 would be $8 per year.[7] Similarly, 8 percent preferred stock

Characteristics of Preferred Stock

---

7. The par value of preferred is similar to the par value of a bond and is used to express the dividend payment (as a percentage of par). The *market value* of a share of preferred is rarely equal to its par value. Market value equals the present value of future dividends on the preferred using the market discount rate (*not* the dividend rate as a percentage of par). For example, assume a $100 par preferred paying an annual 8 percent dividend ($8 dividend = 0.08 × $100), and assume that the preferred is not expected to be called in the future (perpetual dividend). If investors want to earn 10 percent on their investment in the stock, its market value is the $8 dividend discounted at 10 percent, which equals $8 (*P/A*, 10%, ∞) = $8(10.0) = $80. An investor paying $80 for the preferred stock will earn 10 percent annually on the investment as long as the stock is held, assuming that the dividend is actually paid each year.

with a par of $50 would pay $4 (0.08 × $50) in annual dividends. If the preferred stock does not have a par value, the dividend payment is merely stated by itself, e.g., as an annual dividend of $8 per share of preferred stock.

Priority of payment Preferred dividends must be paid before any dividends can be paid to common stockholders. All debt interest takes priority over payments to preferred shares.

Cumulative dividend and participating preferred Usually, a **cumulative dividend provision** is included in the preferred stock agreement which requires that all past unpaid dividends on the preferred stock must be met before any dividends can be declared on the common stock. For example, if the firm has a $10 million (par) 8 percent preferred stock issue outstanding, the annual preferred dividend would be $800,000. Assume that the firm could not pay any dividends in 1975 and 1976, but is considering paying a dividend on the common stock in 1977. Under a cumulative preferred dividend provision, before the common dividend can be paid, the preferred dividends owed for 1975 and 1976, plus the preferred dividend for 1977, must first be paid—a total preferred dividend of $2,400,000 ($800,000 for each of the years 1975, 1976, and 1977).

The cumulative dividend provision is an extremely important protective feature for the preferred stockholders. Since preferred dividends need be paid only when common stock dividends are also paid, without the cumulative provision the firm could greatly reduce payments to preferred stockholders by paying large infrequent dividends on the common stock instead of paying smaller annual dividends. Thus, in the example above but with noncumulative preferred stock, payment of large dividends to common stockholders once every three years would require a payment of $800,000 to preferred stockholders only once every three years; however, to pay even a small dividend to common stockholders each year would require an $800,000 dividend on the preferred every year.

Infrequently, preferred stockholders may participate equally (or up to a stipulated level) with common stockholders in receiving any dividends paid by the firm. Such preferred stock is referred to as **participating preferred.** With fully participating preferred, the dividend distribution involves payment first to preferred stock up to the stipulated amount (e.g., $8 per share on 8 percent $100 preferred), then a dividend payment on each common share equal to that paid on a preferred share, and finally, equal payment of the remaining dividends to the common and preferred stock.

Priority of claim on assets If the firm is in liquidation, the creditors must be completely paid before preferred and common stockholders receive anything. After payment to creditors, the preferred stockholders must be paid the par value of their shares, plus any preferred dividends in arrears or for the current period. Anything remaining goes to the common shareholders.

Voting rights   Preferred stockholders are usually accorded only limited voting privileges. Consent of the preferred stockholders may be required for the issuance of additional securities with an equal or higher-priority claim on the firm's assets or earnings. The preferred stockholders may also be allowed to elect a minority number of directors, e.g., two out of seven. This privilege of electing directors may be contingent upon the failure of the firm to pay preferred dividends for some number of periods.

Other provisions

Callability   The corporation may retain the right to call the preferred shares, generally at a price above par. For example, the firm may be able to call its $100 par preferred shares by paying the shareholders $108 per share, the call premium in this case being $8.

Sinking fund provision   Periodic retirement of the preferred stock under a sinking fund arrangement may be required, although this provision is far less common than it is with bonds. The requirement will generally involve the annual retirement of a given percentage of the total preferred stock issued. The sinking fund payments may be tied to the firm's earnings.

Convertibility   The preferred stock may be convertible into common stock at the option of the holder. The preferred stock may also be issued as a **unit** with warrants to purchase common stock (the unit is the combination of the share of preferred stock and a specified number of warrants). These devices provide the purchaser with the opportunity to benefit from the company's superior performance (by acquiring the firm's common stock), while also containing a safety hedge in the form of preferred stock if the company's fortunes are poor. Convertibles and warrants are discussed in Chapter 20.

Restrictions on the firm   As noted earlier, preferred shareholders may impose certain restrictions upon the firm by exercising voting privileges. In addition, under the preferred stock agreement, the corporation may be required to maintain a specified current ratio or level of working capital before dividends may be paid on the common stock. Also, a limit may be placed on the issuance of additional debt or preferred stock. The primary objective of these conditions is to ensure the ability of the firm to meet preferred dividend payments and to protect the preferred shareholder's investment by limiting additional obligations with an equal or superior claim to the firm's assets.

An actual preferred stock issue   On February 26, 1974, the Appalachian Power Company offered for sale 200,000 shares of 8.52 percent cumulative preferred. The par value of the stock was $100, implying an annual dividend of $8.52 per share (8.52 percent × $100). However, the offering, or selling, price per share to investors was $101 per share, thereby providing them with an actual annual dividend yield of 8.44 percent ($8.52/$101). These terms are shown below.

Shares (000's)	Par value	Annual dividend yield (dividend/par)	Offering price	Actual yield (dividend/offering price)
200	$100	8.52%	$101	8.44%

The stock is callable as a whole or in part at varying prices over time: at $110.28 from issuance through to February 28, 1979; at $108.94 through February 28, 1984; at $105.82 through February 28, 1989; and at $103.59 thereafter. Some of the conditions designed to protect the preferred stockholders' interest were as follows:

1. Consent of the holders of a majority of the total number of preferred shares then outstanding is needed to issue additional preferred stock unless the firm's net income and gross (pretax) income relative to preferred dividends (on old and any new preferred stock) and interest on the firm's debt are at certain specified levels.
2. Consent of the holders of a majority of the total number of preferred shares is required for the firm to issue or assume additional unsecured debt, if the result is to cause the firm's debt burden to exceed a certain specified level.
3. Dividends on the firm's *common stock* will be restricted if the firm's debt-equity ratio exceeds a specified level.

This issue contains most of the provisions that we described earlier.

The Use of Preferred Stock   From the investor's standpoint, preferred stock has the advantage of yielding a relatively safe and steady return. Since dividends received from domestic corporations are 85 percent tax-free to a corporate investor, some firms seeking low-risk returns find the preferred stock of other corporations a desirable investment. Preferred shares are not, of course, risk-free. They may fluctuate in market value, and if the firm's performance is poor, they may not receive any dividends. As with any investment, the desirability of this form of security will depend upon the risk-return preferences of the investor.

From the issuing firm's standpoint, preferred stock has three primary advantages:

1. The preferred shareholder's returns are generally limited so that extraordinary profits of the firm still accrue to the common shareholder.
2. Nonpayment of the preferred dividend does not place the firm into default, as is the case if interest on debt is not paid.
3. Control of the firm remains with the common shareholders.

In merger situations, preferred stock (as well as common stock) has an additional advantage over debt. Suppose firm A is buying firm B and uses the securities of firm A as payment. The use of firm A bonds as compensation to firm B owners would produce a taxable gain to the sellers at the time of sale. On the other hand, if firm A stock (voting preferred or common) were used, the gain would generally not be taxable until the firm B owners were to sell the firm A stock that they received in the merger.

Balancing the advantages of preferred stock are several disadvantages. The dividend payments on preferred, and the preferred's claim to the firm's assets under bankruptcy, take priority over the common shareholders' claims, a disadvantage to stockholders that would not apply if additional common stock were issued. Furthermore, dividends to preferred stock are not tax-deductible as is interest on debt—a disadvantage to the firm. The consequence is that the residual income to stockholders is less with preferred stock than with debt, even if the coupon rate on the debt equals the dividend rate on the preferred.

The lower cost of debt was explained in Chapter 9. To illustrate this point, in Exhibit 19-4, the net income to common shareholders, assuming $5 million of 6 percent bonds outstanding (annual interest of $300,000), is compared with the net income to common shareholders with $5 million of 6 percent preferred stock outstanding (annual preferred dividends of $300,000). The common shareholders' net income is $850,000 with debt, but only $700,000 with the preferred stock, simply because interest is tax-deductible whereas preferred dividends are not.

THE REFUNDING DECISION

Refunding is the issuance of new securities to retire old debt or preferred stock. The old securities may be retired by calling them or by purchasing

Exhibit 19-4.

	Debt	Preferred Stock
Income before interest and taxes	$2,000,000	$2,000,000
Less interest on debt	300,000	0
Income before taxes	$1,700,000	$2,000,000
Taxes (at 50%)	850,000	1,000,000
Income after taxes	$ 850,000	$1,000,000
Dividends on preferred stock	0	300,000
Net income to common stockholders	$ 850,000	$ 700,000

them in the open market. A firm will consider refunding if the cost of borrowing has declined since the old securities were issued. The basis of the gain from refunding and the method of computing the gain will be illustrated below.

As we will see, the refunding problem can be viewed as a firm's investment decision, since it involves obtaining funds (e.g., through borrowing) and then using those funds for a productive purpose (retiring old debt in the refunding case). The refunding is desirable only if the net present value of the resulting aftertax cash flow is positive, as in any investment decision. The initial outlay of the refunding (a cash outflow like the investment outlay under capital budgeting) is the difference between what is paid out to purchase the old securities less what is received from new bond or preferred investors on issuing the new securities. In the case examined below, this initial outlay is equal to (1) the flotation costs of the new security plus (2) the call premium on the old security. The benefits of the refunding operation equal the reduction in aftertax payments to debt (or preferred stock). These benefits must then be discounted to the present to determine their present value. The refunding is desirable only if the present value of the benefits exceeds the initial outlay. In discounting the cash flow benefits, the current aftertax market interest rate on the firm's debt is used as a discount rate. This is the rate that properly reflects the risk involved with the debt-associated cash flows being discounted.

Assume that Vista Corporation has a $100 million, 9 percent (coupon rate) bond issue outstanding, with twenty years remaining to maturity. The bonds were issued five years ago at par ($100 million) with a flotation cost of $2.5 million (Vista netted $97.5 million on the issue). These flotation costs are being charged off for tax purposes as an expense at the rate of $100,000 per year ($2.5 million/25 years).[8] If the bonds are called, the

---

8. Note that the bonds had twenty-five years to maturity when they were originally issued.

unamortized portion of the flotation costs ($2,000,000) will be deductible for tax purposes when the bonds are called. Vista's tax rate is 50 percent. Vista can call the bonds for $107 million. The call premium is therefore $7 million, and this premium is tax-deductible as an expense (like interest) *in the year the bonds are called.*[9] Vista has been informed by its investment bankers that the firm can issue between $95 million and $105 million in new debt at an interest cost of 6 percent. The firm is considering the issue of $100 million of 6 percent bonds which will involve flotation costs of $3 million. Assume for simplicity that the interest on the old bonds was paid right before the refunding and that interest is paid yearly (therefore, the next interest payment on the old debt is due in one year). Given these data, we can compute the net present value of the costs and returns from the refunding.

Initial outlay   The initial outlay equals the aftertax cash outflow to retire the old bonds ($102.5 million) less the net cash inflow from selling the new bonds ($97 million), which equals $5.5 million. The computation is as follows:

Face value of old bonds		$100 million
Call premium	$7 million	
Less tax benefit from deducting call premium	($3.5 million)	
Aftertax call premium cost		$ 3.5 million
Less tax benefit from write-off of $2,000,000 in unamortized flotation costs [tax rate × $2,000,000]		($ 1.0 million)
Cash outflow		$102.5 million
Price of new bonds	$100 million	
Less flotation costs	($3 million)	
Cash inflow		$ 97.0 million
Initial outlay (cash outflow − cash inflow)		$ 5.5 million

Annual savings   Note that both interest and flotation costs are tax-deductible and therefore reduce the taxes paid by the firm. There are two elements that change due to the refunding operation—interest paid on the debt and taxes paid.

9. The $7 million call premium is deductible in the year the bonds are called. Since the firm's tax rate is 50 percent, deducting the $7 million from taxable income reduces taxes by $3.5 million, and this $3.5 million tax saving is subtracted from the $7 million to produce an aftertax call premium cost of $3.5 million.

Interest cost   Recall from Chapter 9 that interest cost equals 1 minus the corporate tax rate times the interest paid since interest is tax-deductible. Therefore, assuming a corporate tax rate of 50 percent:

Aftertax interest expense on old debt	
($100 million × 0.09 × 0.5)	$4.5 million
Aftertax interest expense on new debt	
($100 million × 0.06 × 0.5)	$3 million
Annual savings on interest	$1.5 million

where the 0.5 in the above computation is $(1 - \text{tax rate}) = (1 - 0.5) = 0.5$.

Tax benefits from amortization of the flotation costs   Flotation costs of the new issue are $3 million. This amount may be deducted for tax purposes over the life of the twenty-year bonds in the amount per year of

$$\frac{\$3 \text{ million}}{20 \text{ years}} = \$150,000 \text{ per year}$$

The $150,000 per year may be deducted as an expense. The flotation costs on the old bonds would have been $100,000 per year and would also have been tax deductible. The deduction for flotation costs has therefore increased by $50,000 a year. Since flotation costs can be used as a tax deduction, each added dollar of flotation costs deduction reduces taxes by that dollar times the tax rate. The flotation cost tax benefit of refunding therefore equals[10]

$$\begin{aligned}\text{Tax benefit from increased flotation costs amortization} &= \text{tax rate} \times \text{added flotation costs} \\ &= 0.50 \times \$50,000 \text{ per year} \\ &= \$25,000 \text{ per year}\end{aligned}$$

10. Each dollar of any tax-deductible expense, flotation costs included, reduces taxable income by $1 and thereby reduces taxes by the tax rate × $1. For example, assume that Vista's taxable income before any flotation cost deduction is $1 million and the corporate tax rate is 50 percent. With the old flotation cost deduction of $100,000, taxable income = $1,000,000 − $100,000 = $900,000 and corporate taxes equal the tax rate × $900,000 = 0.5 × $900,000 = $450,000. With the new bonds, the flotation cost tax deduction is $150,000 annually, taxable income = $1,000,000 − $150,000 = $850,000 and corporate taxes = 0.5 × $850,000 = $425,000. The new bonds increase the flotation cost deduction by $50,000 (from $100,000 to $150,000) and therefore reduce taxes by the tax rate × increase in flotation cost deduction = 0.5 × $50,000 = $25,000.

The total benefit per year equals the sum of the aftertax interest saving plus the increased tax saving on amortization of flotation costs, that is,

$$\text{Annual savings} = \$1,500,000 + \$25,000$$
$$= \$1,525,000$$

The savings are realized in each of the forthcoming twenty years.

We now must use the above computations to determine whether or not the stream of benefits is sufficient to warrant the initial cost incurred in refunding. We must compute the net present value of the cash flows. This is done as follows:

Aftertax cost of new debt $= (1 - \text{tax rate}) \times \text{interest rate}$
$$= 0.5 \times 6\% = 3\%$$

Present value factor for a 20-year annuity at 3%
$$= (P/A, 3\%, 20) = 14.877$$

Present value of $1,525,000 per year for 20 years $= 14.877 \times \$1,525,000$
$$= \$22,687,425$$

$$\text{Initial outlay} = \$5.5 \text{ million}$$

Net present value of refunding operation
$$= \text{present value of annual savings}$$
$$- \text{initial outlay}$$
$$= \$22,687,425 - \$5.5 \text{ million}$$
$$= \$17,187,425$$

The net gain from refunding is equal to $17,187,425 over twenty years. It is therefore to the advantage of the firm to refund the existing bond issue rather than to keep it outstanding for the next twenty years. However, these are not the only two alternatives, and a complete analysis of the problem would be to consider not only refunding now, but refunding one year from now, two years from now, etc. The net benefits from refunding one year from now may be even greater than from refunding currently. If, in the above problem, it were expected that interest rates would not fall below 6 percent, refunding currently would likely be the best alternative. However, if the firm anticipated that interest rates in the market would fall significantly below 6 percent, perhaps postponing the refunding decision to a subsequent period would be the best strategy.

It must be emphasized that the reason that refunding was so attractive in the above example was that the firm could call the old bonds for only $106 million. If there were no call provision, the bonds would probably sell for a value that would make refunding unattractive. If the old bonds were viewed by investors (bondholders) as having the same risk as the new debt, the yield to maturity on the old bonds would be approximately 6 percent (the same as the interest rate on the new debt) and their market value would be about $135 million.[11] Without a call provision, the firm would have to pay at least $135 million for those old bonds to retire them by purchasing them in the open market. Refunding under these conditions would clearly not have been a good choice.

The above example involved the refunding of a debt issue. Refunding preferred stock involves a similar computation. Problem 7 at the end of the chapter involves a preferred stock refunding decision.

SUMMARY

Long-term debt and preferred stock are fixed-income securities in that they both provide the investor with a stipulated promised series of payments in the future. The interest and face value are specified for the bonds, and a given dividend rate is stipulated for the preferred stock. Creditors have a prior claim to the company's income and to the firm's assets if the company liquidates. The firm must pay the interest and the maturity value on its debt as agreed upon in the bond contract, or the company defaults and is subject to legal action. In contrast, the firm is not obligated to pay dividends on the preferred stock unless dividends are also paid to common stockholders; i.e., the firm cannot default on preferred dividends. Thus, rather than increasing the probability of bankruptcy, the issuance of preferred stock lessens bankruptcy risk by raising the total assets of the firm, thereby strengthening the capacity of the company to meet its debt obligations.

The value of a bond to investors is the discounted worth of the periodic coupon (interest) payment, plus maturity value. This discounted value may differ from the bond's face or maturity value, depending upon the interest rate investors use in discounting the bond payments. The debt agreement, or indenture, may include provisions to protect bondholders which require the firm to maintain a given working capital position, to restrict dividends, to refrain from issuing further debt of the same class, or periodically to retire part of the debt by buying the bonds in the open market or by purchasing them directly from the bondholders at a specified price. The tax deductibility of interest is a strong encouragement to the use of debt. This incentive does not exist for preferred stock, since preferred dividends are not tax-deductible.

Preferred stock dividends must be paid before any dividends can be paid on the common stock. Dividends are usually cumulative; i.e., before

---

11. $135 million = $9 million ($P/A$, 6%, 20) + $100 million ($P/F$, 6%, 20) = $9 million(11.47) + $100 million(0.3118).

any dividends can be issued on the common stock, there must be payment of all past preferred dividends as yet unpaid. Preferred stock may be participating, in which case preferred shareholders receive dividends on an equal basis with common stockholders.

Financing with debt and preferred stock, rather than with additional common stock, allows existing common stockholders to retain firm control and to retain claim to any extraordinary firm profits; i.e., the rights of ownership are not shared. Debt has the added advantage of interest tax deductibility, whereas preferred stock does not involve the default risk associated with debt. The choice between debt and preferred stock as a method of financing will depend upon the volatility of the firm's income and upon its existing capital structure. Even a relatively stable company may issue preferred stock rather than additional debt if its existing debt burden is great.

QUESTIONS

1. Describe the nature of the promise made to debtholders as opposed to the promise made to stockholders.
2. Explain the financial managers' motivation to use debt.
3. Define: bond, indenture, face value, and coupon rate.
4. Describe how one goes about placing a value on a bond.
5. Why is it that bonds usually do not sell at their face value? Explain fully.
6. Distinguish between debentures and mortgage bonds.
7. What role does the trustee assume when bonds are issued?
8. Under what conditions do you think a firm would call in its bonds?
9. Of what value is the cumulative feature found in preferred stock issues?
10. How can a bond or preferred stock refunding decision be viewed as an investment decision?
11. "In the text of this chapter, the discount rate used to evaluate a refunding decision is the aftertax cost of debt to the firm. I thought the firm's average cost of capital was supposed to be used to evaluate capital budgeting decisions. How come the authors used the rate they did?" Answer this question.

PROJECT

Obtain from a stockbroker a prospectus for a new bond issue. Examine the provisions concerning priority of payment, collateral (if applicable), restrictions on the firm (e.g., on dividends, working capital position, etc.), and any other matters discussed in this chapter.

PROBLEMS 1. Find the value of a bond which matures in twenty years, has a face value of $1,000 and a coupon rate of 8 percent, and pays interest annually. Bonds of similar quality and maturity have a yield to maturity of 10 percent. Show all calculations. [Ans.: $829.72]

2. Find the value of a bond which matures in twenty years, has a face value of $1,000 and a coupon rate of 8 percent, and pays interest annually. Bonds of similar quality and maturity have a yield to maturity of 6 percent. Show all calculations.

3. The Dreyfus Corporation is planning to issue twenty-year bonds with a face value of $1,000 per bond to finance expansion of its plant and machinery. The market rate of interest (yield to maturity) on bonds of the same risk and maturity as the proposed Dreyfus issue is 8 percent.
   a) If Dreyfus issues the bonds with a 10 percent coupon, what price will one bond sell for? With an 8 percent coupon? With a 6 percent coupon? [Partial ans.: price with a 10 percent coupon = $1,196.30]
   b) Provide an explanation for your answers in **a** above.

4. Below is the balance sheet, *before* liquidation, of Sink or Swim Boat Company, Inc. The debt is in the form of A bonds and B bonds. Assume that the firm is liquidated after having defaulted on its debt, and that it receives fifty cents on a dollar (book value) for all of its assets. What would the debtholders be entitled to if there were no subordinated debt (i.e., neither A bonds nor B bonds subordinated to the other)? What would debtholders obtain if the B bonds were subordinated to the A bonds? What do the shareholders get in each case?

Sink or Swim Boat Company balance sheet

Total assets		$250,000
Liabilities:		
A bonds	$100,000	
B bonds	50,000	
Total liabilities	$150,000	
Net worth	100,000	
Total liabilities and net worth		$250,000

5. Arizona Utilities is planning a capital expansion next year to meet the increasing demand for its services. Arizona estimates it will need $2 million and plans to issue preferred stock to finance the expansion. The preferred will have a par value of $50 and a 6 percent dividend. Arizona does not plan to retire the preferred in the foreseeable future. It has found that similar issues of preferred (same risk and maturity characteristics) are yielding 8 percent. Assume that flotation costs are zero.

a) What price can Arizona expect to receive for a share of the pre-ferred?

b) How many shares must it issue to finance the planned expansion? [Ans.: 53,333 shares]

c) What are the advantages of a preferred issue over a bond issue?

6. In 1973 the Seemeenow Swimsuit Company floated a $25 million bond issue scheduled to mature in 1993. Since interest rates were relatively high at the time of issuance, Seemeenow attached a 9.5 percent coupon to the bonds in order to sell them at a par value of $1,000 per bond. Flo-tation costs for the issue were $650,000, which Seemeenow is amortiz-ing over the life of the bond issue for tax purposes. Seemeenow's tax rate is 40 percent. The bond indenture stipulates that Seemeenow may call the bond after 1975 at a price of $1,050 per bond. Recently the prime rate has fallen and Seemeenow's investment bankers have noti-fied the firm that it can now issue $25 million in bonds at par with a coupon rate of 6.5 percent to mature in fifteen years. Flotation costs on the new issue would amount to $787,500. The bankers also mentioned that they do not expect the interest rate to fall lower in the near future. The finance officers of Seemeenow are meeting to determine whether or not they should refinance the old bonds in light of the information given by the investment bankers. What do you advise? (Note: You may round off percents to the nearest $\frac{1}{2}$ percent, e.g., 6.4 percent rounded to 6.5 percent or 7.8 percent rounded to 8 percent, before performing present value computations.) Analyze the problem assuming that the present date is January 1978, just after interest has been paid on the old bonds.

7. Kalamath Utility Services is considering refunding an old preferred stock issue. There are 30,000 shares of the preferred outstanding. Ka-lamath is paying an $8 dividend per year on each share. The par value is $100 per share, and Kalamath can call the stock at $102 per share. Kalamath's financial analysts feel that they can issue 30,000 new shares of preferred at their par value of $100. Since the market rate of interest on similar issues is 7 percent, the analysts feel that if the pre-ferred promises a $7 dividend it can be sold at par, thus saving the firm $30,000 annually in dividends. Flotation costs on the new issue would be $90,000; this $90,000 cost is completely deductible in the current year. Kalamath is in the 40 percent tax bracket. Assume that the call premium on the outstanding preferred stock is *not* tax-deductible.

Should Kalamath refund the preferred stock issue?

convertibles and warrants

In Chapters 18 and 19 we discussed the three types of securities used most often by corporations to raise long-term capital: common stock, bonds, and preferred stock. Two interesting alternatives to those three basic security forms are convertibles and warrants. Convertibles and warrants have the special feature that either can be converted at the will of the owner into the issuing company's common stock. In the two main sections that follow, we will describe the characteristics of these securities and show how they appeal to investors and how they can be used by the firm to obtain additional funds.

CONVERTIBLE

Convertible bonds and preferred stock can be converted at the discretion of the security's owner into the common stock of the issuing firm. The owner may convert at any time or choose never to convert. The investor's decision regarding conversion depends on a number of factors which are discussed below.

Conversion Price and Conversion Ratio

The **conversion price** is the dollars of par value of the convertible security paid per share of common stock acquired through conversion.[1] For example, if the conversion price of the common stock is $50, a $1,000 (par value) bond can be converted into twenty shares of common stock. That is,

$$\text{Conversion price} = \frac{\text{par value of convertible security}}{\text{number of common shares received}} \qquad (20\text{-}1)$$

$$= \frac{\$1,000}{20} = \$50$$

Similarly, if a share of convertible preferred stock with a par value of $100 is convertible into two shares of common stock, the conversion price is $50.

The **conversion ratio** is the number of common shares received for converting the convertible security. In the examples above, the conversion

1. See Chaps. 18 and 19 on par value.

ratio is 20 for the convertible bond and 2 for the convertible preferred stock.

The convertible security agreement may contain a stipulation for a varying conversion price over time; e.g., a bond may be convertible into ten shares of common stock from 1978 to 1980, into $9\frac{1}{2}$ shares of common stock from 1981 to 1983, and so on. Less frequently, the conversion option completely expires after a number of years.

The conversion ratio is adjusted if stock dividends or a stock split is declared. The adjustment ensures that holders of the convertible security will maintain their proportional shares of the firm's common stock. For example, a two-for-one stock split would require a doubling of the conversion ratio. Similarly, a 10 percent stock dividend would result in a 10 percent increase in the conversion ratio.

Investment value of the convertible security The **investment value** (pure security value) of a convertible security is the value that the security would have if it were not convertible but had all its other features. It is the value of the bond or preferred stock as an income-producing asset without conversion into common stock. Investment value equals the present value of the interest plus maturity value of a convertible bond, or the present value of the dividend payments anticipated on a convertible preferred. For example, the investment value of a $1,000 par 5 percent convertible bond with twenty years to maturity is the present value of the coupon interest payments of $50 per year, plus the present value of the $1,000 maturity value received twenty years hence. Assume that the market interest rate on bonds of comparable risk but which lack the conversion option is 7 percent. Recall from Chapter 19 that a bond's coupon rate, 5 percent in the present example, need not equal the market interest rate for computing the bond's market value. The investment value of the bond is therefore[2]

Valuation of a Convertible

$$\text{Investment value} = \frac{\$50}{1 + 0.07} + \frac{\$50}{(1 + 0.07)^2}$$

$$+ \cdots + \frac{\$50}{(1 + 0.07)^{20}} + \frac{\$1,000}{(1 + 0.07)^{20}}$$

$$= \$50(P/A, 7\%, 20) + \$1,000(P/F, 7\%, 20)$$

$$= \$50(10.594) + \$1,000(0.2584) = \$788 \qquad (20\text{-}2)$$

2. Using the factors of Chap. 4, investment value = $50(P/A, 7%, 20) + $1,000(P/F, 7%, 20) = $50(10.594) + $1,000(0.2584) = $788.

A convertible security's market value will generally exceed its investment value. Why is this so? Because the investor not only receives the coupon (interest) payments and the maturity payment (or, with preferred stock, the preferred dividend payments), but also has the *additional advantage* of being able to convert the security into common stock at his or her option. By definition, investment value equals the value of the convertible security as a bond or preferred stock; therefore the market price will be higher than the investment value—how much higher depending on the worth of the conversion option to investors. Only if a conversion option is viewed as worthless (because common stock into which it is convertible is likely to have a permanently low value) will the market value of the convertible security equal its investment value.

Conversion value of the convertible security The **conversion value** of a security is the market value of the stock into which it is convertible. For example, assume that a $1,000 bond is convertible into twenty shares of common stock with a market value of $46 per share. The conversion value of the bond is $920 (20 × $46). That is,

Conversion value = (number of shares of common stock received upon conversion) × (market price per share of common stock)

= (conversion ratio) × (market price per share of common stock)

(20-3)

If the market price of the common stock is high, conversion value can exceed investment value. Conversion value is shown in Figure 20-1; it rises as the market price of the common stock rises. Notice that conversion value can also be less than investment value, if the price of the common stock is low. Recall that our 5 percent bond with twenty years to maturity has an investment value of $788, which in no way depends upon the price of the common stock. But conversion value does depend upon the market price of the common. If that market price were $30 per share, the conversion value would be $600 (20 shares × $30 per share), which is less than the investment value of $788. However, if the price per common share were $50, the conversion of the convertible bond would be $1,000, greater than investment value. Thus, conversion value can be above or below investment value depending upon whether the price of the common stock is high or low.

Market value (market price) of the convertible security We have already decided that the market value of the convertible security cannot be less than its investment value because the convertible security's market value

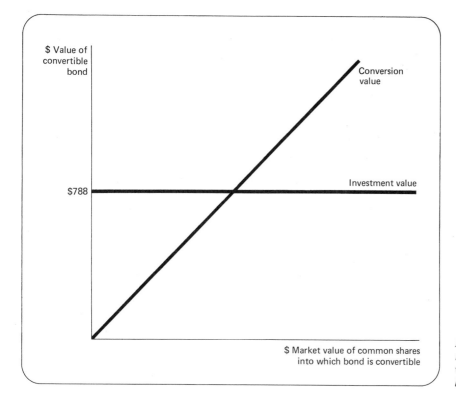

$788

$ Value of convertible bond

Conversion value

Investment value

$ Market value of common shares into which bond is convertible

Figure 20-1. Investment and conversion values of a convertible bond.

equals the investment value of the bond or preferred stock plus the value of the right to convert. It is also true that market value can never be less than conversion value—this is so since the security is always worth at least as much as the common stock into which it can be converted. For example, if we know that we can convert a bond into $920 worth of stock ($920 conversion value), then we know that the convertible bond must be worth at least $920. Therefore, *market value is never less than investment value and never less than conversion value.*

The market value of the convertible security may exceed the floor provided by the investment and conversion values. Since the security also offers the option to convert, a premium above investment value may be paid for the convertible. The market value may also exceed the conversion value, since a convertible security not only offers the stock if one wishes to convert *but also has the investment value floor which common stock does not.*

To illustrate, assume that the convertible bond in the above example has an investment value of $788 and is convertible into twenty shares of common stock with a price of $60 per share; the conversion value of the bond is $1,200, which is equal to the market value of the twenty shares of common stock. But which is better, owning the convertible bond or owning the twenty shares of common stock? Clearly, the bond. The bond can always be converted into the twenty shares of common stock, so must be worth at least as much as the twenty shares of common stock. The bond also has a "floor value," as explained above, equal to its investment value; no such floor exists for the twenty shares of common stock. In other words, the bond is less risky. Thus, if the common stock were to fall to $30 per share, the twenty shares of common stock would be worth $600. However, the convertible bond's value would not fall to $600; it would fall no further than the investment value floor of $788.[3] This added advantage of the convertible security will generally give it a value above the twenty shares of stock into which it can be converted (its conversion value). Of course, if the price of the common stock and of the convertible becomes extremely high, the floor provided by the investment value may become almost irrelevant and the value of the convertible security may approach its conversion value. For example, if the price of the common stock were $100 per share, conversion value of the convertible bond would be $2,000 (20 shares × $100 per share). If it is extremely unlikely that the common stock will fall significantly, the floor provided by the investment value does not provide much of an advantage and the convertible bond's market value will approximate its conversion value.

In summary, the market value of a convertible security will never be less than, and will generally exceed, both its investment value and its conversion value. See Figure 20-2. The excess of market value over the floor provided by the investment and conversion values is referred to as the **conversion premium** (shaded area in Figure 20-2). The conversion premium is the amount by which the market value of the convertible exceeds the higher of its investment and conversion values.

Dilution Effects of Conversion

Conversion will generally lower the earnings per share on the common stock. To understand this, let's look at an example. Assume that the firm has $10 million of twenty-year, 6 percent convertible bonds outstanding (not yet converted), which are convertible into common stock at a conver-

---

3. For the investment value to remain at $788, the market interest rate in Eq. (20-2) must be 7 percent. If the general level of interest rates rises and the stock's price falls, e.g., if the interest rate in Eq. (20-2) rises to 8 percent, the investment value would become $50(P/A, 8%, 20) + $1,000(P/F, 8%, 20) = $705, which still exceeds the $600 value of the shares; the convertible bond would therefore have a market price of at least $705. If the interest rate on the bond were 10 percent in Eq. (20-2), then the investment value would be $50(P/A, 10%, 20) + $1,000(P/F, 10%, 20) = $574; in this case, the convertible bond would be worth at least $600, since the bond's value must be no less than its investment value ($574) or the value of the stock into which it can be converted ($600).

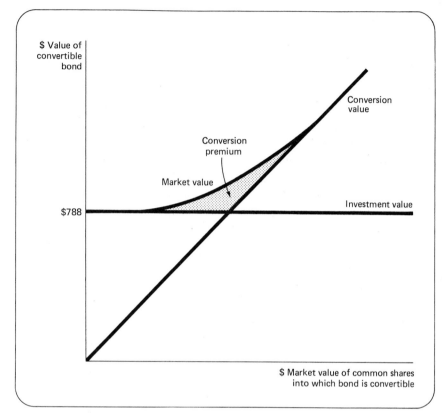

Figure 20-2. Value of a convertible bond. The market value of the convertible bond is never less than the investment value or conversion value. The market value of the convertible approaches investment value if the common stock has a low market value and approaches conversion value if the common stock has a very high market value. The shaded area is the conversion premium, which is the excess of the convertible's market value over the higher of investment value and conversion value.

sion price of $50 (therefore convertible into 200,000 shares of common). The firm also has 1 million shares of common stock outstanding before conversion. From Exhibit 20-1, which summarizes the position of the firm before and after conversion, we see that the earnings per share on the common stock drop from $3.30 to $3 as a consequence of conversion.[4] To see how this same concept works in the case of convertible preferred stock, see problems 3 and 5.

4. It is possible that conversion will lead to a rise in earnings per share. This will occur if earnings per share before conversion are less than added aftertax earnings from eliminating the fixed charges, i.e., interest or preferred dividends on the convertible security divided by the number of new shares due to conversion. For example, assume that in Exhibit 20-1 the firm's convertible bonds were convertible into 50,000 shares of common stock instead of into 200,000 shares. After conversion there are 1,050,000 shares of common stock with earnings of $3.43 per share, which exceeds the preconversion earnings per share of $3.30. This occurred since earnings before conversion of $3 were less than added earnings from eliminating the interest on the convertibles divided by the number of new shares ($300,000/50,000 shares) = $6.

Exhibit 20-1.

	Before conversion	After conversion
Earnings before interest and taxes	$7,200,000	$7,200,000
Bond interest	600,000	0
Earnings before taxes	$6,600,000	$7,200,000
Taxes (at 50%)	3,300,000	3,600,000
Earnings after taxes	$3,300,000	$3,600,000
No. of shares of common stock	1 million	1.2 million
Earnings per share	$3.30	$3.00

Appraisal of Convertible Securities

Many investors find convertible securities attractive because they provide a relatively safe investment income (and therefore an investment value floor) with the possibility of a large gain if the common stock appreciates significantly. However, the investor must make a sacrifice to gain the right of conversion, since the yield on a convertible security is generally less than that on a comparable security without the conversion privilege. Thus, for example, a twenty-year, $1,000 nonconvertible bond of the firm with a coupon rate of 8 percent ($80 per year in interest payments) might sell at its face value of $1,000, whereas a convertible bond with a coupon rate of only 6 percent ($60 per year in interest payments) might also sell at its face value of $1,000. The nonconvertible bond provides a yield of 8 percent and the convertible bond provides a yield of 6 percent. The difference in yield is due to the conversion feature of the 6 percent bond. That is, investors are willing to accept the lower yield on the convertible bond because of the convertibility privilege.

The firm's decision to sell a convertible security must be based, like all financing decisions, on the firm's particular situation and on security market conditions. There is no reason to suppose that convertibles are, on the average, superior to other financing vehicles. It may appear that there is an advantage to the firm because convertible bonds or preferred stock can be sold at a yield less than that required if the securities were nonconvertible. However, whether this ultimately results in a benefit to the firm (and therefore to existing shareholders) depends on the future trend in the company's common stock price. If the firm's stock does not appreciate much in value, then the common stockholders are better off since conversion will never occur. On the other hand, if the firm prospers and the value of its stock does rise, conversion will occur and the convertible security holders will effectively have bought the company's common stock at a bargain price. In this case, the firm's common shareholders are worse off than they would have been if the firm had initially issued nonconvertible securities. Therefore, the company's decision to issue convertibles essentially involves a gamble on the future course of the firm's stock.

Real benefits may be provided by convertibles if the firm wishes to increase its debt (or preferred stock) outstanding in the short run, but to reduce these fixed-charge securities later by replacing them with common stock. If the firm were to issue nonconvertible bonds now and stock later to pay off those bonds, it would incur flotation costs twice—now, and later when the stock is sold. But with convertibles it could issue convertible debt now, which would be converted into common stock at the later date, with flotation costs incurred only in the current period. If a rise in the firm's common stock in a later period is anticipated, so that conversion can be expected to occur, this approach will avoid the refunding costs associated with replacing the nonconvertible debt with common stock.

Generally, convertible issues have a call provision which provides the firm with a means of compelling convertible security holders to convert to common stock. If the conversion value of the convertible security rises above the call price, the firm can merely call the securities and conversion will be forced. For example, assume a $1,000, 6 percent convertible bond convertible into twenty shares of City Corporation common stock. Let the call provision allow the firm to call the convertible for $1,100. Assume that the price per share of City common stock is $65. The conversion value of the bond is $1,300 (20 shares × $65 per share). City Corporation can call the bond, and consequently security holders have the choice of converting or surrendering their bonds for the call price. An investor who does not convert receives the call price of $1,100; an investor who does convert receives twenty shares of common stock with a total value of $1,300. Obviously, investors will convert. In general, to ensure that the convertible security holders will convert and not simply allow the security to be called, management will not call a convertible issue unless the conversion value is somewhat greater than the call price.

WARRANTS

A warrant is an option to buy a specified number of the firm's common stock at a stated price per share. Recall that a convertible security required surrender of the security in exchange for the common stock. A warrant requires a surrender of the warrant, *plus* the payment of additional cash—called the **option price**—in order to obtain the common stock. Warrants are issued by corporations for cash to investors who may exercise them (i.e., buy the stock) or may resell them to other investors. A warrant is like a stock right except that rights are issued free to existing stockholders who may sell them or exercise them by buying new shares (see Chapter 18). Warrants do not have to be exercised when they are bought but generally expire at a given date, although some are perpetual. Alleghany Corporation, Atlas Corporation, and Tri-Continental Corporation are among the few firms that have issued perpetual warrants.

Warrants are often issued with other securities (usually bonds or preferred stock) in a unit or package. The warrants in this case may be "detached" and sold separately by the investor.

Valuation of a Warrant **Theoretical value of a warrant** The **theoretical value** of a warrant equals the market value of the common stock purchased with the warrant minus the total option price paid for the shares. This is analogous to the conversion value of a convertible security. The theoretical value can be expressed as

Theoretical value of a warrant
$$= \text{(market price of common stock} - \text{option price)} \\ \times \text{(number of shares purchased with one warrant)} \quad (20\text{-}4a)$$

or

Theoretical value of a warrant
$$= \text{(market price of stock acquired with one warrant)} \\ - \text{(exercise price paid for share acquired with one warrant)} \quad (20\text{-}4b)$$

For example, assume that Makitbig Company has warrants outstanding each of which entitles the holder to purchase two shares of Makitbig Company stock for $40 per share. These warrants expire on December 31, 1985. If Makitbig common stock were selling for $45 per share, using (20-4a) the theoretical value of the warrant would be

$$\text{Theoretical value of Makitbig warrant} = (\$45 - \$40) \times 2 = \$10$$

By owning a warrant we can buy two shares of stock from the company for $10 less than buying the shares on the open market. The theoretical value can therefore be defined as the discount on the company's common stock that is allowed the warrantholder. If investors buy warrants *for their theoretical value* and exercise them, they end up paying the same price for the company's common stock as they would if they were to buy the common stock directly in the market.

What if the market price of the common stock were equal to or below the option price? Then the theoretical value of the warrant would simply be zero (a warrant will never have a negative value). In some cases, the option price of the common stock varies—generally moving up-ward—over time. For example, it might be $12 per share if exercised in 1976 or 1977, $13 per share if exercised in 1978 or 1979, and so on. Indian Head warrants that expire in 1990 allowed the owner to purchase one share of common stock at $25 per share until May 15, 1975, at $30 per share until May 15, 1980, at $35 per share until May 15, 1985, and at $40 per share until May 15, 1990.

Market value of a warrant Any investor willing to purchase the common stock at its market price will always pay the theoretical value for a war-rant, since it can be immediately exercised and the common stock ob-tained. That is, theoretical value represents the minimum market value of the warrant. Warrants, however, also offer investors the added option of holding the warrant instead of purchasing shares. Holding the warrant is equivalent to holding the common stock, except that the investment in the warrant is less and the warrantholder does not have the rights accorded to stockholders (warrantholder receives no dividends, cannot vote, etc.). To illustrate the advantage of having to invest less in a warrant than in the common stock, we can use the above example. Recall that the warrant en-titles its owner to purchase two shares of common stock at $40 per share. With the Makitbig common at $45 per share, a purchase of two shares would require an investment of $90; the investor could therefore lose up to $90. But if one purchases the warrant for its theoretical value of $10, the most that can be lost is $10. This implies, first, that the investor's maximum loss is less with a warrant than with a common stock. Further-more, for every dollar the common stock rises above $45 per share, the warrantholder makes as much in dollars as the holder of two shares of common. For example, assume Makitbig stock rises from $45 to $50. Both the owner of two shares of common and the owner of a warrant would make a gain of $10 (note that the theoretical value of the warrant would rise from $10 to $20). Of course, if the stock price falls to exactly $40, the stockholder and the warrantholder will each lose $10. The war-rantholder, therefore, earns or loses (up to a loss of $10) dollar for dollar the same amount as the owner of two shares of stock, but the downside loss is minimized to $10 for the warrantholder. It follows that one might prefer to purchase a warrant and not immediately exercise it. This option of not exercising the warrant, in addition to the opportunity of exercising it and immediately obtaining the common stock, has a value. This value is reflected in the market price of a warrant, and consequently the warrant's market price may exceed its theoretical value.

Notice that the advantage of a warrant over common stock is that the maximum possible loss is less than if the stock itself is held (since the warrant is cheaper). If the common stock achieves a very high price, this advantage of holding a warrant rather than holding the common stock becomes less important. For example, if Makitbig stock is selling for $100 per share, the theoretical value of the warrant is $120. By buying the warrant at its theoretical value, the most that can be lost is $120, whereas by buying two shares of the stock, the maximum loss is $200. However, if the likelihood that the common stock will fall as low as $40 is nil, then there is essentially no advantage to holding the warrant. The reason for this is that theoretical value moves approximately dollar for dollar with the two shares of common stock that the warrant entitles the warrantholder to purchase (unless the common stock falls to the option price—in this case $40 per share—at which point the value of the warrant is zero). If Makitbig stock falls from $100 to $90 per share, two shares of stock will fall in value from $200 to $180 and the value of a warrant will also decline by about $20, from $120 to about $100. The loss on the warrant is equal to the loss on the two shares of stock, and there is no advantage to owning the warrant. Generally, therefore, the market value of a warrant will approximate its theoretical value if the price of the common stock is very high relative to the option price. This is illustrated in Figure 20-3.

Appraisal and Use of Warrants

The advantages of warrants for investors relative to directly purchasing the common stock are reflected in the excess of the warrant's market value over its theoretical value. In short, warrants have value beyond their theoretical value because they provide the opportunity of owning the common stock if the warrants are immediately exercised and the alternative of holding the unexercised warrant. As explained in the previous section, one may wish to hold the unexercised warrant rather than the common stock since it involves a smaller investment. Maximum loss is therefore reduced whereas the potential gain is not. The sacrifice is stockholder voting rights and any dividends paid on the common stock that are not received by the warrantholder as long as the warrant is not exercised.

The attraction of warrants for investors has led to their frequent use, especially by small dynamic firms as part of units of bonds, preferred stock, or common stock. A unit might be composed of a bond plus a warrant or of several shares of common stock plus a warrant. Various such combinations have appeared. Although warrants have characteristically been the tool of the smaller firm, in April 1970 AT&T, in a monumental offering, obtained $1.57 billion on an issue of bonds and warrants. This was the first time in over fifty years that the New York Stock Exchange

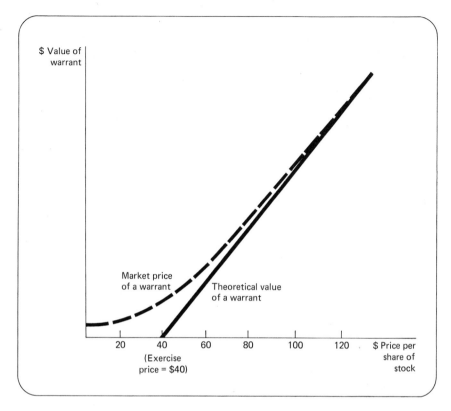

Figure 20-3. Value of Makitbig warrants.

accepted warrants for listing. As it turned out, the price of AT&T stock declined and the warrants became practically valueless, with few of them being exercised at all. Since 1970, other large firms have issued warrants, many of which are also listed on the New York Stock Exchange. Indeed, corporate planners have become increasingly innovative in developing new financing approaches, and warrants may eventually become a standard financing tool.

SUMMARY

A convertible bond or preferred stock can be transformed into the common stock of the corporation at the option of the holder. The value of a convertible as an income-producing security—providing bond interest or preferred dividends—is referred to as its investment value. The market value of the common stock into which the security can be converted is its conversion value. The convertible's market value is the price it sells for in the market, and this value will generally exceed both investment value and conversion value. Conversion increases the number of common shares outstanding and usually decreases earnings per share. It is possible, however, that the earnings per share rise due to conversion since the fixed charges (interest or preferred dividends) on the convertible security are no longer paid by the company. From the standpoint of the investor, a convertible has the advantage of providing a relatively safe return in the form of interest or preferred dividends and, in addition, the potential opportunity to participate in the firm's growth and stock price increase. However, because of the conversion advantage to the investor, the firm can pay a lower interest rate or lower preferred dividend rate than would be the case if the conversion option were not included. Whether a convertible is attractive to a given investor will depend upon the investor's risk-return preferences and expectations regarding the future price of the company's common stock. Similarly, the firm's decision to issue a convertible security will depend upon management's expectations regarding the company's stock price. An advantage of convertible securities is that they allow the firm to issue effectively debt in the short run and stock in the long run (when the convertible is converted into common stock) without incurring flotation costs on two separate issues.

The purchase of a warrant entitles the holder to purchase the company's common stock at a specified price on any date preceding the warrant's expiration. A warrant has a theoretical value equal to the market value of the stock obtained with the warrant less the price paid for the stock upon exercise. The theoretical value is the discount provided the warrantholder on the price of the common stock. The market value of the warrant will at least equal, and will generally exceed, its theoretical value. Warrants are often issued with other securities in the form of units, e.g., one warrant and one bond constituting a unit. Although historically the device of small firms, warrants have recently enjoyed increased popularity as a financing method of larger companies.

QUESTIONS

1. What is the investment value of a convertible security? Explain.
2. Why is it that a convertible security's market price will generally exceed its investment value?
3. If you were confronted with the situation of converting your bonds which are selling at $1,500 apiece into thirty shares selling at $50 each, what would you do?
4. "Convertible securities can be sold with a lower coupon rate than nonconvertible securities. This means that their cost to the firm is less than that of nonconvertible securities." Comment on this statement.
5. What should the holder of a convertible bond do if the bonds are called for redemption and the bond is selling well above call price?

6. Will dilution in earnings per share of common caused by conversion of convertible securities cause a decline in the value of the shares?

7. What are the major differences between a warrant and a convertible security?

8. "If the theoretical value of a warrant is equal to the market price of that warrant, an investor should be indifferent between the purchase of the warrant *and exercising it* and the purchase of the stock." Evaluate this statement, assuming there are no trading costs to consider.

9. Why might it be advantageous to hold a company's warrants rather than its common shares?

PROJECT

Select a convertible bond and obtain quarterly price data for a two-year period (for data, see, for example, the *Wall Street Journal*). For each quarter determine the convertible's investment value, conversion value, market value, and conversion premium. Satisfy yourself that the ideas presented in this chapter are valid for the convertible you selected.

Also obtain two years of quarterly price data for a warrant. Identify the warrant's market price and theoretical value for each quarter. Consider the market price and theoretical value behavior in light of the chapter material.

PROBLEMS

1. If the market price of a common share is $70, and you hold a warrant entitling you to purchase two shares at a price of $40 per share, what is the theoretical value of the warrant? [Ans.: theoretical value = $60]

2. Pluribus, Inc., has outstanding an issue of $1,000, 7 percent subordinated convertible debentures which are callable, mature in fifteen years, and are convertible into common stock at a conversion price of $25. The market price of the common stock is $50. What is the conversion value of the convertible bonds? [Ans.: conversion value = $2,000]

3. A $50 par value preferred stock is convertible into common stock at a conversion price of $40, and the preferred stock is selling in the market at $180 per share. The preferred's investment value is $60. What is the approximate market price of the common stock? Show any calculations you may make. [Ans.: price of common stock = $144]

4. Assume that you own a $1,000, convertible bond of the Smart Company maturing in eight years. These bonds have a 6 percent coupon

rate. The bonds are convertible into twenty-two shares of common stock. In addition, the bonds are callable at a call price of $1,020. The Smart Company straight bonds (i.e., nonconvertible, noncallable) currently sell to yield 7 percent and Smart's stock is selling at $45 a share. The straight bonds have the same risk as the convertibles would have if they didn't have the conversion feature.

a) What is the conversion ratio for the convertible bond?

b) What are the conversion price, conversion value, and investment value?

c) What is the bond's current market value floor?

d) What is the minimum price of the common stock at which shareholders will convert if the convertible bonds are called? (Ignore personal taxes in your computation.)

e) Suppose the stock's price falls to $40 a share. In this case, what would be the bond's market value floor?

5. Automation, Inc., has a $10 million, ten-year, 8 percent convertible bond issue outstanding. The company also has 16,000 shares of 6 percent, $500 par convertible preferred stock outstanding. Both the bonds and the preferred stock are callable. The bond's conversion price is $20 and the preferred conversion ratio is 25. The company is now in a position to call either or both issues. The current year's earnings before interest and taxes are expected to be $10 million. The firm currently has 2 million shares of common stock outstanding. Its tax rate is 50 percent. Show the effect on earnings per share of

a) Conversion of the bonds only.

b) Conversion of the preferred stock only.

c) Conversion of both bonds and preferred stock.

d) Assume that the bonds' conversion price is $66.66 (instead of $20). Show what happens to EPS upon conversion of the bonds only and comment on the result.

6. Consider a $1,000, 6 percent convertible, twenty-year bond maturing ten years from now. The bond is convertible into common stock at a conversion price of $40. The bond is also callable at $1,050. Currently this bond is trading at $880, and the common stock of the same firm sells at $35 a share. Straight bonds of this quality and maturity are currently traded on the market to yield 8 percent.

a) What is the conversion premium paid on the convertible bond?

b) At what common stock price would the holders of the convertible bond be indifferent between surrendering the bond if called or converting? (Ignore personal taxes in your computation.)

c) Suppose that the price per share for the common stock remains at $35, but the going rate of interest falls to 7 percent. What is the minimum possible market value of the bond?

7. A share of Peach Corporation's common stock sells for $60. One warrant will purchase two shares of the common stock at an option price per share of $10. What is the theoretical value of the warrant? [Ans.: theoretical value = $100]

8. A warrant sells for $37 and entitles the owner to purchase four shares of stock at an option price of $4 per share. The common stock sells for $12 per share.
   a) What is the theoretical value of the warrant?
   b) What is the premium at which the warrant is selling?

9. Consider a warrant which is good for purchasing three shares of stock at an option price of $30. The price of the stock is currently $35 a share.
   a) What is the theoretical value of the warrant?
   b) Assume that you purchased the warrant at a $5 premium over the theoretical value. Suppose that a year later the common stock has gone up to $40 a share and that the warrant then sells at a $2 premium over the theoretical value. You then sell the warrant. Assuming that the common stock pays no dividend, compare your rate of return on investment with that on a purchase of three shares of stock. Consider the maximum possible loss in each case and comment.

10. Performance, Inc., needs to raise $1 million to introduce a new engine oil additive. The company would like to sell common stock, but the market is somewhat depressed and management believes that the current $40 a share for its stock does not reflect its true value. Two alternatives are being considered: a) sell $1 million, 6 percent convertible bonds with a conversion ratio of 20 or b) sell 1,000 6 percent bonds, each with twenty warrants attached, with each warrant good to buy one share of common stock at $50. Before adopting a or b, the firm has the following liabilities and equity position:

Short-term loans	$ 500,000
Common stock, $10 par	2,000,000
Retained earnings	500,000
Total claims	$3,000,000

The firm's rate of return on assets before interest and taxes is 25 percent; its tax rate is 50 percent. Thus the EBIT before a or b is adopted is $750,000 (25% × $3,000,000 = $750,000). The rate of return (in terms of EBIT) on investment of any new capital raised under a or b will also be 25 percent.

a) Show the liabilities and equity position of the firm for both alternatives *a* and *b* *after* conversion.

b) Assuming that the firm invests all of its available funds, compute the earnings per share (EPS) for alternatives *a* and *b*. Explain the differences, if any.

c) What considerations other than EPS could be important in reaching a decision as to which alternative to use?

SPECIAL TOPICS

PART

Part 5 discusses several issues relating to some—but not all—business firms. Chapter 21 covers mergers and acquisitions—when they are justified and how management should analyze a potential merger in determining its advisability. Chapter 22 examines the problems faced by companies that conduct foreign trade or that have subsidiaries in foreign countries (multinational companies). The chapter discusses foreign exchange transactions and describes the methods used by firms in financing exports and imports. The last part of the chapter deals with multinational companies and the special problems faced by the financial managers of such firms. Chapter 23 discusses business bankruptcy and how management and creditors cope with business failure.

holding companies, mergers, and consolidations

In this chapter, we will shift our attention from a single corporation to a group organization of corporations. We will consider some *multicorporate* organizations and combinations—holding companies, mergers, and consolidations. In each of these categories, two or more firms are joined under the control of one of the firms or under a single management. The sections that follow will describe the advantages of these kinds of business arrangements, explain how they are formed, and analyze some of the problems they face.

A **holding company** is a corporation which has working control of one or more other corporations, called subsidiaries, through ownership of the subsidiaries' common stock. The holding company may achieve sufficient influence for control with as little as 20 percent, or an even smaller fraction, of a subsidiary's stock. The stock may have been purchased on the open market through a broker (just as an individual investor purchases shares) or through a **tender offer.** Under a tender offer, a company (the holding company in this case) announces that it will purchase, at a specified price, up to a given number of another firm's shares, sometimes all the shares. The specified price is usually 10 to 50 percent above the current market price of the acquired firm's stock; most commonly, it is 30 to 35 percent. The holding company may offer its own shares in exchange for the acquired stock instead of offering dollars. Any existing stockholder of the firm being purchased may tender (offer) his or her shares to the holding company in return for the purchase price indicated in the tender offer.

A holding company can gain control of another firm without the formal approval of the acquired company. The subsidiary is acquired by the direct purchase of its stock. This stock purchase is easily executed, and as noted earlier, only a small percentage of the stock may have to be acquired to achieve effective control of the subsidiary. The holding company and its subsidiary remain as separate corporate entities, and consequently the liabilities of the firms can be kept separate. This is sometimes an advantage; however, it is possible that the holding company's credit will be used to finance the operations of one of its controlled corporations, in which case the opportunity to maintain separate liability is only partially used. (For example, the holding company may use its credit to obtain funds to finance the subsidiary's capital budget, but the holding company may not assume liability for the subsidiary's existing debts.) The holding company structure may result in economies generated by the centralization of management.

Holding companies are subject to an added tax on profits. Fifteen percent of all dividends received by the holding company from the domestic (United States) corporations in which it has an investment are taxed as corporate income.[1] If the holding company and the corporations it controls were merged into a single operation, this added tax on earnings could be avoided.[2]

An additional feature of holding companies is that significant earnings leverage is possible for the stockholders of the holding company. This is illustrated in the example shown in Exhibits 21-1 and 21-2. Holding Company is owned and controlled by stockholders who have invested $200,000 in the firm. Holding Company in turn owns $1 million, or 50 percent, of the stock of its subsidiary, Operating Company. Let us assume

1. For example, if operating company O pays holding company H $100 in dividends, $15 of these dividends would be taxable at the corporate tax rate. If the corporate tax rate were 40 percent, then company H would pay $6 in taxes on the dividends (0.40 × $15).

2. Actually, the tax on 15 percent of dividends can be avoided if the holding company and its subsidiary form all or part of a consolidated group of corporate entities and file a consolidated federal income tax return. One of the requirements for a consolidated group is that the holding company own at least 80 percent of the subsidiary's stock.

Exhibit 21-1. Holding Company and Operating Company Balance Sheets

Holding Company	
Assets	
Investment in Operating Company stock	$1,000,000
Liabilities and owners' equity	
Long-term debt (6% interest annually)	$500,000
Preferred stock (8% interest annually)	$300,000
Common stock (100,000 shares)	$200,000
Operating company	
Assets	
Current assets and plant and equipment	$6,000,000
Liabilities and owners' equity	
Long-term debt (5% interest annually)	$2,000,000
Preferred stock at par	
(dividends at $7\frac{1}{2}$% of par)	$2,000,000
Common stock	$2,000,000

Exhibit 21-2. Operating Company and Holding Company Income Statements under Various Economic Conditions

	Boom	Normal	Recession
Operating Company			
Net operating income	$1,000,000	$800,000	$600,000
Less interest on debt			
(5% × $2,000,000 debt)	100,000	100,000	100,000
Taxable income	$ 900,000	$700,000	$500,000
Less taxes at 50%	450,000	350,000	250,000
Aftertax income	$ 450,000	$350,000	$250,000
Less dividends to preferred			
(7½% × $2,000,000)	150,000	150,000	150,000
Net income to stockholders	$ 300,000	$200,000	$100,000
Rate of return on Operating Company stockholders' equity (net income/ $2 million common stockholders' equity)	15%	10%	5%
Holding Company			
Dividend income from investment in Operating Company (50% of Operating Company's net income to stockholders)	$150,000	$100,000	$ 50,000
Less interest on debt			
(6% × $500,000)	30,000	30,000	30,000
Taxable income	$120,000	$ 70,000	$ 20,000
Less taxes at 7½% of taxable income[a]	9,000	5,250	1,500
Aftertax income	$111,000	$ 64,750	$ 18,500
Less preferred dividends			
(8% × $300,000)	24,000	24,000	24,000
Net income to Holding Company stockholders	$ 87,000	$ 40,750	$ (5,500)
Rate of return on Holding Company stockholders' equity (net income/ $200,000 common stockholders' equity)	43.5%	20.375%	−2.75%

[a] Only 15 percent of dividends (net of expenses) received by a corporation from another United States corporation are taxed; this 15 percent portion of net dividends is taxed at the corporate tax rate, which is 50 percent in the example. The tax is therefore 7½ percent (15% × 50%) of net dividend income. It is assumed in the example that all net income earned by Operating Company is paid to its stockholders.

that this 50 percent interest is sufficient for control of Operating Company. Operating Company is itself "levered" (has non-common stock securities outstanding) since it has debt and preferred stock outstanding with a total face value of $4 million. Thus, the $1 million of equity investment in Operating Company by Holding Company controls $6 million in Operating Company assets. The holding company structure magnifies this leverage since $800,000 of Holding Company capitalization (source of funds) is debt and preferred stock, in amounts of $500,000 and $300,000, respectively. The $200,000 in common stock equity interest shown on Holding Company's balance sheet controls the $1 million of Holding Company assets. The $1 million of Holding Company assets are made up entirely of a 50 percent ownership of Operating Company's stock. The 50 percent of Operating Company's stock provides control of the $6 million of Operating Company's assets. *The result is that the $200,000 of Holding Company stock controls $6 million in Operating Company assets.*

Observe from Exhibit 21-2 that tremendous earnings leverage is provided to the holding company stockholders. If Operating Company is prosperous and has an operating income of $1 million and a net income of $300,000, the rate of return on Operating Company's equity is 15 percent ($300,000/$2 million in Operating Company stockholders' equity), and Holding Company stockholders earn a rate of return of 43.5 percent ($87,000/$200,000). On the other hand, if business is very poor (recession), Operating Company's return on equity is 5 percent ($100,000/$2 million) whereas Holding Company's shareholders suffer a 2.75 percent loss ($5,500 loss/$200,000 equity). What has occurred is that Holding Company has magnified the leverage of Operating Company by issuing its own bonds and preferred stock to purchase the shares of Operating Company. This is conceptually identical to an individual investor's purchases of stock on margin or with money borrowed from a lending institution. The familiar theme that leverage magnifies both prosperity and adversity applies to Holding Company just as it generally does to single corporations and for individual investors.

MERGERS AND CONSOLIDATIONS

A **merger** or **consolidation** is the unification of previously separate companies into a single corporation. Technically, a merger occurs if one of the two or more combining companies survives (e.g., if firm A and firm B merge and the new firm is called firm A). A consolidation is the union of firms into a new firm (e.g., firm A and firm B combine to form firm C). The merger or consolidation of firms which are in similar lines of business, e.g., two food wholesalers or two appliance manufacturers, is referred to as a **horizontal combination.** A **vertical combination** joins firms which are engaged in different stages of production of the same type of product, e.g., an oil producer and a refiner. Another term that joined the vernacular several years ago is **conglomerate.** A conglomerate is any group of firms in different lines of business which are controlled by a single corporation. The controlled firms may or may not be separate corporate entities; the group of companies might therefore constitute either a holding company with subsidiaries or a single large corporation with divisions producing dissimilar products.

Although mergers and consolidations have the technical difference mentioned above, the financial issues involved in these two types of business organization are essentially the same. Therefore, we will simply use the term ''merger'' to refer to either a merger or a consolidation. Also, one of the firms in a merger survives and that firm can be viewed as acquiring the other (nonsurviving) firm; if firm A survives and firm B does not, we will often refer to the merger as the **acquisition** of firm B by firm A.

Merger Procedure and Trends

A merger is initially arranged through negotiations between the managements of the firms concerned. This process is often initiated by one of the companies which buys the other firm by paying cash or securities to the acquired company's stockholders. After a merger agreement has been worked out by the firms' managements, the agreement must then be approved by the companies' boards of directors. For the combination to proceed, approval must be secured from the stockholders of both firms; a majority—and frequently two-thirds—of the outstanding shares of each firm must be voted in favor of the merger. Following this and the filing of any papers with the state governments in which the corporations are domiciled, the exchange of assets or securities is made and the merger is consummated.

During the 1960s mergers and acquisitions in this country reached an historic peak, exceeding the previous high achieved during the boom of the 1920s. As illustrated in Table 21-1, the uptrend in business combinations from the early 1930s to the end of the 1960s was followed by a sharp decline and —in recent years—a recovery. Several factors contributed to the post-1960s decline. Changes in government policy in the form of more vigorous antitrust action and more stringent tax treatment of business combinations tended to dampen the fervor for mergers. This change of sentiment was intensified both by the poor performance of many conglomerates (and the resulting losses to investors) and by the feeling that many businesses had become too large and too powerful. Even without this unfavorable tax and legal climate, the concept of merger as the wellspring of superior growth and performance began to fade as many business combinations proved unsuccessful. It became increasingly clear that expansion through merger could be a serious error, even a disaster,

Table 21-1. Historical trends in mergers and acquisitions

Period	Number of mergers and acquisitions during period
1920–1924	2,235
1925–1929	4,583
1930–1934	1,687
1935–1939	577
1940–1944	906
1945–1949	1,505
1950–1954	1,424
1955–1959	3,365
1960–1964	4,366
1965–1969	8,213
1970–1973	4,147

Source: U.S. Federal Trade Commission.

because anticipated economies of scale and of joint production might not be realized. In addition, during the 1960s, the availability of desirable acquisition candidates declined (and their price rose) as many of these companies were purchased. The intoxication with mergers has been replaced by a reasonable awareness that merger can sometimes produce significant benefits but, like any investment, carries hazards, both discernible and unforeseeable.

A cautious realism toward mergers has evolved out of the hyperemotional enthusiasm of the 1960s and the negativity of the early 1970s. In the 1960s, firms often paid exorbitant prices for acquisitions without carefully considering the ultimate consequences. The result, in many cases, was severe disappointment for the acquiring company. The frequency of such disappointments produced an excessively negative attitude toward mergers in the early 1970s. But by the middle of the decade, a more objective attitude had become apparent. Today, the intuitive and hasty approach is shunned, and acquisition decisions usually follow exhaustive study. Outside experts (particularly commercial and investment banks, CPA firms, and merger specialists) are often used in the merger process. Merger evaluation and analysis will be the subjects of the remainder of this chapter.

Reasons for Merger   Our analyses of investment opportunities for single corporations often focused on the decision to accept or reject a particular investment or choose among several alternatives. In each case, the decision to invest in a new asset would mean *internal* expansion for the firm. The new asset would generate returns raising the value of the corporation. Mergers offer an additional means of expansion, which is *external;* that is, the productive operation is not within the corporation itself. For firms with limited investment opportunities mergers can provide new areas for expansion. In addition to this benefit, the combination of two or more firms can offer several other advantages to each of the corporations: operating economies, risk reduction, and tax advantage.

Operating advantages and synergies Mutual benefits produced by the merger are called **synergies.** Examples are lower costs of production, management, financing, research, and marketing. The most common economies are reductions of duplicate fixed costs of production and management, since fewer plants and smaller total managerial staff may be needed as a result of merger. Even if the merged firms produce different products, it is often possible to reduce accounting and personnel departments and top-level managerial staffs simply by eliminating duplication. Research economies may also be achieved by eliminating similar research efforts and the repetition of mistakes already made by the other firm's researchers. Marketing economies may be produced through savings in advertising (by reducing the need to attract each other's customers), and also from the advantages of offering a more complete product line (if the merged firms produce different but complementary goods), since a wider product line may provide larger sales per unit of sales effort and per salesperson. A major saving often arises from the consolidation of departments involved with financial activities, e.g., accounting, credit, billing, and purchasing. Furthermore, there may be significant economies of scale in acquiring capital through public offerings. Flotation costs per dollar of capital raised drop rapidly as issue amounts increase up to $10 million (see Chapter 16, Table 16-2).[3]

Strategic pricing advantages may also accrue through the acquisition of monopolistic power or something approaching it. However, this advantage involves serious legal risks and is likely to be short-lived because of enforcement of antitrust regulations.

The concept of synergy was the rationale used by many conglomeratiers during the 1960s to justify their ambitious expansion into many unrelated industries. The idea was that by placing many companies under a single management, a cross-fertilization of ideas and managerial expertise would result. In some cases it worked, or at least the conglomerates

3. In a broad study based upon field interviews, Kitching found that synergy from mergers most often results from savings in the finance area, with marketing benefits second in importance, and production and technology the least likely to produce advantages. See John Kitching, "Why Do Mergers Miscarry?" *Harvard Business Review*, 45 (November–December 1967), p. 93.

in question were successful. Notable examples are Textron, ITT, and MCA. But the corporate battleground is strewn with casualties, including such former high fliers as Ling-Temco-Vought, Whittaker Corporation, and Memorex Corporation, all of which expanded into various unrelated fields and suffered large losses. Even Litton Industries, once the archetype of the successful conglomerate, experienced severely deflated earnings and financial difficulties in the early 1970s which necessitated a major overhaul of operations.

The mixed results of acquisition are also reflected in the experience of otherwise successful corporate giants that strayed into unfamiliar areas. Boise Cascade's failure in mobile home and engineering ventures, RCA's enormous losses in computers, and Union Carbide's unprofitable diversification into petroleum, pharmaceuticals, and semiconductors are prominent examples. Lack of success in acquisitions has not been restricted to companies that have diversified into numerous industries. Wolverine Wide World, manufacturer of Hush Puppies, could largely attribute its declining profits in the early 1970s to its acquisition of other shoe companies. Varadyne's expansion within the electronics field was so unsuccessful that its very survival was threatened. Although there are innumerable examples of such failure, the likelihood of achieving synergistic benefits from merger is enhanced if the acquiring company expands into fields with which it is familiar. The senior executive vice president of Interco, one of the more successful conglomerates, has ascribed much of his firm's prosperity to its policy of expanding only into areas that draw on management's existing experience and expertise.

Reduction of risk Through the diversification effects of combination, merger can produce benefits to all firms by reducing the variability (percentage fluctuation) of firm earnings. If firm A's income generally rises when firm B's income falls, and vice versa, the fluctuations of one will tend to offset the fluctuations of the other, thus producing a relatively level pattern of combined earnings. Indeed, there will be some diversification effect as long as the two firms' earnings are not perfectly correlated (both rising and falling together in all cases). The principle of diversification was discussed earlier in Chapter 8.[4] This reduction in overall risk is particularly likely if the merged companies are in different lines of business.

As explained in Chapter 8 (p. 295), reducing the variability of firm earnings can produce benefits ("diversification benefits") if expected bankruptcy costs or cash management costs are reduced. But, if expected bankruptcy costs and cash management costs are insignificant, and if no tax benefits arise from a merger, then a merger which simply reduces the

4. See discussion on pp. 295–299.

variability of total earnings (without increasing expected total earnings) will not produce any benefits for shareholders as long as shareholders can diversify on their own.

If investors in the market can diversify on their own by buying shares in the companies if they were not merged, there is no reduction of risk gain to merging since investors can achieve the same diversification on their own. An investor could buy 1 percent of firm A's shares and 1 percent of firm B's shares, and this would be just as good as buying 1 percent of a merged company made up of firms A and B. That is, investors do not require that the firms diversify since investors can do it for themselves. It has been shown that as long as the transaction costs (e.g., brokerage fees) of trading securities are negligible and there are no significant bankruptcy or cash management costs, diversification through merger will produce no net benefits to shareholders *unless other synergies (e.g., reduced production costs) or tax benefits result from the merger*.[5]

Tax effects   There are two major tax considerations favoring merger. First, the tax treatment of liquidations of stock to raise money to pay estate taxes is particularly generous; thus, for example, the heirs of a company's deceased owner may find it advantageous to sell their inherited stock in the company to another firm. The second tax consideration relates to the offsetting of gains and losses for tax purposes. With merger, the losses of one company can be used to offset the gains of the other, dollar for dollar. The result is that lower taxes or no taxes need be paid by the combined company. Thus, for example, if firm A were earning $3 million per year and firm B losing $1 million per year, a merged company comprising firm A and firm B would have a net income of $2 million per year (assuming no real economies, i.e., synergies, from the merger); without merger, firm A would pay taxes on $3 million of income and firm B would pay no taxes, whereas with merger, taxes would have to be paid only on income of $2 million.[6]

5. See discussion on pp. 295–299, and see L. D. Schall, "Asset Valuation, Firm Investment, and Firm Diversification," *Journal of Business* (January 1972), p. 11.

6. If the firm incurring the loss can carry back its losses against past profits and thereby receive a rebate of past taxes, no gain from merging with a profitable company would accrue. Losses can also be carried forward, so that in future profitable years previous losses can be deducted from the profits, thus reducing taxable income by that earlier loss. However, the firm must wait for this carry forward benefit until it makes a profit. Furthermore, losses can be carried back only three years and forward five years, implying that continuous losses over many years (e.g., due to large research outlays) may never be canceled against profits. In this case of extended losses, a merger with a currently profitable firm would be advantageous.

Internal versus external growth The advantage of synergies, decreased taxes, and risk reduction can affect all members of a merger. In most mergers, however, one corporation is dominant in the merger process in that it wishes to acquire the other firm and thereby take over its operations. Viewed this way, a merger is the purchase of one firm by another. A firm could, of course, build up this operation from scratch through internal investment.[7] However, expansion is more rapid if an existing firm is purchased. In some cases, it may be impossible to duplicate an operation, particularly if a patent or mineral right is monopolized by that company or if the product manufactured has a commanding position in its market. Even if duplication is possible, an attempt to create a similar business operation internally is usually more risky than acquiring a going concern. A newly created operation may not be able to match an existing company's performance record, or acquire similar product markets and staff. This risk element is magnified if the industry of the acquired company already has adequate capacity. Increasing that capacity through internal investment would therefore be profitable only if an existing producer were displaced, whereas a business combination would merely involve consolidating existing capacity. The latter would probably be the less risky alternative.

Keep in mind that, although acquiring an existing firm can have the advantages over internal investment noted above, the stockholders of the takeover candidate will ordinarily demand a price for their stock that reflects the company's value. For the would-be purchaser, this price may be high enough to negate the advantages of combination over internally generated expansion. This is particularly true if several expansionist firms are seeking merger partners, thus bidding up the prices of available candidates. Of course, bargains do sometimes exist. The point here is that, as with most things, the acquiring firm must generally pay for what it gets.

Form of the Property Exchanged The acquisition of one company by another may involve payment of cash or of the purchasing firm's securities, and the property purchased may be the selling firm's stock or only its physical assets. In both cases the buyer is merging the acquired assets with its own. The difference is in how the assets are acquired and what is paid to the seller. Below we examine these alternative forms of exchange.

The property purchased: securities or physical assets The purchase of a firm's physical assets may be simpler than an acquisition of its outstand-

---

7. *Internal investment* should be contrasted with *internal financing of investment,* where the latter refers to the use of retained earnings (cash held by the firm) rather than externally raised funds (through the sale of new stocks or bonds) to finance investment. On internal and external financing, see Chap. 10.

ing stock. Although approval of both the shareholders and the board of directors *of the selling firm* is necessary with an asset sale or a stock sale, for the *acquiring* firm there is an advantage in acquiring physical assets. In contrast with a stock purchase, only the approval of the acquiring company's board of directors, *and not that of the shareholders,* is required. In acquiring another firm's assets, the buying firm will frequently not assume the seller's liabilities, whereas this avoidance of liability is not achieved with a purchase of the seller's stock.[8] Payment for the assets may be cash or the buyer's securities (common or preferred stock or bonds). Some or all of the seller's assets may be acquired; the seller may retain the proceeds from the sale in the company or may distribute the proceeds to the stockholders (after paying the firm's creditors). Thus, the selling firm will survive unless all its assets are sold and the proceeds paid out. If the objective of the seller is only to liquidate some of its assets, it will, of course, prefer an asset to a stock sale. Such a partial sale of assets is not a merger of the buyer and seller, although it partly achieves the merger objective of combining physical assets owned by the two companies.

The acquiring firm may prefer a stock purchase since it requires a smaller investment than an asset purchase in order to achieve control of the selling firm's assets. Only 51 percent (and often less than 51 percent) of the outstanding stock need be purchased for control of the seller firm. Furthermore, achieving merger in the face of opposition by some of the seller's shareholders may be easier through a purchase of most of the selling company's stock than by acquisition of its assets.

The form of payment: cash or securities

Tax considerations Payment for the acquired company may be in cash or in the securities (common stock, preferred stock, bonds, etc.) of the purchasing company. It is the form of payment rather than what is purchased (physical assets or stock) which ordinarily determines the tax consequences of the exchange. If cash or nonvoting securities (e.g., the purchaser's bonds) are used in payment, the transaction will generally be taxable immediately to the seller. Thus, if the owners of the selling firm B originally paid $20 per share for their stock in firm B, and sell these shares to acquiring firm A for $80 in cash per share, $60 of gain is realized and immediately taxable to the sellers (usually at a capital gains tax rate). If, instead of cash, $80 worth of firm A voting common or voting

8. A firm's stock represents the equity interest, which is ownership of the assets less the liabilities which are claims against those assets. Acquisition of stock is therefore acquisition of the net equity claim (residual claim after creditors' claim) against the assets. In contrast, the buyer who simply purchases physical assets from a company, for example, a group of machines, often assumes none of the selling company's liabilities.

preferred stock had been paid for each share of firm B stock, the gain would not be taxable until the firm B stockholders eventually sold their firm A shares received in the exchange. Payment in voting stock therefore produces a tax postponement advantage for the sellers; this is referred to as a nontaxable combination.

A second tax consideration is the depreciation basis of the acquired property once the merger has taken place. As just noted, if the purchase is for cash or the purchaser's bonds, it is taxable when the merger is affected; if voting common or preferred stock is used, it is nontaxable (until the securities received are eventually sold). If the combination is taxable, then the depreciation basis for the assets acquired in the merger is the price paid for the acquired firm. If the combination is nontaxable, the assets have the same depreciation basis as they did for the selling firm. For example, assume that firm A buys firm B for $1 million and that the assets of firm B have a book value for depreciation purposes of $600,000. If the merger is taxable, then acquiring firm A can depreciate the assets using a cost of $1 million as the depreciation base; if, on the other hand, the merger is nontaxable, the depreciation base for firm A will be $600,000 (what it was for B). The greater depreciation deductions—and therefore lower taxable income and lower taxes resulting under a taxable cash purchase of another firm—favor a cash acquisition from the standpoint of the buying company. Of course, this is only one factor and it may be outweighed by other considerations which favor a purchase with the buying company's securities, even though such a purchase would be nontaxable and would result in a lower depreciation basis for the acquired assets.

To summarize, we have seen that if taxes alone are considered and a gain is realized by the seller, the seller would prefer a nontaxable exchange since taxes are postponed; the buyer would prefer a taxable exchange since this provides the acquiring firm with a larger future depreciation deduction and therefore lower future taxes. However, there are also nontax considerations which must be taken into account by both the buyer and seller, and these are considered next.

Nontax considerations   If an acquiring firm has excess cash (more cash than needed to maintain a stable dividend policy), it can purchase another firm with that cash, or it can distribute the cash as dividends and use its stock to buy the other firm. We recall from Chapter 10 that the firm will prefer to finance its investments internally (with the firm's cash) rather than externally (by issuing new securities to obtain investment funds) if the firm's stockholders prefer capital gains income to dividend income. The preference is frequently for capital gains, since capital gains tax rates are lower than the ordinary tax rates applicable to dividends. This principle also applies here; consequently a company with excess cash will usually prefer to use that cash for an acquisition rather than to issue stock for the purchase. In other words, it is cheaper to finance the acquisition through retained earnings than through external financing (issuing stock). Of course, if the acquiring firm does not have surplus cash, or wishes to raise its dividends because its owners desire higher dividends, it may prefer to use stock instead of cash as a means of payment in a merger.

The cash needs of the seller may also be important. The selling firm's stockholders may prefer cash to the acquiring firm's securities if they have an alternative investment opportunity immediately requiring funds. Another factor influencing the means of payment is the relative expectations of the buyer and seller with regard to the purchasing firm's stock. The seller will prefer cash if it feels the buyer's stock is overpriced, and it will prefer stock if that stock appears depressed relative to a reasonable long-run valuation. On the other hand, the buyer will prefer to use its stock in the acquisition if it feels that its shares are inflated, and it will prefer payment in cash if the shares appear to be depressed. As with tax effects, there is obviously a conflict of interests here between the acquiring and acquired firms, and the choice is a matter of negotiation between the parties.

Terms of Merger

The shareholders of both the acquiring and the acquired firms want the merger to improve their wealth positions. Only if the long-run returns per share of common stock of the acquiring firm are improved is the merger acceptable to the buyer. Similarly, the seller is better off only if the cash or securities received in the merger are worth more (i.e., represent a claim to a better stream of returns) than are the securities surrendered. We will now examine the determination of the price paid for an acquired firm. For clarity, purchase with cash and purchase with securities will be examined separately.

Purchase with cash If the payment for the selling company is in cash, then the decision from the standpoint of the buyer can be handled in the same way as any new investment using the capital budgeting methods described in Chapters 7 and 8. Only if the net present value of the aftertax net cash flow from the new assets is positive is the acquisition a good investment. The simplest case is that in which only the assets and not the liabilities of the selling firm are obtained. In this case, the investment in the asset (I) for computing its net present value is simply the cash price paid for the asset.

If the acquisition for cash also involves the assumption of the selling firm's liabilities, the present value of the seller's debt that is assumed must be added to the cost of the assets (cash paid to the seller's stockholders) to determine the initial outlay in computing NPV. The acquisition then would be acceptable to the buyer only if the present value of the future aftertax flow from the acquired firm exceeds the cash paid to the seller's stockholders plus the present value of the seller's debts that are assumed. For example, if firm A merges with firm B by paying firm B's stockholders $1 million in cash, and also assumes firm B's liabilities of $500,000, the computation of the net present value of the acquisition is as shown in Exhibit 21-3. It is assumed in the example that the assets of firm B will generate an aftertax cash flow of $180,000 per year for twenty-five years and that the cost of capital on the new investment is 10 percent.[9] Notice that the situation here is therefore identical to a capital budgeting decision in which firm A buys $1.5 million in assets and finances the acquisition with $500,000 of debt and $1 million in retained earnings (the firm's cash). In both cases, firm A ends up with firm B's assets, and an added debt of $500,000. The Exhibit 21-3 computation produces a NPV of $133,860, implying that the merger is profitable to firm A.

In determining their willingness to sell their shares for $1 million, firm B's stockholders will have analyzed the anticipated future performance of firm B without the merger, tax effects, and other considerations discussed

9. This cost of capital will depend upon the risk of the project. It is assumed here for simplicity that the firm's debt-equity ratio will not be significantly changed as a consequence of the merger. On these points, see Chaps. 6 and 8.

Exhibit 21-3. Evaluating the Purchase for Cash of Company B by Company A

Pretax cash flow from new assets		$300,000
Less taxes:		
Pretax cash flow	$300,000	
Depreciation	60,000	
Taxable income	$240,000	
Tax (0.50 × taxable income)[a]		$120,000
Aftertax cash flow		$180,000
Initial outlay:		
Payment to B's (seller's) stockholders		$1,000,000
Assumption of B's debt		500,000
Total initial outlay		$1,500,000

Applicable cost of capital adjusted for risk of the investment = 10%

$$NPV = \$180,000 \ (P/A, \ 10\%, \ 25) - \text{initial outlay}$$
$$= (9.0770) \times \$180,000 - \$1,500,000$$
$$= \$133,860$$

Conclusion: Merger is profitable since NPV = $133,860.

---

[a] A corporate tax rate of 50 percent is assumed.

earlier. Only those shareholders who want the funds to spend on current consumption, or to reinvest in what they view as better opportunities than firm B, will be satisfied with the merger agreement. This must be a substantial majority of stockholders (depending upon state law) or the combination will not occur. To assure that the selling firm's stockholders will approve the acquisition, the price per share offered by the acquiring firm for the selling firm's stock is often significantly above the stock's premerger market price.

Purchase with acquiring firm's stock   A cash flow analysis such as the analysis of an acquisition using stock could be used to analyze a merger in which stock is issued in payment to the selling firm's stockholders, or in which a new firm's securities are issued under a consolidation to stockholders of both the firms that are being combined. Stockholders will find the merger desirable only if the cash flow to which they have a claim has a higher net present value with the merger than without the merger.

Another more commonly used method of analysis examines present and anticipated future earnings per share with and without merger. Earnings, like cash flow, can be viewed as a measure of the firm's capacity to pay dividends and therefore represent a basis for determining the corporation's value. Generally, the stockholders want an increase in the level of long-run earnings as a result of the merger. Management will therefore try to negotiate merger terms which increase per share earnings. The number of shares that the buying firm (A) will issue in acquiring the selling firm (B) is determined as follows:

1. The shareholders of the acquiring firm will compare the current and anticipated future earnings per share of firm A with and without the merger.
2. The shareholders of the selling firm will compare the current and expected future earnings per share of firm B with the current and expected future earnings per share of the shares that they would receive from firm A under the merger.
3. The managements of firms A and B will negotiate the final terms of the merger in light of **1** and **2**; the ultimate terms of the merger will reflect the relative bargaining positions of the two firms.

The fewer of A's shares that A must pay B, the better off are the stockholders of A and the worse off are the stockholders of B. However, for the merger to be effected, the shareholders of both the buying firm and the selling firm will have to anticipate some benefit from the merger. Generally, for the acquiring and acquired firms' stockholders to gain, there must be an increase in the level of earnings or a reduction in the risk of the earnings generated by the two companies.

To illustrate points 1, 2, and 3 in a simple case (Exhibit 21-4), assume that the expected annual earnings without merger of firms A and B are $200,000 and $100,000, respectively, a total of $300,000 per year. Earnings are expected to remain level in the future. With merger, the expected total annual earnings are $350,000, an increase of $50,000 per year due to the economies generated by the merger. The information missing from Exhibit 21-4 cannot be supplied until the number of firm A's shares to be issued in purchasing firm B is determined. In Exhibit 21-5, the effects of issuing 20,000, 30,000, and 37,500 new shares of firm A in purchasing firm B are shown. With 20,000 new shares there are 70,000 postmerger firm A shares and B's stockholders obtain two-sevenths (20,000/70,000) of the merged firm, i.e., obtain shares worth $1 million ($\frac{2}{7} \times$ $3.5 million postmerger firm value). The merger has no effect on firm B's shareholder wealth, since the value of the firm B stock surrendered is also $1 million. The exchange ratio in column b is the number of new firm A shares issued (20,000) per firm B share obtained (10,000), which equals 2. Firm A's stockholders have shares worth $2.5 million after the merger and are therefore $500,000 better off as a consequence of the acquisition.

If 37,500 new firm A shares were issued, firm B's shareholders would own a fraction $\frac{375}{875}$) of the postmerger firm with a total share value of $1,500,000. Firm A's stockholders would own a fraction ($\frac{500}{875}$) of the merged company's shares worth $2 million. In this case, firm B's stockholders gain and firm A's stockholders neither gain nor lose from the combination. For any number of shares issued between 20,000 and 37,500

Exhibit 21-4. Premerger and Postmerger Financial Data

	Premerger firm A	Premerger firm B	Postmerger firm A
1. Current earnings per year	$200,000	$100,000	$350,000
2. Shares outstanding	50,000	10,000	?
3. Earnings per share [(1)/(2)]	$4	$10	?
4. Price per share	$40	$100	?
5. Price-earnings ratio [(4)/(3)][a]	10X	10X	10X
6. Value of firm [(2) × (4)]	$2,000,000	$1,000,000	$3,500,000
7. Expected annual growth rate in earnings in foreseeable future	0	0	0

[a] The price-earnings ratio equals either [(4)/(3)] or [(6)/(1)].

Exhibit 21-5. Impact of Alternative Numbers of Firm A's Shares Issued to Buy Firm B on the Total Value of Shares Owned by Stockholders of Firms A and B

Number of firm A's shares issued to firm B stockholders (a)	Exchange ratio [(a)/10,000 firm B's shares] (b)	Number of firm A's shares outstanding after merger [50,000 + (a)] (c)	Postmerger fraction of firm owned by firm B shareholders [(a)/(c)] (d)	Value of shares owned by firm B shareholders [(d) × \$3.5 million] (e)	Postmerger fraction of firm owned by original firm A shareholders [50,000/(c)] (f)	Value of shares owned by firm A shareholders [(f) × \$3.5 million] (g)
20,000	2	70,000	$\frac{2}{7}$	\$1,000,000	$\frac{5}{7}$	\$2,500,000
30,000	3	80,000	$\frac{3}{8}$	1,312,500	$\frac{5}{8}$	2,187,500
37,500	3.75	87,500	$\frac{375}{875}$	1,500,000	$\frac{500}{875}$	2,000,000

(e.g., 30,000) both firm A's stockholders and firm B's stockholders benefit from the merger. If less than 20,000 shares were offered to B, B's stockholders would lose in the exchange, and exactly 20,000 shares would leave B's stockholders with no gain or loss. Similarly, an offer of more than 37,500 shares of firm A's stock for firm B would result in a reduction in the wealth of firm A's stockholders, and exactly 37,500 shares would leave A's stockholders no better and no worse off. Since A's and B's shareholders want a gain from the merger, the final bargain must be between 20,000 and 37,500 of firm A's shares paid for firm B.

What will the ultimate bargain produce? That will depend upon the relative bargaining position of firm A and firm B. If firm A has many other merger candidates of equal desirability to firm B, little more than 20,000 shares might be necessary to induce firm B to negotiate. If firms similar to B are rare and B's owners are aware of that fact, and if, in addition, many other merger-hungry firms such as A are seeking merger partners, close to 37,500 shares might be required to buy firm B. This is largely what has happened in recent years. Many small firms were purchased at bargain prices early in the 1960s. As small firms realized that larger companies were counting on actively seeking them for marriage, their offering prices were bid up and bargains became relatively rare.

The above example simplifies the problem in several respects. First, as noted earlier, the stockholders of the two firms may have differing expectations regarding the futures of the firms if left unmerged and if merged. Furthermore, earnings may be growing and not level, as in the above illustration. Thus, for example, firm A might be growing rapidly, firm B growing slowly, and the new merged firm might have an expected growth rate close to that of firm A. In this case, firm B's shareholders would be trading shares with a claim to low growth earnings for shares with rapidly increasing earnings. The greater the growth potential of the new shares of the merged company relative to the old firm B's shares, the fewer the new shares firm A needs to issue to acquire firm B. Indeed, firm B's stockholders might be willing to trade in their shares for new shares with lower current earnings because of the greater growth rate in earnings per share. For example, if current earnings of firm B were $100,000 and growing at 2 percent per year, the owners of firm B might be willing to trade these shares for firm A's shares providing current earnings of only $80,000 but a growth rate of, say, 10 percent per year. In short, future earnings are as important (usually more important) than current earnings in determining the desirability of the merger to the parties concerned.

The emphasis in our illustration has been on earnings because shareholders are primarily interested in a company's ability to pay dividends both currently and in the future, and earnings reflect this dividend payout capacity. Can we infer from this that such considerations as a firm's market or book asset values or holdings of liquid assets are irrelevant in appraising a firm as an acquisition possibility? Book values can be dismissed since they are based upon historical costs and generally do not reflect real economic worth. Any liquid assets acquired in the merger can be added to the purchasing firm's other liquid assets or may be transformed into cash through liquidation of the liquid asset, the cash then being available for reinvestment elsewhere. Of these two choices (holding the liquid assets or liquidating them), the acquiring firm will select the one which provides the more attractive impact on the firm's present and future anticipated earnings and cash flow. The purchased firm may have surplus liquid assets which the acquiring company may sell for cash to be used for other profitable investment opportunities. This may be more economical than purchasing a similar company without surplus liquid resources and borrowing additional funds (or selling new shares) to exploit those other opportunities. In short, the assets of the acquired company can be used or liquidated, and the existence of a firm's excess liquid holdings may make it an appealing merger partner. In any case, however, in evaluating a merger candidate, the acquiring firm will decide how the acquired assets are to be used (including the possibility of liquidation and reinvestment of the proceeds) and then estimate the resulting effect on the firm's earnings and cash flow. This estimate of earnings and cash flow impact will determine the price the acquiring company will pay for the acquired firm.

Accounting Treatment of Mergers

In accounting practice, a merger is recorded as a purchase or as a pooling of interests. The primary difference between the two methods is in the value placed on the assets of the purchased firm for representation on the combined entity's balance sheet and for computing depreciation for the combined firm. *Under the purchase method, the acquired assets are carried at the price paid (in cash or stock) for the selling company's stock plus any liabilities of the selling company assumed by the acquiring firm.*

To illustrate a merger accounted for as a purchase, assume that firm A purchases firm B by paying firm B's shareholders *in firm A stock* worth $1,500,000 (fair market value of the stock) and assume that the purchase method of accounting is used. From the premerger balance sheet in Exhibit 21-6, note that the firm B's owners' equity is only $800,000 and therefore the acquisition involves a $700,000 premium paid to firm B's owners ($1,500,000 in firm A's stock for $800,000 of equity interest). This means that firm B's assets are effectively being valued at $700,000 more than they appear on firm B's books, i.e., are valued at $1,700,000. It is this figure of $1,700,000 at which the acquired assets are recorded on the postmerger books; total assets are therefore $4,700,000 for the combined company ($3 million of firm A's assets + $1,700,000). The depreciation deduction for the merged company in forthcoming years will be computed using the $4,700,000 (less salvage value) as the depreciation base.

Under the pooling of interests approach, the assets are valued just as they were on the acquired firm's books. The depreciation base for the combined company will consequently be $4 million (less salvage value). Thus, if a merger involves payment for a firm's shares in excess of their book value, a pooling of interest involves lower asset values and lower depreciation charges in future periods (and therefore higher income) than does a merger accounted for as a purchase.

It was just noted that purchase accounting will lead to higher recorded

Exhibit 21-6. Premerger and Postmerger Balance Sheets of Firms A and B under the Purchase Method and the Pooling of Interests Methods of Accounting for the Merger

	Premerger balance sheets		Postmerger balance sheet of merged firm	
	Firm A	Firm B	Purchase method	Pooling of interests method
Assets (net of depreciation)	$3,000,000	$1,000,000	$4,700,000	$4,000,000
Liabilities	1,000,000	200,000	1,200,000	1,200,000
Owners' equity	2,000,000	800,000	3,500,000	2,800,000

asset values and therefore greater depreciation deductions and lower income if the purchase price exceeds the book value of the acquired firm. This is an *advantage* of purchase accounting since, with a lower recorded income, taxes are less, and the firm's aftertax cash flow will be greater. For a given price paid for the acquired firm (in cash or stock), the seller is better off the greater is the aftertax cash flow generated in future periods. Income, after the noncash expense, is lower but aftertax cash flow higher, the greater is the depreciation deduction. Recall from Chapter 3 that accelerated depreciation is preferred by firms because it lowers recorded income and taxes and consequently increases aftertax cash flow in the more current time periods. That is, the objective is to maximize the present value of aftertax cash flow, and this is achieved if taxes are lower; a greater depreciation deduction achieves this by lowering taxable income.

We have assumed thus far that the price paid for the acquired firm does not include a premium above the fair market value of the acquired firm's assets if those assets were sold individually. Such a premium is commonly referred to as *goodwill* and arises if the acquired firm has added value from such things as a strong market position, unusually talented personnel, etc. Goodwill is amortized in the financial statements and therefore deducted in computing the earnings reported to stockholders; however, the amortized goodwill is not deductible for tax purposes. This treatment of goodwill is a *disadvantage* of purchase accounting relative to pooling of interests accounting (means lower reported earnings), since the latter records assets at book values rather than at the purchase price.

Opinion 16 of the Accounting Principles Board of the American Institute of Certified Public Accountants specifies the conditions under which a pooling of interests accounting for a merger can be used. If these conditions are not met, the merger is to be treated as a purchase. One condition that must be satisfied for the pooling of interests method to be applicable is that the owners of the acquired firm must maintain their proportionate ownership claim (with voting rights) in the surviving firm. This would occur if they received voting common stock in payment for their stock in the acquired firm, whereas it would not occur if preferred stock, bonds, or cash were exchanged for the selling firm's shares. Use of the pooling of interests approach also requires that the combined entity intends to retain most or all of the purchased assets for at least two years after the merger and that the purchase be effected in a single transaction (no payments contingent upon the firm's future performance).

Because of the form of payment involved, combinations that fulfill the pooling of interests requirements generally are nontaxable whereas those deemed a purchase for accounting purposes may or may not be taxable. The effects of taxability and nontaxability were discussed earlier in considering the method of payment (cash or securities) used in the acquisition.

A holding company is a firm which controls one or more other companies (called subsidiaries) through ownership of the subsidiary firms' common stock. The holding company structure permits the parent firm (the holding company) to control substantial assets with a small investment and also provides earnings that are highly levered. Because of this leverage, the holding company can be a relatively risky enterprise with the opportunity for extraordinary gains if the subsidiaries prosper and large losses if the subsidiaries do poorly.

A merger is the union of two or more firms into a single firm, the situation often entailing the purchase of one company by another. Mergers can produce benefits in the form of production economies, tax reductions, and reduction of risk through diversification. Frequently, however, the purchase price of another company is prohibitively high, thus making internal investment more attractive. A business combination will be particularly advantageous if both firms are too small for efficient operation or if the selling company owns an asset (e.g., a patent) which the buying company cannot obtain through internal investment.

A company can purchase the stock or the physical assets of another firm, and payment is generally in the form of cash or the acquiring company's securities. A purchase is taxable to the selling firm (or its stockholders) if payment is in cash or bonds, whereas the taxes are postponed (a nontaxable exchange) if the voting stock of the purchasing firm is used in payment. From a tax standpoint, the sellers will prefer a nontaxable exchange whereas the acquiring firm will usually prefer that it be taxable. The buying company prefers a taxable purchase because this generally implies a higher depreciation base (higher depreciation deductions for tax purposes) in future years. The choice between payment in voting stock or in cash or nonvoting securities may also depend upon nontax considerations, such as the availability of excess cash in the buying company's coffers, the desire for cash by the selling firm's stockholders, and the expectations regarding the future performance of the acquiring firm's stock that would be used as payment in the purchase.

In a purchase for cash, the decision to sell will be based upon a comparison by the sellers of the cash offered for their firm with the value of the firm being sold. The purchasing firm will treat the purchase as a capital budgeting problem, purchasing the new company only if the net cash flow from the acquired enterprise has a present value exceeding the purchase price. If payment is in the form of stock of the purchasing company, although a capital budgeting approach is still valid, a more common approach is to examine earnings per share with and without the merger. For both parties to agree to the merger, both must feel that there is an improvement in the expected long-run earnings performance of their stock. Particularly if there are real benefits from the merger (for example, production economies or tax benefits), both parties can gain—that is, both can end up with stock worth more than the value without the merger.

SUMMARY

The relative gain achieved by the buyer and the seller will depend largely upon their bargaining positions.

1. Contrast a holding company with a merger and a consolidation.
2. What are the technical differences between a merger and a consolidation?
3. Differentiate between horizontal and vertical combinations.
4. State the steps involved in a tender offer.
5. "Holding companies possess one advantage that a merged firm does not, namely, that only 15 percent of the dividends received from subsidiaries is taxable." Evaluate this statement.
6. Certain production economies can result from mergers. What are some of these economies?
7. How can a reduction in the variability (uncertainty) of firm income occur through merger?
8. Explain when one can regard a reduction in the income uncertainty or variability resulting from a merger as a good thing, that is, as a benefit of the merger? When is it not a benefit?
9. What advantages are there to external growth through merger? Disadvantages?
10. What advantages does the straight purchase of assets have over a merger?
11. From a taxation point of view the form of payment for acquired firms can be important. Explain why. If only tax considerations were important, what form of payment would the seller and the buyer prefer?
12. It has been argued that a prosperous firm can acquire firms with operating losses and thereby incur a tax savings. Explain how this can come about.

PROJECT Find an example of a tender offer being advertised in the *Wall Street Journal*. If you owned 100 shares of stock of the firm for which the tender offer is being made, would you be willing to tender your shares? You should analyze the offer carefully before making your decision (see Appendix A on sources of information about the firms involved).

PROBLEMS 1. Insullatum, Inc. is a holding company which owns 50 percent of Subso Soap Company. The balance sheets of the two firms are shown below:

Insullatum	
Assets	
Investment in Subso	$2,000,000
Liabilities and owners' equity	
Long-term debt (8% coupon rate)	$1,000,000
Preferred stock (9% dividend rate)	$700,000
Common stock (100,000 shares)	$300,000

Subso	
Assets	
Current assets and plant and equipment	$15,000,000
Liabilities and owners' equity:	
Long-term debt (7% coupon rate)	$6,000,000
Preferred stock (8% dividend rate)	$5,000,000
Common stock	$4,000,000

Assume that all of Subso's aftertax income is paid out in dividends and that Insullatum only pays taxes on 15 percent of those dividends. The tax rate for Insullatum and for Subso is 50 percent. Compute the income to Insullatum common stockholders and compute the rate of return on common stockholder equity earned by Insullatum stockholders for each of the following Subso incomes from operations (EBITs): $4,000,000, $3,000,000, and $1,800,000.

2. Explain the tax advantage of merging two firms, Gainer, Inc., and Loser, Inc., where Gainer has a taxable income of $1 million and Loser has a loss of $600,000. Assume a 40 percent tax rate.

3. Cat, Inc., is contemplating the acquisition of Sparrow Company. Cat can acquire Sparrow for $1 million but must pay off Sparrow's $500,000 in liabilities. The pretax cash flow from Sparrow is estimated at $500,000 a year for twenty-five years. The $1 million in Sparrow assets are to be depreciated on a straight-line basis (with no salvage value). The company is in a 50 percent tax bracket, and Sparrow will be operated with no debt. It estimates that investments of comparable risk should yield 10 percent after taxes. Determine whether the acquisition is advisable for Cat.

4. Gargantua Clothing is considering the acquisition of Little Annie Dress Company. Gargantua will pay $2 million to buy Little Annie's assets; Gargantua will assume Little Annie's liabilities of $750,000. The pretax cash flow of Little Annie is estimated at $500,000 a year for twenty-five years. The $2 million in assets are to be depreciated on a straight-line basis (with no salvage value). The company is in a 50 percent tax bracket. It estimates that investment of this level of risk should yield 12 percent. You are asked to determine whether the merger should be made. How would you do this? Show all calculations.

5. Type-It, Inc., is considering a merger with Write-It Pencil Company. The data below are in the hands of both boards of directors. The merger is expected to generate significant production economies and increased earnings. The issue at hand is how many shares of Type-It Write-It should get. Both boards are focusing their attention on earnings per share, for this potentially affects the value of the shares to be received and given. Both boards have agreed that the number of shares to be considered should be 20,000, 30,000, and 40,000. Construct a table demonstrating the potential impact of each scheme on each set of shareholders.

	Without merger		With merger
	Type-It	Write-It	
Earnings per year	$200,000	$100,000	$400,000
Shares outstanding	50,000	10,000	?
Earnings per share	$4.00	$10.00	?
Price per share	$40.00	$100.00	?
Price-earnings ratio	10x	10x	10x
Value of firm	$2,000,000	$1,000,000	$4,000,000

6. Scratch Fur Company is considering a merger with Trap, Inc. The data below are in the hands of both boards of directors. The issue at hand is how many shares of Scratch should be exchanged for Trap. Both boards are considering three possibilities: 40,000, 60,000, and 80,000 shares. Construct a table demonstrating the potential impact of each scheme on each set of shareholders.

	Scratch	Trap	Combined
Current earnings per year	$400,000	$250,000	$750,000
Shares outstanding	80,000	100,000	?
Earnings per share	$5	$2.50	?
Price per share	$60	$30	?
Price-earnings ratio	12x	12x	12x
Value of firm	$4,800,000	$3,000,000	$9,000,000

7. Firm A acquires firm B for $1 million in stock and the assumption of $500,000 in liabilities. The acquired assets have a book value of $800,000. The premerger balance sheets of the two firms are set forth

below. Demonstrate how the balance sheet of the combined firm will look under both the purchase method and the pooling of interests method of accounting.

	Firm A	Firm B
Assets	$5,000,000	$800,000
Liabilities	$2,000,000	$500,000
Owners' equity	$3,000,000	$300,000

The Ups and Downs of ITT

The International Telephone and Telegraph Corporation (ITT) is one of the world's largest and most successful corporations. In 1975 its sales volume ranked it fifteenth among world corporations. It stands as a prize example of profitable growth through merger and acquisition and has been viewed by the business community as an extraordinarily well-managed firm. However to some people, ITT is the outstanding example of a rapacious, immoral, and dangerously powerful corporation—insensitive to the welfare of the citizens of the ninety or so countries in which it operates and outside of the control of any single country. The company has been accused of interfering in the political processes of Chile, of influencing United States policies toward Ecuador, and of obtaining undue favors from officials in the Nixon administration. Regardless of the truth or falsity of the various charges levied against the firm, ITT is an interesting company viewed from a financial perspective.

HISTORICAL BACKGROUND

ITT was one of the first truly multinational corporations. From its founding in 1920 to provide telephone service in Puerto Rico and Cuba, ITT has operated in more than one country. By 1959 it was still basically a telecommunications company, headquartered in the United States, with $765 million in sales from manufacturing and operating telephone equipment in overseas markets. At this time Harold S. Geneen was hired as chief executive for the company. Mr. Geneen was and is considered a business genius. When he left Raytheon, where he was executive vice-president, to join ITT,

Raytheon's stock dropped 6½ points. Arriving at ITT, Geneen set out to transform the company.

Concerned that foreign governments would restrict the growth of an American-based corporation by favoring the products of local companies, Geneen embarked on a program of acquisition and merger on a massive scale. Between 1961 and 1971, ITT acquired 250 firms. In 1971, 75 percent of ITT's sales and revenues were derived from acquisitions made during this period. ITT acquired book publishers and bakers, finance companies and manufacturers of fire-fighting equipment; Sheraton hotels, Avis car rentals, Canteen vending, and Rayonier forest products all became members of the ITT family. By 1973 the $765 million telecommunications company had become a conglomerate giant with $10 billion in sales and $521 million in net income. The average annual growth in earnings per share of common stock was 11 percent per year and earnings increased *every* year from 1957 to 1973. The jewel among the acquisitions was the Hartford Fire Insurance Company, which contributed 24 percent of ITT's 1973 earnings. In 1974 the growth story came to an end, earnings dropped 13 percent, and it was Hartford that did it.

THE HARTFORD STORY

In many ways the acquisition of the Hartford Fire Insurance Company by ITT in 1970 is a story illustrating the proposition that the truth is stranger than fiction. Hartford is the fourth largest fire and casualty insurance company in the United States. The acquisition of this major company by an already enormous ITT set off miniexplosives under the chairs of officials in the antitrust division of the U.S. Justice Department. They immediately started court proceedings to block the merger. After some legal hassles, the Justice Department and ITT reached an agreement. ITT could keep Hartford provided that it got rid of Avis car rentals acquired in 1965 ("No. 2 so we try harder"), Canteen, and two other major acquisitions. ITT also promised to make no acquisitions for the next ten years of companies with assets exceeding $100 million and no "leading companies" with sales over $25 million. Two reactions to this settlement occurred. Democratic members of Congress lambasted the agreement as a sellout by the Nixon administration and the Justice Department to big business. Investors in the stock market were not happy with the cost to ITT, and the company's stock dropped in price. But ITT did obtain Hartford.

The performance of Hartford for the two years following the settlement seemed to validate the critics of the Justice Department. Hartford was a major contributor to ITT's profits in 1971, 1972, and 1973. However, ITT did not "raid" (sell off) Hartford's assets as was feared by some people. Indeed ITT found it necessary to add $93 million in capital (primarily bonds) to the company. In the meantime the Watergate scandals of the Nixon administration came to light. Part of these scandals included suggestions that ITT had improperly tried to influence the Justice Department in the Hartford settlement. Despite the bad public relations that resulted, Hartford still appeared to be the jewel of the companies acquired by ITT. In 1974 came the bad times.

A fire and casualty insurance company is really two businesses. One part of the business is investment in securities and real estate. This part of the business generally shows profits in good times and in bad. The other part of the business is insurance underwriting. For un-

derwriting to be profitable, the company must charge high enough premiums to its customers to cover the losses from fires and accidents that happen. Investment performance in 1974 was poor, and the underwriting business was a disaster. Under pressure from top management at ITT, Hartford had pushed too hard in insuring people and business firms. Hartford cut prices to increase volume and accepted too many high-risk customers. Underwriting *losses* amounted to $123 million in 1974. Investment profits were sufficient for Hartford to show a total profit of $81 million for the year; but this was down 35 percent from 1973. Hartford's decline in earnings coupled with poor performance in some of the other subsidiaries and losses due to changes in foreign exchange rates (see Chapter 22) produced the first drop in earnings for ITT in sixteen years.

In time Hartford will surely recover and become more profitable; but the experience has dispelled the aura of invincibility that once cloaked ITT's top management. The firm's vaunted financial controls were no help in this case. Harold Geneen's credo is "I want no surprises." He got one from Hartford.

CONCLUSION

Ironically, throughout the period of ITT's rapid growth by acquiring other companies, its basic telecommunications business has done extremely well. The European subsidiaries, which are well-established in Britain, France, Germany, and Italy, are highly profitable. In 1974 telecommunication equipment contributed 27 percent of ITT's sales and 39 percent of its profits. The advantage to ITT and its stockholders from combining companies as diverse as the Nancy Taylor Secretarial Finishing School, textbook publishers, billboard advertising companies, car rental agencies, telephone equipment manufacturers, motels, and

Businesses that buy or sell goods and services outside their own country
and businesses that operate in more than one country face a more complex environment than a firm which does business in only one country.
The main complications are of two types. First, monetary units or currencies vary from one country to another. Generally one country's money
cannot be spent in another country. If a United States firm sells goods in
Japan for Japanese yen, the yen must be converted into United States
dollars in order for the firm to buy goods and pay employees in the United
States. The financial manager must consider not only the amounts resulting from a transaction, but also the currency involved. The second
complication is that countries differ in their laws, taxes, business practices, and degree of political and economic stability. Management must
understand and adjust to the operating and financial environment of each
country in which it does business. International financial management is
no simple task.

In this chapter we consider the special problems of international financial management which result from international transactions. The first
section describes the factors influencing the rates of exchange among the
currencies of different countries. Then the methods which have been
developed to finance purchases of goods in international trade are described. The last and major section of the chapter deals with the multinational company, a business firm with branches or subsidiaries in more
than one country.

Suppose you are planning a trip to Germany. You know that you will need
to have German currency, or Deutsche marks (DM), so that you can pay
for purchases while you are there. How many marks can you obtain with,
say, $500? The relationship between the values of two currencies is called
the **exchange rate.** The exchange rate between dollars and marks can be
stated as dollars per mark or marks per dollar; for example, $0.40 per
mark and DM2.5 per dollar are equivalent. At this exchange rate $500
would exchange into (purchase) $2.5 \times \$500 = DM1,250$. Note that one
exchange rate is the reciprocal of the other: $0.4 = 1/2.5$. Exchange rates
of major world currencies, expressed as dollars per foreign currency unit,
are listed in the *Wall Street Journal* each day. The names of several countries' currencies and exchange rates relative to United States dollars are

**CURRENCIES AND
EXCHANGE RATES**

Table 22-1. Selected currencies and exchange rates

Country	Currency	Exchange rates (U.S.$)	
		December 1975	December 1974
Australia	Dollar	1.254	1.317
Austria	Schilling	0.054	0.057
Britain	Pound	2.022	2.329
Canada	Dollar	0.986	1.012
France	Franc	0.224	0.221
India	Rupee	0.111	0.124
Italy	Lira	0.00146	0.00152
Japan	Yen	0.00327	0.00333
Mexico	Peso	0.080	0.080
Netherlands	Guilder	0.372	0.393
South Africa	Rand	1.148	1.447
Spain	Peseta	0.0167	0.0177
Sweden	Krona	0.227	0.239
Switzerland	Franc	0.380	0.384
West Germany	Deutsche mark (mark)	0.381	0.408

Source: *Federal Reserve Bulletin.*

shown in Table 22-1. The information illustrates the wide range of relative currency values that exist at a point in time. In addition, Table 22-1 indicates that precise wording is needed when dealing with foreign currencies. It is not sufficient to say a bushel of wheat sells for $2.50. You must say whether it is $2.50 United States, $2.50 Australian, or $2.50 Canadian. Similarly, more than one country denominates its currency in pounds, in pesos, in francs, in marks, etc.

Not only do the exchange rates between currencies differ, but they also change over time. Comparing exchange rates in December 1975 with those of December 1974, we see that the United States dollar gained relative to most currencies in the sense that a given sum of dollars would purchase more of most of the currencies shown. The exceptions in the table are the French franc which increased in value relative to the United States dollar, and the Mexican peso which stayed the same relative to United States dollars. Note that exchange rates of some currencies such as the South African rand dropped significantly (about 21 percent), whereas others such as the Swiss franc dropped only slightly (about 1 percent).

Changing exchange rates makes international transactions more risky than those which are confined to a single currency. Before looking at how financial managers cope with this risk, we should consider why exchange rates change.

Exchange rates are determined in the foreign exchange market and reflect the supply and demand for each currency. The demand for a given country's currency is based on people's needs to make payments in that currency plus speculative demand, plus government demand. Payments requiring foreign exchange are made for several reasons: purchases of goods being exported from the country, purchases of goods and services by foreign tourists in the country, financial assets being acquired by foreign investors, and direct investments in plant and equipment by foreign corporations establishing productive facilities in the country. Speculative demand for a currency is based on expectations that the currency will appreciate (increase in value) relative to other currencies. Government demand reflects attempts by the government of a country to maintain its currency's value relative to the values of other currencies.

The supply of a currency in the foreign exchange market comes from people who presently own the currency and wish to exchange it for foreign currencies. Importers who wish to pay for goods purchased abroad buy foreign currencies thus supplying their own currency to the foreign exchange market. Tourists exchange their home country's currency for the currencies of the countries they are visiting. Anyone holding currency X who would prefer to hold some other country's currency is a source of supply of currency X. For example, if you are a citizen of country X and are worried about high rates of inflation, political instability, or possible confiscation of your assets in country X, you might prefer to transfer funds out of country X into more secure assets in country Y.

Inflation Although changes in exchange rates result from changes in the supply and demand for currencies, this explanation does not provide a very helpful answer to the question of why exchange rates change. We must look for the more fundamental factors that affect the supply and demand for currencies. One factor is the relative rate of inflation in different countries. If the rate of inflation is 10 percent per year in country X and 1 percent per year in country Y, people will tend to prefer holding the currency of country Y rather than the currency of country X. This is because the value of currency for country Y in terms of the goods and services that may be purchased with this currency is declining at a lower rate than the value of the currency of country X. Therefore, the exchange rate of country X's currency will tend to decline relative to country Y's currency. If people can freely transfer money from one country to another and can freely purchase goods and services throughout the world, the goods and services that can be purchased for $100 in the United States, for example, should be the same as those available in France if $100 is exchanged into French francs. Exchange rates therefore tend to vary so as to provide similar purchasing power in each country. Differences in inflation rates among countries result in changes in exchange rates.

Factors Determining Exchange Rates

Interest rates A second factor influencing exchange rates is relative interest rates. If investors can earn 4 percent interest per year in country Y and 8 percent per year in country X, they will prefer to invest in securities of country X provided that the rate of inflation is the same in both countries. As people buy currency X with currency Y, the exchange rate of country X's currency will appreciate relative to country Y's. The increased demand for securities in country X relative to country Y also tends to reduce the interest rate differential between the two countries. This occurs because the prices of country X's securities rise (reducing their yield to new investors) and the prices of country Y's securities fall (increasing their yield to new investors.)[1]

Government policies and other factors Interest rates and inflation are just two of the many factors influencing exchange rates although these two are very important. Governments often actively intervene in the foreign exchange markets, buying and selling currencies to support the value of their currency relative to others. In some cases governments do not allow their currencies' values to be established in the foreign exchange market. For example, the communist countries are not tied into the international financial system, and their exchange rates are set by government decree. Governments sometimes restrict movements of money out of their country (purchase of foreign exchange) for this reason. The presence of stringent controls on foreign exchange transactions or the prospects of a government's imposing such controls will make foreign investors reluctant to put money into these countries even if interest rates are high there.

There are obstacles to free trade among countries, such as tariffs and quotas, which inhibit the equalization of purchasing power among countries. Generally anything that affects the demand for the currency of a country or its supply affects exchange rates. Many of the factors are the result of governments' actions or are highly influenced by them. Government policies strongly affect the rate of inflation, the level of interest rates, foreign exchange transactions, imports, and exports. The political stability of a country affects the risks of investors in that country. Thus in a sense, the government of each country does determine the rate of exchange of its currency relative to others, not necessarily by controlling the exchange rates directly but through the overall impact of its policies.

Spot and Forward Rates The **spot** rate of exchange between two currencies is today's rate of exchange for currencies being bought and sold for immediate delivery. The **forward** rate of exchange is a rate agreed on today with the actual delivery

---

1. The interest rate (yield) provided by a financial asset is inversely related to its price (see Chap. 5).

of the currency to take place at a *future* time, usually 30, 90, or 180 days from now. Forward exchange rates are therefore prices set today for currency exchanges which will occur in the future.

Forward rates may be greater than the current spot rate (premium) or less than the current spot rate (discount). For example, on March 3, 1976, the following exchange rates were quoted in the *Wall Street Journal* (for transactions on March 2, 1976):

	British pounds (£)	German marks (DM)
	2.0250	0.3887
30-day futures	2.0191	0.3894
90-day futures	2.0084	0.3911
180-day futures	1.9904	0.3942

The first figure shown in each case was the spot rate for that day, $2.025 per pound for example. The other rates are the forward rates for contracts of the time specified. Forward rates on the pound are at a discount from the spot rate, whereas forward rates for the mark are at a premium. This means that the pound is expected to depreciate relative to the dollar (and the mark) in the future and that the mark is expected to appreciate relative to the dollar. Purchase of a forward contract for exchange of £100 into dollars 180 days from March 2, 1976, would assure the purchaser that £100 could be exchanged into £100 × 1.9904 = $199.04 at that time regardless of the spot rate in effect.

Covering investment positions in the forward market Contracts for future exchanges are used to "cover" a position (investment) in a particular currency. For example, suppose interest rates in Great Britain are 10 percent per year and interest rates in the United States are 6 percent per year. You have $10,000 (United States) which you are considering investing in a British security which will mature in 180 days. The spot rate for British pounds is $2; that is, $10,000 will purchase £5,000. If you exchange your dollars into pounds and invest in the British security you will have about £5,250 180 days from now (principal plus 5 percent since the investment is for half of a year). At that time you wish to exchange the pounds back into dollars. You could wait for 180 days and make the exchange at the spot rate prevailing then, whatever it turns out to be. In this case you would run the risk of having the pound depreciate relative to the dollar. That is, instead of being able to acquire $2 for each pound ($10,500), you might only be able to obtain $1.90 per pound or $9,975 ($1.90 × £5,250). Receiving $9,975 in six months' time from an investment of $10,000 is not desirable. You would have been much better off investing at 6 percent per year in the United States if this were to happen. This is called an "un-

Exhibit 22-1. Using a Futures Contract to Cover a Foreign Investment Position

> *Basic Investment*
> $10,000 exchanged at current spot rate of $2 per pound to provide £5,000
>   £5,000 invested at 10% per year to yield £5,250 in 180 days
> *Returns from Uncovered Position*

Spot rate[a]	$2.04	$2.00	$1.96	$1.90
Dollar return[b]	$10,710	$10,500	$10,290	$9,975
Rate of return[c]	14.2%	10%	5.8%	−0.5%

> *Returns from Covered Position*
>   Forward rate (180 days) = $1.98 per pound
>   Dollar return = £5,250 × $1.98 per pound = $10,395
>   Rate of return = 3.95% for 180 days or 7.9% per year

[a] Possible values for exchange rate between British pounds and United States dollars (dollars per pound) in effect 180 days from initial investment.

[b] Dollar value of £5,250 at indicated spot rate.

[c] Annual percentage rate earned on initial dollar investment when returns from British investment are exchanged into dollars.

covered'' position because what you actually earn on the investment depends on future exchange rates. Exhibit 22-1 shows some possible outcomes for different exchange rates.

Alternatively, you could cover the investment by executing a contract in the forward exchange market to exchange £5,250 into United States dollars 180 days from now. The rate of exchange in this contract is the forward rate. Suppose the forward rate is $1.98 on a 180-day futures contract. You would be assured of obtaining $10,395 ($1.98 × 5,250) in 180 days' time. You will safely earn 7.9 percent per year on your investment in British securities as contrasted with 6 percent in United States securities.[2]

Forward exchange markets therefore provide a means for protecting against future changes in exchange rates. They are used by investors in foreign securities, banks, and companies engaged in international transactions. Forward exchange markets also provide a way to speculate on changes in exchange rates. The failure of Franklin National Bank in 1974 was in part due to massive losses from speculation in the foreign exchange markets.

2. This type of transaction is called **covered interest arbitrage.** The net incentive measured by the margin (the difference between 7.9 and 6.0 percent) between the interest returns in the United States and those in Canada and Britain are provided in the monthly *Federal Reserve Bulletin.*

In a typical domestic purchase of goods by one business firm from another, the goods are shipped and the purchaser is billed for their value. The seller provides trade credit to the purchaser as discussed in Chapter 15. However, if the purchaser is unknown to the seller or has a poor credit rating, the seller often will require that the goods be paid for before the purchaser can obtain them. The credit risks are generally greater in international transactions than in domestic ones. Sellers have less reliable information about purchasers in another country, and there is the risk that the government of the purchaser's country will not permit the purchaser to pay for the goods in the seller's currency due to controls on foreign exchange. Shipping times are much greater in international trade; the goods may be in transit for several months. Therefore, the financing burden is much greater because while the goods are on board a ship, for example, neither seller nor purchaser has access to them and yet someone must be financing them.

FINANCING INTERNATIONAL TRADE

Whenever payment is delayed in an international transaction, either the buyer or the seller is exposed to the risk that exchange rates may change in the interim. For example, suppose a United States department store wishes to import 10,000 meters of Thai silk. The seller (exporter) is a silk mill in Thailand, and the current price of the silk is 200,000 baht (Thai currency). The current exchange rate is $0.05 per baht, and so the price in United States dollars is $10,000. Suppose the goods will be in transit for three months and the exporter is willing to extend credit for this period. If the goods are invoiced in dollars (as is quite common) at a price of $10,000, the Thai exporter is exposed to the risk that when final payment is made, $10,000 will not be worth 200,000 baht; that is, the baht may have appreciated relative to the dollar. Of course, if the baht has depreciated, the exporter will get more than 200,000 baht for $10,000. On the other hand, suppose the invoice is in baht, 200,000 baht. Now the importer, the United States department store, is subject to the risk that the dollar has depreciated relative to the baht; that is, it will take more than $10,000 to pay 200,000 baht. Therefore, we see that no matter how the transaction is structured, one party or the other is exposed to an uncertain result when payment is measured in terms of its own local currency and final payment is delayed.

Foreign Exchange Risk

How can this exchange risk be avoided? One way is for the importer to pay on order. In our example above, the department store could purchase 200,000 baht with $10,000 and buy the silk. There is no exchange risk in this transaction; however, the burden of financing is now on the importer, the purchaser of the goods, who will not have them available for use for

Avoiding Exchange Risks

some time. In the meantime the exporter, the seller, has obtained an immediate profit. Competition among exporters for business encourages sales with delayed payment, at least to importers who are known to the exporter and who have good credit ratings.

A second way is to cover the transaction in the forward exchange markets. If the goods are invoiced in the importer's currency, the exporter bears the risk. The exporter can eliminate this risk by selling a forward contract to deliver the importer's currency in exchange for the exporter's currency at the time the sale is made. For example, if the Thai company provides ninety days of credit and invoices the goods at a price of $10,000, it will be receiving $10,000 in ninety days. Suppose the firm sells a contract for delivery of $10,000 in ninety days' time in exchange for baht. If the forward rate on a ninety-day futures contract is the same as the current spot rate ($0.05), the exporter will be able to deliver the $10,000 and receive 200,000 baht in ninety days' time regardless of what happens to the exchange rate in the meantime. If the forward rate is at a discount or premium, the amount of baht to be received will be different from 200,000 but in any case the amount will be known at the time the sale is made. Indeed the price of the goods is likely to depend in part on the length of time for which credit will be extended and the cost of covering the transaction in the forward exchange markets.

If the goods are invoiced in the exporter's currency (baht, for example), then the importer bears the exchange risk. In our example, the United States department store could eliminate the risk of appreciation of the baht relative to the dollar by selling a forward contract to deliver dollars in exchange for baht at a fixed exchange rate. The contract would be for the amount of dollars needed to obtain 200,000 baht at the ninety-day forward rate.

A third method for the importer or the exporter to eliminate risk is to borrow money in the importers' currency and invest the proceeds in securities of the exporter. Notice that the risk, whether borne by the department store or the silk mill, was due to the possible appreciation of the exporter's currency (baht) relative to the importer's currency (dollars). This is so because the fundamental transaction is goods moving from exporter to importer in exchange for money moving from importer to exporter. At some point in time the importer's currency must be exchanged for the exporter's currency. Therefore, the risk is always that the importer's (buyer's) currency will purchase fewer units of the exporter's currency than it did at the time the sale was made. Suppose the goods are invoiced in baht at a price of 200,000 baht. The department store bears the risk that it will take more than $10,000 to acquire 200,000 baht ninety days from now. The department store can avoid this risk by borrowing $10,000 in the United States, converting it to 200,000 baht immediately and investing 200,000 baht in a Thai security (preferably one with a ninety-day maturity). The department store will, of course, pay interest on the loan and receive interest on the investment. The net cost will depend on the difference in the two interest rates. In ninety days the department store can pay the silk mill with the funds already available in baht, so no matter how much the baht has appreciated, the department store is protected. It now has a $10,000 United States bank loan and has paid for the goods. The exporter could use a similar transaction when the goods are invoiced in dollars.

An analysis of the costs of protection against exchange rate risks is complex and beyond the scope of this book. In many instances firms do not choose to protect against the risk, because the costs are too great.

Letters of Credit

As we noted above, immediate payment by the importer (buyer) to the exporter (seller) eliminates the exchange risks of deferred payment and allows the exporter to avoid bearing any credit risk. However, the importer must finance the goods while they are in transit. Moreover, the importing firm owns goods which will not be in its control and available for inspection for some time. The sellers of any product have an incentive (profits) to ease the problems faced by their customers in acquiring those goods. Only when credit or political risks are very great will the seller demand cash in advance. When the parties are well known to each other and the countries involved are stable, sales will be made on open account, as is customary in domestic transactions. Between these two extremes, a variety of specialized financial arrangements have been developed to facilitate international trade. The most widely used arrangement is based on a **letter of credit.** A letter of credit is a written statement made by a bank that it will pay out money if specified conditions are met. There are several different types of letters of credit; here we will describe the one most often used in United States imports—an irrevocable letter of credit issued by a United States bank. (See the suggested readings for descriptions of other types.)

Import letters of credit Let us suppose a United States importer has located a product in a foreign country which he or she wishes to purchase. The importer places an order for the goods, asking the selling firm whether it will agree to ship under a letter of credit. The two parties reach agreement on prices, method of shipment, when the goods are to be shipped, etc. Once the basic terms of sale have been agreed to, the importer applies for a letter of credit from a commercial bank. This letter of credit, sent to the exporting firm, authorizes it to obtain money from a bank in its country (or directly from the United States bank) by presenting the required documents supporting the sale and shipment of the goods. A sample letter of credit such as might be used in a shipment of Thai silk is

Exhibit 22-2. Sample Letter of Credit

CABLE ADDRESS "BANKOFCALA"   IRREVOCABLE LETTER OF CREDIT NO. 00011-2

THE BANK OF CALIFORNIA National Association
OFFICES IN: CALIFORNIA · OREGON · WASHINGTON
P.O. Box 3095, Seattle, Washington 98114   May 3, 1976

Thai Silk Mills Ltd.   Advised through: Bangkok Bank Ltd.
P.O. Box 128   P.O. Box 95
Bangkok, Thailand   Bangkok, Thailand

SPECIMEN

☐ This is the original Credit opened by MAIL.
☒ This is the confirmation of a Credit opened by CABLE today.
It shall be available only for such amount not already availed of under the cable advice and shall not be considered valid unless our correspondent's notification of the cable is attached hereto, both of which shall jointly constitute evidence of the unused amount of this Credit.

Gentlemen:

You are authorized to draw on The Bank of California, N.A., Seattle, Washington   at ------------------- sight
for 100% of the invoice value
for account of Osgood & North, 906 Fourth Avenue, Seattle, Washington 98104

up to an aggregate amount of U.S. $10,000.00--
Ten Thousand and no/100's -- U.S. DOLLARS
Your drafts must be accompanied by:
Signed Commercial Invoice in triplicate;
Certificate of Origin in triplicate;
Packing List in triplicate;
Full set of clean on board ocean bills of lading issued to order of The Bank of
California, N.A., freight collect, notify Osgood & North, 906 Fourth Avenue, Seattle,
Washington 98104 evidencing shipment from Thailand Port to Seattle, Washington of
the following:

10,000 METERS THAI SILK

TERMS: F.O.B. Vessel, Thailand Port

Partial shipments are not permissible. Transhipment is not permissible.

Container bills of lading, unitized, palletized cargoes are acceptable.

Documents must be presented for payment, acceptance or negotiation no later than 10 days
from the on board date of the bills of lading, but within the validity of the credit.

All banking charges outside the United States are for account of beneficiary.

All drafts so drawn must bear the clause: "Drawn under The Bank of California N.A., Seattle, Washington   Letter of Credit
No. 00011-2   dated May 3, 1976   ," and the amount of each negotiation must be endorsed on the reverse
hereof by the negotiating bank.
We engage with drawers, endorsers and bona fide holders that all drafts drawn in compliance with the terms of this Credit shall be honored
upon presentation and delivery of the documents, if drawn and negotiated on or before June 30, 1976

                                                          Yours very truly,

SPECIMEN

                                                          Authorized Signature

This Credit is subject to the "Uniform Customs & Practice for Documentary Credits (1974 Revision) International Chamber of Commerce Brochure No. 290

shown in Exhibit 22-2. A glossary of the terms used in the letter and in international trade is shown in Table 22-2.

Notice that there are four parties involved in this transaction—the importer (Osgood and North), the importer's bank (Bank of California), the exporter (Thai Silk Mills), and the exporter's bank (Bangkok Bank). The

Table 22-2. Definitions of some terms used in international trade[a]

Term	Definition[b]
Accept; acceptance	To agree to pay on a designated date a draft drawn on the party accepting; an acceptance is an accepted draft. (The Bank of California would be the party accepting the draft.)
Beneficiary	Party in whose name a letter of credit has been issued or a draft drawn (Thai Silk Mills).
Bill of lading	Document showing that the goods were received by the carrier ("vessel" in which the goods are to be shipped). A "clean" bill of lading shows no indications of defects in the goods or their packing.
Certificate of origin	Document showing the country where the goods originated (Thailand).
Commercial invoice	The bill for the goods issued by the exporter (Thai Silk Mills).
Confirm; confirmation	To assume an obligation to pay under a letter of credit; a confirmation is the confirming document.
Draft	Instrument by which one party directs another party to make a payment. (Thai Silk Mills would draw a draft against the letter of credit from the Bank of California. The mill might direct the Bank of California to pay $10,000 to Bangkok Bank for the mill's account.)
Free on board (FOB)	A term of sale indicating the point at which the exporter stops paying for transportation costs and the importer begins paying. (Thai Silk Mill would pay all costs involved in getting the silk on the boat. Osgood and North would have to pay for marine insurance and the ocean voyage.)
Open	To establish or issue, as in "to open a letter of credit."

[a] Excluded are those terms defined in the text and included in the glossary at the end of the book.
[b] Remarks in parentheses refer to the text example and Exhibit 22-2.

letter of credit is *irrevocable* by the issuing bank if the *bank* promises to pay the money provided the conditions specified in the letter of credit are met. In such transactions when the importer's bank issues the letter of credit, neither the exporter nor the exporter's bank need have any knowledge of the credit worthiness of the importer. All the credit risk to the exporter is absorbed by the importer's bank, which is in a good position to evaluate the credit of the importing firm. The credit standing of the importer's bank becomes the only concern of the exporting firm and its bank.

THE MULTINATIONAL COMPANY

A multinational company, or MNC, is a company which has direct investments (produces a product or products) in more than one country. The importance of the MNC is highlighted by the fact that *all* the fifty largest (in sales) United States manufacturing concerns are multinationals! There are approximately 200 United States-based corporations with extensive overseas operations and over 3,600 United States companies with at least one foreign subsidiary. As of 1976, the total (United States and foreign) assets of these firms significantly exceeded $200 billion and their sales from foreign operations alone were well over $100 billion. Although the United States is the dominant home of MNCs, Britain, Switzerland, West Germany, Canada, and Japan have, in the aggregate, invested outside their borders nearly as much as has the United States.

The Profit Motive

Four major factors encouraged United States companies to establish subsidiaries abroad. The first—particularly important in the 1950s—was the desire to avoid foreign tariffs against United States goods. For example, to sell its American-made product in France, a cosmetics manufacturer would have to pay a French tariff, but there would be no tariff to pay if the products were manufactured by its subsidiary in France. The decline in trade barriers during the last fifteen years has made this advantage less important.

A second factor encouraging the growth of MNCs has been the lower production costs overseas. As late as the 1960s, very significant labor cost differences made manufacturing abroad much cheaper. However, in recent years, wages in other countries have risen more sharply than have American wages; consequently much of the cost advantage has eroded.

A third force giving impetus to United States expansion overseas was American technical and managerial superiority. This advantage, too, has dwindled in the face of mounting competition from the MNCs of other countries and the increased sophistication of the foreign nations in which the United States MNCs operate.

The fourth factor has been the favorable tax treatment of foreign-source income of United States corporations. However, legislation in 1962 and 1969 eliminated most of the tax benefits. Today, the only major advantage is that no United States taxes need be paid on the income of subsidiaries abroad unless dividends are paid to the United States parent. This feature permits a deferral of United States taxes and is an advantage to operating subsidiaries in countries which have lower tax rates than does the United States.

Because of falling trade barriers, increased foreign labor costs, and increased foreign competition, the rate of return on United States investment abroad has, since the late 1960s, not greatly exceeded the average rate of return on United States domestic investment. This does not imply, however, that foreign investment will cease or even slow down. Investment in underdeveloped areas has consistently generated relatively high profits, and so long as the average return is at least as great abroad as it is at home, capital will continue to flow overseas, barring government restrictions.

The Counterforce: Foreign Investment in the United States

A black limousine speeds through crowded city streets carrying the board chairman to a crucial meeting; the destination is a brainstorming session on how to handle a strike at the Akron, Ohio, plant. The language spoken at the session will not be English, however; it will be Japanese—and the meeting place is Tokyo, not New York.

This vignette reflects a startling change in United States economic relationships with other countries. Whereas the insignia of United States industrial giants have long been familiar to Europeans and Canadians, as well as to the peoples of many less industrialized countries, until recently foreign direct investment in the United States has been less than meager. Now, however, the inflow of foreign investment is accelerating. Britain has been a leader through such English firms as the British American Tobacco Company, the British Land Company, Slater-Walker Securities, Barclays Bank Ltd., and Lloyds Bank Ltd. of London. Switzerland's huge Nestle Alimentana, France's Michelin, and West Germany's Volkswagen are other standard-bearers of the foreign invasion. Total foreign direct investment in the United States was nearly $20 billion in 1975, and it has been rising at over $1 billion annually in recent years.

The Extraordinary Risk of Foreign Investment

Political risks Although few foreign ventures are as ill-fated as Anaconda's copper investments in Chile or some of the international oil firms' holdings in the Middle East, the risk of foreign expropriation—or, at least, controls—are an ever-present threat to multinational enterprises. The danger is particularly great for investments in natural resources in underdeveloped countries, since such resources often represent a large portion of the national wealth and are regarded by the nationals as "part of the country."

To deal with the risk of foreign government intervention confronting United States companies abroad, the United States government has established the Overseas Private Investment Corporation (OPIC). This agency insures against losses due to inconvertibility into dollars of amounts invested in the foreign country or of any income from those investments. Other OPIC programs insure against expropriation and nationalization and against losses due to war or revolution. A number of qualifications restrict the properties that can be insured, and each project must be individually approved for eligibility. The fees charged by OPIC—a specified percentage of the value of the insured property—are the same for all firms and all investments, regardless of risk, but they do vary depending upon whether the coverage is for inconvertibility, expropriation, war, etc.

Exchange rate risk Earlier in the chapter we discussed currencies and exchange rates. The possibility of exchange rate fluctuations is important to the financial planning of an MNC. A change in the international exchange rate between dollars and any foreign currency can have a major impact on a multinational doing business in that currency. For example, Uncsam, Inc., though based in the United States, will be worse off if the francs its French subsidiary takes in fall in value relative to the dollar, since less will be received when the francs are converted to dollars and repatriated to the United States. By the same token, if the franc rises in value, Uncsam will be better off.

Well-managed MNCs take pains to minimize holdings of currencies considered likely candidates for devaluation (fall in value). When the dollar was teetering in the early 1970s, multinational corporations unloaded their Eurodollar holdings (dollars held outside the United States) and purchased German marks, Japanese yen, and other strong currencies. Indeed, one of the major criticisms of MNCs is that their concern about currency values increases the instability of foreign exchange rates. In defense of the MNC, others point out that the MNCs do not cause exchange rate adjustments but only react to weakness in a currency (by selling it) once that weakness has been caused by other factors. Their shifting from the weak to the strong medium of exchange simply speeds up the adjustment process, causing exchange rates to reach a proper level more quickly than would otherwise be the case. The counterargument is that the actions of the MNCs result in an overreaction in one direction or another, thus contributing to market instability. The debate on this issue remains unresolved by either economists or politicians.

Exchange rate changes cause changes in the dollar value of a foreign subsidiary's current assets and current liabilities, and these changes may produce dollar income gains or losses.[3] For example, assume that Blass, Incorporated, has a subsidiary in England with current assets of £100,000. Suppose that the exchange rate is $2 per pound, implying that the dollar value of the subsidiary's current assets is $200,000. That is, the current assets could be sold for £100,000 and then the £100,000 could be

---

3. Only gains and losses due to changes in the dollar values of the subsidiary's current assets and liabilities are recorded on the income statement. This is because long-term assets, liabilities, and equity are not translated into dollars at current exchange rates but at the rates applicable when the long-term asset was acquired, the long-term liability was incurred, or the equity investment was made.

converted into $200,000. If the exchange rate changes to $2.40 per pound, the dollar value of the subsidiary's current assets rises to $240,000, producing a gain in dollars of $40,000 (since the dollar value of the current assets has risen from $200,000 to $240,000). On the other hand, if the exchange rate were to fall to, say, $1.80 per pound, the dollar value of the subsidiary's current assets would fall to $180,000, producing a $20,000 loss. Thus, a rise in the value of pounds in terms of dollars (a fall in the value of a dollar in terms of pounds) raises the dollar value of the foreign subsidiary's current assets. A fall in the value of pounds lowers the dollar value of the subsidiary's current assets.

Similar reasoning applies to liabilities. If the subsidiary had liabilities of £100,000, before the exchange rate change these liabilities would be equal to $200,000. A change in the exchange rate from $2 per pound to $2.40 per pound means that the subsidiary has a debt in dollars of $240,000. That is, to pay off the £100,000 debt using dollars, Blass would have to spend $240,000 instead of $200,000 since it now takes $2.40 to buy a pound. Thus, a fall in the value of a dollar makes a foreign liability larger and therefore a greater burden in terms of dollars. On the other hand, if the exchange rate had fallen to $1.80 per pound, the dollar value of the subsidiary's current liabilities would be only $180,000, $20,000 less than before the exchange rate change.

From the above discussion, we see that a foreign currency's fall in value relative to the dollar produces dollar losses on current assets and dollar gains on current liabilities. A rise in a foreign currency's value relative to the dollar produces gains in current assets and losses on current liabilities. Such gains and losses due to exchange rate fluctuations can be significant to a company with large overseas operations. These gains and losses expressed in dollars are included in the company's consolidated income statement.[4] For example, if a company expects the value of the foreign currency (e.g., the pound) to rise in terms of dollars, it will want to have large current asset balances (for example, a lot of pound deposits) and small current liabilities denominated in the foreign currency (small debts in terms of pounds). The opposite holds if the company expects the foreign currency to fall in terms of dollars. Financial managers of multinational enterprises are very sensitive to exchange rate movements, particularly with the wide fluctuations that now occur under the present system of flexible exchange rates.

The impact on a firm of an exchange rate change depends on the combined effect of the change on the dollar value of the firm's assets and liabilities. To illustrate, assume that World Products has a new British subsidiary with £100,000 in inventories and cash, £60,000 in current liabilities, and therefore a £40,000 net current position (current assets minus current

4. See footnote 3, this chapter.

720

liabilities). If the exchange rate is 1£ = $2, the dollar values of the current assets, current liabilities, and net current position in the British subsidiary are $200,000, $120,000, and $80,000 respectively. These figures are illustrated in Exhibit 22-3. Assume that the exchange rate falls to 1£ = $1.80; that is, the pound is worth less. Notice that the dollar value of the subsidiary's net current position has fallen from $80,000 to $72,000, an $8,000 loss. Of course, if the exchange rate had gone the other way, say to 1£ = $2.20, then the firm would have gained instead of losing since the dollar value of its net investment in Britain would have risen instead of fallen.

Observe from Exhibit 22-3 that it is the net current position that determines the exposure to gains and losses. Recall from the earlier discussion that a given exchange rate change has an opposite effect on the dollar value of the foreign current assets and foreign current liabilities; therefore, if current assets equal current liabilities, the change in the dollar value of the current assets will be exactly offset by an opposite change in the dollar value of the current liabilities. But, if the subsidiary's current assets do not equal its current liabilities, there is a chance to incur dollar gains or losses due to exchange rate changes. If current assets exceed current liabilities, a net dollar gain will occur if the foreign currency rises in value (in which case assets rise in dollar value by more than liabilities rise in dollar value, thereby raising the net current position); a net dollar loss will occur if the foreign currency declines in value (in which case current assets fall in dollar value by more than the current liabilities decline in dollar value, thereby lowering the net current position). Using similar reasoning, if the subsidiary's current liabilities exceed its current

Exhibit 22-3. Impact of an Exchange Rate Change on the Dollar Balance Sheet of a British Subsidiary

	Before exchange rate change (1£ = $2)		After exchange rate change (1£ = $1.80)	
	In pounds	In dollars	In pounds	In dollars
Current assets	£100,000	$200,000	£100,000	$180,000
Current liabilities	60,000	120,000	60,000	108,000
Net current position	£ 40,000	$ 80,000	£ 40,000	$ 72,000

assets (negative net current position), then a rise in the value of the foreign currency will produce a dollar loss (will make the dollar level of the net current position a larger negative magnitude), and a fall in the value of the foreign currency will produce a dollar gain (will reduce the absolute magnitude of the negative net current position).

Asset management   Management of cash balances may in general be handled under the same principles as cash management by domestic firms, but there are some complications. An MNC may hold cash balances in a number of countries. If it has central control over management of cash balances, it may attempt to pool its cash, for the most part, in areas in which safety, liquidity, and yield are highest. Central money pools are usually held in countries which have major money market centers and strong currencies; funds may also be held in countries with low tax rates (tax havens). Obviously, there is an incentive to channel income into the subsidiaries located in tax havens. Exchange restrictions may make pooling impossible in some cases, and they provide one reason that MNCs may wish to deal with large multinational banks which can maintain complete and up-to-date information on worldwide exchange restrictions. Multinational banks can also provide same-day transfers of funds from one office to another, minimizing loss of interest from float time.

With respect to inventories, again the principles developed for domestic inventory management are applicable, with some qualifications. Inventory in transit is part of inventory, and for MNCs inventory may be shipped long distances. Thus it is not likely that MNCs can minimize inventory to the same extent that this is possible for national firms. Moreover, governments which encounter balance of payments difficulties often restrict imports, and MNCs may maintain higher than normal inventories in order to avoid being short of inventory in times of import restrictions.

Management of receivables depends in part on the world economic situation and the need for selling under cash or letter of credit (or cash *and* letter of credit) terms. With cash or letter of credit sales, receivables are minimized. However, competition for customers may force firms to sell on more generous credit terms, and receivables may increase. Since receivables are sometimes in foreign currencies, there may be an exchange rate risk.

Management of debt and equity   Roughly half of the funds used by foreign subsidiaries are provided by the normal internal sources—retained earnings and profits against which depreciation is charged. Since total internal sources of funds for United States domestic firms usually provide about two-thirds of total funds used, it appears that overseas subsidiaries

Managing a Multinational Company

use more external financing. The somewhat smaller share of retained earnings as a source of funds for subsidiaries may reflect the desire of United States parent companies to repatriate funds when possible, in view of the possibility of restrictions on outflows of funds from some countries.

Overseas firms may obtain funds from parent companies in the form of equity, loans, and supplying of inventory and other physical assets without payment within normal time periods. Loans from parent companies to subsidiaries are often more desired than equity investment—partly because foreign exchange controls imposed by governments are likely to make it easier to secure repayment of loans than return of equity. Supplying physical assets is convenient when a subsidiary is assembling products produced by the parent company. Funds are in effect supplied as long as payment by the subsidiary is delayed.

Short-term borrowing by a subsidiary is likely to be conducted in the country in which the subsidiary is operating—from multinational banks in some cases, and from local banks when knowledge of the business situation by the local banks is of advantage. Many United States firms have established finance subsidiaries in foreign countries to raise funds for their industrial subsidiaries. The finance subsidiaries may be based in tax haven countries or incorporated in a state such as Delaware with minimum corporate regulatory requirements.

Finance subsidiaries are likely to borrow in the Eurodollar and Eurobond markets. Eurodollar loans are usually made to prime borrowers, in relatively large amounts (generally $500,000 or more), and on an unsecured basis. Costs are reduced because risk is relatively low, cost per dollar is minimized on large loans, and collateral handling costs are eliminated. Eurodollar loans vary in maturity from one day to as much as fifteen years, although some financial difficulties encountered by banks in 1974 tended to cause them to shorten maturities. Large Eurocurrency loans may be syndicated, with many banks participating and the bank which syndicates the loan seeking participants, structuring the loan, and providing servicing of the loan as needed. The model for such loans is the United States domestic multibank floating rate term loan. The interest rate is stated as a spread above the London interbank offering rate (LIBO rate), with adjustment at predetermined intervals. The LIBO rate fluctuates widely, since the Eurodollar market is a market to which banks turn in time of need of funds.

When long-term funds are needed, borrowing in the Eurobond market may be involved. Bonds are issued, usually in strong currencies such as dollars or Deutsche marks, but sometimes in special currency units. Interest costs are usually lower than for other borrowing in European capital markets, but higher than in the United States. However, disclosure requirements of the Securities and Exchange Commission and costs of such disclosure, which would have to be met for borrowing in the United States, are avoided. It appears from some recent research that voluntary disclosure in the Eurobond market is attractive to investors, and favored by companies since it avoids some onerous requirements of the SEC. Thus when, in early 1974, the United States removed controls on foreign borrowing in the New York market, the Eurobond market diminished in size for a time; however, it revived significantly in 1975 for a record year.

Borrowing in the United States is a final alternative available to foreign subsidiaries, and this may be desirable if dollar funds are needed at a time when Eurodollar rates are very high.

It should be evident that the major difference between debt for domestic United States firms and debt for foreign subsidiaries is that the latter have many more possible sources of funds. Interest rates and marketing conditions vary between sources, and it may be a significant financial task to determine the most suitable sources.

Financial control   The international finance function is more complex than the finance function in domestic firms because of the factors discussed in the preceding sections. There are clearly advantages to centralizing financial control—taxes may be minimized by maximizing profits in certain countries, borrowing may be more advantageous in certain countries, and there are possibilities for eliminating duplication of financial activities. Forms of organization, however, depend heavily on historical factors and may not be as logical as might be desired. Many firms engaged in international activities are in transitional phases, and no form of organization may be precisely suited to their needs. The most that can be said at present is that at least some decisions are typically made at the corporate headquarters level—decisions concerning repatriation of funds, approval of intersubsidiary financing, hedging and currency swaps, and acquisition of funds, especially medium-term or long-term funds.

The Future of MNCs

Unless there is a radical change in economic trends, MNCs will increase their relative importance as a part of the world economy. But increased size will probably be achieved at the price of greater government scrutiny and regulation. Critics have demanded—with some success—that the power of the MNC be curtailed. This pressure has come from labor leaders, senators, economists, crusaders of various sorts, and even from the United Nations. A more vigorous enforcement of antitrust regulations and the appearance of new forms of regulation are likely. Particularly in less developed countries, governments have demanded control and eventual ownership of foreign firms operating within their borders. Only those firms with very limited fixed investment will escape this mounting encroachment, and even in those cases only partially. The rising crescendo of criticism is a natural outgrowth of the very rapid accession of the MNC to a central role in the international system. It seems probable that in most cases the new rules of the game for MNCs will strike a balance between governmental laissez faire and total state control. Failure to achieve such a balance would have regressive repercussions on world economic development.

SUMMARY   When a company conducts part of its business outside its own national boundaries, it faces a much more complicated environment. The financial manager must consider the consequences of a broader range of political and economic risks. One of the most important differences between domestic and international financial transactions is that the monetary units or currencies vary from country to country.

Exchange rates express the relationships between currencies of different countries. The spot rate is the rate on current exchanges of currencies, and the forward rate is the current rate on future exchanges. Differences between spot and forward rates reflect expectations of future changes in foreign exchange rates.

Changes in foreign exchange rates are caused by differences in inflation rates among countries, by differences in interest rates, and by governmental action. Businesses and individuals use the forward exchange market to protect themselves from possible losses due to changes in exchange rates.

The risks are greater in international trade than in domestic trade. Exporting firms are less apt to have reliable credit information about importers in other countries. Due to the long time it takes to ship goods from one country to another, either the importer or the exporter may be exposed to risks of exchange rate changes.

Special financing procedures have been developed to facilitate international trade. The most commonly used financing method is the letter of credit issued by a commercial bank.

Multinational companies—companies with direct investments in more than one country—have assumed enormous significance in recent years. Most major United States firms are multinational. United States companies have invested abroad to avoid trade restrictions and to use cheaper foreign labor and because United States firms have often enjoyed a competitive advantage from superior technical and managerial skills. These factors are becoming less important, and consequently the gap between new United States investment abroad and new foreign investment in the United States has diminished. Investment by foreign corporations in the United States greatly expanded during the 1960s and 1970s.

United States subsidiaries abroad enjoy a tax advantage under United States law since foreign earnings are not taxed until repatriated (paid to the United States parent). Furthermore, foreign income taxes paid are deducted from the United States taxes due (a tax credit).

Foreign investment often involves political risk and risk due to the possibility of exchange rate fluctuations. The financial manager of a multinational enterprise has special problems not encountered by a domestic firm manager. These problems include cash and inventory transfers between countries, use of special credit devices in trade (e.g., letters of credit), raising short- and long-term funds in different countries, and maintaining efficient control over foreign subsidiaries that may be subject to different governmental controls and that follow different commercial practices.

Although there has been sharp criticism of MNCs in recent years, MNCs will almost certainly continue to grow as the world economy expands and becomes more integrated. However, the growth will likely be accompanied by more stringent governmental regulations over MNC activities.

QUESTIONS

1. What risks are present or are greater in international business as compared to domestic business transactions?
2. What factors cause the exchange rate between two countries' currencies to change?
3. What is the difference between the spot rate and the ninety-day forward rate of exchange between two countries' currencies? Be specific and illustrate by means of an example (can be hypothetical).
4. Suppose you are planning to spend a semester at a German university. Six months from now, room, board, and tuition will cost 3,000 marks. What could you do to be sure in advance of the dollar cost of your expenses?
5. In an import letter of credit, what is being financed, who is borrowing the money, and who is lending the money?
6. Is there any exchange risk when imports are financed with a letter of credit? Why or why not?
7. What factors have motivated United States firms to invest abroad?
8. How do changes in exchange rates affect the income of multinational corporations?

PROJECTS

1. Identify a local firm which has some type of international transactions (imports or exports) and interview one of its executives. Find out how the firm handles its financing problem and deals with exchange risks.

2. Pick a large United States corporation and, using its annual report and articles in business periodicals, outline the extent of its international activities. What countries does it do business in, and how much business of what sort does it do there? What percentages of the corporation's sales and profits stem from its international operations? Are its international operations expanding faster or slower than its domestic operations?

3. Interview a local banker regarding the bank's engagement in international activities. What kinds of services does the bank provide for its business and individual customers in the international area? How active is the bank itself overseas?

PROBLEMS

1. Use the foreign exchange rates for December 1975 in Table 22-1 to calculate the amount of United States dollars the following currencies will exchange for.

a) 100 Deutsche marks	[Ans.: $38.10]	
b) 100 Rupees	[Ans.: $11.10]	
c) 100 Pesos	[Ans.: $8.00]	
d) 10,000 Lira		
e) 10,000 Yen		

2. Obtain a recent copy of the *Wall Street Journal* and calculate the currency exchanges of problem 1. How do these figures compare to those obtained in problem 1?

3. Use the exchange rates in Table 22-1 for December 1975 to calculate the following:
   a) How many Mexican pesos can be acquired for $8.00 U.S.? [Ans.: see *c* in table in problem 1]
   b) How many Italian lira can be acquired for $14.60 U.S.?
   c) How many Swiss francs can be acquired for $76.00 U.S.? [Ans.: 200 francs]
   d) How many British pounds can be acquired for $500 U.S.?

4. Use the exchange rates in Table 22-1 for December 1975 to calculate the following:
   a) How many Dutch guilders can be acquired with $100 U.S.?
   b) How many French francs can be acquired with $100 U.S.?
   c) How many French francs can be acquired with 268.8 Dutch guilders?
   d) How many British pounds can be acquired with $100 Canadian?

5. Suppose the *Wall Street Journal* reports the following exchange rates for country Aax whose currency is the zat:

Aax (zat)	1.0000
30-day futures	1.0050
90-day futures	1.0150
180-day futures	1.0250

a) Is the forward rate on the zat at a discount or premium relative to the dollar?

b) Suppose you executed a thirty-day futures contract to exchange 100,000 zat into U.S. dollars. How many dollars would you get thirty days from now? [Ans.: $100,500]

c) Suppose you executed a 180-day futures contract to exchange $100,000 U.S. into zat. How many zat would you get one-hundred eighty days from now?

6. Suppose that interest rates in East No-No are 20 percent per year whereas U.S. interest rates are 6 percent per year. You are considering investing $10,000 for 180 days (one-half year) in East No-No securities but are concerned about exchange rate risk. East No-No's currency is the wombat. You find the following quotations in the newspaper ($U.S.):

East No-No (wombat)	0.0500
30-day futures	0.0490
90-day futures	0.0485
180-day futures	0.0475

a) What is your net gain in dollars U.S. from investing in East No-No securities relative to U.S. securities assuming the exchange rate in 180 days equals today's spot rate. [Ans.: $700]

b) What is your net gain from an uncovered position if the spot rate does not change?

c) Suppose the wombat depreciates 8 percent relative to the dollar in the next 180 days. What is your net gain (or loss) from an uncovered position relative to a U.S. investment? [Ans.: $180 loss]

d) What is your net gain or loss from a covered position? [Ans.: $150]

e) What do you conclude from this analysis? Are there any other factors you should consider before your final decision?

7. McCormick Office Equipment, a United States firm, has a subsidiary in West Germany, Holzwurm Company, which has current assets of 100,000 Deutsche marks (DM) and current liabilities of 60,000 DM. The exchange rate is $1 = 2.5 DM (one dollar worth 2.5 Deutsche marks).

a) What is Holzwurm's net current position (current assets − current liabilities) in Deutsche marks and in dollars? (Ans.: 40,000 DM or $100,000)

b) What is Holzwurm's net current position in Deutsche marks and in dollars if the exchange rate is $1 = 2.0 DM; and what is the gain or loss in dollars due to an exchange rate change from $1 = 2.5 DM to $1 = 2.0 DM?

c) What is Holzwurm's net current position in Deutsche marks and in dollars if the exchange rate is $1 = 3.0 DM; and what is the gain or loss in dollars due to an exchange rate change from $1 = 2.5 DM to $1 = 3.0 DM?

8. Perform the calculations in problem 7 assuming that McCormick has current assets of 100,000 DM and current liabilities of 140,000 DM.

firm failure, reorganization, and liquidation

In each of the preceding chapters, we analyzed the financial affairs of an ongoing firm. That is, in each case, our decisions were based on a firm whose operations generated sufficient revenues to meet its debt obligations and to avoid default. In reality, however, this may not always be true. Some firms do suffer financial distress and must consequently follow certain specific courses of action. The financial manager must know how to act in times of distress, and, as a creditor, must know how to recognize signs of failure in other firms (to minimize the firm's risk in those investments).

We will begin the chapter by explaining what failure means. Then we will examine the historical trends and the most frequent causes of failure. The remainder of the chapter explores how the firm and its creditors deal with financial distress when it arises. Sometimes the firm survives under a voluntary arrangement between the company and its creditors or under a court-supervised reorganization plan. In other cases the company is dissolved, its assets liquidated, and the debt claims partially or wholly repaid.

The failure of a firm can be either economic or contractual.

A firm is an **economic failure** if it does not generate aftertax revenues sufficient to cover its costs of production and to yield a return on investment adequate to justify that investment in the enterprise. In short, the firm cannot be operated profitably. The best solution to economic failure is liquidation of the firm.

Contractual or financial failure occurs when the firm is unable to meet its contractual obligations to its creditors. Contractual failure can occur whether or not a firm is an economic failure. There are two types of contractual failure: illiquidity and insolvency.

Illiquidity occurs when the firm is unable to meet its maturing debt obligations and interest payments, even though the value of the firm's assets exceeds the firm's total liabilities. For example, a firm may be earning $2 million a year before interest and taxes and have assets worth $10 million and liabilities of $5 million. The liabilities may be maturing in the current period and the firm may be unable to pay because of its illiquid position. Clearly, the firm is not an economic failure, but it is in financial distress because of its temporary inability to meet its contractual debt obligations.

DEFINITION OF FAILURE

Insolvency occurs when the firm's total outstanding liabilities exceed the value of the firm. This implies that the firm is not currently able to meet debt commitments. The value of the firm is either the value of the firm's assets as a going enterprise or the value of the assets in liquidation—whichever is larger. Notice that even in this case the firm need not be an economic failure; that is, the productivity of the firm and its assets as a going enterprise may justify its continuation. The problem that exists is merely that the firm owes more than it is worth. In such a case, as we will see, the creditors may gain control and ownership of the company's assets. On the other hand, it may be that the insolvent firm is also an economic failure, in which case the firm will be liquidated and creditors paid off from the liquidation proceeds. These points are explored in detail later in the chapter.

A firm that is an economic failure may terminate and liquidate its assets even if it has not incurred contractual failure. Liquidation means the termination of the firm as a going enterprise and the sale of the assets for the price that they will bring in the market. As long as the firm's value as an ongoing enterprise is less than its value in liquidation, liquidation is justified. Firms in this condition are often referred to as ''being worth more dead than alive.'' For example, a firm may have no debt obligations and be earning $10,000 a year. However, if the liquidating value of its assets were $500,000, the firm would only be earning 2 percent on its capital ($10,000/$500,000 = 2 percent). The firm should liquidate in this case. A firm may also be incurring a loss. If no end to this condition were anticipated, liquidation would clearly be justified. In short, if a firm is an economic failure though not a financial failure, it should be liquidated.

In the remainder of this chapter we will look at firms suffering from contractual failure and perhaps from economic failure. If contractual failure is accompanied by economic failure, the firm will be forced to liquidate by its creditors. If the contractual failure is not accompanied by economic failure, the firm will continue in existence either under a voluntary adjustment or under a reorganization.

A consequence of contractual failure is **bankruptcy.** Bankruptcy is a condition or state in which the firm is unable to pay its debts (is experiencing financial failure) and its assets are surrendered to the court for administration. ''Strict'' bankruptcy involves the liquidation of the firm's assets with the proceeds being used to pay creditors and with any amount left over going to the firm's stockholders. Bankruptcy proceedings, however, may not result in strict bankruptcy and liquidation but may provide for an arrangement or a reorganization under which the firm continues to operate. Bankruptcy proceedings may even be completely avoided if financial distress is remedied before failure occurs. The voluntary remedies used to prevent bankruptcy are discussed below. Then, the bankruptcy process under the National Bankruptcy Act is examined.

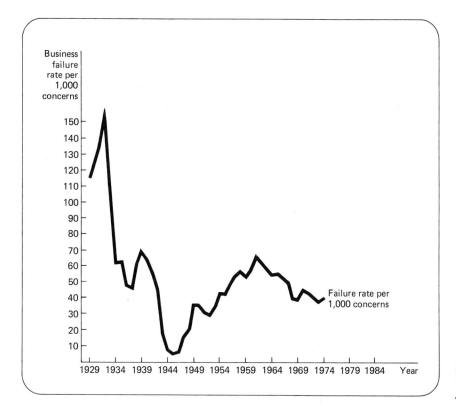

Figure 23-1. Historical business failure rate per 1,000 concerns.

How significant is business failure and what are its causes? Figure 23-1 shows the failure rate of business firms since 1929. Research by Dun and Bradstreet and by others indicates that failure is particularly common among new firms—those that have been in existence less than five years.[1] Furthermore, as might be expected, the failure rate is lower for larger firms and is lower in times of prosperity than during periods of recession and depression. The most important single cause of business failure has historically been the inability of the company to effectively promote the product and generate sufficient sales. Difficulties in collecting on receivables and in controlling operating expenses have also been frequent causes of failure.

FREQUENCY AND CAUSES OF FAILURE

1. Under Dun and Bradstreet's definition of failure, business failures include firms that ceased operations following assignment or bankruptcy; ceased with a loss to creditors after such actions as execution, foreclosure, or attachment; voluntaily withdrew leaving unpaid obligations; were involved in court actions such as receivership, reorganization, or arrangement; or voluntarily compromised with creditors.

VOLUNTARY REMEDIES FOR FINANCIAL DISTRESS

If a firm is unable to meet its commitments to creditors, an agreement to avert bankruptcy may be reached between the firm's creditors and owners. The eventual agreement may take one of several forms, depending upon the circumstances, but it usually results in a continuation of the firm as a going enterprise under existing ownership. In some cases, however, the firm may be terminated if its liquidation value exceeds its value as a going concern. In the discussion of voluntary remedies in this section, we will consider adjustments which allow the firm to survive.

It is important to stress that these agreements are *voluntary*—no court or trustee supervises the settlement. Any creditor who refuses to take part in the agreement may press a claim, blocking the agreement for all creditors. However, this may result in more financial detriment to the creditor than would cooperating in seeking a solution which a majority of the creditors feel will maximize the likelihood of their realizing on their claims. Often small claims—those under $50 or $100—are fully paid, with the creditors having the larger claims remaining as parties to the voluntary agreement. Those creditors participating in the accord with the firm will usually appoint a committee among themselves to handle dealings with the debtor firm. Voluntary solutions to the financial distress of the firm include extension, composition, and temporary assumption of firm control by creditors.

Extension

In an **extension** the creditors agree to *postpone* payments on the debt for a given period in order to mitigate the debtor firm's current difficulties. The extension agreement may specify other measures to strengthen the firm's ability to make future payments, e.g., a discontinuation of dividends to stockholders. To get the creditors to agree to the extension, the firm's owners may have to provide security, such as mortgages on the firm's assets or the personal property of the company's owners (for example, stocks or bonds of another company).

Composition

Under a **composition,** creditors agree *to receive less* than the amount originally owed to them, e.g., 50 cents for every dollar of debt. Part of the settlement may be in promissory notes. Creditors may agree to a composition because they feel that the only other alternative is to force the firm into bankruptcy and liquidation, with the possible result that they would receive even less than under the composition.

Creditor Management of the Firm

If it is felt that existing management is incapable of effectively running the business, an agreement may be reached under which a creditors' committee representing the creditor group assumes temporary control of the firm. The hope is that even if basic problems are not solved, the committee will be able to ameliorate the situation sufficiently for the debts to be retired, after which old management can resume control.

ARRANGEMENTS AND REORGANIZATIONS

The United States Congress has the power to establish laws regulating firms in financial distress. Under the National Bankruptcy Act of 1938, a court-supervised adjustment may be made which provides for survival of the firm but only after significant changes are effected in the firm's capital structure.[2] Liquidation under bankruptcy is also within the purview of the Bankruptcy Act and will be considered later in discussing liquidation.

Arrangement

Chapter XI of the National Bankruptcy Act provides for financial adjustments that are similar to extensions and compositions. An adjustment under Chapter XI is commonly referred to as an **arrangement.** A debtor may petition the court for acceptance of an arrangement under which the firm will eliminate its debts by making only partial or delayed payments to creditors. If the court finds the arrangement equitable, fair, and feasible, and if it is favored by a majority of creditors (in number and in dollars of claim), the plan is implemented. In contrast to a voluntary agreement under which no creditor is forced to comply with the adjustment, all creditors are bound by the terms of the arrangement. Chapter XI of the Bankruptcy Act applies only to unsecured debts; secured debts are unaffected and they must be payed off as originally specified in the loan contract. The court may appoint a receiver to assume control of the firm or may allow existing management to remain. The arrangement may involve the postponement or scaling down of claims (composition) or the issuance of new securities in exchange for the old debt claims. Chapter XI petitions have been filed by firms of varying size and in a variety of industries. Examples in recent years include U.S. Financial, Inc., a large real estate development firm; Autek, Inc., a conglomerate; and Cartridge Television, Inc., a manufacturer of video-tape players.

An arrangement has the advantage of preventing minor creditors from blocking a reasonable plan. The court may appoint an independent trustee or receiver to manage the company. However, the arrangement often allows the old management to continue in control and to establish lines of

2. Chapters X and XI of the National Bankruptcy Act are those of particular relevance here. Chapters I through VII of the act relate to personal bankruptcies, Chapter VIII covers agricultural settlements, and Chapter IX deals with local government readjustments. Chapters XII, XIII, and XIV deal with mortgage readjustments on real property, wage earners' plans, and Maritime Commission liens, respectively. Railroad reorganizations are covered by Section 77 of the Bankruptcy Act and by the Mahaffe Act of 1948; the Interstate Commerce Commission plays an important role in that it approves the trustee, holds hearings, and approves or disapproves the reorganization plan.

credit with new lenders. The legal and administrative expenses are also low due to the relatively simple procedures involved in an arrangement action.

Reorganization Under Chapter X of the National Bankruptcy Act, if a firm is insolvent or incapable of paying its debts as they come due, the corporation itself or three or more of its creditors (with claims aggregating to at least $5,000) may file a petition for reorganization. Chapter X applies to all publicly held corporations, except railroads, and to firms with secured or unsecured creditors. The Bankruptcy Act directs the court to accept the plan of reorganization if it is fair, equitable, and feasible. The plan is fair and equitable if creditors are to be justly and reasonably treated in realizing claims against the firm; e.g., senior claims must be paid before junior claims are met. The plan is feasible if the new payments promised to creditors under the reorganization plan have a high likelihood of being made. The Equity Funding Life Insurance Company and the Four Seasons Nursing Center of America are prominent examples of Chapter X bankruptcies.

A reorganization plan provides for the issuance of new securities to the firm's creditors in order to reduce the firm's fixed debt charge burden. Often, the firm's assets are only sufficient to cover some of the debt claims, in which case the equity claims of stockholders and the claims of some or all unsecured creditors may be completely eliminated, i.e., entirely unpaid and dissolved. New securities are issued to those retaining a position in the firm. These securities may be bonds, preferred stock, or common stock, a guiding principle being that the fixed charges on new claims be sufficiently small that they will be covered by the firm's earnings.

The reorganization procedure After the corporation or its creditors file a petition in court requesting the corporation's reorganization, if the court approves the petition, the court will appoint an impartial trustee who is responsible for preparing the plan of reorganization and then presenting it to the court. The trustee also has responsibility for supervising the firm until the reorganization plan is approved and goes into effect. If the plan is approved by the court, it is submitted to a vote of the firm's creditors and stockholders. If two-thirds of each class of creditor and two-thirds of each class of stock favor the reorganization plan, it becomes binding on all parties whether or not they have supported the plan. If the liabilities of the firm exceed $3 million, the plan must be submitted to the Securities and Exchange Commission, which evaluates the fairness and feasibility of the proposed reorganization. The SEC's role is entirely advisory, but its recommendations are weighed heavily by the court in making its decision.

Once the plan becomes effective, the trustee is discharged and the old management or a newly appointed management assumes supervision of the firm.

Decision to reorganize or liquidate In evaluating the reorganization plan, the court, the security holders, and the SEC must decide whether the firm's going concern value after reorganization will exceed its liquidation value. If liquidation value is greater, then the SEC will recommend liquidation. Reorganization is justified only if the firm is not an irreversible economic failure. If, even after a reorganization, it is likely to be an economic failure, the firm should be liquidated and not reorganized.

To estimate the going concern value, future revenues, costs, and earnings must be forecasted, using available information regarding expected sales, labor and material input costs, and any other factors relating to the firm's operations. Of course, as with any forecast, only rough estimates are possible. The choice between reorganization and liquidation will vary from situation to situation. For example, if the firm were a chain of retail clothing stores which had overexpanded into unprofitable geographical regions, liquidation value of the land and buildings might be very high but the business itself would be an economic failure. Even better management could not generate the sales needed to make the firm profitable. Therefore, liquidation would be preferable to an attempt to reorganize in this case. On the other hand, the firm might be a poorly managed manufacturing firm with good markets for its products and owning specialized equipment with little liquidation value. Reorganization under these circumstances might be more reasonable than liquidation; i.e., the firm might have the potential for being an economic success if property managed whereas the liquidation value of its assets is minimal.

Reorganization and the rule of absolute priority Under reorganization, new securities are issued to some or all of the firm's creditors and perhaps to its preferred and common stockholders, depending upon the value of the firm upon reorganization. The rule of absolute priority, which applies in reorganization procedure, forces the firm to honor senior claims in full before junior claims receive anything. To illustrate the rule of priority in settling the firm's claims, assume that the firm's balance sheet as of the end of the period preceding the petition for reorganization was as shown in Exhibit 23-1. Remember that balance sheet asset figures are at book value ($18 million) and not at liquidation value. Assume that the estimated liquidation value of the firm's assets is $4 million but its going concern value is estimated to be $6 million. The estimated value of the securities to be issued under the new capital structure created under reorganization is $6 million. The total liabilities of $8 million exceed the new value of the

Exhibit 23-1. Balance Sheet

Assets	$18,000,000
Liabilities	
Notes payable	3,000,000
Subordinated debentures[a]	4,000,000
General unsecured creditors	1,000,000
Stockholders' equity	10,000,000

[a] Subordinated to the notes payable. The general unsecured creditors are not affected by the subordination.

firm, and consequently the old stockholders receive nothing under the reorganization. The stockholders' equity interest in the firm has been eliminated because the firm is insolvent (assets of $6 million are less than liabilities of $8 million). Assume that the $6 million in new securities to be issued will be in the form of $2 million in 6 percent bonds, $1 million in $6\frac{1}{2}$ percent subordinated debentures, $1 million in 7 percent preferred stock, and $2 million in common stock. Values of the claims of each creditor and the distribution of the new securities to those creditors are shown in Exhibit 23-2. The holders of the notes receive $3 million in new bonds and new subordinated debentures in satisfaction of their original $3 million claim. The subordinated debenture holders receive new preferred stock and new common stock worth a total of $2,250,000, and the general unsecured creditors receive $750,000 in common stock. Thus, only the note holders receive new securities with a value equal to the original claim against the firm. This is because the notes are repaid before the subordinated debenture holders receive anything.[3]

LIQUIDATION   If the creditors estimate that the going concern value of the firm is less than its liquidation value, they will seek to liquidate the firm's assets and distribute the proceeds among the creditors. There are two procedures that can be used to effect the liquidation: assignment and bankruptcy. Following either of these steps, the proceeds from the liquidation are distributed among the firm's creditors. The remainder of the chapter will explore these topics in more detail.

3. The distribution of securities parallels the distribution of cash under liquidation described in Chap. 19 pp. 640–642, and described in the section below on liquidation.

Exhibit 23-2. Old Claims and New Claims under Reorganization

Old security	Old claim	New claim with reorganization[a]
Notes	$3,000,000	$3,000,000
Subordinated debentures	4,000,000	2,250,000
General unsecured debt claims	1,000,000	750,000

Distribution of new securities
under new claim with reorganization

Old security	Received under reorganization
Notes	$2,000,000 in 6% bonds
	$1,000,000 in $6\frac{1}{2}$% subordinated debentures
Subordinated debentures	$1,000,000 in 7% preferred stock
	$1,250,000 in common stock
General unsecured debt claims	$750,000 in common stock

[a] Recall from Chap. 20 that because the debentures are subordinated only to the notes, the general unsecured creditors are unaffected by the subordination and therefore receive what they would if no subordination agreement existed (per dollar owed this equals the amount contractually owed divided by the dollars available for the debt repayment). Since the securities distributed have a value of $6 million but creditor claims equal $8 million, general unsecured creditors receive 75 percent ($6,000,000/$8,000,000) of their claim, i.e., $750,000 in securities (0.75 × $1,000,000). The remaining $5,250,000 in securities is divided between the notes and subordinated debenture holders; however, since the notes are senior to the debentures under the subordination, they are paid in full (securities worth $3 million) and the remaining $2,250,000 in securities goes to the debenture holders.

Liquidation under Assignment

Under an assignment, the firm and its creditors privately settle the firm's debt. The courts are not involved. A trustee is generally appointed by the creditors to supervise the orderly liquidation of the firm's assets and the distribution of the proceeds. Not infrequently the trustee is the adjustment bureau of a local or national creditors association.

All creditors must consent to the settlement, since any one of them is free to block it and place the firm in bankruptcy through court action. As noted below, the absolute priority rule is applied under a bankruptcy liquidation; i.e., senior claims are fully paid before junior claims are met at all. Therefore, for senior claimants to agree to an assignment they will demand priority treatment. If they are not accorded priority, they will move to throw the firm into bankruptcy. Consequently, the settlement under assignment will generally conform to the absolute priority rule. Since the firm is dissolved under liquidation, creditors receive cash in settlement of their claims in contrast to the new securities received under reorganization. The specific priority ranking of the various claimants will be covered below in examining liquidation under bankruptcy.

Generally, liquidation under an assignment is less costly than under bankruptcy in terms of both legal and accounting expenses and time involved. Furthermore, the creditors have the opportunity to select a trustee who may be more effective than a court-appointed trustee in selling the firm's assets because of greater familiarity with the firm's line of business or greater legal flexibility in handling the sale. However, bankruptcy action may be preferred by one or more creditors. Some creditors may not agree to the proposed distribution of proceeds under the assignment or may feel for other reasons that their rights would be better protected by court supervision of the liquidation. Furthermore, a creditor may prefer to pursue bankruptcy proceedings than to privately seek unanimity of agreement by a large number of creditors under an assignment.

Liquidation under Bankruptcy

Conditions necessary for bankruptcy   Under Chapter X of the National Bankruptcy Act a firm may voluntarily file a petition of bankruptcy. Management may feel that shareholders will be more equitably treated if bankruptcy is initiated voluntarily than if the company's condition deteriorates further and creditors initiate bankruptcy proceedings. An involuntary petition of bankruptcy may be filed by the creditors if the three following conditions are met:

1. If there are twelve or more creditors, at least three with claims totaling $500 or more must join in filing the bankruptcy petition; if there are less than twelve creditors, then only one need file if his or her claim is $500 or more.
2. The firm's debts must total at least $1,000.
3. The debtor has committed an act of bankruptcy within four months of the filing of the petition.

The Bankruptcy Act defines six acts of bankruptcy, one of which is the debtor's admission in writing of an inability to pay debts and a willingness to be adjudged bankrupt. A second and similar act of bankruptcy occurs if the debtor effectively reveals an incapability to pay by having a receiver or trustee take charge of the property while the debtor is insolvent. The remaining acts of bankruptcy relate to the concealment or improper transfer of assets so as to make them unavailable to some or all of the debtor's creditors.

Bankruptcy procedure and distribution of liquidation proceeds   Once the firm is legally deemed bankrupt, the liquidation takes place. (The procedure is the same whether the firm itself voluntarily files for bankruptcy or an involuntary bankruptcy petition is filed by the creditors.) The federal court appoints a referee who then arranges for a meeting of the creditors. At the meeting, claims are proved and a trustee is elected by the creditors. The trustee's responsibility is to liquidate the firm's assets in an orderly manner and to distribute the proceeds to the claimants. Upon completion of the payment to the creditors, the trustee prepares an accounting which is presented to the creditors and to the referee. If no objections arise, the bankrupt firm is discharged and thereby released from any further responsibility for the debts.

Under the rule of absolute priority provided by Chapter X of the National Bankruptcy Act, the distribution of the proceeds from liquidation must conform to the following priority of claims (highest priority first):

1. Expenses associated with preserving, supervising, and liquidating the bankrupt's estate
2. Wages and commissions up to $600 per claimant due to employees of the bankrupt firm and earned within three months prior to the filing of the bankruptcy petition
3. Reasonable expenses of creditors in preventing their unfair treatment by the bankrupt
4. Federal, state, and local taxes that are due
5. Secured and unsecured creditor claims in order of priority
6. Payment of dividends to preferred stockholders
7. Payment of dividends to common stockholders

Item 5 needs some clarification. Secured creditors have first right to that property which was used to secure their claim; to the extent that such property is insufficient to cover the amount owed to them, the secured creditors join the the unsecured creditors in dividing the remaining liquidation proceeds. If the proceeds from the sale of the security property more than meet the secured claims, the remaining funds are used to pay unsecured creditors. If proceeds from sale satisfy creditor claims, then the remaining amount is payable to stockholders.

To illustrate the distribution under the rule of absolute priority, assume that Falling Timber Paper Products, Inc., is to be liquidated. Assume that the liquidation value of the assets is equal to $5.4 million, but that the firm's going concern value under reorganization would be only $1 million. Therefore, liquidation is justified. Also, let the $3 million in notes be secured by a mortgage on the Falling Timber production plant which is sold by the trustee for $2 million. Finally, a total of $400,000 is spent to cover the costs in items 1 through 4 in the list, including those associated with the trustee's expenses in liquidating the estate, wages and commissions to employees, any creditor expenses, and taxes. Therefore, the proceeds available for distribution to creditors and stockholders are $5 million ($5.4 million in proceeds less $400,000 in expenses). The distribution is shown in Exhibit 23-3.

Exhibit 23-3. Distribution of Proceeds Under Liquidation of Falling Timber Paper Products, Inc.

Type of claim	Old claim	Received under the liquidation
Notes (secured by mortgage)	$ 3,000,000	$3,000,000
Subordinated debentures	4,000,000	1,500,000
General unsecured		
debt claims	1,000,000	500,000
Common stockholders	10,000,000	0
Total	$18,000,000	$5,000,000
Computation of the distribution		
Liquidation proceeds available for		
distribution		$5,000,000
Amount paid to secured note holders		
on sale of mortaged property		2,000,000
Available to note and debenture		
holders and general unsecured		
creditors		$3,000,000
Total claims remaining		
($8,000,000 less payment of		
$2,000,000 on secured notes)		$6,000,000
Distribution of remaining $3,000,000 to cover		
total remaining claims of $6,000,000:		

Type of claim	Claim remaining	Claim on liquidation proceeds without subordination	Claim on liquidation proceeds with subordination
Notes	$1,000,000	$ 500,000	$1,000,000
Subordinated debentures	4,000,000	2,000,000	1,500,000
General unsecured creditor claim	1,000,000	500,000	500,000

The funds available for settlement of all claims are $5 million. This amount is less than the debt of $8 million. Therefore, none of the proceeds is paid to the residual common shares, since all creditors must be reimbursed before stockholders receive anything. The mortgage notes have first claim to the $2 million received from sale of the plant representing security on those notes. This leaves $3 million (of the $5 million) for distribution to cover the $6 million of remaining debt ($1 million still owed on the notes, $4 million owed on the subordinated debentures, and $1 million owed to general unsecured creditors). If the debentures were not subordinated to the notes, the $3 million would be distributed by percentage of amount owed to total debt remaining in meeting the remaining $6 million of claims. In this case, each creditor would receive 50 cents for each dollar owed. This is shown in the second column at the bottom of Exhibit 23-3. With subordination, a different distribution occurs. The general unsecured creditors are unaffected by the subordination of the debentures to the notes, and they consequently receive the same amount as they would if there were no subordination, that amount being $500,000. This leaves $2,500,000 for distribution to the notes and subordinated debentures. The notes are fully repaid before the subordinated debentures receive anything. Therefore, $1 million is paid to the note holders and the remaining $1.5 million goes in payment to holders of the subordinated debentures.

Although this example is relatively simple, it illustrates the way proceeds from liquidation are distributed under Chapter X. In all cases, however complicated, the underlying guideline is the rule of absolute priority. Superior claims are paid in full before junior claims receive anything. This procedure is followed regardless of the complexity of the firm's capital structure.

SUMMARY

Failure of a corporation is economic if the company fails to earn a reasonable return on its investments. Failure is contractual or financial if the firm cannot currently meet its commitments to creditors or will default on such commitments in the future because the firm's assets are less than its liabilities (insolvency). A company that is an incurable economic failure (whether or not it is a financial failure) should go out of business and liquidate its assets, since it cannot earn a reasonable return on investment. With contractual failure but no economic failure, the firm will have to make some adjustment in order to satisfy unpaid creditors. This adjustment may involve only postponement of payment on the debt or may require the extreme remedy of a corporate reorganization.

Business failures are more frequent in periods of tight money, recession, and stock market decline. The major causes of failure are general incompetence and lack of experience in management or in the company's particular business line.

Some private agreements between the firm and its creditors to avert bankruptcy are extensions, compositions, or temporary assumption of managerial control of the firm by creditors. Under an extension, creditors accept a postponement of their payments, whereas under a composition the creditors accept only partial payment in satisfaction of the debt.

Adjustments which permit the company to continue in existence may also be effected through court action under Chapters X and XI of the National Bankruptcy Act. Under Chapter XI, firms can petition the court to approve a plan (an arrangement) that provides for settlement of the company's debts. Chapter X of the act covers all public corporations, except railroads, and specifies the steps required for a reorganization. Under reorganization, the old securities of the corporation are retired and new securities are issued to those people with claims against the company. Creditors with senior claims receive securities with a value covering the amount owed to them before junior claimants receive anything (rule of priority). The reorganization may be initiated through court petition by the creditors or by the firm itself. After the court approves the petition, a trustee is appointed to draw up the reorganization plan and to supervise the company's assets until the plan goes into effect. If two-thirds of the creditors and stockholders favor the plan, it becomes effective, in which case the trustee is dismissed and the old management or a new management takes over company operations.

If a company is an economic failure, it will be liquidated. Liquidation may proceed under a private settlement between the company and its creditors or with court supervision under Chapter X of the National Bankruptcy Act. In either case, a general guide in distributing liquidation proceeds is the rule of absolute priority, under which senior claimants are fully paid before junior claimants receive anything.

QUESTIONS

1. Distinguish between economic failure and financial failure.
2. There are two types of financial failure. What are they? In what way or ways are they related?
3. Under what conditions should a firm be liquidated?
4. Describe the general nature of voluntary remedies for financial distress.
5. Distinguish among the three basic types of voluntary remedies of financial distress: extension, composition, and temporary assumption of control of the firm by creditors.
6. What rationale can you give for creditors accepting less than the face value of their claim when a firm is financially distressed?
7. Describe the nature of an arrangement.

8. Reorganization plans must be fair, equitable, and feasible. What is meant by this?
9. On what basis is a decision to reorganize or liquidate a bankrupt firm made?
10. What is the absolute priority of claims rule as it is used in reorganizations and liquidations?

Talk with a lawyer who specializes in bankruptcy cases and inquire about the significance of legal costs, accounting fees, and so on, that are involved in bankruptcy. Ask about the importance of business disruptions caused by creditor (or trustee) takeover if the bankrupt firm is not liquidated but is continued by the creditors as a going enterprise.   **PROJECT**

1. The book value of the assets of Belly-Up Corporation is shown below. The notes are subordinated to the bank loans. The going concern value of Belly-Up is $2 million.   **PROBLEMS**

Belly-Up Corporation balance sheet

Assets		$10,000,000
Liabilities		
Bank loans	$2,000,000	
Subordinated notes	1,000,000	
General creditors	3,000,000	
Total liabilities		$ 6,000,000
Stockholders' equity		$ 4,000,000

    Using the rule of absolute priority, what will each type of creditor and stockholder receive under each of the following assumptions:
a) The firm's assets are liquidated for $6 million.
b) The firm's assets are liquidated for $5 million.
c) The firm's assets are liquidated for $3 million.

2. The book value of the Bad Bag Company's assets is shown below. It is estimated that the liquidation value of the assets is $6 million. Assume a going concern value of $8 million. Also assume the bonds are subordinated to all other liabilities. Bad Bag has defaulted on its debt and is in bankruptcy.

Bad Bag Company balance sheet

Assets		$20,000,000
Liabilities		
General creditors	$7,000,000	
Notes payable	3,000,000	
Subordinated bonds	8,000,000	
Total liabilities		$18,000,000
Stockholders' equity		$ 2,000,000

Using the rule of absolute priority, determine how much the stockholders and each of the creditors will receive.

3. The judge in the reorganization case of Stumble-Tumble Company has determined that the reorganization is fair and equitable. However, he has asked you whether the plan seems feasible. Using the data below of the reorganized company, how would you answer him? Assume the company is expected to have a minimum net income before taxes and interest of $700,000 a year in the foreseeable future.

Security issued under the reorganization	Market value of security
Bank loans, 10%	$ 750,000
Subordinated debt, 8%	$ 500,000
Common stock	$2,500,000

4. The liquidation value of Flop, Inc., is $5.5 million, whereas its going concern value is $1 million. The company voluntarily decided to liquidate. The company has a $3 million mortgage on assets which are sold for $2 million. These assets represent collateral for the firm's mortgage bonds. The cost of the trustee selected to see to the orderly liquidation of the assets is $300,000, and unpaid corporate taxes total $200,000. The list of creditor and stockholder claimants is set forth below. State how much each is entitled to receive in liquidation. Assume the subordinated debentures are subordinated to the mortgage bonds.

Claimant	Balance sheet value of claim
Mortgage bonds	$3,000,000
Subordinated debentures	3,000,000
General creditors	2,000,000
Preferred stockholders	1,000,000
Common stockholders	5,000,000

5. A business fails and is forced to liquidate. Its balance sheet prior to liquidation is as follows:

Cash (deposit)	$ 5,000	Bank loan	$25,000
Inventories	20,000	Accounts payable	25,000
Receivables	10,000	Preferred stock	10,000
Other assets	55,000	Common stock	20,000
	$90,000	Surplus	10,000
			$90,000

The bank loan is secured by the firm's inventories. The following are the liquidating values of the assets:

Cash	$ 5,000
Inventories	8,000
Receivables	8,000
Other assets	19,000
Total	$40,000

a) What are the amounts allocated to each claimant upon liquidation?

b) What would the bank have received if it did not have the lien on inventories.

The Penn Central Debacle

On August 8, 1969, the widely read and highly respected *Commercial and Financial Chronicle* carried a strong recommendation of Penn Central common stock for the long-term investor. Nine months later, on June 21, 1970, Penn Central filed for bankruptcy. A few weeks earlier, the firm's bank creditors had forced the resignation of Penn Central's top officials. The circumstances that led to the railroad's collapse can be summarized in a few words: Penn Central was a marginally surviving enterprise transformed into a disastrous loser by misfortune and gross mismanagement. The tale is an interesting one with a moral or two.

MERGER—A "SOLUTION" TO ALL PROBLEMS

For several years preceding their merger on February 1, 1968, the Pennsylvania Railroad and the New York Central Railroad (NYC) had their own separate problems. When Alfred Perlman took over the NYC in 1956, it was on the verge of folding, and it took a massive reshaping of operations to stave off bankruptcy. As early as 1957, merger between the NYC and the Pennsylvania had been seriously proposed as a solution. Perlman decided instead to try to combine with the Baltimore and Ohio (B&O) and the Chesapeake and Ohio (C&O) railroads. After the latter two lines merged without the New York Central, Perlman turned once again to the Pennsylvania Railroad. This eventually led to merger.

Although it had its troubles, the Pennsylvania Railroad was larger and more successful than the New York Central. The Pennsylvania carried large volumes of bulk commodities with narrow profit margins, whereas the NYC shipped expensive merchandise in low volumes, but with a high per unit profit margin. As we will see, these fundamental differences accounted for many of the postmerger difficulties.

The objective of the 1968 merger was to increase overall efficiency by integrating the two companies. The goal was to eliminate duplication and provide an interflow of ideas, operating strategies, and problem-solving techniques. Economies were to be achieved by improving routes, consolidating facilities, and making changes in physical plant. The figures in the table below, which were presented at the premerger Interstate Commerce Commission hearings, show the savings the railroads hoped to achieve during the first eight years after merger. It was anticipated that over $80 million would be saved in the eighth year. The optimism reflected in the figures no doubt eased ICC approval of the combination.

Year	Savings	Net savings
1	$ 6.7	$ 3.4
2	26.6	14.0
3	51.3	33.7
4	67.2	43.4
5	81.6	68.8
6	81.6	74.1
7	81.6	77.9
8	81.6	78.4
9	81.6	81.1

Note: The difference between the two savings figures represents costs of joint facilities and employee protection agreements.

PREMARITAL ROADBLOCKS

Problems began even before the merger took place. Planning of the combination was hampered by a failure to clearly assign responsibility to the parties involved. In the premerger planning phase, only two officers were identified as part of the postmerger management team—Pennsylvania's chairman Stuart T. Saunders, to be Penn Central's chairman and chief executive officer, and New York Central's Alfred J. Perlman, to be Penn Central's president and chief operating officer. This left the postmerger lines of authority unclear and gave no effective leadership role to anyone in preparing for the merger. Much of the planning was consequently left undone.

Although the original application for the merger was filed with the Interstate Commerce Commission in 1962, final permission was not granted by the ICC until 1966. During the interim of four years, both railroads had deteriorated, and many of the contemplated advantages of merger were lost. The ICC further added to Penn Central's difficulties by forcing the company to absorb and continue to operate the bankrupt New Haven Railroad. Aggravating the problem was an additional two-year delay due to suits by the B&O/C&O and by the Norfolk and Western claiming that the Penn Central combination would create unfair competition. A ruling by the Supreme Court cleared the way for the merger, which finally took place on February 1, 1968. The Pennsylvania Railroad and New York Central Railroad formally combined into the Pennsylvania New York Central Railroad, later to be known as the Penn Central Transportation Company. The Penn Central Transportation Company would become the major subsidiary of the holding company, the Penn Central Company.

BAD BLOOD, CONSTIPATION, AND OTHER POSTMERGER ILLS

Once the merger was consummated, forces intervened which prevented the union from being a success. Old rivalries between New York Central and Pennsylvania employees survived the merger, resulting in personality conflicts and competition rather than the severely needed cooperation. This led to the departure of several executives. Disputes arose between workers over differences in NYC and Pennsylvania procedures. Heated words were even exchanged in trying to decide whether to call the last car on the train a "caboose" (NYC's old name) or a "cabin car" (Pennsylvania's old name).

Also contributing to Penn Central's problems was the 1964 Merger Protective Agreement between the two railroads and the unions. This pact involved major concessions to union employees which significantly reduced the benefits of eliminating duplications and other inefficiencies.

The central cause of Penn Central's eventual demise was its failure to achieve the operating improvements that were the main purpose for uniting in the first place. There were several reasons for this. The sharp differences in operating modes of the two railroads made consolidation difficult. Compounding the problem were general economic recession, inflationary pressures on costs, and bad weather. But the blame cannot be placed solely on dissimilarities of the companies and bad luck; mismanagement played a major role. The integration of the railroads was haphazard and disorganized. Personnel were inadequately trained to deal with new procedures. Incompatible communication and computer systems created delays and train tieups. Employees struggled with a complicated routing system, with railway cars frequently ending up at the wrong destination. Service deteriorated, but customer complaints were ignored or lost in a maze of red tape. Penn Central lost many customers to other carriers, resulting in a further deterioration of the firm's already weak financial condition. During the period from 1967 to the first quarter of 1970, costs rapidly outran revenues, producing large net losses. To quote the president of another large railroad, "Penn Central's illness has been diagnosed as a massive case of constipation. You can feed a lot of cars into their system but nothing ever seems to come out."

DOWNHILL RIDER

Penn Central's capacity to borrow was always somewhat limited because of its heavy debt burden (see figures below for 1967, 1968, and 1969). Cash revenues from operations were inadequate to cover cash outlays for operations and interest on debt. To secure the needed capital, Penn Central had the options of selling additional shares of stock, selling some of its physical assets, liquidating its stock holdings in several of its subsidiaries, or borrowing. It chose the last alternative, with much of the debt issued on a short-term basis. Short-term borrowing was a risky choice, since new funds would soon have to be raised to

repay the maturing short-term obligations. If there were bad news about the company, new borrowing would become very expensive or even impossible. Indeed, this is exactly what happened.

Penn Central's cash drain was principally due to losses on its railroad operations. Adding to the drain was the interest expense on both long- and short-term debt (commercial paper and bank loans). With rising interest rates during the period, short-term borrowing costs mounted. Cash also drained into real estate and other diversification projects. The subsidiaries in which Penn Central was investing were borrowing money themselves, thereby drying up credit lines that might otherwise have been used by Penn Central. The firm exacerbated the cash shortage by maintaining dividends which totaled $55,400,000 in 1968 and $43,396,000 in 1969. The purpose of the dividends was to cultivate optimism about the company, thereby making it easier to borrow. This bluff worked for only a short while.

During the period from February 1968 to June 1970 the cash needs in excess of revenues from operations totaled over $700 million. This was covered by obtaining bank loans and issuing commercial paper and mortgage bonds. By mid-1969, Penn Central was approaching its borrowing limit. Goldman Sachs, which had marketed Penn Central's commer-

	1967	1968	1969
Railway operating revenues	$1,507	$1,514	$1,652
Railway operating expenses	1,236	1,268	1,387
Taxes, equipment, rents, and other deductions	272	293	335
Loss before fixed charges	$ (1)	$ (47)	$ (70)
Fixed charges	85	95	123
Loss on railroad operations	$ (86)	$ (142)	$ (193)

Source: Pennco, Preliminary offering circular, Apr. 27, 1970.
Note: Dollar figures in millions; losses shown in parentheses.

cial paper, indicated it was beginning to have trouble selling new commercial paper to pay off the paper that was coming due. Bad news about the railroad was gradually seeping out, undermining Penn Central's ability to secure additional credit from banks or to sell new bonds. Large losses in the first quarter of 1970 and other gloomy details about the firm caused Penn Central to withdraw a $100 million debenture offering and produced a runoff of the firm's commercial paper. (In runoff, holders of maturing paper want their money and no new investors will buy any of the company's new commercial paper.) On June 8, Stuart Saunders, chief executive officer, and David Bevan, Penn Central's chief financial officer, were forced by creditor banks to resign and Alfred Perlman was relieved of his duties. On June 21, 1970, the Penn Central Transportation Company filed for bankruptcy under Section 77 of the National Bankruptcy Act.

Since the bankruptcy, the Penn Central has been kept alive by infusions of government assistance, principally in the form of loan guarantees. The company's passenger service has been turned over to Amtrak, with Penn Central receiving in return stock in the Amtrak Corporation. But, by 1974, Penn Central was still threatened with liquidation and still losing money at a rate of nearly $200 million a year. The most optimistic of projections places Penn Central in the black by 1984. Others expect death and burial long before that.

GETTING OFF BEFORE THE END OF THE LINE

Sophisticated investors probably became uneasy around mid-1969 about Penn Central's plight, but, as the *Commercial and Financial Chronicle* recommendation noted at the beginning of this discussion reveals, even the "ex-

pert" outsiders were unaware of how bad things really were. The halting of dividends in November 1969 and withdrawal of the $100 million debenture offering in May 1970 unambiguously brought the message home to the public. Some insiders of the Penn Central were apparently a little more nervous a lot sooner and began dumping their shares early in 1969—more than 40,000 shares at prices between $40 and $70 per share, far above the July 1970 postbankruptcy figures of around $5.

Many of those who were fortunate enough to liquidate their holdings before the roof caved in have publicly stated that they sold their stock for "personal reasons" and on the basis of information fully available to the general public. In any case, it is clear that most investors did not anticipate the imminent disaster. Penn Central's decline was very rapid. For many of Penn Central's stockholders, by the time the bad news was received and fully digested, it was too late to get off before the end of the line.

THE MORAL

Penn Central's management was both victim and perpetrator in the disaster. The company was plagued by misfortunes which included labor trouble, bad weather, inflationary pressures on costs, recession, and the Interstate Commerce Commission bureaucracy. But many of these same problems faced other rail lines which survived and even prospered. The profitability of the merged railroad would probably have been in question even with superb management. What chance there was of putting the railroad on a profitable course was totally lost because of poor planning, inadequate controls over operations, and internal dissension. Undoubtedly, Penn Central is not the only firm that failed for some or all of these reasons.

sources of financial information

Information on financial markets, economic trends, and individual companies is available from a wide range of sources. Here we provide a guide to most of the major sources and show how to interpret quotations on stocks and bonds.

DAILY SECURITIES DATA

Most newspapers carry some information on the daily activity in the securities market, but the *Wall Street Journal* (*WSJ*) covers more securities and provides more complete information than almost any other easily available source. The *WSJ* publishes a wide variety of articles on business and financial activities as well as data on commodity prices, foreign exchange rates, bond quotations (including both corporates and governments), and stock quotations. The data are always to be found in the last eight or nine pages of each issue.

Stock Quotations

The location of data on the trading activity of the stock issued by a particular company depends on whether the stock is listed on one of the stock exchanges or not. The *WSJ* provides information on all the listed securities that were actually traded in a given day plus information on the stock of many other companies.

Companies are shown alphabetically (names abbreviated) in three groups, NYSE Composite, Amex Composite, and Over-the-Counter. Therefore, if you are looking for information on a stock and you do not know whether it is listed or not, you must examine all three groups. The NYSE Composite provides information on stocks listed on the New York Stock Exchange and several exchanges, excluding those stocks listed on the American Stock Exchange which are shown under Amex Composite. Other, nonlisted stocks are shown as Over-the-Counter.

An example of the information provided for listed stocks is shown in Exhibit A-1 with an interpretation of the data. An example of a stock traded over-the-counter is shown in Exhibit A-2.

Bond Quotations

The *WSJ* provides very little information on the bonds issued by state and local governments. Your best source of price and related information on

Exhibit A-1. Quotations for Listed Stocks

NYSE Composite Transactions, Monday, May 10, 1976, reported in the *Wall Street Journal,* May 11, 1976

1976 High	1976 Low	Stocks	Div.	P/E Ratio	Sales 100s	High	Low	Close	Net Chg.
$47\frac{1}{2}$	$37\frac{3}{4}$	Abbt Lab	.88	17	73	$45\frac{5}{8}$	$44\frac{3}{8}$	45	$\frac{3}{8}$
$101\frac{3}{4}$	89	Ala P pf	9.44		z10	$99\frac{1}{2}$	$99\frac{1}{2}$	$99\frac{1}{2}$	$1\frac{1}{2}$

Both common and preferred stocks are traded on stock exchanges. The quotation for Abbot Laboratories is a common stock quotation; the Alabama Power stock is a preferred as indicated by "pf" following the abbreviated name for the company. The first two columns show the highest and lowest prices at which the stock had traded during 1976 at the time of the above report. The annual dividend is shown following the company name. Common stock dividends are calculated as four times the most recent quarter's "regular" dividend unless indicated otherwise by a footnote. Footnotes are found at the end of the list of quotations. The price-earnings ratio is the ratio of the closing price to the most recent year's earnings per share reported by the company and is provided only for common stocks, as preferred stockholders generally do not share in earnings after preferred dividends have been paid. Sales, given in hundreds, are the number of shares of the stock that were traded (bought and sold) during the day. There were 7,300 shares of Abbot Lab's common stock traded on May 10, 1976. The "z10" for Alabama Power preferred stock sales indicates that the total number of shares traded on that day was ten. The next three columns give the highest, lowest, and last price at which trading occurred on May 10. The price of Abbot Labs at the close increased $\frac{3}{8}$ of $1 ($0.37$\frac{1}{2}$) from the closing price on Friday, May 7, the previous day of trading.

Exhibit A-2. Unlisted Stock Quotations

Over-the-Counter Markets, Monday, May 10, 1976, reported in the *Wall Street Journal,* May 11, 1976

Stock & Div.	Sales 100s	Bid	Asked	Net Chg.
Am Exprss .80	1,941	$33\frac{3}{4}$	$34\frac{1}{2}$	$-\frac{1}{4}$

Prices in the over-the-counter markets found in the *Wall Street Journal* reflect transactions between securities dealers and may not be those actually paid by investors. American Express was paying dividends at an annual rate of $0.80 per share based on the most recent quarter's dividend. Reported sales were 194,100 shares. "Bid" refers to the price which dealers would pay to sellers of the stock; "asked" refers to the price at which dealers would sell to purchasers of the stock. The "net change" column shows that the stock was down $\frac{1}{4}$, which means that the reported bid price was $0.25 ($\frac{1}{4}$ of $1) less than the bid price reported for the prior trading day, Friday, May 7.

these issues is a local brokerage firm. Information on new state and local issues is provided, however.

Corporate and federal government issues are covered in much greater detail. Corporate bonds may be listed on either the American Stock Exchange or the New York Bond Exchange, and data on listed, traded issues are provided daily. Many listed bonds do not trade every day; therefore often you must look at several days before you will find data on a particular bond. Moody's manuals (see below) indicate the listing of bonds issued by corporations. Exhibit A-3 shows an example quotation and interpretation for corporate bonds. Data on all bonds, notes, and bills issued by the U.S. Treasury, most bonds issued by federal agencies, and some other governmental units are provided in a separate section of the *WSJ*. Exhibit A-4 shows example data for U.S. Treasury issues.

Exhibit A-3. Listed Corporate Bond Quotations

New York Exchange Bonds, Monday, May 10, 1976, reported in the *Wall Street Journal*, May 11, 1976

Bonds		Cur Yld	Vol	High	Low	Close	Net Chg.
Ala P	$10\frac{1}{2}$05	9.9	2	$105\frac{1}{2}$	$105\frac{1}{4}$	$105\frac{1}{2}$	...
Alcoa	$5\frac{1}{4}$s91	cv	34	103	$102\frac{1}{4}$	103	+1
ATT	7s01	8.0	87	$86\frac{1}{4}$	$86\frac{1}{4}$	$86\frac{1}{2}$	+1
ATT	$3\frac{1}{4}$s84	4.4	35	73	$72\frac{3}{4}$	$72\frac{3}{4}$	...

Each bond issue that is listed on the New York Exchange that was traded on May 10, 1976 is shown in the *Wall Street Journal*. Companies such as American Telephone and Telegraph (ATT), have more than one bond issue, and so each one must be identified separately. The identification is by company name (ATT), coupon rate of interest (7s, pronounced sevens, refers to a 7 percent coupon rate), and year of maturity (01, meaning 2001). The current yield is the coupon rate divided by the closing price, not the yield to maturity, which is more relevant to the investor. (Compare the current yields on the two ATT bonds, then consider that the $3\frac{1}{4}$'s will mature in eight years, paying $100 at that time, or a gain of $27 over the current price. The 7's mature in twenty-five years, providing a gain of $14\frac{1}{2}$ at that time.) The "cv" for the Alcoa bonds means that these securities are convertible into common stock and no current yield is provided. The "high," "low," and "close" indicate prices (per $100 maturity or par value) during the trading day (May 10, 1976). "Net change" is the difference between the closing price on this day and the prior day's close. The closing prices for Alabama Power $10\frac{1}{2}$'s due 2005 and ATT $3\frac{1}{4}$'s due 1984 were unchanged from their close on May 7, the previous day of trading.

Exhibit A-4. United States Government Securities Quotations

Monday, May 10, 1976, reported in the *Wall Street Journal,* May 11, 1976

| | U.S. Treasury Bills | | |
| | Mat. | Bid | Ask |
		Discount	
	11–15	5.46	5.34
	5–3	5.78	5.76

| | U.S. Treasury Notes & Bonds | | | | |
Rate	Mat. date		Bid	Asked	Bid Chg.	Yld.
6s	1976	May n	99.31	100.1	...	5.25
$8\frac{1}{4}$s	1990	May	102.10	102.26	−.8	7.92
7s	1993–98	May	91.4	92.4	+.26	7.75

Bills   U.S. Treasury bills have no coupon interest payments; they pay $1,000 per bill to the owner at maturity. All bills have maturities of one year or less; therefore only the month and day of maturity need be shown. For example, 11–15 indicates that the bill will mature on November 15, 1976, and 5–3 indicates that the other bill will mature on May 3, 1977 (since the date of this example is May 10, 1976). Since bill prices are always less than their maturity value, the "bid" and "asked" amounts shown are the annualized discounts from maturity value. These numbers are approximately equal to the annual interest rate earned on the bill if purchased. The bid on the 11–15 bill of 5.46 indicates a discount of approximately 2.73 percent since the bill matures six months from the date of the price quote. The indicated bid price was therefore $100.00 − $2.73 = $97.27 per $100 maturity value.

Notes and bonds   Notes and bonds pay coupon interest and therefore can be identified by their coupon rate and maturity. Shown are 6 percent (6s) and 7 percent (7s) coupon rate securities. The 6 percent security matures in May 1976 and is a note as indicated by the "n" following the maturity date. The distinction between notes and bonds is based on their maturity at original issue and is not important here. The hyphenated maturity for the 7 percent bond means that the bond may be repaid (called) in 1993, but otherwise will be repaid in 1998. "Bid" and "asked" refer to dollar prices per $100 maturity value for these securities and are expressed in $\frac{1}{32}$ of $1; that is, the asked price of the 6 percent note is $100 and $\frac{1}{32}$ per $100 maturity value. "Bid change" is the change in bid price from the previous day's trading in $\frac{1}{32}$ of $1. "Yield" for these securities is the yield to maturity based on the bid price. Yields to maturity for securities usually vary with maturity. Here we see that the 6 percent note due in one year has a much lower yield than the two bonds.

The following is a general guide to financial information. It is organized in two sections. The first section is a quick reference list organized by the type of information. The second section is organized by source and provides a capsule summary of the nature of the information provided in a given source (see page 756).

    Generally, when you are in doubt as to where to find some specific type of financial information, consult the person at the reference desk of your library.

SOURCE GUIDE

Type of information	Sources
Current prices and yields on securities	*Wall Street Journal, Commercial and Financial Chronicle, Bank and Quotation Record, Moody's Bond Record,* stock brokers
Average interest rates on various financial assets	*Wall Street Journal, Federal Reserve Bulletin, Economic Report of the President*
Stock and bond market activity	*Wall Street Journal, Statistical Bulletin of the Securities and Exchange Commission, Commercial and Financial Chronicle*
Aggregate financial data	*Federal Reserve Bulletin, Economic Report of the President*
Individual company data	Annual reports of the company, various manuals of Moody's, *Standard & Poor's Corporation Records, Fitch's Corporation Manuals, Value Line Investment Survey*
General business data	*Survey of Current Business, Statistical Abstract of the United States, Business Statistics*

Selected publications	Type of information
Business Week	General coverage of business affairs
Barron's	Security markets, individual securities, analysis of individual companies
Forbes	Analysis of individual companies, general articles on financial topics
Fortune	General coverage of business affairs, size rankings of major United States and foreign corporations, with summary data
Dun's Reviews	Bankruptcy data, average financial ratios for various industries, general financial articles
The Economist	General coverage of international business
Federal Reserve Bulletin	Wide variety of monetary, banking, and financial statistics; reviews of financial trends
Survey of Current Business	A wide variety of business statistics; see *Business Statistics* for historical data taken from this source
Statistical Bulletin of the Securities and Exchange Commission	Data on stock market activity and corporate securities issues
Monthly reviews of various Federal Reserve Banks	Each Federal Reserve Bank (New York, St. Louis, etc.) publishes a monthly review containing articles on financial and economic activity plus various types of data on national and regional trends

interest tables

Interest rate of 1/3 percent

N	Compound amount — Future value of a present amount F/P	Present value — Present value of a future amount P/F	Annuity compound amount — Future value of an annuity F/A	Sinking fund — Annuity providing a future amount A/F	Annuity present value — Present value of an annuity P/A	Capital recovery — Annuity repaying a present amount A/P	N
48	1.1732	.8524	51.9596	.0192	44.2888	.0226	48
60	1.2210	.8190	66.2990	.0151	54.2991	.0184	60
72	1.2707	.7869	81.2226	.0123	63.9174	.0156	72
84	1.3225	.7561	96.7541	.0103	73.1593	.0137	84
96	1.3764	.7265	112.9185	.0089	82.0393	.0122	96
108	1.4325	.6981	129.7414	.0077	90.5718	.0110	108
120	1.4908	.6708	147.2498	.0068	98.7702	.0101	120
132	1.5516	.6445	165.4714	.0060	106.6477	.0094	132
144	1.6148	.6193	184.4354	.0054	114.2168	.0088	144
156	1.6806	.5950	204.1721	.0049	121.4896	.0082	156
168	1.7490	.5717	224.7128	.0045	128.4777	.0078	168
180	1.8203	.5494	246.0904	.0041	135.1922	.0074	180
192	1.8945	.5279	268.3390	.0037	141.6439	.0071	192
204	1.9716	.5072	291.4940	.0034	147.8430	.0068	204
216	2.0520	.4873	315.5923	.0032	153.7994	.0065	216
228	2.1356	.4683	340.6725	.0029	159.5227	.0063	228
240	2.2226	.4499	366.7745	.0027	165.0219	.0061	240
252	2.3131	.4323	393.9399	.0025	170.3059	.0059	252
264	2.4074	.4154	422.2120	.0024	175.3830	.0057	264
276	2.5055	.3991	451.6360	.0022	180.2613	.0055	276
288	2.6075	.3835	482.2588	.0021	184.9487	.0054	288
300	2.7138	.3685	514.1293	.0019	189.4526	.0053	300
312	2.8243	.3541	547.2981	.0018	193.7801	.0052	312
324	2.9394	.3402	581.8183	.0017	197.9383	.0051	324
336	3.0591	.3269	617.7449	.0016	201.9337	.0050	336
348	3.1838	.3141	655.1353	.0015	205.7726	.0049	348
360	3.3135	.3018	694.0489	.0014	209.4613	.0048	360
∞					300.0000	.0033	∞

N	Compound amount — Future value of a present amount F/P	Present value — Present value of a future amount P/F	Annuity compound amount — Future value of an annuity F/A	Sinking fund — Annuity providing a future amount A/F	Annuity present value — Present value of an annuity P/A	Capital recovery — Annuity repaying a present amount A/P	N
1	1.0033	.9967	1.0000	1.0000	.9967	1.0033	1
2	1.0067	.9934	2.0033	.4992	1.9900	.5025	2
3	1.0100	.9901	3.0100	.3322	2.9801	.3356	3
4	1.0134	.9868	4.0200	.2488	3.9669	.2521	4
5	1.0168	.9835	5.0334	.1987	4.9504	.2020	5
6	1.0202	.9802	6.0502	.1653	5.9306	.1686	6
7	1.0236	.9770	7.0704	.1414	6.9076	.1448	7
8	1.0270	.9737	8.0940	.1235	7.8813	.1269	8
9	1.0304	.9705	9.1209	.1096	8.8518	.1130	9
10	1.0338	.9673	10.1513	.0985	9.8191	.1018	10
11	1.0373	.9641	11.1852	.0894	10.7831	.0927	11
12	1.0407	.9609	12.2225	.0818	11.7440	.0851	12
13	1.0442	.9577	13.2632	.0754	12.7017	.0787	13
14	1.0477	.9545	14.3074	.0699	13.6561	.0732	14
15	1.0512	.9513	15.3551	.0651	14.6074	.0685	15
16	1.0547	.9481	16.4063	.0610	15.5556	.0643	16
17	1.0582	.9450	17.4610	.0573	16.5006	.0606	17
18	1.0617	.9419	18.5192	.0540	17.4424	.0573	18
19	1.0653	.9387	19.5809	.0511	18.3812	.0544	19
20	1.0688	.9356	20.6462	.0484	19.3168	.0518	20
21	1.0724	.9325	21.7150	.0461	20.2493	.0494	21
22	1.0760	.9294	22.7874	.0439	21.1787	.0472	22
23	1.0795	.9263	23.8633	.0419	22.1050	.0452	23
24	1.0831	.9232	24.9429	.0401	23.0283	.0434	24
25	1.0868	.9202	26.0260	.0384	23.9484	.0418	25
26	1.0904	.9171	27.1128	.0369	24.8655	.0402	26
27	1.0940	.9141	28.2032	.0355	25.7796	.0388	27
28	1.0977	.9110	29.2972	.0341	26.6906	.0375	28
29	1.1013	.9080	30.3948	.0329	27.5986	.0362	29
30	1.1050	.9050	31.4961	.0317	28.5036	.0351	30
31	1.1087	.9020	32.6011	.0307	29.4056	.0340	31
32	1.1124	.8990	33.7098	.0297	30.3046	.0330	32
33	1.1161	.8960	34.8222	.0287	31.2006	.0321	33
34	1.1198	.8930	35.9382	.0278	32.0936	.0312	34
35	1.1235	.8901	37.0580	.0270	32.9837	.0303	35
36	1.1273	.8871	38.1816	.0262	33.8708	.0295	36

Interest rate of ½ percent

N	Compound amount — Future value of a present amount — F/P	Present value — Present value of a future amount — P/F	Annuity compound amount — Future value of an annuity — F/A	Sinking fund — Annuity providing a future amount — A/F	Annuity present value — Present value of an annuity — P/A	Capital recovery — Annuity repaying a present amount — A/P	N
48	1.2705	.7871	54.0978	.0185	42.5803	.0235	48
60	1.3489	.7414	69.7700	.0143	51.7256	.0193	60
72	1.4320	.6983	86.4089	.0116	60.3395	.0166	72
84	1.5204	.6577	104.0739	.0096	68.4530	.0146	84
96	1.6141	.6195	122.8285	.0081	76.0952	.0131	96
108	1.7137	.5835	142.7399	.0070	83.2934	.0120	108
120	1.8194	.5496	163.8793	.0061	90.0735	.0111	120
132	1.9316	.5177	186.3226	.0054	96.4596	.0104	132
144	2.0508	.4876	210.1502	.0048	102.4747	.0098	144
156	2.1772	.4593	235.4473	.0042	108.1404	.0092	156
168	2.3115	.4326	262.3048	.0038	113.4770	.0088	168
180	2.4541	.4075	290.8187	.0034	118.5035	.0084	180
192	2.6055	.3838	321.0913	.0031	123.2380	.0081	192
204	2.7662	.3615	353.2311	.0028	127.6975	.0078	204
216	2.9368	.3405	387.3532	.0026	131.8979	.0076	216
228	3.1179	.3207	423.5799	.0024	135.8542	.0074	228
240	3.3102	.3021	462.0409	.0022	139.5808	.0072	240
252	3.5144	.2845	502.8741	.0020	143.0908	.0070	252
264	3.7311	.2680	546.2259	.0018	146.3969	.0068	264
276	3.9613	.2524	592.2514	.0017	149.5110	.0067	276
288	4.2056	.2378	641.1158	.0016	152.4441	.0066	288
300	4.4650	.2240	692.9940	.0014	155.2069	.0064	300
312	4.7404	.2110	748.0719	.0013	157.8091	.0063	312
324	5.0327	.1987	806.5469	.0012	160.2602	.0062	324
336	5.3431	.1872	868.6285	.0012	162.5688	.0062	336
348	5.6727	.1763	934.5392	.0011	164.7434	.0061	348
360	6.0226	.1660	1004.5150	.0010	166.7916	.0060	360
∞					200.0000	.0050	∞

N	Compound amount — Future value of a present amount — F/P	Present value — Present value of a future amount — P/F	Annuity compound amount — Future value of an annuity — F/A	Sinking fund — Annuity providing a future amount — A/F	Annuity present value — Present value of an annuity — P/A	Capital recovery — Annuity repaying a present amount — A/P	N
1	1.0050	.9950	1.0000	1.0000	.9950	1.0050	1
2	1.0100	.9901	2.0050	.4988	1.9851	.5038	2
3	1.0151	.9851	3.0150	.3317	2.9702	.3367	3
4	1.0202	.9802	4.0301	.2481	3.9505	.2531	4
5	1.0253	.9754	5.0503	.1980	4.9259	.2030	5
6	1.0304	.9705	6.0755	.1646	5.8964	.1696	6
7	1.0355	.9657	7.1059	.1407	6.8621	.1457	7
8	1.0407	.9609	8.1414	.1228	7.8230	.1278	8
9	1.0459	.9561	9.1821	.1089	8.7791	.1139	9
10	1.0511	.9513	10.2280	.0978	9.7304	.1028	10
11	1.0564	.9466	11.2792	.0887	10.6770	.0937	11
12	1.0617	.9419	12.3356	.0811	11.6189	.0861	12
13	1.0670	.9372	13.3972	.0746	12.5562	.0796	13
14	1.0723	.9326	14.4642	.0691	13.4887	.0741	14
15	1.0777	.9279	15.5365	.0644	14.4166	.0694	15
16	1.0831	.9233	16.6142	.0602	15.3399	.0652	16
17	1.0885	.9187	17.6973	.0565	16.2586	.0615	17
18	1.0939	.9141	18.7858	.0532	17.1728	.0582	18
19	1.0994	.9096	19.8797	.0503	18.0824	.0553	19
20	1.1049	.9051	20.9791	.0477	18.9874	.0527	20
21	1.1104	.9006	22.0840	.0453	19.8880	.0503	21
22	1.1160	.8961	23.1944	.0431	20.7841	.0481	22
23	1.1216	.8916	24.3104	.0411	21.6757	.0461	23
24	1.1272	.8872	25.4320	.0393	22.5629	.0443	24
25	1.1328	.8828	26.5591	.0377	23.4456	.0427	25
26	1.1385	.8784	27.6919	.0361	24.3240	.0411	26
27	1.1442	.8740	28.8304	.0347	25.1980	.0397	27
28	1.1499	.8697	29.9745	.0334	26.0677	.0384	28
29	1.1556	.8653	31.1244	.0321	26.9330	.0371	29
30	1.1614	.8610	32.2800	.0310	27.7941	.0360	30
31	1.1672	.8567	33.4414	.0299	28.6508	.0349	31
32	1.1730	.8525	34.6086	.0289	29.5033	.0339	32
33	1.1789	.8482	35.7817	.0279	30.3515	.0329	33
34	1.1848	.8440	36.9606	.0271	31.1955	.0321	34
35	1.1907	.8398	38.1454	.0262	32.0354	.0312	35
36	1.1967	.8356	39.3361	.0254	32.8710	.0304	36

Interest rate of ⅔ percent

N	Compound amount — Future value of a present amount — F/P	Present value — Present value of a future amount — P/F	Annuity compound amount — Future value of an annuity — F/A	Sinking fund — Annuity providing a future amount — A/F	Annuity present value — Present value of an annuity — P/A	Capital recovery — Annuity repaying a present amount — A/P	N
48	1.3757	.7269	56.3499	.0177	40.9619	.0244	48
60	1.4898	.6712	73.4769	.0136	49.3184	.0203	60
72	1.6135	.6198	92.0253	.0109	57.0345	.0175	72
84	1.7474	.5723	112.1133	.0089	64.1593	.0156	84
96	1.8925	.5284	133.8686	.0075	70.7380	.0141	96
108	2.0495	.4879	157.4295	.0064	76.8125	.0130	108
120	2.2196	.4505	182.9460	.0055	82.4215	.0121	120
132	2.4039	.4160	210.5804	.0047	87.6006	.0114	132
144	2.6034	.3841	240.5084	.0042	92.3828	.0108	144
156	2.8195	.3547	272.9204	.0037	96.7985	.0103	156
168	3.0535	.3275	308.0226	.0032	100.8758	.0099	168
180	3.3069	.3024	346.0382	.0029	104.6406	.0096	180
192	3.5814	.2792	387.2092	.0026	108.1169	.0092	192
204	3.8786	.2578	431.7973	.0023	111.3267	.0090	204
216	4.2006	.2381	480.0861	.0021	114.2906	.0087	216
228	4.5492	.2198	532.3830	.0019	117.0273	.0085	228
240	4.9268	.2030	589.0204	.0017	119.5543	.0084	240
252	5.3357	.1874	650.3588	.0015	121.8876	.0082	252
264	5.7786	.1731	716.7882	.0014	124.0421	.0081	264
276	6.2582	.1598	788.7312	.0013	126.0315	.0079	276
288	6.7776	.1475	866.6454	.0012	127.8684	.0078	288
300	7.3402	.1362	951.0265	.0011	129.5645	.0077	300
312	7.9494	.1258	1042.4111	.0010	131.1307	.0076	312
324	8.6092	.1162	1141.3807	.0009	132.5768	.0075	324
336	9.3238	.1073	1248.5646	.0008	133.9121	.0075	336
348	10.0976	.0990	1364.6448	.0007	135.1450	.0074	348
360	10.9357	.0914	1490.3596	.0007	136.2835	.0073	360
∞					150.0000	.0067	∞

N	Compound amount — Future value of a present amount — F/P	Present value — Present value of a future amount — P/F	Annuity compound amount — Future value of an annuity — F/A	Sinking fund — Annuity providing a future amount — A/F	Annuity present value — Present value of an annuity — P/A	Capital recovery — Annuity repaying a present amount — A/P	N
1	1.0067	.9934	1.0000	1.0000	.9934	1.0067	1
2	1.0134	.9868	2.0067	.4983	1.9802	.5050	2
3	1.0201	.9803	3.0200	.3311	2.9604	.3378	3
4	1.0269	.9738	4.0402	.2475	3.9342	.2542	4
5	1.0338	.9673	5.0671	.1974	4.9015	.2040	5
6	1.0407	.9609	6.1009	.1639	5.8625	.1706	6
7	1.0476	.9546	7.1416	.1400	6.8170	.1467	7
8	1.0546	.9482	8.1892	.1221	7.7652	.1288	8
9	1.0616	.9420	9.2438	.1082	8.7072	.1148	9
10	1.0687	.9357	10.3054	.0970	9.6429	.1037	10
11	1.0758	.9295	11.3741	.0879	10.5724	.0946	11
12	1.0830	.9234	12.4499	.0803	11.4958	.0870	12
13	1.0902	.9172	13.5329	.0739	12.4130	.0806	13
14	1.0975	.9112	14.6231	.0684	13.3242	.0751	14
15	1.1048	.9051	15.7206	.0636	14.2293	.0703	15
16	1.1122	.8991	16.8254	.0594	15.1285	.0661	16
17	1.1196	.8932	17.9376	.0557	16.0217	.0624	17
18	1.1270	.8873	19.0572	.0525	16.9089	.0591	18
19	1.1346	.8814	20.1842	.0495	17.7903	.0562	19
20	1.1421	.8756	21.3188	.0469	18.6659	.0536	20
21	1.1497	.8698	22.4609	.0445	19.5357	.0512	21
22	1.1574	.8640	23.6107	.0424	20.3997	.0490	22
23	1.1651	.8583	24.7681	.0404	21.2579	.0470	23
24	1.1729	.8526	25.9332	.0386	22.1105	.0452	24
25	1.1807	.8470	27.1061	.0369	22.9575	.0436	25
26	1.1886	.8413	28.2868	.0354	23.7988	.0420	26
27	1.1965	.8358	29.4754	.0339	24.6346	.0406	27
28	1.2045	.8302	30.6719	.0326	25.4648	.0393	28
29	1.2125	.8247	31.8763	.0314	26.2896	.0380	29
30	1.2206	.8193	33.0889	.0302	27.1088	.0369	30
31	1.2287	.8138	34.3094	.0291	27.9227	.0358	31
32	1.2369	.8085	35.5382	.0281	28.7312	.0348	32
33	1.2452	.8031	36.7751	.0272	29.5343	.0339	33
34	1.2535	.7978	38.0203	.0263	30.3320	.0330	34
35	1.2618	.7925	39.2737	.0255	31.1246	.0321	35
36	1.2702	.7873	40.5356	.0247	31.9118	.0313	36

Interest rate of ¾ percent

N	Compound amount — Future value of a present amount (F/P)	Present value — Present value of a future amount (P/F)	Annuity compound amount — Future value of an annuity (F/A)	Sinking fund — Annuity providing a future amount (A/F)	Annuity present value — Present value of an annuity (P/A)	Capital recovery — Annuity repaying a present amount (A/P)	N
1	1.0075	.9926	1.0000	1.0000	.9926	1.0075	1
2	1.0151	.9852	2.0075	.4981	1.9777	.5056	2
3	1.0227	.9778	3.0226	.3308	2.9556	.3383	3
4	1.0303	.9706	4.0452	.2472	3.9261	.2547	4
5	1.0381	.9633	5.0756	.1970	4.8894	.2045	5
6	1.0459	.9562	6.1136	.1636	5.8456	.1711	6
7	1.0537	.9490	7.1595	.1397	6.7946	.1472	7
8	1.0616	.9420	8.2132	.1218	7.7366	.1293	8
9	1.0696	.9350	9.2748	.1078	8.6716	.1153	9
10	1.0776	.9280	10.3443	.0967	9.5996	.1042	10
11	1.0857	.9211	11.4219	.0876	10.5207	.0951	11
12	1.0938	.9142	12.5076	.0800	11.4349	.0875	12
13	1.1020	.9074	13.6014	.0735	12.3423	.0810	13
14	1.1103	.9007	14.7034	.0680	13.2430	.0755	14
15	1.1186	.8940	15.8137	.0632	14.1370	.0707	15
16	1.1270	.8873	16.9323	.0591	15.0243	.0666	16
17	1.1354	.8807	18.0593	.0554	15.9050	.0629	17
18	1.1440	.8742	19.1947	.0521	16.7792	.0596	18
19	1.1525	.8676	20.3387	.0492	17.6468	.0567	19
20	1.1612	.8612	21.4912	.0465	18.5080	.0540	20
21	1.1699	.8548	22.6524	.0441	19.3628	.0516	21
22	1.1787	.8484	23.8223	.0420	20.2112	.0495	22
23	1.1875	.8421	25.0010	.0400	21.0533	.0475	23
24	1.1964	.8358	26.1885	.0382	21.8891	.0457	24
25	1.2054	.8296	27.3849	.0365	22.7188	.0440	25
26	1.2144	.8234	28.5903	.0350	23.5422	.0425	26
27	1.2235	.8173	29.8047	.0336	24.3595	.0411	27
28	1.2327	.8112	31.0282	.0322	25.1707	.0397	28
29	1.2420	.8052	32.2609	.0310	25.9759	.0385	29
30	1.2513	.7992	33.5029	.0298	26.7751	.0373	30
31	1.2607	.7932	34.7542	.0288	27.5683	.0363	31
32	1.2701	.7873	36.0148	.0278	28.3557	.0353	32
33	1.2796	.7815	37.2849	.0268	29.1371	.0343	33
34	1.2892	.7757	38.5646	.0259	29.9128	.0334	34
35	1.2989	.7699	39.8538	.0251	30.6827	.0326	35
36	1.3086	.7641	41.1527	.0243	31.4468	.0318	36

N	Compound amount — Future value of a present amount (F/P)	Present value — Present value of a future amount (P/F)	Annuity compound amount — Future value of an annuity (F/A)	Sinking fund — Annuity providing a future amount (A/F)	Annuity present value — Present value of an annuity (P/A)	Capital recovery — Annuity repaying a present amount (A/P)	N
48	1.4314	.6986	57.5207	.0174	40.1848	.0249	48
60	1.5657	.6387	75.4241	.0133	48.1734	.0208	60
72	1.7126	.5839	95.0070	.0105	55.4768	.0180	72
84	1.8732	.5338	116.4269	.0086	62.1540	.0161	84
96	2.0489	.4881	139.8562	.0072	68.2584	.0147	96
108	2.2411	.4462	165.4832	.0060	73.8394	.0135	108
120	2.4514	.4079	193.5143	.0052	78.9417	.0127	120
132	2.6813	.3730	224.1748	.0045	83.6064	.0120	132
144	2.9328	.3410	257.7116	.0039	87.8711	.0114	144
156	3.2080	.3117	294.3943	.0034	91.7700	.0109	156
168	3.5089	.2850	334.5181	.0030	95.3346	.0105	168
180	3.8380	.2605	378.4058	.0026	98.5934	.0101	180
192	4.1981	.2382	426.4104	.0023	101.5728	.0098	192
204	4.5919	.2178	478.9183	.0021	104.2966	.0096	204
216	5.0226	.1991	536.3517	.0019	106.7869	.0094	216
228	5.4938	.1820	599.1727	.0017	109.0635	.0092	228
240	6.0092	.1664	667.8869	.0015	111.1450	.0090	240
252	6.5729	.1521	743.0469	.0013	113.0479	.0088	252
264	7.1894	.1391	825.2574	.0012	114.7876	.0087	264
276	7.8638	.1272	915.1798	.0011	116.3781	.0086	276
288	8.6015	.1163	1013.5375	.0010	117.8322	.0085	288
300	9.4084	.1063	1121.1219	.0009	119.1616	.0084	300
312	10.2910	.0972	1238.7985	.0008	120.3770	.0083	312
324	11.2564	.0888	1367.5139	.0007	121.4482	.0082	324
336	12.3123	.0812	1508.3037	.0007	122.5040	.0082	336
348	13.4673	.0743	1662.3006	.0006	123.4328	.0081	348
360	14.7306	.0679	1830.7435	.0005	124.2819	.0080	360
∞					133.3333	.0075	∞

Interest rate of 1.00 percent

N	Compound amount — Future value of a present amount F/P	Present value — Present value of a future amount P/F	Annuity compound amount — Future value of an annuity F/A	Sinking fund — Annuity providing a future amount A/F	Annuity present value — Present value of an annuity P/A	Capital recovery — Annuity repaying a present amount A/P	N
48	1.6122	.6203	61.2226	.0163	37.9740	.0263	48
60	1.8167	.5504	81.6697	.0122	44.9550	.0222	60
72	2.0471	.4885	104.7099	.0096	51.1504	.0196	72
84	2.3067	.4335	130.6723	.0077	56.6485	.0177	84
96	2.5993	.3847	159.9273	.0063	61.5277	.0163	96
108	2.9289	.3414	192.8926	.0052	65.8578	.0152	108
120	3.3004	.3030	230.0387	.0043	69.7005	.0143	120
132	3.7190	.2689	271.8959	.0037	73.1108	.0137	132
144	4.1906	.2386	319.0616	.0031	76.1372	.0131	144
156	4.7221	.2118	372.2091	.0027	78.8229	.0127	156
168	5.3210	.1879	432.0970	.0023	81.2064	.0123	168
180	5.9958	.1668	499.5802	.0020	83.3217	.0120	180
192	6.7562	.1480	575.6220	.0017	85.1988	.0117	192
204	7.6131	.1314	661.3078	.0015	86.8647	.0115	204
216	8.5786	.1166	757.8606	.0013	88.3431	.0113	216
228	9.6666	.1034	866.6588	.0012	89.6551	.0112	228
240	10.8926	.0918	989.2554	.0010	90.8194	.0110	240
252	12.2740	.0815	1127.4002	.0009	91.8527	.0109	252
264	13.8307	.0723	1283.0653	.0008	92.7697	.0108	264
276	15.5847	.0642	1458.4726	.0007	93.5835	.0107	276
288	17.5613	.0569	1656.1259	.0006	94.3056	.0106	288
300	19.7885	.0505	1878.8466	.0005	94.9466	.0105	300
312	22.2981	.0448	2129.8139	.0005	95.5153	.0105	312
324	25.1261	.0398	2412.6101	.0004	96.0201	.0104	324
336	28.3127	.0353	2731.2720	.0004	96.4680	.0104	336
348	31.9035	.0313	3090.3481	.0003	96.8655	.0103	348
360	35.9496	.0278	3494.9641	.0003	97.2183	.0103	360
∞					100.0000	.0100	∞

N	Compound amount — Future value of a present amount F/P	Present value — Present value of a future amount P/F	Annuity compound amount — Future value of an annuity F/A	Sinking fund — Annuity providing a future amount A/F	Annuity present value — Present value of an annuity P/A	Capital recovery — Annuity repaying a present amount A/P	N
1	1.0100	.9901	1.0000	1.0000	.9901	1.0100	1
2	1.0201	.9803	2.0100	.4975	1.9704	.5075	2
3	1.0303	.9706	3.0301	.3300	2.9410	.3400	3
4	1.0406	.9610	4.0604	.2463	3.9020	.2563	4
5	1.0510	.9515	5.1010	.1960	4.8534	.2060	5
6	1.0615	.9420	6.1520	.1625	5.7955	.1725	6
7	1.0721	.9327	7.2135	.1386	6.7282	.1486	7
8	1.0829	.9235	8.2857	.1207	7.6517	.1307	8
9	1.0937	.9143	9.3685	.1067	8.5660	.1167	9
10	1.1046	.9053	10.4622	.0956	9.4713	.1056	10
11	1.1157	.8963	11.5668	.0865	10.3676	.0965	11
12	1.1268	.8874	12.6825	.0788	11.2551	.0888	12
13	1.1381	.8787	13.8093	.0724	12.1337	.0824	13
14	1.1495	.8700	14.9474	.0669	13.0037	.0769	14
15	1.1610	.8613	16.0969	.0621	13.8651	.0721	15
16	1.1726	.8528	17.2579	.0579	14.7179	.0679	16
17	1.1843	.8444	18.4304	.0543	15.5623	.0643	17
18	1.1961	.8360	19.6147	.0510	16.3983	.0610	18
19	1.2081	.8277	20.8109	.0481	17.2260	.0581	19
20	1.2202	.8195	22.0190	.0454	18.0456	.0554	20
21	1.2324	.8114	23.2392	.0430	18.8570	.0530	21
22	1.2447	.8034	24.4716	.0409	19.6604	.0509	22
23	1.2572	.7954	25.7163	.0389	20.4558	.0489	23
24	1.2697	.7876	26.9735	.0371	21.2434	.0471	24
25	1.2824	.7798	28.2432	.0354	22.0232	.0454	25
26	1.2953	.7720	29.5256	.0339	22.7952	.0439	26
27	1.3082	.7644	30.8209	.0324	23.5596	.0424	27
28	1.3213	.7568	32.1291	.0311	24.3164	.0411	28
29	1.3345	.7493	33.4504	.0299	25.0658	.0399	29
30	1.3478	.7419	34.7849	.0287	25.8077	.0387	30
31	1.3613	.7346	36.1327	.0277	26.5423	.0377	31
32	1.3749	.7273	37.4941	.0267	27.2696	.0367	32
33	1.3887	.7201	38.8690	.0257	27.9897	.0357	33
34	1.4026	.7130	40.2577	.0248	28.7027	.0348	34
35	1.4166	.7059	41.6603	.0240	29.4086	.0340	35
36	1.4308	.6989	43.0769	.0232	30.1075	.0332	36

Interest rate of 1.25 percent

N	Compound amount — Future value of a present amount (F/P)	Present value — Present value of a future amount (P/F)	Annuity compound amount — Future value of an annuity (F/A)	Sinking fund — Annuity providing a future amount (A/F)	Annuity present value — Present value of an annuity (P/A)	Capital recovery — Annuity repaying a present amount (A/P)	N
48	1.8154	.5509	65.2284	.0153	35.9315	.0278	48
60	2.1072	.4746	88.5745	.0113	42.0346	.0238	60
72	2.4459	.4088	115.6736	.0086	47.2925	.0211	72
84	2.8391	.3522	147.1290	.0068	51.8222	.0193	84
96	3.2955	.3034	183.6411	.0054	55.7246	.0179	96
108	3.8253	.2614	226.0226	.0044	59.0865	.0169	108
120	4.4402	.2252	275.2171	.0036	61.9828	.0161	120
132	5.1540	.1940	332.3198	.0030	64.4781	.0155	132
144	5.9825	.1672	398.6021	.0025	66.6277	.0150	144
156	6.9442	.1440	475.5395	.0021	68.4797	.0146	156
168	8.0606	.1241	564.8450	.0018	70.0751	.0143	168
180	9.3563	.1069	668.5068	.0015	71.4496	.0140	180
192	10.8604	.0921	788.8326	.0013	72.6338	.0138	192
204	12.6063	.0793	928.5014	.0011	73.6540	.0136	204
216	14.6328	.0683	1090.6225	.0009	74.5328	.0134	216
228	16.9851	.0589	1278.8054	.0008	75.2900	.0133	228
240	19.7155	.0507	1497.2395	.0007	75.9423	.0132	240
252	22.8848	.0437	1750.7879	.0006	76.5042	.0131	252
264	26.5637	.0376	2045.0953	.0005	76.9884	.0130	264
276	30.8339	.0324	2386.7139	.0004	77.4055	.0129	276
288	35.7906	.0279	2783.2493	.0004	77.7648	.0129	288
300	41.5441	.0241	3243.5296	.0003	78.0743	.0128	300
312	48.2225	.0207	3777.8020	.0003	78.3410	.0128	312
324	55.9745	.0179	4397.9611	.0002	78.5708	.0127	324
336	64.9727	.0154	5117.8136	.0002	78.7687	.0127	336
348	75.4173	.0133	5953.3856	.0002	78.9392	.0127	348
360	87.5410	.0114	6923.2796	.0001	79.0861	.0126	360
∞					80.0000	.0125	∞

N	Compound amount — Future value of a present amount (F/P)	Present value — Present value of a future amount (P/F)	Annuity compound amount — Future value of an annuity (F/A)	Sinking fund — Annuity providing a future amount (A/F)	Annuity present value — Present value of an annuity (P/A)	Capital recovery — Annuity repaying a present amount (A/P)	N
1	1.0125	.9877	1.0000	1.0000	.9877	1.0125	1
2	1.0252	.9755	2.0125	.4969	1.9631	.5094	2
3	1.0380	.9634	3.0377	.3292	2.9265	.3417	3
4	1.0509	.9515	4.0756	.2454	3.8781	.2579	4
5	1.0641	.9398	5.1266	.1951	4.8178	.2076	5
6	1.0774	.9282	6.1907	.1615	5.7460	.1740	6
7	1.0909	.9167	7.2680	.1376	6.6627	.1501	7
8	1.1045	.9054	8.3589	.1196	7.5681	.1321	8
9	1.1183	.8942	9.4634	.1057	8.4623	.1182	9
10	1.1323	.8832	10.5817	.0945	9.3455	.1070	10
11	1.1464	.8723	11.7139	.0854	10.2178	.0979	11
12	1.1608	.8615	12.8604	.0778	11.0793	.0903	12
13	1.1753	.8509	14.0211	.0713	11.9302	.0838	13
14	1.1900	.8404	15.1964	.0658	12.7706	.0783	14
15	1.2048	.8300	16.3863	.0610	13.6005	.0735	15
16	1.2199	.8197	17.5912	.0568	14.4203	.0693	16
17	1.2351	.8096	18.8111	.0532	15.2299	.0657	17
18	1.2506	.7996	20.0462	.0499	16.0295	.0624	18
19	1.2662	.7898	21.2968	.0470	16.8193	.0595	19
20	1.2820	.7800	22.5630	.0443	17.5993	.0568	20
21	1.2981	.7704	23.8450	.0419	18.3697	.0544	21
22	1.3143	.7609	25.1431	.0398	19.1306	.0523	22
23	1.3307	.7515	26.4574	.0378	19.8820	.0503	23
24	1.3474	.7422	27.7881	.0360	20.6242	.0485	24
25	1.3642	.7330	29.1354	.0343	21.3573	.0468	25
26	1.3812	.7240	30.4996	.0328	22.0813	.0453	26
27	1.3985	.7150	31.8809	.0314	22.7963	.0439	27
28	1.4160	.7062	33.2794	.0300	23.5025	.0425	28
29	1.4337	.6975	34.6954	.0288	24.2000	.0413	29
30	1.4516	.6889	36.1291	.0277	24.8889	.0402	30
31	1.4698	.6804	37.5807	.0266	25.5693	.0391	31
32	1.4881	.6720	39.0504	.0256	26.2413	.0381	32
33	1.5067	.6637	40.5386	.0247	26.9050	.0372	33
34	1.5256	.6555	42.0453	.0238	27.5605	.0363	34
35	1.5446	.6474	43.5709	.0230	28.2079	.0355	35
36	1.5639	.6394	45.1155	.0222	28.8473	.0347	36

Interest rate of 1.50 percent

N	Compound amount — Future value of a present amount — F/P	Present value — Present value of a future amount — P/F	Annuity compound amount — Future value of an annuity — F/A	Sinking fund — Annuity providing a future amount — A/F	Annuity present value — Present value of an annuity — P/A	Capital recovery — Annuity repaying a present amount — A/P	N
40	1.8140	.5513	54.2679	.0184	29.9158	.0334	40
44	1.9253	.5194	61.6889	.0162	32.0406	.0312	44
48	2.0435	.4894	69.5652	.0144	34.0426	.0294	48
52	2.1689	.4611	77.9249	.0128	35.9287	.0278	52
56	2.3020	.4344	86.7975	.0115	37.7059	.0265	56
60	2.4432	.4039	96.2147	.0104	39.3803	.0254	60
64	2.5931	.3856	106.2096	.0094	40.9579	.0244	64
68	2.7523	.3633	116.8179	.0086	42.4442	.0236	68
72	2.9212	.3423	128.0772	.0078	43.8447	.0228	72
76	3.1004	.3225	140.0274	.0071	45.1641	.0221	76
80	3.2907	.3039	152.7109	.0065	46.4073	.0215	80
84	3.4926	.2863	166.1726	.0060	47.5786	.0210	84
88	3.7069	.2698	180.4605	.0055	48.6822	.0205	88
92	3.9344	.2542	195.6251	.0051	49.7220	.0201	92
96	4.1758	.2395	211.7202	.0047	50.7017	.0197	96
100	4.4320	.2256	228.8030	.0044	51.6247	.0194	100
104	4.7040	.2126	246.9341	.0040	52.4944	.0190	104
108	4.9927	.2003	266.1778	.0038	53.3137	.0188	108
112	5.2990	.1887	286.6023	.0035	54.0858	.0185	112
116	5.6242	.1778	308.2801	.0032	54.8131	.0182	116
120	5.9693	.1675	331.2882	.0030	55.4985	.0180	120
∞					66.6667	.0150	∞

N	Compound amount — Future value of a present amount — F/P	Present value — Present value of a future amount — P/F	Annuity compound amount — Future value of an annuity — F/A	Sinking fund — Annuity providing a future amount — A/F	Annuity present value — Present value of an annuity — P/A	Capital recovery — Annuity repaying a present amount — A/P	N
1	1.0150	.9852	1.0000	1.0000	.9852	1.0150	1
2	1.0302	.9707	2.0150	.4963	1.9559	.5113	2
3	1.0457	.9563	3.0452	.3284	2.9122	.3434	3
4	1.0614	.9422	4.0909	.2444	3.8544	.2594	4
5	1.0773	.9283	5.1523	.1941	4.7826	.2091	5
6	1.0934	.9145	6.2296	.1605	5.6972	.1755	6
7	1.1098	.9010	7.3230	.1366	6.5982	.1516	7
8	1.1265	.8877	8.4328	.1186	7.4859	.1336	8
9	1.1434	.8746	9.5593	.1046	8.3605	.1196	9
10	1.1605	.8617	10.7027	.0934	9.2222	.1084	10
11	1.1779	.8489	11.8633	.0843	10.0711	.0993	11
12	1.1956	.8364	13.0412	.0767	10.9075	.0917	12
13	1.2136	.8240	14.2368	.0702	11.7315	.0852	13
14	1.2318	.8118	15.4504	.0647	12.5434	.0797	14
15	1.2502	.7999	16.6821	.0599	13.3432	.0749	15
16	1.2690	.7880	17.9324	.0558	14.1313	.0708	16
17	1.2880	.7764	19.2014	.0521	14.9076	.0671	17
18	1.3073	.7649	20.4894	.0488	15.6726	.0638	18
19	1.3270	.7536	21.7967	.0459	16.4262	.0609	19
20	1.3469	.7425	23.1237	.0432	17.1686	.0582	20
21	1.3671	.7315	24.4705	.0409	17.9001	.0559	21
22	1.3876	.7207	25.8376	.0387	18.6208	.0537	22
23	1.4084	.7100	27.2251	.0367	19.3309	.0517	23
24	1.4295	.6995	28.6335	.0349	20.0304	.0499	24
25	1.4509	.6892	30.0630	.0333	20.7196	.0483	25
26	1.4727	.6790	31.5140	.0317	21.3986	.0467	26
27	1.4948	.6690	32.9867	.0303	22.0676	.0453	27
28	1.5172	.6591	34.4815	.0290	22.7267	.0440	28
29	1.5400	.6494	35.9987	.0278	23.3761	.0428	29
30	1.5631	.6398	37.5387	.0266	24.0158	.0416	30
31	1.5865	.6303	39.1018	.0256	24.6461	.0406	31
32	1.6103	.6210	40.6883	.0246	25.2671	.0396	32
33	1.6345	.6118	42.2986	.0236	25.8790	.0386	33
34	1.6590	.6028	43.9331	.0228	26.4817	.0378	34
35	1.6839	.5939	45.5921	.0219	27.0756	.0369	35
36	1.7091	.5851	47.2760	.0212	27.6607	.0362	36

Interest rate of 2.00 percent

N	Compound amount — Future value of a present amount F/P	Present value — Present value of a future amount P/F	Annuity compound amount — Future value of an annuity F/A	Sinking fund — Annuity providing a future amount A/F	Annuity present value — Present value of an annuity P/A	Capital recovery — Annuity repaying a present amount A/P	N
1	1.0200	.9804	1.0000	1.0000	.9804	1.0200	1
2	1.0404	.9612	2.0200	.4950	1.9416	.5150	2
3	1.0612	.9423	3.0604	.3268	2.8839	.3468	3
4	1.0824	.9238	4.1216	.2426	3.8077	.2626	4
5	1.1041	.9057	5.2040	.1922	4.7135	.2122	5
6	1.1262	.8880	6.3081	.1585	5.6014	.1785	6
7	1.1487	.8706	7.4343	.1345	6.4720	.1545	7
8	1.1717	.8535	8.5830	.1165	7.3255	.1365	8
9	1.1951	.8368	9.7546	.1025	8.1622	.1225	9
10	1.2190	.8203	10.9497	.0913	8.9826	.1113	10
11	1.2434	.8043	12.1687	.0822	9.7868	.1022	11
12	1.2682	.7885	13.4121	.0746	10.5753	.0946	12
13	1.2936	.7730	14.6803	.0681	11.3484	.0881	13
14	1.3195	.7579	15.9739	.0626	12.1062	.0826	14
15	1.3459	.7430	17.2934	.0578	12.8493	.0778	15
16	1.3728	.7284	18.6393	.0537	13.5777	.0737	16
17	1.4002	.7142	20.0121	.0500	14.2919	.0700	17
18	1.4282	.7002	21.4123	.0467	14.9920	.0667	18
19	1.4568	.6864	22.8406	.0438	15.6785	.0638	19
20	1.4859	.6730	24.2974	.0412	16.3514	.0612	20
21	1.5157	.6598	25.7833	.0388	17.0112	.0588	21
22	1.5460	.6468	27.2990	.0366	17.6580	.0566	22
23	1.5769	.6342	28.8450	.0347	18.2922	.0547	23
24	1.6084	.6217	30.4219	.0329	18.9139	.0529	24
25	1.6406	.6095	32.0303	.0312	19.5235	.0512	25
26	1.6734	.5976	33.6709	.0297	20.1210	.0497	26
27	1.7069	.5859	35.3443	.0283	20.7069	.0483	27
28	1.7410	.5744	37.0512	.0270	21.2813	.0470	28
29	1.7758	.5631	38.7922	.0258	21.8444	.0458	29
30	1.8114	.5521	40.5681	.0246	22.3965	.0446	30
31	1.8476	.5412	42.3794	.0236	22.9377	.0436	31
32	1.8845	.5306	44.2270	.0226	23.4683	.0426	32
33	1.9222	.5202	46.1116	.0217	23.9886	.0417	33
34	1.9607	.5100	48.0338	.0208	24.4986	.0408	34
35	1.9999	.5000	49.9945	.0200	24.9986	.0400	35
36	2.0399	.4902	51.9944	.0192	25.4888	.0392	36

N	Compound amount — Future value of a present amount F/P	Present value — Present value of a future amount P/F	Annuity compound amount — Future value of an annuity F/A	Sinking fund — Annuity providing a future amount A/F	Annuity present value — Present value of an annuity P/A	Capital recovery — Annuity repaying a present amount A/P	N
40	2.2080	.4529	60.4020	.0166	27.3555	.0366	40
44	2.3901	.4184	69.5027	.0144	29.0800	.0344	44
48	2.5871	.3865	79.3535	.0126	30.6731	.0326	48
52	2.8003	.3571	90.0164	.0111	32.1449	.0311	52
56	3.0312	.3299	101.5583	.0098	33.5047	.0298	56
60	3.2810	.3048	114.0515	.0088	34.7609	.0288	60
64	3.5515	.2816	127.5747	.0078	35.9214	.0278	64
68	3.8443	.2601	142.2125	.0070	36.9936	.0270	68
72	4.1611	.2403	158.0570	.0063	37.9841	.0263	72
76	4.5042	.2220	175.2076	.0057	38.8991	.0257	76
80	4.8754	.2051	193.7720	.0052	39.7445	.0252	80
84	5.2773	.1895	213.8666	.0047	40.5255	.0247	84
88	5.7124	.1751	235.6177	.0042	41.2470	.0242	88
92	6.1832	.1617	259.1618	.0039	41.9136	.0239	92
96	6.6929	.1494	284.6467	.0035	42.5294	.0235	96
100	7.2446	.1380	312.2323	.0032	43.0984	.0232	100
104	7.8418	.1275	342.0919	.0029	43.6239	.0229	104
108	8.4883	.1178	374.4129	.0027	44.1095	.0227	108
112	9.1880	.1088	409.3981	.0024	44.5581	.0222	112
116	9.9453	.1005	447.2673	.0022	44.9725	.0222	116
120	10.7652	.0929	488.2582	.0020	45.3554	.0220	120
∞					50.0000	.0200	∞

Interest rate of 3.00 percent

N	Compound amount — Future value of a present amount — F/P	Present value — Present value of a future amount — P/F	Annuity compound amount — Future value of an annuity — F/A	Sinking fund — Annuity providing a future amount — A/F	Annuity present value — Present value of an annuity — P/A	Capital recovery — Annuity repaying a present amount — A/P	N
1	1.0300	.9709	1.0000	1.0000	.9709	1.0300	1
2	1.0609	.9426	2.0300	.4926	1.9135	.5226	2
3	1.0927	.9151	3.0909	.3235	2.8286	.3535	3
4	1.1255	.8885	4.1836	.2390	3.7171	.2690	4
5	1.1593	.8626	5.3091	.1884	4.5797	.2184	5
6	1.1941	.8375	6.4684	.1546	5.4172	.1846	6
7	1.2299	.8131	7.6625	.1305	6.2303	.1605	7
8	1.2668	.7894	8.8923	.1125	7.0197	.1425	8
9	1.3048	.7664	10.1591	.0984	7.7861	.1284	9
10	1.3439	.7441	11.4639	.0872	8.5302	.1172	10
11	1.3842	.7224	12.8078	.0781	9.2526	.1081	11
12	1.4258	.7014	14.1920	.0705	9.9540	.1005	12
13	1.4685	.6810	15.6178	.0640	10.6350	.0940	13
14	1.5126	.6611	17.0863	.0585	11.2961	.0885	14
15	1.5580	.6419	18.5989	.0538	11.9379	.0838	15
16	1.6047	.6232	20.1569	.0496	12.5611	.0796	16
17	1.6528	.6050	21.7616	.0460	13.1661	.0760	17
18	1.7024	.5874	23.4144	.0427	13.7535	.0727	18
19	1.7535	.5703	25.1169	.0398	14.3238	.0698	19
20	1.8061	.5537	26.8704	.0372	14.8775	.0672	20
21	1.8603	.5375	28.6765	.0349	15.4150	.0649	21
22	1.9161	.5219	30.5368	.0327	15.9369	.0627	22
23	1.9736	.5067	32.4529	.0308	16.4436	.0608	23
24	2.0328	.4919	34.4265	.0290	16.9355	.0590	24
25	2.0938	.4776	36.4593	.0274	17.4131	.0574	25
26	2.1566	.4637	38.5530	.0259	17.8768	.0559	26
27	2.2213	.4502	40.7096	.0246	18.3270	.0546	27
28	2.2879	.4371	42.9309	.0233	18.7641	.0533	28
29	2.3566	.4243	45.2189	.0221	19.1885	.0521	29
30	2.4273	.4120	47.5754	.0210	19.6004	.0510	30
31	2.5001	.4000	50.0027	.0200	20.0004	.0500	31
32	2.5751	.3883	52.5028	.0190	20.3888	.0490	32
33	2.6523	.3770	55.0778	.0182	20.7658	.0482	33
34	2.7319	.3660	57.7302	.0173	21.1318	.0473	34
35	2.8139	.3554	60.4621	.0165	21.4872	.0465	35
36	2.8983	.3450	63.2759	.0158	21.8323	.0458	36

N	Compound amount — Future value of a present amount — F/P	Present value — Present value of a future amount — P/F	Annuity compound amount — Future value of an annuity — F/A	Sinking fund — Annuity providing a future amount — A/F	Annuity present value — Present value of an annuity — P/A	Capital recovery — Annuity repaying a present amount — A/P	N
40	3.2620	.3066	75.4013	.0133	23.1148	.0433	40
44	3.6715	.2724	89.0484	.0112	24.2543	.0412	44
48	4.1323	.2420	104.4084	.0096	25.2667	.0396	48
52	4.6509	.2150	121.6962	.0082	26.1662	.0382	52
56	5.2346	.1910	141.1538	.0071	26.9655	.0371	56
60	5.8916	.1697	163.0534	.0061	27.6756	.0361	60
64	6.6311	.1508	187.7017	.0053	28.3065	.0353	64
68	7.4633	.1340	215.4436	.0046	28.8670	.0346	68
72	8.4000	.1190	246.6672	.0041	29.3651	.0341	72
76	9.4543	.1058	281.8098	.0035	29.8076	.0335	76
80	10.6409	.0940	321.3630	.0031	30.2008	.0331	80
84	11.9764	.0835	365.8805	.0027	30.5501	.0327	84
88	13.4796	.0742	415.9854	.0024	30.8605	.0324	88
92	15.1714	.0659	472.3789	.0021	31.1362	.0321	92
96	17.0755	.0586	535.8502	.0019	31.3812	.0319	96
100	19.2186	.0520	607.2877	.0016	31.5989	.0316	100
104	21.6307	.0462	687.6913	.0015	31.7923	.0315	104
108	24.3456	.0411	778.1863	.0013	31.9642	.0313	108
112	27.4012	.0365	880.0391	.0011	32.1168	.0311	112
116	30.8403	.0324	994.6754	.0010	32.2525	.0310	116
120	34.7110	.0288	1123.6996	.0009	32.3730	.0309	120
∞					33.3333	.0300	∞

Interest rate of 4.00 percent

N	Compound amount — Future value of a present amount — F/P	Present value — Present value of a future amount — P/F	Annuity compound amount — Future value of an annuity — F/A	Sinking fund — Annuity providing a future amount — A/F	Annuity present value — Present value of an annuity — P/A	Capital recovery — Annuity repaying a present amount — A/P	N
1	1.0400	.9615	1.0000	1.0000	.9615	1.0400	1
2	1.0816	.9246	2.0400	.4902	1.8861	.5302	2
3	1.1249	.8890	3.1216	.3203	2.7751	.3603	3
4	1.1699	.8548	4.2465	.2355	3.6299	.2755	4
5	1.2167	.8219	5.4163	.1846	4.4518	.2246	5
6	1.2653	.7903	6.6330	.1508	5.2421	.1908	6
7	1.3159	.7599	7.8983	.1266	6.0021	.1666	7
8	1.3686	.7307	9.2142	.1085	6.7327	.1485	8
9	1.4233	.7026	10.5828	.0945	7.4353	.1345	9
10	1.4802	.6756	12.0061	.0833	8.1109	.1233	10
11	1.5395	.6496	13.4864	.0741	8.7605	.1141	11
12	1.6010	.6246	15.0258	.0666	9.3851	.1066	12
13	1.6651	.6006	16.6268	.0601	9.9856	.1001	13
14	1.7317	.5775	18.2919	.0547	10.5631	.0947	14
15	1.8009	.5553	20.0236	.0499	11.1184	.0899	15
16	1.8730	.5339	21.8245	.0458	11.6523	.0858	16
17	1.9479	.5134	23.6975	.0422	12.1657	.0822	17
18	2.0258	.4936	25.6454	.0390	12.6593	.0790	18
19	2.1068	.4746	27.6712	.0361	13.1339	.0761	19
20	2.1911	.4564	29.7781	.0336	13.5093	.0736	20
21	2.2788	.4388	31.9692	.0313	14.0292	.0713	21
22	2.3699	.4220	34.2480	.0292	14.4511	.0692	22
23	2.4647	.4057	36.6179	.0273	14.8568	.0673	23
24	2.5633	.3901	39.0826	.0256	15.2470	.0656	24
25	2.6658	.3751	41.6459	.0240	15.6221	.0640	25
26	2.7725	.3607	44.3117	.0226	15.9828	.0626	26
27	2.8834	.3468	47.0842	.0212	16.3296	.0612	27
28	2.9987	.3335	49.9676	.0200	16.6631	.0600	28
29	3.1187	.3207	52.9663	.0189	16.9837	.0589	29
30	3.2434	.3083	56.0849	.0178	17.2920	.0578	30
31	3.3731	.2965	59.3283	.0169	17.5885	.0569	31
32	3.5081	.2851	62.7015	.0159	17.8736	.0559	32
33	3.6484	.2741	66.2095	.0151	18.1476	.0551	33
34	3.7943	.2636	69.8579	.0143	18.4112	.0543	34
35	3.9461	.2534	73.6522	.0136	18.6646	.0536	35
36	4.1039	.2437	77.5983	.0129	18.9083	.0529	36

N	Compound amount — Future value of a present amount — F/P	Present value — Present value of a future amount — P/F	Annuity compound amount — Future value of an annuity — F/A	Sinking fund — Annuity providing a future amount — A/F	Annuity present value — Present value of an annuity — P/A	Capital recovery — Annuity repaying a present amount — A/P	N
40	4.8010	.2083	95.0255	.0105	19.7928	.0505	40
44	5.6165	.1780	115.4129	.0087	20.5488	.0487	44
48	6.5705	.1522	139.2632	.0072	21.1951	.0472	48
52	7.6866	.1301	167.1647	.0060	21.7476	.0460	52
56	8.9922	.1112	199.8055	.0050	22.2198	.0450	56
60	10.5196	.0951	237.9907	.0042	22.6235	.0442	60
64	12.3065	.0813	282.6619	.0035	22.9685	.0435	64
68	14.3968	.0695	334.9209	.0030	23.2635	.0430	68
72	16.8423	.0594	396.0566	.0025	23.5156	.0425	72
76	19.7031	.0508	467.5766	.0021	23.7312	.0421	76
80	23.0498	.0434	551.2450	.0018	23.9154	.0418	80
84	26.9650	.0371	649.1251	.0015	24.0729	.0415	84
88	31.5452	.0317	763.6310	.0013	24.2075	.0413	88
92	36.9035	.0271	897.5868	.0011	24.3226	.0411	92
96	43.1718	.0232	1054.2960	.0009	24.4209	.0409	96
100	50.5049	.0198	1237.6237	.0008	24.5050	.0408	100
104	59.0836	.0169	1452.0911	.0007	24.5769	.0407	104
108	69.1195	.0145	1702.9877	.0006	24.6383	.0406	108
112	80.8600	.0124	1996.5012	.0005	24.6908	.0405	112
116	94.5948	.0106	2339.8705	.0004	24.7357	.0404	116
120	110.6626	.0090	2741.5640	.0004	24.7741	.0404	120
∞					25.0000	.0400	∞

Interest rate of 5.00 percent

N	Compound amount — Future value of a present amount — F/P	Present value — Present value of a future amount — P/F	Annuity compound amount — Future value of an annuity — F/A	Sinking fund — Annuity providing a future amount — A/F	Annuity present value — Present value of an annuity — P/A	Capital recovery — Annuity repaying a present amount — A/P	N
1	1.0500	.9524	1.0000	1.0000	.9524	1.0500	1
2	1.1025	.9070	2.0500	.4878	1.8594	.5378	2
3	1.1576	.8638	3.1525	.3172	2.7232	.3672	3
4	1.2155	.8227	4.3101	.2320	3.5460	.2820	4
5	1.2763	.7835	5.5256	.1810	4.3295	.2310	5
6	1.3401	.7462	6.8019	.1470	5.0757	.1970	6
7	1.4071	.7107	8.1420	.1228	5.7864	.1728	7
8	1.4775	.6768	9.5491	.1047	6.4632	.1547	8
9	1.5513	.6446	11.0266	.0907	7.1078	.1407	9
10	1.6289	.6139	12.5779	.0795	7.7217	.1295	10
11	1.7103	.5847	14.2068	.0704	8.3064	.1204	11
12	1.7959	.5568	15.9171	.0628	8.8633	.1128	12
13	1.8856	.5303	17.7130	.0565	9.3936	.1065	13
14	1.9799	.5051	19.5986	.0510	9.8986	.1010	14
15	2.0789	.4810	21.5786	.0463	10.3797	.0963	15
16	2.1829	.4581	23.6575	.0423	10.8378	.0923	16
17	2.2920	.4363	25.8404	.0387	11.2741	.0887	17
18	2.4066	.4155	28.1324	.0355	11.6896	.0855	18
19	2.5270	.3957	30.5390	.0327	12.0853	.0827	19
20	2.6533	.3769	33.0660	.0302	12.4622	.0802	20
21	2.7860	.3589	35.7193	.0280	12.8212	.0780	21
22	2.9253	.3418	38.5052	.0260	13.1630	.0760	22
23	3.0715	.3256	41.4305	.0241	13.4886	.0741	23
24	3.2251	.3101	44.5020	.0225	13.7986	.0725	24
25	3.3864	.2953	47.7271	.0210	14.0939	.0710	25
26	3.5557	.2812	51.1135	.0196	14.3752	.0696	26
27	3.7335	.2678	54.6691	.0183	14.6430	.0683	27
28	3.9201	.2551	58.4026	.0171	14.8981	.0671	28
29	4.1161	.2429	62.3227	.0160	15.1411	.0660	29
30	4.3219	.2314	66.4388	.0151	15.3725	.0651	30
31	4.5380	.2204	70.7608	.0141	15.5928	.0641	31
32	4.7649	.2099	75.2988	.0133	15.8027	.0633	32
33	5.0032	.1999	80.0638	.0125	16.0025	.0625	33
34	5.2533	.1904	85.0670	.0118	16.1929	.0618	34
35	5.5160	.1813	90.3203	.0111	16.3742	.0611	35
36	5.7918	.1727	95.8363	.0104	16.5469	.0604	36

N	Compound amount — Future value of a present amount — F/P	Present value — Present value of a future amount — P/F	Annuity compound amount — Future value of an annuity — F/A	Sinking fund — Annuity providing a future amount — A/F	Annuity present value — Present value of an annuity — P/A	Capital recovery — Annuity repaying a present amount — A/P	N
40	7.0400	.1420	120.7998	.0083	17.1591	.0583	40
44	8.5572	.1169	151.1430	.0066	17.6628	.0566	44
48	10.4013	.0961	188.0254	.0053	18.0772	.0553	48
52	12.6428	.0791	232.8562	.0043	18.4181	.0543	52
56	15.3674	.0651	287.3482	.0035	18.6985	.0535	56
60	18.6792	.0535	353.5837	.0028	18.9293	.0528	60
64	22.7047	.0440	434.0933	.0023	19.1191	.0523	64
68	27.5977	.0362	531.9533	.0019	19.2753	.0519	68
72	33.5451	.0298	650.9027	.0015	19.4038	.0515	72
76	40.7743	.0245	795.4864	.0013	19.5095	.0513	76
80	49.5614	.0202	971.2288	.0010	19.5965	.0510	80
84	60.2422	.0166	1184.8448	.0008	19.6680	.0508	84
88	73.2248	.0137	1444.4964	.0007	19.7269	.0507	88
92	89.0052	.0112	1760.1045	.0006	19.7753	.0506	92
96	108.1864	.0092	2143.7282	.0005	19.8151	.0505	96
100	131.5013	.0076	2610.0252	.0004	19.8479	.0504	100
104	159.8406	.0063	3176.8120	.0003	19.8749	.0503	104
108	194.2872	.0051	3865.7450	.0003	19.8971	.0503	108
112	236.1574	.0042	4703.1473	.0002	19.9153	.0502	112
116	287.0508	.0035	5721.0151	.0002	19.9303	.0502	116
120	348.9120	.0029	6958.2397	.0001	19.9427	.0501	120
∞					20.0000	.0500	∞

Interest rate of 6.00 percent

N	Compound amount — Future value of a present amount F/P	Present value — Present value of a future amount P/F	Annuity compound amount — Future value of an annuity F/A	Sinking fund — Annuity providing a future amount A/F	Annuity present value — Present value of an annuity P/A	Capital recovery — Annuity repaying a present amount A/P	N
1	1.0600	.9434	1.0000	1.0000	.9434	1.0600	1
2	1.1236	.8900	2.0600	.4854	1.8334	.5454	2
3	1.1910	.8396	3.1836	.3141	2.6730	.3741	3
4	1.2625	.7921	4.3746	.2286	3.4651	.2886	4
5	1.3382	.7473	5.6371	.1774	4.2124	.2374	5
6	1.4185	.7050	6.9753	.1434	4.9173	.2034	6
7	1.5036	.6651	8.3938	.1191	5.5824	.1791	7
8	1.5938	.6274	9.8975	.1010	6.2098	.1610	8
9	1.6895	.5919	11.4913	.0870	6.8017	.1470	9
10	1.7908	.5584	13.1808	.0759	7.3601	.1359	10
11	1.8983	.5268	14.9716	.0668	7.8869	.1268	11
12	2.0122	.4970	16.8699	.0593	8.3838	.1193	12
13	2.1329	.4688	18.8821	.0530	8.8527	.1130	13
14	2.2609	.4423	21.0151	.0476	9.2950	.1076	14
15	2.3966	.4173	23.2760	.0430	9.7122	.1030	15
16	2.5404	.3936	25.6725	.0390	10.1059	.0990	16
17	2.6928	.3714	28.2129	.0354	10.4773	.0954	17
18	2.8543	.3503	30.9057	.0324	10.8276	.0924	18
19	3.0256	.3305	33.7600	.0296	11.1581	.0896	19
20	3.2071	.3118	36.7856	.0272	11.4699	.0872	20
21	3.3996	.2942	39.9927	.0250	11.7641	.0850	21
22	3.6035	.2775	43.3923	.0230	12.0416	.0830	22
23	3.8197	.2618	46.9958	.0213	12.3034	.0813	23
24	4.0489	.2470	50.8156	.0197	12.5504	.0797	24
25	4.2919	.2330	54.8645	.0182	12.7834	.0782	25
26	4.5494	.2198	59.1564	.0169	13.0032	.0769	26
27	4.8223	.2074	63.7058	.0157	13.2105	.0757	27
28	5.1117	.1956	68.5281	.0146	13.4062	.0746	28
29	5.4184	.1846	73.6398	.0136	13.5907	.0736	29
30	5.7435	.1741	79.0582	.0126	13.7648	.0726	30
31	6.0881	.1643	84.8017	.0118	13.9291	.0718	31
32	6.4534	.1550	90.8898	.0110	14.0840	.0710	32
33	6.8406	.1462	97.3432	.0103	14.2302	.0703	33
34	7.2510	.1379	104.1838	.0096	14.3681	.0696	34
35	7.6861	.1301	111.4348	.0090	14.4982	.0690	35
36	8.1473	.1227	119.1209	.0084	14.6210	.0684	36

N	Compound amount — Future value of a present amount F/P	Present value — Present value of a future amount P/F	Annuity compound amount — Future value of an annuity F/A	Sinking fund — Annuity providing a future amount A/F	Annuity present value — Present value of an annuity P/A	Capital recovery — Annuity repaying a present amount A/P	N
40	10.2857	.0972	154.7620	.0065	15.0463	.0665	40
44	12.9855	.0770	199.7580	.0050	15.3832	.0650	44
48	16.3939	.0610	256.5645	.0039	15.6500	.0639	48
52	20.6969	.0483	328.2814	.0030	15.8614	.0630	52
56	26.1293	.0383	418.8223	.0024	16.0288	.0624	56
60	32.9877	.0303	533.1282	.0019	16.1614	.0619	60
64	41.6462	.0240	677.4367	.0015	16.2665	.0615	64
68	52.5774	.0190	859.6228	.0012	16.3497	.0612	68
72	66.3777	.0151	1089.6286	.0009	16.4156	.0609	72
76	83.8003	.0119	1380.0056	.0007	16.4678	.0607	76
80	105.7960	.0095	1746.5999	.0006	16.5091	.0606	80
84	133.5650	.0075	2209.4167	.0005	16.5419	.0605	84
88	168.6227	.0059	2793.7123	.0004	16.5678	.0604	88
92	212.8823	.0047	3531.3721	.0003	16.5884	.0603	92
96	268.7590	.0037	4462.6505	.0002	16.6047	.0602	96
100	339.3021	.0029	5638.3681	.0002	16.6175	.0602	100
104	428.3611	.0023	7122.6844	.0001	16.6278	.0601	104
108	540.7960	.0018	8996.5995	.0001	16.6358	.0601	108
112	682.7425	.0015	11362.3743	.0001	16.6423	.0601	112
116	861.9466	.0012	14349.1103	.0001	16.6473	.0601	116
120	1088.1877	.0009	18119.7958	.0001	16.6514	.0601	120
∞					16.6667	.0600	∞

Interest rate of 8.00 percent

N	Compound amount — Future value of a present amount (F/P)	Present value — Present value of a future amount (P/F)	Annuity compound amount — Future value of an annuity (F/A)	Sinking fund — Annuity providing a future amount (A/F)	Annuity present value — Present value of an annuity (P/A)	Capital recovery — Annuity repaying a present amount (A/P)	N
1	1.0800	.9259	1.0000	1.0000	.9259	1.0800	1
2	1.1664	.8573	2.0800	.4808	1.7833	.5608	2
3	1.2597	.7938	3.2464	.3080	2.5771	.3880	3
4	1.3605	.7350	4.5061	.2219	3.3121	.3019	4
5	1.4693	.6806	5.8666	.1705	3.9927	.2505	5
6	1.5869	.6302	7.3359	.1363	4.6229	.2163	6
7	1.7138	.5835	8.9228	.1121	5.2064	.1921	7
8	1.8509	.5403	10.6366	.0940	5.7466	.1740	8
9	1.9990	.5002	12.4876	.0801	6.2469	.1601	9
10	2.1589	.4632	14.4866	.0690	6.7101	.1490	10
11	2.3316	.4289	16.6455	.0601	7.1390	.1401	11
12	2.5182	.3971	18.9771	.0527	7.5361	.1327	12
13	2.7196	.3677	21.4953	.0465	7.9038	.1265	13
14	2.9372	.3405	24.2149	.0413	8.2442	.1213	14
15	3.1722	.3152	27.1521	.0368	8.5595	.1168	15
16	3.4259	.2919	30.3243	.0330	8.8514	.1130	16
17	3.7000	.2703	33.7502	.0296	9.1216	.1096	17
18	3.9960	.2502	37.4502	.0267	9.3719	.1067	18
19	4.3157	.2317	41.4463	.0241	9.6036	.1041	19
20	4.6610	.2145	45.7620	.0219	9.8181	.1019	20
21	5.0338	.1987	50.4229	.0198	10.0168	.0998	21
22	5.4365	.1839	55.4568	.0180	10.2007	.0980	22
23	5.8715	.1703	60.8933	.0164	10.3711	.0964	23
24	6.3412	.1577	66.7648	.0150	10.5288	.0950	24
25	6.8485	.1460	73.1059	.0137	10.6748	.0937	25
26	7.3964	.1352	79.9544	.0125	10.8100	.0925	26
27	7.9881	.1252	87.3508	.0114	10.9352	.0914	27
28	8.6271	.1159	95.3388	.0105	11.0511	.0905	28
29	9.3173	.1073	103.9659	.0096	11.1584	.0896	29
30	10.0627	.0994	113.2832	.0088	11.2578	.0888	30
35	14.7853	.0676	172.3168	.0058	11.6546	.0858	35
40	21.7245	.0460	259.0565	.0039	11.9246	.0839	40
45	31.9204	.0313	386.5056	.0026	12.1084	.0826	45
50	46.9016	.0213	573.7702	.0017	12.2335	.0817	50
55	68.9139	.0145	848.9232	.0012	12.3186	.0812	55
60	101.2571	.0099	1253.2133	.0008	12.3766	.0808	60
∞		.0800			12.5000	.0800	∞

Interest rate of 7.00 percent

N	Compound amount — Future value of a present amount (F/P)	Present value — Present value of a future amount (P/F)	Annuity compound amount — Future value of an annuity (F/A)	Sinking fund — Annuity providing a future amount (A/F)	Annuity present value — Present value of an annuity (P/A)	Capital recovery — Annuity repaying a present amount (A/P)	N
1	1.0700	.9346	1.0000	1.0000	.9346	1.0700	1
2	1.1449	.8734	2.0700	.4831	1.8080	.5531	2
3	1.2250	.8163	3.2149	.3111	2.6243	.3811	3
4	1.3108	.7629	4.4399	.2252	3.3872	.2952	4
5	1.4026	.7130	5.7507	.1739	4.1002	.2439	5
6	1.5007	.6663	7.1533	.1398	4.7665	.2098	6
7	1.6058	.6227	8.6540	.1156	5.3893	.1856	7
8	1.7182	.5820	10.2598	.0975	5.9713	.1675	8
9	1.8385	.5439	11.9780	.0835	6.5152	.1535	9
10	1.9672	.5083	13.8164	.0724	7.0236	.1424	10
11	2.1049	.4751	15.7836	.0634	7.4987	.1334	11
12	2.2522	.4440	17.8885	.0559	7.9427	.1259	12
13	2.4098	.4150	20.1406	.0497	8.3577	.1197	13
14	2.5785	.3878	22.5505	.0443	8.7455	.1143	14
15	2.7590	.3624	25.1290	.0398	9.1079	.1098	15
16	2.9522	.3387	27.8881	.0359	9.4466	.1059	16
17	3.1588	.3166	30.8402	.0324	9.7632	.1024	17
18	3.3799	.2959	33.9990	.0294	10.0591	.0994	18
19	3.6165	.2765	37.3790	.0268	10.3356	.0968	19
20	3.8697	.2584	40.9955	.0244	10.5940	.0944	20
21	4.1406	.2415	44.8652	.0223	10.8355	.0923	21
22	4.4304	.2257	49.0057	.0204	11.0612	.0904	22
23	4.7405	.2109	53.4361	.0187	11.2722	.0887	23
24	5.0724	.1971	58.1767	.0172	11.4693	.0872	24
25	5.4274	.1842	63.2490	.0158	11.6536	.0858	25
26	5.8074	.1722	68.6765	.0146	11.8258	.0846	26
27	6.2139	.1609	74.4838	.0134	11.9867	.0834	27
28	6.6488	.1504	80.6977	.0124	12.1371	.0824	28
29	7.1143	.1406	87.3465	.0114	12.2777	.0814	29
30	7.6123	.1314	94.4608	.0106	12.4090	.0806	30
35	10.6766	.0937	138.2369	.0072	12.9477	.0772	35
40	14.9745	.0668	199.6351	.0050	13.3317	.0750	40
45	21.0025	.0476	285.7493	.0035	13.6055	.0735	45
50	29.4570	.0339	406.5289	.0025	13.8007	.0725	50
55	41.3150	.0242	575.9286	.0017	13.9399	.0717	55
60	57.9464	.0173	813.5204	.0012	14.0392	.0712	60
∞					14.2857	.0700	∞

Interest rate of 10.00 percent

N	Compound amount — Future value of a present amount — F/P	Present value — Present value of a future amount — P/F	Annuity compound amount — Future value of an annuity — F/A	Sinking fund — Annuity providing a future amount — A/F	Annuity present value — Present value of an annuity — P/A	Capital recovery — Annuity repaying a present amount — A/P	N
1	1.1000	.9091	1.0000	1.0000	.9091	1.1000	1
2	1.2100	.8264	2.1000	.4762	1.7355	.5762	2
3	1.3310	.7513	3.3100	.3021	2.4869	.4021	3
4	1.4641	.6830	4.6410	.2155	3.1699	.3155	4
5	1.6105	.6209	6.1051	.1638	3.7908	.2638	5
6	1.7716	.5645	7.7156	.1296	4.3553	.2296	6
7	1.9487	.5132	9.4872	.1054	4.8684	.2054	7
8	2.1436	.4665	11.4359	.0874	5.3349	.1874	8
9	2.3579	.4241	13.5795	.0736	5.7590	.1736	9
10	2.5937	.3855	15.9374	.0627	6.1446	.1627	10
11	2.8531	.3505	18.5312	.0540	6.4951	.1540	11
12	3.1384	.3186	21.3843	.0468	6.8137	.1468	12
13	3.4523	.2897	24.5227	.0408	7.1034	.1408	13
14	3.7975	.2633	27.9750	.0357	7.3667	.1357	14
15	4.1772	.2394	31.7725	.0315	7.6061	.1315	15
16	4.5950	.2176	35.9497	.0278	7.8237	.1278	16
17	5.0545	.1978	40.5447	.0247	8.0216	.1247	17
18	5.5599	.1799	45.5992	.0219	8.2014	.1219	18
19	6.1159	.1635	51.1591	.0195	8.3649	.1195	19
20	6.7275	.1486	57.2750	.0175	8.5136	.1175	20
21	7.4002	.1351	64.0025	.0156	8.6487	.1156	21
22	8.1403	.1228	71.4027	.0140	8.7715	.1140	22
23	8.9543	.1117	79.5430	.0126	8.8832	.1126	23
24	9.8497	.1015	88.4973	.0113	8.9847	.1113	24
25	10.8347	.0923	98.3471	.0102	9.0770	.1102	25
26	11.9182	.0839	109.1818	.0092	9.1609	.1092	26
27	13.1100	.0763	121.0999	.0083	9.2372	.1083	27
28	14.4210	.0693	134.2099	.0075	9.3066	.1075	28
29	15.8631	.0630	148.6309	.0067	9.3696	.1067	29
30	17.4494	.0573	164.4940	.0061	9.4269	.1061	30
35	28.1024	.0356	271.0244	.0037	9.6442	.1037	35
40	45.2593	.0221	442.5926	.0023	9.7791	.1023	40
45	72.8905	.0137	718.9048	.0014	9.8628	.1014	45
50	117.3909	.0085	1163.9085	.0009	9.9148	.1009	50
55	189.0591	.0053	1880.5914	.0005	9.9471	.1005	55
60	304.4816	.0033	3034.8164	.0003	9.9672	.1003	60
∞					10.0000	.1000	∞

Interest rate of 9.00 percent

N	Compound amount — Future value of a present amount — F/P	Present value — Present value of a future amount — P/F	Annuity compound amount — Future value of an annuity — F/A	Sinking fund — Annuity providing a future amount — A/F	Annuity present value — Present value of an annuity — P/A	Capital recovery — Annuity repaying a present amount — A/P	N
1	1.0900	.9174	1.0000	1.0000	.9174	1.0900	1
2	1.1881	.8417	2.0900	.4785	1.7591	.5685	2
3	1.2950	.7722	3.2781	.3051	2.5313	.3951	3
4	1.4116	.7084	4.5731	.2187	3.2397	.3087	4
5	1.5386	.6499	5.9847	.1671	3.8897	.2571	5
6	1.6771	.5963	7.5233	.1329	4.4859	.2229	6
7	1.8280	.5470	9.2004	.1087	5.0330	.1987	7
8	1.9926	.5019	11.0285	.0907	5.5348	.1807	8
9	2.1719	.4604	13.0210	.0768	5.9952	.1668	9
10	2.3674	.4224	15.1929	.0658	6.4177	.1558	10
11	2.5804	.3875	17.5603	.0569	6.8052	.1469	11
12	2.8127	.3555	20.1407	.0497	7.1607	.1397	12
13	3.0658	.3262	22.9534	.0436	7.4869	.1336	13
14	3.3417	.2992	26.0192	.0384	7.7862	.1284	14
15	3.6425	.2745	29.3609	.0341	8.0607	.1241	15
16	3.9703	.2519	33.0034	.0303	8.3126	.1203	16
17	4.3276	.2311	36.9737	.0270	8.5436	.1170	17
18	4.7171	.2120	41.3013	.0242	8.7556	.1142	18
19	5.1417	.1945	46.0185	.0217	8.9501	.1117	19
20	5.6044	.1784	51.1601	.0195	9.1285	.1095	20
21	6.1088	.1637	56.7645	.0176	9.2922	.1076	21
22	6.6586	.1502	62.8733	.0159	9.4424	.1059	22
23	7.2579	.1378	69.5319	.0144	9.5802	.1044	23
24	7.9111	.1264	76.7898	.0130	9.7066	.1030	24
25	8.6231	.1160	84.7009	.0118	9.8226	.1018	25
26	9.3992	.1064	93.3240	.0107	9.9290	.1007	26
27	10.2451	.0976	102.7231	.0097	10.0266	.0997	27
28	11.1671	.0895	112.9682	.0089	10.1161	.0989	28
29	12.1722	.0822	124.1354	.0081	10.1983	.0981	29
30	13.2677	.0754	136.3075	.0073	10.2737	.0973	30
35	20.4140	.0490	215.7108	.0046	10.5668	.0946	35
40	31.4094	.0318	337.8824	.0030	10.7574	.0930	40
45	48.3273	.0207	525.8587	.0019	10.8812	.0919	45
50	74.3575	.0134	815.0836	.0012	10.9617	.0912	50
55	114.4083	.0087	1260.0918	.0008	11.0140	.0908	55
60	176.0313	.0057	1944.7921	.0005	11.0480	.0905	60
∞					11.1111	.0900	∞

Interest rate of 12.00 percent

N	Compound amount — Future value of a present amount — F/P	Present value — Present value of a future amount — P/F	Annuity compound amount — Future value of an annuity — F/A	Sinking fund — Annuity providing a future amount — A/F	Annuity present value — Present value of an annuity — P/A	Capital recovery — Annuity repaying a present amount — A/P	N
1	1.1200	.8929	1.0000	1.0000	.8929	1.1200	1
2	1.2544	.7972	2.1200	.4717	1.6901	.5917	2
3	1.4049	.7118	3.3744	.2963	2.4018	.4163	3
4	1.5735	.6355	4.7793	.2092	3.0373	.3292	4
5	1.7623	.5674	6.3528	.1574	3.6048	.2774	5
6	1.9738	.5066	8.1152	.1232	4.1114	.2432	6
7	2.2107	.4523	10.0890	.0991	4.5638	.2191	7
8	2.4760	.4039	12.2997	.0813	4.9676	.2013	8
9	2.7731	.3606	14.7757	.0677	5.3282	.1877	9
10	3.1058	.3220	17.5487	.0570	5.6502	.1770	10
11	3.4785	.2875	20.6546	.0484	5.9377	.1684	11
12	3.8960	.2567	24.1331	.0414	6.1944	.1614	12
13	4.3635	.2292	28.0291	.0357	6.4235	.1557	13
14	4.8871	.2046	32.3926	.0309	6.6282	.1509	14
15	5.4736	.1827	37.2797	.0268	6.8109	.1468	15
16	6.1304	.1631	42.7533	.0234	6.9740	.1434	16
17	6.8660	.1456	48.8837	.0205	7.1196	.1405	17
18	7.6900	.1300	55.7497	.0179	7.2497	.1379	18
19	8.6128	.1161	63.4397	.0158	7.3658	.1358	19
20	9.6463	.1037	72.0524	.0139	7.4694	.1339	20
21	10.8038	.0926	81.6987	.0122	7.5620	.1322	21
22	12.1003	.0826	92.5026	.0108	7.6446	.1308	22
23	13.5523	.0738	104.6029	.0096	7.7184	.1296	23
24	15.1786	.0659	118.1552	.0085	7.7843	.1285	24
25	17.0001	.0588	133.3339	.0075	7.8431	.1275	25
26	19.0401	.0525	150.3339	.0067	7.8957	.1267	26
27	21.3249	.0469	169.3740	.0059	7.9426	.1259	27
28	23.8839	.0419	190.6989	.0052	7.9844	.1252	28
29	26.7499	.0374	214.5828	.0047	8.0218	.1247	29
30	29.9599	.0334	241.3327	.0041	8.0552	.1241	30
35	52.7996	.0189	431.6635	.0023	8.1755	.1223	35
40	93.0510	.0107	767.0914	.0013	8.2438	.1213	40
45	163.9876	.0061	1358.2300	.0007	8.2825	.1207	45
50	289.0022	.0035	2400.0182	.0004	8.3045	.1204	50
55	509.3206	.0020	4236.0050	.0002	8.3170	.1202	55
60	897.5969	.0011	7471.6411	.0001	8.3240	.1201	60
∞					8.3333	.1200	∞

Interest rate of 11.00 percent

N	Compound amount — Future value of a present amount — F/P	Present value — Present value of a future amount — P/F	Annuity compound amount — Future value of an annuity — F/A	Sinking fund — Annuity providing a future amount — A/F	Annuity present value — Present value of an annuity — P/A	Capital recovery — Annuity repaying a present amount — A/P	N
1	1.1100	.9009	1.0000	1.0000	.9009	1.1100	1
2	1.2321	.8116	2.1100	.4739	1.7125	.5839	2
3	1.3676	.7312	3.3421	.2992	2.4437	.4092	3
4	1.5181	.6587	4.7097	.2123	3.1024	.3223	4
5	1.6851	.5935	6.2278	.1606	3.6959	.2706	5
6	1.8704	.5346	7.9129	.1264	4.2305	.2364	6
7	2.0762	.4817	9.7833	.1022	4.7122	.2122	7
8	2.3045	.4339	11.8594	.0843	5.1461	.1943	8
9	2.5580	.3909	14.1640	.0706	5.5370	.1806	9
10	2.8394	.3522	16.7220	.0598	5.8892	.1698	10
11	3.1518	.3173	19.5614	.0511	6.2065	.1611	11
12	3.4985	.2858	22.7132	.0440	6.4924	.1540	12
13	3.8833	.2575	26.2116	.0382	6.7499	.1482	13
14	4.3104	.2320	30.0949	.0332	6.9819	.1432	14
15	4.7846	.2090	34.4054	.0291	7.1909	.1391	15
16	5.3109	.1883	39.1899	.0255	7.3792	.1355	16
17	5.8951	.1696	44.5008	.0225	7.5488	.1325	17
18	6.5436	.1528	50.3959	.0198	7.7016	.1298	18
19	7.2633	.1377	56.9395	.0176	7.8393	.1276	19
20	8.0623	.1240	64.2028	.0156	7.9633	.1256	20
21	8.9492	.1117	72.2651	.0138	8.0751	.1238	21
22	9.9336	.1007	81.2143	.0123	8.1757	.1223	22
23	11.0263	.0907	91.1479	.0110	8.2664	.1210	23
24	12.2392	.0817	102.1742	.0098	8.3481	.1198	24
25	13.5855	.0736	114.4133	.0087	8.4217	.1187	25
26	15.0799	.0663	127.9988	.0078	8.4881	.1178	26
27	16.7386	.0597	143.0786	.0070	8.5478	.1170	27
28	18.5799	.0538	159.8173	.0063	8.6016	.1163	28
29	20.6237	.0485	178.3972	.0056	8.6501	.1156	29
30	22.8923	.0437	199.0209	.0050	8.6938	.1150	30
35	38.5749	.0259	341.5896	.0029	8.8552	.1129	35
40	65.0009	.0154	581.8261	.0017	8.9511	.1117	40
45	109.5302	.0091	986.6386	.0010	9.0079	.1110	45
50	184.5648	.0054	1668.7712	.0006	9.0417	.1106	50
55	311.0025	.0032	2818.2042	.0004	9.0617	.1104	55
60	524.0572	.0019	4755.0658	.0002	9.0736	.1102	60
∞					9.0909	.1100	∞

Interest rate of 14.00 percent

N	Compound amount — Future value of a present amount F/P	Present value — Present value of a future amount P/F	Annuity compound amount — Future value of an annuity F/A	Sinking fund — Annuity providing a future amount A/F	Annuity present value — Present value of an annuity P/A	Capital recovery — Annuity repaying a present amount A/P	N
1	1.1400	.8772	1.0000	1.0000	.8772	1.1400	1
2	1.2996	.7695	2.1400	.4673	1.6467	.6073	2
3	1.4815	.6750	3.4396	.2907	2.3216	.4307	3
4	1.6890	.5921	4.9211	.2032	2.9137	.3432	4
5	1.9254	.5194	6.6101	.1513	3.4331	.2913	5
6	2.1950	.4556	8.5355	.1172	3.8887	.2572	6
7	2.5023	.3996	10.7305	.0932	4.2883	.2332	7
8	2.8526	.3506	13.2328	.0756	4.6389	.2156	8
9	3.2519	.3075	16.0853	.0622	4.9464	.2022	9
10	3.7072	.2697	19.3373	.0517	5.2161	.1917	10
11	4.2262	.2366	23.0445	.0434	5.4527	.1834	11
12	4.8179	.2076	27.2707	.0367	5.6603	.1767	12
13	5.4924	.1821	32.0887	.0312	5.8424	.1712	13
14	6.2613	.1597	37.5811	.0266	6.0021	.1666	14
15	7.1379	.1401	43.8424	.0228	6.1422	.1628	15
16	8.1372	.1229	50.9804	.0196	6.2651	.1596	16
17	9.2765	.1078	59.1176	.0169	6.3729	.1569	17
18	10.5752	.0946	68.3941	.0146	6.4674	.1546	18
19	12.0557	.0829	78.9692	.0127	6.5504	.1527	19
20	13.7435	.0728	91.0249	.0110	6.6231	.1510	20
21	15.6676	.0638	104.7684	.0095	6.6870	.1495	21
22	17.8610	.0560	120.4360	.0083	6.7429	.1483	22
23	20.3616	.0491	138.2970	.0072	6.7921	.1472	23
24	23.2122	.0431	158.6586	.0063	6.8351	.1463	24
25	26.4619	.0378	181.8708	.0055	6.8729	.1455	25
26	30.1666	.0331	208.3327	.0048	6.9061	.1448	26
27	34.3899	.0291	238.4993	.0042	6.9352	.1442	27
28	39.2045	.0255	272.8892	.0037	6.9607	.1437	28
29	44.6931	.0224	312.0937	.0032	6.9830	.1432	29
30	50.9502	.0196	356.7868	.0028	7.0027	.1428	30
35	98.1002	.0102	693.5727	.0014	7.0700	.1414	35
40	188.8835	.0053	1342.0251	.0007	7.1050	.1407	40
45	363.6791	.0027	2590.5648	.0004	7.1232	.1404	45
50	700.2330	.0014	4994.5213	.0002	7.1327	.1402	50
55	1348.2388	.0007	9623.1343	.0001	7.1376	.1401	55
60	2595.9187	.0004	18535.1333	.0001	7.1401	.1401	60
∞					7.1429	.1400	∞

Interest rate of 13.00 percent

N	Compound amount — Future value of a present amount F/P	Present value — Present value of a future amount P/F	Annuity compound amount — Future value of an annuity F/A	Sinking fund — Annuity providing a future amount A/F	Annuity present value — Present value of an annuity P/A	Capital recovery — Annuity repaying a present amount A/P	N
1	1.1300	.8850	1.0000	1.0000	.8850	1.1300	1
2	1.2769	.7831	2.1300	.4695	1.6681	.5995	2
3	1.4429	.6931	3.4069	.2935	2.3612	.4235	3
4	1.6305	.6133	4.8498	.2062	2.9745	.3362	4
5	1.8424	.5428	6.4803	.1543	3.5172	.2843	5
6	2.0820	.4803	8.3227	.1202	3.9975	.2502	6
7	2.3526	.4251	10.4047	.0961	4.4226	.2261	7
8	2.6584	.3762	12.7573	.0784	4.7988	.2084	8
9	3.0040	.3329	15.4157	.0649	5.1317	.1949	9
10	3.3946	.2946	18.4197	.0543	5.4262	.1843	10
11	3.8359	.2607	21.8143	.0458	5.6869	.1758	11
12	4.3345	.2307	25.6502	.0390	5.9176	.1690	12
13	4.8980	.2042	29.9847	.0334	6.1218	.1634	13
14	5.5348	.1807	34.8827	.0287	6.3025	.1587	14
15	6.2543	.1599	40.4175	.0247	6.4624	.1547	15
16	7.0673	.1415	46.6717	.0214	6.6039	.1514	16
17	7.9861	.1252	53.7391	.0186	6.7291	.1486	17
18	9.0243	.1108	61.7251	.0162	6.8399	.1462	18
19	10.1974	.0981	70.7494	.0141	6.9380	.1441	19
20	11.5231	.0868	80.9468	.0124	7.0248	.1424	20
21	13.0211	.0768	92.4699	.0108	7.1016	.1408	21
22	14.7138	.0680	105.4910	.0095	7.1695	.1395	22
23	16.6266	.0601	120.2048	.0083	7.2297	.1383	23
24	18.7881	.0532	136.8315	.0073	7.2829	.1373	24
25	21.2305	.0471	155.6196	.0064	7.3300	.1364	25
26	23.9905	.0417	176.8501	.0057	7.3717	.1357	26
27	27.1093	.0369	200.8406	.0050	7.4086	.1350	27
28	30.6335	.0326	227.9499	.0044	7.4412	.1344	28
29	34.6158	.0289	258.5834	.0039	7.4701	.1339	29
30	39.1159	.0256	293.1992	.0034	7.4957	.1334	30
35	72.0685	.0139	546.6808	.0018	7.5856	.1318	35
40	132.7816	.0075	1013.7042	.0010	7.6344	.1310	40
45	244.6414	.0041	1874.1646	.0005	7.6609	.1305	45
50	450.7359	.0022	3459.5071	.0003	7.6752	.1303	50
55	830.4517	.0012	6380.3979	.0002	7.6830	.1302	55
60	1530.0535	.0007	11761.9498	.0001	7.6873	.1301	60
∞					7.6923	.1300	∞

Interest rate of 15.00 percent

N	Compound amount — Future value of a present amount — F/P	Present value — Present value of a future amount — P/F	Annuity compound amount — Future value of an annuity — F/A	Sinking fund — Annuity providing a future amount — A/F	Annuity present value — Present value of an annuity — P/A	Capital recovery — Annuity repaying a present amount — A/P	N
1	1.1500	.8696	1.0000	1.0000	.8696	1.1500	1
2	1.3225	.7561	2.1500	.4651	1.6257	.6151	2
3	1.5209	.6575	3.4725	.2880	2.2832	.4380	3
4	1.7490	.5718	4.9934	.2003	2.8550	.3503	4
5	2.0114	.4972	6.7424	.1483	3.3522	.2983	5
6	2.3131	.4323	8.7537	.1142	3.7845	.2642	6
7	2.6600	.3759	11.0668	.0904	4.1604	.2404	7
8	3.0590	.3269	13.7268	.0729	4.4873	.2229	8
9	3.5179	.2843	16.7858	.0596	4.7716	.2096	9
10	4.0456	.2472	20.3037	.0493	5.0188	.1993	10
11	4.6524	.2149	24.3493	.0411	5.2337	.1911	11
12	5.3503	.1869	29.0017	.0345	5.4206	.1845	12
13	6.1528	.1625	34.3519	.0291	5.5831	.1791	13
14	7.0757	.1413	40.5047	.0247	5.7245	.1747	14
15	8.1371	.1229	47.5804	.0210	5.8474	.1710	15
16	9.3576	.1069	55.7175	.0179	5.9542	.1679	16
17	10.7613	.0929	65.0751	.0154	6.0472	.1654	17
18	12.3755	.0808	75.8364	.0132	6.1280	.1632	18
19	14.2318	.0703	88.2118	.0113	6.1982	.1613	19
20	16.3665	.0611	102.4436	.0098	6.2593	.1598	20
21	18.8215	.0531	118.8101	.0084	6.3125	.1584	21
22	21.6447	.0462	137.6316	.0073	6.3587	.1573	22
23	24.8915	.0402	159.2764	.0063	6.3988	.1563	23
24	28.6252	.0349	184.1678	.0054	6.4338	.1554	24
25	32.9190	.0304	212.7930	.0047	6.4641	.1547	25
26	37.8568	.0264	245.7120	.0041	6.4906	.1541	26
27	43.5353	.0230	283.5688	.0035	6.5135	.1535	27
28	50.0656	.0200	327.1041	.0031	6.5335	.1531	28
29	57.5755	.0174	377.1697	.0027	6.5509	.1527	29
30	66.2118	.0151	434.7451	.0023	6.5660	.1523	30
35	133.1755	.0075	881.1702	.0011	6.6166	.1511	35
40	267.8635	.0037	1779.0903	.0006	6.6418	.1506	40
45	538.7693	.0019	3585.1285	.0003	6.6543	.1503	45
50	1083.6574	.0009	7217.7163	.0001	6.6605	.1501	50
55	2179.6222	.0005	14524.1479	.0001	6.6636	.1501	55
60	4383.9987	.0002	29219.9916	.0000	6.6651	.1500	60
∞					6.6667	.1500	∞

Interest rate of 16.00 percent

N	Compound amount — Future value of a present amount — F/P	Present value — Present value of a future amount — P/F	Annuity compound amount — Future value of an annuity — F/A	Sinking fund — Annuity providing a future amount — A/F	Annuity present value — Present value of an annuity — P/A	Capital recovery — Annuity repaying a present amount — A/P	N
1	1.1600	.8621	1.0000	1.0000	.8621	1.1600	1
2	1.3456	.7432	2.1600	.4630	1.6052	.6230	2
3	1.5609	.6407	3.5056	.2853	2.2459	.4453	3
4	1.8106	.5523	5.0665	.1974	2.7982	.3574	4
5	2.1003	.4761	6.8771	.1454	3.2743	.3054	5
6	2.4364	.4104	8.9775	.1114	3.6847	.2714	6
7	2.8262	.3538	11.4139	.0876	4.0386	.2476	7
8	3.2784	.3050	14.2401	.0702	4.3436	.2302	8
9	3.8030	.2630	17.5185	.0571	4.6065	.2171	9
10	4.4114	.2267	21.3215	.0469	4.8332	.2069	10
11	5.1173	.1954	25.7329	.0389	5.0286	.1989	11
12	5.9360	.1685	30.8502	.0324	5.1971	.1924	12
13	6.8858	.1452	36.7862	.0272	5.3423	.1872	13
14	7.9875	.1252	43.6720	.0229	5.4675	.1829	14
15	9.2655	.1079	51.6595	.0194	5.5755	.1794	15
16	10.7480	.0930	60.9250	.0164	5.6685	.1764	16
17	12.4677	.0802	71.6730	.0140	5.7487	.1740	17
18	14.4625	.0691	84.1407	.0119	5.8178	.1719	18
19	16.7765	.0596	98.6032	.0101	5.8775	.1701	19
20	19.4608	.0514	115.3797	.0087	5.9288	.1687	20
21	22.5745	.0443	134.8405	.0074	5.9731	.1674	21
22	26.1864	.0382	157.4150	.0064	6.0113	.1664	22
23	30.3762	.0329	183.6014	.0054	6.0442	.1654	23
24	35.2364	.0284	213.9776	.0047	6.0726	.1647	24
25	40.8742	.0245	249.2140	.0040	6.0971	.1640	25
26	47.4141	.0211	290.0883	.0034	6.1182	.1634	26
27	55.0004	.0187	337.5024	.0030	6.1364	.1630	27
28	63.8004	.0157	392.5028	.0025	6.1520	.1625	28
29	74.0085	.0135	456.3032	.0022	6.1656	.1622	29
30	85.8499	.0116	530.3117	.0019	6.1772	.1619	30
35	180.3141	.0055	1120.7130	.0009	6.2153	.1609	35
40	378.7212	.0026	2360.7572	.0004	6.2335	.1604	40
45	795.4438	.0013	4965.2739	.0002	6.2421	.1602	45
50	1670.7038	.0006	10435.6488	.0001	6.2463	.1601	50
55	3509.0488	.0003	21925.3050	.0000	6.2482	.1600	55
60	7370.2014	.0001	46057.5085	.0000	6.2492	.1600	60
∞					6.2500	.1600	∞

Interest rate of 20.00 percent

N	Compound amount — Future value of a present amount — F/P	Present value — Present value of a future amount — P/F	Annuity compound amount — Future value of an annuity — F/A	Sinking fund — Annuity providing a future amount — A/F	Annuity present value — Present value of an annuity — P/A	Capital recovery — Annuity repaying a present amount — A/P	N
1	1.2000	.8333	1.0000	1.0000	.8333	1.2000	1
2	1.4400	.6944	2.2000	.4545	1.5278	.6545	2
3	1.7280	.5787	3.6400	.2747	2.1065	.4747	3
4	2.0736	.4823	5.3680	.1863	2.5887	.3863	4
5	2.4883	.4019	7.4416	.1344	2.9906	.3344	5
6	2.9860	.3349	9.9299	.1007	3.3255	.3007	6
7	3.5832	.2791	12.9159	.0774	3.6046	.2774	7
8	4.2998	.2326	16.4991	.0606	3.8372	.2606	8
9	5.1598	.1938	20.7989	.0481	4.0310	.2481	9
10	6.1917	.1615	25.9587	.0385	4.1925	.2385	10
11	7.4301	.1346	32.1504	.0311	4.3271	.2311	11
12	8.9161	.1122	39.5805	.0253	4.4392	.2253	12
13	10.6993	.0935	48.4966	.0206	4.5327	.2206	13
14	12.8392	.0779	59.1959	.0169	4.6106	.2169	14
15	15.4070	.0649	72.0351	.0139	4.6755	.2139	15
16	18.4884	.0541	87.4421	.0114	4.7296	.2114	16
17	22.1861	.0451	105.9306	.0094	4.7746	.2094	17
18	26.6233	.0376	128.1167	.0078	4.8122	.2078	18
19	31.9480	.0313	154.7400	.0065	4.8435	.2065	19
20	38.3376	.0261	186.6880	.0054	4.8696	.2054	20
21	46.0051	.0217	225.0256	.0044	4.8913	.2044	21
22	55.2061	.0181	271.0307	.0037	4.9094	.2037	22
23	66.2474	.0151	326.2369	.0031	4.9245	.2031	23
24	79.4968	.0126	392.4842	.0025	4.9371	.2025	24
25	95.3962	.0105	471.9811	.0021	4.9476	.2021	25
26	114.4755	.0087	567.3773	.0018	4.9563	.2018	26
27	137.3706	.0073	681.8528	.0015	4.9636	.2015	27
28	164.8447	.0061	819.2233	.0012	4.9697	.2012	28
29	197.8136	.0051	984.0680	.0010	4.9747	.2010	29
30	237.3763	.0042	1181.8816	.0008	4.9789	.2008	30
∞					5.0000	.2000	∞

Interest rate of 18.00 percent

N	Compound amount — Future value of a present amount — F/P	Present value — Present value of a future amount — P/F	Annuity compound amount — Future value of an annuity — F/A	Sinking fund — Annuity providing a future amount — A/F	Annuity present value — Present value of an annuity — P/A	Capital recovery — Annuity repaying a present amount — A/P	N
1	1.1800	.8475	1.0000	1.0000	.8475	1.1800	1
2	1.3924	.7182	2.1800	.4587	1.5656	.6387	2
3	1.6430	.6086	3.5724	.2799	2.1743	.4599	3
4	1.9388	.5158	5.2154	.1917	2.6901	.3717	4
5	2.2878	.4371	7.1542	.1398	3.1272	.3198	5
6	2.6996	.3704	9.4420	.1059	3.4976	.2859	6
7	3.1855	.3139	12.1415	.0824	3.8115	.2624	7
8	3.7589	.2660	15.3270	.0652	4.0776	.2452	8
9	4.4355	.2255	19.0859	.0524	4.3030	.2324	9
10	5.2338	.1911	23.5213	.0425	4.4941	.2225	10
11	6.1759	.1619	28.7551	.0348	4.6560	.2148	11
12	7.2876	.1372	34.9311	.0286	4.7932	.2086	12
13	8.5994	.1163	42.2187	.0237	4.9095	.2037	13
14	10.1472	.0985	50.8180	.0197	5.0081	.1997	14
15	11.9737	.0835	60.9653	.0164	5.0916	.1964	15
16	14.1290	.0708	72.9390	.0137	5.1624	.1937	16
17	16.6722	.0600	87.0680	.0115	5.2223	.1915	17
18	19.6733	.0508	103.7403	.0096	5.2732	.1896	18
19	23.2144	.0431	123.4135	.0081	5.3162	.1881	19
20	27.3930	.0365	146.6280	.0068	5.3527	.1868	20
21	32.3238	.0309	174.0210	.0057	5.3837	.1857	21
22	38.1421	.0262	206.3448	.0048	5.4099	.1848	22
23	45.0076	.0222	244.4868	.0041	5.4321	.1841	23
24	53.1090	.0188	289.4945	.0035	5.4509	.1835	24
25	62.6686	.0160	342.6035	.0029	5.4669	.1829	25
26	73.9490	.0135	405.2721	.0025	5.4804	.1825	26
27	87.2598	.0115	479.2211	.0021	5.4919	.1821	27
28	102.9666	.0097	566.4809	.0018	5.5016	.1818	28
29	121.5005	.0082	669.4475	.0015	5.5098	.1815	29
30	143.3706	.0070	790.9480	.0013	5.5168	.1813	30
∞					5.5556	.1800	∞

Interest rate of 30.00 percent

N	Compound amount — Future value of a present amount F/P	Present value — Present value of a future amount P/F	Annuity compound amount — Future value of an annuity F/A	Sinking fund — Annuity providing a future amount A/F	Annuity present value — Present value of an annuity P/A	Capital recovery — Annuity repaying a present amount A/P	N
1	1.3000	.7692	1.0000	1.0000	.7692	1.3000	1
2	1.6900	.5917	2.3000	.4348	1.3609	.7348	2
3	2.1970	.4552	3.9900	.2506	1.8161	.5506	3
4	2.8561	.3501	6.1870	.1616	2.1662	.4616	4
5	3.7129	.2693	9.0431	.1106	2.4356	.4106	5
6	4.8268	.2072	12.7560	.0784	2.6427	.3784	6
7	6.2749	.1594	17.5828	.0569	2.8021	.3569	7
8	8.1573	.1226	23.8577	.0419	2.9247	.3419	8
9	10.6045	.0943	32.0150	.0312	3.0190	.3312	9
10	13.7858	.0725	42.6195	.0235	3.0915	.3235	10
11	17.9216	.0558	56.4053	.0177	3.1473	.3177	11
12	23.2981	.0429	74.3270	.0135	3.1903	.3135	12
13	30.2875	.0330	97.6250	.0102	3.2233	.3102	13
14	39.3738	.0254	127.9125	.0078	3.2487	.3078	14
15	51.1859	.0195	167.2863	.0060	3.2682	.3060	15
16	66.5417	.0150	218.4722	.0046	3.2832	.3046	16
17	86.5042	.0116	285.0139	.0035	3.2948	.3035	17
18	112.4554	.0089	371.5180	.0027	3.3037	.3027	18
19	146.1920	.0068	483.9734	.0021	3.3105	.3021	19
20	190.0496	.0053	630.1655	.0016	3.3158	.3016	20
21	247.0645	.0040	820.2151	.0012	3.3198	.3012	21
22	321.1839	.0031	1067.2796	.0009	3.3230	.3009	22
23	417.5391	.0024	1388.4635	.0007	3.3254	.3007	23
24	542.8008	.0018	1806.0026	.0006	3.3272	.3006	24
25	705.6410	.0014	2348.8033	.0004	3.3286	.3004	25
26	917.3333	.0011	3054.4443	.0003	3.3297	.3003	26
27	1192.5333	.0008	3971.7776	.0003	3.3305	.3002	27
28	1550.2933	.0006	5164.3109	.0002	3.3312	.3002	28
29	2015.3813	.0005	6714.6042	.0001	3.3317	.3001	29
30	2619.9956	.0004	8729.9855	.0001	3.3321	.3001	30
∞					3.3333	.3000	∞

Interest rate of 25.00 percent

N	Compound amount — Future value of a present amount F/P	Present value — Present value of a future amount P/F	Annuity compound amount — Future value of an annuity F/A	Sinking fund — Annuity providing a future amount A/F	Annuity present value — Present value of an annuity P/A	Capital recovery — Annuity repaying a present amount A/P	N
1	1.2500	.8000	1.0000	1.0000	.8000	1.2500	1
2	1.5625	.6400	2.2500	.4444	1.4400	.6944	2
3	1.9531	.5120	3.8125	.2623	1.9520	.5123	3
4	2.4414	.4096	5.7656	.1734	2.3616	.4234	4
5	3.0518	.3277	8.2070	.1218	2.6893	.3718	5
6	3.8147	.2621	11.2588	.0888	2.9514	.3388	6
7	4.7684	.2097	15.0735	.0663	3.1611	.3163	7
8	5.9605	.1678	19.8419	.0504	3.3289	.3004	8
9	7.4506	.1342	25.8023	.0388	3.4631	.2888	9
10	9.3132	.1074	33.2529	.0301	3.5705	.2801	10
11	11.6415	.0859	42.5661	.0235	3.6564	.2735	11
12	14.5519	.0687	54.2077	.0184	3.7251	.2684	12
13	18.1899	.0550	68.7596	.0145	3.7801	.2645	13
14	22.7374	.0440	86.9495	.0115	3.8241	.2615	14
15	28.4217	.0352	109.6868	.0091	3.8593	.2591	15
16	35.5271	.0281	138.1085	.0072	3.8874	.2572	16
17	44.4089	.0225	173.6357	.0058	3.9099	.2558	17
18	55.5112	.0180	218.0446	.0046	3.9279	.2546	18
19	69.3889	.0144	273.5558	.0037	3.9424	.2537	19
20	86.7362	.0115	342.9447	.0029	3.9539	.2529	20
21	108.4202	.0092	429.6809	.0023	3.9631	.2523	21
22	135.5253	.0074	538.1011	.0019	3.9705	.2519	22
23	169.4066	.0059	673.6264	.0015	3.9764	.2515	23
24	211.7582	.0047	843.0329	.0012	3.9811	.2512	24
25	264.6978	.0038	1054.7912	.0009	3.9849	.2509	25
26	330.8722	.0030	1319.4890	.0008	3.9879	.2508	26
27	413.5903	.0024	1650.3612	.0006	3.9903	.2506	27
28	516.9879	.0019	2063.9615	.0005	3.9923	.2505	28
29	646.2349	.0015	2580.9394	.0004	3.9938	.2504	29
30	807.7936	.0012	3227.1743	.0003	3.9950	.2503	30
∞					4.0000	.2500	∞

Interest rate of 40.00 percent

N	Compound amount — Future value of a present amount — F/P	Present value — Present value of a future amount — P/F	Annuity compound amount — Future value of an annuity — F/A	Sinking fund — Annuity providing a future amount — A/F	Annuity present value — Present value of an annuity — P/A	Capital recovery — Annuity repaying a present amount — A/P	N
1	1.4000	.7143	1.0000	1.0000	.7143	1.4000	1
2	1.9600	.5102	2.4000	.4167	1.2245	.8167	2
3	2.7440	.3644	4.3600	.2294	1.5889	.6294	3
4	3.8416	.2603	7.1040	.1408	1.8492	.5408	4
5	5.3782	.1859	10.9456	.0914	2.0352	.4914	5
6	7.5295	.1328	16.3238	.0613	2.1680	.4613	6
7	10.5414	.0949	23.8534	.0419	2.2628	.4419	7
8	14.7579	.0678	34.3947	.0291	2.3306	.4291	8
9	20.6610	.0484	49.1526	.0203	2.3790	.4203	9
10	28.9255	.0346	69.8137	.0143	2.4136	.4143	10
11	40.4957	.0247	98.7391	.0101	2.4383	.4101	11
12	56.6939	.0176	139.2348	.0072	2.4559	.4072	12
13	79.3715	.0126	195.9287	.0051	2.4685	.4051	13
14	111.1201	.0090	275.3002	.0036	2.4775	.4036	14
15	155.5681	.0064	386.4202	.0026	2.4839	.4026	15
16	217.7953	.0046	541.9883	.0018	2.4885	.4018	16
17	304.9135	.0033	759.7837	.0013	2.4918	.4013	17
18	426.8789	.0023	1064.6971	.0009	2.4941	.4009	18
19	597.6304	.0017	1491.5760	.0007	2.4958	.4007	19
20	836.6826	.0012	2089.2064	.0005	2.4970	.4005	20
21	1171.3556	.0009	2925.8889	.0003	2.4979	.4003	21
22	1639.8978	.0006	4097.2445	.0002	2.4985	.4002	22
23	2295.8569	.0004	5737.1423	.0002	2.4989	.4002	23
24	3214.1997	.0003	8032.9993	.0001	2.4992	.4001	24
25	4499.8796	.0002	11247.1990	.0001	2.4994	.4001	25
∞		.0002			2.5000	.4000	∞

Interest rate of 50.00 percent

N	Compound amount — Future value of a present amount — F/P	Present value — Present value of a future amount — P/F	Annuity compound amount — Future value of an annuity — F/A	Sinking fund — Annuity providing a future amount — A/F	Annuity present value — Present value of an annuity — P/A	Capital recovery — Annuity repaying a present amount — A/P	N
1	1.5000	.6667	1.0000	1.0000	.6667	1.5000	1
2	2.2500	.4444	2.5000	.4000	1.1111	.9000	2
3	3.3750	.2963	4.7500	.2105	1.4074	.7105	3
4	5.0625	.1975	8.1250	.1231	1.6049	.6231	4
5	7.5938	.1317	13.1875	.0758	1.7366	.5758	5
6	11.3906	.0878	20.7813	.0481	1.8244	.5481	6
7	17.0859	.0585	32.1719	.0311	1.8829	.5311	7
8	25.6289	.0390	49.2578	.0203	1.9220	.5203	8
9	38.4434	.0260	74.8867	.0134	1.9480	.5134	9
10	57.6650	.0173	113.3301	.0088	1.9653	.5088	10
11	86.4976	.0116	170.9951	.0058	1.9769	.5058	11
12	129.7463	.0077	257.4927	.0039	1.9846	.5039	12
13	194.6195	.0051	387.2390	.0026	1.9897	.5026	13
14	291.9293	.0034	581.8585	.0017	1.9931	.5017	14
15	437.8939	.0023	873.7878	.0011	1.9954	.5011	15
16	656.8408	.0015	1311.6817	.0008	1.9970	.5008	16
17	985.2613	.0010	1968.5225	.0005	1.9980	.5005	17
18	1477.8919	.0007	2953.7838	.0003	1.9986	.5003	18
19	2216.8378	.0005	4431.6756	.0002	1.9991	.5002	19
20	3325.2567	.0003	6648.5135	.0002	1.9994	.5002	20
21	4987.8851	.0002	9973.7702	.0001	1.9996	.5001	21
22	7481.8276	.0001	14961.6553	.0001	1.9997	.5001	22
23	11222.7415	.0001	22443.4829	.0000	1.9998	.5000	23
24	16834.1122	.0001	33666.2244	.0000	1.9999	.5000	24
25	25251.1683	.0000	50500.3366	.0000	1.9999	.5000	25
∞		.0000			2.0000	.5000	∞

suggested readings

The following is a list of readings which can be used to supplement and extend the material covered in this text.

Chapter 1

Anthony, Robert N., "The Trouble with Profit Maximization," *Harvard Business Review,* 38 (November-December 1960), 126–134.

Donaldson, Gordon, "Financial Goals: Management vs. Stockholders," *Harvard Business Review,* 41 (May-June 1963), 116–129.

Schmitz, Robert A., "Facing the New Normalcy in Corporate Finance," *Financial Executive,* 42 (November 1974), 14–21.

Solomon, Ezra, *The Theory of Financial Management.* New York: Columbia University Press, 1963, 1–26.

"The Issues in Social Responsibility," *Financial Analysts Journal,* 27 (September-October 1971), 26–34.

Chapter 2

Dougall, Herbert E., and Jack E. Gaumnitz, *Capital Markets and Institutions.* Englewood Cliffs, N.J.: Prentice-Hall, 3d ed., 1975, 1–26.

Friedman, Milton, "Factors Affecting the Level of Interest Rates," *Proceedings of the Conference on Savings and Residential Financing,* U.S. Savings and Loan League, 1968, 11–27.

Smith, Adam, *The Money Game.* New York: Random House, 1968.

Van Horne, James C., *Function and Analysis of Capital Market Rates.* Englewood Cliffs, N.J.: Prentice-Hall, Inc., 1970, 1–33.

Chapter 3

Maer, C. M., Jr., and R. A. Francis, "Whether to Incorporate," *Business Lawyer,* 22 (April 1967), 127–142.

Meigs, Walter B., *et al., Intermediate Accounting.* New York: McGraw-Hill Book Company, 3d ed., 1974, 753–775.

Prather, Charles L., and James E. Wert, *Financing Business Firms.* Homewood, Ill.: R. D. Irwin, Inc., 4th ed., 1971, 30–55.

Weston, J. Fred, and Eugene F. Brigham, *Managerial Finance.* Hinsdale, Ill.: Dryden Press, 5th ed., 1975, 859–875.

Chapter 4

Grant, Eugene L., *et al., Principles of Engineering Economy.* New York: Ronald, 6th ed., 1976, 25–61.

Chapter 5

Bauman, W. Scott, "Investment Returns and Present Values," *Financial Analysts Journal*, 27 (September-October 1971), 107–118.

Margoshes, S. L., "'Present Value' Techniques of Stock Valuation," *Financial Analysts Journal*, 17 (March-April 1961), 37–42.

Modigliani, Franco, and Gerald A. Pogue, "An Introduction to Risk and Return: Concepts and Evidence, Part I," *Financial Analysts Journal*, 30 (March-April 1974), 68–80.

Soldofsky, Robert M., and Roger L. Miller, "Risk-Premium Curves for Different Classes of Long-Term Securities, 1950–1966," *Journal of Finance*, 24 (June 1969), 429–445.

Robichek, Alexander A., "Risk and the Value of Securities," *Journal of Financial and Quantitative Analysis*, 4 (December 1969), 513–538.

Chapter 6

Brennan, Michael J., "A New Look at the Weighted Average Cost of Capital," *Journal of Business Finance*, 5 (Spring 1973), 24–30.

Brigham, Eugene F., and Keith V. Smith, "The Cost of Capital to the Small Firm," *Engineering Economist*, 13 (Fall 1967), 1–26.

McDonald, John G., "Market Measures of Capital Cost," *Journal of Business Finance*, 2 (Autumn 1970), 27–36.

Solomon, Ezra, "Measuring a Company's Cost of Capital," *Journal of Business*, 28 (October 1955), 240–252.

Chapter 7

Brigham, Eugene F., and Richard H. Pettway, "Capital Budgeting by Utilities," *Financial Management*, 2 (Autumn 1973), 11–22.

Fogler, H. Russell, "Ranking Techniques and Capital Rationing," *Accounting Review*, 47 (January 1972), 134–143.

Lewellen, Wilbur G., H. P. Lanser, and J. J. McConnell, "Payback Substitutes for Discounted Cash Flow," *Financial Management*, 2 (Summer 1973), 17–25.

Mao, James C. T., "Survey of Capital Budgeting: Theory and Practice," *Journal of Finance*, 25 (May 1970), 349–360.

Van Horne, James C., "A Note on Biases in Capital Budgeting Introduced by Inflation," *Journal of Financial and Quantitative Analysis*, 6 (January 1971), 653–658.

Chapter 8

Hertz, David B., "Risk Analysis in Capital Investment," *Harvard Business Review*, 42 (January-February 1964), 95–106.

⸻, "Investment Policies that Pay-Off," *Harvard Business Review*, 46 (January-February 1968), 96–108.

Hirschmann, W. B., and J. R. Brauweiler, "Investment Analysis: Coping With Change," *Harvard Business Review* (May-June 1965), 62–72.

Magee, John F., "How to Use Decision Trees in Capital Investment," *Harvard Business Review*, 42 (September-October 1964), 79–96.

Richardson, L. K., "Do High Risks Lead to High Returns?" *Financial Analysts Journal,* 26 (March-April 1970), 88–99.

Weston, J. Fred, "Investment Decisions Using the Capital Asset Pricing Model," *Financial Management,* 2 (Spring 1973), 25–33.

Chapter 9

Brigham, Eugene F., and Myron J. Gordon, "Leverage, Dividend Policy, and the Cost of Capital," *Journal of Finance,* 23 (March 1968), 85–104.

Donaldson, Gordon, "New Framework for Corporate Debt Policy," *Harvard Business Review,* 40 (March-April 1962), 117–131.

————, "In Defense of Preferred Stock," *Harvard Business Review,* 40 (July-August 1962), 123–136.

Pfahl, John K., *et al.,* "The Limits of Leverage," *Financial Executive,* 38 (May 1970), 48–56.

Sihler, William W., "Framework for Financial Decisions," *Harvard Business Review,* 49 (March-April 1971), 123–125.

Solomon, Ezra, "Leverage and the Cost of Capital," *Journal of Finance,* 18 (May 1963), 273–279.

Chapter 10

Higgins, Robert C., "The Corporate Dividend-Savings Decision," *Journal of Financial and Quantitative Analysis,* 7 (March 1972), 1527–1541.

Millar, James A., and Bruce D. Fielitz, "Stock-Split and Stock-Dividend Decisions," *Financial Management,* 2 (Winter 1973), 35–45.

Porterfield, James T. S., "Dividends, Dilution, and Delusion," *Harvard Business Review,* 37 (November-December 1959), 156–161.

Walter, James E., "Dividend Policy: Its Influence on the Value of the Enterprise," *Journal of Finance,* 18 (May 1963), 280–291.

West, Richard R., and Alan B. Brouilette, "Reverse Stock Splits," *Financial Executive,* 38 (January 1970), 12–17.

Chapter 11

Altman, Edward I., "Financial Ratios, Discriminant Analysis and the Prediction of Corporate Bankruptcy," *Journal of Finance,* 23 (September 1968), 589–609.

Eiteman, David K., "A Computer Program for Financial Statement Analysis," *Financial Analysts Journal,* 20 (November-December 1964), 61–68.

Helfert, Erich A., *Techniques of Financial Analysis.* Homewood, Ill.: R. D. Irwin, 3d ed., 1972, chaps. 1 and 2.

Horrigan, James C., "A Short History of Financial Ratio Analysis," *Accounting Review,* 43 (April 1968), 284–294.

Murray, Roger, "Lessons for Financial Analysis," *Journal of Finance,* 26 (May 1971), 327–332.

Reiling, Henry B., and John C. Burton, "Financial Statements: Signposts as Well as Milestones," *Harvard Business Review,* 50 (November-December 1972), 45–54.

Chapter 12

Kelvie, William E., and John M. Sinclair, "New Techniques for Breakeven Charts," *Financial Executive,* 36 (June 1968), 31–43.

Packer, Stephen B., "Flow of Funds Analysis—Its Uses and Limitations," *Financial Analysts Journal,* 20 (July-August 1964), 117–123.

Raun, D. L., "The Limitations of Profit Graphs, Break-Even Analysis, and Budgets," *Accounting Review,* 39 (October 1964), 927–945.

Reinhardt, U. E., "Break-Even Analysis for Lockheed's Tri Star," *Journal of Finance,* 28 (September 1973), 821–838.

Chapter 13

Chambers, John C., *et al.,* "How to Choose the Right Forecasting Technique," *Harvard Business Review,* 49 (July-August 1971), 45–74.

Helfert, Erich A., *Techniques of Financial Analysis.* Homewood, Ill.: R. D. Irwin, 3d ed., 1972, chap. 3.

Parker, George C., and Edilberto L. Segura, "How to Get a Better Forecast," *Harvard Business Review,* 49 (March-April 1971), 99–109.

Preston, Gerald R., "Considerations in Long-Range Planning," *Financial Executive,* 36 (May 1968), 44–49.

Chapter 14

(Readings for Chapters 14 and 15 indicated by a † are included in Smith, Keith V., *Management of Working Capital.* St. Paul: West, 1974.)

Baxter, Nevins D., "Marketability, Default Risk, and Yields on Money-Market Instruments," *Journal of Financial and Quantitative Analysis,* 3 (March 1968), 75–85.

†Marrah, George L., "Managing Receivables," *Financial Executive,* 38 (July 1970), 40–44.

†Poggess, William P., "Screen-Test Your Credit Risks," *Harvard Business Review,* 45 (November-December 1967), 113–122.

†Reed, Ward L., Jr., "Profits from Better Cash Management," *Financial Executive,* 40 (May 1972), 40–56.

†Schiff, Michael, "Credit and Inventory Management—Separate or Together," *Financial Executive,* 40 (November 1972), 28–33.

†Searby, Frederick W., "Use Your Hidden Cash Resources," *Harvard Business Review,* 46 (March-April 1968), 71–80.

†Snyder, Arthur, "Principles of Inventory Management," *Financial Executive,* 32 (April 1964), 13–21.

Chapter 15

†Conover, C. Todd, "The Case of the Costly Credit Agreement," *Financial Executive,* 39 (September 1971), 40–48.

Daniels, Frank, *et al.,* "Accounts Receivable and Related Inventory Financing—Worthless Collateral?" *Journal of Commercial Bank Lending,* 53 (July 1970), 38–53.

†Diener, Royce, "Analysing the Financing Potential of a Small Business," in I. Pfeffer (ed.), *The Financing of Small Business,* New York: Macmillan, 1967, 211–228.

Donaldson, Gordon, "Strategy for Financial Emergencies," *Harvard Business Review,* 47 (November-December 1969), 67–79.

†Nadler, Paul S., "Compensating Balances and the Prime at Twilight," *Harvard Business Review,* 50 (January-February 1972), 112–120.

†Van Horne, James C., "A Risk-Return Analysis of a Firm's Working Capital Position," *Engineering Economist,* 14 (Winter 1969), 71–88.

Chapter 16

Bloch, Ernest, "Pricing a Corporate Bond Issue," *Essays in Money and Credit.* New York: Federal Reserve Bank of New York, 1964, 72–76.

Hayes, Samuel L., III, "Investment Banking: Power Structure in Flux," *Harvard Business Review,* 49 (March-April 1971), 136–152.

Karna, Adi S., "The Cost of Private Versus Public Debt Issues," *Financial Management,* 1 (Summer 1972), 65–67.

Kelly, Paul S., "New Financing Techniques on Wall Street," *Financial Executive,* 42 (November 1974), 30–42.

Sears, Gerald A., "Public Offerings for Smaller Companies," *Harvard Business Review,* 46 (September-October 1968), 112–120.

Smith, Adam, *Supermoney.* New York: Random House, 1972.

Chapter 17

Bower, R. S., "Issues in Lease Financing," *Financial Management* (Winter 1973), 25–33.

McGugan, V. J., and R. E. Caves, "Integration and Competition in the Equipment Leasing Industry," *Journal of Business* (July 1974), 382–396.

"Rentals and Leasing, A Billion Dollar Business," *Management Review* (July 1969), 63–66.

Smith, Pierce R., "A Straightforward Approach to Leveraged Leasing," *The Journal of Commercial Bank Lending* (July 1973), 19–39.

Chapter 18

Bacon, P. W., "The Subscription Price in Rights Offerings," *Financial Management,* 1 (Summer 1972), 59–64.

Furst, Richard W., "Does Listing Increase the Market Price of Common Stocks?" *Journal of Business,* 43 (April 1970), 174–180.

Lynch, J. E., "Accounting for Equity Securities," *Financial Management,* 2 (Spring 1973), 41–47.

Young, Alan, and W. Marshall, "Controlling Shareholder Servicing Costs," *Harvard Business Review,* 49 (January-February 1971), 71–78.

Zwerdling, G. H., "Stock Repurchase: Financial Issues," *California Management Review,* 11 (Winter 1968), 34–39.

Chapter 19

Brown, Bowman, "Why Corporations Should Consider Income Bonds," *Financial Executive,* 35 (October 1967), 74–78.

Donaldson, Gordon, "In Defense of Preferred Stock," *Harvard Business Review,* 40 (July-August 1962), 123–136.

Elsaid, Hussein H., "The Function of Preferred Stock in the Corporate Financial Plan," *Financial Analysts Journal,* 25 (July-August 1969), 112–117.

Everett, Edward, "Subordinated Debt—Nature and Enforcement," *Business Lawyer,* 20 (July 1965), 953–987.

Pogue, Thomas F., and Robert M. Soldofsky, "What's in a Bond Rating?" *Journal of Financial and Quantitative Analysis,* 4 (July 1969), 201–228.

Chapter 20

Hayes, Samuel L., III, and Henry B. Reiling, "Sophisticated Financing Tool: The Warrant," *Harvard Business Review,* 47 (January-February 1969), 137–150.

Meyer, Anthony H., "Designing a Convertible Preferred Issue," *Financial Executive,* 36 (April 1968), 48ff.

Miller, Alexander B., "How to Call Your Convertible," *Harvard Business Review,* 49 (May-June 1971), 66–70.

Pinches, George E., "Financing with Convertible Preferred Stocks, 1960–1967," *Journal of Finance,* 25 (March 1970), 53–64.

Soldofsky, Robert M., "Yield-Rate Performance of Convertible Securities," *Financial Analysts Journal,* 27 (March-April 1971), 61–65.

Stevenson, Richard A., and Joe Lovely, "Why a Bond Warrant Issue," *Financial Executive,* 38 (June 1970), 16–21.

Chapter 21

Briloff, Abraham L., "The Funny-Money Game," *Financial Analysts Journal,* 25 (May-June 1969), 73–79.

Cohen, Manuel F., "Takeover Bids," *Financial Analysts Journal,* 26 (January-February 1970), 26–31.

Cunitz, Jonathan A., "Valuing Potential Acquisitions," *Financial Executive,* 39 (April 1971), 16–28.

Hogarty, Thomas F., "The Profitability of Corporate Mergers," *Journal of Business,* 44 (July 1970), 317–327.

Shad, John S. R., "The Financial Realities of Mergers," *Harvard Business Review,* 47 (November-December 1969), 133–146.

Chapter 22

Dufey, Gunter, "Corporate Finance and Exchange Rate Variations," *Financial Management,* 1 (Summer 1972), 51–57.

Ewigg, David W., "MNCs on Trial," *Harvard Business Review,* 50 (May-June 1972), 130–143.

Heckerman, Donald, "The Exchange Risks of Foreign Operations," *Journal of Business,* 46 (January 1972), 42–48.

Lietaer, Bernard A., "Managing Risks in Foreign Exchange," *Harvard Business Review,* 48 (March-April 1970), 127–138.

Robbins, Sidney M., and Robert B. Stobaugh, "Financing Foreign Affiliates," *Financial Management,* 1 (Winter 1972), 56–65.

Stahl, Sheldon W., "The Multinational Corporation: A Controversial Force," *Monthly Review,* Federal Reserve Bank of Kansas City, January 1976, 3–10.

Chapter 23

Altman, Edward I., "Corporate Bankruptcy Potential, Stockholder Returns, and Share Valuation," *Journal of Finance,* 24 (December 1969), 887–900.

Gordon, Myron, "Toward a Theory of Financial Distress," *Journal of Finance,* 26 (May 1971), 347–356.

Krause, Sidney, "Chapter X and XI—A Study in Contrasts," *The Business Lawyer,* 19 (January 1964), 511–526.

Walter, James E., "Determination of Technical Insolvency," *Journal of Business,* 30 (January 1957), 30–43.

glossary

Absolute priority	See **rule of absolute priority.**
Accelerated depreciation	Any method of depreciating an asset which produces higher depreciation in earlier years than in later years.
Accounting rate of return	The rate of return on an investment computed as accounting profit divided by some measure of investment; e.g., average profit per year divided by initial investment.
Acid test ratio	See **quick ratio.**
Act of bankruptcy	Any one of the six acts designated by Chapter X of the National Bankruptcy Act which, if performed by the debtor, provides grounds for creditors to file a petition of bankruptcy.
Activity ratio	A financial ratio that indicates how efficiently a firm uses its assets; inventory turnover, average collection period, fixed-asset turnover, and total asset turnover are activity ratios.
After-acquired property clause	A provision in a bond indenture that provides that all property acquired by the firm in the future will also serve as collateral for the bonds.
Agency issue	See **best efforts issue.**
Annuity	A series of equal periodic payments or receipts.
Arrangement	An adjustment under Chapter XI of the National Bankruptcy Act for the settlement of the company's debts; usually covers small- and medium-sized firms.
Authorized shares	Shares authorized under the company's charter for issuance. For example, a firm with 1 million authorized shares may issue up to but no more than 1 million shares unless the corporate charter is amended to increase this number.
Balance sheet method	Forecasts of future financing requirements and available cash based only on forecasted income statements and balance sheets.
Bankruptcy	The condition in which a firm (or individual) is unable to pay its debts, and its assets are consequently surrendered to a court for administration.
Benefit cost ratio	For an investment, the ratio of the present value of its future cash flows to its initial cost. The benefit-cost ratio method uses the ratio to evaluate investment opportunities.
Best efforts issue	Issuing securities without underwriting. Securities are sold on a commission basis by the investment banker with no guarantee of the total amount that will be sold.

Blanket mortgage	A mortgage which covers many assets; e.g., a blanket mortgage covering several buildings in a real estate complex.
Bond	A long-term promise to pay a specified dollar amount; a long-term debt security.
Book value	The original cost of an asset minus total depreciation deductions made to date; this is the value indicated by the firm's financial statements.
Broker	One who arranges the purchase and sale of assets; e.g., a securities (stock) broker, a mortgage broker, and a real estate broker. A broker does not buy or sell the asset but simply brings buyers and sellers together (contrast with **dealer**).
Break-even point	The level of output at which the firm is just breaking even, i.e., earning a zero profit.
Business risk	Risk arising from the uncertainty in the future revenues and expenses (not including debt interest) of a firm (riskiness of the firm's EBIT).
Call premium	The difference between the call price and the face value of the bond.
Call price	The price that the firm must pay per bond to bondholders if the bonds are called (repurchased by the firm directly from bondholders).
Call provision	A stipulation in a bond or preferred stock agreement that the firm has the right to repurchase (call) the outstanding bonds or preferred stock at a given price from the securityholder.
Capital asset	A physical asset (plant and equipment) used by a firm in producing goods or services.
Capital budget	A statement of the firm's planned investments, generally based upon estimates of future sales, costs, production needs, and availability of capital.
Capital gains (losses)	The difference between the original cost of an asset and its selling price. Capital gains (losses) are *realized* when the asset is sold.
Capital income	Income produced from investing money, such as dividends and interest. See also **earned income.**
Capital rationing	The use of funds by the firm in a situation in which the funds are limited, i.e., no additional capital can be obtained regardless of the profitability of the investment opportunity.
Capital structure	The composition of a firm's financing; often refers to the proportions of long-term debt, preferred stock, and common equity on the firm's balance sheet.
Cash budget	Planned cash receipts and payments for one or more future periods.
Cash flow forecasts	Forecasts of cash receipts and payments for one or more periods.
Cash flow from an investment	The dollars coming to the firm (**cash inflow**) or paid out by the firm (**cash outflow**) as a result of adopting the investment.

Certainty equivalent An amount, to be received for certain at a particular point in time, which is equal in desirability to a risky cash flow occurring at the same point in time.

Chattel mortgage A pledge of personal property as collateral on a debt.

Clientele effect The attraction of investors who purchase the company's stock because they prefer the company's policies, such as, the company's long-run dividend policy.

Closed-end mortgage A mortgage which forbids the borrower from using the security (collateral) provided by the mortgage to cover any additional debt unless the additional debt is of lower priority than the existing debt backed by the mortgage.

Coefficient of variation The standard deviation of a variable divided by the variable's expected level, for example, standard deviation of cash flow divided by the expected cash flow.

Collateral Property pledged by a borrower as security on the loan.

Collateral trust bonds Bonds which are secured by marketable securities, inventories, or intangible assets (e.g., patents).

Collection period The time period from the date of sale of the firm's product to the date of collection of cash from the customer.

Combined leverage The combination of operating and financial leverage.

Commercial paper Short-term debt issued by corporations to the public.

Common stock A document which represents the ownership of a corporation.

Compensating balance Money that must be on deposit at a bank to compensate the bank for services; may be a requirement of a loan.

Competitive bid A bid for securities which are ultimately sold to the investment banker which bids the highest price for the issue.

Composition An agreement between the firm and its creditors under which creditors receive less than the amount due to them in satisfaction of the debt (e.g., 50 cents on the dollar).

Compound interest Interest which is paid or received on interest accumulated from prior periods.

Conglomerate A group of firms in entirely different lines of business which are controlled by a single corporation.

Consolidation The combination of two or more firms into a completely new firm (e.g., firm A consolidating with firm B to form firm C).

Contractual (financial) failure Failure to fulfill debt commitments or the likelihood that such failure will occur because firm assets are less than liabilities (insolvency).

Conversion premium The difference between a convertible's market value and the higher of its investment and conversion values.

Conversion price The price, in terms of dollars of par of the convertible security, paid per share of common stock acquired through conversion.

Conversion ratio The number of common shares received for converting the convertible security.

Conversion value The market value of the common stock into which the convertible security can be converted.

Convertible bond A bond which can be converted at the option of the owner into common stock of the corporation.

Convertible security A security (usually a bond or preferred stock) which can be converted at the option of the holder into some other type of security (usually common stock) issued by the same corporation. For example, a convertible bond or a share of convertible preferred stock can be converted by the bondholder or preferred shareholder into the issuing corporation's common stock.

Corporation A business which has been chartered by a state and whose owners are not personally responsible for the business's debts.

Correlation A measure of the degree of statistical relationship between two variables.

Correlation coefficient of two variables A measure of how closely the two variables move together; this covariation is also indicated by the **covariance** of the two variables.

Cost of capital The minimum acceptable rate of return on an investment undertaken by a company; often measured as an average of the rates on the individual securities issued by the company.

Coupon The interest payment to the bondholder made periodically (usually semiannually).

Coupon rate The percentage of a bond's par value that is paid each year as interest to the bondholder (a $1,000 face value bond with a 6-percent coupon rate pays $60 per year in interest).

Covenant A promise by the firm, included in the debt contract, to perform a certain act (e.g., to pay interest on the debt); a **restrictive covenant** is one which imposes constraints upon the firm in order to protect the debtholders' interests (e.g., a restriction on dividends or a requirement that the firm maintain a particular current ratio).

Cover To buy or sell a futures contract in the forward exchange market to protect against a loss which may occur as a result of exchange rate changes.

Cumulative dividends Unpaid preferred dividends from prior years that must be paid before any dividends are paid to common stockholders.

Cumulative preferred stock Preferred stock for which any past unpaid preferred dividends must be paid in full before any dividends are issued on the firm's common stock.

Cumulative voting	A system of electing directors under which a significant minority of the shares is ensured of being able to elect at least one director.
Current ratio	Current assets divided by current liabilities; a measure of a firm's liquidity.
Current yield (on a bond)	The annual interest paid on a bond divided by the current price of the bond.
Dealer	One who is in the occupation of buying or selling some type of asset; e.g., a securities dealer (contrast with **broker**).
Debenture	A long-term debt instrument issued by a corporation which is not secured by specific property but instead by the general credit of the corporation.
Debt capacity	The maximum amount of debt that can feasibly be outstanding for a firm at a given point in time.
Debt ratio	Total firm debt divided by total assets; a measure of a firm's debt burden.
Decision tree analysis	A way of formulating a problem—often represented by a figure that looks like a tree—which involves choosing a best alternative or strategy. Dynamic programming is a solution technique for efficiently solving such a problem.
Degree of combined leverage (DCL)	The percentage change in aftertax earnings per share from a 1-percent change in sales.
Degree of financial leverage (DFL)	The percentage change in aftertax earnings per share from a 1-percent change in EBIT.
Degree of operating leverage (DOL)	The percentage change in earnings before interest and taxes (EBIT) from a 1-percent change in sales.
Depletion	A tax deduction reflecting the using up of a natural resource.
Depreciation	A deduction of part of the cost of an asset from income in each year of the asset's life.
Dilution	The reduction in earnings per share due to an increase in the number of shares outstanding as a result of conversion or the exercise of warrants.
Direct issue	Securities sold directly to investors by the issuing firm.
Discount (bond)	The difference between the face value and market value of a bond if the face value is greater; e.g., the discount is $100 on a $1,000 (face value) bond selling in the market for $900.
Disintermediation	The withdrawal of money from financial intermediaries in order to reinvest it in the securities issued by business firms and governmental units.
Diversification	Investing in more than one risky asset at a time.
Diversification effect of a project's cash flow	The effect of adding the project's cash flow on the variability of the firm's total cash flow (from all firm assets).
Dividend payout ratio	The proportion of earnings paid out in dividends.

Earned income   Income produced by an individual's personal services. See also **capital income.**

EBIT   Earnings before debt interest and income taxes are deducted.

Economic failure   The inability of the firm to earn an adequate return on investment regardless of the company's financial structure.

Economic order quantity   The amount of purchased goods per order which minimizes the cost of inventory.

Equipment trust certificate   Bonds which are secured by equipment.

Equity investment   That portion of firm investment financed from retained earnings or from the sale of equity securities such as common stock or warrants.

Exchange rate   The ratio of the value of one currency relative to another; the rate at which one currency may be exchanged for another.

Ex-dividend   Without a right to a dividend that is about to be paid. A stock is ex-dividend if a new purchaser does not also acquire the right to receive a dividend that will be paid in the immediate future.

Expected cash flow   An average of the possible cash flows in a period; this average equals the sum of all possible cash flows each multiplied by its probability of occurrence.

Extension   An agreement between the firm and its creditors to postpone payments on company debt.

External financing   Raising money by issuing new securities or by borrowing.

External investment   Expansion by acquiring another firm (contrast with **internal investment**).

Extra dividend   A dividend payment, in addition to the firm's regular dividend, which is paid only if the firm has been particularly profitable during the period.

Face value   See **maturity value.**

Factoring   Selling accounts receivable. The purchasing firm is called a **factor.**

Field warehouse   An area set aside on a borrower's premises in which goods used as collateral are placed.

Financial asset   A claim to a present or future payment of dollars; e.g., a corporate bond which is a claim to future interest and principal payments by a corporation.

Financial intermediaries   Financial institutions which borrow money from some people in order to lend it to others.

Financial lease   A lease which is noncancellable (except by mutual consent of both lessor and lessee) and which generally has a duration equal to most of the economic life of the asset.

Financial leverage   The effect of debt financing on stockholder income. Often also used to refer to the use of debt financing by a firm. May also include the impact of preferred stock financing on stockholder income.

Financial ratio A ratio of dollar magnitudes obtained from a firm's financial statements which reflects some aspect of the firm's performance.

Financial risk The uncertainty as to the future returns to a firm's owners resulting from the use of debt or preferred stock.

Fixed charge A payment by the firm required under a contractual agreement; e.g., interest on debt, sinking fund contributions, and lease payments.

Fixed cost A cost which does not change as output changes.

Floor plan Loan agreement used to finance "large-ticket" items such as automobiles and appliances. Each item is separately identified as being collateral for the loan.

Flotation costs The accounting, legal, underwriting, and other costs of issuing securities (new stock, bond, etc.).

Forward rate The rate of exchange as set currently for a transaction to occur at a specified future time.

Funded debt A term used to refer to any long-term debt of the firm.

Funding See **refunding.**

Funds flow The flow of cash (if cash is used to define funds) through the firm; this flow is described by a **sources and uses statement.**

Future value The value at a future date of money which has been paid or received in prior periods.

General lien Claim against all assets of a given type; used to secure a loan.

General partnership A business in which each partner is personally responsible for any debts of the business.

Going public The selling of stock by the issuing corporation to the general public for the first time.

Holding company A firm which owns a controlling interest in one or more other firms (which are referred to as **subsidiaries**).

Horizontal combina-tion The union of firms which are in similar lines of business; e.g., two elec-tronics manufacturers.

Illiquidity The condition in which a firm (or individual) has inadequate funds to meet its obligations.

Income bond A bond that pays interest only to the extent that the firm issuing the bonds has earnings (EBIT) to cover the interest.

Incremental internal rate of return method A method for comparing two or more mutually exclusive investments using the IRR approach. This method examines the IRR on the additional (or "incremental") cash flow produced by one investment relative to any mutually exclusive alternative in order to determine which is more profitable.

Indenture   The contract between the corporation and the bondholders specifying the provisions of the debt agreement.

Insolvency   The condition in which a firm's (or individual's) liabilities exceed its assets.

Interim financing   Short-term loans to be repaid from long-term debt or other financing in the future.

Internal financing   Financing with money earned and retained in the business.

Internal investment   A firm's investment which involves the direct acquisition of productive assets rather than the acquisition of another firm or the productive assets of another firm (external investment).

Internal rate of return   The actual rate of return earned by an investment.

Interrelated investment opportunities   Investments which affect each other's cash flows.

Investment banker   Financial institution specializing in underwriting and selling new securities issues.

Investment company   A company whose primary business is the purchase and ownership of government securities and the stocks and bonds of other firms. Mutual funds, closed-end investment companies, and venture capital firms are investment companies.

Investment tax credit   An income tax credit that is given to firms for investing in plant and equipment.

Investment value   The value that a convertible security would have if it were not convertible but had all its other features.

Lessee   The user of a leased asset who pays the lessor for the usage right.

Lessor   The owner of a leased asset.

Letter of credit   A written statement by a bank that money will be loaned provided conditions specified in the letter are met.

Leverage   The degree of firm borrowing.

Leverage ratio   A financial ratio that measures a firm's debt burden; the debt, times interest earned, and fixed-charges coverage ratios are leverage ratios.

Leveraged lease (or "third party lease")   An arrangement under which the lessor borrows funds to cover part or all of the purchase price of the asset.

Limited liability   A legal term which means that the owner of a business is not personally responsible for its debts; only his investment in the business is available to its creditors.

Limited partnership	A business in which some partners (the general partners) are personally responsible for any debts, but the other partners (the limited partners) are not.
Line of credit	An agreement by a bank to loan money to a customer as needed up to a stated maximum amount.
Linear programming	A mathematical technique for determining the magnitudes of certain variables in order to maximize a particular function assuming the existence of constraints on some of the variables. For example, the problem might be to determine the level of investment in each project in order to maximize net present value given the constraint that only $1 million can be invested in total. Linear programming deals with linear functions whereas nonlinear programming deals with nonlinear functions.
Liquidation	The sale of a firm's assets when the company is dissolved.
Liquidity ratio	A financial ratio that measures a firm's ability to fulfill short-run financial commitments; the current and quick ratios are liquidity ratios.
Listed stock	Stock which is traded on an organized securities exchange.
Lock box	A post office box to which local payments to a company will be sent. A local bank will collect the payments and deposit them in the company's account.
Loss carryback (forward)	Using a business loss in the current year as a deduction from taxable income in prior years (carryback) or future years (carryforward).
Maintenance lease	A lease under which the lessor pays for all maintenance and upkeep of the asset.
Majority rule voting	A system of electing directors under which a majority of the shares has the power to elect the entire board of directors.
Market rate of discount	The rate of discount used by investors to discount returns of a particular level of risk.
Market value (or market price)	The value that an asset (e.g., a security such as a share of stock or a physical asset such as a machine) is bought and sold for in the market.
Matching principle	A principle which holds that the firm should finance short-term needs with short-term sources and long-term needs with long-term sources.
Maturity date	The date on which the firm is to retire a bond by repaying the principal (maturity value); that is, when the bond matures.
Maturity value	The amount the firm promises to pay the bondholder, in addition to interest, when the bond matures. The maturity value is also referred to as the bond's **par value, face value,** or **principal value.**
Merger	The combination of two or more firms with one of them surviving (e.g., firm A merging with firm B with firm A surviving).

Minimum acceptable rate of return	The lowest rate of return that an investment can be expected to earn and still be acceptable; same as the investment's **cost of capital.**
Mortgage	A pledge of specific property given by a borrower as security on a loan.
Mortgage bond	A bond secured by a mortgage.
Multinational company	A company which has direct investments in more than one country.
Mutual fund	A company which invests in securities using money raised from selling shares to individual investors at their net asset value (market value of assets divided by number of shares). Shares will be redeemed by the fund at their net asset value at the request of the investor. Also called ''open-end investment companies.''
Mutually exclusive alternatives	Alternatives or options of which only one can be adopted (adopting one eliminates the chance of adopting any of the others).
Negative pledge clause	A provision in a bond agreement that the firm will issue no new debt which will take priority over the bonds covered by the agreement.
Negotiated under-writing	A process of issuing securities whereby a firm selects an investment banker and negotiates the terms of the deal.
Net lease	A lease under which the lessee pays all maintenance and upkeep of the asset.
Net present value	The present value of the future cash flows of an investment less the investment's current cost.
Net profit	Aftertax net income to stockholders; sometimes also used to refer to the annual annuity that is equivalent to a given net present value.
Note (loan)	Written and signed evidence of a debt.
Note (United States)	A type of United States government security with an original maturity of one to ten years. Similar to a bond but with a shorter maturity.
Open-end mortgage	A mortgage which allows the security (collateral) provided by the mortgage to be used as collateral on additional debt. A **limited open-end mortgage** allows the issuance of further debt up to some specified limit.
Operating lease	A lease which is cancellable by the lessee at any time upon due notice to the lessor; also called a **service lease.**
Operating leverage	The existence of fixed operating costs in the firm's cost structure.
Operating margin	Operating income divided by sales; a measure of a firm's profitability.
Owner of record	The individual recorded on the corporation's books as the owner of the company's outstanding securities.
Par value	The stated value of a security. The par value of a bond is its maturity value, the amount paid per bond at maturity. The par value of a share of preferred stock is the amount on which preferred dividends are paid (a

$100 par value 6 percent preferred stock pays $6 annually in dividends). The preferred's par value is also the amount owed to the preferred shareholder upon liquidation or bankruptcy of the corporation. The par value of common stock is the value of a share of stock set by the board of directors and is generally less than market value; the primary significance of this value is that, in most states, the firm may not pay dividends if such dividends reduce common shareholders' equity in the firm below the total par on all common stock outstanding.

Participating preferred stock   Preferred stock with a provision for increased dividends if the firm's earnings exceed some minimum amount.

Partnership   A business owned by two or more people who agree on how the profits will be divided and who are personally liable for firm debts. See also **limited partnership.**

Payback period   The amount of time required for an asset to generate enough cash flow to just cover the initial outlay for that asset; an asset costing $1,500 and generating an aftertax cash flow of $500 per year has a payback period of three years ($1,500/$500).

Payback period method   A capital budgeting technique which specifies that an investment is acceptable only if it has a payback period less than or equal to some specified time period; e.g., three years.

Personal property   All property other than **real property.**

Pooling of interests method of accounting   A method of accounting for a business combination under which the assets of the acquired firm are subsequently carried on the merged firm's books at the same value that they were carried by the selling firm.

Portfolio   A combination of assets owned for investment.

Preemptive right   The stockholder's right to purchase additional stock of the company before it is offered for sale to outsiders.

Preferred stock   Stock which has a claim against income and assets before common stock but after debt.

Premium (bond)   The difference between the market value and the face value of a bond if the market value is greater; e.g., the premium is $200 on a $1,000 (face value) bond selling in the market for $1,200.

Premium (warrant)   The difference between the market value and the theoretical value of the warrant.

Present value   The value of money at a present date which will be paid or received in future periods. The present date is the earliest date in a problem.

Primary markets   The market in which financial assets are originally issued.

Prime rate   Interest rate charged by banks on short-term loans to large, low-risk businesses.

Principal	The amount on which interest is paid by a borrower or the amount on which interest is received by a lender.
Principal value	The maturity value of a bond.
Private issue	Security issue sold to only a few investors which need not be registered with the Securities and Exchange Commission. Also called **private placement.**
Profitability index	A measure of the profitability of an investment computed by dividing the net present value (or simply present value of future cash flows) by the initial cost of the investment.
Profitability ratio	A financial ratio that indicates the net returns on sales or assets; net operating margin, profit margin on sales, return on total assets, and return on net worth are profitability ratios.
Proprietorship	A business owned by an individual who is personally responsible for all its debts.
Prospectus	Information supplied to potential investors in a new securities issue which describes the current condition and history of the firm.
Protective covenant	See **covenant.**
Proxy	The authorization given by a shareholder to another party to exercise the shareholder's voting rights at a stockholders' meeting.
Public issue	Security issue sold to many investors. Large issues of most types of securities must be registered with the Securities and Exchange Commission.
Public warehouse	A place where goods belonging to other people are stored; sometimes used to maintain control over collateral.
Purchase method of accounting	A method of accounting for a business combination in which the assets of the acquired firm are carried on the merged firm's books at the price paid for them in the merger acquisition.
Pure residual dividend policy	See **residual dividend policy.**
Quick ratio (or acid test ratio)	A measure of the firm's liquidity equal to [(current assets − inventory) ÷ current liabilities].
Rate of return	The interest rate earned on an investment; may be an actual or expected rate.
Real property	Land and buildings.
Realized capital gain	See **capital gain.**
Refunding	The issuance of new securities to pay off outstanding old debt; **funding,** on the other hand, specifically refers to issuing long-term debt to pay off short-term debt.

Reorganization	An adjustment under Chapter X of the National Bankruptcy Act for settlement of the firm's debts; covers all public corporations except railroads.
Residual dividend policy	A policy under which all equity investment is financed first with retained earnings and then, if such earnings are inadequate, by selling additional equity securities such as common stock and warrants. Earnings that are left over after equity investment is made are paid out as a dividend. A **pure residual dividend policy** requires that the above residual policy be followed every year; a **smoothed residual dividend policy** requires following a residual policy over the long run with dividends kept stable from year to year.
Restrictive provisions	Restrictions on various activities of a borrower included as part of a loan agreement to protect the lender. See **covenant.**
Retained earnings	The earnings in a given period which have been retained by the firm rather than paid out as dividends; also refers to the balance sheet account which is the sum of all earnings retained to date.
Reverse split	The reduction in the number of the firm's shares produced by exchanging all outstanding shares for a smaller number of new shares; each shareholder's percentage ownership of the firm is unaffected.
Revolving credit	Legal commitment by a bank to loan money to a customer as needed up to a stated maximum amount. The time period covered by the agreement may extend for several years.
Rights	A privilege offered to stockholders of buying a specified number of additional shares of the company's stock before the stock is offered to outsiders for sale. A stockholder is issued one right per share of stock already owned.
Rights-off	Without the privilege of receiving rights. A share of stock is rights-off if it no longer entitles its owner to a right that is about to be issued by the firm.
Rights-on	With the privilege of receiving rights. A share of stock is rights-on if it entitles its owner to a right that is about to be issued by the firm.
Rule of absolute priority	The principle that senior claims must be fully paid before junior claimants receive anything.
Sale and leaseback	An arrangement under which the user of the asset sells the asset and then leases it back from the purchaser.
Salvage value (residual value)	The price that the firm can receive for an asset after it has used it for an extended period of time (most of the asset's useful life if the term **salvage value** is used).
Secondary market	The market in which previously issued financial assets are traded.
Security market line	The relationship between risk and return on securities bought and sold in the financial markets.

Serial bonds Bonds issued at the same time but which mature at different times in the future. For example, a $50 million serial bond issue may provide for $5 million of bonds maturing in five years, another $5 million of bonds maturing in six years, etc., until all bonds have matured in fourteen years.

Simulation The use of a set of mathematical relationships to duplicate the operations of a system (e.g., a firm), in order to analyze the system. Simulation could be used to analyze the effect of a new project on firm profits.

Sinking fund contribution A periodic payment made by the firm into a fund ("sinking fund") which will be paid to bondholders in retiring the bonds.

Sinking fund provision A stipulation in the bond agreement (indenture) that the firm establish a sinking fund. The fund is used to retire part or all of the bonds by buying them on the open market, calling them, or retiring them at maturity.

Skewness A measure of the nonsymmetry of a probability distribution; **left skewness** and **right skewness** mean that the tail of the distribution is on the left side and right side, respectively.

Small Business Administration (SBA) A federal agency established to aid small businesses.

Small Business Investment Company (SBIC) A financial institution established under certain federal laws to provide financing to small businesses.

Smoothed residual dividend policy See **residual dividend policy.**

Spot rate The current rate of exchange between two currencies; the rate of exchange at which currencies are presently being traded.

Standard deviation A measure of the degree of dispersion of a probability distribution; a higher standard deviation of a cash flow implies a greater uncertainty regarding its level. Standard deviation is the square root of the **variance.** To adjust for scale in making risk comparisons between projects, a useful parameter is the project cash flow's **coefficient of variation,** which equals the cash flow's standard deviation divided by the expected cash flow.

Stated value A value set by the board of directors for no-par stock. Stated value has essentially the same meaning as **par value,** in that dividends may not be paid which reduce shareholders' equity below the stated value of all outstanding shares.

Stock dividend New shares distributed to existing shareholders as a dividend.

Stock exchange A financial institution which provides a central location for the purchase and sale of stocks.

Stock split An increase in the number of firm shares effected by giving stockholders additional shares in proportion to the number of shares already owned.

Subordination Relegation to a lower priority position in receiving interest and principal;

if an issue of debentures is subordinated to other debt, the latter debt is paid the amount due before the **subordinated debentures** receive anything.

Syndicate A group of investment bankers formed to handle a large security issue.

Synergy Benefits from joining two or more economic units; e.g., the benefits from merging two firms if the merger lowers the cost per unit of output.

Taxable income The income of an individual or business on which income taxes are levied as defined by the tax laws. Various deductions are made from total income to arrive at taxable income.

Theoretical value For a warrant, the market price minus the option price of the common stock acquired with a warrant multiplied by the number of shares purchased per warrant; this equals the value of the common stock acquired with a warrant less the exercise price paid for that stock. For a convertible security, theoretical value is the same as **investment value.**

Third party lease See **leveraged lease.**

Trade credit Credit on goods purchased by a company from its supplier.

Treasury bill A security issued by the United States government with a maturity of one year or less, paying $1,000 per bill at maturity with no interest payments.

Treasury stock Shares repurchased from a stockholder by the issuing company.

Trustee In bankruptcy, a court-appointed official who draws up a reorganization plan and supervises the firm's assets until the plan goes into effect. In a public bond issue, an individual or firm who represents the bondholders in dealing with the issuing company.

Underwriting The purchase of securities from the issuing company by an investment banker for resale to the public.

Variable cost A cost which changes as output changes.

Variable rate loan A loan with an interest rate that varies according to the general level of interest rates. The interest rate is not fixed over the period of the loan.

Variance See **standard deviation.**

Venture capital Money invested in a small or new business as an investment by persons not directly managing the business.

Vertical combination The union of firms engaged in different stages of production of the same type of product; e.g., a food retailer and food wholesaler.

Warrant An option to buy a security (e.g., a share of stock) issued by the firm which issued the warrant.

Yield to maturity The rate of return earned on a bond if it is purchased at a given price and held to maturity.

index